SOCIOLOGY OF
SEXUALITIES

SOCIOLOGY OF
SEXUALITIES

KATHLEEN J. FITZGERALD
Tulane University

KANDICE L. GROSSMAN
Columbia College

Los Angeles | London | New Delhi
Singapore | Washington DC | Melbourne

FOR INFORMATION:

SAGE Publications, Inc.
2455 Teller Road
Thousand Oaks, California 91320
E-mail: order@sagepub.com

SAGE Publications Ltd.
1 Oliver's Yard
55 City Road
London EC1Y 1SP
United Kingdom

SAGE Publications India Pvt. Ltd.
B 1/I 1 Mohan Cooperative Industrial Area
Mathura Road, New Delhi 110 044
India

SAGE Publications Asia-Pacific Pte. Ltd.
3 Church Street
#10-04 Samsung Hub
Singapore 049483

Acquisitions Editor: Jeff Lasser
Editorial Assistant: Adeline Wilson
Production Editor: Andrew Olson
Copy Editor: Ellen Howard
Typesetter: Hurix Systems Pvt. Ltd.
Proofreader: Jennifer Grubba
Indexer: Wendy Allex
Cover Designer: Scott Van Atta
Marketing Manager: Kara Kindstrom

Printed in the United States of America

Library of Congress Cataloging-in-Publication Data

Names: Fitzgerald, Kathleen J., 1965– author. | Grossman, Kandice, 1976– author.

Title: Sociology of sexualities / Kathleen J. Fitzgerald, Kandice Grossman.

Description: First Edition. | Thousand Oaks : SAGE Publications, [2017] | Includes bibliographical references and index.

Identifiers: LCCN 2016040645 | ISBN 9781506304014 (pbk. : alk. paper)

Subjects: LCSH: Sex—Social aspects. | Gender identity. | Sex customs.

Classification: LCC HQ21 .F6845 2017 | DDC 306.7—dc23 LC record available at https://lccn.loc.gov/2016040645

This book is printed on acid-free paper.

MIX
Paper from
responsible sources
FSC
www.fsc.org
FSC® C008955

18 19 20 21 10 9 8 7 6 5 4 3 2

BRIEF CONTENTS

DETAILED CONTENTS

ACKNOWLEDGMENTS

It is impossible to acknowledge all the people who have influenced my understanding of the sociology of sexualities, and inequalities more broadly, over the years; but they are reflected in these pages. During my years at Southern Illinois University at Edwardsville when I was working on my master's degree, I was exposed to a committed group of sociologists who were just as interested in teaching as they were in research. Many of them wrote textbooks that were innovative and market leaders at the time, which likely subtly influenced me to try my hand at textbook writing. I am still grateful for the influence of my former graduate professors at the University of Missouri, particularly Mary Jo Neitz, Peter Hall, Ibitola Pearce, Ted Vaughan, and the late Barbara Bank, for their profound influence on my intellectual development. I am thankful for the thoughtful conversations with my graduate colleagues then, and over the years, especially Diane Rodgers, Yngve Digernes, Karen Bradley, and Latanya Skiffer. My late friend and former colleague Pamela McClure still speaks to me in my head about these issues. And thank you to my wonderful new colleagues at Tulane University not just for the intellectual stimulation but for making me feel welcome.

Textbooks are written for a particular audience, of course: students. And so, I would like to dedicate this textbook to the many hundreds of students I have had the pleasure of teaching over the years. It is an undeniable privilege to teach college students, and I know I have been very lucky in my career in that I have encountered so many amazing people.

To the sociologists working in the field of sexuality studies: thank you. It has been a pleasure diving deeply into this scholarship—so many smart people are doing such great work! We wanted this textbook to reflect the best of the field. We hope we succeeded at doing that. Thanks to Jeff Lasser and the folks at SAGE for their enthusiasm and assistance with this project.

And a giant thank-you to Kandice Grossman for enthusiastically jumping on board when I casually mentioned the idea of coauthoring a sociology of sexualities textbook with her. It has been an incredible pleasure to work with her on this project. I knew I could count on her! Finally, my ultimate love and thanks go to my partner, husband, friend, and fellow sociologist, Tony Ladd. His constant love and support has been invaluable. His brilliant mind keeps me sharp, and his big heart make me a better person every day. During the writing of this book, he offered the perfect balance of support and space that was needed. So, this book is dedicated to him.

Kathleen J. Fitzgerald
July 2016

I would like to express heartfelt gratitude to my daughters, Isadora and Madelynn Grossman, for their patience and support throughout this project. They are the light of my life. I would like to thank my two greatest academic influences: Dr. Kathleen Fitzgerald and Dr. Anthony Alioto. For over twenty years, they have both consistently believed in me. It was their teachings twenty years ago that taught me to challenge social ideas and critically evaluate history. It was their encouragement that motivated me throughout this entire writing process. With a most sincere heart, I thank them both for their guidance. And to Kathleen specifically, writing a book with her has been a huge learning experience and pleasure. She is an inspiration and role model in so many ways. I cannot thank her enough for her mentorship.

I want to acknowledge the profound influence I received in my upbringing from my mother, Ginger Mistler, and my grandmother, Bettie Lasley. My gram bore seven children prior to 1960, before there was accessible birth control for women. She was very outspoken about her beliefs in women's rights to reproductive control, choices, and health; this message was imprinted on my mind from an early age. It was her narrative, her story, and her feminist outlook that brought me to the writing of this book. My mother, too, taught me the importance of higher education. This book is a product of their combined efforts at shaping who I am today. Thank you to my sister, Tara Looney, for graciously editing citations and for continued support. Many thanks to Jeff Lasser at SAGE for his enthusiasm for this project.

Kandice L. Grossman
July 2016

PUBLISHER'S ACKNOWLEDGMENTS

SAGE gratefully acknowledges the contributions of the following reviewers:

Sarah A. N. Akers, Washington State University
Lanier Basenberg, Georgia State University
Marni Brown, Georgia Gwinnett College
Angel M. Butts, Rutgers University
Moon Charania, Spelman College
Amanda Czerniawski, Temple University
Barbara Jones Denison, Shippensburg University
Andrea Fitzroy, Georgia State University
Alison Hatch, Armstrong State University
Nicole LaMarre, SUNY Albany
Lisa M. Lepard, Kennesaw State University
Adina Nack, California Lutheran University
Michaela A. Nowell, University of Wisconsin-Fond du Lac
Kathleen O'Reilly, University of Connecticut
Meg Panichelli, Portland State University
Todd Penner, Austin College
Antonia Randolph, Christopher Newport University
Teresa Roach, Florida State University, Appalachain State University
Maura Ryan, Georgia State University
Eryn Grucza Viscarra, Georgia College and State University
Laurie M. Wagner, Kent State University
Kassia Wosick, New Mexico State University
Marik Xavier-Brier, Georgia State University

PREFACE

This textbook takes a sociological approach to the study of sexualities and is designed to be a core text for "Sociology of Sexuality," "Human Sexuality," and similar courses. Taking a sociological approach to the study of sexualities requires an exploration of sexuality as a social construction; the emergence of sexual and gender identities; a focus on intersectionality; historical and current inequalities and discrimination faced by sexual and gender minorities; heterosexual and cisgender privilege; activism/mobilization to challenge such discrimination; and the ways sexuality operates in and through various institutions, such as media, schools, family, religion, sport, and the workplace. Additionally, this text includes chapters on the science of sexuality, from early sexologists to queer theory; coverage of issues facing transgender people; an exploration of sexual health, disability and sexuality, and sexually transmitted infections; and on reproduction. There are chapters on social problems associated with sexuality such as the commodification of sexuality, including pornography, human trafficking, and prostitution; prison sex; and sexual violence. Finally, every chapter includes a boxed insert that explores a global, transnational perspective related to the specific chapter topic.

This text includes the most up-to-date social scientific research on sexuality, as well as coverage of the latest political developments surrounding the issues. It is designed for students to learn the fundamental concepts of a sociological approach to understanding sexualities, but also to integrate such knowledge into their broader understanding of society. An intersectional approach that considers multiple grounds of identity and the ways various modes of oppression intersect and work together in society is consistently woven throughout this book. No sexuality textbook on the market takes such a comprehensive sociological approach to the study of sexualities.

KEY FEATURES OF THE TEXT

- *Sexuality, Inequality, and Discrimination*—This topic is absent from most of the sexuality readers and textbooks, yet this is where students "see" lesbian, gay, bisexual, transgender, and queer (LGBTQ) issues in their daily lives. What is less visible to students is the extent of inequalities LGBTQ individuals historically faced and continue to face, and other forms of discrimination related to sexuality, such as discrimination against pregnant women. Certainly throughout the lifetimes of traditional-aged college students, the issue of marriage equality has been front and center; and, thus, it can appear that the fight for LGBTQ rights has been won. Yet, inequalities remain. Additionally, heterosexual and cisgender privilege remains invisible. When sociologists explore status hierarchies, we look at not only the groups that are disadvantaged but those that reap advantages as well.

- *Activism/Mobilization to Challenge Such Discrimination*—This textbook explores not only inequalities sexual minorities face and heterosexual privilege, but the organized opposition to such discrimination. It is important for students to shake the misconception that progress is "inevitable" and, instead, is the result of decades of organized activism. This text explores LGBTQ activism, from the Compton Cafeteria riots, known as the first transgender riots, to the Stonewall riots, the fight for marriage equality, AIDS activism, and Queer Nation. This book weaves feminist and queer theoretical insights throughout to reveal how challenges to inequality in the streets are reflected and translated in academia, and vice versa.

- *Sexuality and Societal Institutions*—This is the only sexuality textbook on the market that explores the ways sexuality operates in and through institutions such as sports, media, schools, workplaces, family, and religion. By exploring institutions, students again find a way to "see" the inequalities attached to sexuality in their daily lives. For instance, many traditional-aged college students witnessed or participated in battles to allow LGBTQ student organizations (or Gay-Straight Alliances) on their middle-school or high-school campuses. Their generation came of age during significant cultural battles over sex education versus abstinence education. Some of them may work in environments that discriminate against sexual minorities. Some of them come from gay families. They are also the first generation of Americans to come of age as the first gay professional athletes chose to come out of the closet during their athletic careers. This generation of students has also been exposed to a proliferation of gay images in the media, yet simply having gay images does not necessarily mean stereotypes are not being perpetrated.

- *Focus on Transgender People and Issues*—Each chapter of this textbook includes the latest research on transgender people and issues; from the incorporation of intersex and transgender athletes into a gender segregated sports world to discrimination against transgender individuals in the workplace, and epidemic levels of violence directed at transgender people, overwhelmingly transgender people of color.

- *Sexual Identities*—The invention of heterosexuality and homosexuality involved the emergence of sexual identities—for the first time, people's sexual behaviors defined a "kind of person." While this resulted in new forms of discrimination against sexual minorities, it also contributed to the mobilization of LGBTQ individuals to combat their inequality. As just one aspect of how we see ourselves, sexual identities are also understood to intersect with other identities, such as gender, race, and class, informing how individuals see themselves. Much sociological research addresses the ways individuals construct and negotiate multiple identities.

- *Sexual Health*—This text takes a sociological approach to understanding sexual health, including a critical discussion of the emergence of female sexual dysfunction, to an exploration of disability and sexuality, and a discussion of sexually transmitted infections (STIs), including HIV/AIDS, from a sociological perspective. Finally, we explore reproduction, from compulsory reproduction to the commodification of birth, transgender men and childbirth, and the increasing availability of assisted reproductive technologies (ARTs), and what these have meant for LGBTQ families.

- *Social Problems Associated With Sexuality*—This is the arena where sociologists have long contributed to sexuality studies, including research on sexual assault, rape, pornography, sex trafficking, child sexual abuse, and prison sex—with feminist sociologists placing questions of power at the center of such analyses. Additionally, we explore sexual violence targeting the LGBTQ community, intimate partner violence within same-sex relationships, and sexuality and militarism.

- *Global/Transnational Perspectives on Sexuality*—Each chapter includes a boxed insert highlighting a global illustration of one of the issues explored in the chapter. This helps students understand sexuality as a social construction that changes across time and place.

"Sociology of Sexuality," "Sociology of Sexualities," "Human Sexuality," and "Sexuality and Society" courses are increasingly being offered by sociology departments across the nation, often at the behest of students. Sexuality courses tend to be 200 (sophomore) or 300 (junior) level courses, generally with a large population of students who are not sociology majors; thus, having a textbook that takes a sociological perspective is essential. Until now, no textbook on the market took a sociological approach to the subject matter. This text is ideal for courses in sociology of sexualities, gender and sexuality studies, LBGTQ studies, and deviance courses that focus on sexual deviance.

Instructors, sign in at **study.sagepub.com/fitzgeraldss** for the following instructor resources:

- A **Microsoft® Word test bank** is available containing multiple choice, true/false, short answer, and essay questions for each chapter. The test bank provides you with a diverse range of pre-written options as well as the opportunity for editing any question and/or inserting your own personalized questions to effectively assess students' progress and understanding.

- Links to exceptional teaching **resources from A.S.A.'s TRAILS** (Teaching Resources and Innovation Library for Sociology).

THE SOCIAL CONSTRUCTION OF SEXUALITY

LEARNING OBJECTIVES

Upon completion of this chapter, students will be able to . . .

- Explain the sociological approach to the study of sexuality
- Understand what it means to say that sexuality is socially constructed
- Identify key characteristics of a sexual revolution
- Understand sexuality across the life course
- Explain the sexualization of racial/ethnic minorities
- Discuss sexual minorities beyond lesbian and gay

For many, it was an unforgettable image: Michael Sam, an openly gay, African American, male football player, kissing his white male partner on national television, in celebration of being chosen by the St. Louis Rams in the 2014 NFL draft. Upon being drafted, Michael Sam became the first openly gay player in the NFL. Several NFL players openly expressed their unhappiness with Sam's actions, while others cheered the action as evidence of both societal progress and institutional change within the NFL. Former NFL football player Derrick Ward tweeted his discomfort with the image, stating, "I'm sorry, but that Michael Sam is no bueno for doing that on national T.V." Miami Dolphins safety Don Jones tweeted "OMG" and "horrible" after the kissing aired on national television (Yan and Alsup 2014). The Miami Dolphins organization reacted to Jones's comments by fining him and requiring him to attend diversity training.

When Michael Sam was drafted in 2014, he became the first openly gay NFL player.
Source: AP Images. Photo/Jordan Strauss.

Despite the controversy surrounding this event, certainly the image of two men kissing passionately on national television represents progress for lesbian, gay, bisexual, transgender, and queer (LGBTQ) equality, and the fact that this occurred at the NFL draft is also remarkable. Historically, masculinity has been strongly linked with heterosexuality. Football is one of the most masculine sports. Gay male athletes have historically found the sports world an intolerant and hostile place, and maybe the most hostile place is on the football field (see Chapter 6). While Michael Sam did not make the final roster cut as a member of an NFL team, the fact that an openly gay male athlete was drafted by an NFL team was history making in itself.

And yet, this story also provides evidence of how far we still have to go. After the football season ended, Sam commented to Oprah Winfrey that a number of gay NFL players reached out to him personally and commended him for being brave enough to come out, something they were still unwilling to risk.

You are taking this class during a period of unprecedented change for LGBTQ individuals. All state prohibitions on same-sex marriage were overturned in June 2015 with the Supreme Court decision *Obergefell v. Hodges*, making marriage equality the law of the land. Prior to that, in 2013, the Supreme Court declared as unconstitutional the Defense of Marriage Act, which was the federal prohibition on same-sex marriage. High-profile gay, lesbian, and bisexual athletes are coming out of the closet regularly. School policies nationwide are being challenged by the needs and demands of transgender students. And finally, LGBTQ actors and characters are more prolific in the media than ever, including the first transgender character played by a transgender actor, Laverne Cox, on the hit series *Orange Is the New Black*. Daily headlines highlight the ongoing cultural changes surrounding sexuality-related issues, and yet, sexuality is still highly regulated. Prostitution is illegal in all 50 states, for instance (the state of Nevada does allow for prostitution in some of its counties, but it is not legal in the entire state). While the Republican Party remains officially opposed to gay marriage and other rights for sexual minorities, polls show that among younger voters of both parties, gay rights are a given. Despite the significant progress made, LGBTQ individuals still face discrimination and inequality both in the United States and across the globe. These include violence; harassment; legal discrimination in numerous institutions, from the residential sphere to the workplace; and the burden of stereotypical images in popular culture.

Evidence of the undeniable progress, yet the remaining inequalities faced by LGBTQ individuals, includes, but is not limited to:

- In a 2013 issue of *Sports Illustrated,* National Basketball Association player Jason Collins became the first male member of a major American sports team to publicly announce he was gay during his playing career.

- As sexual assaults on college campuses gained increasing national attention, in July 2014, Senator Claire McCaskill (D-MO) announced the results of a national survey that found more than 40 percent of colleges had not conducted a single sexual assault investigation in the past five years—and that is not because there were no charges of sexual assault at those institutions (Vendituolie 2014).
- In July 2014, President Obama signed legislation providing protection for gay, lesbian, and transgender federal workers and their contractors, a move that ultimately affects one-fifth of the U.S. workforce (Pickles 2014).
- The Boy Scouts of America voted to end the ban on participation by openly gay adults in 2015, despite warnings that such a move would result in the demise of the organization; one year later, the Boy Scouts of America are stronger than ever, with a stabilized membership after years of decline (Crary and Mccombs 2016).
- In July 2016, Sarah McBride became the first transgender person to speak at a major political party convention when she gave her invited address at the Democratic National Convention.
- Violence against transgender people, particularly transgender people of color, reached an all-time high in 2015, with 22 murders, nineteen of whom were people of color. As of July 26, 2016, 16 transgender people have been murdered in the United States, and 13 of them were transgender women of color (Fitzgerald 2017).

THE SOCIOLOGY OF SEXUALITIES

In this textbook, we explore sexuality through a sociological lens. This means we approach an otherwise familiar topic from an often unfamiliar angle. Most of us are socialized to think of sexuality as fixed and innate. If asked, most people easily identify their own sexual orientation. However, sociologists view sexuality as more complicated. What defines us sexually? Is it our behaviors, the people we choose to have sex with, or the sexual acts we engage in? Or is it about identity—how we define ourselves along sexual lines? What about our sexual desires and sexual fantasies? Are these the "true" gauges of sexuality? Is there a genetic determinant to human sexuality? Sociologists point to instances where sexual identities, desires, and behaviors are in conflict with one another, rather than the instances where they are consistent, as evidence of how complicated defining sexuality really is.

What does it mean when individuals identify as heterosexual, yet engage in sexual relations with members of their own sex? It might mean that, due to a larger homophobic culture, they are hesitant to accept a gay or lesbian identity despite their actions. It also might mean that they do not have the opportunity to have sex with members of the opposite sex; a situation incarcerated people find themselves in. Researchers identify a sexual practice among black men that is referred to as being on the "down low"; black men who identify as heterosexual, often have wives or girlfriends, yet who engage in sex with other men (Boykin 2005; Collins 2005; King 2004; Snorton 2014). Latino men engaging in similar behaviors are categorized as MSMs, or "men who have sex with men" (Diaz 1997; Gonzalez 2007).

Jessica Taylor and Charlotte Jones married in the summer 2016, something that was not legal in their state prior to the Supreme Court decision in June 2015 that legalized same-sex marriage nationwide.
Source: Photo courtesy of Jessica Taylor and Charlotte Jones; Bron Moyi, photographer.

Sociologist Jane Ward (2015) examines patterns of and meanings behind the sexual contact between straight white men who are not gay. Some scholars use the term ***heteroflexibility*** to describe a broad range of same-sex sexual encounters experienced by heterosexuals in which the actions are understood as meaningless and unlikely to fundamentally challenge a person's presumably fixed sexual identity (Ward 2015). An example of heteroflexibility includes girl-on-girl kissing, whether at fraternity parties or among celebrities, which is generally done for male sexual arousal. Ultimately, identities, desires, and behaviors are not always consistent, thus a simplistic understanding of "sexuality," as based on only one of these criteria, is problematic.

A sociological approach to understanding sexuality requires we understand it as cultural rather than as strictly personal. It is not inaccurate to understand sexuality through an individualistic lens; but that is not the only way to understand it. Sexuality is very much a product of and a reflection of society. While we have learned to view our own sexual desires as quite personal, they are very much a reflection of cultural assumptions surrounding what is natural or unnatural, acceptable or unacceptable, sexually. We understand our sexual desires and behaviors through our social contexts and preexisting cultural scripts. Thus, sexuality is both personal and social. Even further, sexuality is political, as recent political contestation over sexuality-related issues and feminists and LGBTQ activists have repeatedly brought to our attention. Finally, because sexuality is culturally informed, it is important to note that this text will approach the sociology of sexualities primarily through a U.S. lens, with some historical and cross-cultural analyses and comparisons—particularly in the boxed inserts focused on "Global and Transnational Perspectives on Sexuality" found in each chapter.

Sociology is the study of human social behavior, culture, and interaction between individuals and groups. While sociologists do not ignore the importance of biology in sexuality, they instead emphasize the role social forces play in understanding sexuality. A sociological approach to the study of sexuality emphasizes the socially constructed nature of sexuality, the cultural assumptions surrounding sexual behaviors, and the emergence of and significance of sexual identities—all of which will be introduced in this chapter. The rest of the book will focus on the following sociological topics: the science of sexuality; the intersection of gender and sexuality; sexuality as a status hierarchy where one's group membership, either as a member of the privileged group known as heterosexuals or as a member of a sexual minority group, determines one's access to various societal goods and resources; the activism designed to overturn the discrimination faced by LGBTQ individuals; the ways sexuality operates in and through various institutions such as the media, sports, schools, workplace, religion, and family; and sex education, reproduction, disability and sexuality, sexually transmitted infections, and sexual health. Finally, a sociology of sexualities would be incomplete without an understanding of social issues associated with sexuality such as the commodification of sexuality, pornography, prostitution, sex trafficking, prison sex, and sexual violence.

TERMINOLOGY

Some of the terminology used throughout this text is assumed to be straightforward, however, this can be misleading. What does it mean to speak of a ***sexual orientation***, for instance? Sexual orientation refers to an individual's identity based on their enduring or continuing sexual attractions, and may include behaviors and membership in a community of others who share those attractions. Sexual orientation generally falls into four categories: ***heterosexuality***, when one's romantic and sexual attractions are directed at members of the opposite sex; ***homosexuality,*** when those feelings are primarily directed at individuals of the same sex; ***bisexuality,*** when such feelings exist for both members of one's own sex and members of the opposite sex; and *asexuality*, which is broadly defined as having no sexual attraction at all, or being indifferent to sexual activity.

In the current era, the term *pansexuality* has also gained some prominence. It refers to having sexual attractions to individuals, regardless of their sex or gender; a sexual attraction to all sexes/genders. Pansexuality may at first seem similar to bisexuality, except that pansexuality is a more fluid concept than bisexuality, which assumes a gender binary, something we will talk about in great detail throughout this book. Pansexuality rejects the notion of a gender or a sexual binary (the notion of either/or: gay or straight, male or female). *Sexuality* refers to one's sexual desires, erotic attractions, and sexual behaviors, or the potential for these; physical acts and emotional intimacies that are intended to be pleasurable, and that are embedded within larger, socially constructed, body of meanings. For many people, their sexuality is congruent; meaning their identities, desires, and behaviors align. For others, however, this may not be true. Their identities, desires, and behaviors are not always congruent, and instead are inconsistent. They may identify as heterosexual, but desire sexual relations with members of their same sex, for instance. Thus, the definitions we rely on to describe human sexual variation are somewhat problematic, yet we live in a culture that assigns meaning to certain sexual behaviors. The definitions above, limitations and all, reflect those cultural meanings.

Our culture treats sexual categories as real, emphasizing that for each sexual orientation there is a specific set of fixed traits that are associated with it. This is something social scientists refer to as *essentialism.* Essentialist thinking implies a permanence to sexual orientation; that it is static, unchanging, and innate. Essentialism naturalizes differences between groups. As we will see, this is a weakness of the essentialist position on sexuality. Yet, despite such weaknesses, essentialism is the foundation of Western understandings of sexuality. That being said, sociologists do not take an essentialist position on sexuality; instead, we take a social constructionist position, which will be introduced later in this chapter.

This text will rely on the acronym LGBTQ to represent lesbian, gay, bisexual, transgender, and queer individuals and communities. However, that is simply an editorial decision, as there are other, more inclusive, umbrella terms used to refer to the community of gender and sexual minorities. The acronym LGBTIQQAAP (lesbian, gay, bisexual, transgender, intersex, queer, questioning, asexual, allies, and pansexual) is also sometimes used. We have already defined sexual minorities such as bisexuals and homosexuals (male homosexuals are generally referred to as gay while women are referred to as lesbians), but we have not yet defined gender minorities. *Transgender* refers to people whose gender identity is inconsistent with their assigned sex at birth (see Chapter Three). *Queer* is also a label that recognizes the fluidity of sexuality, someone who falls outside the norms surrounding gender and sexuality. Queer is a term that has political origins and emerged during a specific historical era, the 1990s (see Chapter Five). This broad overview of terminology is evidence of the changing cultural understandings surrounding sexuality and thus, should not be understood as fixed.

EVIDENCE OF THE SOCIAL CONSTRUCTION OF SEXUALITY

Sociologists understand sexuality as a *social construction* rather than as something biological. By this we mean that sexuality is defined within particular social and cultural contexts; and, thus, definitions of appropriate sexual behavior change across time and place. Social constructionists emphasize the ways sexuality is learned. British sociologist Jeffrey Weeks (1981) introduces the notion of constructionism as an opposing position to essentialism for understanding sexuality. What is defined as sexually acceptable and natural in our society today has not always been so, just as what some cultures define as appropriate and natural sexual behaviors can be seen as deviant in other times and places. For instance, the Ancient Greeks had a very different sexual order than we do today. In that time and place, adult men were expected to have young, adolescent men as lovers, while at the same time they formed sexual relationships with women. Such behaviors today are viewed not only as deviant but as criminal, due to the ages of the participants.

Sociologists John Gagnon and William Simon (1973) are the first sociologists to question existing essentialist claims of *biological determinism*—the idea that sexuality is determined primarily by our genetics—and instead to emphasize its social nature. Their research challenges psychoanalytic ideas about sexuality popularized by Freud, primarily that there is an innate sexual drive that should be understood as an overwhelming force requiring societal control. Gagnon and Simon emphasize the "everydayness" of sexuality, rather than treating it as special or something separate from everyday life (Jackson and Scott 2015; see Chapter Two).

Our understandings of particular sexual behaviors and physiological reactions, such as virginity loss and orgasms, can also be understood as social constructions. While most of us may think that losing one's virginity is rather easy to delineate, research by Laura Carpenter (2013) finds that it is anything but unambiguous. Virginity loss is generally understood to be the first time a man or woman engages in vaginal-penile intercourse. One problem with this definition is that it is *heterocentric*, centered on and biased toward heterosexuality. Gay men and lesbians are more likely to define their virginity loss as their first time engaging in oral or anal intercourse rather than their first experience with vaginal-penile intercourse. Research also finds that individuals tend to not include coerced sexual experiences, such as rape and sexual assault, as virginity loss. Additionally, if the sexual experience is physically ambiguous in some way or if it is an unpleasant experience, people are less likely to define that experience as virginity loss (Carpenter 2001).

Finally, there is the idea of "secondary" virginity or "born-again" virgins. This refers to people who have lost their "true" virginity, but then decide to abstain from sex until marriage or until some future date when they are in a committed, significant relationship (Carpenter 2013). Secondary virginity is more often found among young, white, conservative, Christian women, particularly those born after 1972. It is linked to the Christian influenced "abstinence-only" educational curriculum that gained prominence in the 1980s (Carpenter 2011; see Chapter Seven). Moreover, this revirginizing phenomenon is gendered because virginity has been socially constructed as more important for women than for men.

Research finds that orgasms can also be understood as social constructions because people learn to understand certain feelings as sexual and pleasurable. While orgasms are physiological reactions, they are not comparable to digestion or sneezing; in fact, orgasms vary considerably across time and across cultures. Female orgasms vary much more than male orgasms. In cultures where women are believed to have less interest in sex, the concept of the female orgasm is unknown (Richters 2011). Much popular media attention is devoted to the issue of the female orgasm. In fact, since the 1960s, women's magazines such as *Cosmopolitan,* under the editorship of Helen Gurley Brown, became notorious for their discussions of women's sexuality, female orgasms, and the radical notion that women should enjoy guilt-free sex. In reaction to the publication of Helen Gurley Brown's book *Sex and the Single Girl* (1962), a male editor of *Life* magazine said, "The assumption that a woman is supposed to get something out of her sexual contact, something joyful and satisfactory, is a very recent idea. But this idea has been carried too far" (Allyn 2000:21).

The idea that sexuality is a social construction challenges how we have been taught to think about sexuality, which is that sexual orientation is innate and that heterosexuality is natural. In the following section, we provide evidence that sexuality is a social construction. We begin by exploring the extent to which sexuality is innate versus the extent to which it is a product of the environment. From there, we analyze the construction of sexual binaries; the invention of heterosexuality and homosexuality; the gendered nature of sexuality and sexual socialization; and finally, the variation in acceptable sexual behaviors cross-culturally and historically.

Nature Versus Nurture

Is sexuality innate? The short answer is, we do not know. Scientists have been unable to identify a genetic marker linked to sexuality. There is no evidence of a so-called "gay gene," or combination of genes, despite considerable scientific efforts directed at this question and much popular interest in the idea. There is somewhat of a cultural preoccupation with the "nature versus nurture" question, not just pertaining to sexuality but also to issues like crime, intelligence, and illness. The "nature versus nurture" question asks: To what extent is homosexuality a result of a genetic predisposition (nature), or is it a reflection of social forces in an individual's environment (nurture)?

Research by Michael Bailey and Richard Pillard (1991) at Northwestern University finds that 52 percent of identical twins of gay men are also gay, compared to 22 percent for fraternal twins, which offers some support for the biological basis of homosexuality. However, since twins are most often raised in the same environment, this research cannot disprove the influence of social factors on sibling sexuality. In 1993, molecular geneticist Dean Hamer and his colleagues at the National Cancer Institute announced that they found a genetic link to male homosexuality on the X chromosome, specifically genetic marker Xq28. By 1999, these findings were seriously challenged by other researchers for lacking *reliability*, the ability to replicate the research findings (replication is a key criterion of science). We will explore other research into the genetic links to homosexuality in Chapter Two.

Ultimately, there is no conclusive evidence that sexuality is genetic. While genetic predispositions to particular sexualities may someday be identified, such findings will still not negate the significance of society on sexuality. Indeed, the "nature versus nurture" frame is far too simplistic. Human experiences like sexuality, intelligence, criminal behavior, and health and wellness are better understood as a result of complex interactions between genes and the environment, rather than as the result of genes *or* the environment.

It is worth considering why we invest so much time and energy into seeking a genetic explanation for homosexuality. Some argue that such research questions reflect a purely scientific pursuit: we seek such knowledge simply for the sake of knowledge; to understand our world and ourselves better. Since the triumph of reason in the Enlightenment era, Western society has widely accepted that science can help us understand the mysteries of nature and society. A more sinister argument could be made: finding a homosexual gene will allow us to address it. In other words, we could find ways to "cure" homosexuality through genetic engineering (Hamer et al. 1993). Such an approach is offensive to the LGBTQ community. Efforts to find a gay gene are also problematic because they limit human sexual agency, the idea that human sexual behaviors are a result of conscious decisions and are not simply genetically determined. However, some members of the LGBTQ community embrace the search for a "gay gene" as a form of *strategic essentialism.* They argue that finding a genetic link to homosexuality makes discrimination against them morally unjustifiable because, if sexuality is innate, then it is inherited in the same way as eye color (Meem et al. 2010).

> ❝
> *"Even if there were a gay gene, it could not possibly explain the varied historical patterning of homosexuality over time, or even within a single culture"* (Weeks 2011:19).

Sexual Binaries

Seeking a genetic explanation for homosexuality (and by default, heterosexuality) supports the idea of a *sexual binary*: the idea that people are either homosexual or heterosexual. That people are either "gay" or "straight" is an integral part of the popular understanding of sexuality today; however, it is a false binary. In fact, the mere existence of bisexuals challenges this idea explicitly. Rooted in the seventeenth-century philosophies of Rene Descartes, also known as Cartesian dualities, the Western world-view is bifurcated—split into two, opposing, categories. Binaries are best understood as pairs of opposing concepts such as nature/nurture, man/woman, gay/straight, black/white, and superior/inferior, among others (Fausto-Sterling 2013). These terms have no meaning in isolation; instead, their meaning emerges from what they are in opposition to. This perspective reduces the understanding of sexuality to an either/or binary, excluding a wide spectrum of diverse sexual experiences and realities.

Research by Alfred Kinsey (1948, 1953) challenges this false "gay or straight" binary by arguing that sexuality should be thought of as a continuum rather than as a binary (see Chapter Two). People who identify as bisexual have difficulties being accepted as bisexual. Too often, they are viewed as insincere—either they are homosexuals who are clinging to their heterosexual privilege or are too homophobic to admit who they really are, or they are heterosexuals who are simply engaging in sexual experimentation. The doubt surrounding the authenticity of bisexuals stems from our cultural understanding of sexuality as binary.

More evidence of the sexual binary is the erasure of bisexuals from the historical record. For instance, while Oscar Wilde has long been identified as a gay icon, he was married to a woman and had children by her. Thus, while he can easily be classified as bisexual, he is instead always referred to as "gay" (Meem 2010:181). A more current example of the erasure of bisexuality is found in the discussion of the film *Brokeback Mountain* (2005). The film is about two male cowboys who engage in a decades-long, on-again off-again, sexual relationship. However, both men are also married to and sexually active with their wives. The film is always referred to as a gay film, yet some argue that it is actually a film about bisexuals (Andre 2006). Whether those characters are truly bisexual or really just gay men who are passing as heterosexual through their marriages is, of course, impossible to answer. But what is obvious with these examples is that we live in a culture that fails to take bisexuality seriously (Meem 2010).

What is the significance of our cultural support for a sexual binary? Reinforcing a clear distinction between "gay" and "straight" ultimately allows heterosexuals to maintain their privileged status. Sociologists view sexuality as one of a number of status hierarchies, where groups can be dominant or subordinate, benefit from privileges or be discriminated against. In terms of sexuality, heterosexuals are privileged and sexual minorities face discrimination and inequality (see Chapter Four). The presence of bisexuals challenges this status hierarchy and those that benefit from it and supports the notion that sexuality is a social construction.

> **"**
> *"The terms heterosexual and homosexual apparently came into common use only in the first quarter of [the twentieth century]; before that time, if words are clues to concepts, people did not conceive of a social universe polarized into heteros and homos" (Katz 1995:10).*

The Invention of Heterosexuality and Homosexuality

Another piece of evidence that sexuality is a social construction is the historical emergence of the concepts of heterosexuality and homosexuality. The terms heterosexual and homosexual emerged in a particular time and place; this implies that prior to that time, the world was not divided into such categories. That does not mean that same-sex sexual behaviors were unheard of or that men and women did not engage in sexual relations with each other. Instead, it means that such behaviors did not define a person.

The concept of heterosexuality did not exist before 1892 (Katz 1995). Men and women formed sexual unions prior to then, but these unions were not referred to as heterosexual. Historian Jonathan Ned Katz (1995) refers to the emergence of the concept of heterosexuality as the "invention of heterosexuality." Prior to his work, heterosexual history had remained taken for granted, "unmarked and unremarked" on (Katz 1995:9). If something is invented in a particular time and place, it can hardly be innate, natural, and timeless, as heterosexuality is understood to be today.

The concept of heterosexuality changes in meaning over the course of the century as well. In its original usage in the 1890s, heterosexual did not refer to normal, male-female sexual relations as we understand the term today. Instead it referred to a kind of sexual deviance, specifically someone with an abnormal sexual appetite. It also referred to individuals with an abnormal attraction to both sexes. This connotation lasted until the mid-1920s among the middle class. Eventually, the term heterosexual came to refer to "normal" and "natural" sexual relations between men and women. This shift occurred as a reflection of a larger cultural emphasis on procreation: heterosexuality is "natural" simply because of its procreative potential. Homosexuality, constructed as the opposite of heterosexuality in this newly emerging sexual binary, is viewed as "unnatural" because it lacks procreative potential.

HETERONORMATIVITY Thus, a cultural ideology known as the procreative imperative paved the way for heterosexuality to become normative throughout the Western world. Previously we discussed the search for a "gay gene." This may cause us to pause and question why the research quest is not for a "straight gene." This is evidence of what social scientists refer to as *heteronormativity*, the idea that heterosexuality is the natural, normal, inevitable, and preferred sexual orientation; it confers privilege on those who conform to the societal norm (Warner 1991). Heterosexuality became synonymous with "sexually normal" by the late nineteenth and early twentieth centuries (Blank 2012). Perhaps surprisingly, heteronormativity even influences gay and lesbian activism, for instance, in the pursuit of the right to marry and adopt children (Schippers 2016). Essentially, gay activists pursuing these agendas are making the case that they are "normal," just like heterosexuals. There are a number of problematic manifestations of heteronormativity. First, it justifies our cultural hatred and fear of homosexuals. Anyone who deviates from the societal norm of heteronormativity risks facing discrimination. Second, it contributes to the invisibility of sexual minorities in media and popular culture (Chapter Six). Finally, it helps perpetuate heterosexual privilege and discrimination against sexual minorities.

COMPULSORY HETEROSEXUALITY An extreme form of heteronormativity is the idea of *compulsory heterosexuality*, a concept first introduced by feminist Adrienne Rich (1980), who argues that women are coerced into heterosexuality and into viewing coupling with men as the only relationship option available to them. Coming from a specifically lesbian feminist point of view, she argues that heterosexuality is not innate to human beings. To use Rich's own words, she questions "how and why women's choice of women as passionate comrades, life partners, co-workers, lovers, community has been crushed, invalidated, forced into hiding and disguise" (Rich 1980:229).

While "coerced" may appear to be a strong term, Rich argues convincingly that a barrage of political, cultural, and legal forces coalesce to limit women's sexual and coupling options. In previous eras or in other cultures, men have had the power to deny women their sexuality through the use of clitoridectomy, chastity belts, the death penalty for female adultery, incarceration in psychiatric facilities for lesbian sexuality, among other punishments. Men force their sexuality on women through rape and sexual assault, but also through the idealization of heterosexuality in literature, advertising, and the media. Women are sometimes coerced into heterosexuality through their limited economic opportunities, which too often make them economically reliant upon men for their survival. Ultimately, male control operates along a broad continuum ranging from violence to control of consciousness, resulting in a culture of compulsory heterosexuality in which men primarily benefit (Rich 1980).

THE INVENTION OF HOMOSEXUALITY Just as heterosexuality is invented in a particular time and place, its opposing concept, homosexuality, is also an invention. The first person to use the term heterosexual, Dr. James Kiernan, is also the first person to use the term homosexual. He defines homosexuals as gender benders, people who rebel against traditional notions of masculinity and femininity. While heterosexuals are viewed by Kiernan as sexual deviants, homosexuals are gender deviants. Homosexuality develops in opposition to heterosexuality. As Jonathan Katz explains, "This inaugurated a hundred-year tradition in which the abnormal and the homosexual were posed as riddle, the normal and the heterosexual were assumed" (1995:55). The science of homosexuality will be explored in more detail in Chapter Two.

Importantly, the emergence of the "heterosexual" and the "homosexual" does more than just place people in categories based on their sexual behaviors. It creates a hierarchy where members of one group are granted favorable status and the other is stigmatized as deviant (see Chapter Four). The emergence of the heterosexual and the homosexual also contribute to the creation of *sexual identities*. For the first time in history, people begin to define themselves and understand themselves in terms of their sexual desires and behaviors. French social theorist Michele Foucault (1978) argues that the creation of gay identities contributes to the emergence of gay and lesbian communities, which eventually led to the gay liberation movement. For Foucault, the emergence of sexual identities is both liberating and constraining, an issue we will explore in more detail in Chapter Two.

The Gendered Construction of Sexuality

One of the most obvious ways sexuality is socially constructed is through gender. While gender will be explored in much greater detail in Chapter Three, here we identify its basic role in understanding sexuality. *Gender* refers to socially created expectations about behaviors associated with one's sex. People defined as "men" are expected to be masculine, while those defined as "women" are expected to conform to norms of femininity. Historically, definitions of homosexuality centered on gender. German physician Karl Westphal uses the term *invert* to describe people with contrary sexual feelings, or sexual feelings toward people of the same sex. He describes these men as "effeminate" and the women as "mannish." This description reveals how sexuality is often understood and explained through the lens of gender.

Expectations surrounding sexual desires, sexual behaviors, and sexual satisfaction are socially created and differ for men and women, as our previous discussion of variation in orgasms and virginity shows. Gendered expectations are associated with the roles we play in our intimate and sexual relationships. In earlier eras, it was accepted knowledge within the medical community that women biologically lacked sexual desire. From today's perspective, we can see this expectation as constructed around gendered ideals of womanhood and femininity, but it is fair to consider how this belief impacts women's actual desire for and experience of sex (see Chapter Three).

Sexual Socialization

Sexual socialization refers to the process by which we learn, through interaction with others, sexual knowledge, attitudes, norms, and expectations associated with sexuality, sexual behaviors, and sexual relationships. The societal belief that men have more sexual urges than women creates a ***sexual double standard***, which refers to greater sexual permissiveness for men and more sexual restrictions for women (Greene and Faulkner 2005; Muehlenhard et al. 2003). This double standard generally prohibits premarital or promiscuous sex outside of love relationships for women, while it encourages similar behaviors for men.

Sociologists Gagnon and Simon (1973) brought the first real sociological analysis to the study of sexuality with the idea of ***sexual scripts***, which emphasize the significance of the meanings people assign to sexual desires and encounters. There are three levels of meaning people use to create their sexual scripts: cultural and historical scenarios, interpersonal experiences, and intrapsychic interactions. We can think of a script as a guide, a blueprint to help us make sense of the sexual. Thus, culture, history, experiences, and self-reflexive interactions all contribute to the role we see ourselves playing in our own sexual desires, interactions, and behaviors. Sexual scripts are learned rather than innate, a major distinction from the Freudian perspective on sexuality. An example of a traditional sexual script is that men should be sexual aggressors and women should be sexually passive.

SEXUAL REVOLUTIONS

Studying sexuality sociologically requires we take context into account. Thus, some eras of history are more significant to the study of sexuality than others. The late nineteenth century, for instance, is known as the Victorian Era, specifically in Great Britain and the United States. In this period of relative sexual repression, doctors believed sexual desire in women was pathological, and masturbation could lead to criminality. The remnants of such attitudes are still with us today, most notably in the sexual double standard. While sexual repression was the dominant sexual ideology of the Victorian Era, counter-ideologies simultaneously existed. For instance, a *free love*, or *sex love,* movement began in the late nineteenth century that espoused the belief that people should have the right to have sex with someone they love, whether or not they are married, and advocated for women to have the same sexual rights as men (Mann 2012). Many early U.S. feminists were free love advocates, primarily because they viewed marriage as a form of servitude for women. Such ideas were groundbreaking for women at the time, since any woman who engaged in a sexual relationship outside of marriage was considered a prostitute (Mann 2012).

Sexual revolutions are an integral part of larger social revolutions, as "the development of new sexual values, scripts, policies, and behaviors is related to all other aspects of social change" (Kon 1995:2). The decades during the 1960s and 1970s in the United States are often referred to as a period of ***sexual revolution***, a period of dramatic social change in sexual norms, mores, and attitudes. In this era there was an increased emphasis on sexual liberation, the introduction of technologies to facilitate sexual liberation, evidence of changing sexual behaviors, as well as a "new candor in American culture, especially the sudden acceptance of nudity in film and on the stage" (Allyn 2000:5). The introduction of the birth control pill in 1960 is an example of a technology that contributed to this sexual revolution. Premarital sex became increasingly normative. Gays and lesbians felt increasingly free to publicly identify as gay. Hippies embraced the phrase "make love, not war" to represent the changing cultural values. In schools that offered sex education courses, they were radically redesigned to avoid scare and fear tactics and instead to approach the subject matter from a rational standpoint (Allyn 2000).

By the late 1970s, a backlash against this culture of sexual permissiveness emerged. Thus, it is imperative to explore the social and cultural context that facilitated the emergence of the sexual revolution during the 1960s and '70s. Sexual revolutions are a form of resistance to sexual repression, particularly resistance to so-called sexual deviance. For example, during the sexually repressed 1940s and 1950s in the United States, "One could go to jail for publishing the 'wrong' book or distributing contraceptive devices to the 'wrong' person, or saying the 'wrong' word aloud in a public place" (Allyn 2000:6).

To understand the social and cultural context that contributes to such dramatic changes in sexual behaviors and understandings, it is helpful to look at different eras also known as sexual revolutions. The United States in the 1920s, for instance, was a period some scholars refer to as our first sexual revolution. During this period in U.S. history, significant changes for women took place in the home, workplace, education, and politics. The concept of the "new woman" was born, which described unmarried women stepping outside of traditional gender roles, becoming icons of changing norms and attitudes about women in society.

BOX 1.1

GLOBAL/TRANSNATIONAL PERSPECTIVES ON SEXUALITY:
THE SEXUAL REVOLUTION IN RUSSIA

The Bolshevik Revolution of 1917 was considered to be one of the most radical revolutions in world history. It sought to abolish all inequality and to transform human nature, specifically by creating a "socialist personality—rational, collectivist, disciplined, and socially oriented" (Kon 1995:2). Sexuality was perceived as an obstacle to such a personality, as it is irrational, individualistic, and undisciplined. By the 1930s, such total control over the personality of citizens involved attempts at desexualizing public and private life, creating a regime of severe sexual repression and even a climate of **sexophobia**, where all sexual activity was considered indecent and unmentionable (Kon 1995). Sex education in schools was nonexistent as was academic sex research. A conspiracy of silence surrounded birth control, promiscuity, homosexuality, infidelity, and sexually transmitted diseases. Criminal penalties for homosexuality were implemented. Erotic art and literature were eradicated. Vladimir Lenin, Marxist leader of the Russian Revolution, described sex and revolution as incompatible: "In the age of revolution, that [sex] is bad, very bad. . . . The revolution demands concentration. . . . It cannot tolerate orgiastic conditions. . . . Dissoluteness in sexual life is bourgeois, is a phenomenon of decay" (Mann 2012:122). Essentially, Soviet society attempted to be asexual from the early 1930s until the beginning of the end of the Soviet Union in the late 1980s (Kon 1995). In fact, "to call the Soviet government puritanical was a gross misstatement; it was afflicted by a paralyzing fear of love and eroticism" (Carleton 2005:1).

Unsurprisingly, sexual freedom became one of the most significant symbols of social liberation (Kon 1995). However, this liberalization came about as a "burst of licentiousness" in a society that lacked an erotic culture, which resulted in many dysfunctional developments (Schwirtz 2010). In Russia, there was an abundance of pornography and increasing numbers of sex shops, yet no sex education in schools. The most common form of birth control was abortion, sexually transmitted diseases were rising rapidly, sexual violence was increasing, and prostitution was one of the most prestigious occupations for women (Kon 1995). While the post-Soviet climate was a dramatically different sexual culture than the Soviet era, some argue that there had been no real sexual revolution in Russia. A sexual shame still lingered from the sexophobic Soviet era. In fact, Russian sexologist Sergei Agarkov described the changes as a sexual evolution rather than a sexual revolution, with people in post-Soviet Russia slowly becoming more comfortable with sex and sexuality (Schwirtz 2010).

Sexual connotations were associated with this liberated "new woman." She rebelled against her mother's generation who still clung to outdated and prudish Victorian Era sexual mores of restraint and repression and began adopting Freudian ideas of sex as pleasurable. The "new woman" included both women on the fringes of society, such as prostitutes, radicals, artists, and lesbians, as well as working- and middle-class women who began exploring their sexuality. There was an increasing acceptance of the idea that women had sexual desires and a questioning of the importance of marriage. Birth control pioneers of this time, such as Margaret Sanger, sought to educate and empower women with the knowledge of how to have sex without fear of pregnancy. Although sexual norms were recast during this revolutionary decade, lesbians still suffered abuse, the sexual double standard persisted, and eventually most "new women" gave up on their youthful ideas and married men.

During this same era, a sexual revolution was underway in Germany as well. There was a radical remaking of sexual norms during the Weimar Republic (1918–1933; Marhoefer 2011). Clinics across Germany opened and began distributing information about birth control and abortion; there was an embrace of sexual liberation; female prostitution was decriminalized; the field of sexology thrived; and the law against male homosexuality known as Paragraph 175 was nearly repealed (see Chapter Four). This movement was cut short by the political turmoil and the rise of the Nazi Party in Germany during the 1930s.

While there was a backlash against the sexual revolution of the 1960s and '70s, it still resulted in several significant cultural changes. First, it destigmatized birth control. Sociologists define **stigma** as an attribute that is deeply discrediting that challenges one's identity (Goffman 1963). Prior to the introduction of the birth control pill, women who used any method of birth control were stigmatized as sexually promiscuous. Since the 1970s, this has changed; the idea that women are sexual beings is less likely to be stigmatized. Abortion is still legal (albeit, under considerable attack by opponents). Second, the sexual revolution weakened the sexual double standard in which the rules about appropriate sexual behavior differ for men and women. Third, it encouraged media acceptance of premarital sex, which means that media representations of cultural behaviors began to more closely mirror actual cultural norms.

SEXUAL RELATIONSHIPS: BEYOND MONOGAMY

Sociologist Steven Seidman (2015) questions whether there really was a sexual revolution in the United States in the 1960s and '70s. While there have indeed been dramatic changes, he argues that some fundamental aspects of American sexual culture remain intact; primarily, monogamous marriage and a cultural emphasis on heterosexual romance. This is referred to as **mononormativity**, the dominant assumption of the normalness and naturalness of monogamy. As sociologist Mimi Schippers (2016) explains, culture teaches us that in order to achieve loving relationships and emotional intimacy, we must be monogamous. Even the passage of marriage equality reinforces monogamy as the dominant, accepted relationship form, albeit for same-sex couples. In this section, we discuss consensual nonmonogamous relationships.

Consensual nonmonogamous relationships need to be distinguished from infidelity, which is when both parties have not agreed to be in a nonmonogamous relationship. Consensual nonmonogamous relationships can take a variety of forms. **Polyamory** refers to people who choose multiple relationships in which participants are sexually and emotionally bound to one another. Open relationships, sometimes referred to as swinging, can involve strictly sexual relationships with other people, without the emotional bonds, and can involve one or both members of a couple (Adam 2006; Barker and Langridge

2015; Jenks 1998). Importantly, polyamorous relationships place an emphasis on gender equality, which differentiates these relationships from polygamy, which tends to be male-dominated (Cascais and Cardoso 2012; Easton and Hardy 2009; Schipper 2016; Sheff 2013; Taormino 2008).

Many who engage in nonmonogamy do so as an explicit critique of mononormativity. They argue that there is nothing natural about monogamy; and, indeed, it is rare among animals and relatively rare among human cultures. Research finds nonmonogamy to be normative among some gay male couples (Adam 2006; Blumstein and Schwartz 1983; Coelho 2011). Some researchers point out that while we have a cultural commitment to monogamy, our behavior is often contradictory. In other words, infidelity is commonplace (Duncombe et al. 2004). Others argue that monogamy is an inherently patriarchal tradition and that women, in particular, benefit from nonmonogamy since it helps protect them from patriarchal oppression (Jackson and Scott 2004). Participants identify some of the benefits associated with nonmonogamy: first, it is a more honest way of relating compared to secret infidelities (Phillips 2010). Second, it is viewed as superior to monogamy in the freedom it allows each participant and the level of communication between the partners (Ho 2006).

Couples who choose nonmonogamy face considerable obstacles. For instance, family and friends often choose not to acknowledge the relationship or one of the partners in the relationship, new partners are perceived as threatening to the existing relationship by outsiders, there is a lack of social support for such relationships, and people in nonmonogamous relationships are falsely assumed to be promiscuous (Barker 2005; Mint 2004; Schippers 2016).

SEXUAL INVISIBILITY

For most of the twentieth century, homosexuals were invisible. While today their visibility is less of an issue, there are still aspects of sexuality that our culture deems unacceptable and thus tend toward invisibility. We have already discussed the invisibility of bisexuality in our culture. In this section, we discuss another example of sexual invisibility: asexuality. Despite our cultural progress on sexuality issues, we still have "blinders on" when it comes to certain aspects of human sexuality.

> "Homosexuals were invisible. They fought in wars, but no one knew; they were everywhere, but no one was aware of them. They were "closeted" or hid their identity for fear of losing their jobs and their families. Homosexuals lived through most of the twentieth century with a hidden identity that imbued their lives with shame and fear" (Seidman 2004:246).

Scientific research has only recently begun to study asexuality, the lack of sexual attraction or indifference to sexual activity. Asexuality was historically viewed as a disorder requiring treatment. Today activists are working to get it accepted as a valid sexual orientation, rather than a disorder, and are addressing visibility and needs for public acceptance (Bogaert 2006; Travis 2007). One such group is known as the Asexuality Visibility and Education Network (AVEN). Despite the simplicity of the definition of asexuality, someone who does not experience sexual attraction, there is actually considerable diversity among people who identify as asexual (Carrigan 2015). Many asexuals, for instance, make a distinction between romance and sex, rather than viewing the latter as the culmination of the former. Some asexuals are sex positive, viewing sex as positive, despite the fact that they have no sexual desire themselves. Others are sex-averse, deeply troubled by both the idea and the act of sex (Carrigan 2015).

SEXUAL PLEASURE

While today we have no trouble understanding sex as pleasurable, this interpretation has not always been the dominant cultural understanding of sexuality. Providing more evidence that sexuality is socially constructed, we can see that in different historical eras, sexual relations served varying purposes. For instance, during the Victorian era, the human sex instinct was viewed as dangerous. Thus, sexual relations were not only confined to marriage but were thought to be for procreative purposes only. This understanding shifts in the early twentieth century, as social scientists, psychologists, psychiatrists, sexologists, and other experts began stepping forward as the authoritative voices on sexuality. These experts shift the discourse surrounding sexuality to one that emphasizes good sexual relations as the foundation for a good marriage (Seidman 2015). It is Freud who shifts our cultural understandings of sex from a procreative ethic to a pleasure ethic (see Chapter Two).

SEXUALITY ACROSS THE LIFE COURSE

While we live in a culture that emphasizes the fixed nature of sexuality, we spent much of this chapter exploring its socially constructed nature and the considerable sexual diversity that exists. We explored the changing nature of sexuality across genders, cross-culturally, and historically. In this section, we extend that analysis to explore the ways sexuality varies across the life course. To understand sexuality across the life span requires we pay attention to both the physiology of sexuality as well as the social construction of sexuality.

Childhood Sexuality

We live in a culture that is not comfortable with the idea of childhood sexuality. In fact, we link notions of childhood innocence to sexuality; and, by extension, when children experience sexual abuse, we describe them as "losing their innocence" or "losing their childhood." We assume children do not and should not know anything about sexuality. Freud is one of the first to challenge the idea of the asexual child (see Chapter Two).

Research on child sexuality generally involves interviews with caregivers (most often mothers) concerning sexual behaviors they observe in their children. This research makes it abundantly clear that children are sexual beings. Both girls and boys engage in what appear to be pleasurable behaviors including genital stimulation, penile erection, and pelvic thrusting as early as infancy (Yang et al. 2005). A wide range of sexual behaviors in children are identified including touching one's own genitals, touching other children's genitals, and masturbating. Numerous studies have concluded that a "substantial proportion" of boys and girls experience their first orgasm before puberty (Crooks and Baur 2011; Janssen 2007). It is risky to assume that childhood sexuality carries the same meanings as adult sexuality, but researchers do believe these are indicators of sexuality in children (G. Ryan 2000; Thanasiu 2004).

Adolescent Sexuality

The physiological changes we go through during adolescence makes it a period in which adults understand children as shifting from an asexual childhood to a sexual adulthood. During this stage of life, young people enter puberty, a period of rapid physical changes, including increasing hormone levels and the development of secondary sex characteristics such as breasts and pubic hair, among others. Menstruation begins in girls. For boys, puberty provides them with the ability to ejaculate, usually around the age of 13, with the initial appearance of sperm about a year later (Crooks and Baur 2011; Janssen 2007; Wheeler 1991).

With these physical changes comes an increase in intimate relationships and sexual behaviors. Masturbation increases in frequency, with rates for females lower than rates among males (Leitenberg, Detzer, and Srebnick 1993). Young people engage in noncoital sex, which refers to a wide range of erotic behaviors that do not involve intercourse such as kissing, manual stimulation, or oral sex. Research finds that rates of oral sex have increased dramatically among teenagers (Brady and Halpern-Felsher 2007; Halpern-Felsher et al. 2006). But the practice of oral sex is gendered. Research finds that adolescent girls are expected to give oral sex and that it can be the path to popularity for them, but boys rarely reciprocate (Orenstein 2016). The preference for oral sex among teenagers is due to multiple reasons. First is the belief that it allows them to engage in sexual behaviors without the health risks. Unfortunately, this is a misunderstanding. While it can help young people avoid pregnancy, it does not reduce transmission rates of sexually transmitted infections, since most sexually transmitted infections can be passed through oral, anal, and genital contact (see Chapter Ten). Second, young people prefer oral sex to traditional intercourse because many believe it maintains their virginity. As we discussed previously in this chapter, our understandings of virginity are social constructions (Crooks and Baur 2011).

In addition to the increase in noncoital sexual behaviors, there has been a dramatic increase in rates of sexual intercourse among American adolescents between the 1950s and the 1970s, with the numbers leveling off since this period. Research finds this varies by race/ethnicity. African American teenagers are more likely to engage in sexual intercourse than either Latino or white teens (Centers for Disease Control 2008). Age at first sexual intercourse is younger for African Americans than for white and Latino adolescents. These differences may be an outcome of poverty since poverty is strongly linked to early sexual activity, and poverty rates are higher among African Americans than among whites. However, Latinos are disproportionately impoverished, which means their poverty rates do not help to explain their age at first sexual intercourse.

> **"Even the most comprehensive sex education classes stick with a woman's internal parts. . . . Where is the discussion of girls' sexual development? When do we talk to girls about desire and pleasure? When do we explain the miraculous nuances of their anatomy? When do we address exploration, self-knowledge? No wonder boys' physical needs seem inevitable to teens while girls' are, at best, optional" (Orenstein 2016:62).**

In addition to variation in adolescent sexuality by race/ethnicity we find that it varies along gender lines as well. The sexual double standard is most forcefully enforced against adolescent girls. Girls' sexual coming-of-age requires them to navigate a highly sexualized culture that tells them they need to be simultaneously sexy and virginal. Today, girls are having sex at younger ages than previous generations, yet for many, their first sexual experiences are not completely voluntary and instead are coerced (Erdmans and Black 2015; Gullette 2011; Orenstein 2016). Research finds that there is a "missing discourse of desire" among adolescent girls (Fine 1988). A discussion of girls' sexual desire is problematically absent from sex education curricula, while the sexual desires of boys are acknowledged (Fine 1988; Tolman 1991, 1994). Girls do not learn to recognize or acknowledge their own sexual desires and instead are taught that boys' sexual desire is more important. Adolescent girls' then interpret their own sexual desires as troubling; they inherit the cultural message that silences their sexual desires and can even lead to disassociation from their bodies (Tolman 1994).

LGBTQ ADOLESCENT SEXUALITY In our heterocentric culture, sexual and romantic relationships are defined along heterosexual lines that leave LGBTQ youth unable to define themselves as sexual beings. As we have already explored, our cultural understandings of virginity are heterocentric. Establishing intimate relationships and engaging in sexual experimentation is important for all adolescents, including LGBTQ youth. Research finds that establishing an intimate relationship helps LGBTQ adolescents find self-acceptance (Silverstein 1981). Establishing a same-sex relationship while still in high school is especially difficult for LGBTQ youth since many fear harassment from their classmates, especially if they are not already out (Sears 1991). Most young people are still in the closet, so it is hard to know who is even a potential partner, a problem straight youth do not have. When LGBTQ youth do have intimate relationships, they are often hidden; thus, they are not celebrated and supported in the same way that relationships involving straight youths are (Savin-Williams 2015). Interestingly, our culture is more accepting of strictly sexual relationships versus romantic relationships among same-sex adolescents. Ultimately, all of this means that sexual minority youth feel isolated and socially excluded at a very vulnerable point in their lives (Savin-Williams 2015).

NOT MY CHILD: PARENTAL VIEWS ON ADOLESCENT SEXUALITY Despite clear evidence of teenage sexual activity, research by Sinikka Elliott (2012) finds that most parents do not believe their children are sexually active. They believe other children are sexual, some even hypersexual, yet they insist their own children are sexually naïve and, thus, asexual. While parents of teenagers view adults as potential threats to their children's sexuality, they also view other teens as sexually active and, thus, as threats to their child. The image of the highly sexual teen is highly raced, classed, and gendered. African American boys' behavior is perceived by many parents as insidious and adult-like (Ferguson 2000). Such stereotypical perceptions of black men as hypersexual and a threat to white women have a long history in the United States. Black and Latina girls are routinely portrayed as sexually opportunistic (Fields 2005; Bettie 2003; Collins 2000, 2004). Young people from poor families are described as not sharing the same values associated with sexuality as their middle-class peers. Parents often describe their sons' female peers as hypersexual and a threat to their less mature sons, despite the fact that research finds girls report feeling pressured by boys to have sex before they are ready. Perhaps unsurprisingly, parents of teenage girls view boys as sexual aggressors and as threats to their daughters (Elliott 2012).

Sexuality and the Aged

Media images portray sexuality as the sole purview of young adults. We are rarely exposed to images of sexually active senior citizens, which results in a warped understanding of sexuality. Even sex research has historically neglected aging (Levy 1994). Despite such cultural and academic neglect, sexuality can be enjoyed throughout the life course. Pharmaceutical companies trafficking in drugs like Viagra and Addyi (known as the "female Viagra") send a mixed message (see Chapter Ten). The first unmistakable message is that aging results in inevitable sexual dysfunction. For men this takes the form of erectile dysfunction while for women it takes the form of an abnormally low sex drive. The second message being sent is that seniors have a right to remain sexually active; that geriatric sex is not a contradiction in terms. Despite this message, too often our cultural narrative portrays youth sex as spectacular and sexuality among the aged as, at best, rare. According to Margaret Gullette (2011), we need to get away from this idea of a glory/

Despite the lack of media images of sexually active senior citizens, sexuality can be enjoyed across the life course.
Source: istockphoto.com/Fang Xia Nuo.

"Decline is taught as a physiological fact in medical settings, textbooks, and feature articles on sex, but when researchers ask new questions of women, decline becomes an artifact of youth bias and assuming that males are the model" (Gullette 2011:138).

decay binary associated with sexuality over the life course and embrace a positive aging story. Research by the Association of Reproductive Health Professionals finds that while desire and sexual frequency decreases with age, sexual satisfaction remains constant from the fifties until the seventies (Gullette 2011).

Our images of sexuality among seniors are gendered—with the assumption being that women lose interest in sex, especially once they are postmenopausal. In other words, the sexual double standard continues into our senior years. Women's sexual attractiveness is perceived as declining as she ages whereas aging men capitalize on a "distinguished" appearance. A 1990 study titled the Midlife Women's Health Survey found that 60 percent of women had not experienced any change in their sexual responsiveness after menopause, while nine percent claim to enjoy sex even more than they did when they were young (Gullette 2011). Importantly, part of having a healthy sex life in one's senior years involves overcoming one's own ageism in order "to consider same-age people and their behaviors sexy" (Gullette 2011:138). A second factor determining women's sexual enjoyment during their senior years involves their empowerment as they age; women become sexual subjects rather than objects (Travis and White 2000). Another variable that determines women's sexual satisfaction in her later years is her overall marital satisfaction (DeLamater et al. 2008).

Some physiological changes do occur as we age that can influence, and potentially interrupt, a healthy sex life (see Chapter Ten). Some men find they struggle to get an erection while others are slower to climax. Many women struggle with vaginal dryness associated with menopause. Some medications can reduce libido. Aging often results in less mobility and flexibility. These changes require adjusting expectations surrounding sex, the necessity of new sexual scripts, relearning effective techniques, and focusing less on orgasm and more on cuddling and flirting (Gullette 2011; Levy 1994).

Like any group of people, there is great variation in the sex lives of the aged. Some research finds gay men report higher satisfaction with their sex lives as they age, despite the fact that frequency of sex declines (Kimmel 1980). One issue sexually active seniors, like sexually active members of any age group, are confronted with are sexually transmitted infections (STIs; see Chapter Ten). Research finds rising incidences of HIV/AIDS among this group according to the Centers for Disease Control and Prevention ("HIV among People Aged . . . ." 2016). For most seniors, being concerned about sexually transmitted infections is new and not something they likely found themselves concerned with during earlier stages of their life when they were more likely to be in a monogamous marriage. It is essential for social scientists who study sexuality not to ignore sexuality among the aged, as this is a growing population. Additionally, the first cohort of the Baby Boom generation (1946–1964) is currently entering their retirement years. This is the cohort that lived through the sexual revolution of the 1960s and '70s, and thus, they are likely to alter our understandings of sexuality and aging in the same way they altered every stage of the life course.

SEXUALIZING RACIAL/ETHNIC MINORITIES

This text takes *intersectionality* into account whenever possible; this means we are attuned to intersecting forms of oppression such as the ways race, class, gender, and sexual orientation intersect, influence, and interact with one another, creating new and unique forms of oppression (Crenshaw 1989). As sociologist Joane Nagel states, "sex matters in ethnic relations, and . . . sexual matters insinuate themselves into all things racial, ethnic, and national" (2003:1).

Some research finds there are a larger percentage of racial/ethnic minorities who identify as LGBTQ than whites. Specifically, a 2012 Gallup Poll found that 4.6 percent of African Americans, 4.0 percent of Latinos, and 4.3 percent of Asian Americans identify as LGBTQ, while only 3.2 percent of white Americans so identify (Gates and Newport 2012; Meyer 2015). Despite this, homosexuality is linked with whiteness. This is because LGBTQ people of color are less visible in the media than white sexual minorities. But it also has to do with the sexualized stereotypes associated with racial/ethnic minority groups in this country. Essentially, by stereotyping people of color as excessively heterosexual, it distances them from homosexuality in the minds of many (Meyer 2015).

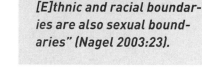

"Sex is the sometimes silent message contained in racial slurs, ethnic stereotypes, national imaginings, and international relations. . . . [E]thnic and racial boundaries are also sexual boundaries" (Nagel 2003:23).

We do not see much variation in sexual attitudes and behaviors between racial/ethnic groups in the current era. In fact, research finds that blacks are more sexually liberal on some measures and more conservative on others compared to whites, but not enough to make any clear distinctions (Staples 2006). However, we do see some differences in sexual outcomes. For instance, African Americans suffer disproportionately from HIV/AIDS, and racial/ethnic minorities have higher rates of teen pregnancy than non-Hispanic whites (see Chapters Nine and Ten). Asian Americans tend to be more reluctant to obtain sexual and reproductive health care (Okasaki 2002). So, while sexual behaviors between racial/ethnic groups tend not to vary, the outcomes of sexual behaviors often do.

Racial/ethnic minority group members in the United States must negotiate their identities, particularly their sexual identities, through a maze of demeaning and sometimes contradictory sexual stereotypes. **Stereotypes** refer to "exaggerated and/or oversimplified portrayals of an entire group of people based upon misinformation and mischaracterizations" (Fitzgerald 2014:114). Stereotypes reflect the dominant group's efforts at maintaining the subordination of minority groups. Stereotypes work to portray a racial/ethnic minority group as deviant, "other," and as potentially threatening to the dominant group. Stereotypes can also negatively affect the identity of those being targeted. Racial/ethnic minority group members may believe dominant group stereotypes about them and, in some cases, even live up to such stereotypes. While these are only stereotypes, their repetition throughout popular culture provides them with legitimacy. Public policies also often reflect these mischaracterizations.

African American men are portrayed as hypersexual, while black women struggle with often contradictory stereotypes that are sexual in nature: mammies, matriarchs, welfare recipients, and the Jezebel (Collins 1991). We can clearly see how social policies reflect sexual stereotypes of black women. The Jezebel, for instance, is a long-standing stereotype associated with black women that has been with us since slavery. A jezebel is a whore, or a sexually aggressive woman. It functions to justify widespread sexual assaults of slave women by white men. While the law protected white women from rape, it did not protect black women during slavery or the Jim Crow era. The welfare mother is portrayed as a woman with low morals and uncontrolled sexuality, which results in her poverty (Collins 1991). Welfare provisions in many states prohibit a woman receiving welfare from having another child while on welfare. Underlying this provision are assumptions about the highly sexual nature and low moral character of poor women who need government assistance. These stereotypes have also justified efforts to control the fertility of black women, through a history of involuntary sterilizations, among other efforts (Roberts 1997; Chapter Nine).

The image of black men as hypersexual, animalistic, sexually immoral, and threatening is deeply rooted in American culture. After slavery ended, American literature and folklore were flooded with images of sexually promiscuous black men as threats to white women (Staples 2006). These became justifications for lynching and the criminalization of black men that remains with us today. These kinds of arguments continue to find resonance with some audiences. Scholar J. Philippe Rushton (1988), for instance, makes the dubious claim that black promiscuity is genetically programmed. However, most scholars do not accept this argument—human behaviors are a complex interaction between genetics and the environment. As we discussed earlier, no genetic link to sexuality has been discovered.

Latinos/as, Asian Americans, and Native Americans face similar sexual stereotypes as African Americans. Latino males are stereotyped as hypersexual, aggressive, and "macho." Another stereotype is that of the "Latino lover" who is seen as more sexually sophisticated and, thus, a threat to white women. Latina portrayals follow a virgin/whore dichotomy: either she is a passive, submissive virgin or she is a sexually aggressive whore (Asencio and Acosta 2010).

Sociologist Rosalind Chou (2012) argues that Asian American sexuality is socially constructed to maintain white male dominance. Asian American women are stereotyped as exotic and eager to please men sexually, specifically white men, yet are also passive and subordinate. Other images of Asian women follow a "dragon lady" script: she is seductive and desirable, but untrustworthy. These stereotypes inform the earliest immigration restrictions in this country. In 1875, the Page Act was passed that excluded "undesirables" from immigrating here. This ban was directed mostly at Asian, and more specifically Chinese, women due to the assumption that they were all prostitutes. During this same era, Chinese men were assumed to be a sexual threat against white women, which justified the implementation of antimiscegenation laws that made interracial marriage between Chinese and whites illegal. Instead of being stereotyped as hypersexual as African American and Latino men are today, Asian American males are portrayed as weak and effeminate, essentially; they are emasculated, as hyposexual, or even asexual (Chou 2012).

For both Latinos and Asian Americans, their immigrant status versus the extent of their assimilation can influence their sexual attitudes and behaviors. Since roughly 39 percent of Latinos are foreign born, this is significant (Asencio and Acosta 2010). Research finds differences in attitudes toward sexuality between Asian American and non-Asian adolescents. For instance, Asian American adolescents tend to hold more conservative attitudes and initiate first sexual activity at a later age than non-Asian American adolescents (Okazaki 2002). The more assimilated Asian Americans are, the more their behaviors start to mirror those of white Americans.

Sexual stereotypes of Native Americans are in many ways similar. For many decades, whites viewed Native Americans as savages and Native women as promiscuous and sexually available to white men. This later morphed into an image of Native women as "dirty little squaws" who slept with married white men, thus threatening white women and their families (D'Emilio and Freedman 2012).

SEXUAL MINORITIES BEYOND LGBTQ

This text operates on the assumption that there is a ***sexual hierarchy*** where the dominant group, heterosexuals, have privileges while subordinate groups, whom we can think of broadly as nonheterosexuals, such as lesbians, gay men, bisexuals, transgender, and queer people face discrimination and inequality (see Chapter Four). The sexual hierarchy is more expansive than this, however. Feminist anthropologist Gayle S. Rubin argues that there is an imaginary line between "good" and "bad" sex and that certain behaviors are at the "top of the erotic pyramid" in that they are the most valued and approved sex acts, while other acts are at the bottom and are disapproved of and often legally sanctioned (1993:11). She uses the analogy of a "charmed circle," in which sexual behaviors that are socially approved of, such as sex for reproduction between heterosexual married couples, are inside the circle and all other sexual behaviors fall outside the circle. In terms of a sexual hierarchy, below the most approved sexual behaviors are unmarried monogamous heterosexual couples, followed by most other heterosexuals. Next on the hierarchy are major areas of contestation, or sex acts that are on the verge of respectability. Here we find long-term, stable, lesbian and gay couples. Sexual activities that fall under the "bad" category include sadomasochism (S/M), fetishism, and cross-generational sex.

Rubin (1993) points out that "most of the discourses on sex be they religious, psychiatric, popular, or political, delimit a very small portion of human sexual capacity as sanctifiable, safe, healthy, mature, legal, or politically correct" (p. 14).

BDSM is a broad term that refers to sexual practices that involve bondage and discipline, dominance and submission, or sadism and masochism, none of which are new sexual predilections. Sexologists during the late 1800s used the terms sadism and masochism to describe some of these behaviors, and Freud put the terms together under the label of sadomasochism (Langdridge 2011). *Sadomasochism* refers to sexual behaviors that involve bondage, humiliation, and infliction or receipt of pain. Historically, these behaviors were considered sick and, thus, required treatment. This medicalization is controversial since sadomasochism is consensual sexual behavior. Today, there is increasing acceptance of this activity. Sadomasochists form their own sexual subcultures of people who engage in similar practices. It is periodically portrayed in film, most recently in the popular *Fifty Shades of Grey* (2015).

Within S/M activities, practitioners establish rules summarized in the phrase "safe, sane, and consensual." Participants agree on a "safe word" before engaging. More than one "safe word" can be created as code words for "stop" or "slow down." Consent is also continually negotiated throughout the sexual encounter, not just at the beginning. The commitment to consent goes so far as to sometimes include verbal or written contracts between participants (Langdridge and Butt 2004). Sometimes participants engage in long term S/M relationships and sometimes participants have never met before they encounter one another at S/M clubs (Langdridge 2011).

Fetishism refers to people who are sexually attracted to objects, situations, or body parts that are not generally viewed as sexual, such as the foot. There is nothing new about this sexual predilection either, as the term originated in the late 1800s. Similarly to S/M, fetishism has faced a long history of medicalization, where the behavior is defined as sick and in need of medical treatment. Some fetishes are considered problematic. For instance, if individuals cannot obtain sexual satisfaction without their fetish, it is considered pathological. If an individual fetishizes a physical disability or skin color of another person, that is potentially problematic due to differential power relations in our society between the able-bodied and the disabled and between people of color and whites (Gerschick 2011; Kong 2002). Interestingly, fetishists are almost always male.

CONCLUSION

Sociologists take a unique approach to the study of sexuality, beginning with the assumption that sexuality is a social construction rather than something that is biologically innate. Research has not found a "gay gene" and even if a genetic link to sexuality were someday to be discovered, that would not negate the vast influence culture has on sexuality.

Evidence of the social construction of sexuality includes the presence of bisexuals and their inability to fit into our binary system of heterosexual or homosexual; the emergence of homosexuality and heterosexuality as concepts; and the gendered nature of our sexual socialization. For sociologists, society influences who we are attracted to, what we view as sexually appropriate and desirable, and what sexual behaviors we ultimately engage in and with whom. We can look across time and see that in different eras, culture was either more permissive toward sexual behaviors and sexual variation or more constraining. We refer to the more liberal eras as sexual revolutions if they have a long-term effect on human sexual behavior.

Sexual relationships in most Western societies tend to privilege heterosexual monogamous marriage; however, other sexual arrangements beyond monogamy exist. Sexuality changes as we move across the life course as well. Some of these changes are an outgrowth of physiological changes while others are social constructions. While sexual attitudes and behaviors do not vary to any significant degree between racial/ethnic groups in a society, it is important to acknowledge the ways stereotypes about racial/ethnic minorities are sexualized and the power of intersecting systems of oppression. Finally, we explore the cultural creation of a sexual hierarchy that divides sexual behaviors into "good" and "bad" categories.

Key Terms and Concepts

Asexuality 5	Homosexuality 4	Sexual identities 10
Biological determinism 6	Intersectionality 18	Sexuality 5
Bisexuality 4	Mononormativity 13	Sexual scripts 11
Compulsory	Pansexuality 5	Sexual orientation 4
heterosexuality 9	Polyamory 13	Sexual revolution 11
Essentialism 5	Queer 5	Sexual socialization 10
Fetishism 21	Reliability 7	Social construction 5
Gender 10	Sadomasochism 21	Sociology 4
Heterocentric 6	Sexophobia 12	Stereotype 19
Heteroflexibility 4	Sexual binary 7	Strategic essentialism 7
Heteronormativity 9	Sexual double standard 11	Stigma 13
Heterosexuality 4	Sexual hierarchy 20	Transgender 5

Critical Thinking Questions

1. What does it mean to say that sexuality is socially constructed? Provide three pieces of evidence that support the argument that sexuality is a social construction. How does understanding sexuality as a social construct alter our dominant cultural understanding of sexuality?

2. Describe sexuality across the life course, identifying sexual changes over the life course that are socially constructed and those that are biological.

3. What is a sexual revolution? Describe key characteristics of past sexual revolutions. Make an argument that we are currently in a historical era that later generations will look back on and describe as a sexual revolution. Now make the counterargument: provide evidence that shows that we are probably NOT currently in a sexual revolution.

Activities

1. Survey ten people who are part of your social circle—classmates, roommates, coworkers, family members—as to whether they perceive sexual orientation to be socially constructed or biologically innate (they may need you to define what it means to say that sexuality is socially constructed). Ask them to support their answer. Write a 2- to 3-page paper answering the following questions: What answers did you get? Are there any patterns to the responses? If so, what are they? Where do these people seem to get their understanding of sexual orientation? Were there any answers that surprised you? If so, why?

2. Check out a gay publication online (such as *The Advocate, Curve, Out, The Official New York City Pride Guide, Pink*). Look over at least three issues. Write a 2-page reflection paper addressing the following questions: What are the main issues facing the gay community, according to your survey of the publications at that particular time? Were these issues you could have identified as being important to members of the LGBTQ community prior to reading these publications? If not, why do you think that is?

Essential Readings

Foucault, Michel. 1976. *The History of Sexuality: An Introduction, Vol. I.* New York: Random House.

Nagel, Joane. 2003. *Race, Ethnicity, and Sexuality: Intimate Intersections, Forbidden Frontiers.* New York: Oxford University Press.

Orenstein, Peggy. 2016. *Girls and Sex: Navigating the Complicated New Landscape.* New York: HarperCollins.

Ward, Jane. 2015. *Not Gay: Sex Between Straight White Men.* New York: New York University Press.

Weeks, Jeffrey. 1986. *Sexuality.* London: Routledge.

Recommended Films

How to Lose Your Virginity (2013). Therese Schechter, Director. The documentary takes an in-depth look at the myths, dogmas, and misconceptions surrounding female virginity in U.S. culture.

Inside Bountiful: Polygamy Investigation (2012). Peter Joseph, Director. This documentary provides an inside look into a community of Canadian polygamists. They are under investigation by authorities, despite being a religious community; yet questions remain about the constitutionality and legality of this practice.

Sex in '69: Sexual Revolution in America (2011). Rob Epstein and Jeffrey Friedman, Directors. This film explores America's second sexual revolution—with a look at the pivotal year 1969. The concept of "free love" was born, "the pill" was becoming more available, *Playboy* magazine exploded onto the cultural landscape, the modern gay rights movement emerged with the Stonewall riots, and San Francisco's hippie culture burst into mainstream America.

Still Doing It: The Intimate Life of Women over 60. (2008). Deirdre Fishel and Diana Holtzberg, Producers and Directors. This film challenges cultural messages that associate sexuality with youth by focusing on the lives of nine diverse women: black, white, single, straight, and lesbian between the ages of 67 and 87. These women discuss their relationships, sex lives, and how they feel about themselves, shattering cultural stereotypes about aging and sexuality.

Suggested Multimedia

Sexuality and U is a Canadian consumer health website providing information on birth control, STDs (sexually transmitted diseases), and sexual health. The website includes an overview of sexuality and child development useful for teachers, parents, and anyone working with children. Retrieved from http://www.sexualityandu.ca/teachers/sexuality-and-childhood-development

THE SCIENCE OF SEXUALITY

LEARNING OBJECTIVES

Upon completion of this chapter, students will be able to . . .

- Explain nineteenth- and twentieth-century theoretical perspectives on sexuality
- Understand the social construction of sexuality
- Explicate the shifting scientific understandings of homosexuality
- Describe the history of sexuality studies in academia
- Debate ethical and methodological issues in sex research

At first glance, Alfred Kinsey seems an unlikely person to become the leading sex researcher in twentieth-century America. Kinsey was born in 1894 into a strict, devout, and sexually repressed Methodist family. He was an entomologist and an expert on gall wasps. Yet, as a faculty member at the University of Indiana in the late 1930s, he was invited to coordinate and direct a new course on marriage and family (what today would be titled a "Human Sexuality" course). The course was immediately popular with students and had a long wait list, despite being restricted to married students. Kinsey's approach to the subject was much more explicit and progressive than that of his predecessor, who taught that masturbation was harmful and condemned premarital intercourse (Bullough 2004). The ignorance concerning human sexuality and the thirst for knowledge among his students inspired Kinsey to make the study of human sexuality not only a scientific endeavor but his life's work.

Kinsey's own life reflects the influence of culture on sexuality that is explored in this book. He was born during the Victorian era into not only a sexually repressed family, but a sexually repressed culture. He grew up feeling shameful about his own sexual feelings and entered his marriage with a PhD in biology, but with minimal understanding of human sexuality. He sought information the way an academic would: through exploring existing scientific research on the subject. He discovered mostly silence among scientists concerning the issue of sexuality. In his marriage and family classes, he confronted a new generation of students who had the same questions and concerns he had upon marriage. Kinsey's research helped shift attitudes about sex in a more permissive direction in the post-World War II era (Bancroft 2004; Bullough 2007).

UNDERSTANDING SEXUALITY THROUGH SCIENCE

Theory is an attempt to explain and understand the world. Theories of sexuality help us understand human sexuality and place it in its proper social and historical context. In this chapter, we explore the science of sex and sexuality, reviewing key early and modern thinkers on the subject. Originating in Europe, *sexology*, or the science of sex, has been a major area of academic and scientific study for the past two centuries. Contributions to sex research have come from the fields of biology, psychology, anthropology, medicine, genetics, sociology, and women's and gender studies. The science of sexology uses systematic, objective methods to gather data about human sexual behavior with the goal of attaining knowledge and understanding more about it. While the goal of scientific research is to remain objective, the scientific process is infused with cultural assumptions. The particular time period and culture in which scientific knowledge emerges is influenced by the dominant ideologies of the era. This chapter explores a wide range of theoretical perspectives and empirical research on sexuality, their underlying assumptions and criticisms, as well as specific ethical and methodological issues associated with sex research.

While the term sexology is no longer in use, there is an abundance of scholarly research related to sex, sexuality, and sexual identity today; and it is an especially burgeoning area in the discipline of sociology. Some examples of recent research in the sociology of sexuality include, but are not limited to, the following:

- Research by Samuel L. Perry (2013) found that persons who attend racially integrated churches are more likely to support same-sex relationships, marriage, and adoption than are those who attend more racially homogenous churches.
- Opposition to pornography has decreased significantly over the past 40 years for both men and women, with women remaining more opposed to pornography than men. In fact, the gender gap in opposition to pornography has widened over this time period as men's opposition has declined faster than women's (Lykke and Cohen 2015).
- Catherine Connell's (2015) research found that gay and lesbian teachers face conflicting expectations between pride and professionalism: being "out" and proud versus the professional norms of the teaching profession that demand sexual neutrality and gender normativity.
- Victims of intimate partner violence (IPV; discussed in Chapter Eight) are unlikely to report the violence to authorities. Research by Xavier Guadalupe-Diaz (2016) finds that LGB people who are nonwhite, male, and had experienced police intervention in a case of IPV previously were the least comfortable with disclosing same-sex IPV to police.

The Early Years: Sex, Morality, and Medicine

Prior to the nineteenth century, sexuality in Western culture was regarded primarily as a moral concern. The dominant authorities on morality, and thereby sexuality, were priests and religious leaders. Rooted in religious theology, sexuality in the West has traditionally been associated with primal, bodily instincts and, according to biblical doctrine, considered sinful. Within the Judeo-Christian tradition, the creation story, as outlined in the book of Genesis, describes the expulsion of Adam and Eve from the Garden of Eden. Eve's disobedient act of eating the forbidden fruit from the tree of knowledge and then persuading Adam to also partake resulted in their awakening to their sinful nature. Both experience shame for their newfound nakedness. God punishes women by creating pain in childbirth and proclaiming that men rule over them, and God punishes men by making them toil and work for their food and survival. This story inspired a range of theological views about gender roles and sexuality, including the ideas that women were temptresses, both men and women were morally weak, and that men should rule over women (see Chapter Eight). Prominent Christian theologians, such as St. Augustine (354–430) and later St. Thomas Aquinas (1224–1274), surmised that sexual intercourse was acceptable only within the bounds of marriage and, even then, only for the purposes of reproduction. Philosophical and religious debates centered on the nature of lust, love, and the human condition ensued throughout history.

Religious views remained the most influential on sexuality until the mid-1800s when the influence of medicine, reason, and science began to gain more credibility and power. The medical profession increased in authority, and physicians came to be seen as experts on sex and sexuality-related issues. While physicians may have taken over as sexual authorities from religious leaders, they often still approached the subject from a moral perspective. As described in Chapter One, the Victorian era (roughly 1830–1890) in both Europe and the United States was generally understood as a cultural period with very specific restrictive ideas about gender roles and sexuality. Victorian ideals encouraged women and men to practice sexual discipline and restraint and engage in sexual activity only in pursuit of procreation and within the bounds of marriage. Moralism combined with scientific investigation resulted in most nineteenth-century physicians treating the primary sexual problems of this era, such as venereal diseases, prostitution, and masturbation, from moral and partisan bias. For example, masturbation, viewed as both a male and female problem, was seen as a deadly disease that needs to be controlled and cured (Laqueur 2004). Another assumption was that men were polygamous by nature whereas women were monogamous; men were more sexual and women were sexually passive, even lacking sexual feeling. These ideologies contributed to cultural expectations that women must help men tame their passionate sexual natures.

This cartoon from the Victorian Era emphasizes the repressiveness of period. Titled "Free Love and Women's Rights," the cartoon depicts a woman asking a bookseller for her-books, as opposed to hymn-books.
Source: Library of Congress. Frank Leslie's illustrated newspaper, vol. 30, April 30, 1870.

Women's bodies and sexualities were largely ignored and misunderstood, as revealed in the prevalent diagnosis of "hysteria" during this time. "Hysteria" was a medical diagnosis in which the symptoms were often consistent with what is now considered the normal functioning of female sexual arousal: anxiety, sleeplessness, irritability, nervousness, erotic fantasy, sensations of heaviness in the abdomen, lower pelvic edema, and vaginal lubrication. Treatment, as prescribed by the doctor, was orgasm, either through sexual intercourse with the woman's husband or by means of massage on the physician's table. The medical invention of the vibrator in the 1880s was created specifically for the purpose of treating hysteria in women. By the twentieth century, "hysteria" was a thing of the past and the American Psychiatric Association formally dropped it as a medical term in 1952 (Maines 1998).

Science of Sex: Sexology

In the early years of sex research, most scientists understood sex to be a fact of nature, a biological driving force, and an essential aspect of humanity. One of the most prominent, early sex researchers was German-born neurologist and psychiatrist, Richard von Krafft-Ebing (1840–1902). Krafft-Ebing wrote *Psychopathia Sexualis* ([1886] 1965), an empirical collection of clinical case studies that became a widely circulated and influential medical text on the subject of sexuality. In this text Krafft-Ebing portrayed nonprocreative sex as pathological and perverse because he considered the ultimate purpose of the human sex drive to be reproduction. He writes, "Man puts himself at once on a level with the beast if he seeks to gratify lust alone, but he elevates his superior position when by curbing the animal desire he combines with the sexual function ideas of morality, of the sublime, and the beautiful" (Krafft-Ebing [1886] 1965:1).

After extensive research into a wide range of cases, Krafft-Ebing identified four primary categories of sexual deviation: homosexuality, fetishism, sadism, and masochism. He defined homosexuality as a contrary sexual feeling and fetishism as the erotic obsession with certain parts of the body or with objects. He defined sadism as gaining sexual pleasure by inflicting pain on another person and masochism as gaining sexual pleasure by inflicting pain on oneself. These were new and revolutionary categories in the fields of medicine, sexology, and psychology. Although these four primary conditions were defined as abnormal, Krafft-Ebing claimed that sadism and masochism were inherent in normal male and female sexuality, the former being associated with the masculine tendencies to be active and aggressive and the latter of a passive and submissive nature (Ooserhuis 2012). Later, partly inspired by Krafft-Ebing's work, Freud coined the now popular term sadomasochism and described it as a component part of the human sexual instinct, as mentioned in Chapter One (Chancer 1992). *Psychopathia Sexualis* was one of the first texts to introduce the term heterosexuality and to equate "heterosexual sex" with "normal sex" (Katz 1995). Despite Krafft-Ebing's attempts to maintain scientific objectivity in his research, his influential views reflected the repressive sexual code of the era, helped define the field of sexology, and influenced the medical and psychiatric professions well into the twentieth century.

In the transition from the Victorian era to the modern era, several physicians and scientists attempted to dispel the misconceptions of the Victorian view of sex and sexuality. By the late nineteenth century, pioneers of this new field began examining and classifying sexual behaviors that had previously been invisible, and a new approach to the study of sexuality developed. More accepting attitudes and objectively researched facts about human sexuality began to gradually infiltrate the science. One of the first physicians to coin the term "sexual science," was German physician Iwan Bloch (1872–1922). His work focused on the history of sexuality, and he might well be called the first *sexologist*, or practitioner who studies human sexuality from a scientific perspective. The new approach used scientific research methods such as case studies, observations, and interviews. The goal of sexology is to discover the laws that govern human sexuality. As the field developed, sexologists questioned why humans have specific sexual instincts, desires, and pleasures.

British sexologist, Havelock Ellis (1859–1939), was a transitional figure between the Victorian and modern perspectives on sexuality. As a physician, writer, and social reformer, Ellis spent decades studying all available information on sexuality and engaging in research, including extensive research on transgender individuals. His research was published in six volumes between 1896 and 1910 titled *Studies in Psychology of Sex*. Ellis was most notably modern in his acceptance of a variety of sexual practices and behaviors and in his recognition of the right of women to sexual satisfaction. He insisted that sexual gratification was necessary for human emotional health. He was one of the first theorists to argue against the notion that homosexuality was immoral and pathological. Ellis is credited with introducing the notions of narcissism and ***autoeroticism***, or satisfaction gained by the subject's own body, and for effecting gradual changes in sexual attitudes over this time period. Overall, his conclusions were radical by Victorian standards and marked a significant shift in the field of sexology away from viewing sex as strictly heterosexual and procreation-based to beginning to understand it from a pleasure-based perspective.

Another prominent sexologist of the era was German researcher Magnus Hirschfeld (1868–1935). In 1919, Hirschfeld founded the first Institute for Sexology in Berlin. The Institute was the first of its kind to accumulate vast research on the subject of human sexual development as well as the treatment of sexual problems. Hirschfeld led the field in objective examinations of homosexuality, transgenderism, cross-dressing, and gender identity. He published one of the first encyclopedic texts specifically on homosexuality, *The Homosexuality of Men and Women* (1914), representing 30 years of research. In it, he attempted to eradicate homophobic discrimination by providing detailed biological information about the orientation, as well as the sociological history of homosexuality. Like Ellis, Hirschfeld was motivated by social reform. He founded the Scientific Humanitarian Committee that undertook research to defend the rights of homosexuals and to decriminalize homosexuality in Germany. He was one of the first in a long tradition of sexologists who sought justice in their scientific pursuits. As a gay, Jewish academic of the Nazi era, Hirschfeld became a target. In 1933, the Nazis took power and attacked Hirschfeld's institute, burning many of its books, as well as its archives.

Clelia D. Mosher, a physician and college professor at Stanford University, was one of the first female sexologists and the first scientist to conduct a sex survey. Her 20-year study addressed sexual and reproductive issues, surveying 45 women born between the years of 1850 and 1890. It was a small sample, but offered a glimpse into Victorian, middle-class, married women's sexual practices and beliefs. Her results revealed a cultural shift in women's views of sex from solely a source of reproduction to a source of personal desire and intimacy. Nearly two-thirds of her respondents acknowledged feeling sexual desire and viewed pleasure as a legitimate reason for sex. One-third reported they always or usually experienced orgasm during sex. Mosher never published or made more than cursory observations of her data. She died in 1940, and the survey was entirely forgotten until Carl Degler accidentally unearthed it in the Stanford University archives in 1973 (D'Emilio and Freedman 2012).

Psychoanalytical Theory: Sigmund Freud

One of the most influential thinkers in shaping Western understandings of sex and sexuality was the founder of psychoanalysis, Sigmund Freud (1856–1939). Freud, like other sexologists of his era, viewed sexuality from a biological perspective and as the driving force in human behavior. He theorized that the sexual drive, or instinct, was unconscious, or beyond conscious personal awareness. Freud's perspective on sex expands significantly on accepted understandings of the era. For instance, unlike other sexologists,

BOX 2.1

GLOBAL/TRANSNATIONAL PERSPECTIVES ON SEXUALITY:
SEXOLOGY IN IMPERIAL JAPAN

Between 1868 and 1945, Japan underwent significant social changes. Emperor Meiji's reign, between 1868 and 1912, brought rapid modernization and dramatic changes in the political, social, and economic institutions, including implementing a constitution, industrialization, and an increase in communication and transportation technologies. The imperial period began in the late 1890s as Japan sought to gain international status and world power through victorious wars against China and Russia and through colonizing Taiwan, Korea, the Philippines, and most of the Pacific Islands.

Japanese sexology developed during this era of colonial expansion and militarization and attempted to establish a normative Japanese sexuality (Fruhstuck 2003). To establish a normative sexuality essentially means to derive a standard of what is "normal" sexual behavior for a particular culture. A society shapes what it deems as "normal" in complex ways. It involves validation from scientific experts, and is influenced by political debates, social control policies, and rhetoric surrounding current issues. During the imperial period in Japan, issues of sex education, prevention of venereal diseases, the problem of masturbation and its alleged consequences, birth control, and prostitution were of central focus.

Scientists studying sex and sexuality in Japan contributed to the management, control, and creation of sexual ideas and norms. One of the more influential sexologists was Yamamoto Senji. In the early 1920s, Senji undertook the first extensive sex surveys of males in Japan, published in the *Kyoto Medical Journal* and titled "Statistical Survey of the Sex Lives of Japan's Male Students" (Fruhstuck 2003). His goal was to discover "normal" and "healthy" sexuality for young males in Japan. This survey's findings went against cultural norms of the time. For example, they found that 33 percent of young men's first sexual experience was with a prostitute and that masturbation was a natural phenomenon and had no negative impact on men's healthy development (Fruhstuck 2003).

Senji's research was less concerned with developing a comprehensive theory of sex and more interested in sexual reform based on scientific knowledge. He developed a sex education course at the University of Tokyo and later attempted to popularize sexological science in journals such as *Sexual Desire* and *Humankind* (Fruhstuck 2003). He believed if the masses gained sex education, it would lead to liberation from outdated and incorrect beliefs about sex. Although his efforts were not welcomed, Senji's research stands as one of earliest and most significant contributions to the field of sexology in imperial Japan.

Freud suggested that the human sexual drive was oriented to pleasure as much as it is the biological urge to reproduce. Because Freud saw the sex drive as pleasure-oriented, this allowed for a much wider range of what he considered "normal" sexual behaviors, including nongenital touching, kissing, caressing, looking, and more—but always with the primary aim of heterosexual procreation.

Freud diverged from others in his field in that he saw the role of society as an important factor in shaping an individual's sexual expressions, or lack thereof. Freud's most influential theory, outlined in several editions of *Three Essays on the Theory of Sexuality* (1906), explained individual, human sexual development from infancy to adulthood, and involved a series of stages of psychosexual adaptations. Freud claimed both sexes faced various psychosexual demands and must accomplish the work of reigning in and controlling their unconscious, biological sexual drives while also abiding by cultural expectations. Freud outlined five primary stages throughout an individual's life, each named after the regions of the body that are most important for sexual gratification during each phase: oral, anal, phallic, latent, and genital. Freud theorized that sexual development begins at birth. Both sexes had similar experiences in several of the stages, but differ drastically in the phallic stage, which occurs around 3 to 5 years of age.

While many of Sigmund Freud's ideas have not held up to scientific scrutiny, Freud challenged repressive sexual norms of the day, primarily by shifting our cultural ideas about sex from a procreative ethic to a pleasure ethic.
Source: istockphoto.com/Grigorios Moraitis.

During the phallic stage, both sexes transfer sexual pleasure to the genitalia, realize their genitalia are different from the other sex, and respond accordingly. For boys, the newfound genital activity results in a sexual longing for their mothers, called the ***Oedipus complex***. In response to discovering girls do not have penises, boys come to fear their penises are removable. Boys experience feelings of competition and hostility toward their fathers over the love for their mothers and, in turn, they fear their fathers might castrate them, resulting in what Freud calls the ***castration complex***. In order to become sexually healthy adults, boys must resolve conflict with their fathers and deny their sexual feelings for their mothers.

Girls' struggles with male-female anatomical differences during the phallic stage are different than boys' struggles, according to Freud. When a young girl realizes she does not have a penis, she also believes it is because it has been castrated and the wound that resulted is her vagina. The clitoris is left, but it is significantly smaller than the penis. Thereby she develops an inferiority complex and an unconscious desire for a penis, something Freud describes as penis envy. Girls also begin to desire sex with and want to reproduce with their fathers, while feeling hostility toward and blaming their mother for their supposed penis castration. Later, Freud claims, as women mature into their fully developed sexual selves, women must learn to redirect their sexual impulses away from their clitorises and toward their vaginas. Freud describes two types of orgasms for women, vaginal and clitoral, with the vaginal orgasm as more mature and superior. Thus, reinforcing the dominant idea of heterosexual sex as normal.

Freud's theories were controversial when he proposed them, and remain so, primarily because they cast women as inferior to men. Many feminist psychoanalytical theorists, including Karen Horney, Nancy Chodorow, and Ellyn Kaschak, have since created alternative theories of personality, sexual, and gender development. Their theories include some of Freud's basic assumptions, but with more contemporary views on sex and gender. Freud's theories are critiqued as biased and inaccurate because he bases his research on observations of the sexual lives of his patients, who were primarily wealthy, Victorian, Viennese women who were seeking long-term psychiatric care. Moreover, sociologists Gagnon and Simon (1973) criticize psychoanalytical theory for relying too heavily on unconscious mental processes, which are difficult, if not impossible, to research with scientific accuracy. They argue that the focus on the inaccessible and unconscious traumas from infancy and childhood as the determining factors of adult sexual desires is deterministic. Despite the sexist bias and controversy, Freud's work has had significant impact on twentieth-century sexologists and Western culture in general. He is credited with being the first to portray sex as being about pleasure rather than reproduction, and he is one of the first to emphasize the social nature of sexuality.

Evolutionary Theory: Charles Darwin

A major nineteenth-century contributor to the scientific understanding of human sexuality is Charles Darwin (1808–1882), specifically in his theory of evolution in *On the Origin of Species* (1859). Darwin was an English naturalist and geologist who, after many years of observing nature, proposed that all species, since the beginning of time, adapt to their constantly changing environments in a process called evolution. He theorized that evolution works by way of a biological mechanism called natural selection. ***Natural selection*** says that inheritable biological traits that are more conducive to survival and reproduction will become more widespread in a population over time. Darwin explains it in simple terms as, "Multiply, vary, let the strongest live and the weakest die" (Darwin 2009:481).

A second characteristic of the process of human evolution is what Darwin calls ***sex selection***. Darwin observed that in most mammals, the female is much more invested in the survival rate of the offspring due to her investment in the process of pregnancy, lactation, and nurturing the young; while males can impregnate a woman with little further obligation. This is referred to as a conflicting parental investment. Because of this biological inequality and conflicting interest, women are what Darwin called "coy," or more hesitant about such a commitment, while men tend to work at convincing the female to partake in sex. In other words, women are more hesitant to engage in sexual intercourse with men because they might become pregnant, requiring years of investment, while men are much more eager to have sexual intercourse because their actual physical investment is only the sexual act itself. This leads to competition between men for sexual access to fertile females (Ryan and Jetha 2010).

In the late twentieth century, several works of evolutionary psychology and evolutionary biology based on Darwin's concept of sex selection became popular. Evolutionary psychology sought to identify which human psychological traits are evolved adaptations. In other words, evolutionary psychology examined how adaptation pressures experienced by ancient human ancestors shape contemporary sex and mating patterns. It assumes Darwin's theory of sex selection of the coy female and the courting, competitive male to be accurate. Questions often asked by evolutionary psychologists include: Are men and women naturally monogamous? Are women choosier about sex partners than men? Do humans model the widespread mammal mating behavior of the aggressive male and coy female? For example, in *The Mating Mind* (2001), Geoffrey Miller theorized that early ancestors choose to mate with people who were smart and innovative in order to create smarter offspring.

While there are feminist evolutionary psychologists and biologists, overall, this approach has been critiqued by many feminists for its essentialist and gendered assumptions about the roles of men and women. Feminists challenge the evolutionary hypothesis that suggests rape is a genetically advantageous behavioral adaptation for men in order to ensure mating (Thornhill and Palmer 2000). Sociologist Martha McCaughey encourages us to question why we see the application of evolutionary theory to explain male behavior, particularly antisocial, "deplorable behavior, such as rape, sexual harassment, and aggression" (2008:2). Other critiques include sociologists who understand sexuality as a social construction, rather than something biological. A social constructionist perspective sees how Darwin's theories are influenced by the particular social and cultural context in which he lives and works, including the assumption that sexuality is natural and innate.

The Kinsey Reports: Alfred Kinsey

In post-World War II United States, there was a significant shift in the study of sexuality toward a focus on the application of scientific methodology with as little researcher bias, assumption, or opinion as possible. One of the most influential sexologists of the midcentury to do this was Alfred Kinsey (1894–1956). Kinsey was an American biologist, entomologist, and zoologist who became focused on human sexual behavior studies in the late 1930s (see opening vignette). Kinsey's extensive research enhanced knowledge about the variety and frequency of human sexual experiences and became foundational to the field of modern sexology. In 1947, he founded the Kinsey Institute for Sex Research at Indiana University, now known as the Kinsey Institute for Research in Sex, Gender, and Reproduction. He and his coresearchers published two tremendously influential books, *Sexual Behavior in the Human Male* (1948) and *Sexual Behavior in the Human Female* (1953), popularly known as the Kinsey Reports. Despite the controversies surrounding their publication, the Kinsey Reports became a tremendous influence on American culture.

The staggering scale of the research was impressive. Kinsey and his team interviewed and collected detailed sexual histories on almost 18,000 people over nearly two decades, compiling a monumental amount of information regarding human sexual behavior in the United States. Their data included such controversial topics as the relative frequency of practices like masturbation, and the extent of premarital, extramarital, and homosexual sex. This research attempted to study and chronicle as much about human sexuality as possible, without judgment.

The Kinsey Reports shocked the American public because they challenged socially accepted views of sex and sexuality and the sexual *norms*, social rules or guidelines that govern every aspect of our behavior, of the day. Kinsey's findings revealed that oral sex,

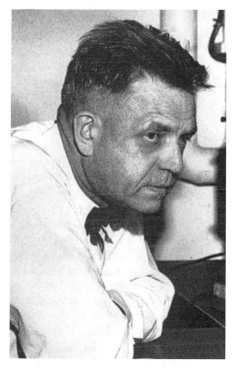

Sex researcher Alfred Kinsey found that sexual behaviors of the mid-twentieth century differed greatly from the sexual norms of the era.
Source: Library of Congress/Corbis Historical/ Getty Images.

premarital sex, same-sex sexuality, and a wide range of sexual fantasies are common. In perhaps their most significant research finding, Kinsey and his colleagues challenged prevailing notions of the sexual binary and instead argued that sexuality ranges along a six-point continuum, from "exclusively heterosexual" to "exclusively homosexual." This became known as the *Kinsey scale*, and it was based on their findings that a substantial percentage of men and women had engaged in same-sex sexual relations. His surveys indicated that masturbation was a common sexual activity. An extremely disputed finding reported that children had sexual feelings and sometimes acted on them, most commonly in form of childhood masturbation.

Kinsey's conclusions were especially contentious in regard to women because they indicated that women enjoy sex. His statistics reported that 50 percent of the women surveyed admit to premarital intercourse, 90 percent to "petting," and 28 percent to homosexual tendencies (Kinsey et al. 1953). Taboos against female sex outside of heterosexual marriage were strong in U.S. culture at this time and this information was met with resistance. His research was the first of its kind to actually verify the double standard of sexuality. For example, by 25 years of age, 83 percent of unmarried men had participated in intercourse, but only 33 percent of women had done so. This gender discrepancy can also be found in the data on extramarital affairs (Kinsey et al. 1948, 1953).

Kinsey was critiqued for ignoring some areas of sexual behavior, such as swinging, masochism, and exhibitionism. He justified this neglect based on the very small number of people practicing such behaviors. He also did not examine pregnancy or the impacts of sexually transmitted disease. Finally, one of the most significant critiques was that he lacked a *representative sample*, which refers to the research sample having the same distribution of characteristics as the population from which it was drawn. The respondents were disproportionately white, educated, Midwestern individuals, which meant his findings were not generalizable. Despite these critiques, Kinsey's work became the standard achievement in the empirical investigation of human sexual practices, heavily influenced public attitudes, and challenged established medical and psychological assumptions about sex and sexuality.

Sexual Physiology Research: Masters and Johnson

In the mid-1960s, William Masters and Virginia Johnson brought the field of sexology to a new level with groundbreaking research focusing on the physiological responses of the human body during sex, specifically, arousal and orgasm. Their controversial research methods involved laboratory-setting observations of volunteers engaging in masturbation and sexual intercourse, while hooked up to biochemical monitors, such as electrocardiographs. Galvanic skin responses, muscle contractions, facial expressions, interviews, and more were analyzed and observed. Their book, *Human Sexual Response* (1966), is a comprehensive summary of their findings, and it quickly became a best seller in the United States. A second important study, *Human Sexual Inadequacy* (1970) addressed problems of sexual performance. This was the first time sexual dysfunction was labeled and explained, with behavioral treatment options. In 1964, they established the Reproductive Biology Research Foundation in St. Louis, Missouri, later called the Masters and Johnson Foundation.

By 1965, Masters and Johnson had observed more than 10,000 episodes of sexual activity in their research. Their physiological studies of sexual stimulation and reactions led them to describe the ***sexual response cycle.*** This cycle consists of four stages from arousal to orgasm, which are respectively called: excitement, plateau, orgasm, and resolution. Their findings revealed that men undergo a waiting period after orgasm, during which they are unable to ejaculate again, while women are capable of multiple orgasms. They described the rhythmic contractions of orgasm by both sexes as occurring in 0.8-second intervals before gradually slowing. Their findings on the nature of the female orgasm were particularly enlightening, and they challenged Freud's ideas of the vaginal orgasm as the mature orgasm. They revealed that the physiology of the orgasm is the same whether women stimulate their clitoris or vagina, essentially proving that women are multiorgasmic. They argued that in most cases, sexual problems for couples were not a result of neuroses or other medical or psychological disorders, but rather a result of conflict in the relationship or poor communication.

Masters and Johnson were the first to conduct research on the sexual responsiveness of older adults, finding they were perfectly capable of orgasms and a healthy sex life, despite cultural assumptions to the contrary. They noted that arousal typically takes longer and requires more genital stimulation with age. In their research on gay men, Masters and Johnson randomly assigned them into couples and discovered that they quickly figured out partner preferences, such as who was receiving anal penetration or giving it, with little discussion. Likewise, with randomly assigned coupled lesbians, one partner quickly assumed sexual control. Between the years of 1968 and 1977, Masters and Johnson treated individuals who were dissatisfied with their homosexuality. They reported a 71 percent success rate in converting homosexuals into heterosexuals over a six-year period (Masters and Johnson 1979). This misconception that homosexuality is something that can or should be treated or changed indicates biases in their research by uncritically incorporating cultural attitudes against homosexuality.

Masters and Johnson's research methodology has faced other criticisms as well. Some argue their data was not representative, particularly in the initial stages, because they studied 145 prostitutes. Then they moved on to primarily white, educated, married couples in their community, which, again, was not a representative sample. Additionally, some critics argue that sexual activity in a laboratory environment is quite different than in the privacy of one's home and probably inhibits some behaviors. The ethical issues associated with assigning arbitrary sexual partners for observation are still hotly debated. Up to this time, it had not been attempted, nor has it been attempted since. Finally, their sexual response cycle has been critiqued for being entirely sequential, linear, physiological, and without consideration of relationship and cultural factors, or even sexual desire. In response, several other models have since developed, including Kaplan's Triphasic Concept (1979), which includes desire and excitement; Whipple & Brash-McGreer's Circular Model (1997), specifically designed for women; and Basson's Nonlinear Model (2001), which considers intimacy and desire, and assumes there is no "normal" in sexual response.

SOCIOLOGY AND SOCIAL CONSTRUCTIONISM

Sociology is a scientific endeavor that emphasizes the careful gathering and analysis of evidence about social life in order to develop better understanding of key social processes. Research methods vary from observations to ethnography, large-scale surveys, census data, interviews, lab experiments, and more. The goal is to discover insights into the social processes that shape human lives and impact personal choices and outcomes. Sociological contributions to sexuality studies did not emerge until the 1960s. Prior to this time, sexuality was viewed as either a natural or psychological phenomenon. Sociology is the first scientific field to theorize sexuality as a social construction.

Social constructionism was introduced by Peter Berger and Thomas Luckmann in *Social Construction of Reality* (1966). This treatise explained that society is formed and organized by human interactions. Concepts and representations of each other's actions, over time, become habitual. These repeated habits create roles people play in relation to each other. These roles then become institutionalized, or embedded in society. Our social processes, habitualized roles and actions, and institutionalized interactions then shape reality and knowledge, and influence how we perceive the world. In other words, reality is socially constructed. Sexuality, Berger and Luckmann note, demonstrates the ever changing adaptability of human conduct. Sexuality, like other roles, is something that is learned and shaped by culture and society.

As described in Chapter One, it was sociologists Gagnon and Simon who began to question the essentialist perspective on sexuality. In addition to studying sociology at the University of Chicago, both researchers studied sexuality at the Kinsey Institute, exploring the social sources of human sexual conduct. They published *Sexual Conduct* (1973), a landmark text in the sociology of sexuality that went on to profoundly influence what is now known as the social constructionist approach to sexuality. Instead of adopting Freud's emphasis on the repression of natural drives as the formation of desire and the sexual self, they focused on how society creates and produces sexuality. Essentially their work challenges biological determinism and claims human sexual behavior is created by society.

Gagnon and Simon argued that sexuality is the result of a complex psychosocial process of development. Acts, feelings, and body parts are not sexual on their own—they become sexual through the application of sociocultural scripts that imbue them with sexual significance. Sexual scripts are not fixed, but are ongoing fluid improvisations. This approach allows for individual change and agency in the development of the sexual self. They claim sexuality is an ongoing action, in which the making and modifying of sexual meaning occurs. In the end, the social constructionist perspective became the dominant paradigm of social science inquiry into human sexuality and is the theoretical foundation behind the ideas in this very textbook.

Despite the work of Gagnon and Simon, during this era, the initial sociological research on sexuality narrowly focused on sexual deviance. Since its inception as a discipline, sociology studied deviant behavior, or the behaviors that violate social norms. By the 1960s, sexual deviance, and what desires and behaviors are defined as sexually deviant, was an ongoing and central focus in the field of sociology. ***Sexual deviance*** refers to behaviors of individuals seeking erotic gratification through means that are considered odd, different, or unacceptable to mainstream society. As social constructionism develops, the question of why some people conform to social expectations, and others do not, began to be understood as something that is influenced by an individual's social experiences and relationships. This emphasis contrasts with the medical and psychiatric focus on the internal states of individuals.

Sociologist Mary McIntosh (1968) was one of the first to question the assumption of homosexuality as deviant. She argued that labeling homosexuality as deviant is a form of social control and segregation and a way to prescribe acceptable heterosexual behaviors. She also critiqued the assumption that it is a "condition," as most criminologists, medical doctors, and psychiatrists of the era proclaimed.

> "
>
> *"The current conceptualization of homosexuality as a condition is a false one, resulting from ethnocentric bias"—Mary McIntosh (1968:182).*

Historian and sociologist of sexuality Jeffrey Weeks is one of the most significant academic voices of the 1970s to challenge essentialism and promote a social constructionist perspective. Weeks's academic work is highly influenced by his political activism, which began with the Gay Liberation Front in the early 1970s in London (see Chapter Five). Weeks's earliest book, *Coming Out: Homosexual Politics in Britain from the Nineteenth Century to the Present* (1977), is a historical analysis of sexuality. Weeks demonstrated how, even though homoerotic behavior most likely existed throughout all of human history, the emergence of the "homosexual" as a distinct category of human identity is a modern phenomenon.

He revealed how identities are changeable and informed by social and historical influences. Yet, at the same time, he proposed that sexuality and sexual identity can be intentionally shaped to benefit individuals and society in the present and future.

Sex in America Survey

In the early 1990s, sociologist Edward Laumann and colleagues decided that in the era of HIV/AIDS, it was imperative we understand sexual behaviors so that we can develop public health approaches that will be effective in changing risky sexual behaviors (Laumann 2011; see Chapter Ten). Despite the studies discussed in this chapter, there is a dearth of sex research, as this is rarely a subject that government and private foundations are interested in supporting (Michael et al. 1994). Most sex research focuses on sexual deviance rather than general sexual practices of the population (Das and Laumann 2015). The sex studies that do exist face methodological shortcomings making their data unreliable, some of which have been discussed in this chapter. Since Masters and Johnson, there have been a few popular reports on sexual practices: the *Playboy* report, *The Janus Report, The Hite Report,* and the *Redbook Report.* All of these studies face methodological problems: they rely on volunteers and their samples are not random, which limits the generalizability of the findings.

Laumann and colleagues (1994) sought to correct this problem. Their project, which was initially called the National Health and Social Life Survey and later became known as the Sex in American Survey, is a scientifically valid, national study, with a random sample of 3,432 adult American men and women of varying ages and races/ethnicities. It includes questions on a wide range of sexual behaviors. Despite the constant bombardment of sexualized images in the media, this research found that American sexual behavior differed remarkably from American sexual norms of the day. Perhaps surprisingly, behaviors were more conservative than the norms. This study found that people in monogamous sexual relationships reported higher satisfaction with their sexual relationships than others,

Americans were less sexually active overall than assumed, and African Americans reported lower rates of oral sex and masturbation than white Americans or Hispanics.

Feminist Contributions to Sexuality Studies

Feminist contributions to sexuality studies at least partially reflects the dramatic shift in social and sexual norms for women in the latter half of the twentieth century. The post-World War II economic boom brought women into the workforce in unprecedented levels and challenged traditional gender roles. Divorce rates began to rise in the early 1960s, changing the dynamics of family structures and intimate relationships. The birth control pill became available in 1960, and the sexual revolution of the 1960s and 1970s encouraged sexual freedom for women. Paralleling the numerous other social movements of the 1960s, a new surge of feminist activism began and formed what is known as the second wave feminist movement, or the women's movement.

The women's movement is a large, varied, and complex social movement that challenges women's relations to power from a variety of different angles. One of its most popular slogans, "the personal is political," implies a standpoint that connects personal experiences with larger social and political structures. This belief questions how gender inequality and sexism impact women's lives in both the private sphere and the public sphere. It brings issues like sexual assault, reproductive health care and rights, sexual harassment, and domestic violence to the forefront of political debate.

Growing out of the women's movement in the 1970s, Women's Studies departments opened in universities across the country. This led to a significant increase in feminist research and theory. Feminist theory contributes a wide array of concepts specific to the science of sexuality, including an exploration of the role of gender in sexuality, heterosexuality as a tool of social control, the concept of intersectionality, the role of violence in sexuality, and the importance of reproductive rights, among others. Feminist academics question the androcentric views of science and its presumption of objectivity; and they seek to engage in new scientific approaches, designed to produce knowledge from the standpoint of women.

There is not one central feminist theoretical position or theory on sexuality. There are a variety of feminist viewpoints that each shed light on the subject. Some feminists believe women hold a unique perspective on sexuality simply because of their gendered experience. For example, Audre Lorde describes, "The erotica is a resource within each of us that lies in a deeply female and spiritual plane, firmly rooted in the power of our expressed or unrecognized feeling" (Lorde 2007:53). Lorde claims this source of power comes from a nonrational knowledge within women and could, if tapped, redefine the way people relate and connect, both sexually and nonsexually.

Luce Irigaray, a French poststructuralist feminist, argues that female sexuality has always been conceptualized on the basis of masculine parameters. Irigaray claims Freud's theory of sexuality, in particular his notions of penis envy and the inferiority of the clitoral orgasm, imply women's sexuality is deficient. If viewed through a Freudian lens, women are "the sex which is not one" (Irigaray 1977:23). She redefines female sexuality and sexual pleasure as a complex set of experiences located in the female body that cannot be reduced to one sexual organ.

African American feminist bell hooks critiques representations of black female sexuality in U.S. culture as objectified, expendable, and the "erotic other" (see Chapter Six). hooks claims that "When black women relate to our bodies, our sexuality, in ways that place erotic recognition, desire, pleasure, and fulfillment at the center of our efforts to create radical black female subjectivity, we can make new and different representations of ourselves as sexual subjects" (hooks 1992:76).

The radical feminist tradition views sexuality as a tool of male dominance and one of the primary sources of oppression for women globally. This tradition claims the relationship between sexuality and dominance is often revealed through acts of violence against women. Examples include sexual harassment in the workplace, domestic violence, sexual abuse, sexual assault, use of rape in war, violence in pornography, and more. Catherine A. MacKinnon (1989b) argues that heterosexuality is defined primarily as an eroticized dynamic of masculine domination and feminine submission and is inextricably linked with violence. Female sexuality, in this context, is defined as something that is to be taken, conquered, achieved, or possessed. MacKinnon argues that forced sex becomes central to the concept of heterosexuality. Thus, "rape is indigenous, not exceptional, to women's social condition" (MacKinnon 1989b:172). She claims that women's sexuality, sexual preferences, and practices are inextricably connected to their social condition of inequality.

Feminist sexology, as an independent field, began growing in the 1970s with a specific focus on topics such as reproductive rights, sex work, LGBTQ identities, pornography, sexual attitudes, and the role of the body (see Chapters Nine and Eleven). In 1976, *The Hite Report*, a revolutionary book by sex educator and feminist, Shere Hite, was published. Building on the physiological studies of Masters and Johnson and the questionnaire approach of Kinsey, Hite asked over one hundred thousand anonymous women, ages 14 to 78, about sex, orgasms, and masturbation. The findings revealed that orgasms are easy for women with clitoral stimulation. The cultural assumption that "good sex" required vaginal penetration is simply that: cultural. Hite's research suggests that heterosexual sex needs to include the stimulation that inspires female orgasms, not just male orgasms.

Hite's methods were highly criticized, due to the fact that her data was not gathered from probability samples and thereby cannot be used to generalize to the population at large. Moreover, the women who responded to her very personal survey may be less concerned about answering sensitive questions about sex than the average woman would be. In other words, the nonresponders are not represented in the sample. Others find her methodology important for studying women's sexuality because it provides an opportunity for women to open up without face-to-face interview pressures or laboratory conditions, which likely inhibits many potential respondents.

INTERSECTIONALITY Intersectionality theory was first introduced by legal scholar and feminist Kimberlé Crenshaw (1989). Intersectionality, as mentioned in Chapter One, is a theoretical approach that considers multiple grounds of identity and the ways various modes of oppression intersect and work together in society. During the 1980s, women of color began to critique feminist scholarship for its primary focus on gender as the most important category for understanding women's subordination and ignoring racial oppression. Women of color have long critiqued the feminist movement for being dominated by white, middle-class women and their issues, which are assumed to apply to all women. They argue that race, class, and sexuality are also crucial aspects of women's lives. An intersectional approach recognizes women's multiple experiences and identities and is also concerned with large-scale, socially constructed systems of power. In other words, it looks at how gender, race, class, and sexuality are systemic forces shaping society.

There is not one specific methodology associated with intersectionality. Researching systemic inequality from an intersectional position is complex and assumes plural *ontologies*, ways of knowing and understanding reality, and *epistemologies*, understandings of *how* we know what we know. From an intersectional perspective, much of what we know stems from our positions in multiple status hierarchies (as women in a patriarchy, for instance, or as heterosexuals in a sexual hierarchy that privileges heterosexuality).

Using intersectionality to study sexuality provides many unique insights. For example, inequality and poverty often intersect in the lives of sexual and gender nonconforming people who experience inequities in education systems and the labor market. Sexuality and poverty intersect with the legal system when laws criminalizing sexual and gender nonconforming behaviors are enforced. This in turn creates social stigma and discrimination and can discourage professionals from working with nonconforming persons and sex workers, out of fear of prosecution (Jjuuko and Tumwesige 2013). This further marginalizes nonconforming persons from social services and protection from structural violence.

Post-Structuralism: Michel Foucault

Most post-structuralists approach the subject of sexuality from the starting point of deconstructing what is considered natural or biological. Sexuality is viewed as a fluid concept that is constantly changing and is relative to each culture, time period, and context. French philosopher and historian, Michel Foucault (1926–1984) explored the relationship between sexuality, power/knowledge, and social control in institutions. In *The History of Sexuality, Vol. 1*, (1978) Foucault challenged the ***repressive hypothesis***, among other things. This is the idea that Western society has historically repressed sexuality, especially during the Victorian era. Foucault argued instead that sexuality was not repressed during this era, but that the modern sexual era was created through a sexual discourse that emerged during the Victorian era. The Victorian era, Foucault counters, was actually the peak of sexual obsession, rather than the repression of it. He dates the discussion of the sinful aspect of sex and sexuality all the way back to early Christian theology practices of confession in the Catholic Church. Psychiatrists, medical doctors, sexologists, and religious leaders have a lot to say about human sexuality in this period; and this obsession led to the modern *scientia sexualis*, or science of sexuality. Foucault claims the process of experts talking about and trying to understand sexuality as something separate from the pleasurable experience of it actually creates what we know of as sexuality. In other words, by creating a discourse focused on discovering the hidden truths of the human sexual instinct, scientists actually fashion human desires, pleasures, and the boundaries of normal and abnormal.

Foucault argues that the process of producing sexual knowledge gives social institutions power. Sexual knowledge produced by medical doctors, psychiatrists, and sexologists operate as forms of social control; they frame people's sexual feelings, behaviors, and identities in ways defined as acceptable and unacceptable. He describes modern Western society and its institutions, including the military, legal and penal system, schools, churches, and medicine, as based on a type of social organization that emphasizes discipline and control. This disciplinary control shapes human beings, including how we view our bodies, identities, and sexuality. Foucault provides a historical analysis for why and how this type of disciplinary control develops in modern society. He sees it as a byproduct of the changing cultural, political, and economic climate of nations toward industrial capitalism, mass education, and literacy, and increasing dependence on government in the seventeenth through the nineteenth centuries. As populations increase, the need to understand and control reproduction, health, and migration become essential, hence the need to control sexuality. Foucault believes it becomes crucial to control and manage sex in order to manage the behavior of citizens, but most importantly to maintain dominant group power.

Institutions rely on ideas and language, or what Foucault calls ***discourse***, to control and maintain power. The language used to discuss sexuality, write laws, and describe medical diagnoses pertaining to sexuality all work to regulate human sexual behavior and expression.

Post-structuralist Michel Foucault explored the relationship between sexuality, power/ knowledge, and social control.
Source: Bettmann/Getty Images.

While he shows the importance of language and social institutions in the process of shaping sexuality and sexual identities, he is critiqued for not addressing other important social components such as gender, class, age, or race. Foucault's work influenced many social scientists in the 1970s and 1980s to argue sexuality was more influenced by society and culture than by biology.

Queer Theory

Queer theory emerged in the 1990s out of poststructuralism, feminist theory, and gay and lesbian studies (Mann 2012). **Queer theory** is a critical analysis of the social construction of sexuality, particularly the ideas of the sexual binary and essentialism; it opposes gender and sexuality classifications as limiting, and instead embraces the concepts of gender and sexuality as fluid, or in flux. In this way, queer theory destabilizes the notion of homosexual and heterosexual identities (Seidman 1997). It seeks to understand what society considers normal, how it comes to be considered normal, who is excluded or oppressed by such understandings, and how the formations of sexual and gender minorities are then created. A founding queer theorist, Eve Kosofsky Sedgwick draws from feminist scholarship and Foucault's writings in her literary critiques of classic works. Sedgwick claims authors such as Charles Dickens conceal homoerotic subplots and work to reveal sexual ambiguities in literature. She coins the term **homosocial** as the relationship between same-sex people and argues it is an important aspect of analysis in order to better understand sexuality.

Queer theory is highly influenced by Judith Butler's seminal work, *Gender Trouble* (1990). Butler critiques the feminist movement for trying to assert that women are a group with common characteristics and interests. She argues that even though the feminist movement rejects the essentialist idea that biology shapes women's destiny, it still divides humans into two groups, men and women, reinforcing the sex/gender binary. She argues that gender, sex, and sexuality are constructed through repetitive performances. Performativity is a stylized repetition of acts, an imitation or miming of the dominant conventions. While it is possible for gender performativity to be subversive, it is not automatic or easy.

Sociologist Mimi Schippers (2016) uses queer theory to understand nonmonogamy, specifically *polyqueer* sex, sexualities, and relationships. She challenges regimes of normalcy attached to heteronormativity and monogamy and argues that when we do this, it allows us to destabilize racial and gender hierarchies as well. In other words, compulsory monogamy is central to heteromasculine domination and white privilege since race, gender, and sexual hierarchies intersect and sustain one another.

THE SCIENCE OF HOMOSEXUALITY

Since the invention of the concept of homosexuality in the late 1800s, understanding same-sex sexuality has been a challenge for physicians, psychologists, and academic researchers. Since the nineteenth century, homosexuality has inspired a wide range of questions, some of which were brought up in Chapter One: Is homosexuality biologically determined? Is there a gay gene? Is it a personal choice? Is homosexuality a result of cultural influences, familial influences, early sexual experiences, or child sexual abuse? Should it be considered deviant? Is it a psychological disorder? Can it be altered? Is it ethical to try to change it? Until recently, most sexologists sought a scientific explanation for the "true" nature of homosexuality while leaving questions of heterosexuality unexplored.

In the Victorian era, medical professionals viewed opposite-sex attraction as normal and same-sex attraction as a perversion and an illness. Same-sex orientation was given the medical term **sexual inversion**, and was based on the medical assumption that gender and sexual orientation were intrinsically connected. The conclusion was that if someone was attracted to a person of the same sex, it was due to gender inversion. Same-sex behavior was labeled as ***sexually degenerate***, or lacking in morality. Victorian doctors were influenced both by Christian teachings that viewed homosexuality as a sin and by criminal laws that pronounced it as illegal. Over the years, electric shock treatments and aversion therapies were often prescribed, as were more drastic measures such as castration, in an attempt to treat or cure homosexuality (see Chapter Four). The terms homosexuality and heterosexuality were not introduced into medical literature until the latter part of the nineteenth century (see Chapter One). By giving opposite- and same-sex sexual behaviors a name and an official identity, the institution of medicine helped to shape and define them.

More current medical and biological approaches to understanding homosexuality have focused on the role of genetics and hormones. Although it is scientifically impossible to establish the exact relationship between genes and behavior traits, the search for a "gay gene" is still pursued (see Chapter One). Due to cultural influences and individual variations in sexual attraction, genes alone cannot explain sexuality. Some biologists suggest that the hormonal chemistry of the mother's body influences the sexual orientation of the embryo in her womb. Other researchers hypothesize that higher levels of the hormone androgen is linked with homosexuality (Balthazart 2011). However, such biological explorations do not have conclusive evidence and are critiqued for the underlying assumption that heterosexuality is normal and homosexuality is a genetic or biological flaw. Finally, biomedical models are criticized for seeking monocausal explanations of homosexuality, abiding within the confines of a binary idea of gender and sex, and for dangerous research testing and medical intervention of homosexual and intersex individuals.

Theorists still exploring homosexuality from a biological perspective, such as Joan Roughgarden in *Evolution's Rainbow* (2013), argue that sexual diversity in nature is common and is an integral part of what makes human beings natural. Her research reveals sexual behavior in many animal species that challenges the traditional assumption that gender identity and sexual orientation correlate and affirms that individuality exists in both humans and animals. Roughgarden reconstructs Darwin's sexual selection theory to emphasize social inclusion and access to resources and mating opportunities, and she insists the scientific approach to understanding homosexuality be reevaluated in light of feminist, gay, and transgender criticisms.

Homosexuality as Mental Illness

The psychological community viewed homosexuality as a mental illness or personality disorder until 1973. Freud believed that human beings were born biologically bisexual, or naturally attracted to both sexes, but that adult homosexuality was a result of childhood trauma or immature sexual development. He viewed heterosexuality as the result of the fully developed and healthy adult. In 1962, Irving Bieber published an influential argument in *Homosexuality: A Psychoanalytic Study*. His research claimed homosexuality was caused by dysfunctional child-parent relationships, primarily a detached father and a domineering mother. Bieber, like other sexologists including Freud and Masters and Johnson, claimed to be able to cure homosexuality. Most psychological explanations of homosexuality are gender biased because the primary emphasis is on male homosexuality. Lesbianism is often viewed as a side topic or simply a reflection of male homosexuality.

The American Psychiatric Association (APA) is the leading professional association of psychiatrists in the United States. It publishes the *Diagnostic and Statistical Manual of Mental Disorders* (DSM), which is written by multiple committees of experts in every area of mental health. Homosexuality was officially classified as a mental illness, or a sociopathic personality disturbance, in 1952. When something is diagnosed as an illness, there is inevitably a focus on finding a treatment or a cure. This is certainly true for homosexuality. The 1950s were a brutal period for lesbians and gay men, as many thousands of them were subjected to incarceration in mental hospitals and treatments such as extended psychoanalysis, electric shock therapy, lobotomies, castration, as well as experimental chemical and pharmaceutical treatments. However, cultural changes and prevailing societal attitudes brought on by the women's and gay rights movements of the 1960s and 1970s urged the psychiatric establishment to reconsider its diagnosis. The APA changed this classification due to changing social and cultural pressures, not new scientific research findings. Thus, in 1973, homosexuality was officially declassified as a mental illness. However, it was not until 2000 that the APA denounced reparative therapies (also known as sexual conversion therapies)—a range of therapies designed to change a person's sexual orientation from homosexual to heterosexual.

Sociology of Homosexuality

In recent decades, social constructionist theories brought an entirely new perspective to the understanding of homosexuality. Sociologists began to inspect the influence of culture and society on homosexual behavior and identity, as seen in Simon and Gagnon's (1973) introduction of the idea of sexual scripts. Ken Plummer, in *Sexual Stigma* (1975), theorized that people learn to be homosexual. Plummer argued that an individual might feel same-sex desires, but the process of identifying as homosexual required learning sexual desires through interacting with both heterosexual and homosexual cultures. Jeffrey Weeks, in *Coming Out* (1977), sought to write a history and sociology of homosexuality. Weeks discovered that there was not a unified experience of homosexuality and that it shifts and changes throughout time and culture, and was influenced by factors such as social class, gender, race, ethnicity, among others.

SEXUALITY STUDIES IN ACADEMIA

Sexuality studies in academia is a fast growing, interdisciplinary field. Feminist, postmodern, lesbian, gay, bisexual, transgender, and queer (LGBTQ) theories all contribute to sexuality studies. Many Women's Studies programs, which developed out of the women's movement in the 1970s, are now called Women, Gender, and Sexuality Studies to incorporate the broader influence of gender and sexuality on the field. Feminist scholars began Women's Studies as a discipline by, about, and for women; but as the field developed, many began to realize that the study of gender and sexuality encapsulated the whole of the field more accurately. By the 1990s, a shift in the names of many academic programs reflected this growing awareness.

> "Lesbian/gay studies does for sex and sexuality approximately what women's studies does for gender . . . . [W]e can still describe lesbian/gay studies by saying that it intends to establish the analytical centrality of sex and sexuality within many different fields of inquiry, to express and advance the interests of lesbians, bisexuals, and gay men, and to contribute culturally and intellectually to the contemporary lesbian/gay movement" (Abelove, Barale, and Halperin 1993:xvxvi).

Lesbian, Gay, Bisexual, and Transgender Studies (LGBTS) scholars specifically focus on sexual orientation, gender and sexual identities, and the historical and contemporary experiences of lesbian, gay, bisexual, transgender, queer, and intersex people and cultures. Born out of the gay and lesbian social activism of the 1970s, this field began with a focus on the history and literary works of gay men and lesbians. Inspired by Women's Studies and African American Studies departments and other identity-based academic fields at the time, LGBTQ studies developed into its own discipline, with departments and degree-earning programs and certificates offered all over the world. Queer studies is an extension of lesbian and gay studies, based on queer theory and topics connected to this field, such as transgender history, sexualities, and LGBTQ legal issues. Just as Women's Studies programs represent the academic arm of the feminist movement, LGBTQ Studies can be seen as the academic arm of the gay liberation movement.

The work of women, gender, and sexuality studies scholars impacts our understanding of sexuality across all disciplines in academia. The role of society and culture cannot be ignored or left out of any analysis of the body, pleasure, desire, or sex. A greater awareness of moral biases, dominant ideologies, norms, and beliefs must be acknowledged and explored for research to be considered valid and credible. This has not always been the case in academic research.

RESEARCHING SEX: ETHICAL AND METHODOLOGICAL CONCERNS

This chapter introduced the leading research in the science of sexuality, from early sexologists to queer theory. Here we explore some key dilemmas surrounding sex research; specifically, ethical and methodological issues unique to sexuality studies. Today, researchers associated with institutions of higher education must obtain subjects' informed consent in order to engage in a research study, are required to follow guidelines that protect human subjects from any physical or psychological risk of injury, and must ensure their privacy and confidentiality. Studying sex and sexuality creates its own set of methodological problems because it is difficult to get people to talk about personal and private matters such as their own sexual desires, behaviors, and fantasies, especially if these entail stigmatized desires and behaviors.

Ethical Issues in Sex Research

The first ethical dilemma concerns whether research on sexual orientation should be done at all. We touch on this topic lightly in Chapter One when we ask why we invest so much time and energy seeking a biological or genetic explanation for homosexuality. Is the goal to find a cure for homosexuality? If so, is that ethical? Clearly, such an approach implies there is something wrong with being gay, lesbian, or bisexual and perpetuates homophobia and discrimination against gays and lesbians. If history is our guide, scientific research on sexual orientation has caused more harm to LGBTQ individuals than good. Even the terminology used by many sexuality researchers belies their homophobic assumptions: homosexuality is often referred to as a disease, a dysfunction, abnormal brain development, or as a result of deficient hormones. For these reasons, some argue that scientists have an obligation to consider the consequences of their research before engaging in it.

A second ethical dilemma tied to sex research involves questions surrounding the researchers and their obligation to disclose their role. One of the most infamous studies concerning this kind of ethical breach in sex research is known as the *Tearoom Trade: A Study of Homosexual Encounters in Public Places* (1970) by sociologist Laud Humphreys. Humphreys studied anonymous sexual encounters between men in public spaces, such as restrooms at rest areas or in urban parks known as "tearooms." In order to gain access to these encounters, he played the role of "watch queen" under the pretense that he was a voyeur who enjoyed watching sexual encounters. Instead, he was a sociologist studying illegal encounters between consenting adults. He wrote down the license plate numbers of the men involved so he could later learn more about the

"Historically, almost every investigation into the causes of homosexuality has aimed at its elimination. . . . The results of such research have been used to force many lesbians and gay men to undergo various procedures to change their sexual orientation, even when there was little reason to think such procedures would have any effect. . . . Such therapies included electroshock treatment, genital mutilation, brain surgery, and lengthy and wrenching psychoanalysis" (Stein 1999:329).

men who participated in these anonymous sexual encounters. A year later, after significantly altering his appearance, he went to their homes and proceeded to engage the men in a fake research study to find out personal information about them such as their marital status, sexual orientation, occupation, and so on. Many of the men who participated in the tearoom trades, he discovered, were married to women, and some were prominent members of the community.

His research is considered unethical because he was not forthcoming about his role as a researcher with his subjects, which could put them at risk; and he violated their right to privacy. They did not consent to his original study, and they were told he was doing a health survey when he came to their homes under false pretenses. He justified his actions by stating he was under no obligation to disclose he was a sociologist engaging in research at the tearoom because he was watching a public act. Despite his justifications, ethical standards guiding social science research today state that researchers are obligated to disclose their research agenda to their subjects, and they cannot mislead subjects about their research. An additional concern with this research is that if his research notes were ever turned over to the authorities, these men's lives could have been ruined. Because sex between men at the time was illegal, they could have been arrested or fired from their jobs, and such information would have certainly disrupted their lives. While it might be difficult to obtain this kind of information any other way, this study remains a primary example of a violation of research ethics.

Kinsey and his coresearchers were also involved in some ethical dilemmas. During the course of their research, the in-depth sexual histories of thousands of men included those of several pedophiles, including a man who claimed to have sexually assaulted and raped dozens of children. They reported the findings in two tables on preadolescent orgasms in their first volume, *Sexuality in the Human Male* (1948). This data became a major source of controversy in the 1990s. Most of the data Kinsey and his colleagues use in the child sexual response charts came from interviewees describing their own sexual experiences as children. But some came from the pedophiles who participated in the research (several were even incarcerated for their sexual crimes at the time of the interviews). It was later discovered that Kinsey recorded the data on child sexual responses in such a way as to protect the anonymity of one of the original sources, the pedophile who reportedly had sex with dozens of children. His decision to protect the privacy of a pedophile and not to turn him over to the authorities was questioned, even though it seems unlikely that this kind of information could have been solicited from a criminal without such assurances of their anonymity.

Methodological Issues in Sex Research

In terms of methodological issues, sex research presents a set of specific issues that standard social scientific research does not face. For instance, survey research seeks to obtain a representative sample. Thus, if researchers wants to study sexual behaviors among today's college students, they must make sure their sample mirrors the college student population along the lines of gender, sexual orientation, age, and race. However, when it comes to sex research, we face the problem of *self-selection bias*, or volunteer bias, in which subjects who agree to participate in sex research tend to be more sexually experienced than those who choose not to participate in such research (Boynton 2003; Plaud et al. 1999). Again, we can turn to Kinsey's research for an example of this. While he and his colleagues took sexual histories of over 18,000 men and women, the representativeness of his sample is questioned: they are all white, better educated, more urbanized, and younger than the population at large, which inevitably limits Kinsey's ability to extend his findings to the population at large. Sampling bias is an ongoing problem in sex research.

Another methodological issue sex researchers face involves the choice of language used to ask questions about sensitive sexual practices. Avoiding highly technical or academic terminology, such as using the term "fellatio" instead of "oral sex," is important to ensure respondent comprehension. Researchers often opt to use more colloquial language and sometimes even slang references to avoid comprehension issues (Das and Laumann 2015).

Stigma and Sexuality Research

Difficulties associated with sexuality research go beyond methodological dilemmas and involve issues of professional stigma and difficulty obtaining research funding. The science of sexuality is often not treated with the same regard as other scientific endeavors and instead, is politicized. Upon release of Kinsey's second book, *Sexual Behavior in the Human Female* (1952), so much outrage ensued that he and his colleagues lost their Rockefeller Institute funding, which was a significant part of their operating budget. In 1991, an act of Congress was used to deny funding for one of the largest surveys of sexuality ever attempted. Congressman Jesse Helms instead preferred funding a survey that supported the "just say no to sex" campaign (Laumann 2011). In the current era, conservative politicians maintain a climate of intimidation and censorship to reduce funding for sex research (Stombler and Jungels 2014). It is especially crucial in the era of HIV/AIDS to better understand sexual practices in order to develop effective strategies of disease prevention, and yet, we still see sex research denied necessary funding.

In addition to funding issues that originate outside of academia, sexuality studies struggle for legitimacy within academic circles as well (Irvine 2015). Sociologist Janice M. Irvine (2015) studied sociologists engaged in sexuality research and found that many report legitimacy questions from colleagues, resulting in academic marginalization. She found sexuality researchers are problematically sexualized by colleagues because of their choice of research topic. Assumptions are made about the researcher's sexual identity and practices simply because of what he or she studies. Additionally, for researchers who are openly LGBTQ, their research is often trivialized as "advocacy" rather than objective science. The *sexuality stigma* attached to sexuality researchers is also gendered; women are more likely to report experiences of stigma than men, and they are twice as likely to have uncomfortable, sexual jokes directed at them, among other issues (Irvine 2015). Essentially, "women sociologists more often perceived that their association with sex research sexualized them and their workplace interactions, producing stereotypically gendered expectations about their desires and availability" (Irvine 2015:122).

In 1970, the American Anthropological Association, encouraged by one of its members, Clark Taylor, adopted a resolution supporting gay and lesbian anthropologists and the right to study gay and lesbian topics. Taylor "spoke eloquently in highly personal language of the discrimination faced by members of the profession who were known to be homosexual or whose scholarly interests focused on homosexuality" (Lewin and Leap 1996:vii). While the resolution passed, it was ignored for many years. Since that time, lesbian and gay academics have formed professional organizations as a way to support LGBTQ scholars and their work. For instance, in 1974, the Anthropological Research Group on Homosexuality was formed; in 1986, its name was changed to The Society of Lesbian and Gay Anthropologists. Such developments are indeed progress, but academia is far from an equal opportunity employer when it comes to sexual orientation. In anthropology, Lewin and Leap state that "Gay men and lesbians continue to find that they must keep a low profile if they are to avoid systematic, although sometimes subtle, discrimination in graduate school and professional life" (1996:x).

CONCLUSION

Sociologists approach the subject of sexuality from a social constructionist perspective. Prior to this approach, most sexologists assumed that sexuality is a natural and fundamental part of being human. Theologians argued sexuality was a primal, sinful drive. Victorian physicians feared homosexuality was a disease. Freud proposed it was an unconscious, psychological drive. Darwin argued sex was an evolutionary drive with the primary objective to propagate the species. Kinsey, Masters and Johnson, and many biologists and sexologists before them, explored the social and physiological dynamics of the experience of sex, still assuming it was a biological and primarily heterosexual drive.

Sociologists and feminists began to theorize sexuality as a learned way of thinking, acting, and feeling—heavily influenced by society and culture and, for feminists, deeply influenced by patriarchal ideologies. Foucault turned common sense assumptions about sexual norms of the Victorian era on their head. It is science that creates the terminology "homosexual" and "heterosexual," designating some sexual behaviors as deviant and others as normal and natural. Kinsey and other modern sexologists were interested in the range of sexual practices people engage in.

The gay rights movement of the 1970s triggered a renewed academic commitment to research on sex and sexuality, with the emergence of lesbian and gay studies and, later, queer theory, and the institutionalization of Gender and Sexuality Studies involving sexuality scholars from across academic disciplines. Sexuality studies influenced research protocols, particularly related to ethical and methodological issues in research. A renewed commitment to the privacy of research subjects, their protection from physical and psychological harm, and their right to consent to research is now expected.

Key Terms and Concepts

Autoeroticism 29	Norms 33	Sex selection 32
Castration complex 31	Oedipus complex 31	Sexology 26
Discourse 39	Ontology 38	Sexual degenerate 41
Epistemology 38	Queer theory 40	Sexual deviance 36
Homosocial 40	Representative sample 33	Sexual inversion 40
Kinsey scale 33	Repressive hypothesis 39	Sexual response cycle 34
Natural selection 32	Self-selection bias 44	Sexuality stigma 45

Critical Thinking Questions

1. Describe the key contributions of early researchers of sexuality. In what ways are their perspectives shaped by nineteenth-century cultural ideologies?

2. Who are some of the main sociological contributors to the social constructionist perspective on sexuality? In what ways are their perspectives shaped by twentieth-century ideologies?

3. How does feminist theory contribute to the science of sexuality? How does intersectionality expand our understanding of sexuality?

4. In what ways do Foucault and queer theorists challenge mainstream ideas of sex and sexuality? What arguments might arise against these perspectives?

Activities

1. Conduct an interview with a sexuality scholar on your campus. Find out which theoretical perspective they favor, if they have experienced any hostility or derision directed at their research subject area. Finally, describe one of their research projects, including their research methodology.

2. Write a one-page description of what the science of sexuality would look like if homosexuality was not historically stigmatized? How would this impact medical and psychiatric views of homosexuality?

3. Find a recent scientific study of sexuality. Describe the research methods and field of study it is rooted in. What contributions does it make to the field?

Essential Readings

Foucault, Michel. 1976. *The History of Sexuality: An Introduction,* Vols. II and III. New York: Random House.

Gagnon, John H. and William Simon. 1973. *Sexual Conduct: The Social Sources of Human Sexuality*. Newark, NJ: Aldine.

Kinsey, Alfred C. 1953. *Sexual Behavior in the Human Female*. Bloomington, IN: Indiana University Press.

Kinsey, Alfred C. 1948. *Sexual Behavior in the Human Male*. Philadelphia: W. B. Saunders Co.

Michael, Robert T., John H. Gagnon, Edward O. Laumann, and Gina Kolata. 1994. *Sex in America: A Definitive Survey*. New York: Little, Brown & Co.

Weeks, Jeffrey. 1977. *Coming Out: Homosexual Politics in Britain from the Nineteenth Century to the Present*. London, England: Quartet Books.

Recommended Films

Kinsey (2005). Barak Goodman and John Maggio, Producers and Directors. Documentary about the Indiana University biologist turned sexologist, Alfred Kinsey, lead researcher and author of the *Kinsey Studies*, a revolutionary, scientific exploration of American sexual behavior in the mid-twentieth century.

Masters of Sex (2013). Michelle Ashford, Sarah Timberman, Carl Beverly, Amy Lippman, David Flebotte, and Judith Verno, Executive Producers. A Showtime television drama series, starring Michael Sheen and Lizzy Caplan, portrays the life and research of scientists William Masters and Virginia Johnson. The series is based off of Thomas Maier's book, *Masters of Sex: The Life and Times of William Masters and Virginia Johnson, the Couple Who Taught America How to Love* (2013).

Suggested Multimedia

The Society for the Scientific Study of Sexuality (SSSS) is an international organization dedicated to the advancement of knowledge about sexuality. SSSS brings together an interdisciplinary group of professionals who believe in the importance of both the production of quality research and the clinical, educational, and social applications of research related to all aspects of sexuality. http://www.sexscience.org/

The Kinsey Institute at Indiana University works toward advancing sexual health and knowledge worldwide. For over 60 years, the institute has been a trusted source for investigating and informing the world about critical issues in sex, gender, and reproduction. http://www.kinseyinstitute.org/index.html

3

GENDER AND SEXUALITY

LEARNING OBJECTIVES

Upon completion of this chapter, students will be able to . . .

- Understand the social construction of gender
- Describe the intersection of masculinity, femininity, and sexuality
- Understand transgender identities
- Recognize intersex and dissolve the assumed sex binary

Our understandings of gender are changing rapidly. As a sociologist who has been teaching women's, gender, and sexuality studies and the sociology of race/ethnicity courses for over twenty years, I rarely find myself completely blindsided by an encounter with students when it comes to these topics. That is exactly the situation I found myself in a few years ago, however. As a sociology professor, I often get asked to speak to campus student organizations. During the fall 2013 semester, a student from our campus gay/straight alliance asked me to speak to their organization about intersectionality. I was happy to do so. On the assigned evening, however, we never got to the scheduled topic.

The organization opened their weekly meeting with a ritual that was new to me. As each member of the organization introduced themselves, they not only stated their name and major, but also identified the pronoun they prefer to be addressed by. I was stunned and, in fact, stumbled when it came time for me to introduce myself. I simply provided a standard introduction: my name and my academic credentials ("Hi, I am Dr. Fitzgerald in the Department of Sociology. I teach courses on inequalities: race, sexuality, gender, and class"). It took me a few minutes to realize how offensive this was—I assumed my gender was obvious and I did not need to specify my preferred pronoun. This was the case for many of the students in the room, but not all. In this instance, I had enacted my cisgender privilege. As a *cisgender* person, someone whose self-identity conforms to their biological gender, I had never been in a situation like this. The student ritual was meant to disrupt the taken-for-grantedness of gender. It was successful at doing so. We spent most of the rest of our time together talking about this ritual and its significance.

This shift appears to be happening across academia. Professor Nyasha Junior of Howard University describes her approach to the issue in an article in *Inside Higher Education* (Junior 2014). On a student sign-in sheet she hands out on the first day of class, she requests students tell her not only their preferred name, which can often differ from their formal name on a course roster, but also their preferred pronoun. When questioned about the request, she responds, "I am also asking for your preferred pronoun because I don't want to make assumptions about how you want to be addressed. You may prefer 'she' or 'he' or something else." While some students seem bewildered by the question, another chimes in with a perfect example of why this is appropriate: "another student raises his hand. In a clear voice, he declared, 'I am married to a trans woman. At work, she is forced to use her government name and to identify as male. At home, she is a woman'" (Junior 2014). Professor Junior declares this one small change opens the door for conversations about differences she feels are essential to making the classroom a more inclusive and comfortable space.

In this chapter, we examine the intersection of gender and sexuality from a sociological perspective. Gender refers to socially constructed patterns of behavior associated with and assigned to biological sex. It is one of the foundational ways in which society is organized. Many aspects of our everyday world, from the use of pronouns in language to designated restrooms, sports teams, and clothing stores are gender segregated. And while it may seem like there are only two gender categories, masculine and feminine, gender is actually a multifaceted, highly malleable phenomenon, constantly changing and adapting. More than just socially defined, it is also an ongoing personal experience that can be individually defined and redefined throughout one's life. For some, gender is an easy category to identify with because it correlates with their biological sex. For others, this is not so clear-cut.

Individuals who do not fit the mainstream norms of sex and gender are increasingly visible, including cross-dressers, gender nonconforming people, transgender individuals, and more. Each of these identities will be further explained and discussed in this chapter. Education about what it means to be transgender has become a growing subject in the news, pop culture, and on college campuses. Interesting and complicated questions about gender identity, sexuality, and society are being raised and discussed, such as: How do we describe or categorize someone's gender if they do not identify as feminine or masculine? Do we need to legally categorize gender? How is gender assigned if someone is born intersex or with ambiguous genitalia? Is there a relationship between gender identity and sexual orientation? New vocabulary and definitions are being constructed by students, teachers, and transgender individuals to describe themselves, their experiences, and their social positions. This chapter seeks to represent the most up-to-date terminology on gender and transgender subjects while also recognizing that vocabulary is historically constructed and subject to change.

In July 2016, Sarah McBride became the first transgender person to speak at a political convention when she addressed the Democratic National Convention.
Source: AP Photo/Bill Clark.

Although education about gender nonconformity and transgender acceptance is increasing in social media, film, television, Internet, and news, transgender people across the globe still face discrimination in nearly every aspect of their lives, which will be discussed further in this chapter. Examples of how transgender and gender issues are making worldwide news include:

- In 2012, in Showtime's series *House of Lies*, the audience first encounters Don Cheadle's 12-year-old son, Roscoe, when he turns up for breakfast wearing a skirt, complaining to his father that he probably won't get the part of Sandra Dee in the school musical because of his assigned gender. The character of Roscoe is one of a growing number of representations in entertainment and news media of gender nonconforming children (Pyne 2014).
- In February 2014, the social media network Facebook began offering over 50 gender identity options for users to choose from. One year later, in February 2015, due to pressure from users for more inclusivity, Facebook added a "custom" gender option for U.S. users to write in their own self-determined identities. (Kellaway 2015).
- On April 2, 2014, the Australian government recognized the existence of a third "non-specific" gender that is neither male nor female. The High Court ruled that not everyone should be forced to identify as a man or a woman, and some people can legitimately be described as gender neutral.
- In January 2015, Oregon begins covering the cost of reassignment surgery for transgender people on Medicaid, including hormone therapy and hormone suppression to halt puberty.
- On February 3, 2015, the *New York Times* published an article titled, "A University Recognizes a Third Gender: Neutral" describing how the University of Vermont now allows students to select their own gender identity and preferred pronoun (Scelfo 2015).

SOCIAL CONSTRUCTION OF GENDER: FEMININITY AND MASCULINITY

Gender, like sexuality, is a social construction. Harold Garfinkle (1967) is one of the earliest sociologists to describe gender as a behavior that is created and produced. Based on his study of "Agnes," a male wishing to appear as, and who later becomes, a female, Garfinkle revealed gender to be a daily, enacted task and performance (Garfinkle 1967). Sociologists Suzanne Kessler and Wendy McKenna (1978) expanded on Garfinkle's work and claim gender is not a reflection of biology, but a social construction that varies across cultures. One of the more significant contributors to understanding the social construction of gender, Judith Lorber (1994), describes gender as something people produce to create identities and statuses, and at the same time, reproduce to create the structure and constraints of the social world.

Gender is socially constructed on a spectrum that is polarized between two ideals: femininity and masculinity, presented as binary, opposing concepts, often referred to as the *gender binary system.* Masculinity and femininity are constructed as opposites and, thus, have no meaning separate from the other. In other words, masculine traits are usually defined as opposite of feminine traits. Masculine traits, or socially assigned qualities associated with being a boy or man, include expectations for men to be unemotional, independent, aggressive, physically strong, logical, and self-confident. Feminine traits, or socially assigned qualities for girls and women, include expectations for women to be emotionally vulnerable, dependent, passive, physically weak, irrational, and self-critical. These gender assignments are based on social ideas that are often unrealistic since most men share many so-called feminine traits and most women have some so-called masculine traits, as they are actually all human traits.

Gender is taught from the moment of birth through interaction with our parents, peers, schools, workplace, and the media, something sociologists refer to as *gender socialization.* By this we mean that we learn what it means to be an acceptable female and an acceptable male. In contemporary U.S. society, hospitals give newborn boys blue hats and girls pink ones. As children, they are expected to play with gender-specific toys: typically, girls are given dolls and boys are given trucks. In school, there is a gendered expectation that boys will be interested in and excel at math and science while girls are expected to be better readers. In high school, teenage men and women are segregated in physical activities: "ideally masculine" males play football and "ideally feminine" females cheerlead. Rarely do high school sports teams allow both males and females on the same team; and in some cases, such as football, there have been efforts to exclude girls altogether.

When young people start dating, very gender-specific dating scripts are taught, such as the expectation that men will be pursuers and women will be passive recipients of attention and sexual desire. This expectation is the same for marriage rituals, in which it is expected that the man propose and the bride-to-be plan the wedding. Within heterosexual marriage and family dynamics, men and women are expected to provide very specific roles: such as men being the protectors and the economic providers while women are expected to be the nurturers and the primary homemakers, even when they also work in the paid labor force. Even the workplace is gendered. Certain jobs, like firefighting and construction work, have traditionally been associated with masculinity, while child care and nursing have traditionally been associated with femininity. Men and women are expected to behave in very specific gendered ways; or the consequences can be social rejection, humiliation, and sometimes violence. All of these expectations can be described as part of the binary, social gender order.

Many people follow their gender assignments their entire lives without question. Moreover, many individuals completely identify with the assigned gender that corresponds with their biological sex. Garfinkle (1967) describes such individuals as "gender normals." A more current term, coined in the 1990s, is ***cisgender***, or someone whose self-identity conforms to their cultural gender assignment. The "cis" in cisgender comes from a Latin word meaning "on this side of." The term cisgender first appeared only in an academic context; but more recently it can be found on the Internet, blogs, and among social activist groups. Sociologists Schilt and Westbrook (2009) describe how cisgender individuals not only identify with their gender assignment at birth but often presume that gender reflects biological sex in all their social interactions, too. In other words, most people assume their personal gender "normalness" reflects the wider society's norms. The emergence of the term cisgender works to disrupt the assumed normality of gender, as the opening vignette of this chapter exemplifies.

Challenging the Gender Binary: Gender in Non-Western Cultures

The binary gender code is not universal or static. Institutionalized gender diversity can be found in cultures throughout the world. Some societies include and accept third and fourth genders. A ***third gender*** is a social category in which an individual can represent gender in a variety of ways: an intermediate state between masculine and feminine, as neither gender, as the ability to cross or swap genders, or another category altogether independent of male/female and masculine/feminine categories. For example, in native North America there were tribes that recognized more than two genders. Anthropologists previously used the term *berdache* to describe third-gender traditions found in many Native American Indian cultures. While this term is no longer in use, the more accepted term coined by Native Americans is *two-spirit* (Jacobs, Thomas, and Lang 1997). In most cases, a two-spirit person is a man who dresses in women's clothing and partakes in women's activities, but it can also describe a woman who dresses or behaves like a man (Jacobs et. al. 1997). Within Native American tribal cultures, the relationship between sexuality and gender is not inextricably connected, as it is in Western cultures; and thus, gender does not always inform sexual preference. Native American cultures generally rely less on the binaries found throughout Western culture; instead of an emphasis on either/or, there is a gender continuum.

Similarly, there are the *fa'afafine*, a third-gender people of Samoa. A fa'afafine is a biological male at birth, who embodies primarily feminine gender traits. The word fa'afafine includes the causative prefix "fa'a," meaning "in the manner of," and the word fafine, meaning "woman." Typically, their behavior is feminine, and they engage in typically feminine work. They have sex almost exclusively with men who are not considered fa'afafine, but sometimes with women, too. The fa'afafine is a commonly accepted and integral aspect of contemporary Samoan culture (Schmidt 2001).

In Thailand, the *kathoey* is a term that refers to a man who is dressing, behaving, or identifying as a female. The word kathoey means a "second-type female" and can include men who exhibit varying degrees of feminine behavior. The common Thai perception is that the kathoey are a third sex. The kathoey are visible in daily work life, media, entertainment, and tourist centers in modern Thai culture; and many tourists describe them as cultural symbols of Thailand. Although there is widespread acceptance, systemic institutional discrimination against the kathoey still exists in Thailand (Winter 2003). The two-spirit of Native American culture, the fa'afaine of Samoa, and the kathoey in Thailand are examples of nonbinary ways individuals express gender and the variations of social acceptance across cultures on the globe.

Gender Identity

The personal experience and performance of gender is often described as an individual's ***gender identity***. Sociologists argue that gender is both externally and internally

BOX 3.1

GLOBAL/TRANSNATIONAL PERSPECTIVES ON SEXUALITY: *THE GUEVEDOCES IN THE DOMINICAN REPUBLIC*

In the 1970s, Julianne Imperato, PhD, of Cornell University traveled to an isolated village in the southwestern region of the Dominican Republic to investigate claims of young girls who started developing male physical features at puberty, including the development of a penis and testes, facial and body hair, and deepening of voice. The locals referred to the phenomena as guevedoces, which means "penis at age twelve" ("The Extraordinary Case of the Guevedoces" 2015). Guevedoces infants are born with female appearing genitalia. Yet, at puberty, their bodies start to transform, and they develop into males. In effect, most guevedoces spend their childhood as girls and adult years as males.

All humans have a set of chromosomes structured in their DNA that indicate sex. Males have XY chromosomes, females have two X chromosomes, and some intersex individuals have mosaic genetics with both XY and XX chromosomes. Dr. Imperato discovered that guevedoces are born with the male XY genotype and are thereby genetically male. However, during fetal development, the internal male sexual organs

develop while the external male organs do not. Female external genitalia of labia and clitoris remain. Imperto's research discovered this is a result of a deficiency in the 5 a-reductase enzyme (Imperato-McGinley et. al 1974). When the testosterone hormone increases at puberty, the body responds and it triggers the development of the male external reproductive organs.

Research has shown this genetic variance to be hereditary and accounted-for 2 percent of births in the 1970s in the southwest region of the Dominican Republic, but is very rare in other parts of the world. Due to the Dominican Republic's isolation and small size of the gene pool, this condition persisted for generations. Due to the prevalence of these births, Dominicans in the area believe in three sexual categories: male, female, and guevedoces. Interestingly, guevedoces are fully accepted in society; and during puberty, when the child makes a physical sex transformation, it is celebrated and appreciated (Kelley 2005). The Dominican Republic stands as an example to the rest of the world of how to approach sex variation with a model of acceptance.

prescribed. Thus, gender identity is a personal and individual process informed by culturally prescribed gender roles, but it is also separate and independent of them. Most people identify with a male or female sex category anatomically, but their sense of self and gender identity is not always so simple. A much wider range of gender experiences exists beyond the traditional social categories of feminine and masculine. For example, a woman may be born as the female sex, but identify with the masculine gender role. Moreover, gender identity is not always fixed or resolute. ***Gender fluidity*** is a term to describe a flexible range of gender expressions that can change over time. A gender fluid person can express gender changes in their behavior or, in some cases, adopt gender fluidity as their gender identity.

Some people identify with and display *both* feminine and masculine gender characteristics. ***Androgyny***, from the Greek word *andro*, meaning "male," and *gyn*, meaning "female," describes an individual who displays and identifies with both gender traits. Famous 1990s U.S. pop singer and cultural sex symbol Prince (1958–2016) exhibited both feminine and masculine gender characteristics in his popular persona. Prince demonstrated femininity in his gestures, dancing, and clothing, but managed to display masculine appeal at the same time particularly through his sexual advances. British pop singer David Bowie (1947–2016) challenged mainstream ideas of gender throughout his entire career with an array of unconventional gender presentations. Bowie was most famous for wearing bold printed bodysuits and brightly colored pant suits, which exemplified and challenged ideals of both femininity and masculinity respectively.

Conversely, an individual can be undifferentiated in terms of gender categorization if they do not identify with or display gender characteristics at all. Undifferentiated is a term coined by psychologist Sandra Bem in her development of the ***Bem Sex Role Inventory*** in 1974. This survey assesses how individuals view themselves psychologically and uses a scale to measure and assign gender personality traits. Bem views masculinity and femininity as two independent dimensions with a neutral dimension in between. If someone scores low on both gender scales, they are what Bem calls undifferentiated. An undifferentiated person is not the same as androgynous because an androgynous person still identifies with both gender categories. This scale has been criticized for its theoretical framework and validity, but it still persists as a helpful tool to understand the range of gender identities and behaviors. A more recent term sometimes used to describe someone who does not identify with any specific gender is ***agender***. Sometimes this can infer that an individual is gender neutral, while for some the term agender is an identity itself.

How do people develop a gender identity? There are many different approaches scholars use to explain how individuals come to adopt a gender identity. Cognitive developmental theorists focus on how humans, particularly children, develop gender identities. Lawrence Kohlberg (1966), one of the most prominent cognitive-developmental theorists, describes gender development as a process of making sense of the world, including one's own body and its relationship to society. For Kohlberg and other cognitive developmental theorists, gender development begins early in life, as soon as girls figure out they are girls and boys figure out they are boys, and progresses into adulthood through a series of stages. Cognitive theorists believe that learning gender involves both a biological and environmental process in which children organize and identify with various social roles, concepts, and attitudes.

Learning theorists emphasize the impact of the social and physical environments on individuals. In this perspective, it is understood that people internalize the norms and practices of gender through their experiences in the world and learn incentives and punishments by behaving in particular ways. Sandra Bem (1983) weaves cognitive and learning theory into an approach she calls ***gender schema theory***. Essentially, she describes an individual's gender schema as a network of associations about concepts of masculinity and femininity that organize and guide an individual's perceptions (Bem 1983). Over time, an individual develops a unique, personalized framework, or gender schema, for understanding the world and its gendered expectations.

Doing Gender

How do we display or express gender? At the most basic level, human beings display their gender through gender cues, which include hairstyle, body language, clothing, and so on. However, gender is more than an external costume presentation. Sociologists West and Zimmerman (1987) describe gender as a social performance or something that we "do." Rather than focusing on how gender is ingrained or developed in an individual, their research emphasizes how we are constantly ***doing gender*** at the interactional level, as a site where gender is invoked, performed, and reinforced. In this context, gender is a verb. They claim individuals perform gender as it is prescribed by society, but under the façade that it is natural. A social accountability structure exists that judges individuals in terms of their success or failure to meet gendered social expectations. In this theoretical understanding of gender, people are in a constant state of learning gender and then "acting" masculine or feminine. Gender then becomes a methodical routine and an ongoing accomplishment.

West and Fenstermaker (1995) apply the same concept to race and class divisions in what they call ***doing difference***, or the ongoing routine of performing social difference. They argue that, like gender, differences between people are reinforced at the interactional level and that a wider social accountability structure is in place to validate and promote such differences. They argue that by revealing how gender, race, and class are accomplished as mass social behaviors, mechanisms of inequality can be revealed.

Some individuals deliberately do gender in ways that are considered atypical for their prescribed gender assignment. This type of behavior is described as ***gender nonconformity***, or sometimes referred to as genderqueer, gender bending, creativity, independence, or variance. Some gender activists deliberately rebel against social expectations to make a statement about the oppressive nature of such expectations. This can be expressed through clothing, pronoun use, appearance, and activities. In some cases, gender rebellion is successful in disrupting the gendered order, or the "naturalness" of gender, and can provoke a momentary crisis in how to categorize people (Lucal 1999). According to Judith Lorber (1994), gender bending, or intentionally breaking the rules and passing between genders, actually preserves gender boundaries. In other words, when a woman dresses as a man, society notices the incongruence between her sex and her gender display, but it does not challenge society's expectations of the two gender categories—masculinity or femininity.

A less researched group of gender nonconformists is children. Often without any conscious or deliberate intent, children violate gender norms in a variety of ways including consistently wearing clothes and playing with toys assigned to the opposite sex, identifying with characters of the opposite sex, expressing a desire to be the opposite sex, or a desire to be both sexes (Pyne 2014). When girls consistently act like boys, they are often called "tomboys" and, for the most part, are accepted. However, this has not always been the case. In the mid-twentieth century, being a "tomboy" was highly stigmatizing. Even today, girls who act like "tomboys" are accepted until they hit puberty. At this point, their behavior becomes more criticized. For boys, there is much less acceptance of gender nonconformity. When a boy periodically or consistently dresses or acts like girls, sometimes referred to as a "pink boy," a social stigma is often placed on him and his family.

Often parents, the education system, and medical and psychological communities address gender nonconformity in children by diagnosing them with a disorder, such as ***gender identity disorder*** (GID), or gender dysphoria, a medical diagnosis given to individuals who experience significant distress with the sex and gender they were assigned at birth. Sometimes parents and authorities try to force young people to conform to traditional gender roles by demanding they wear gender typical clothing. Sometimes children are exposed to verbal and physical abuse by parents and bullying from peers for their nonconformity, and this can cause suffering in the form of anxiety and depression (Pyne 2014). Direct causes or future outcomes of children who display gender nonconforming behavior are still unknown. Sometimes children simply stop gender nonconforming behaviors, sometimes they seek sex changes as adults, and sometimes they go on to continue to represent an undefined middle space in a wide spectrum of gender diversity.

How do we know someone else's gender? Kessler and McKenna (1978) claim that every time we encounter a new person, we make a gender attribution. A ***gender attribution*** is the process of assigning a gender onto a person with or without knowing concretely what gender that person identifies as. It is a process of observing behavior traits and matching them with culturally prescribed gender role expectations. We rely on other people's gender displays to inform how we assign their gender. ***Misgendering*** is a term to describe the process by which people categorize and refer to people's gender, based on perceptions and assumptions, without regard to how the person self-identifies. For example, when a person uses the pronoun "he" to refer to another individual, even though they are not sure if the individual identifies as male. This kind of misperception can cause the misgendered individual to feel anxious or even invisible. Intentional misgendering is a form of abuse and discrimination. The New York City

Commission on Human Rights states that based on existing discrimination laws, employers can be heavily fined if they call transgender employees by the wrong name, gender, or pronoun (NYC Commission on Human Rights 2002).

To avoid misgendering, the social practice of asking what pronouns an individual prefers is becoming a more common practice. The use of the pronoun "they" is a gender-neutral way to refer to someone who may identify as "nonbinary" in gender terms. Due to its new and socially relevant identity, the word "they" was recognized as the Word of the Year in 2015 by the American Dialect Society ("2015 Word of the Year" 2016). Additional gender-inclusive vocabulary is being used on some college campuses including the use of pronoun options "hir," to replace "her/him," and "ze," to replace "he/she." As mentioned earlier in the chapter, in support of the use of new gender terms, in 2014, the social media site Facebook began offering over 50 different gender identity options for users, including gender fluid, agender, and *bigender*, a person who identifies as having two distinct genders.

Gender Roles

Close examination of the social world reveals all the ways gender is socially constructed and organized. Kinship structures, dominant patterns of marriage and family life, and the economy all influence gender and are, in turn, influenced by gender. Personal and intimate aspects of people's lives, such as dating and kissing rituals, are informed by gendered social values and expectations. The social expectation that we will participate in gendered behaviors is called a *gender role*. Gender roles are socially developed and externally prescribed by the specific culture within which we live.

There are a variety of theories on why and how gender roles are established in society. Essentialist theories rely on biological or natural explanations of gender and gender role assignments, such as the explanation that gendered behavior is shaped by sex hormones. Testosterone, which is produced in higher quantities in males, is used to explain aggressive behaviors in male violent criminals and higher risk taking in male financial traders (Coates, Gurnell, and Sarnyai 2010; Dabbs 1995). Evolutionary theory, also based on biological principles, claims human beings are in a constant state of adaptation to their environment in order to ensure survival (see Chapter Two). Thereby, a gendered division of labor develops out of a functional need for the human family to survive. This hypothesis holds that in ancient societies, men were hunters and women gatherers of food, primarily because the demands of pregnancy prevented women from travelling far or away from nursing infants to hunt. Feminist anthropologists critique this theory by suggesting that women often had to travel far to gather food, and they ask the critical question: Even if these roles served a function in history at one time, do they still make sense today?

Materialist and economic theorists emphasize the impact of basic human economic needs in the formation of gender roles. Marxist feminists specifically explore and critique gender roles within the economic system of capitalism. They claim women were historically relegated to reproductive, unpaid domestic labor and excluded from paid, productive labor, supporting the male gender role as head of household. As women began to enter the workforce, traditional patriarchal ideas and sexism prevented women from gaining full, equal economic equality (Hartsock 1987). Feminist economist and writer Charlotte Perkins Gilman (1868–1935) embraced both materialist and evolutionary theories to explain gender roles and inequalities. She argued against Herbert Spencer's theory of social Darwinism, saying it was unnatural that the human female species is completely dependent on the male species; and, in order to progress as a species and a society, the economy required equal divisions of labor.

Gender, Inequality, and Stereotypes

Stereotypes serve the ideological needs of the dominant group in power by justifying inequality. Gender stereotypes justify patriarchy and can negatively impact women's self-perceptions, relationships, and society. Not all stereotypes are overtly negative. For example, women are stereotypically described as being naturally caring, nurturing, and good at mothering. This can be described as a benevolent stereotype, or a form of benevolent sexism. ***Benevolent sexism*** is a way of viewing women stereotypically and in restricted roles, but in a positive or caring tone (Glick and Fiske 2001). Although women can be caring and nurturing mothers, the assumption they are always this way implies they are biologically and naturally suited for motherhood and traditional female gender roles. In reality, many women choose not have children. Does this mean they are not *natural* women? Such descriptions sound positive, but are actually limiting. Benevolent sexist stereotypes often serve to justify and support gender inequality by masking it and making it appear to celebrate women (Glick and Fiske 2001).

Considering the fact that gender inequality is so widespread and pervasive, one might ask if there are any known societies that are gender egalitarian. There are not many examples in existence. Anthropologist Maria Lepowsky (1994) contends that Sudest Island, a small society near Papua New Guinea, represents one of the few gender-egalitarian cultures in the world. A study of its 2,300 inhabitants found equal participation by women and men in decision making, ritual practices, child care, sexual freedoms, and property ownership. Their language does not have any words to describe masculinity or femininity; nor does it have gendered pronouns, such as him or her. In general women are not oppressed, revealing that the subjugation of women is not universal. While Sudest Island comes close to total equality, Lepowsky observes that the genders are not perfectly egalitarian because women spend more time doing housework and men spend more time hunting, with hunting as the more valued social activity (Lepowsky 1994).

Whether egalitarian cultures existed in ancient human history is widely debated among academics. Archeologist Marija Gimbutas (2001) theorizes that prehistoric civilizations were predominantly Goddess-worshipping cultures. This is evidenced through her analysis and collection of a variety of early historical sources, linguistics, folklore, and an examination of thousands of symbolic artifacts, primarily of female statues found across Old World Europe. Historian Riane Eisler (1988) bolsters this theory by arguing that not only did ancient Goddess-worshipping cultures exist, but that they were more than likely egalitarian, or based on what she calls a partnership-centered social network rather than a war-based, hierarchical, dominant-centered culture. Eisler cites archeological evidence from the Paleolithic age, Neolithic agricultural societies, and Minoan Crete civilization in ancient Greece to support her theory. Merlin Stone (1978) claims women's roles were far more prominent in early societies with a Goddess-based religion and that women's status began to decline when patriarchal Judeo-Christian cultures became more prominent. Such theories prove to be pioneering and provocative, but also controversial due to the degree of potential researcher bias and unknown facts about prehistoric life. Despite these efforts to understand ancient religion and gender relations, most historians, anthropologists, and archeologists agree there is little conclusive evidence of prehistoric gender equality.

Gender and Social Institutions

Social institutions, such as education, medicine, and the workforce, play a primary role in defining and shaping gender. Gender roles and expectations within institutions are usually enforced by norms, rules, and regulations. In this regard, institutions can be a source of not only empowerment, but also discrimination in people's lives. Barbara Risman (2004) argues that conceptualizing gender as a social structure can assist in analyzing how gender is embedded in society. Gender is individual, interactional, and institutional, which makes it complex; but seeing it in this way gives it the same social significance as the economy or law.

Gender, as a social structure, intersects with other social institutions. In the U.S. public education system, children are often treated differently based on gender. Research on schools reveals a covert gender curriculum, which refers to an unofficial and unspoken set of norms, behaviors, and values that creates differences between boys and girls and makes gender differences appear and seem natural. A covert gender curriculum can occur in a variety of ways in the classroom, including the amount of and types of attention teachers give to students (Bailey 1993). We still find gender segregation in the workplace and an ongoing gender pay gap, where women earn less than men for the same education, skills, and experience. The medical establishment contributes to the social construction of gender and to gender inequality by allowing cultural ideas of women's bodies to direct medical practice rather than relying on sound medical research (Fausto-Sterling 2000). Traditionally, the male body has been viewed as the standard of normal and healthy, while the female body was viewed as abnormal and unhealthy.

INTERSECTION OF GENDER AND SEXUALITY

Sexuality and gender are intricately intertwined, thus, it is difficult to understand the concepts separately. What makes the matter complex is that, like gender, sexuality operates on two levels: the social and the personal. Additionally, both gender and sexuality are socially constructed and constantly changing. When we talk about the intersection of gender and sexuality, several concepts can be explored including desire, pleasure, and sexual orientation.

Most people seek sexual experiences out of the desire for physical, emotional, or spiritual pleasure. But, what is sexual *desire*? Sexual desire is a desire for sexual intimacy influenced by physical conditions and psychological, social, and cultural influences. While desire is certainly defined on an individual basis, society also teaches us what is desirable. Everything from folklore to social policy can impact what is culturally deemed as desirable.

How do we know if we are desiring something or someone because we choose to or because we have been taught to? For example, why do we find certain perfumes or colognes more arousing or desirable than others? There are a myriad of fragrances that are pleasurable to humans. Our choices of which fragrances we are attracted to are often shaped by cultural values, beliefs, and standards. When a perfume is marketed to females as sexually enticing to males, the decisions made as to why and how it is marketed indicate social influence. Whether we realize it or not, this type of marketing influences our desires about what we find sexually appealing or enticing.

Desires are also gendered. For example, look at the social practice of wearing lingerie. In U.S. culture, lingerie often elicits a sensory response that is steeped in normative social constructions as to what is considered feminine and sexy. In other words, males and females are taught to respond to a woman wearing lingerie in a sexual way because we identify it with sex. Desire is shaped by expectations associated with gender and sex. If a social trend develops that defines masculinity as sexy when a male cracks egg yolks on his head, most people would eventually start identifying egg yolks with masculinity and sexiness. Heterosexual females would be aroused by and desire this act. By deconstructing desire in this way, we can see how it shapes and influences, and in turn is shaped by, gender and sexuality.

Biology also plays a role in individual sexual development, attraction, and desire. Biologists analyze the role of hormones and health in sexual desire. They describe sexual desire as motivated by a biological drive that inspires people to seek out and become receptive to sexual experiences and pleasure. At the most basic level, certainly physical stimulation plays a role in sexual arousal. Physical sensations of pleasure are dictated by the brain's limbic system. Human bodies have erogenous zones that experience physical sensations of pleasure, which then send information to the brain. Pleasure is dictated by the brain's limbic system, which creates sexual urges.

Psychologists offer a range of theories on sexual desire. Freud describes sexual desire as the libido, or the natural, instinctual drive to satisfy sexual urges. Carl Jung (1947) differs from Freud and describes sexual desire as a psychic energy that motivates a range of behaviors, not just sexual. While biological and psychological research on sexual desire and pleasure is important, desire cannot be fully understood without examining the influence of society.

Sociologists explore the role of gender displays in creating desire and organizing sexual attraction. However, gender, biological sex, and sexual orientation do not always correlate. For example, a man displaying very masculine traits may arouse desire in other men or in a women, just as a woman who displays very feminine traits can be found attractive by men or other women. Like gender, sexual attraction and desires are broad and complex experiences that, for some people, change and shift throughout their lives.

Masculinity and Sexuality

Men and women are socialized to think differently about sex, sexuality, and relationships. Men are socialized to embrace the values and ideals of masculinity. Current mainstream values of masculinity in the United States are narrowly defined and focus on heterosexuality, aggression, independence, competition, physical strength, suppression of emotions, and dominance. Men who perform and practice masculinity well receive rewards in the form of power and privilege, while those who do not are ridiculed or stigmatized. Race, class, history, and social context play a role in how masculinity is defined and shaped.

Sociologist Michael Messner and Donald Sabo (1990) describe how men use sports as a cultural space to perform gender and sexuality (see Chapter Six). Messner claims the institution of sport perpetuates *hegemonic masculinity*. Hegemonic is a sociological term to describe the social, cultural, ideological, or economic influence exerted by a dominant group to maintain and legitimate its position of power and encourage all others to consent to its ruling position. Hegemonic masculinity, popularized by sociologist R. W. Connell (1995), embodies the ideals and stereotypes of masculinity, including the claim of authority and privilege. It is constantly perpetuated through almost all social activities and beliefs, such as the sports world, economic sphere, and media. Hegemonic masculinity emphasizes and promotes the dominant social position of men and the subordination and marginalization of women.

Although there is an overarching hegemonic or dominant ideal of manhood, not every man can fit the hegemonic standard; and, in fact, most do not. Connell (1995) describes multiple types of masculinities and the ways each are socially subordinate to hegemonic masculinity in the gender hierarchy. *Complicit masculinity* describes men who do not fit the characteristics of hegemonic masculinity but do not necessarily challenge such ideals either. Often complicit masculine men admire the characteristics of hegemonic masculinity, but do not live up to them. *Marginal masculinity* describes men who sit on the margins of the dominant social groups, such as men of color or men with disabilities. Most marginal masculinities still subscribe to norms of hegemonic masculinity, but in ways defined closer to their specific group's ideals. For example, a disabled man might still rely primarily on hegemonic masculine ideals for sense of self, like physical strength and aggression; but he reformulates such ideals in line with his limitations (Shuttleworth, Wedgewood, and Wilson 2012). *Subordinate masculinity* exhibits qualities that are the opposite of those valued in dominant society. Men who are openly homosexual, emotional, or effeminate can be described as displaying a subordinate masculinity.

While these categories provide a way to understand the complexities of masculinity, Connell emphasizes gender is not a straightforward, fixed character type. Gender is relational, complex, and in flux. Power often overlaps between groups, and influence goes both ways. In other words, subordinate and marginal masculinities have agency and also influence dominant ideals, cultural dynamics, and the role of social privilege (Connell and Messerschmidt 2005). For example, Demetriou (2001) discusses the increasing cultural visibility of gay masculinity in Western societies and its influence on hegemonic masculinity. He claims that gay visibility has made it possible for certain heterosexual men to appropriate certain aspects of gay men's styles and practices and construct a new hybrid configuration of hegemonic masculinity. While hegemonic masculinity is in a constant state of negotiation, male privilege or heteronormativity is never undermined in this process.

Hypermasculinity is a term used to describe the exaggeration of stereotypical masculine behaviors and attitudes. Originally this term was posited to describe exaggerated masculine behaviors including avoiding feminine pursuits, possessing wealth and fame, staying calm in any situation, and exhibiting risk-taking and aggressive behaviors (David and Brannon 1976). More recent research describes hypermasculinity as having four primary dimensions: valuation of dominance and aggression, heterosexual identity, antifemininity, and devaluation of emotion (Corprew, Mathews, and Mitchell 2014). Theorists, such as Mosher and Sirkin (1984) apply this concept to more extreme populations of men who display callous attitudes toward women and believe that violence is manly. Sometimes social institutions and groups foster hypermasculine beliefs and behaviors. For example, the military fosters a hypermasculine culture due to its extreme focus on competition, aggression, violence, fear, and rejection of homosexuality and feminine attributes (Turchik and Wilson 2009).

Masculinity is defined in contrast to femininity and has higher social status with more privileges. This plays out in the way men are taught to view and think about sex. As already mentioned, the sexual double standard encourages men to have more sex, and with more sexual partners, than women. The stereotype that men are less emotional than women sends a message that unemotional sexual involvement is more acceptable for men. Research shows a relationship between the cultural emphasis on male violence within media and the way men define sexuality and sexual behaviors in terms of dominance (Malamuth and Briere 1986). Some feminists argue that the link between aggression, violence, and male sexuality is represented in violence against women in pornography. Pornography often shows men establishing dominance over a woman and sometimes even abusing a woman as pleasurable to both the victim and the perpetrator (see Chapter Eleven). Sexualized representations of women as victims of violence normalizes violence against women and reinforces masculine dominance, male supremacy, and gender/sex inequality (see Chapter Twelve).

Kimmel (1994) claims that rigid and limiting definitions of masculinity lead to fear and hatred of homosexuality and homosexuals. Kimmel claims that American men are taught to be in constant fear of and competition with other men, yet paradoxically are taught not to be afraid of anything because fear is a feminine "sissy" behavior. In *Dude, You're a Fag*, C. J. Pascoe (2007) describes how masculinity, heterosexuality, and homophobia are reinforced among boys in high schools. Her study reveals how masculinity is constructed through interactions and discourse, specifically in what she labels as "fag discourse." Pascoe finds that labeling other boys as fags and joking about being a fag is not only homophobic, but a way to cement young, male, heterosexual identities and relationships. Boys tease one another with the label of fag whenever they appear to care about their clothing, for instance, or when they show weakness. She argues that, in this context, being a fag is a reference to failed masculinity (Pascoe 2007). Pascoe describes this process as repudiation, or rejecting femininity and anything outside the bounds of gender normativity.

MASCULINITY AND RACE/ETHNICITY Race, gender, and sexuality are intersecting structures of oppression. In the race/gender hierarchy, white masculinity is dominant and men of color are marginal. African American masculinity is founded on a history of racist stereotypes and negative characterizations, which have their ideological roots in slavery. Contemporary constructions still work to justify racism and inequality in a number of ways.

Corporate advertising promotes the hypermasculine idealizations of African American men. For example, advertisements by Nike show images of black male bodies with extremely chiseled musculature and physical strength, which do not reflect the average black male body (Carby 1998). Cornel West (1994) describes black male sexuality as being constructed primarily through a process of stylizing their bodies to solicit sexual encounters with women and provoke fear in others. Fear is provoked by displaying aggression or violence and is often directed at other black men, the police, or other authority figures. This form of hypermasculinity values direct confrontation with authority.

In Latino culture, the structures of race, sexuality, and ethnicity inform the construction of masculinities. The term Latino refers to a wide variety of individuals who are from or have ancestors from Spanish-speaking countries, making the construction of Latino masculinities complex. Jennifer Rudolph (2012) coins the term *masculatinidad* to describe Latino masculinity as an ethnically specific gender construct by considering both the cultural interrelationships of different Latino masculinities, such as Puerto Ricans and Chicanos, and how the mainstream norms of U.S. and Latin American cultures inform each other. Most Americans associate Latino males with the term "machismo," which refers to strong masculine pride, sexist, and patriarchal views and often implies high sexual drives (Falicov 2010). Another closely related social construction, often portrayed in media imagery is that of the "Latin lover," who is usually lustful and unfaithful. The "Latin lover" and the machismo male are hypermasculine and hypersexualized images, which are unrealistic and unattainable by most Latin men.

Femininity and Sexuality

Women are socialized to embrace the values and ideals of femininity, which like masculinity, are narrowly defined. Current mainstream cultural expectations of femininity in the United States include passivity, dependence, nurturing, submissiveness, emotionality, irrationality, and heterosexuality. Like masculinity, while overarching feminine ideals permeate, it is not a fixed or rigid typology. It is a layered and complex set of ideals, expectations, and social roles that change over time and across race, class, and cultural boundaries.

The one consistent characteristic of femininity is that it is defined in relation to its position in the gender hierarchy, which guarantees men a dominant position and women a subordinate position. R. W. Connell (1987, 1995) claims this in turn defines the very nature of femininity as compliant to gender inequality. Instead of having an equally opposing position of hegemonic femininity, Connell describes an *emphasized femininity*, or an exaggerated form of feminine gendered behavior oriented toward accommodating the interests and desires of men. Its key features include being overly empathetic and nurturing by tending to male ego and male sexual desires and compliance to expected social roles of wife and mother.

Although Connell claims there is not a hegemonic femininity, sociologist Mimi Schippers (2007) argues that a *hegemonic femininity* exists. It consists of those ideal characteristics defined as womanly that establish and legitimate not only a hierarchical relationship to hegemonic masculinity, as already defined by Connell, but a complementary relationship as well. In other words, there is a symbolic womanly ideal that dominates and rules over other forms of femininity and serves the interest of the gender hierarchy and male dominance. This perspective views the symbolic heterosexual relationship between masculinity and femininity as the central focus in which femininity is shaped.

Hegemonic femininity places value on sexualized female bodies by encouraging women to constantly engage in self-surveillance, spending countless hours and money on their appearance, from a thin body size to appearing perpetually youthful, all to garner heterosexual male attention. Naomi Wolf argues that a woman's preoccupation with thinness promotes her obedience to the gender structure because it symbolizes discipline and conformity to rigid standards of femininity and distracts women from demanding equality in the economic sphere, among other things (Wolf 2002).

Hyperfemininity is a term used to describe the exaggeration of feminine behaviors as they relate to heterosexual relationships. Murnen and Byrne (1991) argue that hyperfeminine women believe their success is determined by maintaining a romantic relationship with a man. Women in this group view their primary value as sexual and thereby use sexual behaviors to obtain and maintain relationships with men. As part of this arrangement, hyperfeminine women view men as always interested in and seeking sex from women. Empirical studies aiming to define and evaluate the extent of hyperfemininity find that women high in hyperfemininity hold more permissive sexual attitudes and have more consensual sexual experiences (McKelvie and Gold 1994). Feminine ideals and expectations are contradictory in that women are encouraged to be sexually submissive to men, but are shamed if they are sexually promiscuous.

When women do not exemplify ideals of femininity and instead enact masculine behaviors such as having sexual desire for other women, being promiscuous, or aggressive, it can be viewed as resisting subordination. Schippers (2007) describes women who engage in these behaviors as exhibiting *pariah femininity*, or behaviors that threaten or contaminate the relationship between masculinity and femininity. Pariah femininities are stigmatized and sanctioned. For example, when a woman is authoritative, instead of being defined as masculine, she is described as a *bitch*. When she is promiscuous, she is not acting like a guy, she is instead a *slut*.

Alternative femininities and masculinities are discursively valued traits and practices in men and women that do not articulate a complimentary relation of dominance and subordination between men and women. Schippers' (2002) research on the social practices of an alternative rock subculture reveals a variety of ways in which the group specifically rejects hegemonic masculinity and femininity in their practices, music, and talk. The group intentionally adopts feminist ideals and creates a different set of meanings, which repudiate the traditional male musician dominating the feminine female groupie, and emphasizes an alternative set of meanings for what it means to be a musician with erotic attraction.

"We inspired a lot of girls then—and boys, I'm sure. And it's not just about playing rock & roll. It's about doing whatever you want to do in life. You've got to fight for what you believe in. If you don't try, you'll always wonder and that's a horrible way to live"
—Joan Jett (Appleford 2013).

An example of a rocker from the '80s who demonstrates alternative femininities is Joan Jett, the cofounder of the all-female rock band *The Runaways* and later *Joan Jett & the Blackhearts*, and the first female artist to own and control an independent record company, Blackheart Records (Fricke 2015). She is often seen in leather-clad, tough girl attire, and her lyrics openly defy gender power structures and feminine expectations. Her music gave direction to the Riot Grrrl movement of the 1990s, which was inspired by third-wave feminism and insisted the women be represented in punk rock.

FEMININITY AND FEMINISM Shelly Budgeon (2014) recognizes the impact the U.S. feminist social movement has on shaping and influencing femininities. The feminist movement is described as occurring in three waves. The first wave began in the mid-nineteenth century when over three hundred women gathered at the Seneca Falls Convention in 1848 to declare women's basic human rights and begin the fight for suffrage, which ultimately led to women gaining the right to vote with the ratification of the Nineteenth Amendment in 1920. Feminine gender roles were largely called into question during this wave as women began challenging the Victorian "cult of domesticity," which insisted women work at home and abide by strict and confining ideals of femininity such as piety, purity, and submissiveness.

Second-wave feminism took place between 1960s and 1990s. It began amid many other social movements at the time including the antiwar, civil rights, and LGBTQ movement (see Chapter Five). It continued to challenge women's inequality by differentiating between sex and gender and recognizing the socially constructed aspects of femininity. Many feminists during this wave denounced conventional feminine practices of beautification and fashion as superficial acts of submission.

In the third wave of feminism, beginning in the mid-1990s, a celebration of femininity occurred with the advent of "girl power," a mainstream cultural trend that celebrates some of the traditional expectations of femininity while also embracing feminist ideals of independence, empowerment, and agency. Third-wave feminists argue that every woman has the right to choose which feminine traditions she wishes to partake in and which not to, as a matter of personal choice and empowerment. Traditional ideals of femininity can now be consciously picked through and performed, instead of being covertly forced on women. In this way, some feminists argue, it destabilizes the gender hierarchy. Some feminists argue that women's socioeconomic progress has advanced to the point that traditional femininity does not pose a threat to women's equality anymore, and so it should not be a central focus for critique (Snyder-Hall 2010).

FEMININITY AND RACE/ETHNICITY The female body is often a place where gender, sexuality, and race are enacted. Patricia Hill Collins (2005) argues that from the period of colonization until now, the black female body has been a source of entertainment and a symbol of animalistic sexuality in Western culture. She argues that the public focus on the bodies of famous black women demonstrate the history of using black women (or any female tinged with "Blackness") as sexual spectacles. In these sexual spectacles, black women's presumed hypersexuality is contrasted with the presumed asexuality of white females. Increasingly, however, women in these spectacles receive an increasing amount of power and money to participate in such spectacles, socially legitimating the focus on their sexualized bodies as sites of worth.

Research by Ingrid Banks (2009) indicates that African American women and girls are often judged using the white female body as the standard. In particular, African American hairstyles are often labeled as "too ethnic" in the workplace or popular media if worn in natural or braided styles. Hair, like the body, is linked not only to race, but also to sexuality. Long hair is typically viewed as more feminine and short hair as less feminine. Black women understand that their hair is an important demonstration of their relationship with the world, particularly concerning their race, gender, and sexual orientation (Banks 2009).

Native American cultures attribute a variety of positive characteristics to femininity that white, mainstream U.S. culture does not. Paula Gunn Allen (2009) describes her personal experience as a Native American woman who is also immersed in mainstream white culture as living in a double bind. In her tribe, femininity is associated with being powerful and strong. Viewing women as powerful is incorporated into tribal traditions, religion, and language. In white culture, femininity is associated with being powerless and weak. Gunn Allen describes how white American schools taught her negative myths about Native American culture and had a negative influence on her ability to self-identify and shape her own gender role.

Asian and Asian American females are often represented in U.S. media as hyperfeminine and the pinnacle of what femininity should be: sexually submissive. Paradoxically, they are also portrayed as hypersexual, subservient, and passive, but women who live to sexually please men. In addition to being stereotyped as docile, Asian women are also viewed as sexually dangerous and seductive; and they have become the targets of sexual and racial fetishization (Pyke and Johnson 2003; see Chapter Six).

TRANSGENDER

Not everyone identifies with the binary, dominant gender order of masculine or feminine. Transgender refers to people whose gender identity is inconsistent with their assigned sex at birth. The term transgender came into widespread use only in the last few decades; and our understandings of transgender people, communities, and issues are still emerging. In

Laverne Cox is the first transgender actress to play a transgender character, on *Orange Is the New Black*. Source: Jon Kopaloff/FilmMagic/Getty Images.

other words, transgender people do not create one uniform, consistent identity. There is great variety among individuals who identify as transgender, which reflects the varied and constructed nature of gender and the complexity of human beings. It is often used as an umbrella term for a broad range of identities including cross-dressers, drag queens and kings, gender fluid, gender nonconformists, and more.

In U.S. society, the term transgender has become somewhat of a "catch all" for anyone who steps outside of the gender norm; and, while the more common use of this term indicates more cultural acceptability, it is also limiting in that the specificity of individuals is often lost. For example, within health care and social services, if a professional is uneducated about transgender issues and concerns, it can impact how they treat their clients; and important medical and social needs can be neglected.

The term ***transsexual*** is a medical term that refers to individuals who are born into one sex, but who identify as the opposite sex and seek to change their sex through body modification, including a medical procedure called sex reassignment. ***Sex reassignment*** can involve taking hormones, undergoing surgical remodeling of the genitals, breast augmentation, gender reassignment therapy, and more. Sex reassignment is a complex process that occurs over a long period of time. Unlike the term transgender, transsexual is not an umbrella term. It is a term used to describe those specifically wishing to modify their bodies to match sex with gender identity. Over time, body modification practices began to be used by transgender individuals. Yet, transgender people do not necessarily identify as transsexual and vice versa. Sometimes the term "trans" is used as shorthand to mean transgender or transsexual. Its meaning is not precise and can cause misunderstanding if not clearly explained.

Transition is a word often used to describe the process an individual goes through when they begin living as the gender they most identify with rather than the one they were assigned at birth. Transition can include medical procedures, legal actions, and personal changes that involve telling friends and family, using a different name, and wearing clothing that aligns with one's gender identity. Transition is different for each individual. *FTM* is an abbreviation for female-to-male transgender person, meaning a person assigned female at birth, but who identifies and lives as male. *Transman* is an identity label sometimes adopted by female-to-male transgender individuals to signify they are male with a history as female. Vice versa, *MTF,* or male-to-female, describes a person born male at birth, but who identifies and lives as a female. *Transwoman* is an identity label sometimes adopted by male-to-female transgender individuals to signify they are women with a history as male. Transitioning is a process, not an event. It often takes years, sometimes an entire lifetime, for an individual to completely transition.

Transgender individuals were traditionally described by the medical and psychological community as having a mental disorder. In 1980, gender identity disorder (GID) was added to the *Diagnostic and Statistical Manual of Mental Disorders* (DSM III) of the American Psychiatric Association (APA) to describe people who experience significant discontent with the sex and gender they are assigned at birth. Traditional treatment therapies aim to reduce gender variance. In 2012, they officially replaced the diagnosis of gender identity disorder (GID) with the term ***gender dysphoria***, a feeling of intense distress that one's body is not consistent with the gender one identifies with. Gender dysphoria is not considered a mental illness, and most current therapies assist individuals in living according to their gender identity and in confronting and coping with the social stigma often experienced by transgender individuals (Glicksman 2013).

The World Professional Association for Transgender Health (WPATH) promotes Standards of Care (SOC) for the Health of Transsexual, Transgender, and Gender Nonconforming People. The SOC are based on the best available science and expert professional consensus. WPATH supports the declassification of GID as a formal medical diagnosis because they argue it pathologizes gender variance and promotes discrimination and stigmatization (*Standards of Care* 2012). While still contested by some, the diagnosis of gender dysphoria is often useful in terms of health insurance coverage. Employers and health insurance companies are only just beginning the process of removing outdated and discriminatory exclusions of transition-related health care to include wider coverage for transgender individuals.

Although transgender individuals struggle gaining acceptance and still experience discrimination on many levels for stepping outside of the expected gender code, many transgender people see their bodies and identities as part of a broader social movement toward social change that disrupts the gender/sex binary, most particularly transgender people in lesbian/gay communities who are attempting to overcome discrimination and oppression (see Chapter Five). Transgender activism seeks to end institutionalized oppression and is represented by a transgender pride flag. It is important to note that not all transgender people see themselves as disrupting gender norms; many transgender individuals are content with the masculine/feminine binary and try to fit within it.

Creator of the Transgender Pride flag, Monica Helms, describes the flag: "The stripes at the top and bottom are light blue, the traditional color for baby boys. The stripes next to them are pink, the traditional color for baby girls. The stripe in the middle is white, for those who are intersex, transitioning, or consider themselves having a neutral or undefined gender. The pattern is such that no matter which way you fly it, it is always correct, signifying us finding correctness in our lives" (Kohner 2015).

A gay pride flag being carried in the Seattle Gay Pride Parade, 2014. This rainbow pride flag became a model for transgender activists who created their own flag with light blue, pink, and white stripes.
Source: istockphoto.com/Pesky Monkey.

Cross-Dressers, Drag Kings, and Queens

Cross-dressers are people who either occasionally or often dress in clothes typically assigned to the opposite sex. This is not to be confused with simply wearing clothes associated with a different sex, as instead it is a deliberate form of gender expression. The term cross-dresser typically refers to heterosexual men who occasionally or regularly wear women's clothes, makeup, and accessories. Cross-dressing does not indicate a wish to permanently change gender or sex. An older term for a cross-dresser was "transvestite." While still used by some, this term, as well as "tranny," "she-male," or "he/she" are considered slurs by most cross-dressers and transgender people today. Some feminists contest how effective cross-dressing is at challenging the sex/gender binary. While an individual is certainly going against gender norms by wearing clothes of the opposite sex, it could be argued that they are simultaneously sending the message of acceptance of the opposite gender norms.

A *drag queen* is a man who dresses up in women's clothes and typically enacts hyperfeminine behaviors for the purposes of entertainment. Drag queens are usually gay performers who perform for mostly straight audiences. Drag shows began in the 1950s and 1960s as a criminal, underground activity, and became popularized in the 1980s and 1990s. A more recent development is the *drag king*, a woman who dresses up in men's clothing and typically enacts hypermasculine behaviors for entertainment. Both the drag queen and king are fundamentally theatrical figures who belong to a political performance culture called "drag." Because drag shows primarily serve entertainment purposes, it is not the same thing as cross-dressing, transgender or even gender-nonconformity.

Drag performances seek to imitate and often exaggerate traditional gender roles in a theatrical act and do not necessarily defy the binary gender system. This supports Judith Butler's (1990) **gender performativity theory** that describes all gender presentations as performances. Butler describes drag queens and kings as acting out gender stereotypes, demonstrating both their hilarity and masquerading qualities. Butler argues that everyone performs gender, whether you are cisgender or transgender, and that our gender identities are produced through repetitive gender performances. Drag performances expose the performance aspect of gender as it relies on imitation and mimicry (Butler 1990). Whether drag performances intentionally seek to disrupt the gender hierarchy or not, Butler claims they destabilize the idea that gender is natural or essential and confirm it is socially constructed.

One of today's more famous drag queens, RuPaul Andre Charles, proclaims, "You're born naked; everything else is drag" (Frank 2015).

INTERSEX

Just as gender is socially constructed on a binary of masculinity and femininity, biological sex is socially constructed on a binary consisting of two opposing categories: female and male, often referred to as the sex binary. For many people, the idea that there are only two sexes is assumed to be a biological fact. Yet, biological sex variation and sex ambiguity has existed throughout human history. **Intersex** is a general term to describe a variety of conditions in which an individual is born with sexual anatomy that does not fit the typical definition of male and female. For example, an intersex infant might be born with female external genitalia, but has male-typical internal anatomy, or sex chromosomes. Sometimes intersex individuals have both male and female external genitalia. Intersex individuals can have any of five different sex chromosome combinations, in addition to being XX or XY, they can be XXY, X, or have both XX chromosome and XY chromosomes. Intersex individuals represent a wide variety of sex variation and can include individuals with physical conditions such as Androgen Insensitivity Syndrome (AIS), which is when individuals are genetically male, but their bodies are resistant to male hormones, so they exhibit the physical traits of a woman (Fausto-Sterling 2000).

Intersex is a socially constructed term that reflects real biological sex variations. An older, more outdated term is hermaphroditism, which has fallen out of favor because it is considered vague, demeaning, and sensationalistic. A more recent medical term for an intersex infant is Disorders of Sex Development (DSD). Georgiann Davis (2015) critiques the use of the word "disorder" to describe intersex because it refers to a condition in need of medical correction or repair. Davis's research reveals that individuals with a diagnosis of DSD are viewed and treated as abnormal and that this view can have a negative long-term impact on individuals' lives. Elizabeth Reis (2007) suggests that the medical terminology be changed to Divergence of Sex Development.

Historically, however, intersex people have been treated as if they have a disorder. In the United States, the response to an intersex infant is typically medical. The standard medical treatment model is to surgically or hormonally "sex" the child as quickly as possible in order to, presumably, prevent the child from experiencing gender confusion or stigma. This approach is chosen because the world is gender segregated. Thus, it is assumed to be easier to make a child fit into the larger gender structure than to raise a child who is intersex in a world where they will not fit in. In this method, parents and doctors decide what sex the infant will be. Physical anatomy and social definitions of the essential components of gender play a role in how the sex is chosen. For example, in the case of an intersex male, surgeons are concerned with the functionality of the penis and whether it will "look right" and "perform satisfactorily" during sexual intercourse (Fausto-Sterling 2000). Parents are encouraged not to tell the child of their intersex origins, or to tell any other family members; to keep it a life-long secret, and to socialize the child according to their new gender assignment.

In the 1990s, the Intersex Society of North America (ISNA) was created out of the intersex rights movement, a social activist group seeking human rights for intersex individuals. ISNA specifically seeks to reform the ways intersex is pathologized in the medical community and society. ISNA advocates for the rights of the child, instead of the needs of the parents; calls for professional mental health care for intersex individuals to deal with social stigma, shame, and trauma often inflicted upon them; and claims honest, open disclosure is the best approach for doctors and parents instead of keeping secrets. ISNA objects to genital surgery in ambiguously sexed infants because it reinforces the idea that sexual difference is unacceptable and damages sexual sensation, thereby impacting the adult's quality of life. Finally, they object to this surgery because sometimes the gender chosen by the doctor is not what the child grows up to identify with.

CONCLUSION

This chapter explores the many facets of gender and how it intersects with sexuality. Much like sexuality, the concepts of sex and gender are socially constructed and thereby in a constant state of flux. Sex, gender, and sexuality are understood in binary terms in Western cultures: male/female, masculine/feminine, and heterosexual/homosexual. This chapter reveals how these binaries and expectations do not accurately capture the complexity of human experience and that inequity exists as certain groups are in dominant social positions, while others are subordinate.

This chapter reveals the ways gender is taught in society through the assignment of gender roles. We also examine how the gender binary code is not universal and the ways some non-Western societies challenge it with the acceptance of third-gender categories. Assigned roles, stereotypes, and social institutions serve to promote, shape, and preserve gender. The inner experience of gender is described as an individual's gender identity and can include a broad range of diverse identities including gender fluid, androgynous, agender, and many more. Gender is an interactive social performance and something that we do in our everyday lives. Some individuals choose to conform to gender norms while others do not.

Gender and sexuality are distinct, yet intimately related concepts. Desire is socially constructed and influenced by gender norms. Heteronormative ideologies emphasize heterosexuality and reject gender displays, which do not clearly point to heterosexual orientation. Masculine and feminine gender norms impact sexual socialization and the way men and women think about and experience sex and relationships. The sexual double standard and sexual objectification of women's bodies reveal inequities within gendered sexual behaviors. The intersection of racial inequality also impacts how gender and sexuality are shaped and reinforced.

With a few exceptions, most cultures do not easily accommodate individuals who do not fit in the binary categories. Transgender is a term for a range of identities of individuals who are attempting to fit into a gender-segregated world. Intersex is a general term to describe a variety of conditions in which an individual is born with sexual anatomy that does not fit the typical definition of male and female. Like transgender individuals, intersex individuals are often considered to have a biological disorder in need of medical treatment. Intersex and transgender activists work to educate society and the medical community about their acceptance of gender/sex diversity and basic human rights.

Key Terms and Concepts

Agender 54	Gender dysphoria 64	Hyperfemininity 61
Alternative femininities 62	Gender fluidity 53	Hypermasculinity 60
Androgyny 53	Gender identity 52	Intersex 66
Bem Sex Role Inventory 54	Gender Identity Disorder (GID) 55	Marginalized masculinity 59
Benevolent sexism 57	Gender nonconformity 55	Misgendering 55
Bigender 56	Gender performativity theory 66	Pariah femininity 62
Cisgender 52	Gender role 56	Sex reassignment 64
Complicit masculinity 59	Gender schema theory 54	Subordinate masculinity 59
Doing difference 55	Gender socialization 51	
Doing gender 54	Hegemonic femininity 61	Third gender 52
Emphasized femininity 61	Hegemonic masculinity 59	Transition 64
Gender attribution 55		Transsexual 64
Gender binary system 51		

Critical Thinking Questions

1. Describe the gender binary system. What are some key socially accepted behaviors associated with femininity and masculinity? How do gender expectations impact our everyday lives. What does it mean to say that gender is socially constructed?

2. How is gender inequality revealed through stereotypes? The sexual double standard? Social institutions? Describe the ways power operates through the gender hierarchy.

3. What does it mean to identify as transgender? What do you think are some of the challenges, barriers, and discrimination transgender people face in our society related to the gender binary?

4. What does it mean to be born intersex? What is the traditional medical response to this condition? In what ways does the Intersex Society of North America challenge this traditional approach?

Activities

1. This chapter teaches us that gender is socially constructed, taught, learned, and performed. Write a short paper describing your activities for an entire day with the central focus on how gender informs your behavior, choices, and expectations. In what ways is your gender experience socially constructed? How do you "do gender" on a daily basis? Have you considered the role of gender in your life before this assignment? If not, why do you think this is so?

2. Research what legal rights transgender individuals have in your state or local area. If there are protective laws, describe them. Using newspapers and other sources, research how and why these laws were enacted.

Essential Readings

Butler, Judith. 1990. *Gender Trouble*. New York: Routledge.

Collins, Patricia Hill. 2005. *Black Sexual Politics: African Americans, Gender, and the New Racism*. New York: Routledge.

Connell, R.W. 1995. *Masculinities*. Berkeley, CA: University of California Press.

Pascoe, C. J. 2007. *Dude, You're a Fag: Masculinity and Sexuality in High School*. Berkeley: University of California Press.

Recommended Films

Barack and Curtis: Manhood, Power, and Respect. (2008). Filmmaker Byron Hurt. A short documentary film examining the contrasting styles of manhood exhibited by then Presidential candidate Barack Obama and rapper/mogul Curtis Jackson, aka 50 Cent.

Be Like Others (2009). Tanaz Eshaghian, Producer and Director; Peter Wintonick, Producer. In the Islamic Republic of Iran, a country with strict social mores and traditional values, sex change operations are legal; yet homosexuality is still punishable by death. Iranian-American filmmaker, Tanaz Eshaghian, accompanies several young men as they contemplate, prepare, and follow through with gender reassignment surgery and transformation.

Growing Up Trans (2015). Miri Navasky and Karen O'Connor, Producers and Directors. Today many children are undergoing gender transition. With new medical options, many are transitioning at younger and younger ages. FRONTLINE takes viewers on an intimate and eye-opening journey inside the struggles and choices facing transgender children and their families.

Intersexion (2012). John Keir, Producer. This is a film that features interviews and stories from several different intersex individuals around the globe. This film looks beyond the shame and secrecy that defines many intersex births and explores how intersex people navigate their way through life, although they do not fit the binary model of a solely male and female world.

Suggested Multimedia

Our Bodies, Our Selves (OBOS) is a nonprofit, public interest organization based in Cambridge, MA, that develops and promotes evidence-based information on girls' and women's reproductive health and sexuality. http://www.ourbodiesourselves.org/

Trans Student Educational Resources (TSER) is a youth-led organization dedicated to transforming the educational environment for transgender and gender nonconforming students through advocacy and empowerment. It provides education for the public on transgender issues and activism. http://www.transstudent.org/

4

SEXUALITY, INEQUALITY, AND PRIVILEGE

LEARNING OBJECTIVES

Upon completion of this chapter, students will be able to . . .

- Understand the significance of institutionalized inequality and privilege
- Identify the various forms of legal discrimination faced by LGBTQ individuals
- Describe the criminalization of sexual behaviors
- Describe the medicalization of sexual behaviors
- Identify examples of violence used to deter sexual deviance
- Pinpoint the ways LGBTQ inequality manifests as privilege by heterosexuals

Many LGBTQ individuals are parents of children they conceived during previous heterosexual relationships. Due to cultural homophobia, this puts custody of their children at risk. In countless instances, the heterosexual parent uses the sexual orientation of the other parent as grounds to sue for custody of the child, arguing that their homosexuality makes them unfit to parent. It is an argument they often win because the law favors heterosexual parents. In one particularly egregious case, a lesbian mother, Mary Ward, found herself in court fighting for custody of her child from the child's biological father. In this case, *Ward v. Ward* (1995), the father was uninvolved in the child's life, did not know what school the child attended, was on his fourth marriage, and had been convicted of and served nine years for murdering his first wife. The judge in this case awarded custody to the father, arguing the child should have the opportunity to live in a nonlesbian household. Filmmakers Katie Carmichael and Edwin Scharlau have made a moving and award-winning documentary about this case titled *Unfit: Ward v. Ward* (2011).

In 1999, David Weigand, a gay father, sued for custody of his son after learning his son called 911 to report his stepfather threatened to kill him and his mother. In this case, the Mississippi Supreme Court ruled 6-3 that the child should stay in the heterosexual household, despite the violence. In a scathing dissent of the ruling, the three judges wrote, "The majority believes a minor is best served by living in an explosive environment in which the unemployed stepfather is a convicted felon, drinker, drug taker, adulterer, wife-beater, and child-threatener rather than live in a home with two men" (Thrasher 2014).

In the current era, discrimination against LGBTQ people seems to be a remnant of previous, less enlightened eras. It appears that journalists, actors, authors, entertainers, and even athletes can be openly gay without experiencing negative consequences to their careers. In June 2015, the Supreme Court struck down remaining state prohibitions on gay marriage, making marriage equality the law of the land. In the face of such undeniable progress, it may be hard to see remaining LGBTQ inequality.

This chapter explores historical and ongoing discrimination and inequality along the lines of sexuality/gender. We specifically explore legal discrimination against LGBTQ individuals including the right to marry; the right to adopt and retain custody of their children; and LGBTQ rights in the military, the workplace, and housing. An analysis of discrimination against pregnant women in the workplace is also reviewed. We investigate the criminalization and medicalization of sexual behaviors as well as discrimination against LGBTQ individuals ranging from violence to *microaggressions*, which refer to daily indignities, whether verbal, behavioral, or environmental, that communicate hostility toward minority group members. Examples of ongoing inequality along the lines of sexuality are as follows:

- The U.S. military dishonorably discharged more than 13,000 gay men and lesbians under "Don't Ask, Don't Tell," a policy in effect between 1994 and 2011.
- In 2010, a lesbian couple in Huntington, West Virginia, was denied the right to rent an apartment because they were lesbians. Denying them the right to rent an apartment was perfectly legal in that city (Cline 2010).
- In 2013, Michael Griffin, a gay teacher at a Catholic School in Pennsylvania, was fired for applying for a marriage license to wed his long-time partner (Matheson 2013).
- A transgender man from Lake Charles, Louisiana, sued his employer, Tower Loan, after his manager discovered he had been born female and insisted that he dress and act as a woman (Grimm 2015).
- In April 2015, Indiana passed a Religious Freedom Restoration Act, causing a storm of controversy because, as written, the law allows for discrimination against LGBTQ people in the name of religion.

THE SOCIOLOGY OF INEQUALITY

Sociologists have long been interested in *social inequality*, the unequal distribution of goods and resources along group lines. An important characteristic about social inequality is that it is patterned, not random. Sociologists refer to this as *institutionalized inequality*, structured inequality between groups of people that is systematically created, reproduced, and legitimated by cultural ideologies (Hurst 2004). The fact that inequality is patterned rather than random tells us there is discrimination against certain groups that results in such patterned disadvantages and advantages.

Karl Marx (1818–1883) is a classic theorist who focused on class inequality specifically during the nineteenth century. Marx was critical of industrial capitalism, particularly for its exploitation of workers. He theorized that in the face of such exploitation, workers would unite and overthrow capitalism. Marx described class conflict as the engine of history. German social theorist Max Weber (1864–1920) is often described as "arguing with the ghost of Marx." He suggests we broaden our understanding of inequality beyond social class to include those of status inequalities. **Status inequalities** are those related to one's economic position, but also are distinct from it; status inequalities refer to group differences in ranking on a community's social hierarchy and reflect lifestyles (Hurst 2004). Research in inequalities along the lines of gender, race, and sexuality emerge out of this line of thought; gender, race, and sexuality are statuses that intersect with social class, but are also distinct from it.

For the first hundred years or so, the discipline of sociology focused exclusively on measuring the extent of social inequalities. Sociologists documented the discrimination directed at minority groups from racial inequality in educational institutions, to women's experiences with discrimination in employment, to LGBTQ people's unequal access to the institution of marriage. The term **social stratification** is used to refer to the systematic ways society ranks groups of people in a hierarchy; some groups have greater status, power, and wealth than other groups. Social hierarchies are not created in a vacuum, but rather intersect and interact with each other constantly. Thus, power and inequality are intricately connected to our understandings of gender, sex, and sexuality.

Toward the end of the twentieth century, after decades researching status inequalities, the investigative lens in sociology shifted toward the study of those privileged by societal status hierarchies. Within any status hierarchy, there are groups who are disadvantaged and groups who are advantaged, or what sociologists refer to as privileged. To be a member of a privileged group means that you receive unearned advantages and benefits because of your group membership. Privileged groups have a disproportionate share of societal goods and resources, yet this is rarely acknowledged and is treated by its recipients as if it is invisible and normal.

An example of the ways status hierarchies intersect is found in the work of Gayle Rubin (1975). She describes the **sex/gender system** as a set of arrangements that turn biological sex into products of human activity, resulting in oppression. Rubin is interested in the psychosocial origins of sexist and heterosexual oppression (Mann 2012). While Rubin suggests that sexism and heterosexism are not inevitable, they are the result of specific social organization, and are thus deeply entrenched hierarchies. Throughout most of the world, gender is organized in a hierarchy; men and masculinity are valued more than women and femininity. This form of inequality shapes the way gender roles are constructed. Those with more power, traditionally men, became defined as more powerful (Firestone 1970).

This book documents the existence of a patriarchy, where women experience sexism and inequality, a racial hierarchy in which racial minorities face systematic disadvantage, and where poor people face disadvantage in relation to the wealthy. But of course the primary hierarchy under investigation in this text is the sexuality hierarchy, a status hierarchy in which LGBTQ people face discrimination and inequality while individuals identifying as, or perceived as, straight benefit from **heterosexual privilege**, the unearned benefits and access to resources associated with the presumption that one is heterosexual. While we may be more familiar with the language associated with the gender hierarchy, known as a patriarchy, the sexuality status hierarchy is referred to as a **heteroarchy**, the system of straight over gay domination (Gilreath 2011).

The cultural ideology that heterosexuality is normal and natural is part of heterosexual privilege. It is a privilege to have your sexuality assumed and not have to "come out" as heterosexual to friends and family. Heterosexual privilege can manifest in economic ways as well. For instance, gays and lesbians are not protected under federal antidiscrimination statutes. Thus, in many places a gay person can be fired from their job just for being gay, unless they are protected by local antidiscrimination statutes that include LGBTQ people, which most municipalities do not have. Heterosexuals do not face the risk of losing their job due to their sexual orientation, which is a manifestation of privilege that has profound financial consequences. Until June of 2015, LGBTQ people's relationships were not formally recognized the way those of heterosexual couples were through the cultural legitimacy associated with legal marriage.

This chapter focuses on inequalities sexual minorities face, historically and currently. Discrimination against LGBTQ people manifests in multiple ways including through legal discrimination, criminalization, medicalization, and violence. After describing the wide range of discrimination sexual minorities' face, we explore how this discrimination provides advantages to heterosexuals; in other words, how it manifests as heterosexual privilege.

LEGAL DISCRIMINATION

Inequality often emerges through legal discrimination: situations in which the law supports and encourages discrimination against some groups. Slavery is a historical example of legal racial discrimination. Slavery was abolished by the Thirteenth Amendment to the U.S. Constitution in 1865; but due to the imposition of Jim Crow laws throughout the South after Reconstruction (1865–1877), it still took nearly one hundred years to make racial discrimination illegal in the United States. The Civil Rights Act of 1964 made discrimination in public accommodations, such as hotels, restaurants, or movie theaters, based on race, color, religion, or national origin illegal; but this legislation does not protect LGBTQ individuals because sexual orientation does not fall within those protected classes.

Lack of legal protection from discrimination often reveals itself in the day-to-day life of a gay person in the form of being denied public services or accommodations. For instance, at Big Earl's Bait House and Country Store, a restaurant in Pittsburg, Texas, a gay male couple were told they were not welcome in the restaurant because the establishment reserves the right to refuse service to anyone. Indeed, on their front door they list the reasons they see as legitimate to refuse service to people, and those reasons include "people wearing baggy pants" and "men that don't act like men and women that don't act like women" (Israel 2014). While most large cities in Texas including Austin, Dallas, Fort Worth, and San Antonio offer legal protections for LGBTQ citizens, the actions taken at Big Earl's are perfectly legal because neither the state of Texas nor the federal government include LGBTQ people in their antidiscrimination clauses.

When it comes to LGBTQ rights, the denial of marriage equality, the ban on serving in the military, and workplace and housing discrimination are examples of legal discrimination. LGBTQ people face discrimination in the public sphere as well, as the previous example illustrates. In all instances, LGBTQ people face discrimination while heterosexuals benefit from these arrangements. We will begin our discussion with the example of same-sex marriage.

Marriage Equality

There are many issues surrounding the right to same-sex marriage that are explored in this text. In this section, we outline why marriage equality is so important; or why not having access to same-sex marriage is a form of discrimination against LGBTQ people. In Chapter Five, we delineate the legal battle that culminated in the Supreme Court decision that made gay marriage the law of the land. In Chapter Eight, we study marriage equality and family formation.

Why is the fight for same-sex marriage so important? After all, tens of thousands of same-sex couples form long-term relationships without the state's recognition. Many of them have their own ritual celebrations, such as a commitment ceremony, to celebrate their union. So why fight for marriage equality? First, there are numerous economic privileges associated with being in a state-recognized union. For instance, there are tax breaks that married couples can access simply as a result of their legal marriage. A married couple can claim Social

The right to legally marry ended some forms of discrimination faced by same-sex couples: same-sex couples could now be eligible for Social Security spousal and survivor benefits, access to a partner's health insurance and other benefits provided by employers, and the right to make medical decisions for a partner in the event they are incapacitated.
Source: istockphoto.com/Alija.

Security spousal benefits and survivor benefits. This is an especially important matter when one spouse makes considerably more money than the other. Other government benefits such as those provided to military personnel and their spouses for education or medical care, for example, are unavailable to same-sex couples based upon one of the partner's military service. Being legally married allows one access to their married partner's health insurance and other employment benefits. Without legal marriage, a surviving member of a same-sex couple does not automatically have rights to inheritance as a heterosexual married couple does.

Second, beyond such financial benefits, being legally married provides a couple with the legal right to make medical decisions for a partner in the event they are incapacitated. Without legal marriage, same-sex couples who have been together for decades find themselves blocked from even being allowed to visit their partner in the hospital, much less being able to make decisions concerning their care. The surviving partner cannot even have a say in funeral arrangements, despite being the person who most likely knows the deceased best. Without legal marriage, a same-sex couple is also disqualified from being able to adopt or foster children. Finally, sociologist Steven Seidman argues that marriage is related to citizenship as well: "[T]he institution of marriage in the United States is invested with national significance . . . . [T]he ideal national citizen is married" (2015:185).

Interestingly, while today same-sex marriage appears to be one of the primary wins for LGBTQ rights, it has not always been a high priority issue for the lesbian and gay activists until the 1990s. Many gay activists felt that issues such as funding for AIDS research and health care, job discrimination, antigay violence, and other issues were more salient to the day-to-day lives of gays and lesbians than the right to marry (Warner 1999). For many lesbians and gays, fighting for marriage equality means embracing an inherently unequal, patriarchal institution (Ettelbrick 1989). It is also part of the "normalizing" of gays and lesbians—they make the claim to being normal, just like heterosexuals, and thus, deserving of the right to marry. Such an argument maintains heterosexual privilege because a heterosexual institution like marriage is portrayed as the norm and, thus, a desired goal. As an institution, marriage is a form of "selective legitimacy," which means that only LGBTQ people who marry and whose relationships mimic the dominant, heterosexual, cisgender culture are acceptable, which is why many gays and lesbians did not support this as the primary gay rights issue (Warner 1999:82). Additionally, it was argued that there are alternative relationship models that could be embraced instead of the institution of marriage.

LGBTQ Adoption

While we talk about LGBTQ families in more detail in Chapter Eight, in this section we outline the discrimination LGBTQ people faced when it came to forming families, In addition to gay marriage bans, many states prohibited same-sex couples from adopting or fostering children. Adopting is regulated at the state level, thus there are no federal guidelines as we find with same-sex marriage. Adoption by LGBTQ single people and couples is legal in every state as of 2016. This is considered progress because as recently as 2006, seven states prohibited LGBTQ adoption: Nebraska, Missouri, Florida, Michigan, Oklahoma, Utah, and Mississippi.

Many adoption agencies refuse to place a child with a same-sex couple for religious reasons that guide their organization, while others are limited by state laws. Some adoption agencies have policies that place a child only into the home of a married couple, which until June 2015, disqualified same-sex couples. Despite these restrictions, an estimated 65,000 children are living with same-sex parents, more than 16,000 in California alone, with gay and lesbian parents raising 4 percent of all adopted children in the country (gayadoption.org).

As the opening vignette to this chapter displays, states that allow single LGBTQ parents to adopt but prohibit same-sex couples from adopting put LGBTQ families

Obtaining the legal right to marry has eliminated some discrimination against same-sex couples pertaining to the right to be adoptive or foster parents.
Source: istockphoto.com/CREATISTA.

in a uniquely precarious position. The issue of the second parent's rights comes up if the adoptive parent dies or if the couple breaks up. In many states, the second parent has no legal rights under the law, while other courts view second parents as "de facto parents" and support their role. Second parents may function as the child's parent for years, only to find that they are treated as legal strangers to the child in a custody battle. Heterosexual adoptive parents do not have to worry about this issue as the law recognizes both of them as legal parents.

Sexuality-Related Discrimination in the Military

Another form of legal discrimination involves the ban on gays and lesbians from military service. Gays and lesbians have not always been banned from the U.S. military, but they have not always been welcomed, either. The military's attitude toward gender- and sexuality-related issues often trails that of the larger culture; in other words, the military has been slower to make changes than the civilian world when it comes to issues related to gender and sexuality. The U.S. military policy during the Revolutionary War imitated the policy of the British in that the act of sodomy, which refers to anal and/or oral sex between men, was criminalized. People were not targeted by this policy, but certain sexual behaviors were cause for discharge. As we have already discussed, the "homosexual" person did not exist until the late nineteenth century. So from the Revolutionary War until World War I, the military prohibited sexual behaviors such as sodomy.

Despite the fact that we did not yet have a term for homosexuals during that era, author Randy Shilts (1993) argues that there is documented evidence of male soldiers in relationships with other males serving during the Civil War. Included in this group was a celebrated Confederate Army General by the name of Major General Patrick Ronayne Cleburne who is believed to have had an intimate relationship with his young adjutant. Other stories involve men passing as women either to avoid service in the Civil War or to marry soldiers serving in the war.

The military ban on sodomy was implemented during World War I, while the original ban on homosexuals serving in the military was implemented in 1940. Thousands of soldiers were imprisoned due to the criminalization of sodomy during WWI. Prior to that time, there was no formal policy banning gays and lesbians from serving in the military. However, during World War II, the Selective Service began setting new standards for qualification for military service. On the advice of psychiatrists, homosexuals were excluded from the service under the rationale that their presence threatened morale and military discipline (Berube 1990).

At the end of World War II, the United States immediately entered the Cold War, and homosexuals were deemed "unfit" to serve. They were perceived as a threat to national security and were seen as weak and, thus, vulnerable to communist infiltration. Psychiatrists developed elaborate screening mechanisms designed to discover and disqualify gay men from military eligibility. As Berube argues, "[T]heir success in shifting the military's attention from the sexual act to the individual had far-reaching consequences" (1990:2). Despite the military's increasing hostility to gay service members, because World War II required such a massive mobilization of volunteers and draftees, tens of thousands of those who served in that war were gay. During the Korean conflict, the Vietnam War, and later the Persian Gulf War, the military enforced the gay ban less stringently in response to shifts in personnel needs (Shilts 1993).

During eras when the gay ban was rigorously enforced, gay military personnel found themselves facing investigation if someone suspected they were gay. There were homosexual purges, dishonorable discharges, and even courts-martial, resulting in considerable mental stress. Female soldiers were subjected to more witch hunts than male soldiers. While women made up one-tenth of the total military personnel, they were discharged three to four times more often than men for being gay (Humphrey 1990).

Intended to be a more progressive policy than the previous military ban on gay men and lesbians serving in the armed forces, "Don't Ask, Don't Tell" in reality was more punitive, resulting in over 12,500 gay men and lesbians being dishonorably discharged from the military between 1994 and 2011.
Source: istockphoto.com/Catherine Lane.

In the 1990s, President Clinton campaigned on ending the ban on gay men and lesbians serving in the military. However, in response to opposition from military leadership, he instead offered a piece of compromise legislation that became known as "Don't Ask, Don't Tell." Under this policy, which was in effect from 1994 until 2011, gay men and lesbians were allowed to serve in the military as long as they kept their sexuality secret. Thus, the policy banned only openly gay service members from serving. "Don't Ask, Don't Tell" was intended to make sexuality a nonissue and to be a more progressive policy than the outright ban on gays and lesbians from serving.

Despite these intentions, it actually became more punitive than the previous policy. Having to pass as straight for an employer is oppressive and not something heterosexuals have to worry about. Over 12,500 gay men and lesbians were dishonorably discharged from the military since the implementation of "Don't Ask, Don't Tell" (Ephron 2009). Careers were destroyed and the cost to the military was significant: millions of dollars in training were wasted when personnel were discharged, and millions of dollars were spent on investigations of suspected gay military personnel (Frank 2009; Shilts 1993). There is even some evidence that "Don't Ask, Don't Tell" actually hindered unit cohesion and, thus, military readiness, despite the claim upon implementation that it was designed to protect unit cohesion (Belkin and Bateman 2003). A cloud of suspicion was cast over all service members; even straight service members were investigated and discharged under this policy (Frank 2009). President Obama ended "Don't Ask, Don't Tell" in 2011; and thus, for the first time since 1940, gay and lesbian service members were free to serve their country openly and without discrimination.

> "The history of homosexuality in the United States armed forces has been a struggle between two intransigent facts—the persistent presence of gays within the military and the equally persistent hostility toward them" (Shilts 1993:3).

The U.S. military declared transgender individuals unfit to serve and banned them in the 1970s; however, that is changing. Prior to 2015, if an active member of the military began to transition, they faced a dishonorable discharge. However, as of June 2015, the Pentagon began the process of ending the ban on transgender service members, expecting this process to last six months—a welcome change to the 15,000 transgender military personnel currently serving their country (Brydum 2015).

SEXUAL HARASSMENT AND SEXUAL ASSAULT IN THE MILITARY Some argue that lesbians in the military are more likely to be victimized by sexual harassment than by homophobia (Shilts 1993). In order to avoid a fruitless attempt to weigh which type of oppression is the most significant, we simply find it safe to say that there is evidence that lesbians serving in the military are victimized by sexual harassment because they are women and by homophobia due to being lesbians; and sometimes the harassment they face is due to an intersection of sexism and homophobia. In fact, rates of sexual harassment in the military are higher than civilian rates, and one type of sexual harassment military women face has been the accusation that they *are* lesbian if they are unwilling to have sex with their male comrades (Hunter 2007). Reports of harassment increase dramatically from women "who did not conform to male expectations of proper gender behavior or who rebuffed or complained about unwanted male attention" (Frank 2009:167). This resulted in some service women not reporting sexual harassment because they feared being labeled homosexual and facing a dishonorable discharge (Hunter 2007). The fact that the military is so intimately linked with masculinity assures that women who join face discrimination and hostility.

Sexual harassment can take two types. The first is referred to as quid pro quo, which refers to a misuse of power where a superordinate lets a subordinate know that their career is reliant upon sexual favors. The second type involves a hostile work environment, where women are made to feel uncomfortable due to the visibility of pornography, or where sexually explicit behaviors or language are common. Sexual harassment in the military has a long history and is described as commonplace. For instance, a survey of female nurses who served in Vietnam found that more than 50 percent reported experiencing inappropriate behaviors such as sexual remarks, touches, and requests for sex (Hunter 2007). The Pentagon's own studies, first conducted in 1977 and then repeated over a 28-year period, find that over half of the 50,000 female military personnel surveyed reported being sexually harassed (Hunter 2007).

Sexual harassment and sexual assault are vastly underreported in both civilian and military contexts for a number of reasons: fear they will not be believed, fear of further victimization by the offender or by the criminal justice system, fear of retribution by the offender's friends, and shame. Military personnel face additional fears that make reporting harassment or sexual violence risky: they are required to report it to their employer, which can result in employment risks if the victim is not believed; they may be accused of fraternizing, which violates policy; and finally, they have to continue working and living in the same environment as their perpetrator. The military does an especially poor job of addressing the sexual victimization of males, as nowhere in the definition of rape are males assumed to be victims. In 1992, the sexual assault of males was included in American military law. For men, reporting sexual assault is risky because they can be accused of being a homosexual and, prior to the end of "Don't Ask, Don't Tell," they faced discharge (Hunter 2007).

Workplace Discrimination

For generations, LGBTQ individuals had no protection against discrimination in the workplace. There has recently been some progress on that issue. In June 2014, President Obama signed an executive order that prohibits employers under contract with the federal government from firing or discriminating against sexual minorities or transgender employees (Hudson 2014). While this order does not protect all employees, it positively affects 28 million workers (Bendery 2014). Equal protection for LGBTQ employees is a patch-work of laws and policies that inevitably result in many individuals still being legally discriminated against. While some states have included LGBTQ individuals in their antidiscrimination clauses, in 29 states it is still perfectly legal to discriminate against LGBTQ employees. Some businesses have voluntarily adopted nondiscrimination policies that protect workers despite their sexual orientation and gender identity. Ultimately, the current configuration of protection can best be described as inadequate (Pizer et al. 2012).

In order to solve this problem of inadequate protection, federal legislation to end all discrimination in the workplace is needed. In an attempt to address this problem, the Employment Non-Discrimination Act (ENDA) has been introduced in nearly every Congress since 1994; but it has yet to pass. Without this kind of legislation, LGBTQ employees are not protected under current antidiscrimination legislation, as sexuality and gender identity are not protected classes. Keep in mind that the legal protection women and people of color currently have under Title VII of the Civil Rights Act of 1964, the Equal Pay Act of 1963, and various other federal Equal Employment Opportunity Laws, from being discriminated against in the workplace due to their sex or their race, is not shared by LGBTQ employees.

In many places of employment in this country, you can still be fired for being gay, lesbian, or transgender; and you would have no legal recourse to challenge that action.

Is there evidence that LGBTQ employees need workplace protection? In other words, do they face discrimination in the workplace? There is overwhelming evidence that LGBTQ employees face workplace discrimination and that it is harmful to them (see Chapter Seven). In 2008, General Social Survey data revealed that 37 percent of lesbians and gays have experienced workplace discrimination within the previous five years and that 12 percent of them have lost a job due to such discrimination. Research also finds that 90 percent of transgender people surveyed experience harassment at work due to their gender identity; and 47 percent of them report discrimination in hiring, promotion, and job retention due to their gender identity (Pizer et al. 2012). Such discrimination negatively affects the financial well-being of LGBTQ employees as well as their mental and physical health.

PREGNANCY DISCRIMINATION Another type of workplace discrimination related to sexuality is pregnancy discrimination. This occurs when women lose jobs or promotions, are not hired, are fired after taking a maternity leave, or some other type of discrimination related to a woman's pregnancy or her intention to become pregnant. Until 1974, schools had mandatory maternity leave policies that required teachers take an unpaid leave after the fourth month of pregnancy. The teachers had no guarantee of reemployment. The Supreme Court ruled in *Cleveland Board of Education vs. LaFleur* (1974) that such mandatory leave policies were unconstitutional and that these policies penalized school teachers for deciding to have a child.

Employers discriminate against pregnant women for a number of reasons, including the fear that the employee will be less productive once she is pregnant or a new mother, or fear that the woman will make demands that the employer will not be able to accommodate. School mandatory maternity leave policies reflect the desire not to have a visibly pregnant woman teaching children. Ultimately, since the vast majority of women will become pregnant

Another type of workplace discrimination that is related to sexuality is pregnancy discrimination. While illegal, this type of discrimination still occurs.
Source: istockphoto.com/Yuri_Arcurs.

at some point during their working years, pregnancy discrimination reflects a male bias in the workplace. Ongoing pregnancy discrimination is the result of the power of traditional gender norms that espouse women's proper role is to be in the home (Brake 2015).

The Pregnancy Discrimination Act of 1978 was passed as an amendment to Title VII of the Civil Rights Act of 1964 that prohibits gender or sex discrimination. The Pregnancy Discrimination Act amends Title VII to "prohibit sex discrimination on the basis of pregnancy," childbirth, and conditions related to pregnancy (Rowland 2004:166). Despite this, however, proving sex discrimination on the basis of pregnancy has been difficult; employers simply claim that the women are fired or not promoted or hired for other reasons, specifically that they are "bad employees" (Rowland 2004).

Cases of pregnancy discrimination reported to the Equal Employment Opportunity Commission (EEOC) rose 66 percent between 1992 and 2007, when the increase in women joining the labor force during those same years was only 22 percent. Additionally, more than 40 percent of gender-based discrimination claims in the past twenty years are related to pregnancy discrimination in hiring (Covert and Konczal 2015). For instance, in 2005 a New York City Catholic school teacher was fired when she told the principal she was pregnant. According to the school administrators, as an unmarried woman, she was fired for violating Catholic morality (Getlin 2005). In 2015, Congress passed the Pregnant Woman's Fairness Act that required employers to accommodate pregnant employees in the following ways: allowing more frequent bathroom breaks, providing a stool to sit on while working, and changing a pregnant worker's job duties so that she does not have to engage in heavy lifting (Covert and Konczal 2015). This research provides an overview of the types of discrimination LGBTQ respondents have experienced, both within the last year and over the course of their lives.

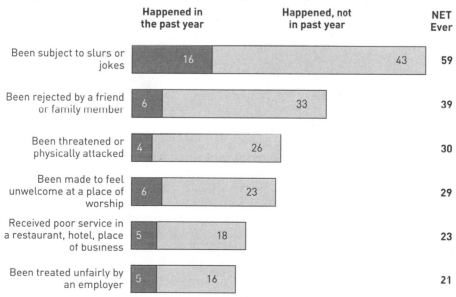

FIGURE 4.1 ■ Perceptions of Discrimination Among LGBTQ Respondents

% saying this ... because of their sexual orientation or gender identity

	Happened in the past year	Happened, not in past year	NET Ever
Been subject to slurs or jokes	16	43	59
Been rejected by a friend or family member	6	33	39
Been threatened or physically attacked	4	26	30
Been made to feel unwelcome at a place of worship	6	23	29
Received poor service in a restaurant, hotel, place of business	5	18	23
Been treated unfairly by an employer	5	16	21

Source: "A Survey of LGBT Americans." 2013. Pew Research Center. http://www.pewsocialtrends.org/files/2013/06/SDT_LGBT-Americans_06-2013.pdf.

Notes: Based on all LGBT (N=1,197). "Net" was computed prior to rounding.

Housing Discrimination

The federal Fair Housing Act does not offer any protection for LGBTQ people seeking to rent or purchase a home, and 30 states do not add protection of LGBTQ people in housing. This begs the question, do LGBTQ people face housing discrimination and need some kind of protection from this type of discrimination? The answer is yes, and the federal government has evidence of LGBTQ discrimination in housing. A 2011 report from the Department of Housing and Urban Development (HUD) found evidence that LGBTQ individuals and families were being denied housing (Burns and Ross 2011). The types of discrimination LGBTQ individuals experience in the housing market include: being treated negatively by real estate agents, landlords, or rental agents when trying to rent or buy a home; being shown less desirable properties; being quoted higher rental prices; verbal harassment by landlords; and outright refusal to allow them to rent or buy properties (Burns and Ross 2011). Transgender people face a much higher risk of being homeless due to their experiences with housing discrimination, and transgender people of color face even higher rates of housing discrimination. These kinds of discrimination will decrease significantly if LGBTQ people are included in the Fair Housing Act coverage. Legislation will not succeed at completely eradicating discrimination, as people break laws all the time. However, it will make discriminating against LGBTQ people risky and will allow for LGBTQ people to take legal action when they are discriminated against.

SEXUALITY AND SOCIAL CONTROL

Homosexuality and homosexual behaviors have long been defined as a form of *sexual deviance*, sexual behaviors that violate societal norms (see Chapter Two). Definitions of deviance change across time and place, as societal norms change, and we can see that with sexual deviance. As this chapter has elucidated, the changing norms surrounding gay marriage are evidence that homosexuality is viewed as less deviant today than in generations past. Sociologists Simon and Gagnon (1967) argue that there are three broad types of sexual deviancy. The first type is normal deviance, behavior that is socially disapproved of, yet is not highly visible. An example of normal deviance is sadomasochism; it is not illegal, but it is not socially approved of either. Second is pathological deviance, such as pedophilia and incest. This type of deviance is relatively rare and violates the law and societal norms. Finally, Simon and Gagnon identify a third type of sexual deviance as deviance that is reinforced by societal norms. The reinforcement ensures that, despite widespread agreement that such behavior is deviant and even the existence of laws against such behaviors, it is likely to continue. A good example of this third type of sexual deviance is prostitution. Laws against prostitution have existed for generations, but such laws have not always been enforced (Tepperman 2006). Prostitution is illegal in all 50 states, yet police are less interested in eradicating prostitution than in containing it to certain undesirable areas of the city (Seidman 2015).

Prostitution has long been defined as the "world's oldest profession" because it has existed throughout history, despite widespread understanding of it as deviant and even, in certain times and places, its criminalization. Gender is deeply embedded in the understanding of prostitution as deviant. In some historical eras, such as Victorian England, prostitution was perceived as a necessary social outlet for men. Even today, while overwhelmingly it is men who purchase sex, female prostitutes bear the brunt of its criminalization. It is prostitutes who are arrested and, in some places, can earn a lifetime label as a "sex offender." In New Orleans, for example, police and city prosecutors use an 1805 law against "unnatural copulation," a term they interpret to mean anal and oral sex, against sex workers. If arrested for breaking this law, sex workers are charged with felonies. If convicted, they face longer jail sentences than a standard prostitution conviction and are forced to register as sex offenders (Flaherty 2010). Thus, a person convicted of prostitution and unnatural copulation faces a lifetime stigma (see Chapter Eleven).

Similar to the social and legal treatment of prostitution, much of the discrimination LGBTQ people face is a result of attempts at social control. ***Social control*** refers to any and all efforts aimed at discouraging deviance and encouraging conformity to social norms. Sociologists distinguish between ***formal social sanctions***, sanctions that are codified, such as laws and rules against certain behaviors, the violation of which can result in punishment. ***Informal social sanctions*** are interactional behaviors, such as shaming, ridicule, or criticism that are used to maintain social control—for example, slut shaming, the act of ridiculing a girl for her presumed promiscuity.

Foucault argues that in the eighteenth century, a new form of power emerged: that of discipline (see Chapter Two). Discipline makes people complicit in their own subjugation. This is particularly true of sexuality. The institution of marriage is a form of social control that disciplines "those outside of it: adulterers, prostitutes, divorcees, the promiscuous, single people, unwed parents" (Warner 1999:89). Foucault is interested in how sexuality becomes a focus of scientific disciplines and thus, how scientific knowledge is used to control, or discipline, sexuality (see Chapter Two).

> ❝
> **"Social regulation is at the heart of the organization of sexuality, producing and shaping sexual patterns as much as controlling them" (Weeks 2012:18).**

Criminalization of Sexual Behaviors

One form of social control involves criminalization, making certain behaviors crimes. Sexual deviance such as adultery, sodomy, and homosexuality, have been criminalized in different historical eras, meaning such behaviors not only violated societal norms, but they also violated laws. The criminalization of homosexuality has primarily taken the form of sodomy laws, laws that define consensual oral and/or anal sex between adults as illegal. Originally, sodomy laws included all nonprocreative sexual behaviors, including masturbation. While the language of sodomy laws does not specifically target homosexuals, as clearly heterosexual couples can and do engage in both oral and anal sex, these laws have been selectively enforced against homosexuals.

The first law outlawing male sodomy was known as the Buggery Act and was passed in England in 1533. At the time, it was considered both a sin and a crime. The original thirteen colonies took their laws from English common law, including the criminalization of sodomy, which was punishable by death. The Puritans considered sodomy to be the most serious sexual sin. Originally, sodomy laws targeted particular sexual behaviors (same-sex sexual behaviors between men) rather than particular people (homosexuals), as we saw with the military example above. As law moved away from religion, sodomy remained a crime, but penalties for violating the law lessened.

As of 1960, every state had antisodomy laws, despite the fact that such laws punished adult, consenting, private sexual behaviors. In 1961, the Illinois legislature revised their criminal code, but did not include sodomy as a crime. This action surprisingly went unnoticed. It was not until 2003 that sodomy laws in the United States were overturned by the Supreme Court case *Lawrence v. Texas* (2003). This decision overturned remaining sodomy laws in Texas and 13 other states, making same-sex sexual behaviors legal throughout the United States. This case also overturned the Court's previous decision in *Bowers v. Hardwick* (1985). In the *Bowers* case, the a defendant had been arrested for engaging in oral sex in his own home, yet the court ruled that long-standing antipathy toward homosexual sex was enough reason to deny a defendant a right to sodomy. In overturning the Bowers case, the Court decided in *Lawrence v. Texas* that a homosexual's private, consensual sexual practices were protected.

Medicalization of Sexual Behaviors

While homosexual behavior has a long history of stigma and criminalization, a specific form of social control of homosexuality emerged in the 1950s: medicalization. The psychiatric community began taking great interest in homosexuality in the 1940s, which resulted in the military ban on LGBTQ personnel, as discussed previously in this chapter. This was a shift away from Freud's understanding of homosexuality as an immature form of sexuality and to an understanding of it as a mental illness. Homosexuality was first included in the *Diagnostic and Statistical Manual of Mental Disorders* in 1952 as a sociopathic personality disorder in which homosexuals were argued to have a pathological fear of the opposite sex. Broadly speaking, the 1950s promoted an extreme culture of conformity. The Cold War was a particularly difficult period for gays and lesbians: Senator Joseph McCarthy included homosexuals in his communist witch hunt—declaring them weak and thus

BOX 4.1

GLOBAL/TRANSNATIONAL PERSPECTIVES ON SEXUALITY: *PARAGRAPH 175 AND THE CRIMINALIZATION OF HOMOSEXUALITY DURING THE NAZI REGIME*

One of the most egregious examples of the criminalization of homosexuality in the modern era is in Nazi Germany. The Nazis were interested in shaping sexual mores in particular ways, criminalizing both male homosexuality and heterosexually promiscuous women (Herzog 2005). The Nazi targeting of gay men was described as "one of the last untold stories of the Third Reich" (Epstein and Friedman 2000). This extreme discrimination directed at gay men was unique in German history at that point. In fact, prior to the Nazis' rise to power, Berlin, Germany, had a thriving gay scene and was the location of the first gay rights movement in the world.

As early as 1938, Nazis were raiding and closing gay bars and organizations. Between 1933 and 1945, over 100,000 men were arrested by the Nazis for the crime of homosexuality. They were punished for violating *Paragraph 175* of the German penal code, which declared "an unnatural sex act committed between persons of the male sex or by humans with animals is punishable by imprisonment; the loss of civil rights may also be imposed." *Paragraph 175* also criminalized heterosexual, promiscuous women (Heineman 2005). Tens of thousands

of gay men were sentenced to prison, while tens of thousands were sent to concentration camps, and many were incarcerated in mental institutions. Ultimately, many were castrated or murdered while incarcerated (Micheler 2005). Transvestites and male prostitutes also faced incarceration under *Paragraph 175*. Similar to the Nazi requirement that Jews wear a yellow Star of David, homosexuals were required to wear a pink triangle for identification.

The law remained in effect for two decades after the war due to ongoing homophobia, with police harassing and arresting gay men through the 1960s. Due to the extreme homophobia of postwar Germany, many gay survivors of Nazi persecution refused to speak about their experiences (Heineman 2005). The first memoir of a gay survivor of Nazi persecution did not emerge until the 1970s. The documentary *Paragraph 175* (2000) interviews most of the remaining survivors (see Recommended Films at the end of this chapter). The gay rights movement of the post-1960s began using a pink triangle as an emblem of gay identity and as a way to commemorate this almost forgotten era of gay history.

susceptible to communist infiltrators. During this period, many LGBTQ individuals were institutionalized in mental institutions in an effort to cure them of their homosexuality. As mentioned in Chapter Two, many gay and lesbian people were subjected to extreme treatments such as lobotomies, shock therapy, castration, chemical treatments, and other tortures under the guise of medical treatment. Thousands of individuals were locked in mental institutions for their entire lives due to being diagnosed "homosexual."

Sexuality, and not just homosexuality, has long been a target of social control. Some of the first forms of sexual discrimination targeted women. For example, men attempted to control women's sexuality through the practice of clitoridectomy and infibulation, also known as *female genital mutilation*. This refers to procedures that involve the partial or total removal of women's external genitalia for nonmedical reasons. These procedures are done to limit women's sexual pleasure and to assure their fidelity in marriage. Over 125 million girls and women alive today have been cut according to the World Health Organization. Also, punishment for female adultery or lesbianism is used to control women's sexuality (Rich 1980). Feminists of the eighteenth century were advocates of *sexual reformism*, a movement that focused on women's right to make their own sexual choices based on rationality, dignity, and autonomy rather than on fear of their husbands or mere conformity to sexual norms (Mann 2012). For sexual reformers, sexual relations were an extension of men's domination over women, with sexual violence as merely one manifestation of such domination.

Homophobia and Hate Crimes

Another way social control manifests itself is in the form of violence. We will discuss the extent of homophobic and transphobic violence in much greater detail in Chapter Twelve. Here we want to introduce the idea because violence is a form of social control, and certainly this is a significant type of discrimination LGBTQ people face. Violence against LGBTQ people is a form of social control because it is designed to let sexual minorities and gender nonconforming people know they are violating the rules and that there is considerable risk involved in that. Much violence directed at gays and lesbians is an outgrowth of *homophobia*, fear and hatred of homosexuals and homosexuality, antigay attitudes, and behaviors. Antigay violence is specifically referred to as *gay bashing*, violence directed at gays and lesbians because of their sexual orientation.

There are many well-known examples of homophobic and transphobic violence. In 1993 in Nebraska, a transman, Brandon Teena, was murdered by two men who had previously raped him in an effort to keep him from testifying against them in court. In 2002 in California, a transwoman named Gwen Araujo was murdered by four men after they discovered she was transgender. One used a *transpanic defense*, an extension of the gay panic defense, where he argued that discovering the victim was transgender so freaked him out that he responded with uncontrollable violence. The brutal beating and murder of Matthew Shepard in Wyoming in 1993 by two men who met Shepard at a bar similarly claimed he made a sexual advance on them that resulted in their violence against him.

Gay bashing is a type of *hate crime*, crimes motivated by prejudice against a social group. President Clinton tried to get lesbian and gay violence added to the hate crime bill, but was defeated by Congress. Eventually, this passed, and LGBTQ victims are included in hate crime statistics. According to the FBI, out of the 6,000 hate crimes in 2013, 20 percent, are based on victims' sexual orientation, second only to race; and 0.5 percent are related to gender identity. Antigay violence is so common that a legal defense known as the *gay panic defense* has been used by defendants, unsuccessfully; they claim that if the gay person shows sexual interest in them, it results in their uncontrollable violence. Many LGBTQ people face *gay bullying*, verbal abuse involving sexual slurs, intimidation, threats of violence, or the use of antigay slogans (see Chapter Seven).

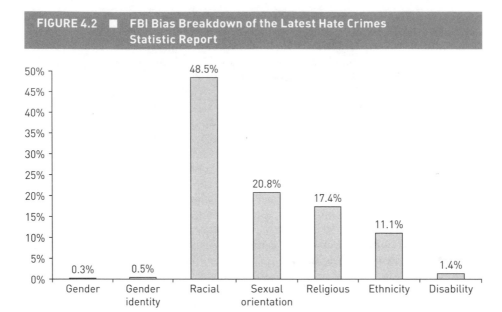

FIGURE 4.2 ■ FBI Bias Breakdown of the Latest Hate Crimes Statistic Report

Source: "Latest Hate Crime Statistics Report Released." 2014. Federal Bureau of Investigation. https://www
.fbi.gov/news/stories/2014/december/latest-hate-crime-statistics-report-released.

TRANSGENDER DISCRIMINATION AND INEQUALITY

Much of the discrimination transgender people in the United States face is similar to that faced by lesbian, gay, and bisexual individuals; yet transgender people also experience unique forms of discrimination specifically related to their status as transgender. Much like homophobia, *transphobia* refers to prejudice, dislike, and hostility toward transgender or transsexual people. Much like lesbians and gays, transgender people face discrimination in their right to marry. Several states (Kansas, Ohio, Texas, and Florida) have recently witnessed court rulings that prohibit transgender people from marrying (Currah, Juang, and Minter 2006). They face discrimination in the job and housing markets and historically have faced discrimination in the military. They face unique discrimination when it comes to family law. Because our world is highly gendered, sex distinctions have legal consequences. They include "whom you can marry, whether you can inherit your spouse's estate, or whether you provide an 'appropriate' role model for your children" (Flynn 2006:33).

> "Transgender family law decisions reflect society's almost fetishistic attitude toward trans individuals, evident in the courts' reductionist tendency to replace substantive analysis (whether Michael is a good parent) with a relentless focus on sexual anatomy (whether Michael has a penis)" (Flynn 2006:33).

Discrimination against transgender people has, until recently, been perfectly legal in the United States primarily because nondiscrimination laws do not specify protection along the lines of sex or gender. Thus, transgender people have fought for inclusion in nondiscrimination laws, with some success (see Chapter Five). The question courts have been left to grapple with is whether discrimination against transgender people is a form of sex discrimination.

In some states, transgender people are banned from using public restrooms. Transgender people face hostility from their employers and are harassed by police. One in five transgender people report being denied care by health care providers due to their gender. In West Virginia, transgender women have been fighting the Division of Motor Vehicles because officials refuse to provide them with a driver's license, claiming they are "misrepresenting" their gender on these official documents (Merevick 2014). While gay and lesbian youth face high suicide rates, one study found that an astonishing 41 percent of transgender people have attempted suicide (Grant et al. 2011).

In addition to the violence transgender people face, they are often unable to turn to police for help, as they experience a disproportionate amount of police violence. The next chapter will discuss police raids of gay bars and transgender establishments in the 1960s and 1970s, yet these are not just events from our past. In March 2003, between 50 and 100 Wayne County Sheriff's department police officers, yelling "hit the floor," raided a private club in Detroit frequented by African American gay men, lesbians, and transgender women. Over 350 people were handcuffed and detained for up to twelve hours. Some were physically abused by authorities, and the police verbally harassed the clientele with statements such as, "Those fags in here make me sick" (Mogul, Ritchie, and Whitlock 2011:46). The police explained that they were responding to complaints pertaining to public safety, which would not normally require a raid at 3:00 a.m. during business hours and the arrest of over 300 patrons. Many transwomen complain of sexual harassment by police officers, resulting in about half the sexual assaults faced by transgender people going unreported. Of those that are reported, in 4.9 percent of sexual assaults of transgender people, police are the perpetrators (Stotzer 2009).

HETEROSEXUAL AND CISGENDER PRIVILEGE

We have spent the bulk of this chapter looking at inequality along the lines of sexuality and sexual orientation, specifically legal discrimination, criminalization, medicalization, and violence against sexual minorities. Inequality is only half the story, however. Whenever one group in a status hierarchy faces disadvantage, the dominant group is going to be advantaged by the arrangement, despite the fact that we rarely acknowledge this. Privilege is often taken for granted. Some speculate that opposition to same-sex marriage may also be about maintaining privilege: "They want marriage to remain a privilege, a mark that they are special . . . some token, however magical, of superiority" (Warner 1999:82).

Some aspects of heterosexual privilege may seem trivial, such as the privilege to show affection to your partner in public without fear of negative sanctions, or being socially accepted by one's neighbors and coworkers. Others are much more serious, such as not facing violence; heterosexuals do not face assault due to their choice of sexual partners. Heterosexuals do not have to hide who they are, or hide their romantic and life partners from coworkers, just to maintain their employment. Heterosexual couples' relationships are validated by the state, and this validation entitles them to financial benefits such as filing taxes jointly, survivor benefits for such things as pensions or inheritance, sharing insurance policies, and the right to access one's loved one in a hospital during emergency situations and to make end-of-life decisions for one's partner. Heterosexuals do not have to worry about losing a job or losing a child custody battle simply due to their sexuality. A heterosexual person can pursue a military career without fearing being outed and dishonorably discharged for who they love. Finally, housing discrimination against LGBTQ individuals results in housing advantages for heterosexuals: they have more housing options, and those options provide them with a significant financial advantage. Finally, being perceived as heterosexual protects you from unwanted attention by police and police harassment. It can also mean the difference between incarceration in a mental hospital and your freedom. Heterosexual privilege manifests in numerous financial, emotional, and social advantages.

CONCLUSION

The chapter begins with an overview of the sociology of inequality. Then it proceeds to explore the inequality LGBTQ people face from the myriad ways they are legally discriminated against to the use of the criminal justice system, the medical profession, and violence as forms of social control. Since the issue of gay marriage has been in the headlines over the past few years, most people are aware of the fact that same-sex couples were prohibited from marrying in all states at some point in time. But the ongoing discrimination LGBTQ parents face in custody battles is less well known, and their recent right to legally adopt children is also an aspect of inequality that tends to be overlooked. Sexuality-related discrimination in the military ranges from the gay ban, to "Don't Ask, Don't Tell," to sexual harassment, and sexual assault. Evidence of workplace and housing discrimination against LGBTQ individuals exists. Attempts to control sexual deviance have taken the form of criminalization, such as sodomy laws, medicalization, and antigay and antitrans violence. Finally, all of this inequality manifests as heterosexual privilege for the dominant group.

Key Terms and Concepts

Female genital mutilation 85	Heterosexual privilege 73	Sexual harassment 79
Formal social sanctions 83	Homophobia 85	Sexual reformism 85
Gay bashing 85	Informal social sanctions 83	Social control 83
Gay bullying 85	Institutionalized inequality 72	Social inequality 72
Gay panic defense 85	Microaggressions 72	Social stratification 73
Hate crime 85	Sex/gender system 73	Status inequalities 73
Heteroarchy 73	Sexual deviance 82	Transpanic defense 85
		Transphobia 86

Critical Thinking Questions

1. What do sociologists mean by the idea of institutionalized inequality? What is a heteroarchy? Why is it important to have a term like heteroarchy?

2. Explain the different types of inequality LGBTQ individuals face or have faced in the United States. Identify at least four ways LGBTQ discrimination manifests as heterosexual privilege.

3. Describe three ways the social control of sexuality has been exercised historically or currently in the United States. Compare and contrast this with another minority group in the United States, historically or currently.

Activities

1. Go to a local history museum (or, if one is not available in your area, visit your state's history museum online). Is there evidence of LGBTQ discrimination in your region commemorated in your museum? What minority groups' stories are being told? What groups' stories are left out? Is there any LGBTQ history presented in your local museum? If so, why do you think this is? If not, why do you think this story is not being told?

2. Read three local/regional newspapers for two weeks (be creative—look for daily city newspapers, weekly newspapers, or newspapers covering minority communities, such as African American newspapers). Count the amount of coverage of LGBTQ issues in those papers over two weeks. Are there stories? What percentage of stories are about LGBTQ issues? Is there a particular narrative that is used when covering LGBTQ issues?

Essential Readings

Berube, Allan. 1990. *Coming Out under Fire: The History of Gay Men and Women in World War Two*. New York: The Free Press.

Fone, Byrne. 2000. *Homophobia: A History*. New York: St. Martin's Press.

Meyer, Doug. 2015. *Violence against Queer People: Race, Class, Gender and the Persistence of Anti-LGBT Discrimination*. New Brunswick, NJ: Rutgers University Press.

Mogul, Joey L., Andrea J. Ritchie, and Kay Whitlock. 2011. *Queer (In)Justice: The Criminalization of LGBT People in the United States*. Boston, MA: Beacon Press.

Shilts, Randy. 1993. *Conduct Unbecoming: Lesbians and Gays in the U.S. Military—Vietnam to the Persian Gulf*. New York: St. Martin's Press.

Recommended Films

Paragraph 175 (2000). Rob Epstein and Jeffrey Friedman, Directors. This documentary interviews gay survivors of the Nazi concentration camps who were incarcerated under Germany's law against male homosexuality, known as *Paragraph 175*.

Freeheld: The Laurel Hester Story (2007). Cynthia Wade, Director. Laurel Hester spent 25 years on the Ocean County New Jersey Police Department before she was diagnosed with terminal cancer. This documentary focuses on her last years of life as she battles to have her lesbian partner receive her pension, something a same-sex couple is able to take for granted.

Before Stonewall (1984). Greta Schiller and Robert Rosenberg, Directors. While LGBTQ people became more visible after the Stonewall riots in 1969 and the emergence of the modern gay rights movement, gay life prior to Stonewall tends to be more obscure. This documentary addresses that void by portraying gay life throughout the first half of the twentieth century in the United States, from conflicts with police, to censorship, World War II, and the emergence of early gay rights organizations such as the Mattachine Society and the Daughters of Bilitis.

The Case against 8 (2014). Ben Cotner and Ryan White, Directors. This documentary film explores the five-year legal battle to overturn Proposition 8, California's ban on gay marriage. This legal battle was, interestingly, spearheaded by conservative attorney Ted Olson.

The Invisible War (2012). Kirby Dick, Director. Award-winning documentary exploring sexual assault in the U.S. military. Features interviews with veterans from multiple branches of the military describing their personal experiences with sexual assault while serving—and their lack of recourse.

Suggested Multimedia

National Report on Hate Violence against Lesbian, Gay, Bisexual, Transgender, Queer, and HIV-Affected Communities, from the National Coalition of Anti-Violence Programs, this report shows the shockingly high rates of violence, especially murders, against lesbian, gay, bisexual, and transgender individuals and the police misconduct experienced when they try to report the violence to authorities. http://www.avp.org/storage/documents/2012_mr_ncavp_hvreport.pdf

GLAD (Gay and Lesbian Advocates and Defenders) is a New England-based organization of LGBT legal advocates formed in 1978. Their mission is to end discrimination based on gender identity and expression, HIV status, and sexual orientation through education, advocacy, and litigation. https://www.glad.org/rights/topics/c/anti-lgbt-discrimination.

5

LGBTQ MOBILIZATION AND ACTIVISM

LEARNING OBJECTIVES

Upon completion of this chapter, students should be able to . . .

- Describe the sociological approach to understanding social movements

- Identify the social and cultural conditions that facilitate the emergence of the gay rights movement

- Differentiate between and identify examples of SMOs (Social Movement Organizations), RSMOs (Radical Social Movement Organizations), and episodes of collective behavior associated with the gay rights movement

- Describe gay rights activism before and after Stonewall

- Identify key moments of transgender activism

On December 10, 1989, hundreds of AIDS activists engaged in a "die-in" at St. Patrick's Cathedral in New York during a Sunday morning service led by Cardinal John Joseph O'Connor, Archbishop of New York. At the time, New York City faced the most serious AIDS crisis in the nation, and yet they could not get the city or the nation to adequately address or even acknowledge the epidemic. An organization by the name of ACT UP (AIDS Coalition to Unleash Power) formed and used direct action, civil disobedience, and demonstrations to draw attention to the AIDS crisis. They saw the Catholic Church as a major cause of the cultural inaction on AIDS. For instance, Cardinal O'Connor discouraged the use of condoms, as they were deemed sinful by the Catholic Church because they were a form of birth control. Members of ACT UP were not all in agreement with the proposed "die-in." Many did not want to offend parishioners, but they did want to make a statement. When Cardinal O'Connor got up to give his homily that morning, hundreds of protesters entered the central aisle and the alter areas of the church and silently lay down on the ground. Others handed out fliers explaining their actions. As the protest continued, some protesters started shouting "Stop Killing Us!" at O'Connor and the Church for what they considered to be their dangerous prohibition on condom use. The police eventually arrested the protesters taking part in the "die-in," while outside over 7,000 other activists continued the protest with picketing and chants. This was one of the most widely covered and memorable campaigns engaged in by AIDS activists in the 1980s and early 1990s (Hubbard and Schulman 2012).

As is evident in the previous chapter's coverage, there has been remarkable progress in terms of LGBTQ rights both in the United States and throughout the world. From a sociological perspective, it is essential to recognize both the human agency behind such social change and the structural constraints that inhibit or facilitate progress. *Agency* refers to the extent to which people and groups have the ability to create and change their own lives. We contrast this with the notion of *structure*, patterned arrangements that are recurring in society, and which inhibit the choices and options people have available to create their own lives. To paraphrase Karl Marx, people make their own history, although it is not always under conditions of their own choosing. By this he means that human agency exists; people's actions do impact their lives. However, there are also larger social structures that exist, which can enable or constrain one's ability to act. For minority groups, racism, sexism, and heterosexism can be understood as structures that constrain the actions of marginalized populations.

Progress on LGBTQ rights has not come about due to the generosity of heterosexuals and cisgender people and their sudden realization that LGBTQ individuals lacked equal rights. Social change is a result of many factors: electoral politics, shifting public opinion,

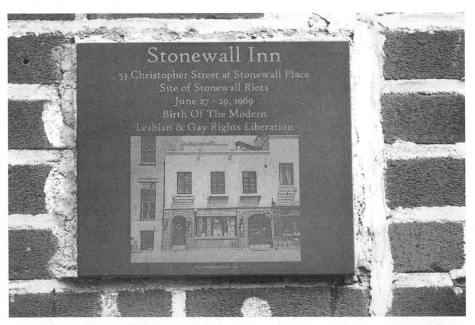

The iconic Stonewall Inn was the site of the 1969 Stonewall Riots, which marked the beginning of the modern gay liberation movement. In 2016, President Obama designated this site a National Monument, the first to recognize LGBTQ Americans.
Source: ©iStockphoto.com/carterdayne.

and especially, social movements and activism. Electoral politics, and particularly ballot measures, have historically not been very effective vehicles for protecting or increasing minority rights, since they are "a mechanism that privileges majoritarianism" (Pierceson 2016:65). Progressive change on gay rights is an outcome of decades of LGBTQ activism against the discrimination and inequality they faced and, in many cases, continue to face.

This chapter explores the mobilization and activism that has resulted in increasing equality for members of the LGBTQ community, as well as the context of that mobilization. We begin with a look at how sociologists understand social movements and their origins; we then look at the social and cultural context that contributed to the emergence of the gay rights movement; and then we look specifically at the gay rights movement from their primary social movement organizations, to some discussion of their tactics and strategies to win equal rights. Evidence of LGBTQ mobilization and activism includes, but is not limited to:

- The Mattachine Society's 1951 Mission Statement establishing the goal of creating a "new pride—pride in belonging, a pride in participating in the cultural growth and social achievements of . . . the homosexual minority" (Eisenbach 2006:20).
- In 1990, a group of New York activists formed Queer Nation, with the goal of challenging LGBTQ discrimination. The group's first activity was a protest called "Nights Out" at a straight bar in New York. They protested the assumption that queers should be restricted to gay bars for socializing and public displays of affection ("Queer Nation NY History" n.d.).
- The National Center for Transgender Equality (NCTE) was founded in 2003 to be a transgender advocacy presence in Washington D.C. to help change laws, policies, and society in order to improve the lives of transgender people.
- In 2012, gay rights activists called for a National Same Sex Kiss Day, essentially a "kiss-in," at Chick-fil-A restaurants across the nation to protest the chain's President's comment that he opposes gay marriage.
- An outgrowth of lesbian feminist activists' efforts to create a vibrant women's culture, the Michigan Womyn's Music Festival was created in 1975 and celebrated its 40th anniversary in August 2015.

THE SOCIOLOGY OF SOCIAL MOVEMENTS

This chapter explores the long history of the gay rights movement and the more recent transgender rights movement. Sociologists define a ***social movement*** as sustained, organized activism to change some aspect of society through the mobilization of large numbers of people. Social movements tend to be composed of marginalized members of society, people who do not feel their grievances are likely to be met through the existing political system. Thus, they organize and demand changes to that system. The gay rights movement can also be understood as a ***grassroots movement***, meaning it emerges from the masses and the actions of ordinary individuals, instead of being organized by elites. Often we look at people who become the face of a movement, like Martin Luther King, Jr., and the civil rights movement, and mistakenly credit them for the movement's origins. The civil rights movement, like the gay rights movement, was a grassroots movement that provided a space for an eloquent, courageous leader like King to emerge, but he was not the movement's founder.

Not all social movements are progressive. Some seek to limit societal changes, to turn back changes that other groups have fought for and won. These are referred to as ***right-wing movements*** and tend to be known for what they are against more so than what they are for (Blee and Creasap 2010; Lo 1982). The activism of the religious right, particularly in their antigay rights platform from the 1980s to the 2000s, is an example of such right-wing activism. The gay rights movement is a left-wing movement because they are "attempting to increase freedom and equality for submerged groups" (Wood and Jackson 1982:9). Right-wing and *left-wing movements* often interact and influence one another. As sociologist Tina Fetner (2008) argues, the gay rights movement eventually became dwarfed by its right-wing opposition, something we discuss in more detail below.

Social movements should not be confused with episodes of *collective behavior,* which refer to spontaneous, short-lived actions of a large group of people, such as riots. When we think of the modern gay rights movement, the organized, long-term efforts by people pushing for social change, we recognize it as being triggered by the Stonewall riots that began on June 28, 1969. The Stonewall Inn was a gay bar in New York. At the time, New York, like most major cities in the United States, had laws that prohibited gay bars from legally operating. This made establishments like the Stonewall Inn susceptible to police harassment and intimidation, most often in the form of raids. Police barge into a club, demand to see ID's, arrest dozens of patrons, and sometimes engage in violence. On this particular night at the Stonewall Inn, some customers who were weary of such harassment fought back. They threw bottles at the police and refused to disperse. Word spread throughout the city; and almost a thousand supporters began gathering in the street, throwing things at the police, and shouting "gay power." Riots and demonstrations continued in Greenwich Village near the Stonewall Inn for days, and the visibility of the Stonewall riots helped trigger mobilization for gay rights activism nationwide.

While the Stonewall riots are the most well-known example of collective behavior by members of the LGBTQ community, they are not the only example. A lesser known ex-ample of LGBTQ collective behavior was the Compton's Cafeteria riots in 1966 in the Tenderloin District of San Francisco. This riot is argued to be the first transgender riot in the United States, and it resulted from similar experiences as those faced by the Stonewall rioters—police harassment. At the time, cross-dressing was illegal; thus, police used it as a reason to raid establishments where transgender people gathered. Compton's Cafeteria was a 24-hour cafeteria and one of the few places transgender people could gather, as they were often unwelcome in gay bars because police used their presence as a reason to raid and close down gay establishments. Similarly, in 1959, riots broke out at Cooper's Donuts in Los Angeles when drag queens and street hustlers fought back against police harassment. These are typical in that episodes of collective behavior often occur as part of a larger social movement, or they can be a catalyst for a social movement.

Social and Cultural Contexts

When sociologists study social movements, they focus on the social context in which organized activism emerges. It takes more than discrimination, inequality, or *relative deprivation*, the minority group members' perception that they face inequality relative to the dominant group, to trigger a social movement (Gurr 1970). The post-World War II (WWII) era witnessed significant social activism. African Americans organized into a civil rights movement, Native Americans mobilized into a red power movement, women engaged in what is now known as the second-wave feminist movement, and lesbians and gays challenged their subordinate status through the gay rights movement. There are a number of social and cultural issues that sociologists look to as facilitating minority protest movements in the post-WWII era, which we explore below. Additionally, there are some factors identified that contribute specifically to the emergence of the gay rights movement, such as the role of WWII, the emergence of gay enclaves and gay bars, the flourishing of a gay press, the Kinsey Studies, and resistance to right wing mobilization, all of which we explore below.

The key characteristics of the post-WWII era that sociologists identify as contributing to the emergence of minority protest movements include: economic growth, increasing educational levels, and increasing urbanization (Farley 2005; McAdam 1982; Morris

1984; Tilly 1974; W.J. Wilson 1973, 1978; Zald and McCarthy 1975). During periods of sustained economic growth, people have the luxury of focusing on more than their just their basic survival needs; they have the freedom to participate in a social movement (Davies 1962; de Tocqueville 1956; Roberts and Kloss 1974). During periods of economic growth, social movements also grow due to increasing access to resources (Jenkins and Eckert 1986; McAdam 1982; Morris 1984; Zald and McCarthy 1975). Also, economic expansion can raise expectations for minority group members (Farley 2005). Since the post-WWII era was an economic boom period, it is unsurprising that so much social activism occurs during this era.

Economic growth combined with increasing educational levels contribute to increasing expectations for many minority group members. Educational levels during the post-WWII era increased for all groups. As people become more educated, their feelings of relative deprivation are likely to increase, and this increases the likelihood that they mobilize to demand an end to the discrimination and inequality they face (Farley 2005). Increasing urbanization results in a surge in activism because as more people live in close proximity to one another, they are able to communicate their grievances and concerns to one another, and are able to help mobilize participants (Farley 2005; Morris 1984). Urbanization also contributes to feelings of dissatisfaction for minority groups and increasing expectations. Finally, social movements feed off of one another, which helps explain the high level of activism during this era. This allowed gay rights activists to borrow strategies and tactics from the civil rights movement, among others, for instance.

Progress on gay rights throughout the twentieth century was anything but a smooth, linear process. For instance, while increasing urbanization in the post-WWII era led to the emergence of gay communities and activism in major urban areas throughout the country, these new gay communities also drew the attention of police. This resulted in LGBTQ people becoming targets of police violence and harassment, as the above examples of the Stonewall, Compton's Cafeteria, and Cooper's Donuts riots exemplify. Also, as previously mentioned, a right-wing backlash against gay rights during the 1980s and 1990s interrupted LGBTQ movement progress, a topic we explore in more detail later in this chapter.

THE INFLUENCE OF WORLD WAR II ON GAY RIGHTS Scholars of gay history emphasize the role of WWII as a specific catalyst for the gay rights movement (D'Emilio 1983). World War II was a massive mobilization of military personnel, unlike anything this country has ever seen. At its peak during this period, the American military included over 12 million men and 150,000 women, most of whom were young, single, and without dependents, a population that D'Emilio (1983) points out is likely to include a disproportionate number of gays and lesbians. Thus, while the military maintained an antihomosexual stance, "The war also created pressures that temporarily suspended the normally harsh military attitude toward . . . homosexuals" (D'Emilio 1983:28). It provided previously isolated gays and lesbians opportunities to meet others like themselves. It also temporarily "weakened the patterns of daily life that channeled men and women toward heterosexuality and inhibited homosexual expression. . . . For men and women conscious of a strong attraction to their own sex but constrained by their milieu from acting upon it, the war years eased the coming out process and facilitated entry into the gay world. Finally, the war allowed men and women who already identified as homosexuals or lesbians to strengthen their ties to a gay life" (D'Emilio 1983:31).

URBANIZATION AND THE EMERGENCE OF GAY ENCLAVES Social movements require *mobilization*, the crucial recruitment of movement participants. World War II mobilized the nation for war, but it also helped mobilize gays and lesbians who found it easier to meet others like themselves in the military. After the war, many gays and lesbians remained in urban areas throughout the country and helped create some of the first *gay enclaves*, or gay neighborhoods known as "gayborhoods," geographic areas of a city where a high concentration of gays and lesbians live and where gay-oriented businesses, such as gay bars, restaurants, bookstores, health care clinics, and bath houses, can be found (Ghaziani 2014). Gayborhoods provide community and support for otherwise marginalized individuals. Gay bars played a significant role early in the mobilization of lesbian, gay, bisexual, and transgender persons because they were places where they could gather, despite the risk of police harassment; and it was in these spaces that they came into overt conflict with the legal system (Thomas 2011). Overt conflict triggered opposition, as the example of the Stonewall riots exemplifies. And, as previously mentioned, urbanization contributed to the emergence of social movements because when people live in close proximity to one another, they are more likely to share their experiences with discrimination and their hopes for social change. When individuals are more isolated in rural areas, they are less able to meet others like themselves or to mobilize large groups of people to change their situation.

In 1966, gay activists in New York took a page from the civil rights movement and organized a "sip in" to protest legal prohibitions on serving alcohol to homosexuals. Organizers invited reporters to follow them to establishments as they ordered drinks and announced they were homosexuals. They were denied service in a known gay bar that had been raided and temporarily closed the previous year. Organizers used this as a legal test case and filed a discrimination complaint against the establishment. While the legal complaint languished, the police commissioner announced several changes in policing policy that resulted in fewer raids and bar closures (Eisenbach 2006).

THE EMERGENCE OF A GAY PRESS While WWII and urbanization undoubtedly played a significant role in the mobilization of gays and lesbians, others argue that the success of the modern gay rights movement can be partially attributed to the emergence of a gay press. "[A] few brave activists set out to challenge a vast antihomosexual matrix of stereotypical media images, discriminatory laws, and repressive social mores" (Eisenbach 2006: vii). Later in this chapter, we discuss the first two gay rights organizations to emerge in the United States, the Mattachine Society and the Daughters of Bilitis. Both organizations published magazines that celebrated gay life and provided a foundation for a new gay press.

Around this same time period, an influential book titled *The Homosexual in America* (1951) was published. Authored by Donald Webster Cory, a pseudonym for Edward Sagarin, a professor of sociology at the City University of New York, this work was the first piece of nonfiction to portray homosexuality sympathetically. Cory challenged the image of homosexuals as sick and morally weak, and he demanded social justice for gays and lesbians. Cory described gay life, encouraged homosexuals to accept themselves, and encouraged society to celebrate the unique contributions of gays and lesbians. He challenged laws that prohibited gays and lesbians from socializing in bars and those that criminalized consensual sexual behaviors, and he encouraged the politicization of gays and lesbians. Cory was especially interested in generating media attention to the serious issues facing the gay community, and he insisted that the mainstream media use actual gays and lesbians in their coverage of gay issues rather than just the voices of psychiatrists speaking for them.

> **Daniel Webster Cory "did not want to surrender the discussion about homosexuality to straights. He called for the right to publish gay books and magazines without the interference of the police. . . . 'We need freedom of expression to achieve freedom of inversion'"** (Eisenbach 2006:16).

Cory's work was an instant success. It was reprinted several times and translated into multiple languages during the 1950s. Despite writing under the pseudonym Donald Webster Cory, the author took considerable risk to publish this book and paid a dear price. His employer discovered Sagarin was the author behind the pseudonym and fired him. Despite the personal price he paid, "as Donald Webster Cory had hoped, by the late 1960s the American mass media had been liberalized to the point that the subject of homosexuality was no longer taboo" (Eisenbach 2006:81).

THE ROLE OF THE KINSEY STUDIES Another factor that influenced gay activism in the post-WWII era was the release of the Kinsey Studies. The Kinsey Studies were widely read upon publication and created a cultural frenzy, as Chapter Two describes. Despite the fact that expert medical opinion defined homosexuality as a sickness during this era, Kinsey's research challenged this position and argued that same-sex sexual behaviors are relatively common, thus, should not be punished. This helped gay men and lesbians to understand themselves as healthy, despite widespread cultural perceptions of them as sick. It also helped them understand they were not alone.

THE INFLUENCE OF RIGHT-WING OPPOSITION MOVEMENTS Once a social movement is underway, another influence on the movement is the opposition that emerges. In the face of a massive right-wing countermovement, the gay rights movement was forced to change its rhetoric and framing of issues, strategies, and goals in order to survive (Fetner 2008). For instance, gay marriage was not a high priority for gay rights activists between the 1970s and the early 1990s. Yet, Republican politicians and right-wing conservatives saw the issue of gay marriage as having strong cultural resonance and as something that would successfully mobilize their voters. While this issue did successfully mobilize conservatives, it also energized lesbian and gay activists to begin fighting for the right to marry. This resulted in a 20-year *culture war*, as it came to be known, which exposed the polarizing nature of gay rights as a political issue. The culture wars referred to the conflict between conservative and liberal values over cultural issues such as abortion, gay rights, and public school history and science curricula, which began in the early 1990s (Hunter 1991). The culture wars initially generated significant political support for right-wingers and the Republican Party; however, they no longer offer the political benefits they once did for the right-wing. In other words, the culture wars are over, and conservatives lost the battle.

Identity-Based Social Movements

Social movement scholars of the late twentieth century began exploring the links between identity, collective identity, and social movements. Social movements of the 1970s were said to mobilize around identity politics, and thus were referred to as *identity-based movements*. That term refers to the idea that social identities, such as race, gender, sexuality, and ability/disability, influence a person's political orientation and motivation for activism (Bernstein 2005). The feminist movement, the Black Power movement, as well as the lesbian, gay, bisexual, and transgender movements are examples of identity-based movements. The concept of *collective identity*, seeing oneself as belonging to a larger political group, helps us understand people's motivations to act collectively and shows how shared grievances and identities are politicized (Taylor 2013; Touraine 1985). Focusing on identity allows sociologists to explain how interest in social movements emerges and what motivates individuals to engage in activism. It helps us understand the cultural effects of social movements, rather than focusing exclusively on a movement's influence on law and policy (Polletta and Jasper 2001). Of central importance to identity-based movements is the "reframing of dominant, stereotypical characterizations and public understandings . . . with the goal of greater self-determination and . . . self-understanding" (Snow 2013: 264).

Certainly one can see developing a positive gay identity as a major objective of the gay rights movement, as our discussion of the emergence of the Mattachine Society, below, and the previous discussion of the emergence of a gay press exemplifies. But coming out as gay and engaging in organized activism for gay rights was incredibly risky, and those who could pass as straight took a lot of risks by visibly engaging in such activism (Eisenbach 2006). Thus, early gay rights activists fought for less stereotypical representations in the media as a way to encourage homosexuals to come out of the closet.

BEFORE STONEWALL: THE HOMOPHILE MOVEMENT

The modern gay rights movement did not emerge out of a void; during the first half of the twentieth century, gay rights activists were laying a foundation for what became the gay rights movement in the latter half of the century. This early gay rights activism began in the immediate post-WWII era and is known as the *homophile movement*. The homophile movement was characterized by gay men and lesbians beginning to see that they were not sick, that instead they were an oppressed minority and, as such, they should challenge their oppression and seek societal acceptance.

All social movements are composed of a variety of *social movement organizations* (SMOs), ranging from those with moderate demands to those with more radical demands. Over the years, social movements can change—sometimes they change their strategies, sometimes they change their goals. There can also be disagreement within a social movement organization over the organization's goals. For instance, during some eras, the gay rights movement pursued an *assimilationist strategy*, which is a rights-based agenda, while at other times, activists and organizations chose a more *liberationist strategy* with a more revolutionary agenda (Rimmerman 2015). The assimilationist strategy can be understood as a fight for a seat at the table. Thus, activists taking this approach generally work within the system, focusing on legal reforms, civil rights, and increasing visibility. Assimilationists are more likely to accept slow, incremental change. The liberationist perspective pursues more radical changes, most often outside the formal political system, such as cultural acceptance, social transformation, and liberation.

While most often the Stonewall riots are cited as the catalyst for the gay rights movement, the origins of the movement can be traced to the organization of the Mattachine Society in Los Angeles in 1951, founded by Harry Hay. The Mattachine Society is recognized as the first gay political organization and is a good example of an SMO. Henry Hay had been a member of the Communist Party and, as such, he organized the Mattachine Society similarly into cells that were designed to protect the identity of the members. Reflecting his Communist Party roots, Hay sought social change through the mobilization of masses of activists willing to engage in militant action. The first step in this process involved homosexuals learning to take pride in who they were and in their culture, rather than internalizing the dominant societal view that they were sinners, sick, and sexual deviants (Eisenbach 2006). In the early years of its existence, the Mattachine Society was interested in changing antigay laws and public opinion (Rimmerman 2015).

Around the same time period, Del Martin and Phyllis Lyon formed a lesbian organization known as the Daughters of Bilitis (DOB) in San Francisco. This organization actually had apolitical roots, in that it was started as a social club for San Francisco lesbians, a safe space where women could meet and talk. Martin and Lyon decided to expand the mission of the organization to include educating the public about lesbianism. This relatively minor shift in organizational objectives was very controversial at the time and resulted in several members quitting the organization over its increasingly political agenda. The DOB was more of a support group for lesbians rather than a mass organization fighting for social change (Eisenbach 2006).

While the origins and objectives of both organizations differed, they employed a similar strategy in that they both published gay-run and edited magazines focusing on gay life. The Mattachine Society published the first issue of *One* in 1953. The U.S. Post Office banned *One* in 1954, declaring it obscene. The Supreme Court overturned this ban in 1958 on the grounds that it is free speech and is thus guaranteed by the First Amendment (Rimmerman 2015). *One* published editorials stating that sexual acts between consenting adults were not sins and should not be crimes. The Daughters of Bilitis began publishing a newspaper called *The Ladder*. This newspaper avoided political commentary and instead focused on poetry, fiction, history, and biography (Eisenbach 2006). Whether political or apolitical, both of these publications provided a space for gay men and lesbians to speak about their lives and to discuss issues of importance to them.

While the Mattachine Society originated as a radical organization, its origins during the McCarthy Era and the fact that it was founded by a member of the Communist Party set it up for serious criticism. Hay and the organization's lawyers were called before the House Un-American Activities Committee. Many rank-and-file members of the organization were concerned with the militant ideology and the organization's association with communism, which ultimately led to a split in the organization. The founder, Harry Hay, was expelled from the organization in 1953, and the new leaders pursued a more assimilationist strategy, seeking integration into the mainstream (D'Emilio 1983:81).

BOX 5.1

GLOBAL/TRANSNATIONAL PERSPECTIVES ON SEXUALITY: *GAY RIGHTS IN RUSSIA*

While gay rights are being won in many places across the globe, Russia still remains a hostile place for LGBTQ people. The Russian government takes a very intolerant stance toward LGBTQ people and homosexuality, often in the name of the Russian Orthodox Church. In 2013, the government passed legislation that banned gay "propaganda," which criminalized even such minor actions such as displaying a rainbow flag or talking about LGBTQ issues with minors. Gay rights activists have petitioned the government to approve a gay pride parade, yearly for the last ten years; the government in Moscow has repeatedly rejected their request. On May 30, 2015, gay rights activists in Russia held a gay rights rally without government approval, and 20 people were arrested ("Russian Gay Activists . . . ." 2015).

Entertainer Elton John has sought a meeting with Russian President Vladimir Putin to talk about gay rights in Russia. Putin declined to meet with him when he visited Moscow for a concert in May 2016 ("Putin Won't Meet . . . ." 2016). One U.S. gay activist organization, Queer Nation (discussed below), led a boycott of Russian vodka to protest Russian antigay laws and violence against LGBTQ people in 2012, known as the "Dump Russian Vodka" campaign ("Queer Nation NY History" n.d.).

The Putin government's hostility has resulted in increasing violence directed at LGBTQ people as well (Fitzgerald and Ruvinsky 2015). Public opinion is not in support of homosexuality or gay rights in Russia, same-sex marriage is prohibited, and LGBTQ people do not have employment protections. Russian gay rights activists are facing the same kinds of hostility, violence, discrimination, and indifference that many LGBTQ activists in the United States faced in the pre-Stonewall era.

AFTER STONEWALL:
THE MODERN GAY RIGHTS MOVEMENT

The post-Stonewall gay rights movement emerged after almost two decades of assimilationist organizing strategies had seemingly made little to no progress. Gays and lesbians were still targets of police harassment, homosexuality was still classified as a mental illness, and gays and lesbians were legally discriminated against in most areas of life including employment and housing. The Stonewall riots were a form of collective behavior that tapped into the direct action protests engaged in by many other movements of the era, such as the civil rights movement, the red power movement, and the antiwar protests, among others. The United States was also in the midst of its second sexual revolution (see Chapter One). Thus, the approach that organizations such as the Mattachine Society took seemed too mild in the post-Stonewall era, and many gays and lesbians turned toward radicalism.

The Gay Liberation Front (GLF) and other more militant organizations emerged across the country as a response to Stonewall. GLF can be classified as a ***radical social movement organization (RSMO)***, a left-wing social movement organization with radical, emancipatory goals rather than goals that are reform-oriented, which is characteristic of most SMOs. RSMOs embrace nonhierarchical leadership structures, participatory democracy, and a radical agenda emphasizing structural change; they also embrace mass actions and innovative tactics (Fitzgerald and Rodgers 2000).

The Gay Liberation Front was formed in 1969 and was the first gay rights organization to use the word "gay" in its title. The rest of the name was taken from the North Vietnam's National Liberation Front and exemplified the group's confrontational, militant, and countercultural approach (Meem et al. 2010). The assimilationist era of gay rights activism that began with the expulsion of Harry Hay from the Mattachine Society in 1953 was over. The GLF was a broad-based movement that sought a complete transformation of society and "attacked the consumer culture, militarism, racism, sexism, and homophobia" (Rimmerman 2015:23). They encourage using the word gay instead of homosexual, which is a more clinical term, as a way to encourage pride among gays and lesbians and to reject the notion of homosexuality as deviant and sick. GLF meetings organize around consensus, emphasize dialogue and participatory democracy, and are antihierarchical (Rimmerman 2015).

The Gay Liberation Front emphasized the emancipatory potential of ***coming out***, a process of acknowledging, accepting, and disclosing one's sexual orientation to those around them (Patterson 1995). In fact, the first gay publication in the post-Stonewall era was titled *Come Out!* Despite the negative stigma still attached to homosexuality at the time and the legal discrimination gays and lesbians faced, encouraging one another to "come out of the closet" rather than to continue to pass as heterosexual was a way to shed light on the discrimination gays and lesbians faced in their daily lives, as well as the heteronormativity of our culture, and some of the subtle ways heterosexual privilege operates. If gays and lesbians begin to come out to their families, friends, and coworkers, then people hostile to gay rights may rethink their position as they discover that people they know are gay. Coming out was treated as a political act during this period, since it increased the visibility of gays and lesbians, and was a way to assert their power. More current research finds that while remaining in the closet is an attempt at capitalizing on heterosexual privilege, coming out can also be understood as an exercise of white privilege, as gays and lesbians from racial and ethnic minority groups are more likely to stay in the closet to avoid shaming the family (Span and Vidal 2003).

The Gay Liberation Front lasted until 1973 and was eventually undermined by internal conflicts. It was replaced by an organization called the Gay Activists Alliance (GAA), a less radical organization that sought both political changes within the system and uses of the mainstream media to their advantage. Their strategy involved influencing electoral politics, which is the foundation of the contemporary mainstream lesbian and gay movements

(Rimmerman 2015). They borrowed direct action tactics from the mainstream civil rights movement. The GAA engaged in "zaps," which are "carefully orchestrated disruptions of public meetings, on city streets, and in offices . . . [using] satirical humor as a way to capture attention" (Cruikshank 1992:77). Zaps are effective at generating media attention and at empowering participants. The goals of the GAA were to repeal sodomy and solicitation laws, end the police entrapment of gay men, end harassment of gay bars and their clientele, and finally, to end workplace discrimination against gays and lesbians (Hunt 1999).

While the Mattachine Society and DOB were relatively small organizations with a handful of chapters in major cities around the country, the modern gay rights movement truly became a national movement by the late 1970s. After six years of planning, the National Gay Mobilizing Committee for a March on Washington launched a National March on Washington for Lesbian and Gay Rights on October 14, 1979, attracting between 75,000 and 125,000 LGBTQ people and/or supporters. The marchers demanded full equal rights for LGBTQ people through inclusion in civil rights protections. The march symbolized the shift from local gay activism to national gay activism (Ghaziana 2008).

Emergence of Lesbian Feminism

During the 1960s and early 1970s, many lesbians were active in both the feminist and the gay rights movements. Despite their shared homosexuality, lesbian feminists felt that the men who made up the gay rights movement were too sexist. They found themselves unwelcome in the mainstream feminist movement when Betty Friedan, President of NOW (National Organization for Women), declared them to be a "lavender menace." Her fear was that having visible lesbians in the movement would hurt the feminist image in the popular consciousness—instead of being seen as an organization that works for equal rights for all women, something most women should be able to support, they were ridiculed as lesbians and "man-haters." Some lesbian activists chose to leave mainstream feminist organizations and form their own lesbian feminist organizations, such as Radicalesbians.

Lesbian feminists fought for women-only spaces. Women's music and women's music festivals such as the National Women's Music Festival and the Michigan Womyn's music festival, emerged out of this notion. Music has long been a crucial part of social movements (Denisoff and Peterson 1972; Eyerman and Jamison 1998). Music helps communicate the ideas of a movement and helps to mobilize participants. These spaces are breaks from the patriarchy—healing spaces for women. The Michigan Womyn's Music Festival has been plagued by controversy in recent years due to their decision to allow only "womyn-born-womyn" on the festival grounds. This has resulted in a number of vendors and artists, such as the Indigo Girls, boycotting the festival. The controversy began in 1991 when a transgender woman was kicked out of the festival. In the face of such controversy, the festival organizer declared the 40th anniversary, August 2015, to be the last Michigan Womyn's Festival.

AIDS Activism

We will talk more about HIV/AIDS in Chapter Ten, but here we explore how the emergence of this disease influenced gay rights activism of the 1980s. It is hard to convey the fear, panic, and uncertainty of the early AIDS era, especially for young gay men in major urban areas such as New York and San Francisco, whose friends were getting sick and dying of mysterious diseases that doctors were unable to explain. People were dying within two years of being diagnosed. In 1981, the Centers for Disease Control first issued a public health warning about the rare pneumonia affecting gay men in the Los Angeles area. The disease was spreading quickly, and by late 1981, the CDC declared it an epidemic.

Despite the fact that this sexually transmitted disease had become an epidemic and had put the bulk of the adult population at risk since most adults are sexually active, the federal government at the time, under the direction of President Ronald Reagan, chose to ignore this public health threat. During President Reagan's eight years in office, he never mentioned AIDS until after the death of actor Rock Hudson in 1985. Perhaps more importantly, he never invested in the necessary research funding required to address a public health epidemic (Shilts 1987).

Such government apathy triggered significant mobilization and activism within the gay community. Two of the most significant social movement organizations to emerge were the Gay Men's Health Crisis (GMHC) in 1982 and the AIDS Coalition to Unleash Power (ACT UP) in 1987. In the face of government inaction and medical uncertainty, one of the first things they did was educate the gay community through the publication of a newsletter titled "Medical Answers about AIDS."

While there is no cure for AIDS, educating people, particularly those in high-risk groups, about safe sex practices was lifesaving. GMHC necessarily avoided the shaming associated with a *sex-negative* approach to safe sex discussions that opposed certain expressions of human sexuality, especially casual sex, same-sex sexuality, prostitution, and other forms of deviant, or non-normative, sexuality. The GMHC also set up a buddy system that consisted of trained volunteers who provided live-in care for those with AIDS. The care was especially important since the fear and panic surrounding HIV/AIDS resulted in many infected individuals facing death alone. Finally, the GMHC established a crisis-counseling hotline and offered legal aid and social work services (Mass 2011). While the organization members directed their services to the New York area, they also worked to influence national AIDS policy.

One of the original five founders of GMHC, Larry Kramer, quit the organization to found a more politically radical organization, ACT UP, in 1987. Their strategy was to use direct action tactics, demonstrations, and civil disobedience to generate media attention to the HIV/AIDS epidemic. They popularized the slogan "Silence = Death." Their first demonstration was on Wall Street and targeted pharmaceutical companies, demanding more access to experimental drugs to fight HIV/AIDS. A demonstration in 1987 protested the high cost of AZT (the only promising approved drug treatment), which cost $10,000 per year, per patient. Other demonstrations targeted the White House, state governments, and airlines that refused to transport PWAs (people living with AIDS). They also targeted New York City government offices for lack of affordable housing for PWAs. ACT UP's 1988 demonstration at the Food and Drug Administration resulted in nationwide news coverage and officially marked a national AIDS movement. ACT UP was visible—they were blocking streets by chaining themselves to each other, getting arrested by the hundreds, chanting slogans, making their demands heard, and through it all, getting mass media coverage. They also used art to send messages that countered those in the dominant culture, such as posters stating, "Kissing Doesn't Kill. Greed and Indifference Do," to address the unfounded fear in the mainstream culture that you could get AIDS from kissing someone.

Both of these organizations not only helped people living with HIV/AIDS and educated others about prevention, but their efforts successfully increased awareness of the epidemic and the lack of government response in the form of medical research funding into treatments and research for HIV/AIDS. Their activism resulted in decreasing costs for AZT, access to experimental drugs, and a speedier drug approval process.

A long-standing critique of the gay rights movement was that it was predominantly a white, cisgender movement. Movement leaders were overwhelmingly white and, more problematically, the movement took on issues affecting white LGBTQ members rather than meeting the specific needs of LGBTQ people of color (Owens 2015). This was less true of AIDS activism, which was much more inclusive than the broader gay rights movement. Since AIDS struck New York City much harder than any other city in America at the outset of the epidemic, the racial diversity of the city assures that racially diverse communities were being targeted by the disease. Thus, organizations like ACT UP were necessarily racially/ethnically diverse. In order to adequately fight HIV/AIDS, activist organizations necessarily focused on more than just white men because the disease disproportionately affects people of color.

AIDS activist organizations were more inclusive than the broader gay rights movement in other ways as well. Throughout the gay rights movement, gay and lesbian activists often formed separate organizations such as the Daughters of Bilitis, the Mattachine Society, and the radicalesbians, with the gender segregation sometimes unintended and sometimes by design. AIDS activism brought gay and lesbian activists together. While lesbians did not face the same risk for contracting HIV/AIDS as gay men did and the lesbian community was not affected as dramatically as the gay male community, they saw government inattention to the disease as an issue affecting all gay people.

Queer Nation

In 1990, gay and lesbian activists in New York wanted to take the energy and tactics of ACT UP and apply them to more multifaceted gay rights issues, rather than just fighting HIV/AIDS. This resulted in the creation of Queer Nation, an organization dedicated to fighting discrimination against gays and lesbians, eliminating homophobia, and increasing the visibility of LGBTQ people. Queer Nation soon had chapters in a half-dozen other cities across the country. At protests members chanted, "We're here! We're queer! Get used to it!" They were particularly interested in fighting to end violence against gays and lesbians. When episodes of antigay violence become known, members of Queer Nation marched through the streets chanting, "Dykes and Fags Bash Back!" They demanded police action and protection as their right. Their desire to increase the visibility of LGBTQ people inspired "Youth Visibility Days" at a local high school.

Undocumented Queer Youth Activism

With an estimated 11 million undocumented immigrants in the United States, it can safely be assumed that there are over 260,000 of them who identify as LGBTQ. Many "undocuqueer" youth have mobilized to fight for justice for both undocumented immigrants and LGBTQ people. One organization, Queer Undocumented Immigrant Project (QUIP), is currently engaged in a campaign titled "Break the Cage," which seeks to end the incarceration and deportation of undocumented immigrants. Undocumented queer organizing began in Chicago in 2001 when Tania Unzuerta was scheduled to testify in support of the DREAM Act on Capitol Hill. Her testimony never happened because of the 9/11 attacks (Lal 2013). After Congress failed to pass the DREAM Act in 2007, undocumented queer youth got together and formed an organization called DreamActivist. This group began a campaign called "Education not Deportation." In 2010, undocumented queer youth activists organized a national "Coming Out of the Shadows" day to bring visibility to immigration laws (Lal 2013).

The Road to Marriage Equality

The quotation on page 104 by Justice Anthony Kennedy is drawn from the U.S. Supreme Court's June 2015 opinion that granted same-sex couples the right to marry and was the culmination of twenty years of activism. The status of same-sex marriage has been complicated for two reasons: first, it is a fast changing issue, and second, each state had the right to determine the specific rights and responsibilities associated with marriage until the Supreme Court ruled on the issue. Once the Supreme Court ruled, that decision became the law of the land. From a conservative perspective, gay rights represent the moral erosion of our society. In conservative political pundit Pat Buchanan's words, it is a culture war "for the soul of America." Progressive people, on the other hand, see gay rights as evidence of societal progress.

One of the earliest court cases challenging the denial of same-sex marriage occurred in Hawaii in 1993. This was not the first time same-sex couples had challenged the prohibition on same-sex marriage, but it is the case that caught the nation's attention. Three same-sex couples claimed they were being discriminated against by being denied the right to marry, and the Hawaii State Supreme Court ruled in their favor—that denying them the right to marry was indeed discrimination. However, the state legislature passed a law that limited marriage to male–female couples only, and 70 percent of the voters in Hawaii voted to amend the state constitution to support the legislation (Pierceson 2016). So, what started out as a fight in the

"No union is more profound than marriage, for it embodies the highest ideas of love, fidelity, devotion, sacrifice, and family. In forming a marital union, two people become something greater than once they were. As some of the petitioners in these cases demonstrate, marriage embodies a love that may endure even past death. It would misunderstand these men and women to say they disrespect the idea of marriage. Their plea is that they do respect it, respect it so deeply that they seek to find its fulfillment for themselves. Their hope is not to be condemned to live in loneliness, excluded from one of civilization's oldest institutions. They ask for equal dignity in the eyes of the law. The Constitution grants them that right"
—Justice Anthony Kennedy's majority opinion in **Obergefell v. Hodges**, *the Supreme Court's 5–4 decision in favor of same-sex marriage, June 26, 2015.*

courts eventually involved both the state legislature and ballot measures, a pattern that was repeated throughout the fight for same-sex marriage.

In 2004, Massachusetts became the first state to recognize gay marriage. In reaction to the initial legalization of gay marriage in some states, the religious right's strategy was to mobilize voters across the country to pass state constitutional amendments that prohibited what they viewed as judicial activism, judges deciding whether denying same-sex couples a marriage license was constitutional or not. By 2004, they succeeded in passing laws against same-sex marriage and same-sex marriage bans in the form of constitutional amendments in 39 states. This legislation also allowed states NOT to recognize gay marriages that were legal in other states, violating the Full Faith and Credit Clause of the Constitution that required states to honor each other's laws. The federal government passed the Defense of Marriage Act (DOMA) in 1996, which allowed states to refuse to recognize same-sex marriages that were granted in states where same-sex marriage was legal.

These actions motivated gay rights activists and organizations to begin fighting for the right to marry. In 2003, Evan Wolfson, a civil rights attorney and gay rights activist, formed an organization called Freedom to Marry to fight for same-sex couple's rights. The goal of this organization was to win marriage equality nationwide, and thus, to eliminate the piecemeal approach to gay marriage. During the late 1990s and early 2000s, the early "wins" for same-sex marriage amount to a few states, such as Vermont and Connecticut, passing civil unions and domestic partnership benefits for same-sex couples rather than allowing them the right to marry. *Civil unions* provide legal protection to a couple at the state level, but do not provide them with access to federal protections or federal benefits, nor are they granted the dignity of a legally recognized marriage. Civil unions are a political compromise—they provide gay and lesbian couples with some protection from discrimination, but same-sex unions are still relegated to a second-class status. Civil unions, for instance, are not recognized in other states in the ways marriages are.

In 2003, a Massachusetts Supreme Judicial Court decision led it to become the first state to recognize gay marriage. The plaintiffs argued in *Goodridge v. Department of Public Health* that civil unions did not protect same-sex couples and their families; thus, not allowing them the right to marry was discrimination. The Court stayed implementation of its ruling for 180 days to allow the state legislature to take action. By early 2004, the majority opinion became final, formalizing the right to gay marriage in Massachusetts. The *New York Times* responded to this by publishing its first wedding announcements for same-sex couples in May 2004. In 2005, California passed a Freedom to Marry bill, which was then vetoed by Governor Arnold Schwarzenegger. In 2006, Arizona was the first state where voters rejected an antigay amendment.

The year 2009 was a big year for gay marriage proponents. The Iowa Supreme Court approved same-sex marriage. The Vermont legislature moved beyond civil unions to an embrace of gay marriage, voting down the governor's veto. Also in 2009, Maine, California, Nevada, New Hampshire, and the District of Columbia embraced marriage

When the Supreme Court ruling in favor of same-sex marriage was announced on June 26, 2015, Barb Sonderman and Martha Pickens immediately headed to their local court house in Columbia, MO, to get married. At this point, they had been together for 17 years and had already had a commitment ceremony. But like many other LGBTQ people, the couple wanted to receive the benefits of a legally recognized marriage. Source: Reprinted with permission. © AP Photo/Columbia Daily Tribune/Nick Schnelle.

equality, although both Maine and California would lose that right before ultimately regaining it. In 2011, President Obama and Attorney General Eric Holder stated that the federal government would no longer defend DOMA. In *United States v. Windsor* (2013), the Supreme Court found DOMA to be unconstitutional under the Due Process Clause of the Fifth Amendment, and it was repealed. This resulted in legal challenges over the next three to four years. More states such as Illinois, Minnesota, Delaware, Washington, and Maryland signed on to marriage equality between 2012 and 2014. A judge in Arkansas struck down that state's ban on gay marriage in 2013. A Louisiana judge became the first judge to support a ban on gay marriage in over a year in 2014, evidence of the shifting winds in this fight ("Winning the Freedom to Marry Nationwide" n.d.).

By the spring of 2015, 37 states, some counties in Missouri (but not the state as a whole), and the District of Columbia had legalized gay marriage. This was a dramatic shift in just one year, as gay marriage expanded by 18 states in 2014 and early 2015. The Supreme Court agreed to hear a case that would either turn back the clock on gay marriage or make it legal nationwide. The decision was announced on June 26, 2015. In *Obergefell v. Hodges*, the Supreme Court legalized gay marriage around the country and struck down all state gay marriage bans, essentially expanding rights to LGBTQ Americans and ending the most significant wedge issue deployed in the culture wars.

TRANSGENDER ACTIVISM AND RIGHTS

Transgender people face unique forms of discrimination. Transgender activism is similarly intertwined with lesbian and gay activism, yet also distinct from it on certain issues.

Early transgender activism focused on fighting invisibility. Much like LGBQ activists, those fighting for transgender rights initially turned to media to fight their invisibility. In 1952, a group of Southern California transgender people published *Transvestia: The Journal of the American Society for Equality in Dress.* Another publication, *Transvestia,* was introduced in 1960 to address issues facing the transgender community. By the 1970s, a New York publication titled *Queens* was on the scene and was more political in nature than previous publications. Today, transgender people are more visible than ever. For example, Laverne Cox, is a transgender actor playing a transgender character on the show *Orange Is the New Black.* The transition of celebrity Bruce Jenner to Caitlyn Jenner has resulted in unprecedented media attention to transgender people, albeit with an unfortunate focus on her physical appearance and clothing rather than the more serious issues facing transitioning.

Transgender people do participate in the gay rights movement. In fact, some argue that the modern gay rights movement was launched by drag queens and transsexuals in 1969, referring to their significant role in the Stonewall riots (Minter 2006). Despite the participation of transgender people in the gay rights movement, there is a distinct transgender movement. Earlier in the chapter we discussed the first transgender riot in American history, the Compton's Cafeteria riot in San Francisco in 1966. The ***transgender movement*** refers to a collection of diverse groups of people, from intersex individuals to drag queens to transgender activists, who share a collective political identity and seek gender self-determination (Currah, Juang, and Minter 2006). Despite the diverse constituencies encapsulated under the umbrella "transgender movement," all of "these groups seek justice and equality for people whose gender identity or expression contravenes social norms" and, thus, are facets of the same movement (Currah, Juang, and Minter 2006:xvi). Transgender activists are fighting for more than freedom of gender expression; they are also fighting for the right to form families, adopt children, freedom to control their own bodies, and access to gendered spaces (as the previous example of the Michigan Womyn's Music Festival exemplifies).

> 66
>
> *Transgender activists have put forth an International Bill of Gender Rights in which they declare that "all human beings have the right to define their own gender identity regardless of chromosomal sex, genitalia, assigned birth sex, or initial gender role" (Currah, Juang, and Minter 2006:xvi).*

Transgender activists are fighting for access to job training programs and housing. Many "wins" for transgender activists have been local. For instance, Minneapolis was the first city in the country to include transgender people in civil rights legislation in 1975. In 2015, West Hollywood, CA, passed an ordinance to implement single-stall unisex facilities in public spaces as a way to make transgender people more comfortable in a world that is otherwise highly gender-segregated. Similar legislation has passed in Washington, D.C., Portland, OR, Austin, TX, and Philadelphia, PA (Smith 2014).

Until recently, most laws prohibiting discrimination do not define sex or gender; thus, transgender people have been at the mercy of the judiciary when they challenge their discrimination. And, as Currah, Juang, and Minter (2006) note, the judiciary has a very poor record on the issue of transgender rights. The exemplary case is *Ulane v. Eastern Airlines* (1984) in which the court found that Eastern Airlines did discriminate against Ulane, but not because she was female. Instead, it was because she was a transsexual. Thus, this judicial precedent found that while it is wrong to fire someone for being a woman, it somehow is not wrong to fire someone for becoming a woman (Currah, Juang, and Minter 2006). Transgender activists fight to have sex, gender, and sexual orientation included in antidiscrimination laws in order to protect them from discrimination on the job, in public accommodations, in housing, and from judicial interpretations such as those in the *Ulane* case.

One of the primary differences between gay activism and transgender activism involves the transgender embrace of medical intervention and treatment. Gays and lesbians fought to have homosexuality removed from the *DSM* (*Diagnostic and Statistical Manual of Mental Disorders*) and to decrease the use of conversion therapies. Transgender activists in the 1960s fought for the creation of health clinics that provide hormone treatments. In 1967, a group of transsexuals formed an organization by the name of COG (Conversion Our Goal). Many activists in the 1970s worked for access to mental health care as well as medical care for transgender people. By 1980, these efforts paid off as the psychiatric community agreed on criteria for a new disorder, gender identity disorder (see Chapter Three). Despite this, transgender people do not approach the medical profession uncritically. Many transgender people face discrimination in the medical field and cannot get the basic health care they need. Thus, transgender activists are fighting for the right to be free from involuntary medical treatments and for access to competent medical care (Currah, Juang, and Minter 2006).

BISEXUAL ACTIVISM

While much bisexual activism falls under the broader umbrella of gay rights activism, there are also some social movement organizations, such as the Bisexual Resource Center and BiNet USA, specifically dedicated to advocacy for bisexuals and the specific issues they face. As Chapter One describes, bisexuals struggle with invisibility and not being perceived as a legitimate sexual identity. Thus, one organization, BiPOL, encourages militant activism to challenge bisexual invisibility and exclusion. One of the founders of BiNet USA, Gary North, claims that one of the major successes of bi activism has been the inclusion of "B" in LGBT (or LGBTQ) in public discussions and campus organizations. He describes this as a subtle but constant reminder of the diverse ways people identify and find pleasure (North 2012).

CONCLUSION

This chapter explores LGBTQ activism and mobilization through a sociological lens. We begin with an analysis of the sociology of social movements: differentiating between social movements and collective behavior; distinguishing between grassroots, left-wing, and right-wing social movements; and exploring the social and cultural conditions that facilitate the emergence of a social movement, paying specific attention to those conditions that facilitated the gay rights movement. We then explore gay activism prior to the Stonewall riots, which includes assimilationist versus liberationist strategies engaged in by social movement organizations (SMOs). The modern gay rights movement emerged after Stonewall and includes many radical gay rights organizations (RSMOs), lesbian feminist organizations, AIDS activism, and queer and bisexual activist organizations. One of the most successful campaigns of the modern gay rights movement has been the fight for marriage equality. Finally, this chapter explores transgender activism, from issues of invisibility to demands for access to appropriate mental and physical health care.

Key Terms and Concepts

Agency 92
Assimilationist strategy 98
Civil union 104
Collective behavior 94
Collective identity 97
Coming out 100
Culture war 97
Gay enclaves 95
Grassroots movement 93

Homophile movement 98
Identity-based
    movement 97
Left-wing movement 94
Liberationist strategy 98
Mobilization 95
Radical social movement
    organization (RSMO) 100
Relative deprivation 94

Right-wing movement 93
Sex-negative 102
Social movement 93
Social movement
    organization (SMO) 98
Structure 92
Transgender
    movement 106

Critical Thinking Questions

1. Identify and explain the social and cultural conditions that facilitated the emergence of the modern gay rights movement. Explain the factors that contributed to the shifts in goals, strategies, and the agenda of the gay rights movement in the 1980s and 1990s. Compare the modern gay rights movement to another social movement of the post-WWII era.

2. Differentiate between a social movement and collective behavior. Explain the role episodes of collective behavior play in the modern gay rights movement, providing detailed examples of such episodes.

3. Explain the ways transgender activism overlaps with lesbian and gay activism, and instances where it is distinct.

Activities

1. Interview someone in your life who has participated in a social movement, asking them about their experiences. Compare what you learn to the chapter overview of the gay rights movement.

2. Go to the Human Rights Campaign website (see below, under "Suggested Multimedia"). Write a 2-page summary of the key

campaigns this organization is involved in. Were any of these issues surprising to you? Are there any issues that are missing? If so, describe them.

3. Identify and describe any social movement tactics or strategies that the gay rights movement borrows from other social movements of the post-WWII era.

Essential Readings

Currah, Paisley, Richard M. Juang, and Shannon Price Minter, eds. 2006. *Transgender Rights.* Minneapolis, MN: University of Minnesota Press.

Eisenbach, David. 2006. *Gay Power: An American Revolution.* New York: Carroll & Graf Publishers.

Fetner, Tina. 2008. *How the Religious Right Shaped Lesbian and Gay Activism.* Minneapolis, MN: University of Minnesota Press.

Rimmerman, Craig A. 2015. *The Lesbian and Gay Movements: Assimilation or Liberation?* 2nd ed. Boulder, Co: Westview Press.

Recommended Films

After Stonewall (1999). John Scagliotti, Director. A sequel to *Before Stonewall* (1984), this film summarizes the gay rights activism of the post-Stonewall era at roughly the 30th anniversary of the Stonewall riots. It explores the rejection of the homophile movement, AIDS activism, Anita Bryant's "Save the Children" campaign, the assassination of Harvey Milk, and the murder of Matthew Shepard.

Milk (2008). Gus Van Zant, Director. A Hollywood portrayal of Harvey Milk's life in the Castro District of San Francisco, when he becomes the first openly gay elected official, and his ultimate assassination.

Screaming Queens (2005). Victor Silverman and Susan Stryker, Directors. A documentary about the transgender women and drag queens who participated in the Compton's Cafeteria riots in 1966 in San Francisco's Tenderloin District to protest constant police harassment. This is known as the first transgender riot in American history, and it occurred three years before the more well-known Stonewall riots.

Stonewall Uprising (2010). David Heilbroner and Kate Davis, Directors. This documentary explores the cultural climate in the pre-Stonewall era, particularly the discrimination and hostility LGBTQ individuals faced, which resulted in the Stonewall riots. The film concludes with a look at the aftermath of the rioting, including the emergence of the modern gay rights movement and gay pride celebrations.

United in Anger: A History of ACT UP (2012). James Hubbard and Sarah Schulman, Directors. An excellent history of AIDS activism from collected oral histories of people involved in ACT UP (AIDS Coalition to Unleash Power). In addition to hearing from the activists, this film presents excellent footage of ACT UP protests and campaigns.

Suggested Multimedia

Queer Undocumented Immigrant Project QUIP (Queer Undocumented Immigrant Project) is part of United We Dream, the largest youth-led immigrant group in the country, composed of over 10,000 youth in 26 states. QUIP works for social justice for undocumented queer youth, their allies, and immigrant queer youth. Using an intersectional analysis, they engage in campaigns to address issues affecting LGBTQ and undocumented immigrant communities. One example of such a campaign is the "Break the Cage" campaign that fights the incarceration and deportation of undocumented LGBTQ immigrants. http://unitedwedream.org/about/projects/quip/

Human Rights Campaign The Human Rights Campaign is the largest LGBTQ advocacy organization in the United States, with over 1.5 million members and supporters. It began in 1980 as the first lesbian and gay political action committee and still engages in political lobbying for LGBTQ causes. They provide financial support for gay political candidates and those who support gay civil rights legislation. They were at the forefront of the fight for marriage equality, ending "Don't Ask, Don't Tell," and winning other key gay rights victories. http://www.hrc.org/

Teaching Tolerance Teaching Tolerance provides teachers and schools with progressive educational curricula. This classroom resource goes beyond traditional discussions of the civil rights movement and includes a discussion of the contributions of LGBTQ African Americans to the movement. The series introduces students to four African Americans, some of whom were LGBTQ while others were advocates for LGBTQ issues: James Baldwin, Lorraine Hansberry, Pauli Murray, and Bayard Rustin. http://www.tolerance.org/LGBT-CRM "The Role of Lesbians and Gay Men in the Civil Rights Movement."

6

MEDIA, SPORT, AND SEXUALITY

LEARNING OBJECTIVES

Upon completion of this chapter, students will be able to . . .

- Recognize sexualized language and imagery in mass media
- Understand the impact sexualized media has on adolescents and children
- Describe representations of gays, lesbians, and transgender people in media
- Identify the various ways sexuality intersects with sport and sport media
- Explain the myriad manifestations of masculinity in sports
- Describe the ways women's sports opportunities have been limited
- Identify issues intersex and transgender athletes face in the sports world

F ew events capture the intersection of gender, sexuality, media, and sport more fully than the 2015 public transition of Olympic gold medalist Bruce Jenner into Caitlyn Jenner. The media campaign surrounding the entire process captivated American audiences and generated landmark levels of public awareness on what it means to be transgender. In April 2015, Caitlyn Jenner, drew 17 million viewers when she spoke about her transition to becoming a woman in an ABC national television news interview with Diane Sawyer. It was a two-hour "20/20" interview, in which she intimately recalls the first time she wore a dress as an 8-year-old boy, her first attempt to transition in the 1980s with female hormones, and her fear of hurting her kids with the truth of her hidden gender identity.

Caitlyn Jenner has been a public figure her entire career. In the 1976 Olympics, as Bruce Jenner, she won a gold medal in the decathlon, which carries with it the title of "world's greatest athlete." At this time in Jenner's life, she represented the embodiment of the ideal

American masculine man. She had chiseled muscles, shaggy hair, and sexual appeal. Then in 2007, while still known as Bruce Jenner, she appeared alongside her then wife, Kris Jenner, in the reality television series, *Keeping Up with the Kardashians*. The show explored the Kardashian-Jenner family dynamics, became wildly popular, and both families became household names. With this level of media attention and visibility, it is not a surprise that, in 2014, Caitlyn hired publicist Alan Nierob to orchestrate a successful public transition story, creating a historic moment in transgender politics (Bernstein 2015).

In July 2015, just a few short months after her nationally broadcast ABC interview, she revealed her new female identity as Caitlyn Jenner on the cover of *Vanity Fair* (Bissinger 2015; Griggs 2015). She wore a cleavage boosting corset and, seated in a sultry pose, she represented the embodiment of ideal femininity. Within weeks, she was awarded the Arthur Ashe Courage Award at ESPN's ESPYs in Los Angeles. And, in that same month, July 2015, E! Network launched the documentary series, *I am Cait*, which chronicles Caitlyn Jenner's life after gender transition.

In this chapter, we begin our analysis of the ways sexuality intersects with various social institutions; the ways sexuality is policed, constrained, and shaped by institutions; and, in turn, the ways those institutions shape sexuality. Here we explore media, sport, and sexuality; and in the following chapters, we extend our institutional analysis to include the workplace, schools, family, and religion. In recent decades, the media and sports worlds have witnessed dramatic changes in terms of LGBTQ representation, with mass media leading

Upon winning the gold medal in the 1976 Olympics in the decathlon, Bruce Jenner was deemed the "World's Greatest Athlete."
Source: AP Photo.

In 2015, Bruce Jenner became Caitlyn Jenner and instantly became one of the world's most famous transgender people.
Source: AP Photo/Charles Sykes.

the change, and the sporting world being much slower to respond to the increasing cultural acceptance of homosexuality and gender nonconformity. These institutions intersect in the form of **sports media**, a term that recognizes that sport is mediated by the media; beyond bringing sports to the audience, the idea of sports media implies that the media frames sports in particular ways for the audience. This is certainly true with respect to gender and sexuality, as this chapter will show.

We begin this chapter with an exploration of sexuality and media, commencing with a fundamental aspect of media: language. From there we explore imagery in media and how this contributes to the hypersexualization and the sexual objectification of bodies. The impact of sexualized media on children and adolescents and representations of LGBTQ in television and film is further explored. We then shift gears to explore the ways sport, gender, and sexuality are framed by the sports media; the heteronormativity of the sports world; and the ways masculinity and femininity play out in men's and women's sports, stigmatizing LGBTQ athletes. We conclude the chapter with a discussion of the role of Title IX in expanding sporting opportunities for women, the gradual opening of the athletic closet, the emergence of the Gay Games, and the challenges surrounding the incorporation of intersex and transgender athletes into a gender-segregated sporting world. Current examples of the intersection of sexuality with the institutions of media and sport include, but are not limited to, the following examples:

- *Fifty Shades of Grey* (2011), a book exploring the erotic story of the world of bondage-discipline-sadomasochism (BDSM), sold more than 100 million copies in the first three years, and then was released as a movie, which grossed over $550 million in its first three months (Child 2015).
- In 2014, Amazon released its television Original Series, *Transparent*, about a middle-aged father transitioning into a woman. In 2015, it won Golden Globe's award for best TV series, and it reveals how transgender issues have become more mainstream.

- In May 2015, American television personality and conservative activist Josh Duggar publicly admitted on Facebook to molesting five underage girls, and to infidelity and pornography addiction. The sex scandal led to the cancellation of his family's TLC reality television series, *19 Kids and Counting*, and his resignation from the Family Research Council, a lobbying group that works against LGBTQ rights, divorce, and porn.
- When the United States Women's National Soccer Team won the World Cup in July 2015, team captain Abby Wambach garnered positive media attention when she ran toward the stands and embraced her wife with a hug and a kiss, a public display of same-sex affection that until recently has rarely been celebrated outside of specifically designated "gay" spaces.
- In August 2015, the first openly gay baseball player, rookie David Denson of the Milwaukee Brewers minor league team, was recognized. Other male professional athletes have waited until their professional sports careers were over to come out.

MEDIA AND SEXUALITY

Media is essentially a term for mass means of communication. Media comes in many forms in today's world, including television, radio, newspapers, magazines, billboards, direct mail, and Internet. Media communication serves a variety of purposes, from local to international news, entertainment, education, advertising, artistic expression, promotional messages, and more. Mass media is woven into our daily lives in a multitude of ways and is a pervasive and powerful tool for reinforcing and shaping social and cultural norms. Sex and sexuality have become primary themes in mass media. Sex scandals involving politicians, celebrities, and public figures are widely covered by news sources. Entertainment media such as television, film, and video are inundated with sexual imagery and storylines revolving around sexual interactions. Even the sexual accounts and inquiries of everyday people can be commonly found in sex advice columns and radio shows.

Media literacy is the ability to access, analyze, evaluate, and create media in a variety of forms and is an essential skill in the twenty-first century. Media literacy helps us understand the role of media in society and how it informs our views of sex and sexuality. In order to analyze and evaluate how media constructs sexuality, it is important to recognize some key principles: audiences negotiate meaning; media is constructed to represent people, places, and events; media contains ideological and value messages; media has commercial implications; and each medium has a unique aesthetic form (Ontario Ministry of Education 1989). In other words, media does not influence all people in the same way; interpretations vary. Media consumption is a negotiated process; we do not simply digest media messages uncritically. Sometimes we reject the message, sometimes we internalize it.

To have commercial implications means that in many cases, media is advertising a product or is supported by advertisers. Media is a dynamic and complex set of genres with a wide variety of messages and values about sex and sexuality. The first two broad forms of sexualized media communication we will analyze are language and imagery.

Sexualized Language in Media

Social constructionist theory views language as a crucial component to understanding reality (Berger and Luckmann 1991). The words we use to define ourselves, others, and the world around us not only organize social life, but shape it too. For instance, as discussed in Chapter Three, language is gendered. Most languages rely on binary gendered pronouns to define people as either male or female, feminine or masculine, boy or girl. Just as language is gendered, it can also be sexualized. Sexualized language can include words that describe and evoke the practice of sexual intercourse, words and labels that define sexual norms, and terms to refer to individuals and groups of people outside the heteronormative sexual mainstream. Popular, mainstream media in the United States uses sexualized language to reinforce and shape cultural assumptions and norms surrounding sexual behaviors.

In Western culture, a wide variety of constantly changing terms are used to describe the practice of sexual intercourse. Most terms for "having sex" imply multiple meanings that make sense in the culture and context in which they are spoken. For example, to "make love," or "to sleep with" implies an intimate relationship between two people. Formal medical terms like "copulation," "coitus," or "mating" are more ambiguous, in that they acknowledge the physical act but provide no clue as to the level of intimacy involved. Other words to describe sex include being "passionate," "intimate," "physical," or even "sensual." Informal terms, or slang words, include "hooking up," "hitting that," or "getting it on." The language media use to frame sexuality reinforces social norms about sex and sexuality. For instance, common sources of information on sexual intercourse are women's and men's lifestyle magazines, which routinely feature stories focused on how to have "great sex." This helps create a common understanding as to what constitutes "great sex," which as we will see in our discussion of disability and sexuality in Chapter Ten, can actually be limiting.

Research on "great sex" editorial advice in popular women's and men's magazines reveals that the content is often presented in ways that promote sexual- and gender-role stereotypes, narrow sexual scripts, and contradictory and conflicting messages about sex (Menard and Kleinplatz 2008). For example, generalizations concerning sexual preferences, desires, and fantasies are gender-stereotyped: men aggressively pursue sex, and women desire sex only in accompaniment with romance. Often readers are advised on how to kiss and caress partners, which positions are the best, and how to perform oral sex—all based on heteronormative sexual scripts (Menard and Kleinplatz 2008). Further, often the language used in sex advice media sources describes sex as risk-free. In other words, sexually transmitted diseases, risk of pregnancy, and sexual violence are often not included in the discussions of "great sex" (see Chapters Nine and Ten).

How much do popular magazines actually shape people's sexual behavior and practices or how they think about sex? This is difficult to decipher. Studies do suggest both adult and adolescent sexual beliefs, attitudes, and behaviors correlate with magazine consumption (Brown 2002; Kim and Ward 2004; Pierce 1993). For example, associations between magazine use and sexual attitudes were explored among 205 female college students. Those who frequently read teen-focused magazines such as *Seventeen* were more likely to endorse stereotypical views of the male sexual stereotype, specifically, the view that men are driven by sexual urges and are fearful of commitment (Kim and Ward 2004).

Just as media promotes and supports language used to describe the practice of sex, it also plays a role in describing what constitutes sexual abuse, assault, and violence. Extensive research has been undertaken to explore the role of language in news media in shaping our perceptions of reality and facts, perceptions of risk, and even how we interpret our own experiences (Kitzinger 2004; Drache and Velagic 2013). Journalists play a powerful role in deciding what stories to pay attention to and the language used to relay the story. For example, reports of sexual assault tend to focus on offences committed by a stranger, and often the offender is labeled as a "monster" or as "evil." Such a frame presents sexual assault as out of the ordinary and the offender as a predatory, deviant person. In reality, the U.S. Bureau of Justice Statistics (BJS) reports that 6 in 10 rape or sexual assault victims say that they knew their perpetrator—most often it was a family member, friend, acquaintance, or an intimate partner (U.S. Department of Justice 2012). A study of sexual victimization of college women found that 9 out of 10 victims knew the person who sexually victimized them (U.S. Department of Justice 2000; see Chapter Twelve).

Moreover, the use of the term "sex" in place of "sexual assault" implies that the offence is primarily about sexual intercourse as opposed to a form of violence, confusing the criminality of the incident. Sexual assault and rape are forms of sexual violence that are subjected on someone else. Language used to describe it should explicitly reveal the nonconsensual nature of the act. To describe a victim as "experiencing" sexual violence shapes readers' perceptions by implying voluntary participation. In recent years, media kits and guides for journalists to help them avoid such mischaracterizations have been offered by nonprofit organizations such as the Minnesota Coalition against Sexual Assault, Chicago Taskforce on Violence against Girls & Young Women, and Dart Center for Journalism and Trauma.

Sexualized Imagery in Media

Social constructionist theory views imagery as powerful representations of society and culture. Like language, images not only represent the culture, they provide meaning and shape society (Berger and Luckmann 1991). Since the birth of photography and film in the last century, images are a fundamental aspect of mass media. In today's world, we are subjected to thousands of media images on a daily basis.

> *"Rape is violence, not 'sex.' Reporting on sexual assault means finding not only the language but the context and sensitivity to communicate a trauma that is at once deeply personal and yet a matter of public policy; immediate and yet freighted with centuries of stigma, silence and suppression. Reporting on sexual violence requires special ethical sensitivity, interviewing skills, and knowledge about victims, perpetrators, law and psychology" (Dart Center for Journalism and Trauma 2016).*

Research reveals that images of men and women's bodies in media are often sexualized (Attwood 2006; Hatton and Trautner 2011; Zurbriggen, Ramsey, and Jawarski 2011). The American Psychological Association describes four possible components to the sexualization of a person or image: when the person's value comes only from sexual appeal, to the exclusion of other characteristics; when a person is held to a standard that equates physical attractiveness with narrowly defined ideals of sexiness; when a person or image is sexually objectified; or, when sexuality is inappropriately imposed on a person (American Psychological Association 2007).

HYPERSEXUALIZATION: MAGAZINES AND MUSIC VIDEOS Popular, mainstream mass media often use sexualized images that reinforce narrowly defined ideas of sexiness and heteronormativity. When images excessively represent narrow ideas of sexual appeal above all other qualities, sociologists refer to them as *hypersexualized*. Feminists have long noticed and critiqued the hypersexualization of women's bodies in media (Gerbner 1978; Tuchman 1978). The hypersexualization the media engages in amounts to the *symbolic annihilation* of women and girls by systematically ignoring, trivializing, or distorting them (Tuchman 1978). hooks (1992) argues African American women are often relegated to sexually wanton representations. An example of a hypersexualized image is a black woman in porn-style clothing, exposing her body and emphasizing the breasts, buttocks, or hips. It reflects a trivialization of her value to emphasize only her sexualized body and it reflects and reinforces sexist and racist ideologies.

Magazines, despite their target audience or content purposes, are full of sexualized and hypersexualized images of men's and women's bodies. A recent study examined the covers of *Rolling Stone* magazine from 1967 to 2009 to measure changes in the sexualization of men and women in popular media over time (Hatton and Trautner 2011). The authors developed a "scale of sexualization" with eleven variables to describe how sexual the cover image was with three primary groupings: nonsexual, sexualized, and images that scored so high they were deemed hypersexual. After analyzing more than 1,000 images, published over the course of 43 years, the authors concluded that representations of both women and men have become more sexualized over time, and women continue to be more frequently sexualized than men.

The majority of male images on the covers of *Rolling Stone* were found to be nonsexual. In the 1960's, 11 percent of men and 44 percent of women were depicted sexually. While in the 2000's, 17 percent of men and 83 percent of women's images were sexualized with 2 percent of men and 61 percent of women's images described as hypersexualized (Hatton and Trautner 2011). This research reveals institutionalized sexism within media representations that promotes the idea that successful female musicians must have sexual appeal, while for males it is less important.

Since emerging in the early 1980s, music videos have become widely viewed and an integral part of the music industry and pop culture. It is estimated young people watch an estimated 30 minutes to 3 hours of music videos per day (Ward 2003). Music videos display sexualized and hypersexualized images of men and women, but women are disproportionately sexualized in this medium (Aubrey and Frisby 2011; Pardun, L'Engle, and Brown 2005; Potter 1998). Music videos, like film, not only show images, but engage in a form of storytelling, which often revolves around sex, sexual relations, and sexualized behaviors.

A content analysis of 40 music videos reveals that not only do men appear twice as often as women, but the videos support gender stereotyping of men as aggressive and dominant, women as sexual and subservient, and heteronormativity, with women as the primary objects of male sexual advances (Sommers-Flanagan, Sommers-Flanagan, and Davis 1993). Overall, the content of music videos portrays a fantasy world in which women are displayed as submissive sexual objects available for heterosexual male's sexual gratification, again, revealing institutionalized sexism within the mass media (Jhally 1990, 1995).

SEXUAL OBJECTIFICATION: ADVERTISING When women and men's bodies are sexualized and hypersexualized in media images, they become sexual objects. ***Sexual objectification*** is the equation of an individual's worth based on body appearance and sexual function. Sexual objectification theories specifically focus on the ways in which women are viewed as sexual objects (Bordo 2004; Dworkin 2006; MacKinnon 1989a). Sexual objectification dehumanizes women by viewing them as passive and inactive rather than as complex, subjective beings. Sexual objectification of women's bodies is pervasive in advertising. Advertising is a $160 billion a year industry, and it is estimated that we are exposed to over 5,000 advertisements every day (Story 2007).

Advertisements, like music videos, not only assert certain ideologies but are designed to sell a product. The feminist concept of the "male gaze" describes how media imagery is designed for the primary looker to be male and the object of the gaze to be female (Mulvey 1999). In advertising, women become objects of sexual desire for men's viewing pleasure, with the objective to sell a product. Thus, the objectification of women's bodies is an extension of the commodification of all goods and services in a capitalist society (Martin 2001). In the case of advertising, women essentially become the commodity being bought and sold. The advertising message is: "buy the commodity, 'get' the woman" (Kilbourne 1999).

Advertising images reinforce distorted and destructive ideals of femininity, including unrealistic expectations of beauty, perfection, and sexuality (Kilbourne 1999). Jean Kilbourne's (1999) research on women's images in advertising reveals they represent mostly young, white, and thin women with unnaturally flawless beauty, and in positions of passivity and dismemberment. Naomi Wolf (2002) claims that media promotes the "beauty myth," a social ideology that promotes unrealistic idealization of feminine beauty. The myth is that beauty is something that can be measured and perfected and that all women should try to attain it; that beauty does not come naturally, but there are cosmetic, diet, and skin care products one must purchase in order to acquire beauty. This myth serves a function as well, in that it has the ability to control women. Wolf argues that chasing the ideals of beauty becomes an obsession that traps modern women in an endless spiral of hope, self-consciousness, and self-hatred, and distracts them from pursuing full equality.

The impact of sexual objectification and standards of unattainable and flawless beauty is that it informs and shapes women's perceptions of and relationships with their own bodies (Spettigue and Henderson 2004). Many actresses are extremely thin, and most female fashion models weigh 25 percent less than the average American woman (Brody 2000). Almost all images in mass media today are mediated through the use of cosmetics, prosthetics, and digital postproduction manipulation, or photoshop, to make women appear even thinner and flawless. It is no surprise that as a result, women are often dissatisfied with their bodies. Constant exposure to images of thinness can lead to the internalization of the thin ideal and, in turn, to the development of distorted body image; preoccupation with shape and size; eating disorders, such as anorexia and bulimia; body dysmorphia disorder; depression; and anxiety (Eyal and Te'eni-Harari 2013).

Eating disorders such as anorexia nervosa and bulimia nervosa disproportionately affect women and adolescent girls. A large-scale national survey found that 0.9 percent of women and 0.3 percent of men reported having anorexia at some time in their lives, and 1.5 percent of women and 0.5 percent of men reported having bulimia (Hudson et al. 2007). Feminist philosopher Susan Bordo's *Unbearable Weight* (2004) theorizes that the physical body can become an instrument and medium of power. In this context she argues anorexia functions as a political terrain through which women negotiate their relationship with sexism and gender inequality. She claims media images and modern diet culture distort women's relationships with their bodies and food and that eating disorders represent a way for women to reclaim control and power, albeit an extremely dangerous and unhealthy one (Bordo 2004).

Research on lesbians and women of color demonstrates that for many women, eating problems are related to trauma (Thompson 2012). Author Becky W. Thompson argues that women who are lesbian, poor, or nonwhite experience eating disorders that are not necessarily primarily linked to the media-constructed "culture of thinness." Instead women in these groups with eating problems trace the onset to oppression in the form of sexual abuse, racism, classism, heterosexism, and sexism. Some minority women are pressured to make their bodies different in order to aid their families' assimilation into a higher-class standing. For these women, their relationship with food was a way to regain control over their lives or to anesthetize the pain of their trauma or oppression (Thompson 2012).

Disordered eating impacts not only women, but also men and children. Eating disorders often develop during adolescence and early adult years, but research indicates the preoccupation with weight begins in childhood (Bryant-Waugh and Lask 2013). Barbie is a cultural symbol of ideal female beauty and serves as a role model for young girls. In a study on the impact of Barbie, girls age 5 to 8 displayed higher levels of body dissatisfaction and a greater desire for thinness after looking at books featuring Barbie dolls compared to ones with larger sized dolls (Dittmar, Ive, and Halliwell 2006).

Increasingly prominent media representations of a muscular male body impact men's relationship with their bodies (Wykes and Gunter 2005). Research shows that males are increasingly developing eating disorders due to body dissatisfaction, but that symptoms are often different than they are in females (Cruz 2014). Instead of thinness, the focus is on muscle enhancement through the use of steroids, supplements, or other muscle-enhancing products. Studies indicate that males who use supplements and other products to enhance their physique are more likely to binge eat and binge drink alcohol (Field et al. 2014). Binge-eating disorder is the most prevalent type of eating disorder in the United States at this time with 3.5 percent women and 2 percent men reporting they experience binge-eating disorder at some point in their lives (Hudson et al. 2007).

Body image plays an important role in sexual health and well-being (Gillen, Lefkowicz, and Shearer 2006). Not only does it impact self-consciousness and sexual self-esteem during sexual encounters, but it can impact expectations about your sexual partner's body

(Wiederman 2000). When bodies are sexually objectified, a narrow conception of sexiness is promoted. The impact of this informs and shapes people's expectations of others and can lead to sexual dissatisfaction. Studies indicate that women who are more satisfied with their body image report more sexual activity, orgasm, and initiation of sex, greater comfort undressing in front of their partner, having sex with the lights on, trying new sexual behaviors, and pleasing their partner sexually than those who are dissatisfied with their body image (Ackard, Kearney-Cooke, and Peterson 2000). Pornography, a fast-growing and powerful source of sexual representation in media, also shapes and informs expectations of bodies and sexuality (see Chapter Eleven).

INTERSECTIONALITY: RACE, CLASS, AND ETHNIC IMAGERY Media images not only reveal, reinforce, and shape our understandings of gender, but they also inform how we perceive racial, ethnic, and class inequalities. Similar to symbolic annihilation mentioned earlier, race and class theorists argue that media engages in a ***structured absence***, when the dominant group has the power to keep certain groups or certain images out of the media (Krabill 2010). For example, healthy black relationships are rarely shown in television and film. Structured absence is not only the lack of representations of people of color, but an omitting of racial sentiments in media content. For example, a lack of regard for the pervasiveness of present-day discrimination or the ways sexual stereotypes impact various race and ethnic groups are invisible in the media.

Sociologist Patricia Hill Collins (2000) describes the use of stereotypes in media as ***controlling images***, meaning these images are a major instrument of power as they work to make racism, sexism, heterosexism, and poverty appear normal and natural. Collins argues that while blacks are incorporated into American culture today, including the media, they are done so in ways that replicate older racial hierarchies. For instance, black sexuality is portrayed as wild and animalistic, which serves the function of helping to perpetuate racial differences and the racial hierarchy. She argues that although the mass media is saturated with sexual imagery, the public dialogue around these portrayals serves to titillate or even repress sexuality rather than to instruct or educate. The media's sexual spectacles often include depictions of black sexuality as deviant and as examples of what not to do. Finally, Collins describes how television talk shows package racist stereotypes of promiscuity among minorities and the poor that suggest cultural, rather than biological, explanations for economic inequality.

Asian females are hypersexualized in media in the form of images of extreme sexual subservience or cunning seductiveness (Hagedorn 1994). The cultural stereotype of Asian women as sexual and exotic objects is historically rooted in the Western colonization of various Asian countries. The long history of U.S. military engagement in the Pacific, including the Philippine Wars, Japan and China during World War II, the Korean conflict, and the Vietnam War, influenced views of Asian women as either sex objects for soldiers to exploit or as the evil, cunning enemy (Chan 1988). Cinema is one of the most influential forms of mass media in modern culture and has a tremendous power to inspire human emotion, attitudes, and behaviors. In films such as *The World of Suzie Wong* (1960) or more recently *X2* (2005), racialized and gendered stereotypes continue. Specifically, Asian women are misrepresented as either sexually subservient or devious. ***Racial fetishism*** involves fetishizing a race or ethnic group by sexually objectifying their bodies based on stereotypes. The individual person has no value, but rather her racial identity is the only erotic factor of worth. Derogatory slang terms to describe white men who fetishize Asian women are "Asiaphiles" who are described as having "yellow fever."

The Walt Disney Corporation is one of the most influential media production companies in North America. Disney films target children and often depict negative gender, racial, and ethnic stereotypes. In Disney's film *Pocahontas* (1995), violence and brutality associated with colonization and conquest is sanitized and made to seem invisible. A racist notion of white superiority over native "savages" is supported most obviously in the lyrics of the song "Savages." The film tells the historically inaccurate story of a romantic relationship between the Native American female character, Pocahontas, and English settler, John Smith. Images of Pocahontas are sexualized with her scantily dressed and modelesque physical features. This depiction of a Native American woman reinforces a long tradition of Native American women being misrepresented as the "Indian Princess" stereotype, or as inferior, lustful, and deeply committed to some white man (Pewewardy 1997).

Children, Sexualization, and the Media

There is growing concern about young people's exposure to sexual content in media and its potential effects on their sexual attitudes, beliefs, and behaviors. Extensive research has been conducted to understand young people's daily media exposure, its specific content and message, and the impact on young people concerning sexuality. Children's media exposure is higher than ever in the digital era. Not only do most U.S. and Canadian children have easy in-home access to television, films, and video games, but the Internet is easily accessible via computers and mobile electronic devices on a daily basis. "Generation M2: Media in the Lives of 8- to 18-Year-Olds" is a large-scale, nationally representative survey conducted by the Kaiser Family Foundation in 2010 about young people's media use. This study shows 8- to 18-year-olds devote an average of 7 hours and 38 minutes per day to using entertainment media. And since young people often use more than one media source at a time, or are "media multitasking," young people are actually managing to get a total of 10 hours and 45 minutes of media content into those 7.5 hours (Rideout, Foehr, and Roberts 2010).

In recent years, governments and large research organizations investigated the sexualization of children in media, including the UK Home Office's "The Sexualization of Young People" (Papadopoulos 2010), the American Psychological Association Taskforce Report on the Sexualization of Girls (APA, 2007), and the Australian government-led research project, "The Sexualization of Children in Modern Media" (Commonwealth of Australia 2008). Findings reveal media images adultify images of children while infantilizing images of adult women, which blurs the lines between sexual maturity and immaturity and essentially displays children as sexual objects and adult women as children. Clothing advertisements target young girls with displays of child models dressed in erotically provocative clothing: fishnet stockings, kiddie thongs, and padded bralettes are promoted to girls as young as ten years old (George 2007). The reality television show on child beauty pageants, *Toddlers and Tiaras*, which debuted in 2009, released controversial footage of a three-year-old contestant dressed as the prostitute played by Julia Roberts in the 1990 film *Pretty Woman* (Henson 2011).

How do young people respond to the sexualization of culture? Obviously an individual child's age and level of cognitive and emotional development are significant; but research reveals that many young people internalize media and advertising images, and the results impact their relationships with their bodies and their sexual behaviors (Levine and Kilbourne 2008). It can also hinder their ability to form healthy sexual relationships with marriage partners later in life (Durham 2008). Next to adolescent's parents and peers, mass media is the primary source of information regarding sexual norms (Durham 2008). Televised media has a high prevalence of sexual talk and portrayals of sexual behavior. A link between the amount of television watched and the likelihood of a young person to have sexual intercourse at an earlier age is found to be correlative (Collins et al. 2004). Moreover, teens rely on media for sex education (see Chapter Ten).

Sociologists asked 71 pre-teen girls to record media video diaries about their everyday engagement with popular culture

"*Here's what lots of girls don't know. Those 'pretty women' that we see in magazines are fake. They're often photoshopped, air-brushed, edited to look thinner, and to appear like they have perfect skin. A girl you see in a magazine probably looks a lot different in real life,*" wrote 14-year-old activist Julia Bluhm (2012).

(Jackson and Vares 2015). They specifically examined girls' responses to hypersexualized performances by female pop celebrities. What they found is that girls negotiate meanings of a sexually saturated pop culture in complicated and contradictory ways, which often reflect the binaries of "good girl" versus "bad girl," "slut" versus "nonslut," associated with expectations of female sexual behavior. Jackson and Vares (2015) encourage feminists who want to engage with girls on the subject not only to encourage political, gender-focused critiques of hypersexualized media, but to take it a step further by engaging in conversations about alternative, noncommodified meanings of sexuality. In this way, the development of a pleasurable, embodied sense of sex and self is possible.

LGBTQ REPRESENTATIONS IN TELEVISION AND FILM

Similar to symbolic annihilation and structured absence mentioned earlier, representations of LGBTQ individuals and groups in television are widely neglected or distorted. In fact, throughout television's first four decades, gays were virtually invisible (Becker 2006). This invisibility promotes heteronormativity, as well as cisgender and heterosexual privilege. Commercial demands shape LGBTQ images in television and film; for instance, advertisers fear offending mainstream audiences, so when LGBTQ people are portrayed, they generally fit mainstream stereotypes.

In the 1970s, gay rights activist groups, such as the Gay Activist Alliance (GAA), began to address the issues of visibility and the portrayal of homosexuality on television (Montgomery 2006). As a result, there has been a steady increase in the representation of gays and lesbians in film and television.

Sociologist Joshua Gamson (1998) warns of the visibility trap that LGBTQ people find themselves in: increasing visibility creates particular dilemmas for marginalized populations. The desire for increased visibility for these populations is understandable; being recognized and affirmed can "lay the groundwork for political change" (Gamson 1998:213). Yet, television and film sensationalize "other" sexual minorities and gender nonconformists and increasing visibility is likely to result in a conservative backlash.

From Invisibility to Stereotypical Images: Lesbians and Gays on Television

Gay television characters first emerged in the 1970s on shows such as *Soap* (1977–1981) and *Dynasty* (1981–89). Introduced in 1998, NBC's comedy *Will and Grace* featured television's first gay male lead character, Will Truman. The show was highly successful in ratings and generated profits for advertisers well into the 2000s. Many other shows began featuring gay characters, such as Stanford Blatch, the gay best friend of Carrie Bradshaw in the Emmy-award-winning HBO series *Sex and the City* (Netzley 2010). Often gay male characters are portrayed as the best friend to a straight woman or in secondary or supporting roles.

Specifically gay-themed programming on U.S. network television really began in the 1990s. *Queer as Folk* was a groundbreaking show introduced by Showtime in 1999; every character was gay and every episode was gay themed (Chambers 2009). Between 1994 and 1997, hit shows like *Roseanne* and *Friends* included gay jokes and references; nineteen network series included recurring gay characters; and perhaps most surprising, over 40 percent of all prime time network series had at least one gay-themed episode (Becker 2006:3). *The L-Word* (2004–2009), a lesbian-themed show, emerged at the same time as media hype around "lesbian chic" in the early 1990s emphasizing the trendiness of lesbianism (Beirne 2008). Importantly, the increasing presence of gay and lesbian characters and issues on television exposed heterosexual privilege—the taken-for-grantedness of heterosexuality and heterosexual images in the media (Becker 2006). As a whole, despite successes in television, in 2011–2012, LGBTQ characters still represented only 2.9 percent of all scripted characters on U.S.-based broadcast television networks (GLAAD 2012).

Lesbian, Gay, and Bisexual Images in Hollywood Cinema

Cinema shares a similar story. Traditionally, representations of gays, lesbians, and transgender individuals are altogether neglected or marginalized. In a groundbreaking book, *The Celluloid Closet*, Vito Russo (1987) analyzed Hollywood films from the 1890s to 1980s. He argued that lesbians and gays are often completely left out; and when portrayals are included, they are from a homophobic standpoint. Russo described how the voluntary Motion Picture Production code, also known as the Hays Code, applied a set of moral guidelines and censorship to film production. If filmmakers wanted their films shown in mainstream cinemas they had to follow these guidelines. The Hays Code prohibited all mention of homosexuality from the silver screen until the 1950s. When gay and lesbian characters were finally openly made visible in films in the 1960s, they were primarily defined by their sexual orientation and often lacked any complex character development (Russo 1987).

Like television, since the 1990s, film has increased visibility and improved its portrayal of LGBTQ characters. The success and popularity of such films as *Philadelphia* (1993), about a gay man living with HIV/AIDS; *Flawless* (1999), about a homophobic cop who befriends a drag queen; and *In & Out* (1997), a film about a former school teacher who questions his sexuality, among many others, led to the production of more films in the 2000s. In 2005, *Brokeback Mountain,* a film about the secretive, sexual relationship between two cowboys, achieved mainstream commercial success.

Despite such success, LGBTQ characters and storylines are still often avoided. Between 1990 and 2005, research reveals that film award campaign ads continually avoided LGBTQ imagery while promoting heteronormative themes, even in ads for LGBTQ films (Cabosky 2015). For example, in the first three months of the advertising campaign for *Brokeback Mountain*, the ads displayed heterosexual imagery of the main male characters with their wives (Cabosky 2015). It was not until the final months of its marketing campaign, notably after it had earned an Oscar nomination, that images of gay intimacy began to appear in relation to the film in advertisements (Cabosky 2015).

In addition to issues of visibility, when LGBTQ characters are incorporated into film and television, stereotypes and misrepresentations are enforced. One of the most prevalent stereotypes about gay male characters is they possess the gender character traits assigned to women: highly feminine, submissive, and emotional. The archetype of "the sissy" brings amusement to audiences and is not threatening, as it represents weakness (Russo 1987). In this way gay male characters are often appreciated primarily for their comedic value, and are not portrayed as complex human beings. Gay men are also often portrayed as hypersexual, infected with HIV/AIDS, sexually promiscuous, and otherwise immoral (Hart 2000; Herman 2005). Lesbians, on the other hand, are often portrayed and defined by their level of embodied sexual desirability and ideal femininity, shaped by heterosexual norms (Jackson and Gilbertson 2009). In other words, most lesbians in media are thin, attractive, and objects of heterosexual desire. Lesbian sex scenes are shown twice as often as gay male sex scenes. When lesbians are sex objects for the male gaze, it can make lesbian sexual relations appear to be a performance for others (Jackson and Gilbertson 2009).

Transgender Images and Issues in Media

Gender-variant people have long been part of a media spectacle in the form of freak shows. Most cities had laws against cross-dressing well into the 1960s (see Chapters Four and Five). In the first half of the twentieth century, when cross-dressers, intersex, and transgender people found themselves arrested, freak show producers would bail them out in exchange for them joining their freak shows. The "bearded woman" and other "freaks" were "othered" and became entertainment for the mainstream (Sears 2008). In recent years, transgender individuals have become more visible in the media and are being seen in a more positive light. CNN describes 2015 as "America's Transgender Moment" (CNN.com 2015). In addition to the attention Caitlyn Jenner's transition attracted, transgender models such as Andreja Pejic appeared in *Vogue* magazine and Carmen Carrera in *W* Magazine (Gregory 2015).

In television, transgender roles are steadily increasing, such as the role of actress Laverne Cox as a transgender prison inmate in *Orange Is the New Black*, a transgender gym coach on the final season of *Glee*, and an entire show about an aging father who begins life as a woman, in *Transparent*. Children's books about acceptance of and the experiences of transgender people are popular, including *I Am Jazz* (2012), a story of a transgender child based on the real-life experience of Jazz Jennings. Jennings is a *YouTube* star and spokesperson for trans kids; and she is featured in a TLC reality show about her life called *All That Jazz* (2015).

"I would say that 2014 was a watershed moment for visibility, but the record unemployment rates, homicide rates and discrimination that we experience has not changed. So we need more of what's happening in the media in terms of visibility to affect policies and how we treat transgender folk," —Laverne Cox (Berenson 2015).

While visibility is a tremendous step toward greater equality, the transgender community is still often viewed in a negative light. Gay and Lesbian Alliance against Defamation (GLAAD) research on transgender characters in scripted television over a decade reveals that 54 percent are negative representations, 35 percent are problematic, and only 12 percent are considered fair and accurate. This research is comprehensive in that it looks at television, including all the major networks and seven cable networks. Stereotypes and misrepresentations are frequent, often portraying transgender characters as victims, villains, and as sex workers. Finally, antitransgender slurs, language, and suggestions were present in 61 percent of scripted dialogue (GLAAD 2012).

SEXUALITY AND SPORT

Few institutions expose the intersection of gender and sexuality better than sport. David Coad (2008) introduced the term **sports sex**, to refer to how traditional mythologies about sex and gender are created and perpetuated through sports culture. Sports scholars have long identified sport as a heterosexist and homophobic institution that manifests not only in a rejection of homosexuality but in an embrace of hyperheterosexuality (Anderson 2002; Connell 1995; Griffin 1998; Hekma 1998; Pronger 1990; Sartore and Cunningham 2009). Notions of masculinity are particularly linked to our understandings of heterosexuality, particularly the jock culture that surrounds sport. **Jock culture** refers to an environment that encourages many unhealthy behaviors by athletes, particularly machismo, hypercompetitiveness, violence, bullying, aggression, male supremacy, and female subordination (Coad 2008; Lipsyte 1975). Jock culture "propagates gender myths, insisting on the 'natural' differences between men and women and, finally, it relies on the heterosexual myth" (Coad 2008:6). Jock culture is so pervasive that the idea of a gay athlete often comes across as an oxymoron (Anderson 2005).

Sport Media

Media scholar Sut Jhally (1984) uses the term **sports/media complex** to describe the commercial and ideological interdependence of the institutions of sport, mass media, and advertising. Sports are mediated events; "what viewers see, then, is not the actual event, but a mediated event, in other words, a media event" (Eitzen and Sage 2003:251). Thus, sportscasters help create listeners' and viewers' sport experiences through camera angles, narratives, and especially what information and images are revealed and which are concealed about specific athletes or the game itself. Broadcast teams choose what to highlight based on what is considered to be good television and what is perceived as keeping people tuned in. Male sporting events dominate television broadcasting, which reinforce our ideas about gender, sport, and masculinity. How male athletes and their bodies are portrayed in sport media reinforces Western cultural understandings of masculinity. Research by Nick Trujillo (1995) finds that NFL broadcasts regularly reproduce three images of the male body—as an instrument, a weapon, and an object of gaze.

Sports media, then, helps marginalize women's sports. While women's rates of sport participation have skyrocketed since the passage of Title IX, they are still only a fraction of sports media coverage (Messner, Duncan, and Willms 2007). In collecting data over a 15-year period, Messner, Duncan, and Willms (2007) found that in 1989, only 5 percent of television network time was devoted to women's sports. Ten years later, it increased to a mere 8.7 percent. By 2004, the proportion of news coverage devoted to women's sports had *fallen* to 6.3 percent, and by 2009 it had fallen to 1.6 percent (see Figure 6.1). Because of the assumption that audiences prefer male bodies and, thus, they will not be able to sell advertising during a women's sporting event, women's professional sports teams were unable to secure a major national TV network contract until 1996 when a new women's basketball league finally got one. As Messner and colleagues state, "In the past three decades we have witnessed an historic sea change in sport's gender dynamics. But one would never know this, if one simply got one's sports information from the network affiliates' evening and late-night news shows, or from the sports highlights shows on ESPN and Fox. The mass media's continued marginalization of women's sports serves to maintain the myth that sports are exclusively by, about, and for men" (Messner, Duncan, and Willms 2007:158).

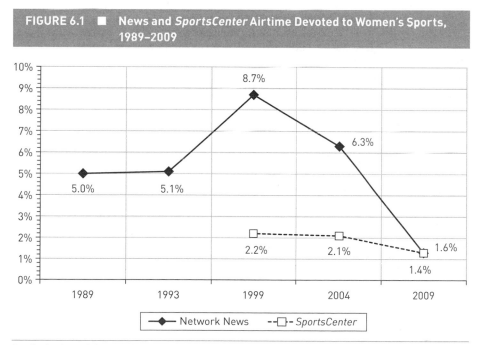

FIGURE 6.1 ■ News and *SportsCenter* Airtime Devoted to Women's Sports, 1989–2009

Despite the dramatic increase in women and girls' athletic participation, there has not been a corresponding increase in media attention to women's sports. In fact, media coverage of women's sports has declined since its peak in 1999.

Source: "Gender in Televised Sports: News and Highlight Shows, 1989-2009." 2010. Michael Messner and Cheryl Cooky. http://dornsifecms.usc.edu/assets/sites/80/docs/tvsports.pdf.

In addition to the marginalization of women's sports, sports media sends problematic messages to male athletes. Some researchers argue the sports media provides a *televised sports manhood formula* that presents "boys with narrow and stereotypical messages about race, gender, and violence" (Messner, Dunbar, and Hunt 2007:141). Television coverage of men's sporting events, programming such as *SportsCenter*, and the commercials that accompany these sports programs all provide seamless messaging to men and boys about what it means to be a man. This involves messages concerning the appropriateness of aggression, violence, playing to win, avoiding being perceived as "soft," and the idea that beautiful women are their prize for success on the athletic field.

Masculinity and Sport

The linkage between masculinity and sports has a long history. Competitive team sports gained significant popularity in the United States simultaneously as the nation was faced with a crisis of masculinity in the early twentieth century (Anderson 2009; Anderson, McCormack, and Ripley 2013). During this era, the United States was industrializing, urbanizing, and modernizing. People's lives were changing dramatically. Instead of men engaging in the physical demands of farm labor, most men were employed in factories. There was also an active women's movement that challenged traditional gender roles (Filene 1975; Messner 1992). Sigmund Freud, a significant thinker of the era, noted that an outcome of the increased urbanization was an increase in same-sex sexual activity. This resulted in a *moral panic*, an extreme societal response to a perceived erosion of morals due to social changes (Cohen 1972). Freud argued that this occurred because with men working outside the home, boys lacked male role models. Sport was proposed as a solution to this dilemma. Thus, competitive organized sports were designed as a masculinizing agent in boy's lives (Anderson, McCormack, and Ripley 2013). Masculinity can never be taken for granted; it is something men must continually prove, and the sports world is a perfect venue for this.

As we describe in Chapter Three, masculinity and femininity are opposing concepts. Masculinity requires rejecting all things feminine; and since competitive sports originated as a masculinizing agent, it is unsurprising women were marginalized from competitive sports for so long. Homophobia and misogyny are used to construct masculinity (Anderson 2005). This explains why the sporting world maintained its commitment to homophobia well into the turn of the millennium, whereas societal attitudes toward gays and lesbians in the rest of society began to shift in the 1990s (Anderson, McCormack, and Ripley 2013). As Griffin argues, "Sport is more than games. As an institution, sport serves important social functions in supporting conventional social values. In particular, sport is a training ground where boys learn what it means to be men" (1998:16).

Homophobia in the sports world manifests in a number of ways. First, through the use of homophobic language to motivate men to excel, such as being called a faggot, pussy, wuss, gay, or fag by teammates or coaches, or when such terms are used to deride opposing teams. Scholars emphasize the role of language in establishing dominance and masculinity among male athletes (Adams, Anderson, and McCormack 2010). Research finds homophobic language is present in all types of men's sports, although it seems to be declining, mirroring the declining cultural homophobia (Anderson 2002; McCormack 2014).

> "Sport can be seen as one of the last bastions of traditional masculinity, where men can prove themselves as 'real' or 'inferior' men and differentiate themselves from women" (Symons 2007:140).

Another manifestation of homophobia in sports is the invisibility of gay athletes. Because of the interconnectedness between sport and masculinity and the extreme homophobia in sport, gay men have yet to make tremendous strides in the sports world. The dearth of gay male athletes is particularly evident in the four major professional sports in the United States: football, baseball, hockey, and basketball. There are 3,496 athletes on professional rosters of the four major North American leagues; and only one openly gay man was among them until he retired in 2014, Jason Collins of the NBA (Ogawa 2014). Of course there are gay male athletes, as the story of Michael Sam in the opening vignette of Chapter One shows, but most of them have chosen to remain closeted due to homophobia and the value placed on masculinity among athletes. We will discuss the recent and measured emergence of the gay athlete below.

SPORTS, MASCULINITY, AND SEXUAL ASSAULT We will explore sexual violence in greater detail in Chapter Twelve, but here we discuss *sports rape*, or rapes committed by athletes—a sexual assault as an extension of the dysfunction of jock culture (Coad 2008). There is nothing legally distinct about sports rape, of course. It is still rape, a felony. But sports rape is unique in the extent of institutional cover-up often engaged in by universities, athletes, media, and sometimes even the victims themselves.

While media coverage of rape charges against celebrity athletes such as Darren

In 2014, Jason Collins was the only openly gay male professional athlete competing in one of the four major sports (basketball, football, baseball, and soccer).
Source: AP Photo/Tony Dejak.

Sharper, Jameis Winston, Kobe Bryant, and Mike Tyson proliferate, research finds that sports rape is not limited to a handful of celebrity athletes (Benedict 1997, 2004; Benedict and Yaeger 1998). In fact, it is found across cultures, with disturbing frequency. Athletes must continuously prove their manhood, masculinity, and heterosexuality. Heterosexual conquests, both consensual and nonconsensual, help athletes establish and maintain their masculinity in jock culture. Importantly, when charges are filed against an athlete for rape or sexual assault, most of the players are never convicted of a crime (Benedict 2004; Coad 2008).

In *Missoula: Rape and the Justice System in a College Town,* Jon Krakauer (2015) exposes five rapes or attempted rapes that occurred at the University of Montana in Missoula, MT, between the years 2010 and 2012. Several members of the UM football team were among those accused of sexual assault. What he finds are disturbing patterns of disrespect and disinterest by the local police and prosecutors, and assumptions that the women are making false accusations. The women who pressed charges or spoke publicly were attacked in the press and on local football fan websites.

Sexuality, Femininity, and Sport

The fact that sport is a masculinizing agent in the lives of boys and men should not lead us to conclude that it does not hold a significant influence on the sporting experience for women. First, because sport has long been linked to men and masculinity, women athletes are perceived as trespassers on male terrain (Bryson 1990; Griffin 1998). If women can be athletic, competitive, and muscular, then how is masculinity distinct from femininity?

Second, the linkage of sport with masculinity has limited women's opportunities to compete in sports. The ancient Greek Olympics allowed only male competitors, and women were not allowed to even watch the competition. It was not until 1920 that the United States sent a women's team to compete in the Olympics (Griffin 1998). In the early 1900s, women became interested in sports such as golf, tennis, and bicycling. The 1920s were an era of expanded opportunities for sports participation for women due to the growth of women's colleges. Critics argued strenuous activities could damage women's reproductive organs and participation in sport would lead to "mannishness" in women; essentially, they feared female athletes would acquire masculine characteristics. Of primary concern was the fear that women would develop what were assumed to be male sexual characteristics and interests; specifically, it was feared that women's sexual inhibitions would decrease. By the 1930s, however, the concern shifted. Instead of fearing women's sport participation would lead to excessive heterosexuality, it was feared that it would lead to a failed heterosexuality; in other words, the new fear was that the female athlete might prefer women. In the post–World War II era, this fear transitioned into the stereotype of the "mannish lesbian athlete" (Cahn 2007).

The linkage of female athleticism with lesbianism becomes a powerful stigma, the "bogeywoman" of sport (Cahn 2007). Homophobia discourages many girls and women from playing certain sports and causes parents to steer daughters away from sports or programs that they believe attract lesbians (Eitzen and Sage 2003). Some women's collegiate athletic programs even practice a form of *negative recruiting* in which coaches encourage high school players to sign with their program because it is free of lesbians. This practice was most explicit in the women's basketball program at Penn State under coach Rene Portland (Mosbacher and Yacker 2009). Portland's well-known "training rules" were: no drinking, no drugs, and no lesbians. While such discrimination against lesbian athletes was well-known on campus, Portland maintained the practice throughout her 27-year career as a college basketball coach until she retired in the late 1990s. Negative recruiting does not happen in men's sports due to the heteronormativity of sport culture. Male athletes are assumed to be heterosexual, whereas the association of sports with masculinity means female athletes are assumed to be sexually deviant.

Linking female athleticism with lesbianism influences how women athletes present themselves on and off the field. Women's professional sport organizations overtly emphasize the heterosexual femininity of their players as a way to avoid the lesbian stigma, which they assume will decrease fan interest and attendance. Some women's teams have taken this so far as to enact a closeted atmosphere similar to the military's former "Don't Ask, Don't Tell" policy (Eitzen and Sage 2003). Advocates of women's sport respond to the lesbian stigma "by insisting that sport participation increased women's heterosexual appeal. They worked hard to project an image of happy and enthusiastic heterosexuality among women athletes" (Griffin 1998:35). Both lesbian and heterosexual athletes work to manage their identity within the context of sport by presenting themselves as ultra-feminine in the same ways that male athletes embrace hypermasculinity (Melton 2013). For instance, female athletes often wear full makeup and feminine hairstyles during athletic competition.

This feminization of female athletes was clearly seen during World War II, when professional men's baseball leagues were suspended so the men could serve in the military. Philip Wrigley, owner of the Chicago Cubs, formed a women's professional baseball league in its place. The league enforced a "femininity principle" as a way to ensure that the players were normal, white, heterosexual girls, which was believed to appeal to their desired fan base. Players were chosen as much for their looks as for their athletic abilities; and they were required to adhere to hair, makeup, and dress codes, including competing in a skirted uniform rather than pants (Cahn 1994; Griffin 1998).

The lesbian stigma also justifies the lack of media coverage of female sports. Research clearly shows the disproportionate amount of media attention devoted to male sporting events compared to women's athletics. Televised male sports send particular messages to viewers about gender and sport, including "sports is a man's world" and "women are sexy props or prizes for men's successful sport competition" (Messner, Dunbar, and Hunt 2007). Such images reinforce the lesbian stigma by emphasizing the heteronormativity of sport (Melton 2013). Additionally, sportscasters continually emphasize the marital and motherhood status of heterosexual female athletes, while remaining silent about the relationship status of nonheterosexual athletes. This is why the international television coverage of Women's

National Soccer Team player Abby Wambach running to her female partner and kissing her in celebration of the U.S. World Cup victory in July 2015 was a radical shift away from the extreme heteronormativity of past media coverage of women's sports.

Perhaps most problematically, lesbian athletes and coaches play and work in constant fear of being outed, experiencing what scholars refer to as *minority stress*, the stress associated with being a member of a stigmatized group and being devalued in your society and in your field (Meyer 2003). Scholars note female athletes' physical and psychological well-being is inhibited due to minority stress (Sartore and Cunningham 2010). Other research finds women's psychological health declines when they are in unsupportive athletic environments, leading to low self-esteem, low confidence, high stress levels, and even substance abuse (Krane 1997). While homophobic environments take their greatest toll on lesbian athletes and coaches, heterosexual female athletes are also negatively affected. "Homophobia affects all women; it creates fears, pressures women to conform to traditional gender roles, and silences and makes invisible the lesbians who manage, coach, and play sports" (Eitzen and Sage 2003:246).

Despite the destructiveness of homophobia in women's sports and the lesbian stigma attached to women athletes, it is a mistake to paint the picture as entirely bleak. Sport can also be an accepting environment for lesbians. Many lesbians find a supportive community among women athletes and, as Pat Griffin states, "many lesbians in and out of sport describe the network of friends and ex-lovers whom they feel safe with and affirmed by as *families of choice*. . . . They also create an opportunity for lesbians in sport to meet and fall in love" (1998:190).

TITLE IX Opportunities for women in sports expanded dramatically with the passage of Title IX in 1972. The legislation was intended to provide women with equal educational opportunities as men. In the language of the legislation, "no person in the United States

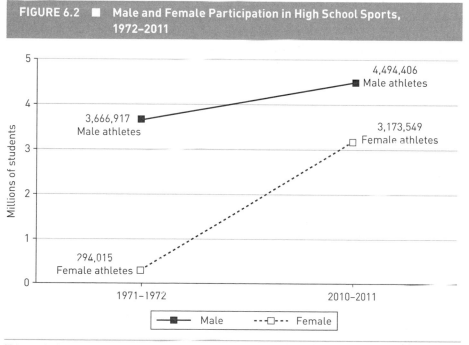

FIGURE 6.2 ■ Male and Female Participation in High School Sports, 1972–2011

This graph shows the dramatic increase in female participation in high school sports since the passage of Title IX legislation.

Source. "Title IX and Athletics." National Federation of State High School Associations. http://www.ncwge .org/TitleIX40/Athletics.pdf.

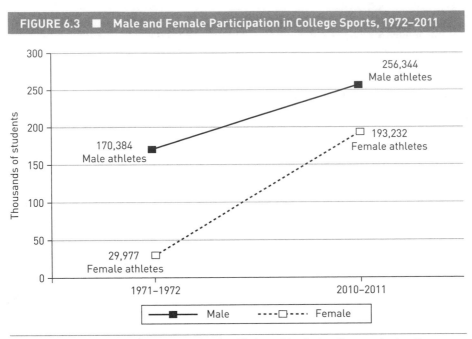

FIGURE 6.3 ■ Male and Female Participation in College Sports, 1972–2011

This graph indicates the dramatic increase in female athletic participation in college sports since the passage of Title IX.

Source: "Title IX and Athletics." NCAA Sports Sponsorship and Participation Report, 1972—2011. http://www.ncwge.org/TitleIX40/Athletics.pdf.

shall, on the basis of sex, be excluded from participation in, be denied the benefits of, or be subjected to discrimination under any education program or activity receiving federal financial assistance" (Hogshead-Makar and Zimbalist 2007). Unintentionally, this legislation opened up incredible sporting opportunities for women at all levels, yet "despite the law's promise, athletic departments remain one area of resistance to equity for men and women in higher education" (Hogshead-Makar and Zimbalist 2007:1).

The effect of Title IX on women's sport participation is undeniable. In 1971, 294,000 girls played on a high school sports team, compared with 3.7 million boys. By 2011, 3.1 million girls played high school sports compared with 4.5 million boys (see Figure 6.2). Women's participation in collegiate sports and the Olympics has also increased dramatically since the passage of Title IX (Messner 2007; see Figure 6.3). The 2016 Olympics hold the distinction of having the most female Olympians ever, with women making up 45 percent of the participants (Baciglupi 2016). Despite such progress, there is nowhere near gender parity in sports. Boys sports programs are better funded, offer players the opportunity to play for better coaches and better-paid coaches; girls have substandard athletic facilities; male athletes have more scholarship dollars; and the vast majority of colleges and universities are not in compliance with Title IX.

COMING OUT OF THE ATHLETIC CLOSET

This chapter portrays the athletic world as one hostile to LGBTQ athletes and coaches, primarily due to the conflation of sport with masculinity, which results in invisibility for gay male athletes and stigma for female athletes who are presumed to be lesbian. In the early 1980s, no lesbian athlete was publicly out. Women's professional sports organizations such as the Women's Tennis Association and the Ladies Professional Golf Association sought to keep lesbian athletes in the closet for fear of losing fans and commercial endorsements

(Griffin 2014). Despite the declining degree of homophobia in the mainstream culture, and the increasing visibility of LGBTQ people and issues in the media, the athletic closet continues to remain shut; LGBTQ professional athletes remain closeted or come out only after their athletic careers end. Eric Anderson (2005) became the first openly gay male coach when he came out in 1993 as a running coach at a conservative high school in California. He shares the dramatic change in how he was perceived: "Overnight I had gone from being known as the hilarious teacher and revered coach to the faggot teacher and the faggot coach. My athletes went from being the pride of the school . . . to the shame of the school, affected by a guilt-by-association process relating to my stigma" (2005:2). As of 2014, there was only one openly gay NCAA coach, Sherri Murrell of Portland State University (Griffin 2014).

Gay athletes exist at every level of the sport, from high school to college and professional athletics, of course. Rather than being repelled by the homophobia of sport, some research finds that gay men are drawn to sport because it is a perfect cover for their homosexuality (Pronger 1990). For this reason, many gay male athletes are uninterested in coming out. While female professional athletes in the 1980s were often "outed" against their will, by the early 2000s, professional athletes were coming out as lesbian on their own: from tennis player Amelie Mauresmo in 1999, to WNBA players Sheryl Swoopes in 2005 and Brittney Griner in 2013, homophobia against lesbian athletes appears to be decreasing to some extent (Bullingham, Magrath, and Anderson 2014). In 1999, Massachusetts high school football player Corey Johnson's coming out was covered in the *New York Times*. Ultimately, his coming out experience was one of acceptance. Most athletes who come out describe feeling an immense sense of liberation (Anderson 2005).

Gay Games

Gay athletes have sometimes formed their own self-segregated sporting opportunities, such as the Gay Games. There is a Gay and Lesbian Athletic Foundation, and increasing numbers of gay sports organizations have established gay sports spaces rather than focusing on assimilating LGBTQ people into mainstream, heterocentric sports organizations. In response to the marginalization of LGBTQ athletes, and with the goal of creating more inclusive sporting opportunities for LGBTQ athletes, former Olympic decathlete Tom Waddell founded the Gay Games in 1982. Through the Gay Games, Waddell hoped to unite the gay and lesbian communities, which were quite divided at the time, to challenge myths about gay men as feminine, and to normalize gay and lesbian people through sport competition (Symon 2007). The Gay Games mark a shift in gay liberation away from an emphasis on LGBTQ oppression toward focusing positively and publicly on expressing pride in one's gay identity (Pronger 1990; Symons 2007). This international athletic competition and cultural event occurs every four years, and it sometimes draws more participants than the regular Olympic Games (Griffin 1998). The first competition was in 1982 in San Francisco. Another international competition emerged in 2006, the World OutGames, which are held every four years. This event is currently a competitor to the Gay Games, and there are talks of the two merging by 2022.

CREATING SPACE FOR INTERSEX AND TRANSGENDER ATHLETES

Since most competitive athletic programs in this country are gender-segregated and based on an assumed gender binary, many athletes, including those who are intersex, transsexual, and transgender, have to fight for the right to participate in organized sports. In the face of such demands, some sporting organizations struggle to adopt appropriate policies. One of the first widely known disputes occurred in 1977 when Renee Richards, who had been

Salviatore Lamia, an Algonquin Shinnecock American Indian, won medals in the triple jump and the long jump at the Gay Games in 2006.
Source: AP Photo/M. Spencer Green.

born male but transitioned to female, challenged the U.S. Tennis Association's requirement that athletes must possess two X chromosomes to compete in the women's U.S. Open. The assumption behind her exclusion was that as someone who was born male, she must have some kind of competitive advantage over the other women. In other words, the policy was based not just on a gender binary but on a gender hierarchy; it was assumed that males were athletically and physically superior to females.

Following this logic, male athletes do not face sex verification testing in international competition the way women have. It is assumed an athlete born female would not have any competitive advantage over athletes who had been male their entire lives. The assumption of female athletic inferiority prompts sex verification at the highest levels of competition. In 1968, the International Olympic Committee (IOC) shifted from a visual inspection of female genitalia to chromosome testing to determine athletes' eligibility. Simply seeking to make sure competitors have a second X chromosome is not going to solve the problem; while women typically have two X chromosomes, there are a number of chromosomal variations that can and do occur (see Chapter Three). Importantly, mandatory sex verification was initially implemented for political reasons. During the Cold War, Western nations feared Communist nations would engage in "gender fraud to dominate women's sport in the service of nationalist objectives" (Buzuvis 2013:59).

By 1996, the IOC no longer required sex verification of female athletes. However, it is still done on a case-by-case basis when there is cause for suspicion. Rather than relying on a chromosome test, an athlete declared suspicious faces a panel of medical and psychological experts conducting more holistic tests. South African athlete Caster Semenya faced such a panel in 2009 (see Box 6.1). They concluded that while she did have elevated levels of testosterone, it did not disqualify her from women's sport. Since 2011, the IOC has allowed female athletes to compete as long as their testosterone levels are below the normal range for a male or if they have androgen insensitivity syndrome (which essentially means their bodies cannot use the testosterone they make). In Semenya's case, there is an assumption

South African athlete Caster Semenya faced suspician and humiliating challenges to her eligibility to compete as a woman at many international athletic competitions.
Source: AP Photo/Anja Niedringhaus.

she has no competitive advantage over other female athletes (Buzuvis 2013). While this policy is an improvement over previous era's sex verification testing, it also faces critique. For instance, why should sport emphasize the level of natural occurring hormones someone has as the only competitive advantage worthy of disqualifying an athlete? Women who are naturally taller have a competitive advantage in many sports, yet that does not disqualify them from competition (Buzuvis 2013).

When it comes to transgender athletes, the IOC has been at the forefront of policies to determine participation, implementing a policy in 2004 that allows transsexual/transgender athletes to participate with their transitional sex. There are three criteria that a transsexual/transgender athlete must meet, however:

(1) Surgical and anatomical changes must have been completed, including external genitalia and gonadectomy;

(2) Legal recognition of their assigned sex has been conferred by the appropriate official authorities; and

(3) Hormonal therapy appropriate for the assigned sex has been administered in a verifiable manner and for a sufficient length of time to minimize gender-related advantages in sport competitions [later defined as a minimum of two years from the time of surgery]. (Buzuvis 2013).

Numerous other sporting organizations followed the IOC in adopting this policy for transsexual/transgender athletes, including one high school sporting organization, the Connecticut Interscholastic Athletic Association (Buzuvis 2013). However, many are urging against adoption of the IOC policy. Specifically, critics argue that the requirement that the person have sex reassignment surgery to participate in youth sports is unrealistic since surgery is not recommended for people under eighteen years of age.

As of 2007, the Washington Interscholastic Athletic Association (WIAA) decided to allow high school and middle school athletes to compete on a team that is consistent with the athletes' gender identity, irrespective of their officially assigned gender. They do not require any medical evidence to support the student's claim. Advocates praise this policy for its inclusiveness. The NCAA allows transgender athletes to play according to their identified sex rather than their birth sex (Buzuvis 2013). As many states and municipalities begin to include gender identity and expression in their antidiscrimination clauses, colleges and universities are starting to be proactive to avoid discriminating against transgender athletes.

Trans Inclusion in the Gay Games

While the International Gay Games are designed to be an inclusive sporting event, they somewhat ironically struggled with the inclusion of transgender athletes. The Gay Games IV in 1994 were the first games to have a specific transgender policy (Symons and Hemphill 2006). The Federation of Gay Games (FGG) sought to develop an inclusive policy that included persons who were living fully as members of the sex they had transitioned to. Their policy did not require athletes to have completed sex reassignment surgery, which can be financially unattainable for many and medically prohibited if the individual has other medical conditions such as HIV, herpes, or Hepatitis C. Despite attempts at inclusiveness, many transgender people felt the policy was discriminatory because it relied on the authority of experts stating the person was transgender. For many, this was problematic

BOX 6.1

GLOBAL/TRANSNATIONAL PERSPECTIVES ON SEXUALITY:
*SOUTH AFRICAN SPRINTER CASTER SEMENYA AND SEX
TESTING IN INTERNATIONAL SPORTS*

Caster Semenya is a South African athlete whose eligibility to compete in international competitions was threatened when people questioned her sex, specifically whether or not she was a female. When she won the 800 meter race in 2009 at the World Championships in Berlin, competitors immediately began questioning her sex. She was banned from international competition for a year; a decision that was reversed in 2010. Even before she experienced official gender verification testing, she used to have to go to the bathroom to show a member of the competing team that she was female before a race (Levy 2009). She went through sex testing to prove she was female, and the results were leaked. She did not have a uterus or ovaries, despite the fact that she was brought up as a girl and has female external genitalia. She was born with undescended testes, which results in her having three times the amount of testosterone as the average female; this was felt to put her at an advantage over other females.

The International Association of Athletics Federation (IAAF) chooses to use testosterone levels to distinguish between males and females, but that is arbitrary. Due to this, Semenya has been forced to undergo treatment, the exact nature of which remains undisclosed, but likely involves hormone therapy and monitoring (Greenfield 2012). Since this controversy erupted, Semenya consciously altered her appearance so she looks more feminine. Some are critical of this, calling it a "policing of femininity." For women who are exceptional athletes, the first question to emerge is whether or not they are even a real woman.

because it made their gender identity pathological (Symons and Hemphill 2006). Despite this opposition, "the gay games of 1994 appears to have been the first international sports event to include transgender participants within its policy and procedures, including those who were in transition or who could not complete their sex change for financial and/or medical reasons" (Symons and Hemphill 2006:118).

By 2002, the Gay Games VI were held in Sydney, Australia. The FGG had established the most inclusive gender policy by defining gender in terms of social identity and not requiring medical authorization of one's gender. The policy also went "beyond Western conceptions of sex/gender/sexuality, as traditional indigenous transgender identities were included. . . . Indigenous Australian Sistergirls, Indonesian Waria, Thai Kathoey, South Asian Hijra and Samoan Faafafine" (Symons and Hemphill 2006:123).

CONCLUSION

This chapter examines how two powerful institutions, media and sport, interact to shape and inform sexuality and are, in turn, shaped by sexuality. Language and imagery are fundamental aspects of communication. Both are sexualized in mass media in a variety of ways, often leading to discrimination against women, sexual minorities, and gender nonconforming people. The tendency to hypersexualize and objectify bodies in the media can influence an individual's sexual relationships with others, contribute to a negative body image, and in extreme cases, lead to disordered eating. The impact of sexualized media on children and adolescents reveals media can and does have the power to shape their beliefs and understandings about sex and sexuality. Representations of LGBTQ individuals and groups in television and cinema have been traditionally neglected and negatively stereotyped. With progress in recent years, equality in representation is still needed.

Few institutions expose the intersection of gender and sexuality better than sport, and the sport media plays an important role in reinforcing heteronormativity. The intersection of masculinity in sport marginalizes female athletes and gay athletes. While women have made significant progress in sports since the passage of Title IX, the sports media has not kept up with these cultural changes. Gay athletes have faced the option of assimilating into mainstream, homophobic sports institutions or segregating into gay sports spaces. Finally, sports remains one of the most rigidly gender-segregated institutions in society. This presents transgender and intersex athletes with some serious dilemmas. International athletic competitions have attempted to address these issues through different forms of sex verification tests since the 1960s. Today, many high school and college athletic programs are establishing policies that allow for the inclusion of transgender and transsexual athletes in sports.

Key Terms and Concepts

Controlling images 118	Moral panic 124	Sports rape 125
Hypersexualized 115	Negative recruiting 126	Sports sex 122
Jock culture 122	Racial fetishism 118	Structured absence 118
Media 113	Sexual objectification 116	Symbolic annihilation 115
Media literacy 113	Sports media 112	Televised sports manhood
Minority stress 127	Sports/media complex 122	formula 124

Critical Thinking Questions

1. Describe how language is sexualized in media. How is imagery sexualized in media? What potentially dangerous impacts can these have on women and girls? What impacts do these have on men and boys?

2. Describe representations of LGBTQ individuals in media. How are stereotypes perpetuated? What messages do stereotypes send? What impact might they have?

3. Explain the intersection of masculinity and sport and the affect this has on gay and female athletes. What role does sports media play in reinforcing masculinity in sport?

4. Explain the two paths LGBTQ athletes have taken to enter the sports world: assimilating into mainstream sports organizations or forming separate, gay sports spaces. What are the pros and cons associated with each approach? What affect does each approach have on the wider society? How is this similar to LGBTQ political activism described in Chapter Five?

Activities

1. Describe a transgender character you have seen portrayed in television or film. How are they depicted? What social norms or values are reflected?

2. Watch a major men's sporting event on television and write down evidence of masculinity being reinforced (paying attention to the broadcaster's comments, camera angles, etc.). Imagine if, instead, this sporting event involved female athletes (if you are watching men's basketball, reimagine it as women's basketball, for instance). Take the evidence you compiled and see how it applies (or fails to apply) to a sporting event involving the opposite sex. What does this tell you about sports media and the frame through which we see sports?

Essential Readings

Anderson, Eric. 2005. *In the Game: Gay Athletes and the Cult of Masculinity.* Albany, NY: State University of New York Press.

Griffin, Pat. 1998. *Strong Women, Deep Closets: Lesbians and Homophobia in Sport.* Champaign, IL: Human Kinetics.

Messner, Michael A. 2007. *Out of Play: Critical Essays on Gender and Sport.* Albany, NY: State University of New York Press.

Russo, Vito. 1987. *The Celluloid Closet: Homosexuality in the Movies.* New York, NY: Harper & Row.

Wolf, Naomi. 2002. *The Beauty Myth: How Images of Beauty Are Used against Women.* New York, N.Y.: HarperCollins Publishers.

Wykes, Maggie and Barrie Gunter. 2005. *Media and Body Image: If Looks Could Kill.* Thousand Oaks, CA: Sage.

Recommended Films

Celluloid Closet (1995). Rob Epstein and Jeffrey Friedman, Directors. A documentary narrated by Lily Tomlin that reviews various Hollywood screen depictions of homosexuals and the attitudes behind them throughout the history of North American film.

Killing us Softly Series: Advertising's Images of Women (2010). Jean Kilbourne, Writer/Director. This highly influential and award-winning series by Jean Kilbourne examines over 160 print and television ads and reveals sexist and misogynistic images and messages and a restrictive code of femininity that disempowers girls and women.

Tough Guise: Violence, Media, and the Crisis in Masculinity (1999). Sut Jhally, Executive Producer/Director. Narrated by antiviolence educator Jackson Katz, this film explores how U.S. media and pop-cultural imagery shapes the social construction of masculine identities, particularly a violent masculine ideal.

Training Rules (2009). Dee Mosbacher and Fawn Yacker, Directors. This documentary investigates the Penn State women's basketball program under Coach Rene Portland and specifically her "training rules" which involved "no lesbians." Through interviews with former players, the harm caused by this homophobic athletic environment is exposed.

Suggested Multimedia

Center for Media Literacy (**CML**) is an educational organization dedicated to promoting and supporting media literacy education as a framework for accessing, analyzing, evaluating, creating, and participating with media content. http://www.medialiteracy.com/new-you

Gay and Lesbian Alliance against Defamation (**GLAAD**) is an organization that works with print, broadcast, and online news sources to highlight stories from the LGBT community. GLAAD works with writers and producers to bring LGBT characters and plotlines to entertainment media. www.glaad.org

Gay and Lesbian International Sport Association is a group whose goal is to nurture and grow LGBTQ sports worldwide, to make associations with mainstream sport and human rights organizations, and to organize the World OutGames every four years. Originating in 2006, this event is a competitor to the Gay Games, and there are talks of the two merging by 2022. http://www.glisa.org/outgames/aboutglisa/

SEXUALITY, SCHOOLS, AND THE WORKPLACE

LEARNING OBJECTIVES

Upon completion of this chapter, students will be able to . . .

- Provide evidence of schools as agents of social control, particularly pertaining to sexuality
- Identify the various approaches to creating safe schools for LGBTQ youth
- Describe the shifts in sex education over the last 50 years
- Understand the two types of sexual harassment and the extent of this in the workplace
- Discuss the types of discrimination LGBTQ employees face

For LGBTQ students, schools are often not safe spaces; they face harassment and violence, they are exposed to biased language from fellow students and often from faculty and staff, and many cannot count on support from the administration if they report harassment and bullying. Some students and their families have filed lawsuits against their schools for failing to protect LGBTQ students.

The first of these was the case of *Nabozny v. Podlesney.* Student Jamie Nabozny filed a suit against the principal of his former middle school and high school in Ashland, Wisconsin. The harassment began when Jamie was in seventh grade. What began as cruel teasing rapidly progressed to physical violence. In one incident, a group of male students pretended to rape him while another group of students watched. When the school principal was informed of this, he responded by telling Jamie that that was what he should expect if he was going to be openly gay at school. He had objects thrown at him, was beaten in the boys' bathroom, and once experienced a beating so severe that he suffered internal bleeding and had to be hospitalized. Despite reporting every incident to school authorities, none of the perpetrators were ever punished. The violence and harassment so traumatized Jamie that he attempted suicide a number of times and eventually dropped out of high school for his own safety. Afterwards, he was diagnosed with posttraumatic stress disorder stemming from the abuse.

While a lower court ruled that school officials could not be held responsible for the abuse, a federal appellate court overturned that decision. Following his subsequent trial, a jury awarded Jamie $962,000, "setting the precedent . . . that schools are constitutionally obligated to protect all students, regardless of sexual orientation, from harassment" (Miceli 2005:38). This case and the publicity it received sent a clear message to schools across the country that they have an obligation to protect their LGBTQ students from harassment and violence (Biegel 2010; Miceli 2005). Despite this obligation, schools still continue to fail many LGBTQ students.

This chapter explores the ways sexuality intersects with and influences two significant institutions: schools and the workplace. Educational and employment institutions are both sites where LGBTQ people, pregnant women, and pregnant teens face or have historically faced discrimination and inequality. Discrimination and inequality in both institutions can be addressed through some of the same policies, such as including LGBTQ people in the Civil Rights Act and in nondiscrimination clauses; yet policies alone do not result in a bias-free environment, as our discussion in this chapter shows.

There are some significant differences between these two institutions and the way they intersect with sexuality. First, schools are much more conservative on sexuality-related issues than employers are. Second, they involve individuals at different stages of the life cycle: most students are minors, thus, not legal adults in the eyes of the law; and most employees are adults. Despite progress for LGBTQ students and employees, inequality remains. Evidence of the inequality LGBTQ students and employees continue to face include, but are not limited to the following:

- In 2008, Lawrence King, a gender-nonconforming student of color in a Southern California public school was shot twice in the head by a 14-year-old classmate only days after he came out as gay (Biegel 2010).
- In 2010, a lesbian student sued her school, the Itawamba County Agricultural High School, in Fulton, MS, for discrimination when they canceled their senior prom after she requested to bring her girlfriend as her date and to wear a tuxedo. School officials argued that it violated their policy against same-sex couples and that only boys could wear tuxedos.
- In 2010, Rutgers University freshman Tyler Clementi committed suicide three days after images of him having sexual relations with another male surfaced on the Internet (Strauss 2012).
- Vandy Beth Glenn was fired from her job with the Georgia General Assembly after her boss found out she was transgender (Burns and Krehely 2011).
- In 2012, high school junior Reuben Lack lost his position as student council president after he introduced a resolution to change the titles from Prom King and

Prom Queen to more gender-neutral titles in order to help make the prom a more welcoming environment for LGBTQ students.

- Despite other gay rights gains, there remains overwhelming pressure for LGBTQ employees in the workplace to remain closeted (Miller, C. 2014).
- A 16-year-old transgender high school girl, Taylor Alesana, committed suicide in 2015 after being bullied at school (Branson-Potts 2015).

SCHOOLS, SEXUALITY, AND SOCIAL CONTROL

Schools are inherently conservative institutions, particularly when it comes to sexuality-related issues. As mentioned in Chapter Four, married, pregnant teachers were sent home until the 1973 Supreme Court case brought by a teacher, Jo Carol Lafleur, put an end to school discrimination against pregnant teachers. Pregnant and parenting teens were dismissed from school as well, until it was convincingly argued in 1972 that under Title IX, these young women had a right to access a public education.

School dress codes reinforce gendered messages about sexuality as well, specifically reinforcing the sexual double standard. In one high school, the dress code declared that girls could not show their belly button or midriff, while boys had to wear their pants at their waistline, without exposing underclothes or skin (Pascoe 2007). Such dress codes are focused on curtailing girls' sexuality, while the boys' restrictions are instead a reaction against urban, "street" fashion (Orenstein 2016). In other research on girls' perceptions of school dress codes, Raby (2010) found that it is girls' clothing that is perceived as problematic when it is revealing, since it is viewed as distracting boys. Schools' conservative approaches to sexuality-related issues result in LGBTQ students, faculty, and staff still struggling for acceptance and acknowledgement, with some schools more welcoming than others.

Children are thought of as innocent and asexual; thus, schools, especially elementary schools, are institutions charged with protecting that innocence. By junior high and high school, the attitude shifts to one where schools are charged with containing what is perceived to be an otherwise out-of-control sexuality among their young student body. This image of junior high and high schoolers as sexual powder kegs is part of the reason why so many schools have resisted allowing gay student organizations on campus, have been hesitant to accept openly gay teachers, or have refused to include discussions of same-sex sexuality as part of healthy sexual expression in sex education courses. However, in the face of bullying and violence experienced by sexual minority and gender-nonconforming youth and increasing LGBTQ youth mobilization, schools are being forced to become safe spaces for all students.

Coming Out in School

Research finds that LGBTQ people are coming out, coming to an acknowledgement and an acceptance of their homosexuality, which often involves openly declaring it to family, friends, coworkers, and classmates, at younger ages than in previous eras (Patterson 1995; see Chapter Five). Through the 1980s, it was assumed that people came to an understanding of a gay or lesbian identity in their late teens and early twenties, with men coming to terms with it at younger ages than women. The average age of coming out today is between 14 and 16 for boys and girls (Orenstein 2016). A similar pattern exists for transgender youth as well, as they are recognizing and acknowledging their gender identities at much younger ages. Two decades ago, the pattern was for transgender people to come out in middle age. Today, we are witnessing the first generation of transgender teens who see themselves as transgender teens (Beemyn and Rankin 2011). Thus, LGBTQ youth and their needs really did not become an issue for schools until well into the 1990s (Miceli 2005).

Coming out is difficult for teenagers who face the threat of violence and harassment in schools and often know of no supportive places to turn for guidance (McDermott, Roen, and Scourfield 2008; Walls et al. 2008). LGBTQ youth who face family rejection are over eight times as likely to attempt suicide and are at significantly greater risk for depression (Ryan et al. 2009). This is the impetus behind the "It Gets Better" campaign started by author Dan Savage and his partner Terry Miller in 2010 in response to a rash of gay youth suicides. It involves YouTube videos of adult LGBTQ people pointing out that life gets better, emphasizing that things are not going to remain as dark as they may seem for many LGBTQ youth during their middle school and high school years. It is simply a message of hope to young people. This is also why many middle schools, junior highs, and high schools across the country are attempting to make their schools safer for LGBTQ youth, something we explore in great detail below.

This chapter focuses mostly on LGBTQ student's K–12 educational experiences for two primary reasons: first, college students are adults: thus, they can make choices more freely pertaining to their education. If they attend a college or university that does not provide a safe environment, they can transfer to another school, something that is less of an option for students in their K–12 years. Second, most of the research studying the bullying, harassment, and violence faced by LGBTQ youth in schools are of the K–12 population. That being said, in many ways higher education has led the way for creating a safer space for LGBTQ students. The fight for the right to form gay student organizations began on college campuses and later spread to middle schools, junior highs, and high schools. Also, colleges and universities often have courses or programs in LGBT studies, queer studies, and sexuality studies; in addition, they sometimes have an Office of Gender and Sexual Diversity at the administrative level, showing an institutional commitment to creating a safe and welcoming place for sexual minority and gender-nonconforming students.

LGBTQ Students' Experiences of Harassment in Schools

The most recent data available, the 2013 National School Climate Survey by the Gay, Lesbian, and Straight Education Network (GLSEN), finds most schools in the country are actually hostile places for sexual minority students. LGBTQ students avoid certain school spaces because they feel unsafe or uncomfortable (see Figure 7.1). They face alarming rates of harassment, violence, and *bullying*—aggressive behavior directed at a classmate who is perceived to have less power—and are exposed to homophobic and transphobic remarks from fellow students, faculty, and staff. Specifically, 71 percent of LGBTQ students regularly heard the word "gay" used in a negative way and were distressed by it (Ciancotto and Cahill 2012).

Harassment occurs at all levels, from elementary school to middle school to high school. In elementary school, harassment takes the form of homophobic slurs but is usually directed at gender-nonconforming students. While we differentiate between LGB youth and transgender youth, some of the harassment they experience as young people conflates the two topics. For instance, research finds that LGB youth report being victimized for their gender nonconformity while in elementary school; specifically, boys are called sissies and girls are called tomboys beginning around the age of 8 as gender becomes increasingly salient to children (Cianciotto and Cahill 2012). Verbal taunts such as "fag" and "gay" proliferate in elementary schools, even if children are unclear of the sexual meaning of the slurs.

Anti-LGBTQ violence and harassment increases dramatically in middle school, junior high, and high school; and more research exists on the bullying and harassment that goes on at this level. According to GLSEN's 2013 research, more than 71.4 percent of LGBTQ middle school, junior high, and high school students report they frequently or often heard "gay" used in a negative way, 64.5 percent heard other negative homophobic remarks, and 56.4 percent heard negative remarks about gender expression, while 51.4 percent of students at some point heard homophobic remarks from faculty or staff members (Kosciw et al. 2014). Ultimately, 55.5 percent of students feel unsafe at school due to their sexual orientation and 37.8 percent feel unsafe at school due to their gender expression (Kosciw et al. 2014). According to research by the

FIGURE 7.1 ■ Percentage of LGBT Students Who Avoid Spaces at School Because They Feel Unsafe or Uncomfortable

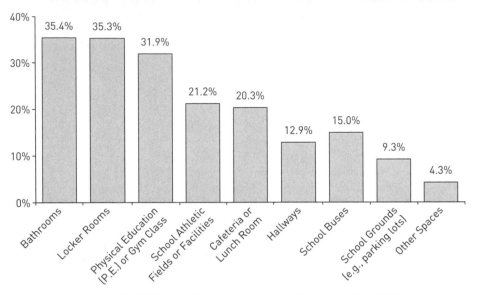

Source: Figure from GLSEN's 2013 National School Climate Survey. Kosciw et al. 2014. GLSEN.org/nscs.

National Institute of Mental Health, 24 percent of LGB youth were threatened with violence, 11 percent were physically assaulted, 2 percent were threatened with weapons, and 5 percent were sexually assaulted (Cianciotto and Cahill 2012). Much of the verbal harassment experienced by LGBTQ students in high school qualifies as sexual harassment (see Chapter Four). High school girls who identify as gay or lesbian are more likely than heterosexual girls to be sexually harassed, through offensive name-calling or being touched or grabbed in a sexual way.

Cyberbullying, which refers to using electronic media to intentionally and aggressively harass someone, disproportionately affects LGBTQ youth. Research finds that 94 percent of teens go online, and 63 percent of them do so daily (Lenhart et al. 2010). Because social media is so new, there is very little research on the impact of cyberbullying on children, or LGBTQ youth in particular; but one study found victims of cyberbullying to have higher levels of depression than other bullying victims (Strauss 2012). Cyberbullying is important to talk about in the context of education because it is generally young people who engage in this practice; and when these behaviors are present during school, it is disruptive to their education (Strauss 2012).

IMPACT OF HARASSMENT The harassment and violence LGBTQ students face in school manifests in higher dropout rates, poorer academic performance, higher rates of depression, increased risk of PTSD and substance abuse, and more absenteeism (see Figure 7.2). Studies consistently show that gay and lesbian youth attempt suicide at much higher rates than their heterosexual peers (Cianciotto and Cahill 2012). Bullying and harassment can result in students curtailing their educational aspirations: LGBTQ students are half as likely to pursue secondary education or attend college than a national sample of heterosexual students. Research also finds that due to the stress related to their victimization and their isolation, they are more likely to engage in risky and unprotected sexual behaviors, increasing their risk of contracting sexually transmitted diseases (Cianciotto and Cahill 2012). Importantly, the majority of LGBTQ students do not report the assault and harassment they face in school, either because they feel school personnel and administrators will not do anything about it or because they fear it might make the situation worse.

Transgender Students' Experiences of Harassment in Schools

Transgender students experience harassment similar to LGB students, while also experiencing unique forms of discrimination. Schools are somewhat gender segregated, which results in dilemmas for transgender and gender-nonconforming students—specifically in terms of access to certain spaces such as restrooms and locker rooms. While a simple solution would be to offer gender-neutral restrooms and at least one space where a student can change clothes behind closed doors, most schools have been slow to adapt to the needs of transgender students. According to GLSEN, transgender students feel less safe at school and experience higher rates of harassment and assault compared to cisgender LGB students. For example, 73.6 percent of transgender students reported being verbally harassed based on gender expression sometimes, often, or frequently at school, compared to less than one in three cisgender LGB males and females (29.2 percent and 27.3 percent respectively) (Kosciw et al. 2014).

The first reported lawsuit against a school for discriminating against a transgender student was in 2000. The 15-year-old plaintiff began wearing women's clothing and makeup in seventh grade. During her eighth-grade year, the school principal required that she report to him every morning so he could evaluate whether or not her attire was appropriate; if it was too feminine, he sent her home to change. Eventually, she stopped going to school altogether. The plaintiff and her grandmother filed a lawsuit against the school district. The court eventually determined that she had been discriminated against and that she "must be allowed to express her self-identified gender while attending school," further explaining that "to force her to wear male clothing would be to stifle her selfhood 'merely because it causes some members of the community discomfort'" (Cianciotto and Cahill 2012:18). The First Amendment and due process clause of the Constitution give transgender students the right to dress according to their gender identity rather than according to their sex assigned at birth.

Transgender students also have unique privacy concerns. For instance, whether or not they choose to be "out" as a trans person is often questioned. If they are not living as their assigned birth sex, do they have a right to keep that information to themselves, or is keeping such information private actually a form of deception? Young people who are transitioning often change schools in order to start over with their new identity at a new school. Transgender youth are generally presenting as one gender but still have the physical and biological body of the other because they are too young for sex reassignment surgery and, if they are under the age of sixteen, are still too young for hormone treatments. Transgender youth do have one medical option at their disposal. That is the use of ***hormone blockers***, which can "pause" the onset of puberty. This allows transgender youth to present as one sex, without experiencing bodily changes that challenge their presentation of self, while also not making the kinds of permanent, irreversible changes that medical treatments such as hormones result in.

School personnel need be aware of the types of stressors that transgender youth often experience in their homes that can affect their performance in school. Many are facing intense opposition from their parents, family, and friends; "it can be argued, in fact, that transgender persons are among the most misunderstood of any identifiable group in existence today" (Biegel

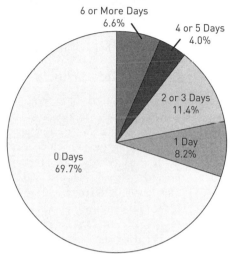

FIGURE 7.2 ■ Frequency That LGBTQ Students Missed Days of School In The Past Month Because of Feeling Unsafe or Uncomfortable

6 or More Days 6.6%
4 or 5 Days 4.0%
2 or 3 Days 11.4%
1 Day 8.2%
0 Days 69.7%

Source: Figure from GLSEN's 2013 National School Climate Survey. Kosciw et al. 2014. GLSEN.org/nscs.

2010:180). Research indicates that transgender youth are much more likely to be involved with substance abuse, running away, homelessness, and prostitution than their cisgender peers (Biegel 2010). In 2004, the school board in Orange County, California, expanded their definition of "gender" in order to provide antidiscrimination protection to gender-nonconforming youth in the state's public schools. One city in that region, Westminster, risked losing state funding for its refusal to comply with the new regulations. One board member opposed to expanding protections for transgender youth claimed that she felt accepting the policy would promote homosexuality, transsexuality, and cross-dressing, and that boys would claim to be girls just to get into the girls' restroom (Biegel 2010). There is no evidence to support such fears. First, she erroneously conflates homosexuality and transgender issues. Second, knowing the extreme harassment transgender students face, it is far-fetched to imagine that high school students would engage in cross-dressing, even to get into the girls' restroom.

Creating Safe Schools

A range of solutions have been incorporated to help make schools safer for LGBTQ students including: establishing high schools specifically for LGBTQ students, introducing LGBTQ-inclusive curriculum, creating support organizations such as Gay-Straight Alliances (GSAs), implementing antibullying policies and programs, and challenging the institutionalization of heterosexuality in schools. These efforts have hardly been without controversy. For instance, protesters verbally harassed students on their first day of classes as they entered the first gay high school in the country, Harvey Milk High School in New York City (Colapinto 2005). In 1984, a Los Angeles high school started a gay rights organization called Project 10 in response to a gay student dropping out due to bullying and violence. Project 10 was soon implemented district wide and became a nationwide model. Since Project 10 was implemented in 1984, a very socially conservative era, merely being a gay student support organization resulted in its becoming a lightning rod of controversy and a target of the religious right who claimed it posed a danger to children. In this case, the school district supported Project 10 and did not cave to the pressures of the religious right (Connell 2015).

Harvey Milk High School in New York City was the first school in the country designated specifically for lesbian, gay, bisexual, transgender, queer, and questioning youth.
Source: AP Photo/Mary Altaffer.

GAY-FRIENDLY SCHOOLS One of the solutions to the harassment and bullying gay students face at school has been the creation of schools specifically for LGBTQ students. New York City's Harvey Milk High School is the first high school of this kind, a public school designated specifically for lesbian, gay, bisexual, transgender, queer, and questioning youth. Harvey Milk High School first opened in 1985 and became a fully accredited public school in 2002. With its current enrollment of 52 students in grades 9–12, it provides a safe space and a path to graduation for students bullied out of other schools due to their sexuality and/or gender nonconformity. Eighty percent of the students at Harvey Milk are black or Latino and are from some of the poorest parts of New York; essentially, these are some of the most at-risk adolescents in the city.

Establishing a gay school as a solution to the bullying, harassment, and violence gay students face is problematic for a number of reasons. First, this is clearly not a solution for all LGBTQ students. There are 300,000 New York City high school students, 10,000 of whom are likely LGBTQ, conservatively estimated; and Harvey Milk High School currently enrolls 52 students. Additionally, there are only three gay-friendly high schools in the United States, Harvey Milk in New York, Pride School in Atlanta, and Alliance in Milwaukee, Wisconsin. While Harvey Milk and Alliance are public schools, Pride School in Atlanta is a private school, with a yearly tuition of $13,000. Most school districts are unlikely to entertain the idea of opening such a school for any number of reasons, from cost concerns to fear of a backlash from religious and political conservatives. The Chicago public school district discussed opening a gay high school, and the hostility they received from religious conservatives stalled the plan (Calefati 2008).

Second, segregating gay students from straight students does not solve the problem of homophobia and bullying in schools; it merely protects some students from such treatment. Bullies are the ones who need to change their behaviors rather than having their victims segregated in their own schools. Constitutional law professor Jonathan Turley argues that this is a problematic precedent reflecting the era of "separate but equal" educational systems (Colapinto 2005). While admittedly not an ideal solution, defenders argue we should not expect students to endure harassment and bullying while we attempt to change the behaviors of bullies. Some have argued that gay schools are a cop-out solution for school districts. Turley, for instance, maintains that training teachers, monitoring classrooms, and punishing prejudicial students for their homophobic harassment and violence is actually far more difficult and expensive for school districts than opening a segregated gay high school (Colapinto 2005).

Third, while LGBTQ schools address sexuality, they are less successful at effectively addressing other issues of marginalization such as race, class, and gender. Some research finds that transgender racial minority students at a gay high school do not experience the school to be a safe space for them (Gutierrez 2013). There are no transgender teachers at the school, so they do not have an adult mentor to turn to who intimately understands their issues. Transgender issues are invisible in the curriculum; and the students experience threats, harassment, and even violence from not only their peers but also from teachers, principals, and even campus security guards.

Opposition to the Harvey Milk High School even includes a lawsuit that seeks to have the school's $3.2 million dollars in taxpayer funding revoked on the grounds that it is a waste of money due to the low numbers of students being served by the school and the fact that it violates New York's law prohibiting discrimination in school admissions on the basis of sexual orientation (Colapinto 2005). While this lawsuit has not yet been resolved, it appears there are some settlement negotiations in process. For instance, the school's website no longer includes any language pertaining to the school being for LGBTQ youth. Instead, the school is described vaguely as a small, safe, educational environment that promotes a diverse, confident, and self-respecting community.

QUEERING THE CURRICULUM The traditional, formal, curriculum in schools tends to ignore LGBTQ people and their experiences while heterosexuality is reinforced in both subtle and overt ways. In order to feel like they belong, both in the school and the larger world, students need to see themselves in the curriculum. Part of the ***hidden curriculum***, the unintended or unofficial lessons students learn in schools in addition to the formal curriculum such as math, social studies, English, history, and so on, is heterosexuality and gender conformity (Vaccaro, August, and Kennedy 2012). This can be specifically understood as an ***informal sexuality curriculum***, where institutional policies and practices, relationships between students and teachers, and school

"These kids are volatile, aggressive, hostile, as a way to protect themselves . . . . They've been harassed and bullied and beaten up so often, they have a thick armor. We're trying to teach them how to manage difficult emotions, how to be confident in who they are. We help them with coming-out issues, and the struggle of identity" (Colapinto 2005).

rituals all contribute to the construction of and reinforcement of heterosexuality in schools (Pascoe 2007; Trudell 1993). Despite their proclaimed avoidance of sex and sexuality-related issues, schools are actually highly sexualized and gendered institutions, and these messages certainly come through in the curriculum where heterosexuality and gender conformity are reinforced in subtle and overt ways (Pascoe 2007).

According to recent research by GLSEN (Kosciw et al. 2014), only 18.5 percent of LGBTQ people were ever taught positive aspects of LGBTQ history, while 14.8 percent of them were actually taught negative content about LGBTQ people and topics. In elementary school curricula, LGBTQ people and experiences are almost totally absent; however, this is partially because sexuality-related topics are almost completely absent from the curriculum. Yet, one could include LGBTQ topics in the curriculum without it being a discussion of sex. For instance, a standard part of an elementary school curriculum involves a unit on the family. While diverse families are emphasized, gay families are still ignored and thus invisible in the curriculum (Vaccaro et al. 2012). In secondary school classrooms, students may read poetry by Walt Whitman, yet his sexuality is never mentioned; history courses cover the civil rights movement, but not the gay rights movement.

In some places, this is changing. The state of California passed educational reforms known as the Fair, Accurate, Inclusive, and Respectful (FAIR) Education Act, which requires public schools to include the contributions of LGBTQ individuals. However, resistance remains in other locales. Some states have mandated the inclusion of anti-LGBTQ messages in their state's health curriculum, either requiring that they emphasize that the state prohibits same-sex relationships or requiring that they relay the message that homosexuality is deviant and dangerous (Vaccaro et al. 2012). While LGBTQ-related content is not mandated in most states, it is important to remember that such content is protected under the First Amendment (Biegel 2010). Parents have a right to *not* allow their children to receive certain information and ideas, but the courts have generally not sided with them in such cases. In *Mozert v. Hawkins County Board of Education* (1987), a group of parents sued the school district claiming that a wide range of materials in the basal readers being used at their children's schools were in violation of their rights as Christians. The court ruled against the families on the grounds that "mere exposure in the public schools to ideas that might offend a family's religious beliefs does not constitute a violation of that family's rights under the Free Exercise clause of the First Amendment" (Biegal 2010:82).

Queering the curriculum involves including LGBTQ people and experiences as an integrated part of the mainstream curriculum, rather than as a separate unit. Using "queer" as a verb like this allows us to shift the discussion away from queer as an identity and instead understand it as a stance or a position (Springer 2008). Adding LGBTQ-themed books to a school library is one way to create a more inclusive curriculum. Additionally, teachers can add LGBTQ-themed examples to their existing lesson plans, such as including a discussion of the Stonewall riots in a section on history and social change. The idea is to make sure examples used in class are not heterocentric and instead are inclusive of LGBTQ history and experiences. The California Safe Schools Coalition found that 83 percent of their schools included LGBTQ issues in their tolerance curriculum in high schools, 64 percent in middle schools, and 54 percent in elementary schools (Cianciotto and Cahill 2012). After the implementation of the new curriculum, students, both gay and straight, reported feeling safer in schools with LGBTQ-inclusive curricula. Students reported they were made fun of less, that they were less likely to hear of mean lies being spread about them, and that overall there was less anti-LGBTQ bullying in their school (Cianciotto and Cahill 2012:92).

Despite this progress, the majority of textbooks used in the United States pay little to no attention to LGBTQ history or issues. A content analysis of high school and college level textbooks published between 1992 and 2005 found LGBTQ invisibility. Specifically, 95 percent of the pages included no discussion of same-sex sexuality at all, with many defining sexuality as heterosexual; and 80 percent of the time same-sex sexuality was described in a negative context (Macgillivray and Jennings 2008). According to GLSEN, most students do not have access to LGBTQ-related curricula or resources, and this is particularly true for students in rural areas and those in the South (Kosciw et al. 2014).

"Even teachers who describe themselves as social justice advocates fail to challenge homophobic and transphobic language and images in many early childhood settings" (Vaccaro et al. 2012:86).

GAY STUDENT ORGANIZATIONS Gay student organizations are designed to support sexual minority and gender-nonconforming youth, educate the campus community about homophobia, and advocate for gay rights on campus and nationwide (Miceli 2005). Despite the fact that gay student organizations are now found in many middle schools, junior highs, and high schools throughout the country, research by GLSEN (2014) finds that only approximately half of the LGBTQ students surveyed report that their school had a Gay-Straight Alliance (GSA) or similar gay student organization; which, of course, means that about half of American LGBTQ students attend a school that does not have such an organization (Kosciw et al. 2014). Advocates for gay student organizations, such as teachers and school counselors, were initially motivated by U.S. Department of Health and Human Services 1989 research that found that between 20 and 30 percent of youth suicides were linked to sexual orientation, which helped to frame LGBTQ youth as an at-risk population (Miceli 2005:26).

While students in middle school, junior high, and high school are on the frontlines of the battle for gay student organizations today, the initial demands for these began at the college level in the early 1970s and were an extension of gay activism in the post-Stonewall era. The first litigation involving a Gay Student Organization (GSO) involved the University of New Hampshire in 1973. While the university recognized the organization, the media attention surrounding a dance sponsored by the GSO resulted in the Board of Trustees suspending GSO-sponsored events (Biegel 2010). At Georgetown University, gay and lesbian students sued the University for refusing to allow a gay student organization on campus. The University claimed that since it was a Jesuit institution, such an organization violated their religious rights, an argument the courts agreed with (Miceli 2005). While these institutions made headlines in the 1970s, college students across the country began quietly establishing gay student organizations on their campuses (see below).

The first high schools to establish gay-straight alliances (GSAs) were private boarding schools in Massachusetts, Phillips Academy and Concord Academy. These early GSAs were focused on increasing the visibility of LGBTQ students and improving the climate for sexual minority students. Establishing "gay-straight alliances" instead of gay student organizations is intended to communicate that LGBTQ issues affect everyone, and thus, student organizations should include straight and gay students (Miceli 2005). These organizations soon spread to public schools in Massachusetts by the early 1990s. GLSEN formed in 1990, and one of their primary objectives was to help local schools establish GSAs across the nation. By 2004, there were over 2,000 GSAs across the country; by 2011, there were more than 4,000 (Hartinger 2011).

GSAs are not evenly distributed across the country, however, as only 2.3 percent of schools in the South have them (Miceli 2005). Research finds that many factors influence the likelihood of a school having a GSA, including region of the country; whether the school is in a suburban, urban, or rural area, with suburban schools having the greatest likelihood of having a GSA and rural areas having the least; teacher/student ratio, where the lower the ratio, the greater the likelihood; racial demographics, with GSAs more likely to be found in schools with a larger percentage of white students; and socioeconomic status of the student body, with the more poor students a school has, the less likely it is to have a GSA (Fetner and Kush 2003). An additional factor is whether or not the GSAs are in states that include sexual orientation in their nondiscrimination policy (Miceli 2005).

Students protesting the denial of a gay-straight alliance at their Texas high school in 2011.
Source: AP Photo/Todd Yates/Corpus Christi Caller-Times.

Despite this progress, the opposition to GSAs has remained intense. In 1995, the Salt Lake City School Board, for instance, banned all school clubs as a way to prevent the formation of a GSA. In 2015, students at Brandon High School in Rankin County, Mississippi, attempted to form a GSA, but the school board prohibited it. In 2016, an attempt to form a GSA at a rural Tennessee school aroused community opposition, with one person comparing the presence of a gay-straight alliance with a campus terrorist organization, specifically claiming that if this organization was not stopped, schools would establish "F.I.M.A. (Future ISIS Members of America)" (Ring 2016).

Such opposition has resulted in students and families suing schools. There have been two types of lawsuits: one is against schools for their failure to protect students from harassment and discrimination, an example of which is described in the opening vignette. The second type of suit challenges the schools on Equal Access grounds; specifically, schools have been sued if they refused to allow GSA organizations while at the same time supporting other student organizations. Both types of lawsuits have been successful (Miceli 2005).

While the kind of changes discussed here would not have happened without the mobilization and courage of LGBTQ youth, some argue that the GSA movement would have been much less successful without the incorporation of straight allies, both teachers and fellow students (Miceli 2005). Simply on the basis of numbers alone, it is unlikely that a youth movement that relied exclusively on LGBTQ students would have been as effective at influencing school policies. This is partially due to homophobia and the stigma associated with homosexuality that limited the sympathy gay youth garnered (Miceli 2005).

GLSEN (2014) finds that the presence of a GSA or similar organizations on campus results in a more accepting climate for LGBTQ students ("National School Climate . . ." 2014). For instance, on campuses with such organizations, LGBTQ students are less likely to hear racial slurs and homophobic remarks; and when they hear such remarks, students are more likely to report them to authorities, which is evidence that they expect something will be done about it. Additionally, LGBTQ students feel safer, experience lower levels of victimization for their sexuality and/or gender nonconformity, and feel more connected at their schools when they have a gay student organization.

POLICIES AND PROGRAMS Creating safe schools for LGBTQ students includes establishing specific policies and programs that penalize discrimination and bullying; such policies exist at the federal, state, school district, and classroom level. At the federal level, students can rely on the equal protection clause of the U.S. Constitution, Title IX of the Education Amendments Act of 1972, and the Equal Access Act of 1984 (Cianciotto and Cahill 2012). As we saw in the opening vignette, federal courts have ruled that public schools are obligated to protect all students, including those who are sexual or gender minorities, from harassment and discrimination. According to Title IX, a school is required to protect a student from harassment once they have been notified it has occurred; schools can be found liable for monetary damages if they were found to be "deliberately indifferent" to a history of pervasive harassment (Cianciotto and Cahill 2012).

While these protections are helpful, more needs to be done at the federal level. For instance, passing the proposed Safe Schools Improvement Act that would require states that receive ESEA (Elementary and Secondary Education Act) funds to establish comprehensive student conduct policies that prohibit bullying and harassment along the lines of race, color, national origin, sex, disability, sexual orientation, gender identity, and religion. The proposed Act also would require that states report data on bullying and harassment and provide Congress with a report on the data every two years. Introduced yearly since 2007, this legislation has yet to pass Congress.

The state is the second level where nondiscrimination policies and programs to protect LGBTQ students exist. Most states have laws that prohibit discrimination and bullying in schools; but most of these laws do not explicitly include sexual orientation or gender identity as protected categories, which leaves LGBTQ students in many states vulnerable. According to GLSEN, currently LGBTQ students are included as protected categories in only 18 states. Thirteen states and the District of Columbia include sexual orientation and gender identity in their nondiscrimination clauses, with Wisconsin including only sexual orientation but not gender identity.

However, some states actually have laws that *negatively* affect LGBTQ students. An example are the **no promo homo laws** that prohibit teachers from discussing gay and transgender issues, including issues pertaining to sexual health and HIV/AIDS, in a positive light. Some go so far as to require teachers to portray LGBTQ people negatively. Currently eight states have such laws (see Figure 7.3). Most are in the South, the region of the country with the fastest growing rates of HIV/AIDS (see Chapter Ten).

In states that do not protect LGBTQ students, school districts can establish their own policies and programs to protect sexual minority and gender-nonconforming students, with the exception of states that have "no promo homo" laws in place. School districts can extend protection to LGBTQ students by including them in their nondiscrimination clause or specifically including them in their antibullying policies. Beyond this, schools can follow the lead of Massachusetts, which launched the nation's first safe schools initiative 20 years ago. This involved developing policies to protect sexual minority youth from harassment, violence, and discrimination; to offer school personnel training in violence and suicide prevention; and to provide counseling for family members of lesbian and gay students (Cianciotto and Cahill 2012). In 2007, New York City followed with the implementation of its Respect for All initiative that included training for teachers and school staff; mandated reporting and investigation of bullying, harassment, and violence; and required school principals to develop and review their antibullying plans in their overall school review.

Teacher and staff training are essential for creating a safe environment for LGBTQ students. Such training does two things: first, it provides teachers and staff with the necessary tools to help students who are coming to terms with a gay or lesbian identity. Second, it provides them an opportunity to work through their own personal biases surrounding issues of sexual orientation and gender nonconformity. Many gay rights advocates and organizations, from the ACLU (American Civil Liberties Union) to NCLR (National Center for Lesbian Rights) to GLSEN, offer training workshops to school districts on how to prevent anti-LGBTQ bullying

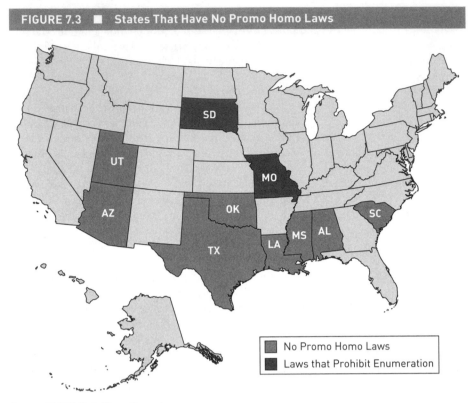

FIGURE 7.3 ■ States That Have No Promo Homo Laws

No Promo Homo Laws
Laws that Prohibit Enumeration

Source: GLSEN State Maps. From glsen.org.

and harassment (Cianciotto and Cahill 2012). In schools where faculty and staff lack such training, too often bullying and harassment of LGBTQ students is ignored (Pascoe 2007).

Finally, antibullying policies can be implemented in individual classrooms. Teachers can make it perfectly clear, for instance, that using the terms "gay" or "fag" will not be tolerated. They can explain why such language is harmful and wrong and punish violators. This type of change will require teachers to quit ignoring the current rampant use of such terms and address what is a blatant form of harassment in their classrooms (Pascoe 2007).

CHALLENGING INSTITUTIONALIZED HETEROSEXUALITY A *heterosexualizing process* refers to the ways young people are taught to perceive heterosexuality as normal and natural; it sends distinct messages about the appropriateness of heterosexuality and the inappropriateness of same-sex sexuality. The heterosexualizing process happens as early as elementary school and continues through high school. For example, school rituals, such as homecoming courts, are composed of male-female "couples." Also, interaction patterns between teachers and students, including homophobic bantering and "coupling up" male-female students for in-class examples are part of a heterosexualizing process (Pascoe 2007). This is an example of heterosexual privilege in educational institutions that marginalizes nonheterosexual students.

While including LGBTQ people and issues in the mainstream curriculum, establishing gay-straight alliances, and implementing antibullying policies are all ways to make schools safer for LGBTQ students, some argue these do not go far enough. They argue that we need to change school culture, specifically by challenging the institutionalization of heterosexuality in schools (Payne and Smith 2012). Antibullying programs are limited in their effectiveness because they focus on individuals instead of the school culture that privileges gender and sexual conformity. Schools also must emphasize empathy, solidarity,

Institutionalized heterosexuality is obvious in this image of a high school Homecoming court.
Source: istockphoto.com/Brian McEntire.

and social justice and be an environment of adults willing and able to talk to and listen to children talk about gender and sexuality-related issues ("Queering Schools" 2014).

COLLEGE AND UNIVERSITY CAMPUSES So far our discussion has focused on K-12 classrooms, but many college campuses have worked to make their campuses safer for LGBTQ students as well. This begins simply with making nondiscrimination clauses inclusive of sexual and gender minorities. When institutions take that step, they become a more attractive place for LGBTQ faculty, which means that LGBTQ students will be more likely to have mentors and role models on campus. As recently as 1970, there was not one openly gay or lesbian professor on a college campus in this country (Biegel 2010).

As has already been discussed, colleges and universities were the first campuses to fight for the right to have gay student organizations, although many still face opposition when they attempt to establish such organizations, especially in more conservative regions of the country. In addition, colleges and universities can be safe spaces for LGBTQ students by offering courses in queer theory, sexuality studies, or LGBT studies. But many campuses are going beyond such basics. Tulane University, for instance, has a Sexual and Gender Diversity Office as part of its Office of Multicultural Affairs, signaling an institutional commitment to LGBTQ students on that campus. This office offers a "Trans 101" workshop multiple times per year for faculty and staff that provides a basic overview of acceptable terminology, a discussion of issues transgender students and faculty face, and a forum for faculty and staff to ask questions.

Despite such progress on some campuses, research finds that many college campuses are not safe spaces for LGBTQ students. LGBTQ student perceptions of their *campus climate*, the cumulative attitudes and behaviors of employees and students pertaining to the inclusion of, and level of respect for, individual and group needs, are reported as "positive" as long as nothing bad happens. This is more accurately described as a neutral environment (Rankin 2005; Tetreault et al. 2013). Such findings exemplify that LGBTQ students may come to campus expecting to experience bullying, harassment, and violence. A 2004 national study of the campus climate at 14 institutions that included 1,000 students and 669 staff, faculty, and administrators, found that 34 percent of students hid their sexual orientation or gender orientation on campus and 19 percent were concerned with physical safety (Rankin 2005; Tetreault et al. 2013). Additionally, 32 percent of LGBTQ people of color reported harassment compared to 28 percent of white LGBTQ students (Tetreault et al. 2013).

According to the National Consortium of Higher Education LGBT Resource Professionals, 641 colleges and universities today have LGBTQ resource centers on campus; up from 175 in 2011. However, simply having resources available is not enough, as they do not seem to significantly affect LGBTQ students' perceptions of their campus climate (Tetreault et al. 2013). More efforts need to be made, such as matching students with LGBTQ-friendly roommates and having an LGBT alumni group (Lipka 2011). Students can evaluate their campus through the Pride Index, a national listing of LGBTQ-friendly colleges and universities.

While many college campuses are leading the way on transgender issues, there are always improvements that still need to be made. Implemented in 1996, the University of Iowa was the first college in the country to have a trans-inclusive nondiscrimination policy; now almost one thousand campuses include "gender identity" in their nondiscrimination policies (Beemyn 2015). Many institutions now offer gender-inclusive housing, where students can have a roommate of any gender; they allow students to use their chosen first name rather than their legal name on campus records; and some ask students their preferred pronouns so these can be included on course rosters. In Oregon, two fraternities have changed their bylaws to allow transgender men as members (Nashrulla 2016). Despite these improvements, the "vast majority of college students, classroom faculty, student affairs educators, and administrators have a tremendous amount to learn about gender diversity" (Rankin and Beemyn 2012).

One of the problems with most of the changes described above is that they do not address the needs of transgender students who identify as **nonbinary**, those who choose not to identify as male or female. In a study of 111 nonbinary transgender college students from 62 colleges, all but one of the students felt that their colleges were not doing enough to support them, even though many of the institutions had made many of the changes described above and are considered "trans friendly" (Beemyn 2015). One of their biggest complaints included being misgendered in class and on official documents. Their needs also include gender-inclusive restrooms that students of any gender can use. Sometimes state laws interfere with the rights of public colleges and universities to support sexual minority or gender-nonconforming students. For instance, in March of 2016, North Carolina passed the *Public Facilities Privacy and Security Act* that required public restrooms to be used only by people whose biological, assigned birth matches the sign on the restroom door. This law denies public colleges and universities in that state the opportunity to be more accommodating to transgender students, faculty, and staff by implementing policies that would allow transgender students to use the restroom aligned with their gender identity (Logue 2016).

Colleges and universities can solve some of these problems by allowing students to choose a preferred pronoun, including gender-neutral options such as "they" and "ze," when they enroll. That pronoun is then listed on course rosters so that instructors are able to accurately address the student (see Chapter Three). On official records, students should also be able to use their chosen name, which may differ from their legal name; currently, only about 150 colleges and universities offer this option. Finally, it is imperative that institutions of higher learning make an effort to educate their cisgender faculty, staff, and student body about transgender issues (Beemyn 2015).

INCLUSION OF TRANSGENDER STUDENTS AT WOMEN'S COLLEGES Women's colleges face some of the biggest struggles with including transgender students since their mission is to educate women. While transgender students' numbers may be small, "their presence has become a lightning rod for a renewed examination of the mission, history, and future of women's colleges" (Marine 2011). Female students are applying to and being admitted to women's colleges. Then over the four years of their collegiate career, some begin the transition from female to male. Thus, while most women's colleges are not accepting male applicants, they nevertheless are finding themselves with male students in classrooms and dormitories. Despite such dilemmas, transgender students find women's colleges attractive because they are safer, both physically and psychologically (Padawer 2014).

Single-sex institutions have taken a wide variety of responses to this new challenge to their institutional identity and are evidence of the ongoing contestation surrounding transgender college students. Hollins University, a small, women's college in Virginia, has established a policy that they will confer diplomas only on women. Thus, if students at their institution begin the transition to male, they are expected to transfer to a different institution in order to graduate. For Wellesley, and most women's colleges, they require only that their applicants be female. Thus, if any of their students begin to transition to male, they can stay at the institution. This has not been an unproblematic solution, however. For many women at Wellesley, to have a transman in a position of campus leadership undermines the mission of the women's college, which is often the primary reason students choose to attend women's colleges. Use of the word "sisterhood," once prominent on these campuses, is now being changed to "siblinghood" to reflect these campus demographic changes, a change that has been controversial. How instructors refer to the student body (using "she" instead of "he," for instance) is also perceived as problematic by some. And while some women's colleges are allowing transmen, most are still resistant to allowing transwomen (people raised as male who go on to identify as women). Mills College became the first women's college to admit transwomen, even if they have not yet transitioned to female when they come to campus. A final example is Mount Holyoke College, which broadened its admissions policy to include all academically qualified students, except for those who are biological males at birth and who still identify as male (Padawer 2014).

History and Experiences of LGBTQ Teachers

Schools are not only populated with LGBTQ students, but with sexual minority and gender-nonconforming administrators, teachers, and staff. While there have been some progressive changes, schools have not historically been welcoming places for gay employees. Schools have historically constructed child welfare in opposition to gay rights. Thus, for decades LGBTQ teachers could not get a job if they were out and would be fired if their sexuality was discovered (Biegel 2010). While sexual minority teachers face hostility, transgender teachers experience even higher rates of opposition. In 1978, a California politician sought to ensure that homosexuals were barred from teaching in the state's public schools under Proposition 6 (known as the Briggs initiative), an idea Supreme Court Justice Antonin Scalia agreed with in his dissent of *Lawrence v. Texas* (2003). According to PEW Research Center data, as of 2007, 28 percent of Americans still agreed with the Briggs initiative and believe that school boards should be able to fire teachers known to be gay (Biegel 2010). While many conservatives still hold this view, more people today argue that having LGBTQ teachers, staff, and administrators can provide a source of support for LGBTQ students in schools that are otherwise hostile places for them.

LGBTQ teachers struggle reconciling two contrasting identities—their sexual identity and their occupational identity. LGBTQ teachers of the modern era came of age in the era of gay pride, where they have been encouraged to be out and proud as a way to show their acceptance of themselves and to demand cultural acceptance for homosexuals. However, their professional identity dictates they be more circumspect about their personal and, especially, their sexual lives (Connell 2015). LGBTQ teachers manage this by presenting as sexually neutral and gender-normative, especially those who wish to avoid the *glass closet*, where they are inadvertently outed as gay or lesbian due to their nonconforming gender performance (Connell 2015).

Teachers are hesitant to come out even in relatively progressive schools and regions of the country because that information can change the classroom dynamic, as they become the "gay teacher." *A hypersexualization* of gay teachers happens when administrators and parents fear the teacher will want to focus on sexuality-related topics and that it will cause students to ask invasive and personal sexuality-related questions (see Chapter Six). LGBTQ teachers struggle to balance presenting their sexuality and addressing sexuality-related issues in schools without hypersexualizing or hypersanitizing the topic (Connell 2015).

Alternative schools like Harvey Milk, Pride, and Alliance are not just havens for LGBTQ students, but they can be refuges for LGBTQ teachers as well. Christian Zsilavetz, founder of Atlanta's Pride School, taught for 25 years and says he "never felt truly open or supported by administrators while teaching in public schools and wanted that to change. He wanted LGBTQ students and teachers to be able to openly discuss who they are in a school setting without fear" ("Groundbreaking High School . . ." 2016).

College Campuses: From "In Loco Parentis" to the "Hook-Up" Culture

Through the 1960s, college campuses had strict rules and regulations, many specifically intended to limit sexual fraternizing between students. Most universities required females to live on campus until they were 21 years of age. Dorms were sex segregated, visitation was restricted, and there were strict curfews. At Barnard College, and many others, when a man visited a woman in her dorm room, the "three-foot rule" applied: three of their four feet had to be touching the floor at all times. Most colleges enforced dress codes that banned female students from wearing pants or shorts and males from wearing T-shirts and jeans (Anderson 2012). Essentially, colleges and universities did not treat students like adults, as would be an appropriate reflection of their chronological age; instead, these institutions operated *in loco parentis*, Latin for "in place of the parent."

These kinds of restrictions resulted in student activism in the 1960s, specifically materializing as the Free Speech Movement at the University of California–Berkeley in 1964 and spreading to campuses across the country the following semester. Part of the demands of the New Left student activism that emerged during this era included full civil rights for all citizens, equal opportunities, and personal liberties, including successfully challenging the rule of in loco parentis. Campus administrators responded by liberalizing or eliminating most of the oppressive rules and regulations (Anderson 2012).

College campuses are described as hook-up cultures, where coeds engage in sexual encounters with friends, acquaintances, or strangers, with no expectations of a commitment.
Source: istockphoto.com/abishome.

Today, college campuses are described as ***hook-up*** cultures, where coeds engage in sexual encounters with friends, acquaintances, or strangers, with no expectation of a commitment. A hook-up is, essentially, a sexual encounter with no strings attached. Research by sociologist Kathleen Bogle (2008) finds that the concept of hooking-up has been around since the 1980s, despite the fact that the terminology did not emerge until 2000. The emergence of a hook-up culture reflects college students' more liberal attitudes about sex and sexual behaviors, which are an outgrowth of the sexual revolution of the 1960s. College students no longer date in the traditional sense of the term. Instead, they have casual sexual encounters during their college and young adult years, with the intention of establishing long-term relationships in the future. The decline of traditional dating is due to a number of reasons, including the fact that people are marrying later and the fact that such a large percentage of young people spend their young adult years on a college campus (Bogle 2008).

In Bogle's research, she finds that as freshman, both males and females embrace hook-ups because they were uninterested in being "tied down" in a relationship. After freshman year, things begin to change. While men still enjoy hooking-up, women begin to want something more and hope their hook-ups can progress into a relationship (Bogle 2008). Men hold a lot of the power on a college campus because women outnumber men on most college campuses; thus, the status quo, a hook-up culture, remains.

SEX EDUCATION

In the first half of the twentieth century, the United States was considered the world leader in sex education; by the second half of the century, Scandinavia replaced the United States as the world leader, and the United States was engaged in international campaigns to restrict sex education (Zimmerman 2015). In the early twentieth century, organizations such as the American Federation for Sex Hygiene were dedicated to eradicating venereal disease and prostitution through education. From the beginning, it was thought by many that schools were the perfect institution for educating Americans about sex. However, this idea was and still is controversial. For many conservatives, the home is the best place to teach sex education. Others feel that schools are the appropriate institutions for teaching about sex education, especially since so many families will simply avoid teaching their children about sex education (Luker 2006). Despite this push, sex education varies tremendously across the country.

The controversy surrounding sex education today is between two broad approaches to teaching sex education: abstinence-only sex education and comprehensive sex education. Federally funded abstinence-only education emerged in the 1980s in the form of conservative state laws and policies. Abstinence-only education teaches young people not to have sex at all, at least not until they are married. They emphasize that abstinence is the only way to absolutely avoid pregnancy and sexually transmitted diseases. This approach does not mention safe sex, pregnancy prevention, or reproductive health. They emphasize that contraception can and does fail, that abortions leave lasting emotional scars on women, and that having sex can cause death (HIV/AIDS). Opponents find this fear-based approach problematic, while proponents laud it for its emphasis on sexual morality (Luker 2006). Sex education in schools has historically reflected the "twin assumptions that American teens are too innocent to know about sexuality and too sexual to be trusted with the information" (Pascoe 2007:29).

Abstinence-only education emerged in a socially conservative era, reflecting conservative religious values. However, this was also the era of the HIV/AIDS epidemic (see Chapter Ten). In 1987, Surgeon General C. Everett Koop advocated using education to fight HIV/AIDS. In his 1986 report on HIV/AIDS, he called on schools to start teaching about the disease as early as the third grade, which outraged conservatives. At the time, only three states and the District of Columbia mandated sex education; but by 1992, all but four required or recommended it (Zimmerman 2015). However, one in three American school districts was teaching abstinence-only sex education. In a national survey conducted in 1997, nearly two-thirds of the high school–aged girls said they learned about the topics of birth control, contraception, or preventing pregnancy from magazines (Sutton et al. 2002). Under President George W. Bush, the United States spent over a billion dollars promoting abstinence (Boonstra 2007).

Comprehensive sex educators believe that knowledge is power. If students have the knowledge and the right values, they can be counted on to make informed, healthy decisions about their sex lives, and thus, avoid sexually transmitted infections, teen pregnancy, and sexual violence. Comprehensive sex education teaches students about same-sex sexuality and masturbation; contraception, including abortion; and safe sex; but it also teaches that abstinence is an option for young people.

Despite the fact that surveys find that 93 percent of Americans support teaching sex education in high schools, and 84 percent feel it should start even younger, in middle school and junior high, only a minority of schools actually offer comprehensive sex education courses (Haffner and Wagoner 1999). Schools have not responded to these demands and instead, have accommodated conservatives in their opposition to sex education in schools, especially comprehensive sex education.

BOX 7.1

GLOBAL/TRANSNATIONAL PERSPECTIVES ON SEXUALITY: *AMERICAN SEX EDUCATION GOES GLOBAL*

The United States is known for its cultural exports: American films attract worldwide audiences. We also literally export American cultural values and ideologies through funded development programs and nongovernmental organizations. Perhaps surprisingly, sex education has been one of our exports, particularly "abstinence until marriage" education. This is not an accident. Western experts, through NGOs (nongovernmental organizations), have been influencing sex education programs throughout the developing world since the 1940s (Zimmerman 2015).

As part of President George W. Bush's campaign to fight HIV/AIDS in Africa, the President's Emergency Plan for AIDS Relief (PEPFAR), the United States provides funding to 22 nations to help them fight HIV/AIDS. As we explore in Chapter Ten, sub-Saharan Africa is the epicenter of the HIV/AIDS epidemic. However, this funding is linked to

a particular message known as the ABC approach—abstain, be faithful, and use condoms. No funds can be used to provide condoms; however, they can educate people about condom use, except for teens under the age of 15, who are prohibited from even receiving information about condoms (Boonstra 2007).

Not only is Africa the epicenter of the HIV/AIDS epidemic, but the great bulk of the people living with the disease are young people. Thus, sex education in schools is viewed as the best way to educate the population about HIV/AIDS. HIV/AIDS education is being included in science, history, economics, religion, and math classes in Botswana and Kenya, and throughout sub-Saharan Africa. But, echoing the moralism of American abstinence education programs, "whatever the subject, almost all such lessons ended with the same advice: abstinence, except in marriage" (Zimmerman 2015:121).

SEXUALITY AND THE WORKPLACE

Workplace culture differs from school culture in that there is no expectation that it be sexually neutral. While many employers may try to restrict sexual fraternizing between employees, or between management and employees, sexual relationships between coworkers are hardly unusual and "sexual bantering, flirting, and dating are commonplace at work" (Williams, Giuffre, and Dellinger 1999). While sociologists have paid more attention to sexual harassment in the workplace than to sexual consent, both are prevalent and will be discussed in this chapter. From there we explore the experiences of LGBTQ employees in the workplace, including discrimination against LGBTQ employees, the pink ceiling, and challenges associated with a gay-friendly workplace.

Heterosexual Relationships in the Workplace

As mentioned, sociologists have not paid much scholarly attention to employee relationships in the workplace. What research we do have finds that 15 percent of people report meeting their current sexual partner at work (Laumann et al. 1994). Most research focuses on heterosexual workplace relationships and neglects LGBTQ workplace relationships. Despite the commonality of workplace sexual relationships, many employers prohibit such fraternizing; and employers face no legal restrictions on their enforcement of prohibitions against fraternization between coworkers (Massengill and Peterson 1995). Women are more likely to be penalized for workplace sexual relationships because they are more likely to occupy a lower-level position in the organization. Thus, they are more vulnerable and are considered replaceable (Williams, Giuffre, and Dellinger 1999). Courts have not found this to amount to discrimination against the subordinate, female, employee.

Some businesses, such as family businesses, actually encourage the formation of sexual relationships. Colleges and universities, particularly those in rural areas, have found it beneficial to employ family members (Ferber and Loeb 1997). And certain industries, such as natural foods and high tech, are also more accepting of dating and fraternizing and therefore do not attempt to limit such fraternizing. Ultimately, most workplaces fall somewhere in the middle—accepting some types of relationships and limiting others (Williams et al. 1999).

Some work cultures are more highly sexualized—such as the restaurant industry and operating rooms. Employees argue that such sexual banter helps them deal with their stress; others argue that the sexualized culture benefits them financially in terms of tips (Giuffre 1997; Williams et al. 1999). Context matters; behaviors that will get you terminated in one context may be perfectly acceptable in another.

Sexual Harassment

One of the most common types of workplace discrimination is *sexual harassment*, a violation of Title VII of the Civil Rights Act of 1964 (see Chapter Four). Despite the fact that anyone can be a victim of sexual harassment, it is disproportionately experienced by female employees, with nearly half of all working women experiencing sexual harassment during the course of their working lives (Ilies et al. 2003). Women are especially likely to face sexual harassment in male-dominated work environments, such as the military, where between 65 and 79 percent of women experience harassment annually (Bastian, Lancaster, and Reist 1996; Buchanan et al. 2014). Workplace sexual harassment can result in decreased productivity, depression, and increased stress.

There are several key organizational characteristics that predict sexual harassment. The first refers to *organizational climate,* how individuals perceive their workplace; specifically, its policies, practices, and procedures (Parker et al. 2003). A positive organizational climate decreases rates of sexual harassment, and decreases retaliation against those who report harassment. A second organizational characteristic is *job gender context*, where the proportion of men significantly outnumbers women in an organization, which increases the risk of sexual harassment. Finally, *organizational tolerance of sexual harassment* (OTSH) is the third important factor in determining the extent of sexual harassment in an organization. The OTSH is high when victims of sexual harassment are punished for complaining, perpetrators are not punished for harassment, and complaints are not taken seriously (Buchanan et al. 2014; Hulin, Fitzgerald, and Dragow 1996). The Equal Employment Opportunity Commission has established guidelines for effective sexual harassment policies as a way to decrease OTSH and rates of sexual harassment overall.

LGBTQ Employment Experiences

LGBTQ employees do not have the same workplace protections that other protected groups do under Title VII of the Civil Rights Act. The Employment Non-Discrimination Act (ENDA) is legislation that has been introduced to address this as we explored in Chapter Four. LGBTQ employees often suffer from **tokenism**, meaning they generally account for fewer than fifteen percent of their work group and this heightened visibility results in their being subjected to stereotypes about their group (Kanter 1977). Much like schools, work settings also institutionalize heterosexuality. This happens in three ways: implementing policies that privilege nuclear family arrangements, permitting a climate that stifles discussion of LGBTQ relationships, and tolerating coworker interactions that stigmatize homosexuality (Hearn and Parkin 1987).

HOMOPHOBIA IN THE WORKPLACE Homophobic work environments can result in minority stress for LGBTQ employees; minority stress refers to the strain minorities experience resulting from oppression and the view that they are inferior (Brooks 1981; see Chapter Six). Meyer (1995) found that gay men suffered significant mental health issues due to minority stress in their workplace. Even after the NFL drafted its first openly gay player in 2015, LGBTQ employees generally remain closeted in corporate America, and there are very few openly gay chief executives in the 1,000 largest corporations (Miller, C. 2014). The barriers sexual minority employees face to executive offices and corporate boardrooms are referred to as a **pink ceiling**. This is despite the fact that 91 percent of Fortune 500 companies include sexual orientation in their nondiscrimination clause, proving that more than policies are needed.

Closeted employees report a range of negative outcomes in the workplace that can interfere with an LGBTQ employees' advancement, from avoiding certain clients and coworkers they may fear are homophobic, to skipping social events, and difficulty finding mentors (Miller, C. 2014). Due to the heteronormativity of most workplaces, LGBTQ employees feel uncomfortable bringing their same-sex partners to social events, displaying a photo of their loved one on their desk, or describing weekend plans to coworkers. A heteronormative climate means employees are assumed to be heterosexual. These are all workplace issues heterosexual employees do not have to concern themselves with.

Even more than their experiences with heteronormativity, LGBTQ employees deal with blatant discrimination due to their sexual orientation. The discrimination can take two forms: **homophobic behaviors** that include homophobic jokes, comments, and threats; and **prejudicial behaviors** that include unequal treatment and practices (Buddel 2011). Research finds that between 25 and 66 percent of LGB individuals have experienced workplace discrimination in the United States, from ostracism to termination, limited career mobility, and even violence (Beatty and Kirby 2006). Sometimes the discrimination occurs in the hiring process. Research finds that 90 percent of respondents at a baked goods company in the Southwestern United States said they would not hire anyone they thought was homosexual and would be unlikely to promote someone who was gay or lesbian (Embrick, Walther, and Wickens 2007).

COMING OUT AT WORK While most LGBTQ individuals come out during their school-age years, coming out is a process, not an event. Thus, it occurs numerous times throughout the course of one's life, including in the workplace. Many LGBTQ individuals opt to pass as heterosexual at their jobs in order to avoid facing discrimination and harassment (Buddel 2011). Remaining closeted results in significant stress for LGBTQ employees.

Researchers have identified a scale to measure workplace identity management strategies LGBTQ employees engage in. As this scale shows, identity management in the workplace is more complicated than just whether or not someone is "closeted" or "out." A person can *pass* as heterosexual, which involves managing one's identity in order to appear heterosexual, or be *explicitly out*, which involves openly identifying as gay or lesbian. But they can also engage in *covering*, which is when they censor information that would imply they are gay or lesbian. Finally, they may also be *implicitly out*, which involves being honest about one's life without applying gay, lesbian, or bisexual labels (Anderson et al. 2001; Buddel 2011; Griffin 1992).

> " *We are bearable as long as we 'cover' and do not 'flaunt' ourselves. Taboo behaviors include placing pictures of our loved one on our desk, and mentioning our same-gender companion in conversations"* (Hill 2009: 38–39).

Disclosing one's sexuality in a safe workplace can provide some benefits. For instance, LGBTQ employees may experience supervisor support, coworker support, and organizational support upon coming out—all of which contributes to increased career satisfaction for LGBTQ employees. Research has found that out employee satisfaction was 50 percent higher than for those who are closeted at work. This difference can be explained by the amount of time, effort, and energy closeted persons put into keeping their secret; all of that is time, effort, and energy they are not able to put into their work. Being closeted also inhibits employees' ability to bond with and build personal networks with professional colleagues.

CHALLENGES OF A GAY-FRIENDLY WORKPLACE While many workplaces are hostile toward LGBTQ employees and potential employees, a relatively new type of work environment has emerged. The *gay-friendly workplace* is defined as a work setting that attempts to eradicate homophobia and heterosexism by going beyond a mere tolerance of LGBTQ workers to an acceptance and welcoming of them (Giuffre, Dellinger, and Williams 2008). The entertainment, fashion, advertising, retail sales, and hospitality industries are broadly considered to be gay-friendly. Some use the term gay-friendly workplace to describe organizations that are gay-owned and/or serve the LGBTQ community; others use the term to signify that their predominantly heterosexual coworkers do not discriminate against them due to their sexuality. In order to qualify as a gay-friendly workplace, it takes more than gay-friendly policies. Research has found that gay men working in organizations with gay-friendly policies describe facing discrimination and hostility when they disclose their sexuality to their supervisor (Tejeda 2006). While research finds that LGBTQ employees are grateful to work in a gay-friendly environment where they can be comfortably "out," they also describe differential treatment based on their sexuality including stereotyping, sexual harassment, and gender discrimination (Giuffre et al. 2008).

One of the stereotypes LGBTQ employees face even in a gay-friendly workplace involves the stereotypes surrounding the presumed hypersexualization and promiscuity of sexual minorities. This translates into coworkers asking inappropriate questions about LGBTQ employees' sex lives or family arrangements, things they would be unlikely to ask of their straight and cisgender colleagues. As a way to combat stereotypes about LGBTQ people, some employees intentionally restrain their behavior at work in order to avoid fueling such stereotypes. For instance, gay men sometimes report that they intentionally avoid acting "campy" at work.

A second type of discrimination LGBTQ employees face specifically in gay-friendly workplaces involves specific forms of sexual harassment. Examples include sexual comments pertaining to "conversion" from heterosexual clients or coworkers and unprofessional conduct from coworkers specifically directed at the LGBTQ employee because they are LGBTQ (Giuffre et al. 2008). Straight people may be sexually harassed in the workplace, of course, but the type of discrimination we are speaking of here is specific to the fact that some workers are LGBTQ. For instance, a lesbian employee may be asked by a female coworker if she is interested in threesomes, something the coworker is unlikely to randomly ask of a heterosexual colleague. Some research finds that lesbians face unwanted sexual advances from their heterosexual male colleagues who insist that their attraction to women is a result of their not having had a sexual experience with a "real" man (Dunne 1997). Such discrimination limits LGBTQ workers' full incorporation into the workplace.

A final type of discrimination faced by LGBTQ employees in a gay-friendly environment is gender discrimination directed at them because of their sexuality. This type of gender discrimination is based on the stereotype that gay men and lesbians are gender nonconforming; that lesbians are masculine, and gay men are feminine (Giuffre et al. 2008). One woman explained that because she was a lesbian, her male coworkers made sexual remarks about other women, assuming she would be on board with such sexual objectification of women. Unlike a heterosexual woman in the workplace, this person did not feel like the remarks were directed at her, but instead that she was expected to go along with them (Giuffre et al. 2008).

CONCLUSION

Despite significant progress for LGBTQ rights over the last 30 years, schools still remain hostile places for lesbian, gay, bisexual, transgender, and queer youth. They experience verbal harassment and bullying, physical threats and assault, and are too often not protected from such violence. Many schools are working to become safe spaces for LGBTQ students, through establishing gay high schools and gay student organizations, implementing more inclusive curriculum, and adopting antibullying policies that prohibit discrimination and provide victims recourse against perpetrators. While all of these developments signal progress, they are not enough. Schools need to challenge institutionalized heterosexuality in order to truly become safe spaces for all students.

In many ways, colleges and universities have led the way in creating safe campuses for LGBTQ students. The first gay student organizations were established on college campuses; many offer courses in LGBT studies, queer theory, and/or sexuality studies; some are making changes to accommodate transgender students such as allowing students to choose their preferred pronouns and choose how their names will appear on course rosters; and women's colleges have faced some of the most significant challenges adjusting to the presence of transgender men on their campuses, responding in a wide variety of ways.

Importantly, schools are also workplaces employing administrators, teachers, and staff, some of whom are LGBTQ. Research finds that the risk that LGBTQ teachers will encounter the glass closet, being outed against their will, increases if they are gender-nonconforming. Also, the sexually neutral climate of schools implies that they should not be out. Many of the changes that are made to help create a safe space for LGBTQ students also benefit LGBTQ administrators, teachers, and staff.

The perception of schools as conservative institutions has also influenced our approach to sex education, which is still overwhelmingly focused on abstinence. Even in the face of the HIV/AIDS epidemic and the popularity of comprehensive sex education, schools remain overwhelmingly committed to abstinence-only education. We even export it to developing nations of the world as part of funding for HIV/AIDS prevention development projects.

The workplace is not a sexually neutral institution in the same way that schools are. There is plenty of flirting and dating that goes on between coworkers, which results in approximately 15 percent of people marrying someone they meet at work. However, many employers attempt to restrict sexual fraternizing between employees, or between subordinates and superordinates. One of the most common forms of discrimination in the workplace is sexual harassment, and women are the most jeopardized by this illegal practice. LGBTQ people experience discrimination and homophobia, including the pink ceiling, in the workplace—and most cannot count on legal protection from such discrimination. Finally, there has been an emergence of a new type of workplace, the gay-friendly workplace, in which LGBTQ people may feel more comfortable, but in which they also experience specific kinds of discrimination related to the fact that they are LGBTQ.

Key Terms and Concepts

Bullying 140
Campus climate 149
Covering 157
Cyberbullying 140
Explicitly out 157
Gay-friendly workplace 157
Glass closet 151
Heterosexualizing
  process 148

Hidden curriculum 143
Homophobic
  behaviors 156
Hook-up 153
Hormone blockers 141
Hypersexualization 151
Implicitly out 157
Informal sexuality
  curriculum 143

In loco parentis 152
Nonbinary 150
No promo homo laws 147
Pass 157
Pink ceiling 156
Prejudicial behaviors 156
Sexual harassment 155
Tokenism 156

Critical Thinking Questions

1. To what extent does the research on hook-up culture on college campuses reflect your experiences? Is hook-up culture gendered?

2. Compare the sex education you received to the types of sex education discussed in the text. Would you describe your sex education as "comprehensive"? Was anything missing?

3. Explain the various solutions to the inclusion of transgender students at women's colleges. Which of these seem the most appropriate and why? Can you think of any other solution to the dilemma of inclusion these institutions are facing? Can you think of any similar examples in history?

4. Explain the various ways workplaces are sexualized environments. In these sexualized environments, what groups of people can be considered privileged and what groups of people can be considered disadvantaged, based on the research presented in this chapter?

5. Identify the benefits LGBTQ employees experience by coming out at work. What are some disadvantages they face by coming out? How is the coming out process evidence of heterosexual privilege? Compare coming out in school to coming out at work. What might be some advantages and disadvantages provided by each environment?

Activities

1. Find out more about LGBTQ rights on your college campus. Are sexual minorities and gender-nonconforming people protected in your institution's anti-discrimination clause? If so, how long has this been the case? If not, have there been attempts to make this happen? Talk to three professors about this—do they think this is an issue they should be concerned with? Why? Is there a gay student organization on campus? Are there campus activities focused on LGBTQ people and their issues?

2. Find out more about LGBTQ rights at your workplace (if you do not have a job, use your parent's employer or a major employer in your city). Are sexual minorities and gender-nonconforming people protected in their antidiscrimination clause? Peruse their website—do they highlight the importance of diversity? If so, do they include sexual and gender diversity in this discussion?

3. Go to your college or university Human Resources Department webpage and read over the sexual harassment policies listed. Give examples of what constitutes sexual harassment at your institution. Ask one of your professors about any sexual harassment training he or she may have been required to attend.

Essential Readings

Biegel, Stuart. 2010. *The Right to Be Out: Sexual Orientation and Gender Identity in America's Public Schools*. Minneapolis, MN: University of Minnesota Press.

Bogle, Kathleen. 2008. *Hooking Up: Sex, Dating, and Relationships on Campus*. New York University Press.

Connell, Catherine. 2015. *School's Out: Gay and Lesbian Teachers in the Classroom*. Berkeley, CA: University of California Press.

Luker, Kristin. 2006. *When Sex Goes to School: Warring Views on Sex—and Sex Education—Since the Sixties*. New York: W.W. Norton & Company.

Miceli, Melinda. 2005. *Standing Out, Standing Together: The Social and Political Impact of Gay-Straight Alliances*. New York: Routledge.

Snyder, C. 1995. *The Lavender Road to Success: The Career Guide for the Gay Community*. Berkeley, CA: Ten Speed Press.

Recommended Films

It's Elementary: Talking about Gay Issues in School (1996). Debra Chasnoff, Director, and Helen S. Cohen, Producer. This documentary addresses antigay prejudice by providing adults with lessons on how to talk to children about LGBTQ people. Shot in first- through eighth-grade classrooms across the United States, the film argues that antigay prejudice and violence can be prevented if children have the opportunity to learn these things when they are young.

The Education of Shelby Knox (2005). Marion Lipschutz and Rose Rosenblatt, Directors. Documentary tells the story of Shelby Knox, a Southern Baptist teenager who joined a campaign for comprehensive sex education in Lubbock, TX. Lubbock is a city with some of the highest teen pregnancy and STD rates in the country, yet the solution to these problems was abstinence-only education.

Philadelphia (1993). Jonathan Demme, Director. This Hollywood film stars Tom Hanks as a gay attorney, who is fired when the partners at his powerful Philadelphia law firm discover he is HIV+. He sued the firm for discrimination.

Suggested Multimedia

Beyond Tolerance: A Resource Guide for Addressing LGBTQI Issues in Schools This resource guide is designed to help students and educators address homophobia, transphobia, and heteronormativity in schools. http://www.nycore.org/wp-content/uploads/Beyond%20 Tolerance.pdf

It Gets Better Campaign Beginning in 2010, this campaign is intended to help young LGBTQ people see that there is hope, and to help inspire them to make the changes necessary to make the world a better place. This has become a worldwide movement with over 50,000 user-created videos that have been viewed over 50 million times. The website also contains a timeline showing how things have become better for LGBTQ people since this project began in 2010. http://www.itgetsbetter.org/pages/about-it-gets-better-project/

Gay-Straight Alliance Network GSA Network was founded in 1998 to help establish gay-straight alliances in schools across the country. It has expanded to become a social justice organization that trains youth in leadership development, so they can go on to work to create safer schools and communities. https://gsanetwork.org/

GLSEN has over 35 chapters in local communities and a national network of activists and resources for educators and students. https://www.glsen.org.

8

RELIGION, FAMILY, AND SEXUALITY

LEARNING OBJECTIVES

Upon completion of this chapter, students will be able to . . .

- Understand the social role of religion in shaping views on sex, gender, and sexuality

- Analyze Christian, Jewish, and Muslim beliefs on women's sexuality, homosexuality, and transgender identities and their impact

- Describe religious feminist and LGBTQ reformist views and interpretations

- Define gay families and explain why their emergence has caused some to perceive them as a social problem

- Understand the historical and current discrimination LGBTQ families face

- Explain the opposition to gay parenting and identify the primary critiques of those arguments

- Identify specific issues LGBTQ victims of intimate partner violence face

n 2009, Uganda passed a law known formally as the Uganda Anti-Homosexuality Act and more popularly known in the Western press as the "Kill the Gays" bill since the original version included a death penalty clause (the version of the bill that passed substituted life in prison instead of the death penalty). Laws against homosexuality have existed in Uganda since the British colonial era. The laws were originally designed to punish locals who engaged in "unnatural sex," since at the time some Ugandan warriors took boys as brides, a practice similar to what existed in Ancient Greece. While hostility toward homosexuality is found throughout Africa, U.S. evangelical Christian leaders who were in Uganda as part of the Family Life Network conference were influential in the development of the 2009 Anti-Homosexuality Act. The evangelicals led a seminar on the "homosexual agenda" in which they argued that homosexuals were a threat to the African family, specifically, a threat to children, marriage, and society. Some of the information presented included research by Paul Cameron that claimed gays were more likely to molest children; research that has been soundly refuted as faulty science. In fact, due to Cameron's sloppy science, he has since been expelled from the American Psychological Association and the American Sociological Association.

One of the speakers, Don Schmierer, was a board member of Exodus International, an organization that claims to be able to cure people of homosexuality through the power of Jesus Christ. Another speaker, Scott Lively, author of books opposing homosexuality, met with Ugandan government officials to promote his pro-family and antigay agenda directly (Gettleman 2010). While the evangelical leaders who inspired this bill later distanced themselves from it due to the extreme punishments associated with it, these evangelicals have a history of missionary work in Africa and have been criticized for their influence on public policy: "Human rights advocates in Uganda say the visit by the three Americans helped set in motion what could be a very dangerous cycle. Gay Ugandans already describe a world of beatings, blackmail, death threats like 'Die Sodomite!' scrawled on their homes, constant harassment, and even so-called correctional rape" (Gettleman 2010).

Religion plays a very important role in shaping ideas about gender, sex, and family values. Much of the homophobia and discrimination faced by LGBTQ people emerges out of beliefs associated with organized religion. Religious opposition to homosexuality is broad, but almost always comes back to the idea that homosexuality is unnatural and a threat to the family. Thus, this chapter will explore the intersection of sexuality with two fundamental societal institutions, religion and the family. We begin with some current examples of the ongoing discrimination faced by LGBTQ people within religious institutions and the family:

- The *New York Times* printed the first same-sex wedding announcements on May 23, 2004, after Massachusetts became the first state to recognize gay marriage.
- In June 2013, Pope Francis asked, "Who am I to judge gay people?" This was viewed as a breakthrough for a church that condemns homosexuality. However, since that statement Pope Francis has not changed church doctrine that declares homosexuality sinful (Gallagher and Burke 2016).
- In 2015, President Obama announced support for a national ban on gay conversion therapies that have been promoted through Christian ministries since the 1980s, which argue homosexuality is a curable disease (Merritt 2015).
- In 2015, seven members of Women's Ordination Worldwide (WOW), a Catholic organization working toward the ordination of female priests, were arrested while protesting the ban on women priesthood in the Catholic Church (Mosendz 2015).
- The Supreme Court ruled in favor of a lesbian mother who had been denied adoption rights by the state of Alabama. The mother had been the child's legal adoptive mother in her former state of Georgia, but when she moved to Alabama, she found her parental rights denied her (Farias 2016).
- In March 2016, a federal judge struck down Mississippi's prohibition on adoption by gay couples, the last law in the country to ban same-sex couples from adopting.

RELIGION AND SEXUALITY

The first half of this chapter examines the intersection of sexuality and religion. Contemporary sociological analyses of religion are not necessarily about theological belief systems; instead, the primary focus is on religious traditions, attitudes, and behaviors and their role in constructing society. As you already learned in previous chapters, gender, sexuality, and sexual desires are shaped by particular social and cultural contexts. Religion plays a significant role in shaping attitudes about sex and sexuality. In fact, sex, gender, and sexuality have always been and still remain central topics in all of the western religions.

In the following sections, we will specifically examine the traditions, attitudes, and behaviors toward women's sexuality and LGBTQ sexualities and identities in the three major Abrahamic religious traditions: Christianity, Judaism, and Islam, as practiced in the United States. The Abrahamic religions all come from the same belief that the Hebrew patriarch Abraham, and his descendants, played a key role in the development of each tradition. Each of these traditions is complex and multidimensional. There is not one single definitive view on sexuality in any of these traditions. Questions arise when religious doctrine resists changes in society; sometimes a clash occurs between those who wish to maintain older traditions and those who want to embrace new ones. Some of the major questions being asked by all three religions are whether forbidden sexual relationships are still important, whether the sexual and spiritual experience is connected, if the relationship between sexuality and reproduction is as relevant as it used to be, and whether new traditions need to be reformed to adhere to modern issues, such as the rights of gender-nonconforming and transgender people.

Christianity

Christianity is a religion centralized around the life, death, and resurrection of Jesus, who was a Jew that lived around the first-century CE in ancient Israel. The primary belief is that Jesus is the Son of God who came to earth, lived, and died to save humanity from their sins. The primary Christian text is the Bible, which is comprised of two primary parts, the Old Testament and the

---

FIGURE 8.1 ■ LGBTQ Perceptions of Gay-Friendliness of Religious Organizations

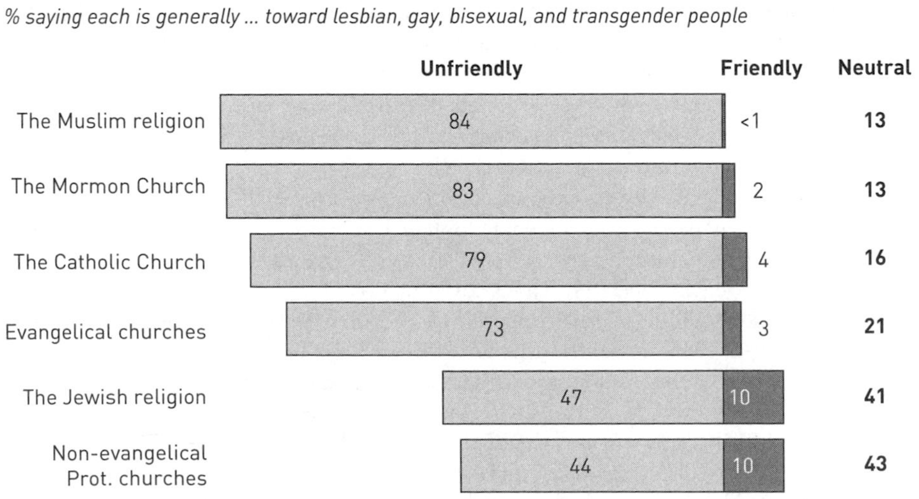

% saying each is generally … toward lesbian, gay, bisexual, and transgender people

	Unfriendly	Friendly	Neutral
The Muslim religion	84	<1	13
The Mormon Church	83	2	13
The Catholic Church	79	4	16
Evangelical churches	73	3	21
The Jewish religion	47	10	41
Non-evangelical Prot. churches	44	10	43

Source: "A Survey of LGBT Americans." 2013. Pew Research Center. http://www.pewsocialtrends.org/files/2013/06/SDT_LGBT-Americans_06-2013.pdf.

Notes: Based on all LGBT (N=1,197). Those who didn't answer not shown.

New Testament. The Old Testament includes the five books of the Jewish Torah and other ancient Israelite writings. The New Testament tells the story of Jesus and was written nearly one hundred years after his death. There are many disagreements over interpretations of the Bible leading to many different Christian denominations; the two primary denominations are Catholicism and Protestantism.

Catholics continue to uphold the tenants of the historical Church of Rome headed by the Pope. Distinctive Catholic practices include devotion to the saints, use of the rosary, practice of confession, and a belief in Purgatory. Protestants reject many practices and beliefs of Catholics and emphasize the importance of reading the Bible and salvation through the faith of the individual. The United States has the largest population of Christians in the world. According to Pew Research Center (2014) 70.6 percent of the population identified as being Christian with 46.5 percent identifying as Protestant and 20.8 percent as Catholic. Christianity plays an immensely important role in shaping cultural ideas about gender, sex, and sexuality.

Pope Francis surprised many when he announced in 2016 that Christians should apologize to gays and lesbians who have been discriminated against by the church.

Source: Franco Origlia/Getty Images News/Getty Images.

CHRISTIANITY, SEX, AND GENDER Traditional Christian ideologies are gendered. The God-language used in the Bible is masculine, and the majority of biblical stories are by and about men. Christianity is traditionally aversive toward feminism and promotes patriarchal family values, in which the father is the head of household and leader in all family and religious matters. Many passages in the Bible suggest *protective paternalism*, or the idea that it is men's spiritually ordained duty to protect women. Women are portrayed as the weaker sex in need of guidance and protection.

Complementary gender roles, or the belief that men and women have God-ordained different, but complementary, roles in religion, family, marriage, and society are practiced by many Christians. For women, virginity, marriage, and motherhood are highly emphasized. The Virgin Mary is one of the only female symbols in the church. She represents a biologically unattainable reality for women, being simultaneously a virgin and a mother, but is nevertheless held as a role model for women. Women cannot be ordained as Catholic priests or hold positions of leadership in the Catholic Church; and, among fundamentalist Protestants, women are taught to be submissive to their husbands. The exclusion of female clerics and the discrimination against women is described by scholars as *misogyny*, or the contempt or prejudice against women (Alioto and McHale 2014). In recent decades, as gender roles in society changed bringing women out of the private sector and into the public sector, many Christian movements sprung up to enforce complementary gender role segregation and revive "traditional family values." For example, starting in the early 1990s, the nation-wide Christian, evangelical group, The Promise Keepers, sought to affirm essentialist gender roles and to reclaim male authority in the home. A male-exclusive revival movement, it promoted a masculine spirituality in which men are taught how to be leaders in the home and that their wives should submit to their leadership.

In regard to sex and sexuality, the Catholic Church is full of restrictive teachings for both sexes; but due to women's position as the weaker sex, women's sexuality is even more restricted. Catholics believe it is sinful and morally wrong to engage in premarital sex, extramarital sex, and masturbation; and use of birth control, abortion, sterilization, assisted reproductive technologies, and any sexual intimacy other than heterosexual sex. ***Celibacy,*** or abstaining from marriage and sexual relations, is required of all priests and clergy. Sex within marriage is considered legitimate only when the primary function is procreation. The body itself is viewed as a vessel of flesh that is gendered and sexed; for males it is in a constant state of sexual lust, and for females it is a source of temptation for male lust, both to be controlled and managed at all times. Research shows that while these ideas on sexuality are still fundamental tenants of the Catholic belief system, most Catholics do not adhere to most of these restrictions (Cavendish 2003).

A purity ring symbolizing "True Love Waits," a purity movement that promotes abstinence before marriage.
Source: AP Photo/Daniel Miller.

Protestant views on sex vary greatly. Right-wing, evangelical Christians tend to be more fundamentalist in their beliefs about sex and restrict sexuality in much the same way as Catholics. The ***sexual purity movement*** is an evangelical movement that promotes abstinence for young Christians. Active since the 1990s, two of the most popular sexual purity movements today are True Love Waits, a Bible study program to help students understand their sexuality in light of the gospel, and Silver Ring Thing, a virginity pledge program. Sara Moslener, in *Virgin Nation: Sexual Purity and American Adolescence* (2015a), claims sex purity movements are not about promoting a biblical view of sexuality, but rather explaining and coping with the cultural crises of changing gender roles and sexual norms. She demonstrates how the social moments in which these movements emerge are also times when conservative evangelicals are trying to exert political power. When asked what was the most important message of her book, Moslener says, "Sexual purity isn't about what Abby and Brendan do on a Friday night, it's about constructing a view of the United States as a nation in distress and claiming that evangelical Christianity can not only best explain the crisis, but save us from our demise" (Moslener 2015b).

Reformist, liberal Christians tend to view sex as a positive and healthy aspect of human life. Protestants often grapple with the question of whether sex is inextricably linked to reproduction. While for Catholics, it is the only permissible correlative. Christian ***feminist theology*** is the study of God that seeks to reinterpret the Bible to include a female perspective and a focus on reclaiming women's roles in Christian history. Their goal is not only to critique Christianity for its oppression against women but to revise Christianity to be more gender egalitarian. Many feminist theologians seek to reclaim women's sexuality in a way that is healthy and empowering while still remaining situated in Christian principles.

CHRISTIAN VIEWS ON HOMOSEXUALITY The morality of homosexuality continues to be a heated debate for many Christians. The Catholic Church opposes same-sex relationships because they do not fulfill the procreative purpose of sex (Cavendish 2003). Catholics believe procreation is the essential aspect of human sexuality, so every sexual act must be open to it as a possibility. For this reason, Christianity has traditionally forbidden ***sodomy,*** sexual intercourse involving anal or oral copulation, and often parallels it with homosexuality. Official Catholic teachings suggest individuals with same-sex attractions live a life of chastity and sexual abstinence. Despite this intolerance, paradoxically, the Catholic Church teaches that LGBTQ individuals deserve respect, compassion, and understanding from all Christians. In a groundbreaking moment in 2016, Pope Francis announced all Christians should apologize to gays who have been offended or discriminated against by the church (Gallagher and Burke 2016). Mixed messages abound on this topic.

Protestant views vary. Liberal, reformist Christians view homosexuality as biologically natural and thereby not a sin, since sin is viewed as something humans choose. Right-wing, evangelical Protestant Christians believe God designed human beings to be heterosexual and it is a sin to be homosexual. They view homosexuality as a personal choice, a lifestyle, or even a sickness that must be healed or cured in an individual. Transformational Christian ministries, such as Living Hope Ministry, seek to "heal" same-sex attractions. Living Hope claims pastoral counseling, mentoring, support groups, and training on how to create a more intimate relationship with Jesus Christ will create sexual expression and desire for monogamous heterosexuality (Living Hope Ministries 2016). Christian homophobia varies by region. In *Pray the Gay Away* (2012), Bernadette Barton argues the Bible belt, a term usually used to describe conservative Christian states like Arkansas, Mississippi, Tennessee, and North Carolina, lags behind more progressive areas in the United States on acceptance of LGBTQ individuals. Barton describes how Christian institutions in these regions contribute to passive and active homophobia.

Many right-wing positions on homosexuality point to biblical passages as evidence God is opposed to it. Contemporary Biblical scholars argue the specific historical and cultural contexts in which supposedly restrictive passages were written are not only difficult to interpret, but outdated according to how same-sex relations are understood in today's context. Historian John Boswell argues many passages taken today as condemnations of homosexuality can be translated as condemnations of prostitution, and passages in which same-sex acts are described as unnatural or immoral can be translated as "out of the ordinary" (Boswell 2005).

IMPACT OF RELIGIOUS CONDEMNATION ON LGBTQ PEOPLE The impact of religious condemnation is immense. Some LGBTQ individuals who have been openly rejected by their religion and taught that God, the ultimate source of truth and love, does not approve of their sexuality become severely depressed and even suicidal. When the family of origin rejects LGBTQ youth for religious condemnation or homophobic reasons, there is a significantly higher likelihood of depression and suicide (Ryan et al. 2009). Suicide is the second leading cause of death for youth in the United States between the ages of 15 and 34, according to the Centers for Disease Control and Prevention (2014). Lesbian, gay, and bisexual youth are four times more likely to attempt suicide than their heterosexual peers (Russell 2003). And while more research is still needed, some reports show nearly half of all transgender individuals attempt suicide at some point in their lives (Grossman and D'Augelli 2007).

Some LGBTQ individuals develop what is called ***internalized homophobia***, which is when they adopt and internalize the homophobic attitudes about lesbian, gay, bisexual, or transgender people perpetuated in mainstream society. It is sometimes referred to as self-hatred as a result of being socially stigmatized (Lock 1998). Researchers say it can correlate with a number of psychological and medical outcomes, including depression, shame, substance abuse, and dangerous sexual behaviors. One of the most damaging impacts of internalized homophobia is ***horizontal oppression***, or when an LGBTQ person discriminates against other LGBTQ people. Sometimes this can manifest when deeply closeted politicians or religious leaders, who have significant impact on influencing the views of large groups of people, discriminate against the LGBTQ community.

For example, Ted Haggard, the former pastor of the 14,000-member New Life Church, one of President George W. Bush's advisors on evangelical issues, and president of the 30-million member National Association of Evangelicals that represents more than 45,000 evangelical churches across the United States, openly and publicly condemned homosexuality and opposed gay rights for most of his career. In 2006, he resigned from all positions when a former prostitute, Mike Jones, said the pastor had paid him for sex over a three-year time period. After publicly denying these allegations, later Haggard admitted to having gay sex after unsuccessful attempts to change his orientation through counseling (Merritt 2015). This is one of many examples in the media of powerful people who internalized homophobia and displayed horizontal oppression.

LGBTQ CHRISTIANS The emergence of the gay liberation movement in the 1970s brought about many challenges and divergent movements within Christianity. Some gay and lesbian Christian believers insist on the compatibility between spirituality and homosexuality. Others reject the church entirely based on its views of homosexuality. Those who believe the basic tenants of Christian faith are inclusive and accepting of all people, no matter their race, gender, or sexual orientation, seek to reform the church from within. *Liberation theologies* are comprised of activists who employ religious beliefs and sacred texts to focus on social justice issues and work toward greater equality.

Gay and lesbian theologies, which place the gay and lesbian experience at the center of the theological process, arose in the 1970s in response to discrimination (Stuart 2003). They claim a person's sexuality can be a starting place for a relationship with God. This position assumes sexual identity is a stable place where knowledge can be created (Stuart 2003). Gay and lesbian theologians differ in their beliefs on how sexual identity is formed, whether it is biological or socially constructed; but they argue it is a stable enough place to build the study of God. While some find empowerment from this approach, it is criticized for being essentialist because experiences among individuals vary so greatly.

The Metropolitan Community Church (MCC) first began in Los Angeles in 1968 and has since launched into an international movement of churches known as the Universal Fellowship of Metropolitan Community Churches (UFMCC). It is a Protestant Christian movement started by gay activist and human rights advocate, Reverend Troy Perry. UFMCC views its Christian mission as seeking social justice for LGBTQ people. UFMCC has been a leading force in the development of *queer theology*, or the study of God that destabilizes all sex, gender, and sexual orientation categories. Queer theology questions whether gender and sexual orientation are categories by which humans should identify or be defined by in the Christian community. Queer theology questions whether the family unit is the best site for Christian practice and commitment, as is traditionally assumed. Finally, queer theology claims sex is an act of unity, no matter orientation or gender; and unity is a spiritual Christian principle (Rudy 1998).

Other LGBTQ Christian reformists seek to be incorporated equally into existing theologies. Dignity USA is a gay and lesbian Catholic movement founded in 1969. With local chapters across the United States, it works toward increasing respect and justice for LGBTQ individuals within the Catholic Church.

A similar organization, the Catholic Association for Lesbian and Gay Ministry seeks to affirm and provide inclusive pastoral care and ministry to LGBTQ individuals and their families. It encourages the participation of lesbian and gay Catholics within the Church and communicates and serves as a model to other Catholic organizations in order to create openness and change on the current confusion about and discrimination against LGBTQ people. The Black Lives Matter movement has a spiritual philosophy rooted in Christian foundations, but dismissive of centralized, male-dominant leadership. Black Lives Matter openly accepts LGBTQ people on the front lines of the movement. Rooted in *black liberation theology,* or the spiritual philosophy that Christianity is a tool of empowerment for the oppressed, the intersection of LGBTQ and black civil rights issues are of central focus in this movement.

Some LGBTQ Christians use art to express their desires for reform. Christian artist Douglas Blanchard and author Kittredge

> " Dignity USA made a public statement challenging the Catholic position on homosexuality saying, "We believe that gay, lesbian, bisexual and transgender Catholics in our diversity are members of Christ's mystical body, numbered among the People of God. We have an inherent dignity because God created us, Christ died for us, and the Holy Spirit sanctified us in Baptism, making us temples of the Spirit, and channels through which God's love becomes visible. Because of this, it is our right, our privilege, and our duty to live the sacramental life of the Church, so that we might become more powerful instruments of God's love working among all people" (Dignity USA 2016).

Cherry created an illustrated story of a young, gay Jesus in a modern city in *The Passion of Christ: A Gay Vision* (2014). The book takes the story of Jesus' life and re-envisions it with Christ as queer and his persecutors as fundamentalists. It is profound because it insists Jesus does not belong to one particular group of people, such as heterosexuals, or any particular time period. Instead of Christian values being used as a justification for LGBTQ discrimination, this book suggests the Christian principles of solidarity and compassion be embraced as part of the larger movement toward greater equality.

SAME-SEX MARRIAGE AND THE CHURCH In the Catholic Church, marriage is considered a holy sacred union between a man and a woman; as a sacramental duty and a rite of passage (Grove 2011). Marriage is a term often used to describe the spiritual union between the soul of a Christian, the "bride," and Jesus Christ, the "bridegroom." The human family is viewed as an extension of this marriage. In 2015, when the *Obergefell v. Hodges* Supreme Court case ruled in favor of same-sex marriage in the United States, Catholic churches were officially opposed. The Catholic Church refuses to authorize religious wedding ceremonies for same-sex couples.

Protestants are torn on their position on same-sex marriage. Some Protestant churches openly endorsed same-sex marriage before it was legal, while others adamantly opposed it both before and after the Supreme Court ruling. For example, the Unitarian Universalist congregations and clergy have recognized and celebrated same-sex marriages since the 1970s. Whereas the Episcopal Church approved gay marriages only in 2015; but clergy can still decline to officiate, and a bishop still has the authority to forbid his clergy from officiating gay marriages (Conger 2015). Churches that take supportive stands on LGBTQ issues and celebrate same-sex weddings are sometimes called "welcoming churches" or "affirming churches." There are still many Protestant churches, such as the Church of Jesus Christ of Latter-day Saints and the Southern Baptist Convention, that refuse to officiate or recognize same-sex marriage.

TRANSGENDER AND CHRISTIANITY Conservative, evangelical Christians openly reject transgender individuals. Most evangelicals believe sex and gender are the same thing and do not understand the complexity of transgender identity (Green 2015). And, further, when evangelicals refer to their church communities for education about transgender issues, it is biased against transgender identity, perpetuating confusion and even transphobia. While some religious organizations are content to teach and promote their beliefs about sex and gender to their congregations only, others attempt to mold civil law to reflect their beliefs. A political debate over the "Bathroom Bills" that erupted in 2016 brought many Christian viewpoints on transgender issues to light in the United States. Some states began to question the legality of bathroom access for transgender and gender-nonconforming individuals in public life. As mentioned in Chapter Seven, in March 2016, the Republican-controlled North Carolina general assembly passed House Bill 2, or the *Public Facilities Privacy and Security Act*, a law that requires transgender people to use bathrooms based on their sex at birth rather than their gender identity. North Carolina legislators claim it is protecting people who feel their privacy is violated, and they claim it protects girls and women from potential sexual predators.

In response, in May 2016, the Obama administration issued over 100,000 letters to U.S. public schools offering guidance and direction on transgender federal rights and specifically on their right to use public restrooms matching their gender identity. The U.S. Justice Department and the state of North Carolina issued dueling lawsuits over the issue, with the Justice Department arguing the North Carolina bill was a violation of civil rights. LGBTQ activist groups across the country openly protested the bill. The nationwide chain Target publicly announced it would allow transgender employees and customers to choose the bathroom that corresponds with their gender identities.

Despite opposition, evangelical Christian supporters from all over the country openly and publicly defend North Carolina's bill. President of the Billy Graham Evangelistic Association and of the Christian international relief organization Samaritan's Purse Franklin

Graham said, "The fact is, gender identity isn't something we choose or feel. We are the sex God created us to be—male or female. How a person feels doesn't change the facts" (Hallowell 2016). This perspective challenges the medical, psychological, and sociological understanding of transgender people and issues.

On the other hand, some Christians, like the United Church of Christ and the Unitarian Universalists, have issued specific statements of inclusion of transgender individuals both as church members and in ordination. Overall, there is not a unified Christian stance on transgender equality.

Judaism

Judaism is one of the oldest religious traditions, dating to nearly 1000 BCE in ancient Israel. The core belief is of a covenantal relationship between God and the children of Israel, or Jews. The sacred foundational text is the *Torah*, which is comprised of the same first five chapters as the Christian Bible. A key supplemental text is a collection of oral teachings and laws called the *Talmud*. Judaism consists of a rich variety of beliefs and practices around the world, but the three primary denominations in the United States are Orthodox, Conservative, and Reform Judaism.

Orthodox Judaism adheres strictly to traditional laws and customs. They believe the Torah is the direct word of God, delivered in its entirety to Moses at Mount Sinai. They view it as unchanged and authoritative. Conservative Judaism believes the Torah was not written by God, but instead was transmitted by humans and that while the moral codes are absolute, the laws are adaptable to time and culture. Reform Judaism, the most liberal of the three, believes the Torah was written by humans and that laws are constantly evolving and changing. Approximately 2.2 percent of the U.S. population is Jewish. Yet, 5 million of the world's 13 million Jews live in the United States, making it the second largest Jewish-populated nation—the first being Israel.

JUDAISM, SEX, AND GENDER Judaism is often described as one of the most sexist religions. This is because of its belief in one male, sexless deity, who has no female counterpart, making divine female imagery and language nearly invisible in Jewish theology. It is also considered sexist because women are generally not included in the important stories in the religious texts and were traditionally excluded from the study of religious texts, leadership positions, and from participating in important rituals. Moreover, strict gender divisions apply to most sacred rituals and practices. Most of these restrictions are still upheld in Orthodox Jewish practices, while Reform Judaism greatly modifies gender-segregated customs to be more inclusive and accepting of women.

Ancient rabbinic teachings view women as highly sexual beings who must be controlled by men. Jewish feminists have been significantly influential in shifting this view. While Jewish feminists appreciate that women's sexual desire is acknowledged, they have worked steadily against traditions that suggest women should be kept in private spheres due to their sexual temptations. Judith Plaskow is a Jewish theologian who engages in the practice of *midrash*, the Jewish practice of interpreting religious stories to find possible meanings from a feminist perspective. Her "Coming of Lilith" (2005) midrash reinterprets the Genesis creation story while also exploring questions about women's sexuality. In it, a wise and brave character, Lilith, is Adam's first wife who refuses to be sexually submissive to Adam and leaves him. Later Lilith becomes a close friend with Adam's second wife, Eve. It is a story about sexual equality and female solidarity.

Sex itself is, for the most part, viewed as natural and healthy in Judaism. While some Orthodox traditions forbid sexual behaviors such as masturbation, homosexuality, premarital sex, adultery, and sexual relations with non-Jews, most Reform Jews do not uphold such views. Monogamy and marriage is emphasized, but premarital sex and divorce have long been an acceptable tradition in Reform Judaism. While procreation is celebrated and encouraged, as part of continuing the Jewish tradition, birth control and abortion are both permitted without controversy.

JEWISH VIEWS ON HOMOSEXUALITY AND BISEXUALITY The same few passages on homosexuality in the Old Testament for Christians exist in the Torah. And, similarly, they are up for interpretation. Hebrew Scriptures are thousands of years old and are products of a culture radically different from modern society. Sexual orientation, as we understand it today, did not exist. For instance, same-sex intimacy for women or bisexuality is never addressed in the Torah.

For most of history, homosexuality was rarely mentioned publicly among Jews, and there was an assumption Jews did not have same-sex attractions (Alpert 2003). Heterosexual, monogamous, procreative sex was viewed as the ideal human relationship and fulfillment of the Jewish covenant with God. With the gay liberation movement of the 1970s, Jewish gays and lesbians began openly identifying with their sexual orientation. At first, synagogues did not accept gays and lesbians; but as the decades passed and society became more accepting, Reform Jewish synagogues openly accepted them. Gay synagogues can be found in numerous places throughout the country, and gay clergy and same-sex marriage are accepted in both Reform and Conservative Jewish practices. Most Orthodox movements are still opposed to homosexuality and same-sex marriage.

Most Reformist Jews believe same-sex attraction is not something chosen, but is instead a natural variation of human nature (Alpert 2003). Interestingly, bisexuality is not considered in the same way. Bisexuality tends to be viewed as a choice and is often rejected by Jews, even gay Jews. Bisexual individuals are often viewed as promiscuous, indecisive, and confused because they can't decide on which gender to be attracted to or are too selfish to narrow down (Eisner 2013). These are examples of *biphobia*, or aversion toward bisexual individuals or groups. Some argue Judaism is *monosexist*, or assumes sexual orientation naturally fixates on one sex (Robinson 2002). Bisexuality is a reminder of the complexity of sexuality and insists the binary of gay/straight be challenged.

TRANSGENDER AND JUDAISM Because of its highly gendered traditions and rituals, gender variance poses theological and practical problems in Judaism. Orthodox Jews consider cross-dressing, hormone treatments, and sex reassignment surgery forbidden and point to sacred Hebrew Scripture as justification of this view. However, in 2015, the Union for Reform Judaism approved a resolution on the rights of transgender and gender-nonconforming people. The resolution insisted on changes such as referring to transgender individuals by their chosen identity, making liturgical language more gender neutral, providing gender-neutral bathrooms, and increasing training on sensitivity (Perez-Pena 2015). This resolution is the most considerate of transgender individuals and rights of any major religion in the United States to date.

Islam

The last of the Abrahamic faiths, Islam, emerged in the seventh century CE in the Arabian Peninsula. Its primary belief centers on Muhammad, who lived around 600 CE, as the final prophet of Allah, the Arabic name for God. The primary sacred text is the **Qur'an**, which was revealed to Muhammad over a period of 23 years. The **Hadith** is a supplementary text made up of Muhammad's sayings. There are five basic tenets for obedient Muslims: testimony of faith, prayer, giving alms, fasting, and a pilgrimage to Mecca in Saudi Arabia.

There are two primary branches of Islam: Sunni and Shia. While both branches share the same fundamental beliefs of Islam, there are some variations in practices. One of the primary differences is that Sunni Muslims do not believe spiritual leaders are a higher-privileged class, and they tend to be more liberal overall. Shias believe Imams, or leaders, are supreme and inherit some of Muhammad's inspiration; and they tend to be more conservative overall. Pew Research Center estimates that Muslims made up approximately 1 percent of the U.S. population in 2015, with the majority being Sunni Muslim.

ISLAM, SEX, AND GENDER Traditional Muslim values teach that women should be submissive to men. Gender roles have traditionally been very separate and strictly defined. Women's isolation was historically practiced in many Muslim countries; and if a woman were to go out in public, it was expected she be fully veiled. In modern times, the issue of veiling is debated. In the United States, approximately half of all Muslim women wear the veil (Khalid 2011). Some feminists argue the veil is a symbol of control over women's sexuality and freedom, while others argue it is a symbol of freedom of choice and religious devotion. Some defenders of the veil claim it elevates women's position by not making them sexual objects of desire (Marvasti and McKinney 2004).

Islam views sex and sexuality positively. Unlike Christian views that sexual needs and desires are sinful, Islam recognizes sex as a natural part of being human. Marriage and procreation are highly emphasized, and sexuality is viewed as intrinsic to these aspects of life. However, many feminists argue this positive viewpoint is primarily a masculine, heterosexual affirmation (Wadud 1999). In fact, women's sexuality is barely mentioned in the Qur'an while men's is referred to on many occasions, including the heterosexual pleasures men will find in paradise after death. A woman's sexual purity is highly emphasized in Islam, and virginity is expected until marriage.

ISLAM AND HOMOSEXUALITY Traditionally in Islam, sexual contact between men is not permissible, is stigmatized, and in some countries like Yemen and Saudi Arabia, criminalized and punishable by death (Bearak and Cameron 2016). Sodomy is repeatedly described as a sin in the Qur'an. Homosexuality is usually viewed as something an individual chooses. Same-sex relations among women are viewed as immoral based on the law that sex outside of marriage is wrong. Otherwise, lesbians are overlooked. In the United States, while a heteronormative view of sexual orientation is still strongly upheld in Islamic faiths, greater tolerance and acceptance has been growing in recent decades. For example, Muslims for Progressive Values (MPV) founded Unity Mosques in Atlanta, Georgia, Columbus, Ohio, and Los Angeles, California; and the Muslim Alliance for Sexual and Gender Diversity (MASGD) works to support and connect LGBTQ Muslims.

Same-sex marriage is a difficult topic for many Muslims. While their beliefs are that marriage is a contract between men and women only, there is a strong belief that marriage should be free to be defined by particular groups in the way they wish outside of government regulation (Brown 2015).

TRANSGENDER AND ISLAM In the Hadith, or the sayings of Muhammad, the term *mukhannathun* is used to describe gender-variant individuals, usually effeminate male individuals, or males who like to dress and behave as women (Bolich 2008). In other words, transgender individuals have been recognized since the beginning of this religion. Modern Muslims continue to recognize the presence of transgender individuals, although acceptance is still not entirely sanctioned. It is more acceptable than same-sex relations because transgender "conditions" are viewed to be something an individual is born with, while homosexuality is chosen. Transgender surgical operations have been legal in Iran since 1987. It is the first country in the Middle East to allow them and second to Thailand in the amount of sex reassignment surgeries performed in the world.

In 2013, in what is considered a landmark moment for the transgender community, Egyptian law recognized gender identity disorder (GID) as a legitimate medical condition and permits gender reassignment surgery for those who are diagnosed. Some argue that despite the rate of reassignment surgeries in places like Iran and Egypt, transgender individuals are still rejected socially and culturally by Muslims around the world. One argument is that the primary reason for the surgeries being allowed is to try to force people into heterosexual categories of male and female, not to celebrate gender diversity or gender fluidity.

Transgender Muslims in the United States battle discrimination and hostility on two fronts: transphobia and *Islamophobia*, or hatred and fear of Muslims or their politics and culture. In 2016, one of the deadliest shootings in the United States took place at a gay nightclub in Orlando. The suspect was an American Muslim who pledged allegiance to the terrorist group ISIS the night of the shooting, although there is some debate surrounding the shooter's motives and the extent to which they were homophobic (see Chapter Four). Many queer Muslims spoke up on social media sites after the attack about their sadness regarding the tragedy, but also their fear of being caught between homophobic and Islamophobic cross-fire. Islamic studies professor Amanullah De Sondy writes that Muslim Americans and LGBTQ Americans are both marginalized, and they should unite (Sondy 2016).

Amanullah De Sondy writes, "The challenge for Muslim communities around the globe today is to find and appreciate differences and pluralism and to support the lives of believers who do not fit societal norms. It is imperative if we want to support those on the margins who are hurt and damaged" (2016).

LGBTQ FAMILIES

Family is one of the most significant institutions in society. Like any other institution, it is influenced by changes in the larger society. But changes in the family are often met with greater resistance than other institutional changes because the family has a sacredness not assigned to the economic, political, or educational spheres. Family formation is a legal contract, in that states legally recognize marriages and the dissolution of them; set laws concerning who can marry and at what age they can legally marry; and who can legally adopt; and recognize children and parents as legally related on official documents such as birth certificates. But for many, it is also a deeply significant religious ritual; many people get married in churches, mosques, temples, or synagogues; have their children baptized there; and even follow religious teachings concerning marital dissolution.

There has been considerable family change over the last 50 years that has resulted in much consternation about what this means for the American family. Increasing divorce rates and out-of-wedlock births, a retreat from traditional gender roles as more women with children enter the paid labor force, and, of course, the legal right to same-sex marriage and growing numbers of LGBTQ families are all examples of family changes viewed by some as cause for concern. This half of the chapter explores some of these key ideas: family change, defining gay families, same-sex marriage, LGBTQ parenting, children of LGBTQ parents, and intimate partner violence.

The Changing Family

From a sociological perspective, family change is unsurprising. Exploring families historically and cross-culturally allows us to see there is no one family form constant across time and place. In other words, there is nothing traditional about the so-called **traditional family**, which is a term often used to describe the family form dominant in the 1950s. Specifically, the *traditional family* refers to a nuclear, heterosexual,

The definition of a gay family is contested, but most often refers to a same-sex couple and their children.
Source: istockphoto.com/DGLimages.

As sociologist Judith Stacey eloquently puts it, "love, marriage, and baby carriages are all the rage among lesbians, gay men, and transgendered people . . . , and yet, despite these mind-boggling changes, the word family continues to conjure an image of a married, monogamous, heterosexual pair and their progeny" (2011:4).

white, married couple who maintain traditional gender roles, and their children. All other family forms, including gay families, are perceived as deviant or at best alternative (Ferguson 2011). While sociologists view family change as expected, in mainstream culture, the "demise" of the traditional family has been perceived as a *social problem*. A social problem refers to a phenomena regarded as bad or undesirable by a significant number of people or a number of significant people who mobilize to remedy it (Heiner 2015). Thus, family change associated with gay rights and the emergence of gay families has generated significant opposition. Some of the opposition to gay marriage was discussed in Chapters Four and Five. We will explore opposition to gay parenting later in this chapter.

Defining Gay Families

While family diversity is not new, the demands of various family types, beyond the traditional family, to be recognized and accepted is not only new but unprecedented; thus, much of the debate over the changing family today is about the legitimation of diverse family forms (Coontz 2011). This is certainly true for *gay families.* What is a gay family? Most often that phrase implies a same-sex couple and their children. However, the term can actually refer to any family with a gay family member: parent, child, or sibling (Stacey 1996). Nancy Mezey defines LGBTQ families as "two or more people related by birth, law, or intimate affectionate relationships, who may or may not reside together, and where the LGBT identity of at least one family member impacts other family members in some meaningful way" (2015:5-6). While LGBTQ families have experienced increased visibility in the last two decades, this visibility does not extend equally to all gay families. Referring to them as invisible families, sociologist Mignon Moore (2011) argues the family lives of gay women of color tend to be ignored in scholarship on gay and lesbian families and in scholarship on black families, contributing to their marginalization.

The typical gay family differs from the typical heterosexual family in a few key ways. First, gay families are more likely to reside in urban areas, with over one-half of them concentrated in 20 cities, including "gay meccas" such as San Francisco. They tend to be more educated, less likely to have children than heterosexual households, and more egalitarian than traditional families that tend to be patriarchal, or male dominated (Allen and Demo 1995). The egalitarian nature of LGBTQ families often emerges intentionally, as members of the family unit consciously work to maintain equality in their households. LGBTQ families have the luxury of not being bound by tradition and thus have the freedom to create new family forms.

To speak of a "typical gay family" can be misleading, however. There is great diversity among gay families, specifically along racial/ethnic and social class lines. Moore (2011) argues, for instance, that low-income, African American lesbians negotiate motherhood within a different cultural context than white lesbians as a result of racism and a politics of respectability. For these women, becoming a mother is often the only source of status they have, and there is a certain "recognition, reverence, and respect that is associated with being a heterosexual mother . . . [which] can be disrupted when they reveal themselves as gay" (p. 118). The price of reproductive technologies, which we explore later in this chapter and in Chapter Nine, means social class is a significant determinant of the likelihood of whether a same-sex couple can even become parents. Diversity among gay families also falls along gender lines: gay male couples and their children face some issues lesbian couples and their families may not face, and vice versa. For instance, cultural biases that portray women as more nurturing than men serve to discriminate against gay men who are parents and hope to maintain custody of their children or those seeking to become parents through adoption or foster parenting (Downs and James 2006; Lev 2004; Mallon 2004).

EXILES FROM KINSHIP The modern gay rights movement of the 1970s encouraged LGBTQ people to come out of the closet, as we have already discussed. Coming out often symbolized an exit from the family; coming to terms with one's homosexuality often meant being kicked out of one's home and disowned by family members. Additionally, as much as families rejected their LGBTQ family members, gay people in turn rejected families, to the extent that Kath Weston (1991) referred to gays and lesbians of this era as *exiles from kinship*. Much like women's liberationists of the 1960s and 1970s, the family as an institution was critiqued by gays and lesbians as patriarchal and oppressive; marriage and family were viewed as an abhorrent extension of compulsory heterosexuality (Rich 1980; Sullivan 2011). At the beginning of the modern gay rights movement of the 1970s, gay people generally felt their options were to be openly gay or to be a parent, but not to be both. LGBTQ people who had children from previous, heterosexual relationships struggled to maintain custody of those children and were rarely openly gay parents (see below).

MARRIAGE EQUALITY We discussed the political mobilization, opposition, and fight for marriage equality in Chapters Four and Five. Here we explore the connection between marriage and family formation, the meaning of marriage for same-sex couples, and the mononormativity of marriage equality.

Marriage has historically been the primary way to create families, and almost every known group of people used some form of marriage to organize kinship—albeit with considerable variation in the forms and meanings associated with marriage (Mezey 2015). Despite the variation, marriage serves many functions: it is a way to legitimize sexual relationships, raise children, establish rights to property and inheritance, establish economic relationships, and dictate living arrangements (Mezey 2015). All that being said, despite the near universality of the institution of marriage, all of these functions could be met by other social arrangements.

Research on those who took advantage of San Francisco Mayor Newsome's call to begin offering marriage licenses to same-sex couples in 2004 offers three explanations for their desire for the right to marry: some viewed same-sex marriage as a political statement, others saw it as a way to secure legal rights, while still others saw it as a means to gain social recognition, although men and women spoke differently about these things (Kimport 2014). The women interviewed were more suspicious of the institution of marriage than were men. Men and women were interested in different legal rights associated with marriage, specifically with men citing hospital visitation and rights of partner inheritance while women were more interested in parental rights afforded through marriage (Kimport 2014). Marriage equality was certainly a victory for the LGBTQ community. That being said, it bears emphasizing that marriage equality reinforces mononormativity, the normality of monogamy.

LGBTQ PARENTING The shift from an anti-family position to a pro-family one began in the late 1970s and early 1980s as LGBTQ people began seeking ways to create families of their own (Sullivan 2011). In this period there was a lesbian baby boom; and by the 1990s, there was a full-blown *gayby boom*, an explosion of LGBTQ individuals and couples seeking ways to become parents and an increasing visibility of gay families. Today, research by the Williams Institute finds 37 percent of LGBTQ-identified adults have a child at some point in their lives; 3 million LGBTQ adults have a child, and 6 million people have an LGBTQ parent (Gates 2013).

While many LGBTQ people have children from previous heterosexual relationships, one of the most significant developments of the gayby boom era is that same-sex couples are choosing to form families. Thus, the intentional nature of LGBTQ parenthood is significant. Four things facilitated the increase in gay families: the gay liberation movement, the second-wave feminist movement, the HIV/AIDS epidemic, and the development of new

BOX 8.1

GLOBAL/TRANSNATIONAL PERSPECTIVES ON SEXUALITY:
MARRIAGE EQUALITY ACROSS THE GLOBE

The United States made marriage equality the law of the land with the June 2015 Supreme Court decision *Obergefell v. Hodges*. How does the U.S. timeline on marriage equality compare with the rest of the democratic industrialized world? Do we lead the world on gay rights or are we global laggards? In May 2016, the Italian Parliament approved civil unions for same-sex couples. While we have already discussed the differences between civil unions and marriage equality (see Chapter Five), this is considered a victory for LGBTQ Italians since it is a country where the traditional family is still prominent and it is dominated by the Roman Catholic Church, an institution that prohibits homosexual behavior (Povoledo 2016).

According to the PEW Research Center, almost two dozen countries allow gay marriage. Ireland, another predominantly Catholic country, legalized gay marriage in 2015 through a popular vote, with 62 percent of voters supporting same-sex marriage. Same-sex marriage was approved in France, New Zealand, England, and Wales in 2013 and in Scotland in 2014. The

Netherlands, famous for their political tolerance, was the first nation to approve same-sex marriage in 2000, with Belgium following suit in 2003, Canada and Spain in 2005, and South Africa in 2006. Norway and Sweden also legalized gay marriage in 2005, although Sweden had allowed civil unions for same-sex couples since 1995. The Lutheran-affiliated Church of Sweden began allowing their clergy to officiate at same-sex ceremonies in 2009.

There is a very clear trend toward increasing access to marriage for same-sex couples across the globe and the United States has not exactly led the way on this issue. However, in the United States, gay marriage was originally treated as a state issue. By that measure, the first state to allow gay marriage was Massachusetts in 2004. Germany remains one of the only countries in Western Europe that does not allow same-sex couples to legally marry, and Chancellor Angela Merkel has said it is not a priority for her administration (Terkel 2015). Germany has allowed civil partnerships for same-sex couples since 2001 ("Gay Marriage around the World" 2013).

reproductive technologies (Mezey 2008, 2015). The gay liberation movement helped LGBTQ people develop positive self-images as they challenged the dominant cultural portrayal of homosexuals as mentally ill and deviant (Chapter Five). Once they learned to see themselves as not sick and to demand cultural acceptance, those with a desire to become parents began to see themselves as worthy parents. The second-wave feminist movement contributed to the emergence of LGBTQ families, specifically through encouraging the development of a feminist consciousness among women that encouraged them to explore their sexuality and to take control of their bodies, including their fertility (Mezey 2008, 2015).

The HIV/AIDS epidemic dramatically increased homophobia (see Chapter Ten). Additionally, the epidemic exemplified the second-class status of LGBTQ people, as thousands of gay and bisexual men died alone; while for others, their partners were prohibited from visiting them in the hospital by family members who disapproved of their relationship. Issues related to next of kin, hospital visitation rights, and decisions about medical care all led to a glaring recognition of their lack of relationship status in the eyes of the law. There is also some evidence LGBTQ people sought to become parents in the 1980s as a way to counteract the deaths from HIV/AIDS the gay community was experiencing (Lewin 1993; Mallon 2011;

Mezey 2015; Moraga 1997; Weston 1991). Finally, advances in reproductive technologies made becoming parents a more realistic option for same-sex couples (discussed below).

An LGBTQ person can become a parent through a number of ways: having their own biological children through previous heterosexual relationships, through adoption and foster parenting, and through assisted reproductive technologies. Despite the fact that courts have historically privileged biological parents when it comes to custody, all four approaches to gay parenting have faced restrictions, including LGBTQ people who have their own biological children. As the modern gay liberationist movement increased LGBTQ visibility, it triggered opposition movements, and much of this opposition focused on homosexuals' supposed threat to children. In the 1950s in Boise, Idaho, and Sioux City, Iowa, for instance, gay men were incarcerated in large numbers simply on the belief they were a threat to children (Rivers 2013). In this climate of fear, many LGBTQ people lost rights to their biological children.

In 1977, former Miss America and actress Anita Bryant led a campaign against an ordinance that passed in Dade County, Florida, which prohibited discrimination based on sexual orientation in housing, employment, and public accommodations. The campaign was titled "Save Our Children" and garnered massive support from the newly politicized Christian right. The campaign portrayed homosexuals as a threat to the traditional family and Christian values, with Bryant specifically arguing that homosexuals sought to recruit children through molestation. This was the first organized opposition to the modern gay rights movement, and it had some significant short-term success. Not only was this particular ordinance repealed, but also LGBTQ activism inspired opposition to similar ordinances in other cities across the country.

Anita Bryant led a campaign titled "Save the Children" to oppose a gay rights ordinance that has passed in Dade County, Fl, in 1977. The campaign portrayed homosexuals as a threat to the traditional family and Christian values, specifically arguing that homosexuals attempted to recruit children through molestation.
Source: AP Photo/Anonymous.

LGBTQ PARENTS AND THEIR BIOLOGICAL CHILDREN Before the 1960s, most LGBTQ parents remained closeted out of fear that if their homosexuality were discovered they would face persecution and lose custody of their children (Rivers 2013). While the gay rights movement improved the situation for LGBTQ parents, between 1967 and 1985, lesbian and gay parents "lost more court battles than they won" (Rivers 2013:53). Despite the judicial precedent of support for biological parents, courts have significant discretion when it comes to awarding child custody (Larson 2010). Once they began using the "best interests of the child" as the rather subjective barometer, they were able to avoid the question of whether a gay or lesbian person was an unfit parent (Rivers 2013). This has allowed judicial bias to cloud outcomes. One particularly egregious example was the case of *Weigand v. Houghton* (1999), where a judge ruled against awarding custody of a 15-year-old boy to his gay biological father and his partner in favor of leaving the child with the mother and her abusive, unemployed, and drug-addicted boyfriend (Larson 2010). It was common for judges to decide it was in the best interest of the child to live with the heterosexual parent in order to avoid stigmatization and ridicule from their peers.

In addition to the "best interest of the child" standard, in custody cases since the Victorian era, courts generally relied on a "maternal preference" standard, assuming children were always better off in the custody of their mothers. The rise of lesbian mothers and increasing divorce rates in the 1970s challenged this judicial reasoning. Since lesbians were perceived as deviant, their lesbianism trumped their womanhood. Judges often operated on the assumption that lesbians and gay men were child molesters, which meant it was not in the child's best interest to be living with the gay parent. Due to these judicial biases, it became very difficult for lesbian or gay biological parents to win custody of their children; thus, attorneys often recommended their clients avoid a trial and settle (Rivers 2013).

If LGBTQ parents were granted custody, they faced restrictions divorced heterosexual couples rarely faced. In countless cases, gay and lesbian parents had to agree through a legal affidavit never to have their same-sex partners and their children in the home at the same time. Sometimes same-sex parents were forced by custody court judges to repudiate their sexual orientation and undergo regular psychiatric examinations testifying to this. Many were granted custody only if they refrained from any gay rights activism, which essentially denied them their Constitutional rights to free speech and assembly. Often the gay parents were limited to supervised visitation with their children, out of fears the gay parents would molest the children if they had the opportunity (Rivers 2013).

ADOPTION AND FOSTERING In May of 2015, the last state restriction on gay adoption was overturned, as courts reversed Mississippi's ban. But in the not too distant past, most states in the United States prohibited same-sex couples from adopting children (see Chapter Four). Some estimates find same-sex couples are more willing to adopt a child than heterosexual couples are. Adoption is often a last choice for heterosexual couples and a first choice among same-sex couples (Mezey 2015).

Despite these restrictions, an estimated 65,000 children are living with same-sex parents—more than 16,000 in California alone—with gay and lesbian parents raising 4 percent of all adopted children in the country (gayadoption.org). It is estimated that approximately 4 percent of adopted children in the United States are adopted by same-sex couples and 6 percent of all foster children in the United States are living with gay men or lesbians (Baumle and Compton 2015; Gates et al. 2007).

Today adoption is a more affordable route to parenthood than use of assisted reproductive technologies (discussed below). Despite changes in the law, some adoption agencies still refuse to work with same-sex couples; in many cases, this is an "informal or quiet policy" (Mezey 2015). In conservative states, some agencies and social workers hide the gender and sexual identity of their clients as a way to allow them to adopt or foster—but not to do so openly and, thus, challenge the conservative values of the region. The foster care system in the United States currently has 104,000 children who are eligible for adoption.

Prior to the legalization of gay marriage, same-sex couples who chose to become parents had to take an extra legal step that heterosexual, married couples did not: they had to go through a legal procedure known as a **second parent adoption.** This is a legal procedure that allows both parents to be recognized, making sure the partner who did not give birth or legally adopt the child can make a legal claim to that child. For a married, heterosexual couple, the "second parent" automatically becomes the legal father to the child. Being a legal second parent means that if something were to happen to the birth parent, the second parent is the child's legal guardian. As essential as these are for LGBTQ families, not all states and sometimes not every judge allowed second parent adoptions (Mezey 2015).

ASSISTED REPRODUCTIVE TECHNOLOGIES Technological advances, such as **assisted reproductive technologies (ARTs),** which refer to using technologies such as egg donation, surrogacy, artificial insemination, or in vitro fertilization to conceive a child, have made same-sex family planning possible. While ARTs open the door to family formation for many same-sex couples, these technologies are very expensive. Thus, they privilege professional same-sex couples and are not realistic options for low-income or working-class couples. They also have not always been available to same-sex couples. Donor insemination has been in use since 1884, but traditionally was only used to help infertile heterosexual couples (Ehrensaft 2008). Today, the fastest growing group of women turning to assisted reproductive technologies are women "who have absolutely nothing wrong with their bodies but are missing a body to have a baby with—that would be lesbian couples and lesbian single women" (Ehrensaft 2008:162). In addition to the child and the parents, many ARTS involve a ***birth other***, or outside parties such as sperm donors, egg donors, surrogates, or gestational carriers who help the person or couple have a child (Ehrensaft 2008). The increasing use of ARTs has radically transformed family life.

WHAT ABOUT THE CHILDREN? Opponents of gay parenting offer several arguments for their disapproval. The first is that children of gay parents are more likely to suffer confusion concerning their gender and sexuality and, thus, are more likely to become gay themselves (Richman 2009). Another argument is that homosexual parents are more sexually promiscuous and, thus, more likely to molest their own children. A third argument is that same-sex couples are unstable and likely to separate. A final reason offered is children of gay parents are more likely to be stigmatized and ostracized by their peers, thus, not allowing LGBTQ people to parent will protect children from this potential discrimination (Stacey and Biblarz 2001; Wardle 1997).

All of these arguments lack empirical support and are easily refuted. First, there is no evidence the sexuality of a parent determines the sexuality of their children. If that were the case, one would have to ask how so many LGBTQ individuals come from heterosexual parents. The second argument is wrong on many levels. First, there is no evidence that lesbians and gay men are more promiscuous than heterosexuals. Second, it conflates two very different things: promiscuity and pedophilia. Third, most pedophiles are heterosexual men, not gay men, so this fear is clearly misplaced. The argument that same-sex couples are more unstable and, thus, likely to separate cannot be supported by the evidence, either. With divorce rates for heterosexuals at 48 percent for first marriages, and as high as 62 percent for second marriages, one can hardly make the case that heterosexuality is conducive to relationship stability. Finally, making the case that LGBTQ people should not be allowed to parent because their children will face ridicule from their peers due to homophobia is problematic. Perhaps instead of denying same-sex couples the right to parent, we should address homophobia.

Despite how easily these arguments are refuted, all of these arguments have been used by judges to justify transferring child custody from lesbian or gay parents to heterosexual parents (Stacey and Biblarz 2001). Despite the fact that more and more courts are allowing gay and lesbian parents to maintain custody of their children, discrimination against LGBTQ parents still exists. This is particularly true for the most marginalized members of the LGBTQ community—impoverished gays and lesbians, transgender parents, and transgender parents of color (Crozier 2012). In general, race and class privilege can facilitate parenthood for LGBTQ people (Mezey 2008, 2013).

CHILDREN OF GAY PARENTS What do we know about the outcomes of children raised by LGBTQ people? Does parents' sexual orientation matter? The American Psychological Association (APA) argues that no known studies have found children of gay parents to be disadvantaged compared to children of heterosexual parents (Gates 2015). The American Sociological Association (ASA) filed an amicus brief (a "friend of the court" brief) arguing that social scientific research finds children raised by same-sex parents do just as well as children raised by opposite-sex parents (Gates 2015).

Sociologists Judith Stacey and Timothy J. Biblarz (2001) evaluated the findings of 21 psychological studies published between 1981 and 1998 concerning the effect of parental sexual orientation on children. As stated, most research finds no differences in child outcomes; in other words, children of gay parents are "just like everyone else." Stacey and Biblarz, however, somewhat controversially found the sexual orientations of parents can matter, particularly on issues related to gender and sexuality. They argue that children with lesbian or gay parents are more likely to be less gender-typed and more likely to be open to homoerotic relationships (Stacey and Biblarz 2001).

Children in gay families may deal with different experiences than children in heterosexual families. In *Families Like Mine*, Abigail Garner (2005), whose own father came out as gay after he and her mother divorced, interviewed more than 50 grown sons and daughters of LGBTQ parents. Her book focuses on the primary issues that come up when kids of LGBTQ parents get together and talk about their families, including: what it is like to be in the spotlight with so much attention being paid to children of gay parents; why coming-out is a necessary and ongoing process in gay families; how to navigate homophobia; the sexual orientation of children; and the impact of HIV/AIDS on gay families, among others.

INTIMATE PARTNER VIOLENCE

We discuss sexuality-related violence in more detail in Chapter Twelve, but here we focus on a specific kind of violence: intimate partner violence. When family violence started getting the attention it deserved, it was often referred to as "wife battering." While women are disproportionately victimized and males are disproportionately the perpetrators of family violence, the scope of the problem is much broader than the term "wife battering" captures. The term intimate partner violence is more inclusive of the phenomenon. *Intimate partner violence* is defined as "any form of psychological/verbal (e.g., name calling, threats, manipulation), financial (e.g., controlling access to monetary resources), physical (e.g., the use of physical force), or sexual (e.g., verbal and/or physical coercion to engaging in unwanted sexual activity) violence directed at another individual" with whom one shares an intimate relationship (Barrett and St. Pierre 2013:2).

The extent of LGBTQ intimate partner violence is highly contested; we do not know if same-sex couples experience more or less violence than heterosexual couples experience. Some research finds that rates of intimate partner violence experienced by lesbians range from 8 to 60 percent and for gay men it ranged from 11 to 44 percent (Turell 2000). Clearly, such varying rates lead to us to question the data. The best research we have is by Tjaden and Thoennes (2000). Their findings indicate that lesbians experience domestic violence less than gay men and less than women in heterosexual relationships. Specifically, 11 percent of women who were in a live-in relationship with another woman report experiencing violence, whereas 30.4 percent of women who live with a man as part of a couple reported such violence at the hands of their husband or boyfriend. For gay men, 15 percent report experiencing intimate partner abuse while only 7.7 percent of men living with a female partner or spouse experience such violence. Despite debate about the numbers, intimate partner violence is a serious issue in the LGBTQ community.

Explaining the potentially varying rates of violence between heterosexual couples and same-sex couples requires we turn to research by sociologist Michael P. Johnson (1995). He introduced two types of intimate partner violence: situational violence and patriarchal terrorism. *Situational violence* refers to occasional outbursts of violence by either spouse. *Patriarchal terrorism* involves systemic male violence where women are physically and emotionally terrorized (Johnson 1995). Patriarchal terrorism helps us understand why men are more likely to be perpetrators of domestic violence and women are more likely to be victimized. Ultimately, this type of violence emerges out of a society that allows men to control women, even in the home.

When it comes to intimate partner violence between lesbian partners, research by Claire Renzetti (2011) finds there are several factors that correlate with abuse. The first is the partners' relative dependency on one another. Perhaps surprisingly, the batterers appear to be more dependent on the partners they victimize. This intense dependency manifests as jealousy and sometimes involves alcohol and substance abuse. An imbalance of power in the relationship contributes to abuse. Another influential factor in understanding intimate partner violence between lesbians involves a personal family history of violence. Children who grow up in families with violence either become abusive or are drawn to abusers.

The second-wave feminist movement of the 1960s and '70s demanded wife beating be taken seriously and treated as a crime the way assaults between nonintimate partners were.

Feminists spent considerable time and energy establishing safe places for victims of domestic violence, particularly through establishing women's shelters across the country. Despite these efforts, today it is clear that battered lesbians and gay men experience great difficulty obtaining the help they need. First, LGBTQ intimate partner violence tends to be invisible. Sometimes this is because same-sex relationships are not taken seriously, while other times there is a perception that lesbians do not engage in the kinds of power struggles that exist in heterosexual relationships (Mezey 2015). Second, police and shelter workers too often lack training for addressing LGBTQ intimate partner violence. Some may even be homophobic. Third, with same-sex abuse, too often it is assumed to be mutual battering, rather than a clear perpetrator and victim. Fourth, most shelters are safe spaces only for biologically born women as a refuge from male perpetrators, which means that gay and bisexual men, transgender people, and lesbians cannot use standard shelters as a refuge from an abusive partner (Douglas and Hines 2011; Greenberg 2012; Mezey 2015; Renzetti 2011).

CONCLUSION

In conclusion, religion and family are powerful institutions in society that shape ideas about sex, gender, and sexuality. In this chapter, we look at the intersection of sexuality in the three Abrahamic religions: Christianity, Judaism, and Islam. An analysis of traditions and beliefs reveals a bias against women's sexuality in all three traditions and a heteronormative, patriarchal expectation for families. An analysis of views on homosexuality and transgender issues was explored for each tradition, with little acceptance among the more conservative denominations and faster-growing acceptance among the liberal, reformist religious groups. Feminists and LGBTQ religious individuals are steadily working to reform outdated and homophobic practices in all the traditions.

The family has always changed in response to larger, structural conditions, including religion, and the current era is no exception. Some of the most significant changes have surrounded LGBTQ people and their rights to family formation. The last few years have witnessed the legalization of same-sex marriage, and the final barrier to adoption by LGBTQ people and couples was overturned. Despite such progress, LGBTQ people still experience discrimination in keeping their children, or having children, or just being perceived as capable of successfully raising a child. Finally, the increasing visibility of LGBTQ families has resulted in increasing visibility of violence within those households as well. Shedding light on this problem can help to address it.

Key Terms and Concepts

Assisted reproductive technologies (ARTs) 178
Biphobia 171
Birth other 178
Black liberation theology 168
Celibacy 165
Complementary gender roles 165
Exiles from kinship 175
Feminist theology 166
Gay and lesbian theologies 168
Gay families 174

Gayby boom 175
Hadith 171
Horizontal oppression 167
Internalized homophobia 167
Intimate partner violence 180
Islamophobia 173
Liberation theologies 168
Midrash 170
Misogyny 165
Monosexist 171
Mukhannathun 172
Patriarchal terrorism 180

Protective paternalism 165
Queer theology 168
Qur'an 171
Second parent adoption 178
Sexual purity movement 166
Situational violence 180
Social problem 174
Sodomy 166
Talmud 170
Torah 170
Traditional family 173

Critical Thinking Questions

1. In what ways have each of the major religious tradition discussed in this chapter condemned homosexuality? Describe the potential impact of religious condemnation on LGBTQ individuals.

2. Describe gay and lesbian theology. Describe queer theology. What are the differences between each?

3. Explain the significance of our changing understanding of family violence and particularly the shifting language from "wife beating" to "intimate partner violence." What other types of family violence exist?

4. Looking over the data in the Global Perspectives box, speculate on why the United States did not lead the world in the legalization of same-sex marriage.

Activities

1. If you belong to a religious organization, do a scripture study of 1 to 3 passages on homosexuality or passages suggestive of control over women's sexuality. Investigate language translations of the passage and its specific, historical context. Ask your religious leader their interpretation of the passages. Analyze whether the religion's overall message of God and human behavior is consistent with the interpretations. Write about your findings in a short paper.

2. Watch one of the suggested films listed below. Write a reflection paper on what you learned and how it bolstered one of the main lessons in this chapter.

Essential Reading

Burke, Kelsy. 2016. *Christians under Covers: Evangelicals and Sexual Pleasure on the Internet*. Berkeley: University of California Press.

Garner, Abigail. 2004. *Families Like Mine: Children of Gay Parents Tell It Like It Is*. New York: Perennial Currents.

Mezey, Nancy J. 2015. *LGBT Families*. Thousand Oaks, CA: Sage.

Moore, Mignon R. 2011. *Invisible Families: Gay Identities, Relationships, and Motherhood among Black Women*. Berkeley: University of California Press.

Renzetti, Claire. 1992. *Violent Betrayal: Partner Abuse in Lesbian Relationships*. Newbury Park, CA: Sage.

Weston, Kath. 1991. *Families We Choose: Lesbians, Gays, Kinship*. New York: Columbia University Press.

Suggested Films

A Sinner in Mecca (2015). Parvez Sharma, Director and Producer. This film explores Islamic Mecca for the world's largest pilgrimage: the *Hajj*. Filming in Saudi Arabia presents two serious challenges: filming is forbidden in the country, and homosexuality is punishable by death.

Fatherhood Dreams (2007). Julia Ivanova, Director and Producer. This documentary is about four gay fathers and their children. These are men who had always wanted to be fathers, and each one takes a different path to fatherhood explored in the film: adoption, surrogacy, and coparenting.

Fish Out of Water (2009). Ky Dickenson, Director. Highlights the Bible verses most used to condemn homosexuality and same-sex marriage. The documentary speaks to ministers on both sides of the religious debate over homosexuality and gay marriage.

For the Bible Tells Me So (2007). Daniel G. Karslake, Director. This documentary looks at how the religious right has used the Bible to stigmatize the gay community and at how those members of the Christian community who have out children are affected by this homophobia.

Gayby Baby (2015). Maya Newell, Director. This Australian documentary follows four children raised by same-sex parents and explores the ways growing up as a "gayby" has affected them.

The Case against 8 (2014). Ben Cotner and Ryan White, Directors. This HBO documentary film explores the five-year legal battle to overturn Proposition 8, California's ban on gay marriage. This legal battle was, interestingly, spearheaded by conservative attorney Ted Olson.

Unfit: Ward v. Ward (2011). Penny Edmiston, Edwin Scharlau, and Katie Carmichael, Directors. This film explores the custody battle between a lesbian mom and her ex-husband, a convicted killer. The lesbian mom is deemed "unfit" by the courts and loses custody of her child.

Recommended Multimedia

All Children, All Families. The Human Rights Campaign offers information and resources for same-sex couples hoping to become parents. They also promote cultural competency among child welfare agency workers. http://www.hrc.org/resources/professional-organizations-on-lgbt-parenting

The Trevor Project. Founded in 1998 by the creators of the Academy Award®-winning short film TREVOR, The Trevor Project is the leading national organization providing crisis intervention and suicide prevention services to lesbian, gay, bisexual, transgender and questioning (LGBTQ) young people ages 13 to 24. http://www.thetrevorproject.org/

Institute for Judaism and Sexuality. An organization working toward a complete inclusion and welcoming of LGBTQ Jews in communities and congregations. www.huc.edu/ijso

Muslims for Progressive Voices. An inclusive community rooted in the traditional Qur'anic ideals of human dignity and social justice. www.mpvusa.org

Gayadoption.org This organization offers legal help for LGBTQ individuals hoping to adopt a child. Since adoption laws vary by state, it is essential to get the right legal information for each state. http://gayadoption.org/facts-supporting-gay-adoption/

9

SEXUALITY AND REPRODUCTION

LEARNING OBJECTIVES

Upon completion of this chapter, students will be able to . . .

- Understand the concept of compulsory reproduction
- Explain how the body is socially constructed
- Clarify issues of pregnancy and childbirth for cisgender and transgender males
- Challenge narratives surrounding teen pregnancy and childbirth
- Describe the history and current social issues surrounding birth control
- Define sexual and reproductive rights and choice
- Explain the ways assisted reproductive technologies are gendered, classed, and raced

Former Arkansas Governor and former Republican presidential candidate Mike Huckabee spoke about contraception and female sexuality at the 2012 Republican National Convention in Tampa, Florida. His views reflect right-wing, conservative, Christian thinking on these issues. He said Democrats tell women "they are helpless without Uncle Sugar coming in and providing them a prescription each month for birth control because they cannot control their libido or their reproductive system without the help of government" (Coscarelli 2014). To put it more simply, he believes women can and should control their libido all on their own through abstinence, the only legitimate form of birth control. The role of men in the reproductive process is ignored in such statements.

Huckabee speaks for an entire group of constituents, politicians, and corporate owners who believe **contraception,** or prevention of reproduction, is immoral because all sexual intercourse should have the primary goal of reproduction. Huckabee and those who share similar beliefs oppose government family-planning services and believe that employers should be able to decide whether female employees should have access to birth control under their work-provided health insurance plans. Those who adhere to anticontraceptive beliefs argue that if a woman takes birth control measures, she will engage in risky sexual behaviors and is more likely to have sex with multiple partners. Even though research disproves these notions, the presumptions still persist (Peipert et al. 2012). This view disregards the fact that many women take birth control for a variety of medical reasons. And, most especially, it does not see birth control for what it is: a way for women to take control of their reproductive health, economic security, and family-planning decisions.

Instead, it stigmatizes women's sexuality. And, it doesn't stop with birth control. In 2012, Huckabee said women were worse at multitasking during their menstrual cycles. In 2012, he defended Missouri Republican Representative Todd Akin's descriptions of a "legitimate rape," when Akin falsely claimed women rarely get pregnant from rape because "the female body has ways to shut the whole thing down" (Kane and Henderson 2012). In 2015, Huckabee supported the decision to deny an abortion to a 10-year-old rape victim in Paraguay. The case drew worldwide attention after the victim was raped by her stepfather in a country that prevented the girl from receiving an abortion (Marcotte 2015). Overall, Huckabee represents a perspective that leads many feminists, activists, and everyday people to describe as nothing short of a war against women's reproductive rights.

This chapter examines sexuality and **reproduction,** or the process of creating a new human individual. Reproduction is traditionally the product of sexual activity, or procreation; but with the invention of new technologies, there is now an array of options for human reproduction. Yet, the female body still remains the most crucial component of the process. Pregnancy, childbirth, and motherhood have been at the core of feminist discourse about women's rights since the onset of the women's movement. As early as the 1860s, feminist pioneer Elizabeth Cady Stanton began advocating for women's "right to self-sovereignty," or the right to take deliberate measures to avoid pregnancy. Stanton argued against the popular belief that pregnant women should rest and stay indoors during pregnancy, and insisted on more physical freedom during pregnancy and childbirth for women. Stanton openly spoke out for greater sexual freedom for women at a time when sexual and social mores were very restrictive for women.

One hundred years later, feminists were still fighting for very similar things. In the 1970s, the right to abortion and access to sexual and reproductive health came to the forefront of the feminist movement and remain as top concerns to this day. **Reproductive health** is defined as a state of physical, mental, and social well-being in all matters relating to the reproductive system, at all stages of life. Good reproductive health is when an individual has a satisfying and safe sex life; and, if so desired, the capability to reproduce, deciding when and how often, and the freedom to decide not to. It also means safe, effective, and affordable methods of family-planning and health care services to prevent pregnancy and birth or to progress through the process.

The role of medical, legal, and commercial developments in the area of reproduction shape social perceptions and act as forms of control over female sexuality and reproduction. In this chapter, we will look at the perception of reproduction as compulsory and the ways such expectations impact primarily women, but also transgender individuals. The body is very much a social space and carries meanings and social implications that will be explored. Medical institutions play a large role in constructing ideas about what is healthy and unhealthy reproduction, and those ideas will be analyzed throughout the chapter. All reproductive processes will be analyzed from a sociological perspective, including menstruation, pregnancy, childbirth, breastfeeding, birth control, sterilization, and infertility.

Examples in recent years of how issues of sexuality and reproduction have made mainstream news are:

- In 2010, Thomas Beatie became known as the "pregnant man" because he was the first publicly recognized transgender man to give birth. Beatie has since given birth to three children.
- In 2013, North Carolina paid victims of forced sterilization $10 million. It is estimated the government of North Carolina sterilized more than 7,000 people between 1929 and 1974 (Cohen 2013).
- In 2014, a woman was banned from breastfeeding in a Victoria's Secret store in Austin, Texas. After the story made national news, the company apologized.
- In 2015, antiabortion activists falsified undercover videos depicting Planned Parenthood staff selling fetal tissue and body parts, influencing several states to defund the sexual health organization, resulting in multiple state investigations—all of which turned up no sign of wrongdoing.
- In 2016, the Indiana Court of Appeals overturned a prior feticide conviction of Purvi Patel, who had previously been sentenced to 20 years in prison after allegedly taking abortion-inducing drugs (Liss-Schultz 2016).
- In 2016, at the start of Transgender Awareness Week, THINX, the maker of "period panties" that absorb menstrual blood, launched a boyshort line to appeal to the transgender community, specifically transmales who still have functioning female reproductive organs.

COMPULSORY REPRODUCTION

Reproduction is not just a biological experience. It is also a socially constructed phenomenon. ***Compulsory reproduction*** is the idea that individuals, especially women, are socially coerced into viewing reproduction as a necessary and obligatory part of the human experience. It is related to Rich's (1980) concept of compulsory heterosexuality, which is the idea that women are coerced into heterosexuality and into viewing coupling with men as the only relationship option available to them (see Chapter One). Rooted in essentialism, compulsory reproductive ideology naturalizes reproduction and assumes human beings are designed to procreate naturally. Such assumptions arise from a variety of traditional, cultural beliefs including Judeo/Christian/Islamic religious ideals that promote the idea that human beings are naturally heterosexual and are ordained to further the human species as part of their covenant with God (see Chapter Eight). Less religious and more scientific beliefs support the idea that humans are biologically wired to propagate and are thereby driven by hormones and chemicals. A popular social belief is that reproduction and parenting give meaning to life and provide a way for people to become fulfilled and feel "complete."

Compulsory reproduction impacts the sexes in different ways due to different gender identity and role expectations. For men, the pressure to reproduce is often not felt as intensely. Fatherhood is secondary to their primary identity as a man, while women feel intense pressure to reproduce as a primary source of their womanly identity. Many feminists refer to the societal pressure for women to reproduce as **compulsory motherhood**, or the idea that women are socially coerced into viewing motherhood as a necessary and obligatory part of the female experience. Sociologist Charlene Miall (1994) finds that motherhood and fatherhood are not experienced in the same way. Both men and women overwhelmingly believe that women want children more than men do and that they experience biological and social pressures to reproduce that men do not. As a result, men and women experience infertility differently, which reveals gendered assumptions of compulsory reproduction (discussed in more detail below).

As already mentioned, until recent technological advancements in the twenty-first century, reproduction was limited to sexual activity between men and women. In today's world, a variety of reproductive advancements exist; and while sperm and egg are still required, heterosexual relations are not. Parenthood is readily available to LGBTQ couples (see Chapter Eight). More research is needed on how gay and lesbian identities are impacted by compulsory reproduction and how lesbian women confront social ideals of compulsory motherhood. Compulsory reproduction is an idea that has long-term and serious consequences; new life is brought into the world every day under this unrecognized obligation.

THE BODY AS A SOCIAL CONSTRUCTION

Like reproduction, the human body is socially constructed. This may seem like a strange idea at first. Most people think of physical bodies as purely biological. And while they are definitely shaped by biology, bodies are also constructed by society. Environmental factors like health, illness, nutrition, exercise, and stress can impact the actual physiological make-up of the body. Social factors like gender, race, sexual orientation, and class influence men and women's bodies and their body self-image (see Chapter Three). For example, big, strong muscles are equated with masculinity; and some men go to great lengths to attain this image, including extreme body building and use of steroid supplements. The fact that individuals undergo complete, medically guided, physical sex changes reveals the malleable and constructed nature of the human body.

Most relevant to this chapter's subject of sexuality and reproduction is how medicine shapes and influences the body. The medical profession is a social institution responsible for treating illness and promoting health in society. Categories such as health and illness, or normal and abnormal, are defined and determined within specific cultural contexts. Meanings are negotiated, change over time, and can vary widely from society to society. Views on the root causes of illness or the primary ways to heal can be vastly different across time and place. The medical establishment holds great power over determining what is defined as and treated as a medical condition. Most medical providers and hospitals are working for profit. Moreover, health care is reliant on the use of drugs produced by pharmaceutical companies, which are also working for profit. The profit motive can skew intentions and reasons for various treatments.

Medicalization is the process by which human conditions and problems come to be defined and treated as medical conditions, and become the subject of medical study, diagnosis, prevention, or treatment. Reproduction is medicalized. Everything from sexuality to menstruation, childbirth, menopause, and infertility are considered medical conditions with a wide range of diagnoses, interventions, and treatments available. Each of these topics will be explored in varying degrees throughout this chapter. In the following passage we will take a deeper look into menstruation, both its biological and socially constructed realities.

Menstruation as Biological Reality

While most women are aware that menstruation, ovulation, and fertility are related somehow, most are unaware of exactly how and why. In a 2014 online survey of a cross-sectional sample of 1,000 women, approximately 40 percent were unfamiliar with the ovulatory cycle (Lundsberg et al. 2014). A 2016 study of women ages 18 to 51 years, with over 52 percent Hispanic and 70 percent living in poverty, reveals startling facts: 49.6 percent do not know the average number of days for a regular menstrual cycle, 47.2 percent do not know what ovulation is, 67.2 percent do not know ovulation timing, and 79.2 percent do not know the number of eggs released from an ovary each month (Ayoola, Zandee, and Adams 2016). For far too many Americans, basic reproductive knowledge is lacking.

The **menstrual cycle** is the monthly process of ovulation and menstruation that almost every woman experiences. The average age to start menstruation in the United States is 12.5 years, with African American girls menstruating about six months earlier (Steingraber 2007). The menstrual cycle ends for women during **menopause**, the time when reproductive processes stop functioning, between the ages of 45 and 55. Most menstrual cycles are approximately 28 days in length, in which female reproductive hormones undergo several changes to prepare for pregnancy. The first two weeks of the cycle begin with an increase in estrogen; at approximately day 14, the ovaries create an egg. One egg then leaves the ovaries, travels down the fallopian tubes to the uterus, creating **ovulation**. A woman is most likely to get pregnant during the 3 days before or on the day of ovulation. If a woman's egg comes into contact with male sperm, it can become fertilized. If not, the uterine lining is shed, resulting in menstrual blood. Most women spend approximately 35 years menstruating once every month. It is perhaps the most commonly shared female experience.

If a woman does not want to reproduce, is her menstrual cycle necessary? Certain contraception, like the birth control pill, can suppress menstruation. Many physicians approve of this technique and advise women to forgo their cycle. Some menstrual activists challenge this approach and claim menstruation is a healthy bodily process and can be an indicator of overall health. Menstruation can provide important information about the body. For example, if a young woman's menstrual cycle stops, this can indicate illnesses such as thyroid disease or an eating disorder. Or, if a menstrual cycle is irregular, it can indicate disease or infection.

Menstruation as Social Construction

Although menstruation is a biological reality, societal values help construct its meaning, experience, and management. In U.S. patriarchal culture, menstruation holds a status of shame, secrecy, and silence. Advertisements for menstrual-oriented products frame it as something that restricts physical and social activities, brings physical discomfort, and is unhygienic (Vostral 2008). Women are asked to conceal, clean, and control their menstruation at all times. This can have a negative impact on girls' and women's attitudes and experiences of menstruation. Negative attitudes and expectations about menstruation can lead to body shame, self-objectification, and lack of agency in sexual decision making (Stubbs 2008). Transgender males often still have female reproductive systems and monthly menstrual periods. They have to manage not only negative societal messages about menstruation, but also the confusing feelings of having a female biological experience while identifying as male.

Menstruation is medicalized and, thus, often requires treatment—particularly in regard to the condition known as **premenstrual syndrome** (PMS), a group of physical and mood-based symptoms that women can experience prior to menstruation. There is no medical or scientific consensus on the exact definition, cause, or treatment of PMS. A research review published in 2012 reveals there is no scientific support that validates PMS as a legitimate or widespread condition, as the medical community has previously tried to portray. Instead, it is part of a larger myth that links menstruation with negative emotions (Romans et al. 2012). Feminists do not negate the correlation of mood changes with menstruation but argue that too often women are blamed for certain behaviors because of PMS. This is in line with essentialist views that confine women's abilities and options to the "natural" workings of the female body.

In *The Woman in the Body* (2001), Emily Martin studied medical metaphors used for women's reproductive processes and compared them to women's own views of their reproductive processes and experiences. She found that medical texts describe the female reproductive system using metaphors that treat it as an information-transmitting system within a hierarchical structure. Basically the body is a replication of modern industrial society, with female reproductive organs as the factory and pregnancy as the product. Menstruation represents failure to produce new life, and menopause represents the end of one's reproductive life. In her interviews with 165 women, Martin found that middle-class women internalized and explained menstruation in medical terms, but they experienced a bifurcation between their actual experience and "the mechanics." She found working-class women did not adopt medical views of menstruation, and they explained it in terms of subjective experience, such as "you bleed to clean out your insides" (Martin 2001:110). Only four of Martin's interviewees reported PMS symptoms, leading Martin to view PMS as a culturally constructed disease used to justify sexism. Moreover, she argued that medical views of menstruation as something to be "treated" reflects the intensive work discipline of industrial society and its inability to adjust to natural human cyclical processes.

PREGNANCY AND CHILDBIRTH

Pregnancy and childbirth in the United States is medicalized. Before the nineteenth century, most women called on a midwife to assist in labor and childbirth at their home. Today, most women go to the hospital to receive care from certified, medical doctors—something described as the *medicalization of childbirth*. The modern medical approach has been remarkably effective at saving lives. Overall, the rates of maternal death and infant mortality have plummeted in the last 100 years, much of which is due to medical advances and improved sanitation. However, the medical model of pregnancy and childbirth has its drawbacks, primarily in regard to access to maternity care, the commodification of birth, and the technocratic model of birth.

Access to Maternity Care

Access to health care is an ongoing issue in the United States because health insurance is privatized; and citizens must get it through their employers, or have enough income to purchase insurance in the market, or simply pay cash for health care. Prior to 2014, approximately 47 million Americans were uninsured. In 2011, 62 percent of women in the United States covered by private health insurance plans, not through an employer, lacked maternity coverage. In 2014, the U.S. Congress implemented the Affordable Care Act (ACA) that attempted to reform the health care system by providing more people with affordable health insurance. ACA especially works in terms of affordability, access, and quality of women's maternity care. All health insurance plans in the United States are now required to cover essential maternity benefits such as prenatal, birth and postpartum care, newborn care, breastfeeding supplies, contraceptive services, sexually transmitted disease screening, domestic violence screening, and more (Assistant Secretary for Public Affairs 2015). Without adequate access to preventative measures and basic health care, pregnant women and infants are at risk for many complications. These can range from premature birth, to fetal disorders, to death.

Race and income inequality intersect to create disparities in health care for pregnant and birthing women. African American and Native American women and children are at much greater risk during pregnancy, childbirth, and infancy than whites due to lack of access to or substandard care. *Maternal mortality* is the death of a woman while pregnant or within 42 days of termination of pregnancy from any cause related to or aggravated by the pregnancy or its management. For the last four decades, death rates for black women during pregnancy and childbirth complications have been approximately four times white women's death rates in the United States (Tucker et al. 2007). According to the Centers for Disease Control (CDC) Pregnancy Mortality Surveillance System, during 2011 and 2012, the number of

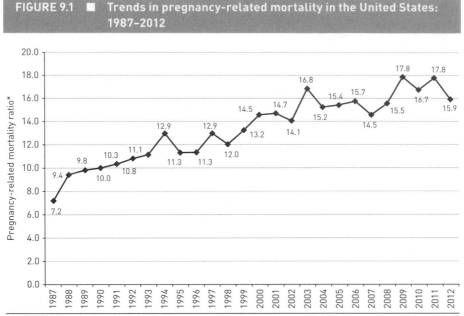

FIGURE 9.1   ■   Trends in pregnancy-related mortality in the United States: 1987–2012

The number of pregnancy-related deaths in the United States is alarmingly high for a wealthy, developed country. Most disturbingly, pregnancy-related deaths have been on an upward trend since 1987.

Source: CDC, Division of Reproductive Health. http://www.cdc.gov/reproductivehealth/maternalinfanthealth/pmss.html.

*Note: Number of pregnancy-related deaths per 100,000 live births per year.

reported pregnancy-related deaths was 11.8 deaths per 100,000 live births for white women and 41.1 deaths per 100,000 live births for black women (Pregnancy Related Deaths 2013).

Black mothers are also twice as likely to have costly premature births due to factors including poor access to health care, existing health problems, and greater susceptibility to stress (Giscombe and Lobel 2005; O'Donnell 2016). **Infant mortality** is the death of a child under the age of one year. The infant mortality rate of black infants is more than twice that of white infants (Mathews and MacDorman 2008). According to the CDC, in 2013 the infant mortality rates for whites was 5.06 deaths per 1,000 births; and for African Americans, it was 11.11 deaths per 1,000 births. Both infant mortality rates and maternal mortality rates are measures of the overall health of a society; the more babies and pregnant/birthing women who live, the healthier a society must be.

Commodification of Birth

Giving birth in the United States is big business. Prenatal care and delivery are expensive, costing an average of $20,000 for an uncomplicated birth. According to a report by Truven Health Analytics, between the years 2004 and 2010, the prices that insurers paid for childbirth rose 49 percent for vaginal births and 41 percent for caesarean sections (Truven Health Analytics 2013). The average total price charged for pregnancy and newborn care was about $30,000 for a vaginal delivery and $50,000 for a cesarean section. Even with insurance, women pay out-of-pocket copays and expenses, averaging $3,400. In contrast, women in other western industrialized countries spend almost nothing for childbirth, and are offered postpartum care and maternal education for little or no cost. The United States is the most expensive place to give birth in the world (Rosenthal 2013).

The cost of birth continues to rise because health care in the United States is a for-profit system. Health care used to be a humanitarian function of society; now it is a profitable industry. One way this plays out is in the medical billing process. All aspects of maternity and birth care are billed item by item, and nothing goes unnoticed or is too small. Two decades ago,

FIGURE 9.2 ■ Infant Mortality Rates, by Race and Hispanic Origin of Mother: United States, 1999–2013

| | | Race and Hispanic origin of mother[1] | | | | |
| | | | Not Hispanic or Latina | | | |
Year	Total[2]	Hispanic or Latina	White	Black or African American	Asian or Pacific Islander	American Indian or Alaska Native
		Infant deaths per 1,000 live births[3]				
1999	7.04	5.71	5.76	14.14	4.73	9.35
2000	6.89	5.59	5.70	13.59	4.79	8.19
2001	6.84	5.44	5.72	13.46	4.65	9.67
2002	6.95	5.62	5.80	13.89	4.66	8.67
2003	6.84	5.65	5.70	13.60	4.68	8.72
2004	6.78	5.55	5.66	13.60	4.55	8.62
2005	6.86	5.62	5.76	13.63	4.77	8.31
2006	6.68	5.41	5.58	13.35	4.40	8.64
2007	6.75	5.51	5.63	13.32	4.60	9.38
2008	6.61	5.59	5.53	12.67	4.39	8.66
2009	6.39	5.29	5.33	12.40	4.28	9.17
2010	6.14	5.25	5.18	11.46	4.17	8.65
2011	6.07	5.15	5.07	11.45	4.18	8.52
2012	5.98	5.11	5.04	11.19	3.97	8.74
2013	5.96	5.00	5.06	11.11	3.90	7.72

| | | Detailed Hispanic origin of mother[1] | | | |
Year	Mexican	Puerto Rican	Cuban	Central and South American	Other and unknown Hispanic or Latina
		Infant deaths per 1,000 live births[3]			
1999	5.51	8.35	4.64	4.67	7.24
2000	5.43	8.20	4.57	4.64	6.88
2001	5.22	8.53	4.25	4.97	6.02
2002	5.42	8.19	3.74	5.06	7.15
2003	5.49	8.18	4.59	5.04	6.66
2004	5.47	7.82	4.57	4.65	6.72
2005	5.53	8.31	4.45	4.69	6.44
2006	5.34	8.02	5.06	4.52	5.78
2007	5.42	7.72	5.21	4.57	6.41
2008	5.58	7.29	4.88	4.76	5.86
2009	5.12	7.19	5.75	4.47	6.06
2010	5.12	7.09	3.81	4.43	6.09
2011	4.99	7.84	4.34	4.35	5.41
2012	5.02	6.86	4.99	4.14	5.59
2013	4.90	5.92	3.04	4.30	5.88

[1] Persons of Hispanic origin may be of any race. Starting with 2003 data, some states reported multiple-race data. The multiple-race data for these states were bridged to the single-race categories of the 1977 Office of Management and Budget standards, for comparability with other states. See Appendix II, Hispanic origin; Race.
[2] Includes all infant deaths not shown separately.
[3] Infant is under age 1 year.

Infant mortality rates are a measure of the overall health of a country. They are distressingly high in the United States, particularly so for racial/ethnic minorities, as this data exemplifies.

Sources: CDC/NCHS, National Vital Statistics System, public-use Linked Birth/Infant Death Data Set. See Appendix I, National Vital Statistics System (NVSS).

Notes: Rates based on a period file using Weighted data. Also see Table 10.

most fees were covered under one general hospital fee. Today, items such as use of the delivery room, the birthing tub, epidural, or even the removal of the placenta can be given a separate charge. The lack of transparency in health care costs is problematic, as most women simply receive an un-itemized bill after birth. The Affordable Care Act creates more transparencies, but overall the medical system is designed in a way that costs patients and benefits insurance companies, pharmaceutical companies, hospitals, and medical device companies.

Technocratic Model of Birth

Birth in the United States is based on a ***technocratic model***, meaning it is a process controlled by doctors and scientists who claim to have the most knowledge about it (Davis-Floyd 2004). The modern technocratic approach to birth strongly encourages women to see an ***obstetrician***, a medical doctor who specializes in the management of pregnancy, labor, birth, and, most specifically, reproductive surgery. Obstetricians are highly skilled and tend to view birth as a medical service, with technology, pain management, and time management as high priorities. The technocratic model heavily relies on common labor interventions, such as artificial labor induction, electronic fetal monitoring, forceps, and vacuum extractors. There is a focus on the doctor as the "deliverer," not the mother; and it is often the doctor who is thanked for the birth, rather than the mother.

Many attribute the technocratic model of birth for the increase in the amount of cesarean sections in the United States. A ***cesarean section*** is a surgical operation for delivering a child by cutting through the wall of the mother's abdomen. The overall cesarean delivery rate in the United States increased 60 percent from 1996 through 2009, from 20.7 percent to 32.9 percent (Osterman and Martin 2014). In many cases, cesarean sections are necessary due to clinical issues such as uterine rupture. In some cases they are chosen if a woman is high risk because she is older, overweight, or diabetic. However, for low-risk women, the American College of Obstetricians and Gynecologists finds that cesarean delivery poses a greater risk of maternal morbidity and mortality than vaginal delivery and argues that all measures should be taken to prevent it (The American College of Obstetricians and Gynecologists and Society for Maternal-Fetal Medicine 2014). Neonatal mortality rates are higher among infants delivered by cesarean section (MacDorman et al. 2006). When compared to other developing countries, the United States has one of the highest cesarean section rates and maternal and infant death rates (Kim and Saada 2013).

Many doctors and low-risk women choose cesareans because it offers the false notion of more control because it can be scheduled and timed, unlike unpredictable vaginal births. ***Designer birth*** is a new term to describe a planned cesarean surgery in which a tummy tuck is done immediately after the delivery. Some women prefer this approach for the added cosmetic surgery and elect to have cesarean sections just for this purpose. Serious consideration of the significant risks involved are encouraged for both doctors and low-risk pregnant women.

FIGURE 9.3 ■ Overall Cesarean Delivery and Low-Risk Cesarean Delivery: United States, final 1990–2012 and preliminary 2013

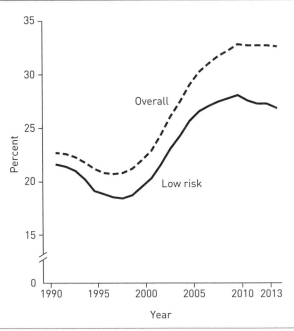

Source: Current data: CDC, National Center for Health Statistics, 2016. https://www.cdc.gov/nchs/data/nvsr/nvsr63/nvsr63_06.pdf.

Note: Low risk is defined as nulliparous, term, singleton births in a vertex (head first) presentation.

More and more women prefer and are demanding a more holistic model in which care is woman-centered. Many women seeking holistic care hire a midwife instead of an obstetrician. ***Midwives*** are trained professionals with expertise and skills in the area of pregnancy and childbirth. They focus on supporting women by offering individualized care that is suited to a woman's unique mental, emotional, physical, and even spiritual needs. In 1979, sociologist Barbara Katz-Rothman was the first to define the difference between the medical model and midwifery model of care. The ***midwifery model*** is based on female perspectives and experiences, with a view of the female body as healthy, and an overall

BOX 9.1

GLOBAL/TRANSNATIONAL PERSPECTIVES ON SEXUALITY:
GIVING BIRTH IN AFGHANISTAN

Afghanistan is deemed by UNICEF as one of "the worst places in the world to give birth" (Nebehay 2009). It has one of the highest maternal and infant mortality rates in the world. Decades of war and oppressive rule from the Islamic fundamentalist group, the Taliban, devastated Afghanistan's health care infrastructure. The Taliban (1994–2001) banned women from receiving maternity care from male doctors; so with few female doctors available, most births occurred without skilled attendants. By 2002, Afghanistan's maternal mortality ratio was one of the highest in the world: 1,100 deaths to every 100,000 live births (World Health Organization 2015). Compare this to the United States, which had a maternal mortality rate of 21 deaths to 100,000 live births in 2010 (Central Intelligence Agency 2010).

Further compounding the problem is women's low social status and lack of education and literacy in Afghanistan. Many young women marry very young and have their first pregnancy at a young age, increasing chances for prenatal and birth complications. Adding to these issues, some conservative religious views make women feel ashamed of being pregnant because it is a public acknowledgement they had sex with their husbands. They are too ashamed to get health care or even go to a hospital during labor complications.

For every woman who dies, twenty more survive; and because they are unattended

by skilled professionals, many have complications such as obstetric fistula. An ***obstetric fistula*** is a hole between the vagina and rectum or bladder that is caused by prolonged, obstructed labor. If a woman's labor becomes obstructed, she can be in horrific pain for days before the baby is finally born. Often the infant dies from lack of adequate blood flow, and the mother is left with an obstetric fistula. The fistula almost always causes fecal or urinary incontinence. And often she is rejected by her husband and village due to her foul smell. Obstetric fistula is considered a disease of poverty, as it occurs only in poor countries where women have no assistance with getting the baby out and have no surgeon to sew up the hole afterward. It is entirely preventable.

To reverse maternity deaths and cases of obstetric fistula, health officials and international partners have sought to train midwives and female surgeons. A variety of two-year training programs have increased the number of skilled midwives in Afghanistan. Organizations such as the Fistula Foundation offer 75 free surgeries per year and educational materials to women. Conditions for women have slowly improved over the last decade, but there still remains a very acute need for more maternity care. As of 2011, nearly 60 percent of all births were still not attended by a health care professional (Kakissis 2011).

trust in the body, nature, and birth processes. In this approach, time is irrelevant, and birth requires patience from everyone involved. This is in direct contrast to the technocratic model, which is critiqued for being male centered, with the female body viewed as unsafe and defective, and the entire process in need of control and management through technology.

The technocratic model views pain during childbirth as inevitable and unacceptable. Narcotic-type drugs for pain are almost always administered in a standard medical birth and complete spinal anesthesia is common. Dr. Grantly Dick-Read (1942, republished in 2013), in *Childbirth without Fear*, was one of the first to argue that the pain of birth is primarily a result of social attitudes. As already described, the body is a social space with specific symbolic meanings and representations. A birthing woman's body is embedded with cultural ideas that associate birth with excruciating pain. United States culture promotes fear in girls and women about birth from a very early age. The midwifery model of care does not necessarily view pain entirely as socially created, but it does view it as something that can be naturally managed with techniques such as guided imagery, breathing, movement, or hydrotherapy. An example of the midwifery model can be found in the work of internationally renowned Dr. Ina May Gaskin, founder of the Farm Midwifery Center in Tennessee, who has practiced midwifery for over 41 years. Author of numerous books, Gaskin promotes a focus on joy during birth, rather than fear and pain. In *Spiritual Midwifery* (2002), Gaskin shares how she witnessed many women experience painless childbirths, and in some cases, she witnessed women experience orgasms during birth.

BREASTFEEDING

Breast milk is the most ideal nutrition for newborn human infants. It is the perfect blend of vitamins, protein, fat, and antibodies for an infant to grow and fight off viruses and bacteria. Breast milk is easily digested and lowers the risk of infants developing asthma and allergies. Research confirms that an infant who is breastfed exclusively for the first six months of life has fewer ear infections, respiratory illnesses, and digestive issues. The skin-on-skin bonding and eye contact that takes places during breastfeeding helps infants feel love and security. The progesterone released in a woman's body while breastfeeding makes her feel relaxed. Long-term benefits are just as rewarding. Children who are breastfed have been linked to fewer issues with obesity and a lower risk of diabetes. All around, breastfeeding is the best choice for infants, and the great majority of health care providers agree.

It hasn't always been this way though. There was a time in U.S. history when health care providers and doctors told new mothers that the best food for their newborn was infant formula. Until the end of the nineteenth century, the only substitute food given to newborns was animal's milk—and only rarely, under extreme circumstances, or when a **wet nurse**, a woman hired to breastfeed another woman's infant, could not be found. The first formula to be patented and used was in 1883, and it was a starchy, sugary compound lacking in nutrients and vitamins. By the 1940s and 1950s, corporations had concocted a more nutritional blend of fortified cow's milk and were aggressively marketing it to doctors. Consequently, infant formula came to be seen as a safe substitute for breast milk, and by the 1970s was the primary way mothers fed their infants in the United States (Stevens, Patrick, and Pickler 2009).

Infant formula is still widely used in the United States today. Research links its usage to the development of several common childhood illnesses, such as allergies, diabetes, and obesity (Stevens et al. 2009). More and more health care providers encourage breastfeeding to increase the health of mothers and children, and the trend is finally reversing. The Centers for Disease Control and Prevention approximates that in 2013, 77 percent of mothers initiated breastfeeding at birth, and 49 percent were still breastfeeding at six months (Division of Nutrition, Physical Activity, and Obesity 2013).

Breastfeeding as Taboo

Part of the resistance surrounding women's decision whether or not to breastfeed has to do with the fact that in the United States, breastfeeding in public is a social *taboo*. Even if the woman's breast is covered up completely, it is too often described as indecent, scandalous, and inappropriate. Women are often asked to leave public places if seen breastfeeding. It is viewed as a private act that should be hidden from view. This is primarily because women's bodies, most especially her breasts, are sexualized. Women and their breasts are seen as sex objects before they are seen as mothers. This reveals how powerful gender constructions can be, despite biological designs.

Imagery of sexualized breasts abound in U.S. media and marketing; through such imagery, it becomes clear that they are intended for the sexual pleasure of men. If a woman's breast or nipple is revealed while breastfeeding her infant she is often accused of trying to seduce or titillate males around her. Most breastfeeding women would argue this is the farthest idea from their mind. Breasts are so sexualized in U.S. culture that the more politically correct term for breastfeeding in corporate settings and public policies is now "nursing," because even to say "breast" is to imply something sexual or dirty. Breastfeeding advocates work to protect, promote, and support women who choose to breastfeed. And while more and more women are finding acceptance, many are still met with numerous cultural, institutional, and commercial barriers.

Costs of Breastfeeding

One argument made by breastfeeding activists is that it saves money. They also argue it saves taxpayers' money in the long term due to the social costs of obese children and adults, which are attributed to infant formula feeding. While breastfeeding is virtually free and infant formula is very costly, breast milk is not entirely free. Research shows that breastfeeding mothers lose earnings. The longer a woman breastfeeds, the more income she loses (Rippeyoung and Noonan 2012). Moreover, long-term breastfeeding, while medically encouraged, is class biased, because poor and working-class women are not usually in occupations where they have the autonomy needed to be able to breastfeed a child. Most women who breastfeed longer than six months are white, college educated, and married to college-educated men who can financially cover the woman's loss of income while she breastfeeds (Rippeyoung and Noonan 2012).

More and more employers are trying to be more work friendly to nursing mothers. The Affordable Care Act requires employers to provide break times and space for women to pump breast milk at work. It also requires that breast pumps be covered by health insurance. Many women in the United States choose to pump since there is no federally mandated "paid" maternity leave. It is a financial challenge because most doctors recommend women breastfeed for six months, but they are offered only 12 weeks of leave, which employers are not required to pay. If a mother decides to breastfeed, there are many hidden costs.

"Breasts are a scandal because they shatter the border between motherhood and sexuality" —Iris Marion Young (2005:88).

TRANSGENDER AND GENDER-NONCONFORMING PREGNANCY

Cultural ideologies like compulsory reproduction and compulsory motherhood make pregnancy and childbirth an expectation for women. A pregnant body implies the acceptance or rejection of such social norms and is an expression of power relations. When a transgender or gender-nonconforming individual is pregnant, they go against society's expectation that pregnancy is a feminine experience assigned for females only. Individuals assigned male at birth do not have the anatomy needed for pregnancy. As of today, there are no successful uterine transplants or ***extrauterine pregnancies***, meaning a pregnancy outside the uterus and in the abdominal cavity, for transwomen and cisgender males. However, transmen and gender nonconformists with the sex assignment of female at birth, can and often do reproduce.

Most transmen retain their female reproductive organs after having socially and/or medically transitioned, and are thereby able to achieve pregnancy. Typically, the progression of pregnancy and birth is the same for transmen as it is for cisgender females. However, a pregnant transman is often greeted with suspicion and hostility from health care providers (Henig 2014). Negative social, emotional, and medical experiences are commonplace for pregnant transgender men. Often this is because health care professionals still do not understand fluid gender identity and expression and are not comfortable with patients outside the gender binary. A review of transgender experiences during pregnancy and childbirth reveals that greater awareness to the specific needs of transgender pregnancies are needed, such as ways to deal with their reported increasing experiences of gender dysphoria during pregnancy, discussions of options for chest (breast) feeding, and how and when to reinitiate testosterone (Obedin-Maliver and Makadon 2015).

Gender-nonconforming individuals struggle with similar issues. In A. K. Summers' graphic memoir, *Pregnant Butch: Nine Long Months Spent in Drag* (2014), she describes how her masculine identity was challenged by pregnancy. She found it difficult to accept her pregnant feminized body and describes how the entire pregnancy and childbirth process is feminized in society and defined by strict feminine gender roles. She describes pregnant women's subordinate position in society as revealed through various cultural practices, such as when people feel confident commenting on or even touching a pregnant body just because it is pregnant. Gender-affirming policies and behaviors in both the medical and social world are important for bringing greater equality to the process of pregnancy and birth for all.

TEEN PREGNANCY AND BIRTH

Like transgender pregnancies, teen pregnancies go against social norms. When a teenager is pregnant, she is often socially shamed, blamed, and criticized for lack of responsibility or for what is perceived as sexual promiscuity. By blaming teen mothers exclusively, the fathers and their responsibility escape much of the social commentary and concern, while the larger social issues that contribute to teen births also go unexamined. The blame approach impacts policies and programs, which tend to focus on changing the behaviors of teens, especially female teens, instead of addressing what it is they need to prevent pregnancy and birth or to be successful parents (Erdmans and Black 2015).

In 2014, the birth rate for babies born to teens, ages 15 to 19, was 24.2 per 1,000 births. This is a historic low for the United States, declining by two-thirds from the teen birth rate in 1991, despite the fact that we continue to treat teen pregnancy as an epidemic (Erdmans and Black 2015). While the U.S. teen birth rates are lower than they have ever been, they are substantially higher than all other developed nations. Sociologists Mary Patrice Erdmans and Timothy Black (2015) describe systemic inequalities rooted in patriarchy, poverty, and racism that impact young teen mothers' lives before they get pregnant. They argue that teen birth is often preceded by a complex set of experiences including family life stress, sexual abuse, neglect, domestic violence, and lack of education.

Race differences in teen births are enormous. In 2014, black and Hispanic teen birth rates were more than two times higher than the rate for white teens, and Native American teen birth rates more than one and a half times higher (Hamilton et al. 2015). Intersecting the lives of people of color is concentrated poverty, which is the single most important predictor of teen pregnancy. Areas of high unemployment and poverty give few options for higher education or professional employment, lowering incentives for teens to postpone parenthood (Raley 2008). Teen daughters of teen mothers are more likely to become teen mothers (Hoffman and

Maynard 2008). Teens in child welfare systems are at higher risk, and teens living in foster care are more than twice as likely to become pregnant than those not in foster care (Boonstra 2011).

Once a poor teen mother becomes a parent, the chances that she will continue to live in poverty are extremely high. Only half of teen mothers receive a high school diploma by age 22. Fewer teen mothers decide to marry, going against heteronormative messages that pregnancy should come after marriage or at least be accompanied by it. Many teen fathers follow gendered expectation that the mothers should take on most of the parenting responsibilities, and the fathers have minimal involvement (Nylund 2006). Single teen mothers often rely on federal social aide programs, including health care and food stamps. Children of teen mothers are more likely to have more early developmental delays, problems with school achievement, higher placements of foster care, and are three times more likely to be incarcerated during adolescence than children of mothers who delay parenting (Hoffman and Maynard 2008).

Yet, it is important to emphasize that not all teen births have negative outcomes. Patriarchal values tend to view an unmarried, young mother as immature, irresponsible, and immoral. But, in some cases early childbearing can be a positive adaptation to stressful economic and family conditions and can actually promote and propel women into life situations they otherwise would have thought unattainable (Geronimus 1991). Sometimes young women are simply resilient enough to survive and thrive despite, or even because of, having a child while a teenager. So, while negative experiences often lead to teen birth, teen motherhood is not a unanimously negative experience. Moreover, the issue is multilayered and complex. Popular political rhetoric shapes negative ideas about teen mothers that are often assumptions and leave many questions unanswered. For instance, it is assumed that if an impoverished young woman delays childbearing until her early twenties, poverty will not necessarily be her fate. This assumption deserves to be challenged, though, since most poor people remain poor; there is very little social mobility (Luker 1997).

Comprehensive sex education and access to birth control make a huge difference in rates of teen pregnancy and birth. Numerous studies released in 2014 revealed that increased access to birth control is responsible for the largely increasing decline in abortion and teen pregnancy rates (Birgisson et al. 2015; Parks and Peipert 2016; Secura et al. 2014). The Centers for Disease and Prevention claims that there are huge differences in state-by-state teen birth rates. The states with the fewest teen pregnancies, such as New Hampshire, Massachusetts, Maine, and Connecticut, are proactive on the issue. They provide access to family-planning services and birth control, access to comprehensive sex education, and generally promote a cultural message of understanding of teen sexuality (Fox 2014). A 2009 study correlates states whose residents have more conservative religious beliefs and promote abstinence-only sex education programs, such as Mississippi and Texas, with higher rates of teen births (Strayhorn and Strayhorn 2009).

BIRTH CONTROL

Throughout most of human history, sex and reproduction have been inextricably linked. It was only until the invention of contraception, the practice of preventing reproduction through deliberate use of artificial methods, that nonreproductive heterosexual sex became possible. This did not stop the immense influence of cultural notions of compulsory reproduction or compulsory motherhood. However, it did make "family planning" possible and gave human beings much greater control over when and how often reproduction occurs. In the following section, we will look at the history of birth control, primarily in the United States; the gendered nature of birth control; and how race and class inequalities intersect in the use, forced use, and distribution of contraception.

History of Birth Control

Methods to prevent pregnancy and venereal disease have always been a part of the human story. A historical review of barrier methods, or condom use, reveals the first use dates back to King Minos of Crete in 3000 BCE who used a goat's bladder (Kahn et al. 2013). The Egyptians used linen sheaths, the Romans animal intestines, and the Chinese silk (Kahn et al. 2013). So the idea of using something like condoms to prevent pregnancy is not new. Prior to modern technological advancements, however, they were not readily available, and men and women had to primarily rely on behavioral methods such as withdrawal, fertility awareness, or abstinence. These methods have high failure rates.

The history of birth control in the United States dates to the nineteenth century when changes in the manufacturing of rubber produced more effective and comfortable condoms, and the diaphragm was invented. Although these two forms of birth control were effective and available, this did not mean that they were widely accepted. In fact, in 1873, the U.S. government passed the *Comstock Laws*, also referred to as the "chastity laws," that declared any control of reproduction obscene. Advertisements, information, or distribution of birth control was prohibited. The postal service was allowed to confiscate birth control sold through the mail, and the punishment for having or selling pornography was imprisonment or a very large fine. Birth control activist Margaret Sanger fought for women's reproductive rights by opening the first birth control clinic in the United States and was arrested under the Comstock Laws for her efforts. In 1936, in the *United States v. One Package* case involving Margaret Sanger, a reversal on the federal ban of birth control was issued, ending the Comstock era and paving the way for the legitimization of birth control in the United States.

It was not until the 1960s that the Comstock-style approach to contraception fully subsided. The first oral contraceptive, the birth control pill, was approved by the FDA in 1960, and it became the harbinger of a reproductive revolution. In 1968, the FDA approved the sale and use of intrauterine devices (IUDs). Over time, more options became available. In 1990, the first contraceptive implant, Norplant, was offered for women. In 1990, the first injectable method, *DepoProvera*, was introduced; and, in 1993, the first female condom was developed. In the 2000s, the hormonal patch, *Ortho Evra*, and the vaginal ring, *Nuvaring*, were introduced. In 1999, an emergency contraception pill, *Plan B*, was approved by the FDA. It is a form of birth control used after sex to prevent pregnancy. It can be taken up to five days after unprotected sex.

Today, for the first time in history, large numbers of women have access to relatively safe and inexpensive birth control. This is nothing short of revolutionary. This newfound freedom brings with it new opportunities to pursue higher education and advanced careers. Legal policies slowly caught up with this social revolution. In 1965, in the Supreme Court case, *Griswold v. Connecticut*, married couples, under the right to privacy in the U.S. Constitution, gained the right to use birth control. This reveals an assumption behind compulsory reproduction that married couples do not need birth control because they are supposed to be having children. In 1972, the Supreme Court legalized birth control for all citizens regardless of marital status in *Baird v. Eisenstadt*. By the early 1970s many young, single women were using contraception in increasing numbers. Today, more than 60 percent of women of reproductive age, from 15 to 44, are using contraception in the United States (Jones, Mosher, and Daniels 2012). The increasing rates of women gaining college degrees and careers since the 1960s are directly correlative to women's ability to control their reproductive lives (Goldin and Katz 2002).

Gendered Contraception

As you might have noticed, the entire history of birth control primarily resides on woman-controlled methods, besides behavioral methods and the male condom. The hormonal methods mentioned above, such as the birth control pill, implants, injections, patches, and rings all rely on the delivery of hormones into the female body. In most cases, progesterone and estrogen are released to suppress ovulation or thicken the cervical mucus, blocking sperm penetration. While most are over 92 percent effective, they do not prevent against sexually transmitted diseases, and come with a variety of side effects, some potentially dangerous. Women began noticing such side effects early on.

In 1970, the U.S. Senate began hearings on the safety of the birth control pill. The primary concern was the risk of estrogen causing cancers. Feminists from the D.C. Women's Liberation group vocally raised concerns and challenged the medical-pharmaceutical establishment who marketed it. As a result, the formulation of the birth control pill was drastically changed by significantly reducing the level of hormones used, and an insert with information about potential side effects became required. This was the first time information was issued with prescription drugs; it is now a requirement for all pharmaceuticals in the United States. This did not mean the side effects stopped. The Centers for Disease Control and Prevention released a report on the use of contraception between 1982 and 2008 (Mosher and Jones 2010). They estimate 45 million women used the birth control pill at least once in their lives. Of those, 30 percent (or 13.6 million) had discontinued the pill because they were dissatisfied with it. About two out of three (64 percent, or 8.6 million) of the 13.6 million women who stopped using the pill stopped because of side effects. Hormonal birth control methods, while liberating, have their drawbacks.

Where is the male birth control pill? While dozens of hormonal contraceptives have been introduced for women since 1960, not a single new contraception has been developed for men in over 100 years (Shapiro 2015). Birth control is highly gendered. Attitudes of both men and women toward a male contraceptive pill and their trust in the effective use of the pill reveal gender stereotypes and the sexual double standard (Eberhardt, van Wersch, and Meikle 2009). Women are expected to be sexually passive and thereby thwart sexual advances and, by extension of this, prevent pregnancy. Masculinity is built on exhibiting fertility rather than preventing it. Femininity is associated with care of one's own health and that of others. Despite gender barriers, many men are interested in a male birth control pill option. Several cross-cultural studies reveal that the majority of male participants expressed willingness to use a contraceptive pill (Heinemann et al. 2005; Martin et al. 2000).

The medical and scientific communities are influenced by and contribute to socially constructed ideas of gender and gender stereotypes. In medicine, traditionally, the male body is viewed as the baseline for "normal" while the female body is viewed as "abnormal" and in need of medical intervention (Fausto-Sterling 2013; Martin 2001). Therefore it follows that women's bodies are the primary site of invasive medical inventions, especially in regard to sexual and reproductive interventions (Shapiro 2015). Traditionally, the reproductive patient is female, not male. Oudshoorn (2003) describes this as the invisibility of male reproductive bodies in scientific medicine. There is a commonly accepted medical viewpoint that although it takes both sexes to create an embryo, because it is a woman's body that is specifically capable of carrying through with the reproduction, contraceptive and reproductive responsibility should thereby be primarily placed on her. In order for science and research to invent and market a male contraceptive pill, social scripts have to expand and male bodies be considered.

One medical option available and increasingly popular for men is ***vasectomy***, a form of contraception in which the tubes that transport sperm from the testicles to the penis are surgically cut or blocked. It is minimally invasive, has few side effects, and a very low failure rate. It is considered a form of ***sterilization***, or a permanent end to reproductive ability. For many women and feminists, vasectomy has come to symbolize a solution to the problem of gender inequality in contraception in heterosexual relationships (Lowe 2009).

Forced Sterilization and Eugenics

For women, sterilization is offered in the form of ***tubal ligation***, or the surgical cutting or blocking of the fallopian tubes, which prevents the egg from moving down to the uterus where it can potentially be fertilized by sperm during sexual intercourse. A nonincision form of tubal ligation is when a microinsert is placed in the fallopian tubes, which causes natural tissues to grow, blocking the tubes. Sterilization is the most common contraceptive method utilized by couples in the United States (Bartz and Greenberg 2008). It is safe, effective, and most importantly, a choice.

Unfortunately, the United States has a history of **forced sterilization**, the process of permanently ending someone's ability to reproduce without his or her consent. Forced sterilization is backed by government policy. In 1927, the U.S. Supreme Court ruled, in *Buck v. Bell*, that forced sterilization of the "unfit," including the intellectually disabled, does not violate the Constitution. Forced sterilization laws were passed in 30 states, and approximately 70,000 U.S. citizens were sterilized based on this ruling (Cohen 2016). This decision has never formally been overturned. It is a legal mandate highly influenced by the once popular **eugenics movement**, a racist social philosophy advocating the improvement of human genetic traits through the promotion of reproduction for people with desired traits and reducing the reproduction of those with undesired traits, usually through sterilization. Undesired traits, such as sexual promiscuity or "feeblemindedness," were vague, unspecific, and extremely subjective.

Birth control activist and founder of Planned Parenthood Margaret Sanger.
Source: Bettmann/Getty Images.

Eugenics influenced a racist, pseudoscience movement that presented a range of faulty studies attempting to justify such political views as that the United States should reduce immigration and that "undesirables" are unsafe for society (Davis 1981). Even birth control activist Margaret Sanger worked with the eugenics movement in an effort to reduce the number of births among the lower classes (Sanger 2007). The eugenics movement went out of social favor in the 1940s, specifically after the Nazi movement used eugenic ideology in its justification for committing genocide across Europe.

Despite the demise of the eugenics movement, forced sterilizations occurred well into the 1970s, and racial/ethnic minority women were particularly targeted. In the 1960s and '70s, it started to become known that many poor women of color were forced to undergo involuntary sterilization. By 1970, an estimated 20 percent of all married black women were permanently sterilized, with black women the targets of 43 percent of federally subsidized sterilizations (Davis 1981). In the south, poor black women were sometimes given hysterectomies or tubal ligation while under anesthesia during childbirth (Scully 2004). A "Mississippi appendectomy" was a term used to describe an unnecessary hysterectomy on black women, done as practice for medical residents (Roberts 1997). Women would wake and not know they had been sterilized, sometimes for years. The state of North Carolina sterilized more than 7,000 people between 1929 and 1974 (Cohen 2013). In North Carolina, it was legal for anyone to simply request another person be sterilized, upon which a medical board would review and decide on forced sterilization. Additionally, "in 1974, an Alabama court found that between 100,000 and 150,000 poor black teenagers had been sterilized each year between 1930 and 1970" (Smith 2009).

In some cases Latina immigrant women, who could not speak English, were forced into signing consent forms for tubal ligation, when in reality, they did not know what they were agreeing to (Lira and Stern 2014). Even women whose first language was English were coerced into signing consent forms. They were pressured by hospital staff, sometimes while they were in labor; and often they were not told the procedures were irreversible. Consent forms were described as a "farce" by investigators (Caron 2008). High rates of forced sterilization were reported from Native American women, receiving care under of the federally funded Indian Health Services (IHS), and in Puerto Rico, under the care of U.S.-funded health care policies. By 1976, an estimated 25 percent of Native American women of childbearing age were sterilized (Davis 1981; Jaimes and Halsey 1992).

Unfortunately, forced sterilization is still an issue. According to the Center for Investigative Reporting, female inmates were coercively sterilized between 2006 and 2010 by doctors under contract with the California Department of Corrections and Rehabilitation (Schwarz 2014). In response, in 2014, California passed a bill prohibiting forced sterilization in prisons. This is a reproductive justice issue.

SEXUAL AND REPRODUCTIVE RIGHTS AND CHOICE

Human rights are rights inherent to all human beings regardless of nationality, sex, sexual orientation, gender, ethnicity, race, religion, language, or other status. Basic human rights are defined by various national laws, international laws, human rights groups, and consensus documents. The Universal Declaration of Human Rights proposed by the United Nations in 1948 declares all humans have the right to the highest standard of physical and mental health. An essential component to this is *sexual and reproductive health rights (SRHR)* that are the rights to sexual and reproductive health care and the right to sexual and reproductive autonomy and decision making. The 1994 International Conference on Population and Development (ICPD) Programme of Action (United Nations 2014) developed the most important international objectives regarding reproductive health rights. These are to ensure access to affordable, voluntary, and informed family-planning, prenatal, and childbirth services; and to meet the changing reproductive needs over the life cycle, in ways sensitive to diverse cultures. SRHR are important because access to reproductive health care can determine a woman's social and economic status. This is a transnational and a national concern.

SRHR were called into the forefront of U.S. politics by the Women's Health Movement (WHM) that emerged during the 1960s and the 1970s. The primary goal of WHM was to improve health care for all women, but they gave special attention to reproductive health rights (Nichols 2000). WHM and feminists across the country spoke out for women's *reproductive control*, which is the ability to choose when and how often to reproduce. This brought the issue of a woman's right to have an *abortion*, the deliberate termination of a human pregnancy, to the level of a national debate. In 1973, the U.S. Supreme Court landmark case, *Roe v Wade*, legalized the right for women to have an abortion across the country. However, state legislatures do have the right to specify: the time period during which a woman can have an abortion, the procedures used, whether there is state funding for and private insurance coverage of, required waiting periods, required counseling or not, and whether parental involvement is required for minors.

Abortion is a safe and healthy option for *unintended pregnancy*, or pregnancy that is mistimed or unwanted. Research shows that most Americans want an average of two children (Guttmacher Institute 2016). In order for this to happen, a woman spends approximately five years pregnant, postpartum, or trying to become pregnant. Most women are fertile between the ages of 15 and 44. This leaves 25 years trying to prevent pregnancy. In 2011, 45 percent of the 6.1 million pregnancies in the United States each year were unintended (Finer and Zolna 2016). Unintended pregnancies are most common among women and girls who are poor (Finer and Zolna 2016). The economic stressors of an unintended child cost not only the mother, but the state. In 2010, 68 percent of the 1.5 million unplanned births were paid for by public insurance programs, primarily Medicaid (Guttmacher Institute 2016). In 2011, 42 percent of unintended pregnancies ended in abortion (Finer and Zolna 2016).

Greater reproductive control and access to reproductive health care provide the option for motherhood as voluntary, not compulsory.

Women of Color and Reproductive Justice

Angela Davis, Dorothy Roberts, and other black feminists critiqued the WHM in the 1970s for being primarily composed of white, middle-class, feminist activists who left out concerns and specific issues faced by women of color and working-class women (Davis 1981). While primarily white, middle-class feminists had been fighting for the right to abortion and access to birth control, black women in the United States have been fighting for the right to have children. They have referred to their fight as a fight for ***reproductive justice*** instead of a fight for reproductive rights, shifting the discussion away from abortion and toward a more holistic understanding of women's reproductive lives and concerns.

As Deborah Roberts says in *Killing the Black Body*, "regulating Black women's reproductive decisions has been a central aspect of racial oppression in America" (1997:6). During slavery, black women were treated as human breeders and often were expected to have as many children as possible, but often were denied the right to mother them. In the 1990s, the stereotype of the black welfare mother portrayed her as having too many children. Roberts' research reveals how some young black women were coerced into accepting Norplant right after childbirth as a means to "alleviate poverty."

In addition to biases within the WHM, there exist wider ***health disparities***, or differences in health status among disadvantaged groups in the reproductive health care system. Because of inequities, women of color and poor women have less access to reproductive health care and often report negative experiences with it (Nsiah-Jefferson 2003). Services such as abortions and prenatal screening are often unavailable in rural areas, prisons, public hospitals, and on Native American reservations. Or, if they are available, often the costs prohibit access. Because poor women and women of color are less likely to work in jobs with benefits that cover reproductive health, many go without. This also means lack of access to affordable contraception. Hence, there are higher rates of unintended pregnancies among poor women, who will likely lack adequate prenatal care as well. Ironically, it is low-wage jobs without benefits that often pose the greatest health threat and negative consequences for mothers and fetuses. For immigrants and natives for whom English is not a first language, it is difficult to find reproductive health and abortion services with bilingual services and some cultural sensitivity training.

The attack on Planned Parenthood "is part of an ultra right-wing attempt to restore the basis of patriarchy or a male-dominant system and the necessity of a long-term racist system which is controlling reproduction. And to control reproduction, you have to control the bodies of women."
—Gloria Steinem (2015).

When doctors and medical practitioners negatively stereotype poor and minority women, an array of injustices can occur. Women have reported how doctors deliberately withhold information, lie about procedures, coerce them into sterilizations, or use the ideology of "fetal rights" against them. Women of color and poor women deserve both access to good reproductive health care and protection from injustices within the health care system. There have been calls for a nationally coordinated women of color movement, with a focus on dismantling white supremacy and colonialism in order to achieve reproductive health equality (Davis 1981; Nsiah-Jefferson 2003; Roberts 1997; Smith 2009).

Disability Rights and Reproductive Rights

The sexual and reproductive rights movement emphasizes women's right to have an abortion, while the disability rights movement emphasizes the right *not* to have an abortion. Disability rights activists have fought for disabled women's right to bear children and be mothers since the 1960s and '70s (see Chapter Ten). Effective medical and rehabilitation services contributed to this activism and effectively increased disabled women's ability to have children. While discrimination still exists, many disabled women can now enjoy motherhood.

A more modern concern of disability activists is addressing new technologies that allow for the practice of prenatal screening of any potential disabilities in the fetus, such as Down's syndrome, spina bifida, muscular dystrophy, among others. When a fetus is found to have disabilities, medical professionals encourage selective abortion. Disability rights activists insist that in some cases selective abortion for fetuses with disabilities could be called "eugenic abortion," or an attempt by the medical community to eradicate all disability (Saxton 1998). Anthropologist Rayna Rapp (2000) claims that the women, for the first time in history, have the "moral" choice to decide which babies are born or not. The disability rights movement seeks to emphasize the rights of all women to maintain control over reproduction while also untangling sexist, racist, and ableist ideologies (Saxton 1998).

Institutional Sexism, Racism, and Reproductive Rights

Historically, social institutions have exercised enormous power over women's bodies through controlling their sexuality and reproduction; specifically, politics, religion, and corporations influence women's access to reproductive health care and shape ideologies about women's health and bodies. We will take a brief look at how each of these social institutions impacts women's access to reproductive rights.

POLITICS The highly contested issue of abortion is a prime example of how women's reproductive rights are a site of political contestation and control. United States politicians are expected to take a stand as either antiabortion, often called "pro-life," or proabortion, often called "pro-choice." Many right-wing, conservative politicians argue that the unborn fetus has rights, hence the right to a life, while left-wing, liberal politicians argue that only the woman has legal rights, hence it is her right to choose if she wishes to carry the fetus in her body. This creates a political environment in which politicians have to choose from two extreme options: individual choices versus fetal rights. This problematically oversimplifies a subject that is far more complex.

This binary view of abortion tends to neglect several relevant and complex social perspectives. For example, it is important to remember that it is exclusively females who get pregnant and experience childbirth. In a society with a long history of institutionalized sexism, this must not be overlooked. Women in the United States earn less than men, experience more sexual violence, are not equally represented in politics, receive an average of only six weeks of maternity leave, and are not provided with any kind of publicly funded day care. Research conducted at six U.S. colleges and universities found that individuals who endorse sexist beliefs are linked with antiabortion attitudes (Begun and Walls 2015). The binary argument over abortion marginalizes women of color, poor women, and women with disabilities by not recognizing the intersectionality of oppression. When a simplistic model is used to create legal policy, it is limiting. A more complex perspective is more helpful to understanding unintended pregnancies and how diverse populations of women deal with it.

RELIGION The Catholic Church is openly opposed to any form of contraception, other than Vatican-approved "natural" methods or abstinence, and is vehemently opposed to abortion (Alioto and McHale 2014). It could be described as **_pronatalist_**, the practice of encouraging the bearing of children. The Catholic Church, like all religions in the United States, is sovereign in its right to worship practices, theology, and requirements of membership. But, when it attempts to influence government policy, these beliefs can have tremendous impact on women. For example, many right-wing, conservative politicians are Catholic and base their antiabortion and anticontraceptive stances on their religious belief system, even though their contract as a public servant is to a secular government. Following a Catholic belief entails opposition to state funding for family-planning assistance and insurance policies that cover contraceptive drugs and devices. And while only 22 percent of the U.S. population identifies as Catholic, 31 percent of the current Congress is Catholic, and there are six Catholic justices, out of nine total, on the Supreme Court (Berenson 2015).

The Catholic Church also provides public health services in various Catholic-funded hospitals across the country. These hospitals do not offer contraception or abortion services. Often times, these hospitals serve low-income communities. Lack of access to contraception increases the rate of unintended births. The more children a woman gives birth to, the higher her chances of complications. A controversial situation in 2009 involved a terminally ill woman who was 11 weeks pregnant with her fifth child and was admitted to Catholic-run St. Joseph's Hospital and Medical Center in Phoenix, Arizona. The only way to save her life was to abort the pregnancy (Hagerty 2010). Although the hospital is antiabortion, it relied on Directive 47 in the U.S. Catholic Church's ethical guidelines for health care providers—that allows, in some circumstances, abortion if it will save the mother (United States Conference of Catholic Bishops. 2009). The woman lived.

Unfortunately, Sister Margaret McBride, chief administrator of St. Joseph's hospital, was excommunicated, the most serious penalty the church can levy, for approving this decision. In comparison, no priest accused of pedophilia in the Catholic Church has ever been excommunicated (Hagerty 2010). The example reveals not only the limiting access women have to reproductive rights, but a gendered double standard in how the Church handles what is perceived as immoral and controversial (see Chapter Eight).

"The exemption sought by Hobby Lobby and Conestoga would . . . deny legions of women who do not hold their employers' beliefs access to contraceptive coverage . . . . Would the exemption . . . extend to employers with religiously grounded objections to blood transfusions (Jehovah's Witnesses); antidepressants (Scientologists); medications derived from pigs, including anesthesia, intravenous fluids, and pills coated with gelatin (certain Muslims, Jews, and Hindus); and vaccinations?"
—Ruth Bader Ginsburg, Dissent from Hobby Lobby Contraception Decision (2013).

CORPORATIONS Corporations have a primary motive of making profit, not necessarily sustaining reproductive health or rights. Pharmaceutical companies have been criticized for downplaying potential side effects and risks for certain drugs, especially birth control. Depo Provera was the subject of debate in the 1970s and '80s on whether it was safe for public use after many users claimed extreme side effects (Gold and Willson 1981; Kline 2010). Thousands of liability lawsuits were filed against the drug company, Merck, maker of the NuvaRing contraceptive, claiming women were harmed by using the product. Most say that the product put them at risk of life-threatening blood clots, and that they were not adequately warned of this risk. In 2014, Merck agreed to pay out $100 million to settle such law suits.

Corporations are influenced by government policies and religious ideology. A classic example of how policy, religion, and corporations intersect to restrict women's reproductive rights is in the 2014 Supreme Court *Burwell v. Hobby Lobby Stores Inc.* ruling in which a religious exemption was granted to the bosses of Hobby Lobby to deny contraceptive health care coverage to its employees. In other words, if a form of contraception violates an employer's religious beliefs, they do not have to provide coverage of it for their employees (Dockterman 2014). All three female Justices dissented, arguing that this ruling limits women's rights.

Assisted Reproductive Technologies (ARTs)

Just as medical technology provides ways to control reproduction, it also provides ways to increase chances of reproduction. As already mentioned in Chapter Eight, assisted reproductive technologies (ARTs) developed in recent decades include in vitro fertilization, intrauterine insemination, ovarian stimulation, and intracytoplasmic sperm injection. In vitro fertilization (IVF) was first performed in 1978 with the world's first "test tube baby." Since then, it has become a worldwide practice. ARTs are medical methods that aid conception; but they are also very much social experiences, specifically influenced by class, race, sexuality, and gender. In the following section, we will examine the gendered experience of infertility and unequal access to ARTs.

ARTS, INFERTILITY, AND GENDER ARTs benefit individuals and couples who face *infertility*, the inability to conceive after regular unprotected sex, and can assist same-sex couples. Infertility is a complex condition that can be caused by a range of factors, such as genetics, age, abnormal ovulation, sexually transmitted diseases, body weight disorders, environmental toxins, use of hormonal contraception, and even emotional distress. Gender and infertility are inextricably linked. In U.S. society, compulsory reproduction and compulsory motherhood are woven into the cultural fabric. The feminine gender role is constructed around the idea of fertility and nurturance. For this reason, infertility can be a psychologically devastating experience for women. It can lead to depression and feelings of self-blame, isolation, and grief (Raque-Bogdan and Hoffman 2015). Just as more pressure to prevent and control reproduction is placed on women, the same can be said for the pressure to reproduce. In highly patriarchal and pronatalist countries, motherhood is a way for women to ensure social status, power, and marital security (Mumtaz, Shahid, and Levay 2013). Even today, a childless woman in the Unites States is often stigmatized for being an "old maid," a lesbian, or even mentally unstable.

Infertility is often blamed on women, despite the fact that male infertility is just as common. According to the Centers for Disease Control and Prevention, approximately 6 percent of married women from 15 to 44 years of age in the United States are unable to get pregnant after one year of unprotected sex, and 12 percent have difficulty getting pregnant or carrying a pregnancy to term, regardless of marital status (Chandra, Copen, and Stephen 2013). For men, ages 25 to 44, 12 percent reported some type of infertility. In other words, this is a problem for both sexes. Yet, more emphasis is placed on women's infertility than men's, both socially and in medical contexts (Greil, Slauson-Bevins, and McQuillan 2010).

ARTS AND INCOME DISPARITIES Income disparities exist in terms of access to treatment for infertility. Effective and affordable fertility treatment and access to ARTs is challenging in the United States, where ARTs are not subsidized in most states, and private insurance rarely covers all of the costs associated with them. Many treatments are restricted to those who can pay "out of pocket." The average cost of IVF treatment in the United States is $19,000 (American Society for Reproductive Medicine 2015). Often, couples will need multiple treatments and additional medications to conceive. Obviously this restricts low-income couples from access.

Racial and ethnic minorities in the United States have less access to ARTs than non-Hispanic whites (Bitler and Schmidt 2006). In Massachusetts, a state with mandated insurance coverage of ARTs, the majority of individuals receiving fertility services are white, highly educated, and wealthy (Jain and Hornstein 2005). Research on the comparison between utilization of infertility services by minorities in the military versus the civilian population reveals that when traditional barriers are reduced, minorities seek more care. African Americans in the military had a four-fold increase in ART services than African American civilians (Feinberg et al. 2006).

ARTS AND OLDER MOTHERS Women are having children at an older age than ever before in history. The Centers for Disease Control and Prevention reports that the average age of a new mom is 26. Many women in the United States have their first child in their 30s or later. There are several social trends that explain later births. First, the availability of birth control and reproductive rights allows women more choices. The second explanation is that more women want to attain a college education and establish careers before having children. In earlier generations, both of these options were unavailable. The new and increasing fertility available through assisted reproductive technologies makes it easier and safer for older women to reproduce. Historical data suggests that the overall risk for infertility increases with age and can be as high as 64 percent for women between ages 40 and 44. Yet, with ART options, women are willing to wait. This is changing the social landscape of gender, motherhood, and families.

CONCLUSION

In conclusion, reproduction is as much a biological as a socially constructed experience. Compulsory reproduction, heterosexuality, and motherhood are influential in society's views of sex, sexuality, gender, and families. Like reproduction, the body is socially shaped. Women's reproductive processes, such as menstruation, pregnancy, childbirth, breastfeeding, and infertility are medicalized. Women do not have equal access to health care for a variety of reasons including racism, sexism, and income inequality. The commercialization and technocratic models of birth restrict women's options financially, physically, mentally, and—some might even argue—spiritually. Transgender and teen births push the limits of what is viewed as socially acceptable, and are both in need of further research and understanding from both the medical world and social policies.

Contraception is gendered in our culture, with the primary responsibility placed on women. Access to contraception has been an ongoing battle for women. Poor women, women of color, and women with disabilities face challenges gaining access to birth control and having the right to reproduce; and they have experienced a range of discriminatory policies, including forced sterilization. Abortion is an ongoing and contested issue for women, but regardless, it provides an option for women who experience unintended pregnancy. Sexual and reproductive rights are essential to all women in order to ensure access to affordable, voluntary, and informed family-planning, and prenatal and childbirth services; and to meet the changing reproductive needs over the life cycle and in ways sensitive to diverse cultures. Institutions like medicine, politics, and corporations often prevent access to sexual and reproductive rights.

Assisted reproductive technologies create new options for reproduction, but they are also very much centered in social experiences of class and gender. While allowing for greater access to parenthood for LGBTQ families and older mothers, access is still limited for low-income individuals.

Key Terms and Concepts

Abortion 201
Cesarean section 192
Compulsory
    motherhood 187
Compulsory
    reproduction 186
Contraception 184
Designer birth 192
Eugenics movement 200
Extrauterine
    pregnancy 196
Forced sterilization 200
Health disparities 202
Infant mortality 190

Infertility 205
Maternal mortality 189
Medicalization 187
Medicalization of
    childbirth 189
Menopause 188
Menstrual cycle 188
Midwife 189
Midwifery model 193
Obstetric fistula 193
Obstetrician 191
Ovulation 188
Premenstrual
    syndrome 188

Pronatalist 203
Reproduction 185
Reproductive control 201
Reproductive health 185
Reproductive justice 202
Sexual and reproductive
    health rights 201
Sterilization 199
Taboo 195
Technocratic model 191
Tubal ligation 199
Unintended pregnancy 201
Vasectomy 199
Wet Nurse 194

Critical Thinking Questions

1. What is compulsory reproduction? Provide three examples in which reproduction is emphasized and expected.

2. Describe two ways in which the body is socially constructed. How is menstruation viewed in society, and can it impact women's experiences with it?

3. Compare the technocratic model of birth with the holistic model. What are the risks and benefits of each?

4. When was the birth control pill put on the market in the United States? What was the status of contraception prior? What has been the impact of birth control on women's lives?

5. What role do institutions play in women's access to reproductive health and rights, going beyond the examples in the chapter? Describe an example of ways in which they are prohibitive.

Activities

1. Research and find an example in history of a female, reproductive-based experience that was deemed a medical condition in need of treatment, only later to be deemed healthy and normal. Research further and try to find what cultural ideologies shaped the medical and scientific community's position.

2. *Teen Mom* is a reality television series that premiered on MTV in 2009. Watch a few episodes, and analyze whether you

think it is a good prompt for discussion on sex education, teen pregnancy and birth, birth control, and romantic relationships. Could it be an effective teaching tool? Why or why not?

3. Find out where the closest Planned Parenthood is in your state. Describe the services it offers for patients. Has your state issued any restrictions that limit its ability to offer patients full reproductive care?

Essential Readings

Eig, Jonathan. 2014. *The Birth of the Pill: How Four Crusaders Reinvented Sex and Launched a Revolution*. New York: W. W. Norton & Company.

Erdmans, Mary Patrice and Timothy Black. 2015. *On Becoming a Teen Mom: Life before Pregnancy*. Oakland: University of California Press.

Kaplan, Laura. 1997. *The Story of Jane: The Legendary Underground Feminist Abortion Service*. Chicago: University of Chicago Press.

Martin, Emily. 2001. *The Woman in the Body: A Cultural Analysis of Reproduction*. Boston: Beacon Press.

Miller, Patricia. 2014. *Good Catholics: The Battle over Abortion in the Catholic Church*. Oakland: University of California Press.

Roberts, Dorothy. 1997. *Killing the Black Body: Race, Reproduction, and the Meaning of Liberty*. New York: Vintage Books.

Recommended Films

Birth Story: Ina May Gaskin and the Farm Midwives (2012). Sara Lamm and Mary Wigmore, Directors. Tells the story of Ina May Gaskin and her spirited friends, who taught themselves midwifery while living on their entirely communal, agricultural society called The Farm. Their social experiment created a model of care for women and babies that changed a generation's approach to childbirth.

Breeders: A Subclass of Women (2014). By the Center for Bioethics and Culture. This documentary explores the issue of surrogacy through talking to surrogates, physicians, psychologists, and activists involved in the issue. Explores the question of the commodification of childbirth in this way, and the impacts of surrogacy on the surrogates and the children born from surrogacy.

Google Baby (2009). Zippi Brand Frank, Director. A documentary that spans three continents telling what the baby production industry looks like from a global perspective. It sheds light on the outsourcing of surrogacy.

Little Man (2005). Nicole Conn, Director. A documentary by and about Nicole Conn and her partner, Gwendolyn Baba, who decide to adopt a child in 2002. When their surrogate mother turns out to have serious undisclosed medical issues, the couple chooses to have Nicholas born 100 days early, leaving the under-one-pound infant with a very small chance of survival. Nicole and Gwendolyn battle to keep Nicholas alive, while the stress of the medical emergency tests their relationship.

Silent Choices (2010). Faith Pennick, Director. Explores black women's experiences with abortion, a topic generally shrouded in silence. Abortion has long been viewed as a "white woman's issue" in the African American community, despite the fact that abortion rates for black women are two to three times higher than for white women. Both African American women who support abortion and those who oppose it are interviewed, as are experts such as Dorothy Roberts. Additionally, the film explores the idea that abortion is the latest attempt at black genocide.

The Business of Being Born (2008). Abby Epstein, Director. Ricki Lake recruits filmmaker Abby Epstein to explore the maternity care system in the United States. Focuses on several couples in New York City who are trying to give birth on their own terms. The film questions if birth should be viewed as a natural life process, or as a potential medical emergency. Explores the U.S. maternity care crisis and the emergence of "designer births."

The Pill (2003). Chana Gazit, Producer and Director. This PBS documentary looks at the history of the birth control pill in the United States and the enormous impact of its availability for women. Offers insights into U.S. history including eugenics, feminist activism in the 1960s, the role of medicine and pharmaceutical companies, and women's changing roles in society.

Suggested Multimedia

Guttmacher Institute is a leading research and policy organization committed to advancing sexual and reproductive health and rights in the United States and globally. https://www.guttmacher.org/

Margaret Sanger Papers Project is maintained and created by the New York University Department of History. It contains information about Sanger, including samples of her writing. http://www.nyu.edu/projects/sanger/

National Women's Health Network (NWHN) is supported by a national membership of consumer advocates seeking to shape policy and support women's consumer health decisions. https://www.nwhn.org/

The Farm Midwifery Center provides a very special service for mothers, babies, and their families. For 40 years they have practiced, treating with love and respect and empowering them to fulfill their desire for natural childbirth in a sane and safe home setting. http://thefarmmidwives.org/

SEXUAL HEALTH

LEARNING OBJECTIVES

Upon completion of this chapter, students should be able to . . .

- Understand the meaning of sexual health and the primary forms of sexual dysfunction for men and women

- Describe the disability/ability status hierarchy and specifically discuss sexual ableism and the effects of erotic segregation

- Explain the origins of the HIV/AIDS epidemic and the moral panics of the early years

- Describe some of the key social consequences of HIV/AIDS globally

In January 2011, a judge in the United Kingdom ruled that a 41-year-old intellectually disabled man, referred to as Alan, was prohibited from participating in sexual relations with his male partner, referred to as Kieran. Both men lived in public housing. In his ruling, the judge noted that their relationship included anal sex, oral sex, and mutual masturbation. One of the concerns the judge listed was his presumption that Alan was unable to understand the threat of sexually transmitted diseases he was facing by engaging in sex (Gill 2015). While we cannot say for sure whether this judge's decision was motivated by homophobia, researchers say there is a strong heterosexual bias in educational materials designed to teach intellectually disabled people about sexuality (McCarthy 1999). People with intellectual disabilities who have same-sex attractions are referred to as "an invisible group" (Lofgren-Martenson 2009).

In 1994, a 7-year court battle ended in the nonconsensual sterilization of a Philadelphia woman, Cindy Wasiek, because she was "severely retarded" and her mother feared she would be raped and impregnated (her medication prohibited her from using hormonal birth control methods).

In this case, the mother's fears dominated the arguments, and Cindy was "prevented from being an active participant in the life decisions that concerned her" (Block 2007:167). While most people have the privilege of keeping the most intimate details of their lives private, people with disabilities do not have such privilege. In fact, their sex lives quite often become topics of discussion in courts and in the press.

Caregivers, policy makers, and parents argue that people with intellectual disabilities need to be protected from harm and abuse (Fyson and Townson 2015). Indeed, this is a very real threat, as people with disabilities are at much greater risk of physical and sexual violence (Gerschick 2011). At the same time, others argue that we must recognize the sexual agency of people with disabilities.

We have treated sexuality as a given so far in this text; physical acts and emotional intimacies that are intended to be pleasurable, which are embedded within a larger, socially constructed, body of meanings. Up to this point, we have taken for granted the "physical" aspects of sexuality. This chapter on sexual health will rectify that. We discuss what is meant by healthy sexuality, explore the challenges associated with sexual expression for people with physical and mental disabilities, and conclude with a look at sexually transmitted diseases. The stories introduced in the opening vignette exemplify some key points related to the primary themes this chapter will explore, including: the surveillance of people with disabilities such that even their sex lives are publicly scrutinized and controlled by others, the intersection of homophobia and discrimination against people with disabilities, and the importance of understanding one's risk for sexually transmitted infections. As the following exemplify, these are topical issues:

- According to the Centers for Disease Control and Prevention, in 2008, one in four teenage American girls had a sexually transmitted infection, the most common of which was human papillomavirus (HPV), which can cause cervical cancer ("One in 4 Teen Girls . . . " 2008).
- The fourth season of the hit television series *American Horror Story: Freak Show* (2014) controversially turned its lens on our cultural marginalization of "freaks," people whose bodies do not conform to the norm. Some regarded it as voyeuristic; others saw it as a powerful cultural challenge to the invisibility of disability.
- In 2014, African Americans made up a little over 12 percent of the population, but accounted for 44 percent of HIV/AIDS diagnoses; Latinos made up 17 percent of the population, and accounted for 23 percent of HIV/AIDS diagnoses, according to the Centers for Disease Control and Prevention.
- A 2014 UK newspaper poll found that 44 percent of respondents said they did not think they would have sex with a person with physical disabilities (Quarmby 2015).
- The FDA approved the use of female Viagra in August 2015; known as Addyi, this is the first drug approved to treat sexual dysfunction in premenopausal women (Whiteman 2015).

UNDERSTANDING SEXUAL HEALTH

Sociologists focus on the ***social construction of illness***, a perspective that emphasizes how the meaning and experience of illness is shaped by cultural and social systems. A social constructionist approach does not deny the medical reality of disease; instead, disease is viewed as a biological condition while illness is understood as the social meaning of the condition (Conrad and Barker 2010). This chapter focuses on a few key issues related to **sexual health**, a term that the World Health Organization defines as "a state of physical, emotional, mental, and sexual well-being related to sexuality" (Sadovsky and Nussbaum 2006:3). Sexual health includes identifying and treating sexual dysfunction, sexually transmitted infections, and sexual satisfaction, specifically related to people with physical and intellectual disabilities.

The range of sexual problems women can face include lack of interest, lack of orgasm, and pain during sex; for men it includes erectile dysfunction, premature ejaculation, lack of interest, and failure to achieve orgasm. Men and women can suffer **sexual aversion disorder**, where they fear sex and experience a range of feelings from discomfort to disgust, anxiety, and panic at the thought of sexual contact. Women can experience **persistent sexual arousal disorder**, which is unwanted, intrusive genital arousal, in the absence of sexual interest and where even having an orgasm does not relieve the sensation of discomfort (Leiblum and Goldmeier 2008). Men and women can experience severe and ongoing pain during intercourse, although this is more common for women.

Male Sexual Dysfunction

The most common male sexual dysfunction is **erectile dysfunction** (ED), also known as impotence, when the penis consistently fails to become erect or an erection cannot be maintained, making intercourse impossible. ED has generated significant attention since the introduction of Viagra in 1998. Viagra became pharmaceutical giant Pfizer's top-selling drug from 2003 through 2015, and erectile dysfunction drugs are expected to reach $3.4 billion in sales by 2019, declining from $4.3 billion in 2012 ("Erectile Dysfunction Drugs . . . " 2013). Erectile dysfunction is caused by both physical factors, such as diabetes or the side effects of medications, and psychological factors, such as performance anxiety. While 20 percent of men over the age of 20 experience ED, prevalence increases with age, where a man in his 50s is twice as likely to experience ED.

"Sexual virility—the ability to fulfill the conjugal duty, the ability to procreate, sexual power, potency—is everywhere a requirement of the male role, and thus 'impotence' is everywhere a matter of concern" (Tieffer 1995:141).

Keep in mind our discussion of masculinity and its links to sexuality (Chapter Three). In the face of phallocentric discourse, for a man to be unable to achieve and maintain an erection is perceived as a disastrous affliction, a "failure to stand up and be counted as a 'real' man" (Potts 2000:90). According to research, middle-aged and older men denied the significance of the link between masculinity and sexual performance. However, men with ED were more likely to equate ED with a "troubled masculinity." Additionally, men who believed strongly in traditional masculine ideologies were more likely to equate sexual performance with masculinity (Thompson and Barnes 2013).

Female Sexual Dysfunction

The drug Addyi, known commonly as the female Viagra, is the first FDA-approved drug to treat female sexual dysfunction. Viagra had been on the market 17 years before a similar version was made for women. **Female sexual dysfunction** refers to a medical problem with biological, psychological, and social components, which is age-related and believed to be highly prevalent, affecting anywhere from 30 to 50 percent of women (Berman et al. 2001).

The most common statistic cited is that 43 percent of women experience sexual dysfunction (Lauman, Paik, and Rosen 1999).

Many people question this statistic, however. In order to have been counted as experiencing sexual dysfunction, a woman had to answer yes only to experiencing one of seven problems for two months or more during the past year, including, lack of desire for sex, anxiety about sexual performance, difficulties with lubrication (Moynihan 2003). Critics have said that simply experiencing lack of desire should not constitute a disease. While there is a place for the medical treatment of sexual dysfunction, these critics think such treatments should be offered in conjunction with treatment for emotional and relationship issues, which are often the foundation of women's sexual dysfunction. Those critics have promoted a woman-centered understanding of sexual problems as, "'discontent or dissatisfaction with any emotional, physical, or relational aspect of sexual experience,' with four categories of causes: sociocultural, political, or economic; relationship-related; psychological; and medical" (Moynihan 2003:47).

While measuring sexual dysfunction in men has been rather straightforward and focused on their ability to obtain and maintain an erection, for women, it is more difficult to identify and quantify. Diagnoses involve "measurement of hormonal profiles, vaginal pH, and genital vibratory perception thresholds, as well as the use of ultrasonography to measure clitoral, labial, urethral, vaginal, and uterine blood flow" (Moynihan 2003:46). Some specifically focus on ***female sexual arousal disorder***, which refers to the inability to attain or maintain the lubrication-swelling response, which is a woman's first physiological response to sexual arousal, or lack of or diminished feelings of sexual excitement or pleasure. Essentially, any deviation from the four successive phases of sexual response, identified by Masters and Johnson in 1966, can count as female sexual dysfunction: excitement, plateau, orgasm, resolution (see Chapter Two).

Some have argued that this is the most recent example of "the corporate sponsored creation of a disease" rather than the identification of a new disorder, or what sociologists would call the social construction of illness (Moynihan 2003:45). Researchers working in collaboration with pharmaceutical companies have been trying to develop "a new category of human illness" designed to target women, an untapped market since the spectacular success of Viagra, which was introduced in 1998 (Moynihan 2003:45). While many women struggling with sexual dysfunction may welcome this research and treatment option, others may simply welcome the subtext of such research: that women are, indeed, sexual beings who deserve sexual fulfillment. While ideologies of masculinity make male impotence "everywhere a matter of concern," for women, assumptions about women's sexuality, specifically, that women really aren't very sexual and do not have sexual desires, meant that concerns about women's sexual dysfunction went unaddressed for a much longer period of time (Tiefer 1995:141).

SEXUALITY AND DISABILITY

This text has primarily addressed the sexual status hierarchy, where heterosexuals are the dominant, privileged group and LGBTQ folks face discrimination and inequality (Chapters Four and Five). We have also explored ways the sexual hierarchy intersects with the gender hierarchy and the racial hierarchy. In this chapter, we explore what is perhaps the least understood status hierarchy: ability/disability. As a society, "we are simply far behind when it comes to disability awareness" (Rainey 2011:83). We live in a world that privileges the able-bodied, cognitively unimpaired.

> **"The assertion that able-bodiedness is the foundation of sexiness might seem self-evident. After all, the sexiest people are healthy, fit, and active: lanky models, buff athletes, trim gym members brimming with energy. Rarely are disabled people regarded as either desiring subjects or objects of desire"** (Mollow and McRuer 2012:1).

The term used to describe this is ***ableism***—the discrimination, inequality, or oppression of people or groups with physical and/or intellectual disabilities, from denial of rights to denial of access, who face stigma, hatred, and "othering" by able-bodied people and cultures. As with all other status inequalities, the ableist hierarchy intersects with other status hierarchies, such as homophobia, to create unique forms of oppression, as the opening vignette exemplifies (Gill 2015). Ableism can be seen in our attempts to eradicate the disabled through eugenics policies, to eradicate disabilities through medical treatments and cures, or to assure the invisibility of people with disabilities in popular culture (Rainey 2011).

Who qualifies as a person with a ***disability***? Generally, a *disability* refers to a wide range of physical and psychological impairments that impose limits on the person in one or more major life activities (Rothstein, Martinez, and McKinney 2002). We commonly understand disability/ability as binary constructs. However, it is more helpful to think of them as two ends of a continuum, since aging is a disabling process that makes anyone who is not currently disabled "temporarily able-bodied" (Gershick 2011). Disability has historically been defined in medical terms, as a deficiency or a pathology requiring medical intervention (Gershick 2011).

A specific type of ableism will be the focus of this section of the chapter, ***sexual ableism.*** *Sexual ableism* refers to the denial of sexual agency to individuals "based on criteria of ability, intellect, morality, physicality, appearance"; and it generally includes the idea that people with disabilities should not reproduce (Gill 2015:3). **Sexual citizenship** refers to the rights related to sexual agency and expression that are sanctioned and legitimated by the state (Richardson 2000). As Michael Gill (2015) asks, should sexual citizenship depend on IQ?

This image should encourage you to think about the idea of sexual citizenship; specifically who has rights related to sexual agency and expression and who is denied those rights.
Source: istockphoto.com/shironosov.

Or particular bodily capabilities? Some disability theorists argue that even though people with disabilities are no longer forcibly segregated in institutions away from their able-bodied peers (see below), "the cultural taboo against disabled/nondisabled intimate relationships is a form of *erotic segregation,* similar to the social taboos placed on interracial relationships" (Rainey 2011:3). While our culture is saturated with sexualized images, when it comes to images of disabled sexuality and intimacy, there is invisibility.

Because we lack images of people with disabilities and healthy sexuality in popular culture, it can be difficult for people with disabilities to develop positive self-esteem and self-worth. In other words, they internalize their oppressor; they believe the negative stereotypes about them that they are undesirable and unlovable (see Chapter Eight). We have already discussed how there is a missing discourse of desire for adolescent girls (Chapter One); this idea can be extended to people with disabilities as well. In fact, "disabled populations are not viewed as acceptable candidates for reproduction or even capable of sex for pleasure" (Tepper 2000:285). While low sexual desire or lack of orgasm are generally defined as sexual problems, this is not the case for people with disabilities because they are not assumed to have sexual desires and needs (Tepper 2000).

What does privilege look like in this arena of inequality? Sexual ableist privilege includes not only the privilege of sexual agency, being assumed capable to make decisions about your own sex life, but also the assumption that your physical body is a sexual body, and the privilege to not have your consensual sexual activity subjected to oversight and regulation. People with disabilities are constantly subjected to invasions of their privacy in ways the able-bodied do not have to fear. Finally, sexual ableist privilege includes the assumption that able-bodied people have the right to sexual pleasure.

In response to the discriminatory treatment of people with disabilities, a *disability rights movement* emerged in the 1960s that sought to end discrimination, inequality, and oppression of people with disabilities and to change society by ending the stigma associated with disability. Part of the agenda of that movement was to recast disability as a normal part of life. Some use the term "nondisabled" to describe the able-bodied because it disrupts the

This image of a woman in a wheelchair at an ACLU Gay Pride March captures the intersection of disability and sexuality.
Source: istockphoto.com/andipantz.

privilege associated with ableism and challenges the normativeness of nondisabled bodies (Rainey 2011). The movement was slow to address issues of sexuality, focusing initially on access and employment issues (Gerschick 2011).

The disability rights movement seeks to shift us away from the **medical model of disability**, where medical professionals attempt to fix those who are differently abled and make them "normal," to a **social model of disability** that "views the physical and social environment as the problem. Inaccessible buildings and transportation, prejudice, and fear of people with disabilities cause poverty, isolation, and depression—not the impairment itself. The solution, then, is to change the built environment and to shift attitudes" (Rainey 2011:16). The 1990 *Americans with Disabilities Act*, which makes discrimination against people with disabilities illegal, requires that employers provide reasonable accommodations to disabled employees, and requires accessibility requirements in public accommodations, is an example of the social model.

Sexuality and People With Physical Disabilities

Some research finds that people with physical disabilities have difficulty establishing and maintaining intimate relationships (Howland and Rintala 2001; MacDougall and Morin 1979; Taleporos 2001; Taleporos and McCabe 2001, 2015). Other studies, however, find that many people with physical disabilities lead active sexual lives (White et al. 1993). Research indicates that physically disabled men have more difficulties establishing relationships than do physically disabled women. People with physical disabilities are less likely to suffer from depression if they are in a relationship, and physically disabled people who are single experience lower sexual well-being than those who are in a relationship. For people with physical disabilities, the highest sexual satisfaction rate is for those who are in a relationship, but not living together. Researchers theorize that is because when living together, the nondisabled partner becomes the primary caregiver and the intimate partner, which is added stress on the relationship (Taleporos and McCabe 2015).

We have certain cultural beliefs about sex that interfere with our ability to imagine physically disabled people as sexual beings capable of intimate relationships. They are, instead, stereotyped as dependent, asexual, and a burden; someone who is dependent is childlike and, thus, the caring they require is desexualized (Rainey 2011). It is often assumed that people with physical disabilities have a lower sex drive than able-bodied people or that their disability makes sex impossible. Beliefs about the appropriateness of certain sexual positions, like the missionary position, which often for a person with physical disabilities is not possible, contribute to the problem. We lack images of physical diversity in our culture, and that limits our ability to imagine sex with anyone other than an able-bodied partner. Additionally, there is a heterosexual "script" that is repeated throughout popular culture, where sex is a progression toward penis-vagina intercourse, which is the "real" thing, and that "other forms of sex are perverse, unsatisfying, or pathetic" (Rainey 2011:144). For some people with disabilities, penis-vaginal intercourse is not possible, while oral sex or hand manipulation, or the use of sex toys is possible. Thus, in order to understand sexuality and physical disability, we have to break free from our understandings of what counts as "good sex."

> "" Sex therapist Tuppy Owens's (2014) book **Supporting Disabled People with Their Sexual Lives** *includes a discussion of "sex toys suitable for people with different impairments. These include vibrating cushions, remotely controlled masturbation devices, and vibrators with long handles . . . ."* (Quarmby 2015).

Another challenge is getting beyond the notion of caring for a physically disabled person as desexualized. In other words, the care of a physically disabled person often involves exposure and sometimes touching of the sex organs, as they need help with bathing, dressing, and using the toilet. Yet caregivers are trained to not perceive these body parts as sex organs or as capable of arousal; instead care is desexualized. Research on disabled/nondisabled couples finds that they actually eroticize care activities and that this enhances their intimacy. This is because "by giving care, the nondisabled partner (and disabled partner) received physical sexual closeness . . . the giving and receiving were mutual and simultaneous" (Rainey 2011:146). The partners feel they are even closer than before the disability or closer than their nondisabled married friends, because the caregiving involves such intimacy and knowledge about otherwise private aspects of life (Rainey 2011). Based on her research, Sarah Rainey (2011) believes that disabled/nondisabled sexuality is "truly 'queer' in the 'queer theory' sense of the word . . . . [Because] nonheteronormative ways of expressing love and sexual desire are common in disabled/nondisabled relationships" (p. 152).

Sexuality and People With Intellectual Disabilities

Our cultural discomfort with the thought of people with intellectual disabilities as sexual beings is a product of twentieth-century ideas and policies. People with intellectual disabilities are perpetually infantilized, or treated as if they are children, which erases their physical maturity. Similarly to children, this becomes the justification for denying them the rights of full citizenship, including sexual citizenship (Monk and Townson 2015).

"Disability and impairment can invigorate sexuality, and disrupt our standard norms of gender and sexuality. Disabled bodies give us the chance to think outside of the box, outside the vision of penetration, the Hollywood view of sex," says sociologist Kirsty Liddiard (Quarmby 2015).

People with intellectual disabilities have historically been assumed to be excessively sexual, and their sexual activities deemed risky and inappropriate (Gill 2015). During the early twentieth century, when eugenics ideologies were popularized (see Chapter Nine), concerns with mental deficiencies, described as feeblemindedness, and the effects these could have on societal progress took hold. As eugenics philosophies spread throughout the Western world, several extreme solutions were implemented: segregating the "mentally defective," as they were referred to, into institutions, and involuntary sterilization (Chapter Nine). Institutions for the "mentally defective" enforced strict segregation in order to limit the contact between the sexes and the risk of sexual interactions (or at least heterosexual interactions). The solution of institutionalization stemmed from the understanding of intellectually disabled people as perpetual children who were eternally dependent. "Defectives" were prohibited from marrying in the United States, Denmark, Norway, and Sweden (Monk and Townson 2015).

The United States became the first nation to engage in the forced sterilization of intellectually disabled people when Indiana legalized compulsory sterilization in 1907 (see Chapter Nine). The use of sterilization began with castration, which was intended to stop inmates from masturbating. Soon afterwards it was used to halt reproduction of degeneracy, or the "unfit," a broad category that included not only the feebleminded, but criminals and rapists as well (Monk and Townson 2015). Canada, Denmark, Norway, Sweden, Switzerland, and Germany all followed the United States in legalizing compulsory sterilization of the "unfit."

"Asexual, hypersexual, perverse, and contaminated: These four damaging tropes from history combine to form a bitter legacy for disabled people" (Quarmby 2015).

Disability and Sex Work

The dearth of cultural images of disabled people as sexual beings has opened up somewhat controversial opportunities for the commodification of disabled sexualities. In this section, we explore the role of sex assistants and sex surrogates for disabled people and the role of people with disabilities in disability pornography (see Chapter Eleven).

SEX ASSISTANTS AND SEX SURROGATES Across the globe, organizations exist to connect sex workers with disabled people (Quarmby 2015). In Holland and Denmark social workers will even suggest sex workers to their disabled clients and the government may even pay for a limited number of visits. These sex workers are referred to *sex assistants,* a trained person who sexually assists a person with physical (and sometimes mental) disabilities. While similar, this is distinct from prostitution, in that prostitution is illegal in most countries, and even where it is legal, it can still be stigmatized; and sex assistants specifically focus on people with disabilities. Sex assistants are legal in some countries, such as Sweden and Israel, and have been the source of considerable debate in other countries, such as France (Quarmby 2015). In the United States, where the practice is not legal, some advocates argue that it should at least be decriminalized, "because some people with disabilities cannot obtain sex without paying for it, they should be exempt from any penalties" (Quarmby 2015).

The core of the idea is that people with disabilities are sexual beings as well, and if they have their other needs addressed (medical, psychological, etc.), why should their need for a sexual outlet go unmet? Opponents argue that it is society that needs to change; by allowing disabled people to hire sex assistants, we are reinforcing the view that they are too abnormal for able-bodied people to love. There are also issues of consent, particularly in terms of people with intellectual disabilities. The issue of consent becomes controversial when sex assistants are working with a person who is unable to speak, for instance. Sex assistants must learn to read the person's facial cues and other signals. Finally, some argue that the focus on sex is short-sighted in that most people, even people with disabilities, are looking for a relationship, not just a sexual encounter; and sex assistants obviously cannot help with that issue (Quarmby 2015). Of course, that argument is mononormative, assuming the naturalness and normativity of monogamy (Chapter One). It is possible that some people with disabilities are interested in a sexual relationship, or multiple sexual relationships, and are not interested in a long-term intimate relationship.

Sex assistants are similar to *sex surrogates* who are hired to assist someone who experiences sexual dysfunction and to empower clients "to be able to engage in meaningful and satisfying relationships" (Rosenbaum, Aloni, and Heruti 2014:322). Sex surrogacy was first promoted by Masters and Johnson (see Chapter Two) as a way for people to learn sexual intimacy through experiencing it; and it gained interest after the release of the film *The Sessions* (2012). Sex surrogacy is controversial, and the extent of the practice worldwide is unknown (Rosenbaum et al. 2014). Surrogate Partner Therapy (SPT) is a type of sex therapy that involves a therapist, a surrogate, and a client.

Sex surrogacy is distinct from prostitution, despite the fact that in both cases, a person is paid for sexual services. The differences amount to the fact that with sex surrogates, approximately 87 percent of the time is spent in nonsexual activities such as education, relaxation, and emotional support (Noonan 1984). Also, surrogates take an active role in the therapeutic process, whereas prostitutes are interested only in the monetary exchange for gratifying specific sexual desires (Rosenbaum et al. 2014).

DISABILITY PORNOGRAPHY The invisibility of disabled sex extends into pornography, despite how ubiquitous pornography is in our society (see Chapter Eleven). While there is a proliferation and normalization of pornography in the dominant society, "to say that you specifically like porn with amputees, little people, or people in wheelchairs is definitely something to hide" (Rainey 2011:40).

Disability porn is a contested issue. Thus, while "making sexualized images of people with disabilities can help correct the image of asexual or childlike people with disabilities . . . , the tone of such portrayals often remains that of a perverse fetish . . . , encouraging the objectification of people with disabilities (especially women)" (Rainey 2011:41). While for the most part, people with physical disabilities are stigmatized and thus, struggle finding intimate partners, they also face the paradoxical situation of being desired by fetishists for their disabilities. This is particularly true for women amputees (Gerschick 2011). Websites, magazines, and forums exist where men can meet women with physical disabilities. While many of these forums are controlled by women with disabilities, and thus, their experience is empowering, questions of exploitation still surround these because of the larger power differentials between the able-bodied and the disabled. Physically disabled sex worker Ellen Stoll described how she felt when she posed for *Playboy;* she viewed it as a celebration of her sexuality and that it was a way to oppose the restrictions society placed on her because of her disability (Cummings 1987). The complicated nature of the issue is captured by Thomas J. Gerschick: "While some women with disabilities experience a positive effect, these communities simultaneously sexually objectify women with disabilities" (2011:80).

Disability, Sexuality, and Homophobia

As mentioned in the opening vignette, while sexuality and disability tends to be invisible, LGBTQ people with disabilities are the truly invisible group. While some research finds that few people with disabilities identify as LGB, this may be due to the fact that many are unaware alternative sexualities exist (Abbott and Howarth 2007; Bennett and Coyle 2007; Burns and Davies 2011; Thompson 2003). In one study, 74 percent of female, intellectually disabled respondents gave a completely incorrect answer to the question "What is homosexuality?" However, 93 percent were able to give at least a partially correct answer when asked what being gay meant (Burns and Davies 2011). Other research has found people with intellectual disabilities hold negative views toward homosexuality (McCabe 1993; McCabe and Schreck 1992; Murphy and O'Callaghan 2004).

Other researchers have pointed out that such negative perceptions of homosexuality may be changing as people with disabilities are gaining access to sex education and as societal views seem to be changing (Servais 2006). Research finds that women with intellectual disabilities have less personal exposure to gay people, which likely contributes to their higher levels of homophobia. Additionally, women with intellectual disabilities tend to adhere to more traditional gender roles, which correlate with negative attitudes toward same-sex sexuality (Burns and Davies 2011).

Heteronormativity among caregivers and families of people with disabilities contributes to their lack of diverse options; in other words, it can "silence the opportunities for understanding people's hopes and experiences of positive sexual expression—in all its diversity" (Higgins 2010:254). For instance, caregivers asking, "Do you have a boyfriend or girlfriend" rather than "Do you have a partner" reinforces heteronormativity among clients with disabilities (Higgins 2010).

Scholars concerned with the homophobia and heteronormativity surrounding disability, particularly among their caregivers and families, propose a *diversity framework,* beyond the medical and social models discussed earlier. A *diversity framework* moves beyond "difference" to a recognition of and a celebration of diversity, including sexual diversity, gender identity, and relationship status (Higgins 2010; Mackelprang and Salsgiver 1999).

SEXUALLY TRANSMITTED INFECTIONS

Significant threats to any sexually active person's sexual health are ***sexually transmitted infections (STIs),*** which refers to a collection of diseases that are transmitted through sexual contact, including vaginal intercourse, oral sex, anal sex, or any nonpenetrative genital contact. In the past, STIs were referred to as sexually transmitted diseases (STDs) or venereal disease (VD). Over 15 million Americans contract an STI each year (Nack 2008). STIs include syphilis, chlamydia, HIV/AIDS, genital herpes, human papillomavirus (HPV), and gonorrhea. Some, like HPV and herpes, are chronic conditions. STIs are a major public health crisis in the United States because people can transmit the viruses without knowing they are infected, and infection can result in severe reproductive health complications, including the risk of infertility (Centers for Disease Control and Prevention 2016).

Who is at the greatest risk for STIs? Young people between the ages of 15 and 24 made up 50 percent of the 20 million new infections in 2014, according to the CDC ("CDC Fact Sheet . . ." 2016). Women are also disproportionately affected by STIs, including HIV/AIDS (discussed below). Women are at greater risk than men for contracting STIs for anatomical reasons. The vagina is covered in a mucous membrane that allows bacteria and viruses to pass through rather easily, and the environment is warm and moist, which encourages the growth of the bacteria and viruses, thus, increasing their risk for STIs. Young women are particularly vulnerable to STIs because their anatomy changes over the course of their lives. In young women, their epithelial cells, those lining the passage from the vagina to the uterus, extend out over the vaginal surface of the cervix and are not protected by cervical mucus; thus, they are more vulnerable to sexually transmitted infections. These cells recede as women age, making older women less vulnerable to STIs (Eng and Butler 1997). Pregnant women are at greater risk for STIs than women who are not pregnant, with the potential for more severe consequences for the woman and her baby. Racial/ethnic minority women are at greater risk for STIs than white women. The explanations for these variations are social, not biological. For instance, racial/ethnic minorities are disproportionately impoverished in this country. Poverty can contribute to early sexual activity, more exposure to illegal drug use, poor nutrition, and lack of medical care.

Common STIs

In this section, we explore the most common STIs, based on the latest information available through the Centers for Disease Control and Prevention (2016). *Syphilis* is a STI that is simple to cure with antibiotics if caught, but it can wreak havoc on one's body if left untreated. It can be contracted through sexual contact, or a mother can pass it on to her child during birth, according to the CDC. There are three stages to syphilis in adults: primary, secondary, and latent. In the primary stage, a painless sore appears at the location where syphilis enters your body: on the hand, genitals, mouth, or anus. The sore generally lasts for three to six weeks; yet its disappearance is not an indicator that the virus has left the body.

The secondary stage is characterized by lesions or skin rashes on your mouth, vagina, or anus. The rash can be on the palms of the hand or on the bottoms of the feet, and is rough and reddish-brown. A collection of symptoms can co-occur with the rash and sores, including fever, swollen glands, sore throat, headaches, and fatigue. The latent stage appears 10 to 30 years after the initial infection and occurs if a person never is treated for the disease. It is characterized by paralysis, blindness, and dementia. It can also damage your internal organs, causing death.

Genital herpes is a common STI in the United States, infecting 1 in 6 people between the ages of 14 and 49, according to the CDC. It is caused by one of two viruses, herpes simplex type 1 and herpes simplex type 2; and is passed in body fluids through anal, oral, or vaginal sex. Symptoms, such

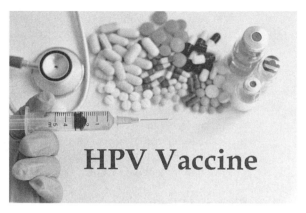

A vaccine to protect against the most deadly strands of the most common sexually transmitted disease, HPV, was made available in 2006. Source: istockphoto.com/jarun011.

as sores or blisters around the mouth, rectum, or genitals, and generally mild flu-like symptoms often go unnoticed. Infected people generally experience frequent outbreaks of symptoms, especially during the first year. While there is no cure for herpes, there are treatments that prevent or shorten outbreaks. Herpes increases one's risk for HIV because the open sores bleed easily, increasing the likelihood of infection if your partner is HIV+.

Gonorrhea is another very common sexually transmitted infection among young people aged 15 to 24, according to the CDC. Similar to syphilis, men and women can get gonorrhea through anal, oral, and vaginal sex; and it can be passed from a mother to a child during birth. Symptoms for men and women include a burning sensation when urinating. If the rectum is infected, symptoms include anal itching, bleeding, discharge, and painful bowel movements. Men's symptoms include a white, yellow, or green discharge and painful testicles. Other women's symptoms include increased vaginal discharge and vaginal bleeding between periods. Most of the time, gonorrhea can be cured with the right treatment; however, there are new strains that are drug resistant. Untreated gonorrhea can cause permanent health problems including infertility, pelvic inflammatory disease, and ectopic pregnancy.

Chlamydia is a sexually transmitted infection that affects men and women. Most people with chlamydia have no symptoms. For those who do, symptoms for women include vaginal discharge and a burning sensation when urinating; and for men include discharge from their penis, burning when urinating, and swollen testicles. If left untreated, it can inhibit a woman's chances of becoming pregnant and can increase a woman's odds of having a fatal ectopic pregnancy, according to the CDC.

Human papillomavirus infection (HPV) is the most common sexually transmitted infection in the United States. It is so common, according to the CDC, that almost all sexually active people will get it at some point in their lives. There are many different strains of HPV, some cause genital warts and others cause cancer. Most strains of HPV do not cause long-term damage and go away on their own, while others are deadly as they cause cervical cancer, throat cancer, and cancer of the anus, penis, vagina, or vulva. In 2006, 9,710 women were diagnosed with the most invasive cervical cancers, and 3,700 died from it (Nack 2008).

A historic public service announcement warning of VD, specifically syphilis. Source: Work Projects Administration Poster Collection/Library of Congress.

The best way for women to be protected from HPV is to get screened for cervical cancer regularly. There is also a vaccine, Gardasil, that the CDC recommends all boys and girls aged 11 to 12 get. This vaccine does not protect against all strains of HPV, only the four most deadly types, which are associated with 70 percent of cervical cancers (Nack 2008). Because of the stigma associated with STIs (see below), Gardasil has not been marketed as a "HPV vaccine." Instead, it has been marketed as a "cervical cancer" vaccine. Conservative organizations, like the Family Research Council, expressed concern that the vaccine would inspire young people to engage in premarital sex, which is possibly why Merck pharmaceuticals chose to market it as a "cervical cancer" vaccine. Since the vaccine does not protect against all strains of HPV, even women who have had the vaccine still need to practice safe sex and have regular gynecological exams (Nack 2008).

STIs and Stigma

STIs are stigmatized illnesses, but perhaps more so for women. People diagnosed with STIs feel a sense of shame, and often feel "dirty," irresponsible, naive, or like "damaged goods," or someone who will never be healthy, whole, and loveable again (Nack 2008). STIs are a threat to an individual's **sexual self**, "individuals' self-evaluations of their own sexual desirability and how they think of their own imagined and experienced erotic sensuality" and include perceptions of one's body as healthy or unhealthy (Nack 2008:7). STIs can result in a **spoiled sexual self**, self-loathing characterized by a sense of unattractiveness, due to medical conditions, ability/disability, or feeling certain sexual behaviors are immoral (Nack 2008). People with STIs must negotiate their stigma in interactions with others, which can result in a spoiled sexual self. Now we shift gears and talk about the most stigmatizing sexually transmitted infection: HIV/AIDS.

HIV/AIDS

The Human Immunodeficiency Virus is the virus that causes AIDS. It targets the immune system, to the point that people infected with HIV gradually become immunodeficient, and unable to fight infections and cancers that a healthy body otherwise would. AIDS (Acquired Immune Deficiency Syndrome) refers to the advanced stage of HIV infection, which usually emerges 2 to 15 years after initial infection, and is characterized by the presence of key infections or cancers and severely depressed immunity, according to the World Health Organization ("HIV/AIDS Fact Sheet . . ." 2016). There are only four ways HIV can be transmitted: through sharing needles with an infected person; sharing bodily fluids (semen, blood, or vaginal fluid) with an infected person; a transfusion of infected blood; or an HIV-infected mother can infect her baby through pregnancy, birth, or breast feeding if she is not being treated for the disease.

THE ORIGINS OF AN EPIDEMIC The disease was first identified in 1981, although it was not referred to as AIDS until 1982. The first death from what was later learned to be HIV was a Danish doctor, Grethe Rask, in 1977. She had been experiencing unexplained fatigue and malaise for two years, was losing weight, had severe diarrhea, and swollen glands. After a year or two of this, her mouth became covered in yeast infections; blood tests revealed staph infections; and medical tests showed her T-cell count was down, which meant her immune system was barely functioning. After she died, an autopsy revealed the presence of *Pneumocystis carinii,* a rare pneumonia that was generally not fatal (Shilts 1987).

Dr. Rask was one of the first non-Africans to die of what became known as AIDS, and scientists believe she contracted the disease while working in a hospital in the mid-1960s and early 1970s in Zaire (now known as the Democratic Republic of the Congo). According

Knockout HIV offers free HIV testing in communities across the country.
Source: Photo by Kathleen J. Fitzgerald.

to scientists, there was nothing new about this virus; it originated around 1908 in Africa and is generally believed to have been passed from chimpanzees, likely by a hunter who was infected while processing a chimpanzee (Wolfe 2012). Thus, the HIV/AIDS epidemic is not so much a story of a new virus, but instead is the story of the social and cultural conditions that contributed to the emergence of an epidemic.

In the late 1970s, dozens of people in the United States were dealing with the same mysterious illness that killed Rask. In addition to the symptoms she experienced, a rare skin cancer, *Kaposi Sarcoma*, dementia symptoms, night sweats, and persistent fevers were found in many. In the United States, it was almost all men, mostly gay men, who were infected. Confounding medical professionals across the country, otherwise healthy young men were dying within months of becoming symptomatic from a disease no one understood or even had a name for. In the beginning it was called GRID (Gay-Related Immune Disorder) because of the population of people primarily being affected.

By 1982, the CDC had changed the name of the disease to AIDS (Acquired Immune Deficiency Syndrome), since it was discovered that the disease was affecting more than gay men. Hemophiliacs, IV drug users, Haitians, and heterosexual women in Africa were now counted among the infected. Epidemiological research revealed that the disease was likely sexually transmitted, which meant that all sexually active people were at risk, and the blood supply was likely infected. (Prior to 1985, some people got HIV from

> " *Those who are responsible for this epidemic are men and women who are continuing to engage with a wide variety of partners in sexual acts that have been defined as deviant and sinful by the Judeo-Christian community for over 2000 years now"* (Fitzpatrick 1988:34).

blood transfusions, since HIV+ people who did not know they were infected donated blood, which infected the blood supply. A test to screen donated blood for HIV was implemented in 1985). While the spread of HIV/AIDS was not initially understood, it was eventually discovered that it can be passed from person to person through blood, semen, or breast milk. Anal sex and IV drug use were found to be the riskiest behaviors, resulting in the highest rates of transmission. By 1983, there were 2,807 known cases of AIDS and 2,118 deaths from the disease; by 1986, almost 25,000 people had died from the disease ("Thirty Years of HIV/AIDS . . ." 2016). It became an epidemic. By 1987, the first drug to treat HIV, AZT, was available; it was the most expensive drug in history at $10,000 per year to treat one infected individual.

MORAL PANICS SURROUNDING HIV/AIDS Between 1981 and 1987, 40,000 people died of a disease no one had ever heard of just six years before (Hubbard and Schulman 2012). This resulted in panic—50 percent of Americans at the time felt that people with AIDS should be quarantined (Hubbard and Schulman 2012). The first 10 years of the AIDS epidemic were accompanied by moral panics, irrational responses that involve spreading fear among a large number of people that something specific, in this case HIV/AIDS, was a threat to the social order (Cohen 1972; see Chapter Six). The moral panic involved an antigay backlash, campaigns to close bathhouses in San Francisco, and fears that casual contact with infected individuals would spread the disease.

ANTI-GAY BACKLASH While certainly the exploding HIV/AIDS epidemic was a growing public health concern, and remains one today that warrants concern, our societal reaction was largely irrational. A rational response would have included a federal infusion of millions of dollars to the CDC and other appropriate recipients to fight the disease, funding both research and prevention education through public service announcements, at a minimum. The Reagan administration was not interested in spending tax dollars fighting HIV/AIDS; many speculated that this was because the groups being infected were persecuted minorities: gay men, IV drug users, and Haitian immigrants.

Fundamentalist Christian and Orthodox Jewish sects viewed AIDS as divine punishment, for violating God's laws, particularly prohibitions on homosexuality (Doka 1997). Even though there were "innocent victims" of the epidemic, such as hemophiliacs, the presence of HIV/AIDS was still considered to be evidence of a society that was tolerating too much sin (Doka 1997). There are religious leaders who claim to this day that AIDS is a homosexual disease and God's punishment for such immorality.

BATHHOUSE BATTLEGROUND Since the Gay Liberation movement had proudly affirmed gay sex, promiscuity and the commercialization of gay sex exploded in the form of bathhouses, where thousands of same-sex sexual, and often anonymous, encounters between men occurred nightly. As journalist Randy Shilts explains, the "businesses serviced men who had long been repressed . . . and were perhaps now going to be extreme in exploring their new freedom. It would all balance out later, so for now, sex was part and parcel of political liberation" (1987:19).

Sexual liberation was not limited to the gay male community; it was a key characteristic of the 1960s hippie counterculture that advocated "free love." The ideologies of the counterculture quickly spread, resulting in a "Sexual Revolution" (Chapter One). The erosion of norms surrounding sexual behaviors, "unsettled mainstream America. The sexual constraints of the postwar years, such as the cultural ideal of a woman maintaining virginity until marriage or the social restrictions on unmarried couples living together, fell away as people experimented with freer sexual forms" (Bloom and Breines 2015:275).

Bathhouses were significant institutions in the 1960s and '70s gay community, as they were gay-owned businesses, gathering places where gay people could meet in a nonstigmatizing environment, where they were not going to be arrested for engaging in sex, and where even voter registration sometimes occurred (Doka 1997). In 1984, there was a campaign to close bathhouses in San Francisco because they were perceived as fueling an epidemic of sexually transmitted diseases, especially HIV; and a similar campaign followed in New York the following year (Shilts 1987).

Many gay rights activists were vocally opposed to the closing of the bathhouses, claiming the sex would only go underground, and, thus, such action would not solve the problem. They also demanded that the government appropriately fund research and prevention education rather than closing the bathhouses; the solution felt particularly punitive and homophobic. A judge ruled that instead of closing the bathhouses, there would be restrictions on the sexual activity that occurred in them; for instance, private rooms were eliminated, which deterred many people from coming to the bathhouses for sexual encounters. The new restrictions and the fear of AIDS led to financial ruin for many, although bathhouses still exist in many cities.

As discussed previously, the HIV/AIDS virus had already been in existence for decades. The epidemic was a result of a particular confluence of social changes: the counterculture movement's advocacy of "free love"; the Gay Liberation movement's proud affirmation of gay sex; and globalization, the increasing ease of travel. The dramatic increase in the numbers of people traveling across the globe and the sexually transmitted nature of the disease resulted in a global pandemic.

FEAR OF CASUAL ENCOUNTERS The moral panic extended to fears that drinking from the same water fountain, or using the same toilet seat as an infected person could result in transmission of the virus. It was feared that hugging or touching someone with HIV could spread the disease. Thus, based on such unfounded myths, children with HIV were harassed at school to the point that they were forced to quit going. People who were found to be HIV+ were fired from their jobs out of fear that casual contact could result in infection. Today, persons living with HIV/AIDS are protected from discrimination by the *Americans with Disabilities Act* in employment, housing, and public accommodations; but these protections were not a given and had to be won through court battles during the early years of the epidemic.

The fear of casual contact and the stigma of HIV/AIDS resulted in many dying AIDS patients being treated poorly by medical professionals and being abandoned by their families. Ruth Coker Burks, a 25-year-old Arkansas woman, spent much of 1984 in a Little Rock hospital with a friend who had cancer. While there, she noticed the door to a patient's room covered with a giant red, plastic bag and the nurses avoiding the room. When it came time to check on the patient, the nurses would draw straws and the loser would have to go in the room (Koon 2015). She correctly assumed it was an AIDS patient.

Ignoring the moral panic that had gripped the country and the nurses at that particular hospital, she entered the room and talked to the dying man, who probably weighed less than 100 pounds. He asked her to bring his mother to visit him. When she mentioned that to the nurses, she was told his mother was not coming, and he had not had any visitors for his entire six-week stay. When Burks called the man's mother, she was told that her son was a sinner and that not only would she not come to visit him, but she would not be claiming his body when he died either. This was the beginning of a mission for Burks. Between 1984 and the mid-1990s, she took care of hundreds of people with AIDS: taking them to doctor appointments, picking up their medications, helping them fill out necessary paperwork, talking to them, and holding their hand as they took their last breath. Sometimes she paid for their cremation. She buried over three dozen people herself when families refused to claim their bodies (Koon 2015).

HIV/AIDS TODAY Medical treatments for HIV/AIDS have improved considerably. While there is no cure yet, most people with access to medical treatment are living for decades after diagnosis; it is no longer an immediate death sentence as it was in the 1980s and 1990s. Despite progress, HIV/AIDS remains a serious pandemic, with 44,000 new infections per

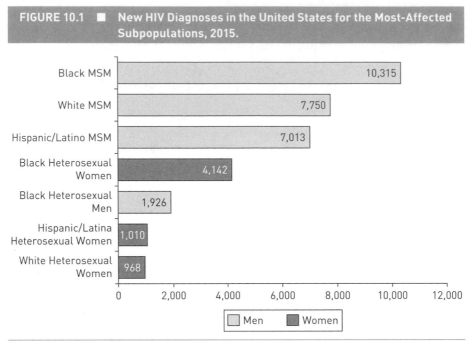

FIGURE 10.1 ■ New HIV Diagnoses in the United States for the Most-Affected Subpopulations, 2015.

New HIV diagnoses in the US are concentrated among men, and found disproportionately among black and Latino men.

Note: MSM stands for men who have sex with men.

Source: CDC, Estimated. http://www.cdc.gov/hiv/statistics/overview/ataglance.html.

year in the United States and 2.3 million worldwide, according to the Centers for Disease Control and Prevention. More than 1.2 million Americans are living with HIV, and 1 in 8 of them are unaware they are infected. Over the past decade, the number of new diagnoses fell by 19 percent. But that decline has been uneven.

While everyone who is sexually active and having unprotected sex is at risk of contracting HIV, the risk is greater among some populations (see Figure 10.1). Gay and bisexual men (classified by the CDC as MSMs, men who have sex with men) are at the greatest risk, with African American MSMs at the highest risk. Between 2005 and 2014, diagnoses among white gay and bisexual men declined 18 percent while they increased 24 percent among Latino gay and bisexual men. For African American gay and bisexual men, HIV rates increased by 22 percent between 2005 and 2010, but have leveled off since.

The most astonishing change has been the explosion of new infections among young African American gay and bisexual men, ages 13 to 24, who have experienced an 87 percent increase since 2005 and 2010, with a 2 percent decline in the six years since. According to the CDC, this astounding statistic is explained by the following facts: African Americans are already disproportionately infected and are most likely to have sex with other African Americans; lack of awareness of HIV; stigma associated with it; and the problems associated with being disproportionately impoverished, including lack of health care. African Americans and Latinos are disproportionately infected with HIV, as mentioned above; and HIV diagnoses are concentrated in the southern United States (Centers for Disease Control and Prevention 2016).

GLOBAL PANDEMIC One of the primary themes associated with the HIV/AIDS pandemic is inequality, as the statistics in the preceding paragraph exemplify. This inequality is also global. According to the World Health Organization, there were 36.7 million people living

BOX 10.1

GLOBAL/TRANSNATIONAL PERSPECTIVES ON SEXUALITY:
THE CONSEQUENCES OF HIV/AIDS ON AFRICA

The epicenter of the HIV/AIDS pandemic is sub-Saharan Africa, which accounts for two-thirds of the world's new infections, according to the World Health Organization (WHO). Africa, the least developed region of the world, is home to 70 percent of the world's HIV+ people (Baylies, Bujra, with the Gender and AIDS Group 2000). And the most vulnerable people, women and children, are particularly at risk. Since the primary mode of transmission of HIV in Africa is through heterosexual contact, some argue that halting the spread of HIV/AIDS will require "far-reaching transformation in the relations between men and women" (Baylies, Bujra, with the Gender and AIDS Group 2000:xi).

Women are more likely to be blamed for the transmission of HIV/AIDS in Africa, whether through prostitution or through childbirth (Baylies, Bujra, with the Gender and AIDS Group 2000). African women are more vulnerable to infection for many reasons including the fact that there is greater cultural tolerance for men's sexual promiscuity, both before and after marriage, and also because women "are often expected to give but not receive pleasure" (Baylies, Bujra, with the Gender and AIDS Group 2000:7).

Children are at particular risk for HIV infection. At the end of 2013, there were 3.2 million children living with HIV/AIDS and 91 percent of them were in sub-Saharan Africa ("Children and HIV/AIDS . . ." 2016). African children are at particular risk due to poverty, poor nutrition, and lack of medical care, which increases the likelihood of a mother transmitting the virus to her child. Another explanation is sexual abuse in the home. While sexual abuse is found in every culture in the world, children are particularly vulnerable to sexual exploitation in Africa because of the perpetuation of an ancient myth that sexual intercourse with a virgin will cure certain diseases. This myth has resulted in the rape of young girls and even babies (Kelly 2003).

The civil conflicts found in many parts of Africa also put children at greater risk for HIV/AIDS because these conflicts result in forced migration, the disruption of communities, poverty, and the breakdown of law and order, which often includes the rape of children (Mustapha and Gbakima 2003). Due to the HIV/AIDS epidemic, there are over 15.1 million orphans in Africa, and the vast majority are due to AIDS ("Children and HIV/AIDS . . ." 2016). Because of the stigma associated with the death of their parents from AIDS, most orphans are abandoned, ostracized from their extended family, and excluded from schools and their communities (Patterson 2003).

There are some positive developments, however. Between 2000 and 2015, new HIV infections fell by 35 percent, according to the World Health Organization, and there was a 58 percent reduction in the number of children under the age of 15 accounting for new HIV infections ("Children and HIV/AIDS . . ." 2016).

with HIV in 2015, and only 17 million were on antiretroviral therapy. While HIV/AIDS has disproportionately affected men in the United States, globally, women make up the majority of HIV/AIDS cases. It is the leading cause of death among women of reproductive age, and young women are twice as likely as men to be newly diagnosed in poor nations (McKinney and Austin 2015). While life expectancy is increasing across the globe, in many poor nations, HIV/AIDS is contributing to decreasing life expectancy, especially for women (Baylies, Bujra, with the Gender and AIDS Group 2000; McKinney and Austin 2015; Neumayer 2004; Riley 2005).

CURRENT SOCIAL CONSEQUENCES OF THE HIV/AIDS CRISIS While one could explore any number of social consequences associated with the HIV/AIDS epidemic, we want to focus on three: the retirement crisis facing many infected gay and bisexual men; the potential and pitfalls associated with a new drug treatment model known as pre-exposure prophylaxis; and the linkages between HIV/AIDS, women, and ecological destruction in poor nations.

RETIREMENT AND THE HIV/AIDS CRISIS HIV/AIDS has had a devastating effect on the gay male community. One aspect of the disease that people are facing today involves retirement. There are at least 1.5 million LGBTQ people aged 65 and older in the United States today, and this number is expected to double by 2030 ("Discrimination" n.d.). As of 2015, 50 percent of all people living with HIV in the United States are over the age of 50 (Heinemann and Schegloff n.d.). While thousands of men died of HIV early in the epidemic, many also lived. But with the specter of what appeared to be inevitable early death lingering over their life, "many long-term AIDS survivors . . . talked about poor financial decisions they made in the 1980s and 1990s . . . and are now paying for as they enter retirement" (Sweet 2014). People who don't expect to live a long life, generally don't prepare financially to do so. Additionally, while many infected people survived the epidemic, they spent many of those years too sick to work, which also inhibited their ability to save money for their retirement.

NEW DRUG TREATMENTS: POTENTIAL AND PITFALLS In 2012, the FDA approved a new drug, Truvada, not only for HIV treatment but for prevention as well; a pre-exposure prophylaxis, PrEP. Studies find pre-exposure prophylaxis to be an astounding 96 to 100 percent effective (McNeil 2014). Such effectiveness can extend beyond individuals to entire cities when approached through a public health model; "by treating enough inhabitants, the whole 'viral load' of a city can be lowered. That protects everyone—just as cities used to slow down smallpox outbreaks by rapidly vaccinating thousands of inhabitants" (McNeil 2014:7). While Truvada does not cure HIV/AIDS, there is reason for optimism that it can slow the pandemic.

Despite the optimism, there is also cause for concern. The first concern is economic. Truvada costs $13,000 per year. Thus, unless individuals are insured or independently wealthy, they are unlikely to have access to this drug. As mentioned previously, gay black and Hispanic men are the highest risk groups for HIV, yet they are the least likely to have health insurance. This can also contribute to ongoing global inequalities associated with this disease—for economic reasons, these kinds of treatments are not even being promoted in poor countries throughout the world where the epidemic is the most severe. Essentially, in order to end the epidemic, all 35 million people who are infected with HIV will need to be on PrEPs (McNeil 2014).

HIV/AIDS, WOMEN, AND ENVIRONMENTAL DEGRADATION Researchers have also identified links between environmental degradation, women, and HIV/AIDS prevalence in poor nations (McKinney and Austin 2015). Environmental destruction—including deforestation; increasing salinity of soil; and air, water, and soil depletion—limits food production. This results in malnutrition; great susceptibility to infectious disease, including HIV/AIDS; and less ability to fight disease (Beisel 1996; Scrimshaw 2003; Scrimshaw and SanGiovanni 1997; Stillwaggon 2006). Severe hunger also increases women's likelihood of engaging in risky sexual behaviors in exchange for food (Heimer 2007). Environmental degradation contributes directly to the intensification of hunger, a reduction in the availability of clean water, and an increasing rate of HIV among women across less developed nations. Ultimately, this research finds that "women bear the brunt of environmental declines . . . [including] the increased likelihood of contracting life-threatening infections and associated reductions in life expectancy" (McKinney and Austin 2015:541).

CONCLUSION

This chapter explores the intersection of the physical body and sexuality, including explorations of sexual health, sexuality and disability, and sexually transmitted diseases. A sociological approach to these issues involves taking a social constructionist approach to illness, understanding the ability/disability status hierarchy, and the ways ableist privilege plays out, particularly in terms of sexuality. Additionally, we explore the intersection of homophobia and ableism, the stigma attached to STIs, the moral panics surrounding HIV/AIDS, the national and global inequalities surrounding HIV/AIDS, and some of the key current social consequences of the AIDS epidemic.

Key Terms and Concepts

Ableism 214
Disability 214
Disability rights
movement 215
Diversity framework 219
Erectile dysfunction 212
Erotic segregation 214
Female sexual arousal
disorder 213
Female sexual
dysfunction 212

Medical model of
disability 215
Persistent sexual arousal
disorder 212
Sex assistant 217
Sex surrogate 218
Sexual ableism 214
Sexual aversion
disorder 212
Sexual citizenship 214
Sexual health 212

Sexual self 221
Sexually transmitted
infections 219
Social construction of
illness 211
Social model of
disability 215
Spoiled sexual self 221

Critical Thinking Questions

1. Identify the ways the ability/disability status hierarchy is similar to the sexuality hierarchy. In what ways are these distinct?

2. Speculate on why sex assistants and sex surrogates are illegal in many countries (including the United States). Should these professions be legal? What benefits would come from legalizing sex assistants and surrogates? What problems might arise from such legalization?

3. Explain what is meant by sexual health. Give two specific examples of where our cultural images of sexual health come from.

4. Explain the moral panics surrounding HIV/AIDS in the early years of the epidemic. Identify some remnants of these moral panics in our cultural understandings of HIV/AIDS today. Identify a current moral panic (that may or may not be related to sexual health).

Activities

1. While watching television or surfing the Internet, take notes on the number of commercials for erectile dysfunction that you encounter. What are the primary themes in these advertisements? Do they indicate anything about masculinity in American society?

2. Look for images of sexuality and disability in popular culture. To what extent do they challenge the stereotypes discussed in this chapter. If they challenge stereotypes, speculate on why.

3. Go to the Centers for Disease Control and Prevention website and explore the

section on STIs and college students. Then design a quick survey to find out what your college classmates know about STIs and the college population. Get twenty students to complete the survey. Are your campus colleagues aware of the extent of STIs or not? Why might this be? What contributes to their awareness, or what is likely to be inhibiting their awareness?

4. Have you had sexual education (sex education) at some point in your life? If so, did it cover sexual health, sexual dysfunction, disability and sexuality, and STIs? Speculate on why some of these issues were covered and why others were ignored.

Essential Readings

Gill, Michael. 2015. *Already Doing It: Intellectual Disability and Sexual Agency*. Minneapolis, MN: University of Minneapolis Press.

Nack, Adina. 2008. *Damaged Goods? Women Living with Incurable Sexually Transmitted Diseases*. Philadelphia, PA: Temple University Press.

Rainey, Sarah Smith. 2011. *Love, Sex, and Disability: The Pleasures of Care*. Boulder, CO: Lynne Rienner Publishers.

Shilts, Randy. 1987. *And the Band Played On: Politics, People, and the AIDS Epidemic*. London: St. Martin's Press.

Recommended Films

And the Band Played On (1993). Roger Spottiswoode, Director. This Hollywood film, based on the best-selling book of the same name by Randy Shilts, is centered on the epidemiological work of the Centers for Disease Control and Prevention in the first 10 years of the epidemic. It explores the origins of the HIV/AIDS epidemic, from its mysterious emergence among gay men in the United States and its devastating effects on that community, to the understanding that the disease was sexually transmitted, to conflicts between French and American scientists over who should get credit for discovering the disease, and to the rising death toll as it became a global pandemic.

Deep South (2012). Lisa Biagiotti, Director. This documentary explores the often-overlooked and silent HIV/AIDS epidemic in the rural South. Due to certain cultural characteristics associated with the American South, such as high rates of poverty and religiosity, it has become fertile ground for the HIV/AIDS epidemic. This film focuses on three Americans who are struggling to survive the epidemic in the rural South.

Sick: The Life and Death of Bob Flanagan Supermasochist (1997). Kirby Dick, Director. This documentary explores the life of Bob Flanagan, who after being diagnosed with cystic fibrosis, turned to masochism for both sexual pleasure and to help him cope with the constant pain he was in every day. His self-torture routines became avant-garde, live performances. The film also explores Flanagan's intimate relationship with a dominatrix.

The Sessions: (2012). Ben Lewis, Director. Based on the life of Mark O'Brien, a journalist who was paralyzed from the neck down as a result of having polio as a child. After a writing assignment on sex and the disabled, he decided to turn toward a sex surrogate to experience sex for himself.

We Were Here: The AIDS Years in San Francisco (2011). David Weissman and Bill Weber, Directors. This powerful San Francisco-based documentary explores the shift from the celebratory, safe-haven, LGBTQ community in the 1970s to the shock, fear, and grief as it became the epicenter of the AIDS epidemic in the early 1980s. Explores love and loss through the stories of five people who experienced it firsthand.

Want (2007). Loree Erickson, Director. Short, autobiographical film exploring her goal of being seen as more than her disability, and making visible queer "crip" sexuality. Toward that goal, the film contains scenes of Loree having sex with a female partner and her being cared for by friends.

Suggested Multimedia

Centers for Disease Control, HIV in the United States. Go to the CDC website and get an overview of HIV/AIDS in the United States. To what extent was the HIV/AIDS epidemic visible to you prior to reading this chapter? Whether it was visible or invisible, speculate on why that is. Go beyond HIV data and explore the section on STIs and college students. Does the data on the extent of STIs among college students surprise you? Why or why not? http://www.cdc.gov/hiv/statistics/overview/ataglance.html

The Love Lounge, part of enhance the uk, an organization working to change the way society views disability. The "Love Lounge" website offers sex and relationship advice to people with disabilities. This includes an Undressing Disability campaign designed to increase sexual health and sexual awareness among disabled people. http://enhancetheuk.org/enhance/the-love-lounge/

COMMODIFICATION OF SEX

LEARNING OBJECTIVES

Upon completion of this chapter, students will be able to . . .

- Understand what it means to commodify sex and sexuality
- Discuss the legalities and social issues surrounding pornography
- Describe the legalities and social issues regarding prostitution
- Understand the impact of globalization on the sex trade
- Explain sex trafficking, sex tourism, and the role of military prostitution

Craigslist.com is a free, classified advertisement website with sections for jobs, housing, items wanted, services, items for sale, and so on. There is also a "personals" section in which "women seeking women," "men seeking men," "men seeking women," or even "missed connections" can be explored. While the site is considered a particularly useful site for dating and connections for gays and lesbians who live in conservative areas, it is also a controversial site. Most of the ads found in these sections are not your typical advertisements for dating.

Ad after ad includes photographs of scantily clad men and women in suggestive poses or pictures of genitalia. There is a very specific lingo and terminology used and a range of shorthand terms including M4M, meaning "men for men," MHC, meaning "married Hispanic couple," HWP, meaning "height and weight are proportionate to body size," RTS, short for "real time sex," and many more. Many ads offer massages, undefined services, or are seeking "generous men." Although Craigslist is supposed to rid advertisements placed by prostitutes, it is still a site for advertising prostitution, which is illegal in the United States. In addition to coded paid sex ads, Craigslist is one of the most popular sites for seeking anonymous sex. Under the tab "casual encounters," you can find endless opportunities for "no strings attached" sexual hookups.

Carmine Sarracino and Kevin Scott (2009) describe Craigslist as an example of how U.S. culture has become ***pornified***; or put into other words, mainstream culture has become inundated with sexual themes and explicit imagery. They argue that we no longer have to purchase pornography because we increasingly *live* porn in our daily lives. Craigslist normalizes the selling and shopping for sex by lumping it together with other kinds of shopping and by substituting negative or stigmatized terms with positive terms, like "casual encounters." Sarracino and Scott predict that when porn is totally absorbed into a culture, its vocabulary and behaviors become completely normalized and are no longer even visible as porn. While we are not at the point of total absorption, Craigslist and other online sex sites reveal how the commodification and pornifying of sex is becoming increasing commonplace.

In this chapter, we examine the commodification of sex from a sociological perspective. ***Commodification*** is a term that means to turn something into a commodity, or a marketable product or service to be bought and sold. In capitalism, a commodity is sold on the market at a certain price, generally based on supply and demand. When sex and sexuality are commodified and become saturated in the economy, sociologists call it the ***sexual economy.*** In the current sexual economy, large market and social forces shape the identity and value of sex commodities more than the subjects involved. For example, when the physical act of sex is turned into a marketable service, its value is more about profit and less about physical intimacy. When the image of a nude body is a commodity to be purchased and consumed, it becomes more of an object and less of a subject. The sexual economy occupies a central and increasingly prominent position in U.S. economy and culture. The intersection of race, gender, age, and class inequalities significantly shapes the complex dynamics of the sexual economy and will be analyzed throughout the chapter.

Essential to this subject is an exploration into the ***commercial sex industry,*** or the economic enterprise that offers adult sexual entertainment and services, including pornography; all forms of prostitution, from street prostitution to massage brothels; strip clubs; phone sex; and more. An in-depth sociological analysis of the legalities, social debates, and societal impact of both pornography and prostitution is provided. In the United States, prostitution is illegal, except in some counties in the state of Nevada; thereby most prostitution takes place in the underground criminal economy. The sex industry is also globalized where sex and sexuality is bought and shared across borders, and the costs and benefits are not evenly distributed. We explore the historical exploitation of colonialism, which contributes to unequal globalization, as well as the current trends of economic exploitation, sexual oppression, and international migration associated with neocolonialism. Three primary aspects of the global sex economy analyzed are sex trafficking, sex tourism, and military prostitution.

Recent examples of how the commodification of sex is a mainstream feature in U.S. culture include:

- In 2014, Texas Attorney General Greg Abbot declared the Super Bowl the single largest human trafficking incident in the United States. In the anticipation of the 2015 Super Bowl, FBI and local law enforcement agencies arrested 360 sex buyers and 68 sex traffickers, and recovered 30 juvenile victims of sex trafficking (Gaillard 2016).

- In 2015, Jared Fogle, TV spokesperson for Subway, was arrested for possessing child porn and repeatedly having sex with minors. The case involved interstate travel to pay minors for sex, as well as at least 400 child pornography videos. He received a 15-year jail sentence (Oritz and Bogert 2015).
- In 2015, federal agents raided the offices of Rentboy.com, a male escort website operating unchallenged for the past 18 years in New York City. Assets were seized, the website shut down, and employees charged with promoting prostitution (Dienst 2015).
- In September 2015, a Florida couple was prosecuted for running a sex tourism business in which they sent travelers to the Dominican Republic and then paired them with prostitutes. They dealt in email and phone inquiries and advertised on Backpage.com (Cutway 2015).
- In 2015, North Carolina prosecuted a teenage couple for making child porn because they had naked pictures of themselves on their phones. This led to intense criticism and discussions in the legal and academic community on whether consensual "sexting" is a crime (Miller 2015).

PORNOGRAPHY

A fast growing and widely popular aspect of the commercial sex industry is *pornography*, or sexually explicit material, such as videos, photos, or words, designed to be sexually arousing to the viewer. Pornography has been in existence, in some form, for centuries and finds popularity in almost every culture on the globe. In the United States, it began as images of nudes on playing cards in the late eighteenth century and has adapted to each new changing technology every decade since. Today pornographic magazines can be found on newsstands and pornographic books and films in adult bookstores in almost every city.

The most popular and accessible form of pornography today is found on the Internet through websites and adult chat rooms. It is estimated that there are over four million pornographic websites online, which is 12 percent of all websites; 68 million daily search engine requests for pornographic materials; and that 42.7 percent of Internet users watch porn (Kimmel et al. 2015). It is estimated that every second, $3,075.00 is being spent on pornography, which means it is a multibillion dollar industry (Kimmel et al. 2015). While increasingly popular among both men and women, it seems men watch porn more than women. In a recent study of 813 university students, 87 percent of young adult males use pornography and 31 percent of young adult females (Carroll et al. 2008).

Technology and the Rise of Amateur Porn

Pornography is transformed and influenced by technological advancements. In the new millennium, the adult sex porn industry largely shifted toward web-based content. Web-based pornography comes in two primary formats: preproduced video scenes and live web cam performances (Tibbals 2013). Preproduced sex scenes can be produced and uploaded by professionals or amateurs. Revenues are then split between the web space owner and the owner of the content. Live, interactive sex shows are made possible through the technological invention of web cams. In this format, consumers can chat "cam to cam" via a video chat network. Performers can be professionals, but are most often amateurs, who create a profile on a streaming site and benefit from the site's consumer traffic and marketing. This technology has given rise to the proliferation of amateur porn.

Porn chat rooms are spaces in which ordinary people can participate in the creation of pornography, mainly in the form of *cybersex*, or having imagined sex, in real time, with a partner or partners in the chat room. In addition to web cams, the everyday use of digital video cameras and cell phones with video capability enable ordinary people to record their own sexual activities and post the results via their computer on a dedicated website. This has significantly increased the amount of amateur porn available online. While paper magazines and DVDs are still on the market, digital mediums are by far the more popular and more affordable option. Most pornography websites are now provided online for free and can be accessed and consumed by anyone with an Internet connection.

Legalities and Debates

Pornography is legal and protected as a freedom of expression under the First Amendment to the U.S. Constitution, unless it is found to be obscene. **Obscenity** is a legal term for materials that are socially offensive by generally accepted standards of decency. For example, sex with animals or children is generally considered obscene in our culture. In the case of children, it is very clear cut: it is a federal crime to have, make, sell or distribute, or look at child pornography in the United States. Across the globe, it is universally agreed on that it is obscene and unethical for children to be in pornography. In all other cases, pornography is subjective. This is where things can become confusing. In 1964, Supreme Court Justice Porter Stewart simply defined obscenity as, "I know it when I see it." What is considered to be sexually arousing differs from individual to individual, is socially constructed, and changes over time—as do views of what is socially acceptable, vulgar, or immoral. In other words, some people's ideas of obscenity are different than others'. There are ongoing debates as to whether pornography is inherently obscene or immoral.

The liberal perspective on pornography views it as bringing harmless pleasure to the consumer and society. This side argues pornography should be treated as a cinematic genre like any other—an artistic medium open to interpretation by the viewer (Church Gibson 1993; Lehman 2006; Williams 1999). Similarly, a cultural studies perspective proposes a "radical context" model in which pornography is seen as a complex cultural artifact with symbolic meaning to be analyzed, not morally relegated (Attwood 2002; Sullivan and McKee 2015). The conservative point of view is that pornography threatens the moral values of a society. This side often argues pornography encourages people to commit adultery and engage in deviant sexual behaviors. Pornography is viewed as synonymous with the corrosion of traditional family and religious values.

Many feminists are critical of pornography because of its sexist portrayals of women, the emphasis on male dominance, female submission, and the focus on pleasing men exclusively. However, not all feminists agree on these points. Described as the **Porn Wars** of the 1980s, feminists came down to a "for or against" debate about pornography. Radical feminists against pornography argued that not only is porn inherently sexist, but it is a primary source of oppression and violence against women. Antipornography feminists argued pornography is a form of prostitution because women's bodies are commodified. They often cite how the word *pornography* derives from a Greek word meaning "writing about prostitutes" (Spector 2006). At the height of these debates in the 1980s, two of the most outspoken feminists, Andrea Dworkin (1993) and Catherine MacKinnon (1989a), sought to codify and criminalize pornography. They defined pornography as a form of sexual discrimination and created criteria for identifying it: when porn exemplifies sexual submission by a woman, presents women as sexual objects, or when women are penetrated by objects.

Those in favor of pornography, or anticensorship feminists, believe that pornography does not cause women's subordination. This side argues that focusing on a single source of oppression, such as pornography, downplays sexism within more powerful social institutions, including judicial, legal, familial, occupational, scientific, and religious. Some in favor of pornography began a movement called **sex positive feminism**, and maintain that sexual freedom is an essential component to women's overall freedom. This side argues pornography actually opens up discussion about sex and sexuality and can be an educational tool for women.

The feminist debate over pornography continues; but less focus is on whether it should be legal and more concern toward issues of consent, labor rights, and expanding understandings of desire and pleasure. In this context, consent refers to giving permission for a sexual experience, or for the sharing of a recording of a sexual experience or a nude image. In the age of digital video recording, many individuals are being recorded without their awareness, and then exploited online. The goals of labor rights advocates are diverse; but they generally aim to ensure fair treatment, equal pay, and health and safety standards for sex workers in the porn industry.

Violence and Pornography

Arguments that claim pornography is harmful to society lead many sociologists to study if and how pornography shapes actual sexual behavior and attitudes. One of the greatest concerns is whether pornographic images of violence and domination increase acts of sexual violence. In the 1970s and '80s, several studies concluded that the majority of pornographic films reveal scenes of women being dominated and exploited by men, include physical aggression and depictions of rape, and that these violent depictions lead to assault and acts of hostility (Cowan et al. 1988; Malamuth, Reisin, and Spinner 1979). Ybarra and Mitchell (2005) describe the relationship between pornography and sexual violence as complex. Their research indicates men who have no previous convictions for sexual offences can frequently view pornography with no effect. However, men who have predispositions toward aggressive sexual behavior have four times higher sexual aggression when repeatedly exposed to pornography (Ybarra & Mitchell 2005). The problem, of course, is we do not always know who has a predisposition toward violence until they commit an act of violence.

Research on male intimate partner violence offenders supports the idea that men who utilize pornography and strip clubs exhibit more controlling behaviors, engage in sexual abuse more often, and are more likely to use sexual violence against their partners (Simmons, Lehmann, and Collier-Tenison 2008). Conversely, Todd Kendall's (2006) controversial investigation into the relationship between exposure to pornography and sexual violence analyzed statistics on rape and Internet usage from multiple states. Kendall's findings indicate easy access to pornography actually reduces instances of sexual violence. The states that adopted the Internet earlier show larger declines in rape. The issue with Kendall's research is that it does not take into account other variables, which may be influencing the reduction of rape.

Similarly, there have been two Presidential Commissions on the topic of pornography that reached similarly contradictory conclusions. The 1970 U.S. Commission on Pornography and Obscenity found no conclusive links between pornography and sex crimes. In 1986, the Attorney General's Commission on Pornography, or the "Meese Commission," concluded pornography is dangerous, causes sex crimes, increases aggression in males, inspires sexism against women, and encourages pedophilia. In the face of such contradictory evidence, whether porn directly influences violent behavior is unresolved at this point. What we do know is pornography generally depicts heterosexual sex as a violent act against women. Women are repeatedly slapped, spit on, choked, and depicted to be in pain during sex. Unlike BDSM where forms of rough or violent sex are consensual and practiced with clear communication about boundaries and rules, violent sex in pornography is unregulated and appears to be the norm.

Gender, Race, Class, and Sexuality

Pornography comprises a complex and vast array of content that capitalizes on existing asymmetrical power relations in society, including gender, race, sexuality, and age. The majority of pornography is produced for white, heterosexual, male consumers (Albright 2008). Content analysis of objectification, power, and violence in 400 popular pornographic Internet videos from the most visited pornographic web sites reveals a high prevalence of images of male domination, female submissiveness, and the sexual objectification of women's bodies (Klaassen and Peter 2015). Most porn is geared toward an emphasis on male pleasure, not only in the actual sex act, but for the assumed male viewers. Even mainstream lesbian porn is generated for male viewing pleasure. An example of this is the focus on penetration, often with a sex toy, as the way to achieve orgasm. Penetration symbolizes male dominance and mimics heterosexual male penetration of the female negating sexual pleasure between two women outside of a heterosexual context (Day 2009).

Watching porn can have a long-lasting impact on the emotional health of women, men, and their relationships. A study of 15,246 respondents in the United States who had intentionally viewed or downloaded porn revealed it had negative consequences (Albright 2008). Women reported more negative consequences, including lowered body image, partners critical of their body, increased pressure to perform acts seen in pornographic films, and less actual sex. Men reported being more critical of their partners' body and less interested in actual sex (Albright 2008).

Like violence, sociologists ask whether sexist depictions in porn actually cause sexist behaviors and attitudes in reality. Researchers at the University of Copenhagen and the University of California-Los Angeles studied the impact of pornography on sexist attitudes among heterosexuals (Hald, Malamuth, and Lange 2013). Results show, among men, increased past pornography consumption was significantly associated with less egalitarian attitudes and more hostility toward women. Another study indicates both men and women who watch porn are less likely to support affirmative action for women (Wright and Funk 2013). Theoretically, these results support the perspective that pornography may support gendered scripts for social behavior that may be applied to judgments beyond sex or sexual activity.

In response to the seemingly inherent sexism found in porn, in recent years, there is an up-swing in "female-friendly" porn that depicts sex that is a mutually enjoyable experience between men and women instead of entirely male-pleasure-focused. **Feminist porn** is a genre of pornography that explores alternative representations of beauty, desire, pleasure, and power and is committed to gender equality and social justice. Most feminist porn attempts to be ethically produced porn, which means that performers are paid fairly and that their consent, safety, and well-being are considered in the production process.

Gail Dines (2010) argues porn racializes bodies and sexual behaviors with degrading titles and plot lines that emphasize subordination, inferiority, and stereotypes. She cites porn video

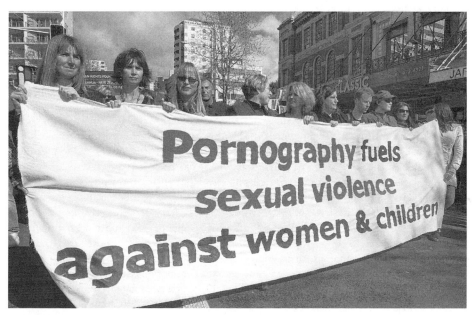

An anti-pornography march in 2008.
Source: Hannah Peters/Getty Images Entertainment/Getty Images.

titles like "Oh No! There's a Negro in My Mom" as an example of how most people working in the production end of the business are white and come from a white, and often racist, perspective. Such titles contribute to the racial fetishization of racial minorities. Dines argues women of color are often relegated to genres that lack any plot and hold no glamour, security, or status. Often hard-core porn depicts black men and white women having sex, with the emphasis on the size and power of the black man's penis. *Hustler*, one of the most widely distributed hard-core pornography magazines in the world, regularly depicts caricatured black men as having oversized penises but undersized heads, thus signifying mental inferiority and supports the racial stereotype that black men are sexual savages apt for sexual misconduct (Dines 2010).

In contrast to the hypersexualized black male, Asian men rarely appear in heterosexual pornography. When portrayed at all, they most frequently appear in gay porn as a feminized "other" to a masculinized white male (Han 2015; Shimizu 2013). The gay, Asian, male roles represent a submissive, feminine, often young, stereotype (Fung 1991). Racializing sexualities not only promotes false stereotypes, but constrains definitions of sexual norms and limits understandings of sexual diversity (Shimizu 2013).

Intersex and transgender individuals are degraded in porn videos with titles like "tranny" or "hermaphrodite" that perpetuate stereotypes and use stigmatizing language. The two categories are often lumped together as freakish, fantasy porn. Research reveals that most representations of transgender individuals in porn are hypersexualized, with more focus on transwomen than transmen (Davy and Steinbock 2012). Some argue this representation stems from the medical conception of transsexuality as something that only happens to hypersexual individuals (Davy and Steinbock 2012). Despite the slow cultural acceptance of transgender individuals in mainstream society, transgender porn has been steadily increasing in popularity in recent years. Some view this as a good sign that acceptance is increasing, while others see it as a fleeting porn trend (Morris 2015).

Impact of Pornography on Young People

A debate exists over pornography, children, and the Internet, primarily about restriction and regulation of pornography viewing by children. Research suggests the Internet is accessible to 95 percent of 12- to 17-year-olds in the United States (Madden et al. 2013). While it is obvious that more computer access can lead to greater access to pornography, it is not so obvious how much porn young people are exposed to or have access to. A national survey on risk, impact, and prevention revealed that 42 percent of youth between the ages of 10 and 17 had unwanted exposure to sexual pictures on the Internet, challenging the assumption that young people are seeking out porn (Mitchell, Finkelhor, and Wolak 2003).

When older teens were asked how they believe porn impacts young people, 59 percent responded that viewing pornography encourages young people to have sex at an earlier age, 49 percent felt that the Internet promotes negative attitudes toward women, and 49 percent said pornographic images may promote the idea that having unprotected sex is safe (Ybarra and Mitchell 2005). Evidence that exposure to *sexually explicit websites* (SEWs) significantly increases adolescent attitudes and behaviors about sex has been found in several studies. In one study, youths who sought out pornography also reported instances of delinquency and substance abuse in the prior year (Ybarra and Mitchell 2005). Adolescents exposed to frequent SEWs were more likely to have multiple lifetime sexual partners, to have had more than one sexual partner in the last three months, to have used alcohol or other substances at their last sexual encounter, to have higher sexual permissiveness compared with those never exposed, and to have engaged in anal sex. In a sample of 30 juveniles who had committed sex offenses, exposure to pornographic material at a young age was common (Wieckowski et al. 1998).

Age-centered themes are prevalent throughout pornography. Young girl or teenage content is a popular genre of porn that features young-looking performers. Often pornography video titles feature teens who are "barely legal." The illusion of youth is conveyed via clothing, hairstyles, and props and is usually acted by 18- and 19-year-old performers. While young females are marketed toward heterosexual male consumers, young-looking men, sometimes called "twinks," are also marketed toward gay male consumers (Tibbals 2013). While the videos are illusions and fantasy, it does lead sociologists to argue pornography is contributing to the sexualization of children (see Chapter Six).

Child Pornography

Any visual depiction involving the use of a minor engaging in sexually explicit conduct is considered *child pornography.* Visual depictions can be in the form of photographs, film, or video. Sexually explicit images means actual or simulated sexual intercourse, masturbation, or images of the genitals or pubic area. As mentioned earlier in this chapter, child pornography is considered obscene and is illegal under federal law in the United States. Child pornography is a steadily increasing problem, primarily through the accessibility of the Internet. The web provides a level of anonymity for perpetrators that makes it difficult for them to be caught. Law enforcement reports that in 2009, an estimated 1,910 arrests were made for crimes that included child pornography production; this is five times as many as in 2000, and double the arrests made in 2006 (Wolak, Finkelhor, and Mitchell 2012). It is a problem that seems only to be getting worse. People who watch, produce, share, or even those who are aware of child pornography and do not report it are committing a sex-based crime and, if convicted, will be considered a registered sex offender and predator.

Youth sexting is not gender neutral. "While equal numbers of boys and girls may sext voluntarily, girls are twice as likely to be among those who were pressured, coerced, blackmailed, or threatened into it—fully half of teen sexting in one large-scale survey fell into those categories . . . . Among the girls I met, the badgering to send nude photos could be incessant, beginning in middle school" (Orenstein 2016:22).

There are many studies that attempt to understand why a person engages in child pornography. In all of them, offenders report sexual arousal as the primary reason; but other explanations include curiosity, substance abuse issues, and as a way to prevent child sexual abuse (Merdian et al. 2016). There is not a consensus on whether child pornography leads to sexual child abuse or prevents it. More details on sexual abuse and pedophilia are discussed in Chapter 12.

Youth Sexting

With the advent of smart phone technology, people can now send images and messages instantaneously to each other. Human beings are sexual creatures, so not surprisingly, it didn't take long for people to begin *sexting*, or sharing sexual images and messages. For sexually consenting adults, sexting is legal and a form of sexual expression and connection. And, many adults engage in it. According to an online survey conducted by Drexel University, eight in ten adults reported having engaged in some form of sexting in the prior year (Grinberg 2015). For minors though, sexting is a problem. In today's world, most young people have their own cell phones, and they are navigating their first sexual experiences in a digital environment in a way that has never been done before. Learning how to do this safely is an ongoing process, and there are many debates on the legalities of youth sexting.

Exactly how many youths engage in sexting is not exactly clear. According to a 2009 online survey conducted by The Associated Press, MTV, and Knowledge Networks, one in three youth, ages 14 to 24, said they engaged in some form of sexting. This report found it is more prevalent among young adults than teens. In the survey, sexting could include sending or receiving naked photos or videos, or receiving texts or online messages with sexual words (Magid 2009). A telephone poll in the same year by the Pew Research Center's Internet and

> *"I believe in the empowered sex worker . . . . I was one. But the empowered sex worker isn't representative of the majority of sex workers"* (Bazelon 2016b).

American Life Project found that five percent of teens ages 14 to 17 had sent naked, or nearly naked, photos or videos via cell phone (Hoffman 2011).

Concerned parents, school officials, lawmakers, and police question if sexting by minors should be considered child pornography. Each state has its own unique approach to handling sexting. It is illegal in all states to possess a sexually explicit image of a minor, or to distribute, or promote that image. Some states have amended the laws against child pornography to make sexting among youths a misdemeanor instead of a federal offense. In other states though, sexting has not been addressed; and the state will defer to child pornography laws. In such states, teens have been charged with one or more felony offenses and, when convicted, are required to register as sex offenders. In those jurisdictions, it does not matter if the nude selfie was sent consensually. Of course, in regard to coerced sexting, sexual privacy violation, sharing sexual photos without permission, or sending sexual photos to an unwilling recipient, there is no doubt these are sexual crimes. Within the states without updated laws, victims are often fearful to report such crimes for fear they will also be charged with the same offense as the perpetrator. Many argue that the laws need to be amended to keep up to date with changing technology.

PROSTITUTION

Prostitution is the act of engaging in sexual activity for some form of commercial payment. It is one of the oldest occupations, tracing back to ancient civilizations, and one of the most controversial (Ringdal 2004). It is traditionally regarded as women's work in service of heterosexual men, but prostitutes can also be males or transgender people and service all range of sexualities. The term prostitute is historically associated with immorality, sinfulness, and shame. Negative slurs commonly used to describe prostitutes, such as whore, reveal gendered and negative social associations, most often about those providing the services rather than those purchasing the services.

There is a long-standing controversy on the moral and ethical standing of prostitution, which partially plays out in a debate over how to describe the work. The debate boils down to the central question: Is prostitution sexual labor or sexual exploitation? The term *sex worker*, first coined by Carol Leigh in the 1970s, describes someone who works in the commercial sex industry. Some prostitutes prefer the term sex worker because it refers to income-generating work and a legitimate profession rather than a class of immoral women (Leigh 1997). The term sex worker implies a prostitute has agency and freely chooses her field of work. The term sex worker also "hinges on an ideological conviction—the belief that the criminal law should not be used here as an instrument of punishment or shame, because sex work isn't inherently immoral or demeaning" (Bazelon 2016a:38).

Some opponents of decriminalization call themselves abolitionists, as they align their fight for equality with that of the battle to end sex slavery (Bazelon 2016b). Some feminists and former prostitutes take this position because they see prostitution as sexual exploitation, an extension of sex and gender inequality, and a result of lack of choices for women (Dworkin 1997). From this perspective, prostitutes are viewed as coerced victims of a larger economic and sexually exploitative system. This divide will be further explored in the discussion on legality later in this chapter.

The prevalence of prostitution varies significantly and is very hard to estimate due to a range of factors including transnational migration and variations in legality. A global "Sexual Exploitation" report from Fondation Scelles (2014) estimates there are from 40 to

42 million prostitutes in the world, and that three-quarters of them are between the ages of 13 and 25—80 percent of whom are female. In many countries in Europe, and in Canada, prostitution is legal, which increases its social acceptability; but it is still associated with criminal activity and thereby statistics are difficult to reliably collect. In the United States, prostitution is illegal, except in some counties in the state of Nevada. The FBI's Uniform Crime Report lists 78,000 arrests for prostitution and commercialized vice in 2007, but this accounts for only those who are arrested (Chen 2009). While the exact number is hard to pin down, experts suggest that over one million people have worked as prostitutes in the United States, or about one percent of American women (Chen 2009). A definite number is nearly impossible to calculate due to its illegal status, underground criminality, and the fact that many people drift in and out of prostitution.

Most prostitutes are women. Streetwalkers are prostitutes who can be found walking the streets and engaging in sexual activity in cars and various outdoor locations. Although the image of the streetwalker is most often associated with prostitution, in fact, streetwalkers only make up approximately one-fifth of all prostitutes (Weitzer 2012). Most prostitution occurs indoors in places such as brothels, escort services, bars, and massage parlors (Weitzer 2012). It is a highly class-stratified form of work with street work at the lowest stratum, and the most stigmatized, and call girls at the highest stratum (Weitzer 2012). Where a prostitute works, either on the streets or indoors, can influence the risks and dangers of the job. Street prostitutes are at the highest risk of violence such as rape, assault, and robbery. Call girls, escorts, and massage parlor workers still face many dangers; but typically, they have regular, lower-risk clients and are in better positions to screen for potentially violent customers (Lever and Dolnick 2000).

In order to understand who becomes a prostitute and why, it is important to make the distinction between forced child and adolescent prostitution and adult women who choose to become prostitutes. Sexually exploiting children is inherently nonconsensual. The age of consent is the age at which a person is considered to be legally competent to consent to sexual acts. Age of consent laws vary across different state jurisdictions in the United States, but most set the range between 14 and 18. Sexually exploiting children is a type of sexual abuse. The exact number of victims is not known, and estimates of children at risk vary. The FBI's research claims the average age of entry into child "prostitution" is 12 years old, while girls as young as 9 years old have been known to be exploited. Child sexual exploitation is illegal everywhere in the world under the United Nation's international law, established under the "Optional Protocol to Convention on the Rights of the Child on the sale of children, child prostitution and child pornography" in 2002. More discussion on forced sexual exploitation will be covered in the human trafficking discussion later in this chapter.

There are many different sociological explanations for why a teen might be exploited through prostitution. There is a direct correlation between teens who experience abuse, run away from home, become homeless, and prostitution (Flowers 2001). Many argue prostitution may become a survival strategy option for those with experiences of childhood sexual abuse, incest, or physical abuse (Nadon, Koverola, and Schludermann 1998). Childhood sexual and physical abuse has been found to be a precursor to prostitution in numerous studies since the early 1980s (Bagley and Young 1987; Silbert and Pines 1981; Simons and Whitbeck 1991; Widom and Kuhns 1996). In a recent survey of prostitutes in Vancouver, out of the 100 prostitutes interviewed, 72 percent reported experiencing childhood physical abuse (Farley, Lynn, and Cotton 2005).

Economic vulnerability, often homelessness or poverty, can be contributing factors. Sometimes women face emergency situations such as escaping a violent partner, losing a job, having children with special needs or health problems; and they seek prostitution as a financial solution to these problems. For many, prostitution seems like their only option. High levels of debt and low levels of education and employment skills are often characteristics of women who get into sex work. Moreover, there is a strong link between substance abuse and prostitution (Brawn and Roe-Sepowitz 2008). Many individuals enter a life of prostitution to support alcohol or drug addiction (Flowers 2001; Maxwell and Maxwell 2000). Some studies indicate prostitution work instigates or amplifies substance dependency (Chase and Statham 2005).

Racial inequality can intersect with economic inequality to increase vulnerability. In the African American community, researchers describe how prostitution is rooted in what they call a black underclass, a culture of poverty supported by an underground economy built on illegal drug sales and prostitution (Carter and Giobbe 1999). At its core, the black underclass is built on racism and the legacy of slavery. They describe how most black women in prostitution were born into the black underclass where racism and sexism intersect. While poverty and race inequalities are explanations for why some women turn to prostitution, they are not the complete story. Individuals who go into prostitution come from diverse racial, class, age, gender, and socioeconomic backgrounds. There is not a profile for the prostitute.

Johns and Pimps

Prostitutes, or sex workers, engage in sexual and social situations in which a range of other people are involved. Most notably, the customer, sometimes called a "john," a client, or a "trick." In countries where prostitution is illegal, this person is a criminal. In cases where the customer engages in sexual activity with someone under the age of consent, that person is a criminal and a pedophile. The primary customers of prostitution are men. Some are critical of criminalizing clients of prostitutes because they fear it forces clients to take greater risks, such as going to a very remote place in order to have sex and avoid being arrested, which puts the prostitute at greater risk for potential sexual violence (Bazelon 2016b). Research, public policy, and law enforcement have traditionally focused attention on the prostitutes instead of the customers or the pimps.

There are differing views on exactly who the male customers are. Some views indicate that male customers are disproportionally attracted to exploitation and violence (Dworkin 1993; Hunter 1994). Melissa Farley's research indicates the attitudes of male sex buyers dehumanize and commodify women, and reveal a lack of empathy for the prostitutes they hire, and feelings of anger and hostility toward them (Farley et al. 2015). Others argue the main customers of prostitution are regular, everyday men often in regular marriages (Raymond 2004). Kingsley Davis (1937) in his classic sociological thesis on prostitution argued that prostitution existed to serve a social function of fulfilling men's sexual needs. This theory can easily be understood as an extension of the sexual double standard. In a 2005 national sample, one study found male customers of female street prostitutes less likely to be married, and more likely to be unhappy, to express greater sexual liberalism, and to engage in other aspects of the sex industry more frequently than men in general (Monto and McRee 2005).

The number of male customers in the United States is difficult to assess. Kinsey's research on male sexuality in the 1940s supported the idea that a majority of men in the United States patronized prostitution, with approximately 69 percent based on a convenience sample of 18,000 men. In 1964, Benjamin and Masters (1964) estimated that closer to 80 percent of U.S. men had hired a prostitute. More recent reports from the 1992 National Health and Life Survey found only 16 percent of men in the United States had ever hired a prostitute (Michael et al. 1994). The exact number is difficult to pin down because, like all crimes, it is an underground activity difficult to research and quantify.

While some prostitutes are independent entrepreneurs, many are controlled by a pimp. A pimp is usually a male who controls the actions and proceeds of one or more prostitutes. In the United States, pimps call themselves "players" in the "game," or some describe themselves as "business managers" (Dank et al. 2014). Pimps manage most of the pre-transaction preparation, such as marketing, finding clients, choosing a location, setting the price, and scheduling the time for the sex act. Pimp-controlled prostitution is the most common form of street-level prostitution in the United States, with some estimates that

80 percent of prostitutes become involved with pimps over time (Dalla 2002; Williamson and Cluse-Tolar 2002). Often pimps have a "bottom girl," a prostitute who runs the "business" if the pimp travels or is busy. Often the bottom girl aids in managing the prostitutes and is a personal assistant to the pimp. Pimps can sometimes be women. Most often women who manage prostitutes are madams, or the managers and owners of brothels.

Pimps typically target specific women for prostitution, specifically, young, desperate, homeless women. Sometimes poor women of color are specifically targeted by pimps because of their exotic quality (Dank et al. 2014). For example, in a study of eight major U.S. cities, pimps in California described targeting Asian and Asian American females for prostitution work because their clientele specifically sought after them, making them a "hot commodity" (Dank et al. 2014). Pimps are often abusive and attempt to control and exploit women through the use of physical violence, sexual assault, manipulation, isolation, verbal abuse, torture, threats of violence, and even murder. Some pimps claim to protect prostitutes by making sure customers pay and don't physically harm them, although pimp violence is often just as much of a reality (Norton-Hawk 2004).

Male and Transgender Prostitutes

Most sociological research concentrates on female prostitutes, and much less is known about male and transgender prostitutes. Males made up 34 percent of prostitution arrests from 21 states in a cross-national study in 2001 (Vandiver and Krienert 2007). Similar to females, male prostitutes are stratified into street and indoor work, such as massage, bar, escort, and "call boy" services (West 1993). In a review of various studies, Weitzer (2005) concludes that there appear to be some differences in the way males and females experience prostitution. These include the tendency for males to be involved in prostitution in a more sporadic and transitory way, less dependent on it as a primary source of income, more compelled to define their sexual orientation, less likely to be abused as children, less likely to have been coerced into prostitution, less likely to have a pimp, and more likely to experience sexual gratification from their work.

Research on male and transgender prostitution tends to focus on risky sexual behavior and rates of HIV. Transgender prostitutes report experiencing significantly higher rates of HIV infections when compared to male and female sex workers (Boles and Elifson 1994). For example, in a study of 53 transgender prostitutes in Atlanta, 68 percent were found to be HIV positive (Elifson et al. 1993). Transgender individuals are often more economically vulnerable, and needs can trump safety when customers are willing to pay more for unprotected sex (Sausa, Keatley, and Operario 2007). Transgender prostitutes often have urgent financial needs, stemming from transphobia and the inability to find employment, as well as costly procedures of gender transition, which make them more susceptible to unprotected sex and at higher risk for HIV (Nemoto et al. 2004). Transgender prostitutes occupy the lowest stratum of the prostitute hierarchy and are the most stigmatized (Weitzer 2005).

Debates Over Legalities

Just as there is controversy over exactly how to describe prostitution, there is also a long-running debate as to whether it should be legalized or criminalized. At one end of the spectrum is the legalization argument, which states that prostitution is a valid form of work and should be legal and regulated like all other forms of business. This side argues prostitutes, or sex workers, willingly choose their line of work and that it should be treated like any other legitimate form of employment: taxed, regulated for employee and customer safety, meet employment laws concerning work hours, and contribute to social security so employees can eventually retire. At the other end of the spectrum is the criminalization, or abolitionist, position that states prostitution is inherently violent and harmful to women and should be treated like a crime. This side argues women do not choose to become prostitutes but instead are coerced, either directly or indirectly by people in their lives or by dire circumstances.

Various national organizations and individuals in the United States call for legalization of prostitution. One such group is *Call Off Your Old Tired Ethics* (COYOTE), an organization initiated by one of the first U.S. sex workers' rights campaigns in the 1970s. They call for the laws prohibiting prostitution, pimping, and pandering to be repealed and replaced by labor laws. Very large international organizations such as Amnesty International, Human Rights Watch, and the World Health Organization agree prostitution should be decriminalized based on the indication that criminalization reinforces discrimination and places prostitutes at higher risk of harassment, disease, and violence (Purtill 2015). Decriminalization will lead to a decrease in the transmission of HIV, for instance, because the profession will be regulated and sex workers will be tested regularly. It can also free governments to focus on sex trafficking (discussed later in this chapter) and child sexual exploitation rather than wasting time and resources arresting and prosecuting consenting adults (Bazelon 2016b).

The World Charter for Prostitutes' Rights was adopted in 1985 by the International Committee for Prostitutes' Rights (ICPR), demanding legalization, and made a clear distinction between adult prostitution that results from individual decision and self-determination versus forced prostitution and trafficking of persons. There is no agreement as to how to define voluntary prostitution, and there are disagreements as to how much the health of sex workers should be regulated. The primary focus of the legalization position is on reducing the stigma associated with prostitution, safety, personal freedom, and the removal of moral condemnation from the law. Critiques of this position are that these ideologies are built on class and race privilege. In other words, most prostitutes who choose sex work and argue for decriminalization are white and middle class (Bazelon 2016b).

The criminalization position calls for prostitution to be illegal based on its coercive and exploitive nature, intrinsic violence, association with other criminal activities, illegal drug use, and physical and emotional health risks. Radical feminist perspectives view prostitution as a form of male domination over women, or an extension of sexism (Dworkin 1993; MacKinnon 1993). It is a sexually exploitive institution that allows men unconditional sexual access to women, limited solely by ability to pay. Kathleen Barry's (1996) classic work defines prostitution as a political condition in which women's subordination is the base from which discrimination and victimization is enacted. Socially supported tactics of power and control facilitate the recruitment or coercion of women and children into prostitution and effectively impede their escape. These tactics include economic marginalization, child sexual abuse, rape, violence, double victimization, as well as racism, classism, and heterosexism.

> "Women like myself who were forced by nobody need to find our voices and assert that this does not mean we were forced by nothing. It is a very human foolishness to insist on the presence of a knife or a gun or a fist in order to recognize the existence of force, when often the most compelling forces on this earth present intangibly, in coercive situations. My prostitution experience was coerced. For those of us who fall into the 'free' category, it is life that does the coercing" (Moran 2013:224).

Those who adhere to this position argue that the distinction between forced and voluntary prostitution is impossible to detect because coercive tactics are always involved, even if the prostitute is not aware of how. They claim violence is intrinsic to prostitution and cite high rates of violence as proof. For example, women in prostitution have a death rate that is 200 times higher than women who are not involved in prostitution and are much more likely to be raped than nonprostituted women (Potterat et al. 2004). In Farley's 2005 survey, 90 percent had been physically assaulted in prostitution, 78 percent had been raped in prostitution, and 72 percent met DSM-IV criteria for posttraumatic stress disorder. This position has been critiqued for being essentialist because it makes sweeping claims about all types of prostitution over large periods of time and across cultures.

GLOBALIZATION AND SEXUALITY

The global economy and the sexual economy are deeply intertwined. *Globalization* is a term that refers to the worldwide integration of economies through free trade and free flow of capital; and the cultural exchange of ideas through the transnational migration of people, information, and consumer culture. An important and distinguishing historical feature that shapes the modern global economy is colonialism. *Colonialism* varies throughout time and across regions, but it is understood as an exploitive system of rule in which a dominant, powerful country occupies another and controls land and resources in that country. When a country is colonized, the colonized people and indigenous populations are denied political, economic, and even cultural autonomy. European colonialism, which took place between the sixteenth and the mid-twentieth centuries, affected the entire world and dramatically transformed international relations—particularly because in addition to the economic exploitation, it was founded on a false sense of moral and racial superiority that deeply influenced sexuality and sexual norms.

Postcolonialism is a term to describe the process of decolonizing the world, which began in the mid-twentieth century as more and more former colonies began adopting democracy and capitalism, while still dismantling the residual political, socioeconomic, and psychological effects of their colonial history. In the decolonization process, some of the dominant gendered, racialized, sexual, and economic structures of domination and exploitation remained. *Neocolonialism* is a term used by sociologists to describe the continuation of the exploitive economic model of colonialism after a colonized territory has achieved formal political independence. This can come in the form of using capitalism or cultural imperialism to influence a country to adopt practices that primarily benefit the more dominant powerful country or normalize the more dominant culture's beliefs.

Colonialism, in all its forms, influences and organizes systems of sexual power. Historically, colonialism took sexual autonomy away from colonized people by influencing and shaping their sexual norms and beliefs. Current global sexual politics and the global sexual economy are still influenced by these norms. Europeans viewed "uncivilized" or indigenous cultures as sexually backward or exotic, idealized heterosexuality and heteropatriarchal gender norms, and attempted to supplant their ideals on colonial regions. *Heteropatriarchal* is a term used to describe the expected social arrangement of heterosexuality with the father or male as head of household with primary power over women and family. Kamala Kempadoo (2013) describes how colonialism in the Caribbean shaped the sexual-economic relations and created a hierarchy with European ideas of sexuality as superior and progressive, and colonized people's ideas of sexuality as uncivilized and inferior.

As countries around the world integrate into the global economy, the transformation impacts their sexual economies in a variety of ways. In some areas, it increases industrialization and thereby increases the migration of people for labor and, in turn, the demand for women's sexual labor. Economic downturns cause some women and girls to migrate for better work, making them more vulnerable to sex trafficking. Globalization brings with it faster and easier communication and travel, which increases the growth of sex tourism and the migration of people to areas where the sex industry is thriving. Finally globalization promotes militarism across the world, and military bases become sites for the sexual exploitation of women. The following sections of this chapter will explore three aspects of globalization and sexuality: sex trafficking, sex tourism, and militarism.

Sex Trafficking

A tragic characteristic of globalization is the practice of trade in human beings, or human trafficking. Human trafficking is a worldwide phenomenon in which a person is forced into slave labor. An offshoot of human trafficking in the global sex trade is *sex trafficking*, a form of modern sexual slavery in which someone uses force, fraud, or coercion to cause

Anti-trafficking activists have sometimes used billboards to generate attention to this social problem.
Source: AP Photo: Jay Pickthorn.

a commercial sex act with an adult, or anytime someone causes a minor to commit a commercial sex act. **Commercial sex acts** include prostitution, pornography, or sexual performance in exchange for anything of value including money, shelter, food, clothes, and more. Under the *U.S. Victims of Trafficking and Violence Protection Act of 2000*, all sex trafficking is a violation of federal law; and anytime a minor, or someone under the age of 18, is used in a commercial sex act, that person is considered a victim of trafficking, regardless of their willingness or desire to engage in the sex act (U.S. Congress 2000).

Sex trafficking is the fastest growing business of organized crime and one of the largest criminal enterprises in the world. The majority of sex trafficking is transnational, with victims being taken from less developed countries to more developed countries. It is also domestic and regional and occurs in almost all countries on the globe, including the United States. Globally, the International Labor Organization estimates there are 4.5 million victims of forced sexual exploitation in the world, with approximately 21 percent children. Of that 4.5 million, 98 percent are women (ILO Global Estimate 2016). Exact estimates on how many people are sex trafficked in the United States are impossible to figure at this point. What we do know is that the National Human Trafficking Resource Center reported they received 5,544 calls on human trafficking issues: 74.6 percent of them concerned sex trafficking, and 91.4 percent of the victims were female (National Human Trafficking Resource Center 2015).

The root causes of sex trafficking are various, complex, and often differ from one country to another. Sex trafficking is driven by social, economic, and cultural factors specific to location. With that said, there are some overarching trends. The most consistent is migration. Sex trafficking is more prevalent in areas where there are groups seeking to migrate. In many cases, the potential victim is seeking a better location due to local conditions of poverty, lack of social or economic opportunities, violence or conflict, political instability, or natural disaster. Migration is a common characteristic of globalization, especially when there is economic growth in newly industrializing countries; people move for better work. The rapid expansion of the Internet and all forms of media across the globe promotes images and normalcy of wealthier countries. This increases people's desire to want to migrate to more developed countries. When victims are seeking or are in migration, they are destabilized and displaced, making them more vulnerable to being exploited by offenders who might offer false promises of work and security.

According to the Louisiana Human Trafficking Report (2014), the state of Louisiana, specifically New Orleans and Baton Rouge, has a significant problem with sex trafficking. Conditions in New Orleans make it a prime location for trafficking because it is a transportation hub, with an influx of migrant laborers in the years since Hurricane Katrina. It is also a city well known for its sexual entertainment services. Moreover, Louisiana ranks as one of the poorest states in the country with nearly 20 percent of its population living in poverty in 2012. Youth homelessness is one of the worst cases in the country, ranking 46th out of 50 in 2010 for risk of child homelessness. Between 2009 and 2012, the Rescue and Restore Coalition Louisiana, funded by the U.S. Department of Health and Human Services, identified 140 victims of sex trafficking in the New Orleans and Baton Rouge areas. The youngest confirmed victim was six years old (Louisiana Human Trafficking Report 2014).

Sex trafficking usually involves three primary phases: recruitment, transport, and exploitation. Some traffickers offer to pay for the victim's transportation and recruitment to a specific job but purport incurred debt, enslaving the women in an ongoing and obscure ***debt bondage***, in which her labor is repayment for the incurred debt. Interest is accrued for food, shelter, and clothing, and often the victims are never able to get out of debt. They are sometimes threatened with violence if they try to leave. If a sex trafficking victim is illegally in a foreign country where she cannot speak the language, she is often unwilling and unable to seek help or go to law enforcement. Porous borders between countries, corrupt government officials, weak immigration laws, and the involvement of transnational organized criminal groups make the issue of migration and sex trafficking difficult to manage.

Sex trafficking experts often talk about push and pull forces that propel or lure vulnerable people into situations of forced sexual exploitation. An example of a push/pull factor is intimate partner violence. When a woman attempts to escape violence, often she flees to temporary housing, can lose employment, and experiences high levels of stress that can make her vulnerable to becoming trafficked. On the other hand, when a woman tries to leave sex trafficking, she is also at risk, due to her lack of resources and support, and can become a prey to an abusive intimate partner (Leidhold 2013). The overwhelming majority of sex trafficking victims are women and girls. Sexism devalues women and girls across the globe and increases their vulnerability to trafficking. With that said, males and transgender individuals are also trafficked. Once victims are enslaved in sex trafficking, they lose human agency and freedom. They often do not receive any of the income from the commercial exchange. They are reduced to commodities.

A major push/pull factor is poverty. In some cases, parents sell their children into sex trafficking. Sometimes this is for direct cash as a desperate measure to alleviate poverty, but it can also be because parents are hoping the child will eventually find a better life with more opportunities somewhere else. For example, some mothers in Cambodia who reported as sex traffickers of their own daughters claimed they felt forced to sell their daughters due to poverty and debt (Haworth 2014). Cambodia is both a transit and a destination country for women and children who are trafficked from Vietnam and China for sexual exploitation. Cambodia's recent history of the brutal Khmer Rouge regime from 1975 to 1979, combined with poverty and corruption, make it specifically vulnerable to sex trafficking. UNICEF estimates that children account for a third of the 40,000 to 100,000 people in Cambodia's sex industry, and it is considered the global center for pedophiles.

Revenue from trafficking people can be very large. It is estimated to be a multibillion dollar per year industry. It is illegal work, and sex traffickers face risks—including losing financial operational costs, and, most obviously the risk of being caught and punished (Wheaton, Schauer, and Galli 2010). Financial risks include expensive transportation costs, including falsified documents and travel fees, and sometimes paying family members fees for the child being trafficked. Yet, even with these dangers, traffickers are not being swayed to stop. It is a fast-growing industry with high profits.

BOX 11.1

GLOBAL/TRANSNATIONAL PERSPECTIVES ON SEXUALITY:
NATURAL DISASTER AND CHILD SEX TRAFFICKING IN NEPAL

It is a tragic fact that where natural disaster strikes in the world, child trafficking increases. Examples of this correlation can be found in Haiti after the 2010 earthquake, in the Philippines after the 2013 typhoon, and in Indonesia after the 2004 tsunami (Branigan 2013; Evans 2010; Nwe 2005). In Nepal, in 2015, two earthquakes hit 16 days apart, both over 7.3 magnitude, instantly killing thousands and leaving over half a million people homeless (Barry 2016). Many children became orphaned. Since the double disaster, the estimated rates of child sex trafficking in Nepal have been steadily increasing (Childs 2016). Nepal already had a trafficking problem. It is estimated that 12,000 Nepalese children are trafficked to India every year, according to a 2001 International Labor Organization study (Kumar, Gurung, and Adhikari 2001).

Nepal is considered a source country for girls and women to be internationally trafficked, primarily to India, but also to Saudi Arabia, Malaysia, and United Arab Emirates, for prostitution, sex work, forced labor, domestic servitude, and more. Oftentimes, women and girls are lured with promises of work or marriage. According to the United Nations, approximately one-third of the Nepalese population works abroad, so migration is common (Chen 2015). The Trafficking in Persons Report (TIP) compiled by the U.S. State Department rates Nepal as Tier 2, which means the government does not fully meet the minimum standards for eliminating trafficking, although the report does recognize efforts are being made (Trafficking in Persons Report 2016).

Many nongovernmental organizations, such as UNICEF, are working to protect children in Nepal by checking interception points along traveling routes between the borders of India and China for trafficking victims, and finding shelters and safe homes for orphaned children. Shakti Samuha, an organization in Nepal established in 1996 and run by survivors of sex trafficking, works to empower returning trafficking survivors by providing shelter, legal aid, and therapy. Shakti Samuha is working on a specific project to educate adolescent girls and women in the 14 earthquake-affected districts about the dangers of trafficking (Shakti Samuha 2016).

"Employers" of trafficked victims can be owners of a wide range of businesses, including online pornography sites, sex parlors, or brothels. Like the trafficker, their primary interest is profit. With a slave, the labor is nearly free. Moreover, because it is underground and illegal, employers do not have to be concerned about employee rights, safety laws, or benefits for workers. Finally, the consumer is also often a criminal, in countries where prostitution is illegal, seeking the highest benefit for the lowest cost. The demand for commercial sex is high, which is why traffickers keep up the supply of victims. In some cases, the consumer does not know the prostitute or sex worker is being held in bondage against their will.

FEMINIST RESPONSE The controversy over whether prostitution should be legal or illegal discussed earlier in this chapter is drawn into debates on how to stop sex trafficking. Feminists who view prostitution itself as a violation of human rights view sex trafficking as an extension of this violation. In other words, all prostitutes are victims of trafficking. These feminists often refer to themselves as abolitionists, or feminist activists fighting modern-day sex slavery. They believe prostitution should be abolished and protection should be enhanced for victims of sex trafficking. Research conducted by Seo-Young Cho, Axel Dreher, and Eric

Neumayer (2013) supports the claim that countries where prostitution is legal experience more reported human trafficking. Feminist critics of the abolitionist movement argue prostitution is not inherently violent or exploitive. They believe that grouping prostitution and trafficking is promoting unrealistic stereotypes of all prostitutes as victims, and they criticize this position for promoting a moral crusade (Weitzer 2007). This view promotes the decriminalization and legalization of prostitution as a solution to the problem of sex trafficking. This side also focuses on the rights of all trafficked persons and sex workers and on sexual and economic justice (Kempadoo 2013; Lobasz 2009).

The legalization versus criminalization debate surrounding prostitution is not meant to leave us at an impasse. Instead, it is meant to make us realize prostitution cannot be understood outside of larger, structural issues such as sexism, racism, and global inequality. As Kamala Kempadoo (2013) argues, context matters. By reducing the cause of sex work down to a single issue, such as violence against women or sexism, the complex variety of socioeconomic conditions and cultural histories specific to each location and group are lost. At this point, legalizing prostitution advantages mostly women who freely choose to enter the profession and are able to leave it when they please. As long as the gender wage gap is alive and well, and women are too often the sole providers of their children, some women will be economically coerced into sex work. Women must have viable employment options and must earn enough money to support their families. For women of color, the gender wage gap is even greater. Women of color must also share in these economic and employment opportunities. As long as globalization privileges wealthy nations at the expense of poor nations, Third World women of color will be forced into sex work. Until we have greater social equality, the debate over legalization versus criminalization of sex work cannot be resolved.

MAIL-ORDER OR INTERNET BRIDES A mail-order or Internet bride is a woman who is marketed as a bride to economically privileged American, European, or Asian men seeking marriage. The term "mail order" comes from the pre-Internet era when women listed themselves in bride catalogs. Today, they are listed on various Internet sites, most of which are brokered by commercial companies called the *international brokerage marriage (IBM) industry*. In some cases men seek brides online because there is a shortage of women in their areas due to migration or son preference, which can lead to practices of prenatal sex selection and a shortage of female births. Most women who are willing to migrate as brides are in poverty, and Internet marriage is a way to escape. Others, including young girls, are forced, or trafficked, as mail-order brides. In the United States, it is estimated that the IBM industry is growing, with nearly 500 services who match between 9,500 and 14,000 foreign women with U.S. men (Lindee 2007). Proponents of the IBM industry claim it facilitates interculturalism and opportunities, by giving women in poor areas the experience of living in wealthier countries.

Critics of mail-order brides claim women who find themselves in these situations are more susceptible to violence. This is partly because of cultural differences, language barriers, lack of support and networks, and complete reliance on the consumer spouse for economic support (Sico 2013); but, more so, because the process of buying a bride is a form of commodifying a human being. When a human is commodified, "it" is seen as an object and is more vulnerable to being abused. In most cases, the men are seeking women who comply with traditional gender stereotypes of submissiveness and subordination and who will uphold the traditional family model of subservient wife and mother. Traditional gender expectations are often used as justification for gender-based violence. Racial stereotypes and ideologies are often placed on the foreign brides, creating unrealistic expectations, power imbalances, and inequality. The U.S. Congress passed the *International Marriage Broker Regulation Act of 2005*, requiring international marriage brokers to provide prospective brides with information packets about domestic violence and the criminal histories of male clients, including any records from the National Sex Offender Public Registry.

Sex Tourism

Globalization makes worldwide communication and transportation easier. In turn, travel for sexual purposes increases. *Sex tourism* is a term used to describe travel to a foreign country with the intent to engage in sexual activities with a sex worker. Sex tourism is a significant contributor to the global tourism industry. Growing populations of people around the world have enough income and time to take entire vacations oriented around sexual pleasure activities. Sex vacations, or holidays, are taken primarily by men who come from industrialized countries, such as the United States, United Kingdom, Canada, Germany, Japan, or Kuwait. Sometimes sex tourism takes place while an individual is simultaneously on a business or work-related trip. Sex tourism is found across the globe; but popular destinations are Brazil, Thailand, The Netherlands, Philippines, Dominican Republic, and Cambodia. It is legal in some countries, such as The Netherlands, and illegal in other countries, such as Brazil.

Many sex tourist destinations are in economically disadvantaged areas with very high levels of poverty. Viewing sex tourism from an economically exploitive position, Julia O'Connell Davidson (2005) argues sex tourism is the activity of individuals who use their economic power to attain powers of sexual command over others. Sex tourists view their actions as something they have a right to, viewing the entire transaction from an entirely self-interested perspective. An awareness of how racism, colonialism, global economic inequalities, sexism, and other social dynamics benefit them while disadvantaging others seems to be limited (Leuchtag 2003). Combining the disadvantages of poverty with the exploitive demands of sex tourism creates an environment in which women and girls are more susceptible to sex trafficking and child sex exploitation. The *commercial sexual exploitation of children (CSEC)* is the sexual abuse of a child by an adult and remuneration in cash or kind to the child or a third person. CSEC can take the form of sex trafficking, pornography, or child sex tourism.

Child sex tourism is the sexual exploitation of children by an adult, or pedophile, who travels in order to have sexual contact with children. Child sex tourism is illegal in all parts of the world. Despite this fact, it is still a feature of the informal, underground sex market and a driving force in the commercial sex trade industry, as it is highly lucrative. A study by UNICEF on the high rates of commercial sexual exploitation of children in the coastal areas of Kenya reveals that the disparity between a family's capacity to generate goods and income and what can be earned in sex work encourages children to seek out tourists (Jones 2006). Some ten to fifteen thousand girls, up to 30 percent of all 12- to 18-year-olds in the coastal areas, are involved in casual sex work (Jones 2006).

Countries with more sex tourism have higher rates of HIV. Evidence shows that in low- and middle-income countries, HIV prevalence among sex workers is 12 times greater than among the general population. The highest rates of HIV are found in sub-Saharan Africa (see Chapter Ten). An analysis of 16 countries in sub-Saharan Africa in 2012 showed a pooled prevalence of more than 37 percent HIV rate among sex workers (Kerrigan et al. 2013). UNAIDS' "Gap Report" (2014) is a cumulative global study of HIV among sex workers that found stigma and discrimination, violence, and punitive legal and social environments are key determinants of increased HIV vulnerability. Punitive environments have been shown to limit the availability, access to, and use of HIV prevention, treatment, care, and support for sex workers and their clients. In some areas, such as across sub-Saharan Africa, there are very few programs designed to educate, prevent, or treat HIV. For example, a review of 54 projects found most included small, local-level efforts that provided condoms and only occasionally included HIV testing (Dhana et al. 2014).

FEMALE SEX TOURISM: "THE CARIBBEAN BEACH BOYS" The bulk of sex tourism is defined by heterosexual relations between male sex tourists and female sex workers, but there is a significant amount of female sex tourism that remains less studied by sociologists. Growing numbers of white, wealthy European and North American women seek male sex workers in the Caribbean islands (Herold, Garcia, and DeMoya 2001). Some researchers claim female sex tourism is different than male sex tourism because often the men they have sex with are not considered prostitutes, but rather "beach boys," as they are called in Barbados. A beach boy is a companion and "boyfriend" and often accepts only gifts in exchange for sex, rather than money. Pruitt and LaFont (1995) termed the exchange *romance tourism*. This implies women are primarily interested in an emotional relationship on these excursions. Other sociologists argue that female sex tourism is intimately tied to having greater economic power. In other words, it is the same as male sex tourism in that women are motivated by the exploitive opportunity to have sexual and economic power over another, with the primary difference being it provides a form of gender emancipation for women they can't normally find in their home cultures. Women, like men, are also motivated by racialized sexual fantasies of hypersexual men from faraway, exotic cultures (de Albuquerque 1998).

GENDER, RACE, AND ETHNICITY IN SEX TOURISM Gender, race, and ethnicity factor intricately into the global sex tourism economy and shape ideals and fantasies about what is sexually exotic. Racialized sexualities and fetishes make some groups attractive to tourists looking for an exotic, sexual adventure. Joane Nagel (2000) describes sex tourism as *ethnosexual*, or the intersection and interaction between ethnicity and sexuality. Ethnosex is defined and shaped by specific cultural constructions of race, ethnicity, sex, and power that are built into and around commercial sex tourism enterprises all over the world. Fantasies of the ethnic exotic "other" are both created by and sold to consumers, whether it be the untouched, native, virgin female, who is simultaneously hedonistic and sexually advanced, or the hypersexualized, dark skinned, savage male. Nagel (2000) describes some sex tourist consumers as "ethnosexual adventurers," who seek recreational sexual encounters, and some as "ethnosexual invaders," who sexually assault "others" across ethnic boundaries, raping and enslaving, as a means of sexual domination and colonization.

Bangkok, Thailand, also referred to as "sexual Disneyland," is one of the largest sex tourism destinations in the world. Asian women have long been eroticized in the West as sexually submissive and docile, and this is part of the appeal for sex tourism in Thailand. Sunny Woan (2008) describes how white sexual imperialism, through a history of rape and war, created the hypersexualized stereotype of the Asian woman (see Chapter Three). This stereotype, in turn, fosters the over-prevalence of Asian women in pornography; the Asian fetish syndrome; and worst of all, sexual violence against Asian women. In Bangkok, more than just reducing women to mere objects and commodities, an array of very strange and exotic sexual displays and offerings can be found in its Red Light District. Many of these sexual displays are regarded more as sexual perversions, or even torture, as women are reduced to grotesque objects engaging in absurd and often harmful sexual performances, such as putting live turtles into their vaginas, dancing on a pole, and then ejecting the turtle into an aquarium; or inserting razor blades into their vaginas (Guzder 2011). Sex tourism is inextricably structured along lines of gender, race, ethnic, and class inequality.

Sexuality and Militarism

Countries where war or armed government forces have a strong presence are described as living under a system of *militarism*. The U.S. government has approximately 800 military bases in foreign countries around the globe (Vine 2015). There has never been a nation or empire in history with this many bases in foreign lands (Vine 2015). Many would describe this as global militarism. According to the Center for Women's Global Leadership, militarism can also be defined as a set of values rooted in heteropatriarchal gender constructions, in which violent masculinities are idealized and misogynistic, homophobic, and transphobic behaviors are normalized (Center for Women's Global Leadership 2015). An example of misogyny, or the contempt or prejudice against women, is the practice of U.S. military bases coordinating with government authorities to provide servicemen with sex provided by trafficked women or local sex workers. This practice is rooted in the idea that men have a high sex drive that must always be met. Also rooted in this practice is a historically accepted view within the military that "sexual recreation" is vital to the well-being and morale of troops (Enloe 2014).

Research finds U.S. bases in South Korea were a hub for transnational sex trafficking of women from the Asia Pacific and Eurasia to South Korea and the United States (Hughes, Chon, and Ellerman 2007). The U.S. military has 83 bases in South Korea (Vine 2015). Three specific types of trafficking were found connected to U.S. military bases there: domestic trafficking of Korean women to clubs around the military bases, transnational trafficking of women to clubs around military bases, and transnational trafficking of women from South Korea to massage parlors in the United States (Hughes, Chon, and Ellerman 2007). In 2014, 122 South Korean women, who describe themselves as former Korean "comfort women" for U.S. troops, sued the South Korean government. The women claim the South Korean government violated their human rights by training them to work as prostitutes and coordinating with pimps to run a sex trade through the 1960s and 1970s for U.S. troops (Park 2014).

In areas experiencing war, women are at an even greater risk for sex trafficking. The former Yugoslavia and the Balkans region is an example of how a combination of war, economic transition, and globalization-related factors pushes women into sex trafficking. The entire region is a transit and major destination for trafficked women. The International Organization for Migration claims that 120,000 women and children are being trafficked into the European Union each year, mostly through the Balkans (Nikolic-Ristanovic 2003). Traffickers take advantage of the market demand and women's need to find jobs in a disrupted economy. Many women seek migration out of violent or dangerous areas only to become trafficked into the sex industry (see Chapter Twelve).

In 2016, activists formed a Korean "comfort women" foundation called the "The Foundation for Justice and Remembrance for the Issue of Military Sexual Slavery."
Source: AP Photo/Kyodo.

CONCLUSION

This chapter explores what it means to commodify sex and sexuality. When bodies and sex are viewed as objects and commodities, they are bought and sold in what we call the commercial sex industry. Two main areas of the U.S. sex industry discussed are pornography and prostitution. The rise in popularity of porn in today's Internet culture leads some to view our entire culture as pornified. Debates surrounding the legal aspects of consent and labor rights of porn actors are still ongoing. Themes of violence and gender, race, and sex inequality within porn are commonplace; and this chapter explains some of the reasons for this, and how it impacts men, women, relationships, and young people. While the negative consequences of pornography are vast, it can also be a positive expression of sexual pleasure and desire, as in the case of feminist porn. In the case of child pornography, it is child sexual abuse and a criminal offense. The modern dilemma of youth sexting on digital devices is discussed, and the struggle to decide whether it should be considered child pornography is still ongoing.

Prostitution is thoroughly explored in this chapter. The different dynamics of prostitution are analyzed and all the players involved, including johns and pimps, are reviewed, instead of just focusing on female sex workers, as often happens in discussions about prostitution. The debate on legalization versus criminalization of prostitution is explained on both sides. In the global economy, the commodification of sex is structured on older social and political structures of colonialism and on current trends of global economic exploitation. A modern form of slavery, sex trafficking, is explained in the global and national context and a feminist response explored. The dangers of internationally brokered marriages through online sites are explored including the risk of sex trafficking, partner violence, and lack of support for the brides. Sex tourism is explained as a further example of how globalization shapes the sex industry in favor of the wealthy and powerful as exploitive. Finally, militarism shapes commodified sexual relations in various regions around the world and perpetuates traditional ideologies of masculinity, male sexual dominance, and the sexual double standard.

Key Terms and Concepts

Child pornography 239
Child sex tourism 250
Colonialism 245
Commercial sex acts 246
Commercial sex industry 233
Commercial sexual exploitation of children (CSEC) 250
Commodification 233
Cybersex 234
Debt bondage 247

Ethnosexual 251
Feminist porn 237
Globalization 245
Heteropatriarchal 245
International brokerage marriage (IBM) industry 249
Militarism 251
Neocolonialism 245
Obscenity 235
Porn Wars 235
Pornified 233

Pornography 234
Postcolonialism 245
Prostitution 240
Romance tourism 251
Sex positive feminism 235
Sex tourism 250
Sex trafficking 245
Sex worker 240
Sexting 239
Sexual economy 233
Sexually explicit websites (SEWs) 238

Critical Thinking Questions

1. What does it mean to commodify sex? Describe three examples in society in which sex is commodified? Who are the commodities and who are the consumers? What is the role of gender in all examples?

2. Describe what it means to say porn has become mainstream? What sexual

images and expectations are connected to watching porn?

3. Describe the criminalization and the legalization arguments over prostitution.

4. How is sex trafficking different from prostitution? How does the debate on

legalization of prostitution factor into discussions of sex trafficking?

5. What is sex tourism? How do gender, race, ethnicity, and the global economy factor into sex tourism?

Activities

1. Visit a local business or event where sex is commodified. This can be a burlesque show, a sex toy shop, an adult video store, an exotic dance club, or even a pole dancing class. Write a 3-page, self-reflective paper on your personal responses to the experience. Connect your experience with a few of the key concepts you learned in this chapter. This exercise is designed to encourage students to observe, reflect, and connect ideas from the chapter.

2. Up to this point in your life, what have you been taught about prostitution from your family, school, peers, and media? How does this impact your opinions and feelings about sex work? Reflect on how this chapter impacts your views on sex work, if at all. Write about these reflections in a 3-page paper.

Essential Readings

Grant, Melissa Gira. 2014. *Playing the Whore: The Work of Sex Work*. London, England: Verso Books.

Kara, Siddharth. 2009. *Sex Trafficking: Inside the Business of Modern Slavery.* New York: Columbia University Press.

Moran, Rachel. 2015. *Paid For: My Journey through Prostitution*. New York: W.W. Norton.

Rivers-Moore, Megan. 2016. *Gringo Gulch: Sex, Tourism, and Social Mobility in Costa Rica*. Chicago: University of Chicago Press.

Sarracino, Carmine and Kevin M. Scott. 2009. *The Porning of America: The Rise of Porn Culture, What It Means, and Where We Go from Here*. Boston: Beacon Press.

Recommended Films

American Courtesans (2013). James Johnson, Director. This documentary dives into the lives of high-end American escorts. It is a sex-positive view of prostitution by women who love their vocation.

Hot Girls Wanted (2015). Jill Bauer and Ronna Gradus, Directors. A documentary about young women who have been drawn into the sex trade and how easy it is for our current Internet culture to become involved in making porn.

In the Name of Love (2003). Several young "Russian mail order brides" are followed over a three-year period as they meet, date, and, in some cases, marry the American men. Several issues are explored including male chauvinism, poverty, culture shock, and love.

Mala (2015). Dan Sickles and Antonio Santini, Directors. Explores the transgender community in Puerto Rico including interviews with a hairstylist, a prostitute, an activist, and more. Captures the discrimination and hardship that can come with the journey through discovering one's identity.

Very Young Girls (2014). Nina Alvarez, Director. A documentary focused on former-prostitute-turned-activist Rachel Lloyd and her support center, Girls Educational and Mentoring Services. The film gives an in-depth look into her work with young girls who are victims of sex trafficking.

Suggested Multimedia

Coalition against Trafficking in Women (CATW) is a nongovernmental organization that works to end human trafficking and the commercial sexual exploitation of women and children worldwide. http://www.catwinternational.org/

Human Trafficking Search is a global research database and resource hub on human trafficking for the purpose of educating and raising awareness of the issue. http://www.humantraffickingsearch.net/

Sex Workers Education Network is a website that contains academic, political, and occupational safety/health information about sex work. http://www.bayswan.org/

The Code (short for "The Code of Conduct for the Protection of Children from Sexual Exploitation in Travel and Tourism") is an initiative to provide awareness, tools, and support to the tourism industry in order to prevent the sexual exploitation of children. http://www.thecode.org/

SEXUAL VIOLENCE

LEARNING OBJECTIVES

Upon completion of this chapter, students will be able to . . .

- Discuss the significance of gender and sexuality in sexual violence
- Describe the primary social problems concerning rape and sexual assault
- Understand the dynamics and problem of child sex abuse
- Explain the extent of and the racialized nature of homophobic and transphobic violence
- Describe carceral sexualities and why prison sexuality should be of concern

Every Valentine's Day, millions of women around the world organize to dance, strike, perform, and speak out in defiance against violence against women and girls. These efforts are part of an ambitious campaign called "One Billion Rising." It is launched by V-Day, a global activist movement to end violence against women and girls, including rape, sexual battery, incest, female genital mutilation, sex trafficking, and sex slavery. V-Day was started in 1998 by playwright and activist, Eve Ensler, author of the groundbreaking play, *The Vagina Monologues*, which addresses women's sexuality, rape, and sexual abuse. The play inspired such intense reactions from women all over the world, it led to the creation of V-Day. The play itself is performed royalty-free every year as part of the campaign. The "V" in V-Day stands for Victory, Valentine, and Vagina (www.v-day.org).

Launched in 2012, V-Day's One Billion Rising campaign is the "the biggest mass action to end violence against women in human history" (www.v-day.org). The name "One Billion" comes from the United Nations estimate that one in three women on the globe will be raped and beaten in her lifetime, and with approximately 3 billion women in the world, the number of victims comes to 1 billion. In 2015, millions of activists in over 200 countries gathered on Valentine's Day and posted videos on social media and to a streaming feed on the campaign's website. Every year the campaign focuses on a theme. In 2016 it was revolution, and in 2014 it was justice. A range of issues are focused on, based on the specific needs addressed by the grassroots organizers in the various countries involved. For example, in 2014, risings in Bangladesh and Hong Kong focused on labor rights in addition to sexual violence (Khaleeli 2015).

1 Billion Rising, an international campaign to end violence against women, was started by Eve Ensler, the author of "The Vagina Monologues."
Source: AP Photo/Sipa.

All participants are asked to gather and dance in public. The message is that women and survivors of sexual violence do not need to be ashamed of their stories or their bodies. Ensler says, "When you are raped, you are forced to leave your body because it is a landscape of terror and pain. It feels contaminated and polluted. Just the act of releasing your trauma when you dance can make you feel part of a community" (Khaleeli 2015).

UNDERSTANDING SEXUAL VIOLENCE

Sexuality and violence are, unfortunately, intimately connected. **Sexual violence** is a broad term to describe any sexual act committed against someone without that person's freely given consent. It includes all unwanted sexual activity, including rape, sexual assault, incest, sexual harassment, exposure, stalking, peeping, any unwanted or inappropriate sexual contact, and even experiences that do not involve physical contact between a perpetrator and a victim. Women and girls are far more likely to be victims of sexual violence than men, although boys and men are also victims. In all circumstances, sexual violence is a crime. While sexual violence is outwardly viewed as unacceptable, in many ways, U.S. culture ignores, trivializes, and normalizes sexual violence. This led feminists in the 1970s to label U.S. culture as a **rape culture,** or a culture in which rape is so widespread it is normalized (Harding 2015). Since the 1970s, the term has broadened to include a wide variety of cultural practices and beliefs that encourage male sexual aggression and violence against women and make sexual violence seem natural and inevitable.

In the following sections, we discuss several different aspects of sexual violence including rape, child sex abuse, transphobic and homophobic violence, and prison rape. The mythology surrounding rape and sexual assault, its prevalence, and issues with its exact definition will be explored. We will analyze the role of consent, victimization language, and double victimization in regard to rape in U.S. culture. A more specific look at campus, wartime, and prison rape and sexual assault are explored, as well as a review of feminist theoretical perspectives on the causes and prevention of sexual assault. We investigate child sexual abuse, a highly prevalent form of sexual violence, specifically focusing on the challenges associated with reporting and the stigma associated with child sexual abuse. We then use the lens of intersectionality to look specifically at violence against LGBTQ people, and specifically LGBTQ people of color. We conclude this chapter with an exploration of prison sexuality, particularly exploring prison rape and sexual assault. Prisons are environments where the normalization of sexual violence is unsurprising. However, this chapter shows how sexual violence is normalized throughout our entire culture. Examples of the normalization of sexual violence include:

- In 2003, Congress unanimously passed the *Prison Rape Elimination Act* (PREA), which estimates that 13 percent of U.S. inmates will be raped while incarcerated. At least one million inmates had been raped in American prisons in the previous 20 years (Jacobs 2009).
- In 2012, Jerry Sandusky, former assistant football coach for Penn State football, was convicted of sexually assaulting 10 boys during 15 years. Known as the "Penn State Child Sex Scandal," this case led to the firing of Hall of Fame football coach Joe Paterno and the questioning of many other campus authorities who might have known about and ignored Sandusky's abuses (Drape 2012).
- In 2014, President Obama issued a White House task force to investigate college sexual assault, in which colleges conducted "campus climate" surveys nationwide. Guidelines were later developed to encourage campuses to more aggressively tackle sexual assault (Steinhauer 2014).
- In a classic example of victim blaming, in a 2014 CNN interview with Joan Tarshis, a woman who accused Bill Cosby of sexually assaulting her 45 years ago, the CNN host, Don Lemon, asked her why she didn't use her teeth to bite his penis in order to stop her rape (Taibi 2014).
- In 2016, former Stanford University swimmer, Brock Turner, was given a six-month jail sentence for sexually assaulting an unconscious woman. Critics across the country protested that this sentence was too lenient, including Vice President Joe Biden, who wrote an open letter to the victim expressing his outrage over the case (Scott 2016).
- On June 12, 2016 Omar Mateen killed 49 people and wounded 53 in a mass shooting at Pulse, a gay nightclub in Orlando, Florida. This is one of the largest acts of mass murder in U.S. history, and it was directed specifically at the LGBTQ community of color, as it was "Latin night" at the club.
- The body of a nurse, African American, transgender woman Dee Whigham, was found in a hotel room near Biloxi, Mississippi, on July 23, 2016. She was the 16th transgender person murdered in the U.S. in the first seven months of 2016 (Brighe 2016).

Rape

Rape is a serious problem in U.S. culture. It is problematic not only because of its high prevalence, but also due to its historically ambiguous and changing definition, and to decades of false cultural mythology surrounding it. Statistics presented by the National Sexual Violence Resource Center on the incidence of rape are staggering. One in five women in the U.S. will be raped at some point in their lives (National Sexual Violence Resource Center 2015). Gender is one of the most important characteristics of the rape epidemic. While 9 percent of victims of rape and sexual assault are males, 91 percent are female (National Sexual Violence Resource Center 2015). Rape is a gender-based crime primarily perpetrated by men against women. Additionally, despite our cultural narrative of "stranger danger," eight out of ten rape victims know their offender, and one in ten women has been raped by an intimate partner in her lifetime (National Sexual Violence 2015). As mentioned earlier in the chapter, these figures lead many to call the U.S. a rape culture.

The precise definition of rape has been a source of contestation and debate for years by feminists, politicians, legal scholars, and those in the criminal justice system. Variability in precise sex crime terminology, such as rape, leads to problems in the court system, reporting, and data collection on the incidence of rape. Since 1927, the FBI's Uniform Crime Report had defined "forcible rape" as "the carnal knowledge of a female, forcibly and against her will" (The United States Department of Justice 2012). This outdated definition was gendered and too narrow. In 2012, under the advice of the Attorney General, the FBI adopted a new definition of *rape* as "the penetration, no matter how slight, of the vagina or anus with any body part or object, or oral penetration by a sex organ of another person, without the consent of the victim" (The United States Department of Justice 2012). For the first time in U.S. history, the federal criminal justice system has a working definition of rape that is gender neutral. Moreover this definition recognizes rape can happen with objects, not just genitalia; and it emphasizes consent. Despite this progress, the legal definition of rape still varies state to state and creates confusion.

In some states, like New Jersey, rape is described as a sexual assault. *Sexual assault* is a more broad term to describe any type of forced or coerced sexual contact or behavior that happens without consent. It includes rape, attempted rape, incest, child sexual abuse, sexual harassment, fondling, and all other forced sexual behaviors against another person. For some states, the shift toward calling rape a "sexual assault," is a way to shift the focus from the sexual to the violent aspect of the crime. In South Carolina, rape is referred to as "criminal sexual conduct," and in Florida, "sexual battery" (Palmer 2011). Many feminists support the shift away from the word "rape" because they argue the word has cultural implications as a crime of sexual passion and tends to focus attention and blame on the victim, not the offender. While the term "sexual assault" gives the act of rape more serious gravity in the courts, it can also be confusing because while rape is always sexual assault, sexual assault is not always rape. Others argue the word "rape" adds severity to the act and should still be used. The debate is ongoing.

In the 1970s, sociologists and feminists introduced the concept of *rape myths*, or widely held attitudes and inaccurate beliefs about rape that serve to deny, justify, and perpetuate male sexual aggression against women (Edwards et al. 2014). Susan Brownmiller (1975) was one of the first feminists to assert that historically rape was viewed as a crime against property and that the continuance of sexual violence against women was perpetuated by outdated patriarchal ideologies of gender and sex inequality. Research over the past 40 years indicates a direct correlation between the ongoing epidemic of sexual violence and rape myths (Edwards et al. 2014). Rape myths are false, tend to blame the victim, minimize the assault, and fail to address the realities of rape. Some of the most prominent rape myths are that husbands cannot rape their wives, women enjoy rape, women ask to be raped, women lie about being raped for revenge or attention, rape doesn't happen often, rape is committed by strangers, and the way a woman dresses causes rape.

Unfortunately, rape myths can influence laws. For example, a common rape myth is that husbands cannot rape their wives. Rape laws historically did not protect married women, as it was a general assumption that marriage automatically implied consent to all sexual relations. Challenges to this began in the 1970s and by 1993, the marital rape exemption, as it was known, was overturned in all 50 states.

Acceptance of rape myths happens at the individual and institutional levels. There are a variety of ways to measure the endorsement of rape myths in individuals. In one study, between 25 and 35 percent of male and female respondents reported they believed the majority of rape myths (Edwards et al. 2014). A review of a variety of studies on the acceptance of rape myths shows men are more likely to believe rape myths than women; people who believe rape myths are more likely to be sexist, racist, and homophobic; and victims who believe rape myths feel guilty and responsible for the assault (Burrowes 2013).

Institutions such as the media and the criminal justice system often endorse rape myths. Studies of media headlines reveal rape myths are prevalent and shape public attitudes toward rape (Franiuk, Seefelt, and Vandeloo 2008). The belief in rape myths by jurors has been shown to influence decision making in rape cases, specifically in wrongful acquittals in sexual assault trials (Hildebrand and Najdowski 2015). Police officers who believe rape myths can be insensitive to a rape victim and even blame the victim. This is known as *double victimization*, or exposure to the initial crime and then later negative exposure to an errant criminal justice worker or system that serves as a second victimization. Sometimes police accuse women of lying about being raped and even go so far as to accuse victims of seeking vengeance or attention through their false accusation. Social scientists who study false reporting find the prevalence of false allegations is between 2 percent and 10 percent for rape (Lisak et al. 2010).

Racism and classism intersect with rape myths creating even more layers of deception and violence. The myth of the black rapist of white, middle- or upper-class women is a racist myth that dates back to the Reconstruction era after slavery was abolished in the United States (Davis 2015). The myth of the black male rapist gave rise to lynching and became interwoven in legal institutions—resulting in violent, discriminatory legal practices, including castration and execution of black men during this era. Today the myth that black men are more apt to rape white, middle- and upper-class women still lingers and impacts public views and juries, despite the fact that contemporary data reveals the majority of sex offenders are white and most victims of sex crimes are white (Wheeler and George 2005).

CONSENT In the context of sexual activity, *consent* is when a person agrees to engage in a sexual act with another person. While the exact legal definition varies state to state, most laws require that in order to give consent, a person has to be mentally capable of making that decision. In other words, they cannot be experiencing some form of natural or induced impairment that inhibits them from making clear decisions. Examples of things that can disable one's ability to consent range from alcohol intoxication to accidents that cause brain trauma. In order to give consent, a person has to be of a certain age. Age of consent laws vary state to state, but most set the range between 14 and 18. Youths below the age of consent cannot legally consent to having sex. *Statutory rape* is a sex crime in which sexual relations take place between an adult and young person below the age of consent. Punishments for statutory rape vary across states, depending on the factors involved, including the age of the victim and the age difference between the victim and the perpetrator.

Debates surround expressions of consent. Until very recently, a person's "attitude of willingness" or performance of "nonverbal consenting behaviors" was enough to indicate consent for sexual intercourse in a court of law. However, nonverbal consent creates confusion, and lawmakers are trying to find ways to bring greater clarity. Consent has been shown to be especially contentious when it comes to marital rape, or rape between two people who are married; or *date rape*, or *acquaintance rape*, terms that describe the rape of an acquaintance or while on a date. Date rape and acquaintance rape are crimes that happen between two people who know each other and are willingly spending time together. Sometimes perpetrators use a

The University of Tennessee, Knoxville, included this image of "Defining Consent" in its alumni magazine in 2015, showing their campus commitment to ending rape.
Source: Image courtesy of the University of Tennessee, Knoxville.

date rape drug, or an incapacitating agent. This last type of rape is also called incapacitated rape or drug-facilitated sexual assault; and it can happen between acquaintances, or the perpetrator can be a stranger (Brown, Testa, and Messman-Moore 2009). Consent is often debated in court in cases regarding date rape because the perpetrators will often claim the victim "acted" consensual or that there was simply a misunderstanding. The perpetrator will use the fact that the victim willingly went on a date with him as proof that she was sexually interested.

In the face of this confusion, a new standard of consent has emerged, known as the affirmative consent standard. The *affirmative consent standard* states that the person who initiates sexual contact must receive a verbal "yes" or affirmation from the other person before engaging in sexual activity, or when moving from one sexual activity to another. Consent must be ongoing throughout the sexual experience. For instance, a person may consent to oral sex, but have no intention of or desire to engage in anal sex. Their original consent cannot and should not be interpreted as a carte blanche. This standard is intended to reduce any ambiguity surrounding consent. Many college campuses have adopted the affirmative consent standard in their policies on sexual assault (see more on campus rape below). In 2014, California adopted "yes means yes" legislation that requires affirmative consent in all sexual encounters (Keenan 2015). While these measures are meant to protect women, some argue the government should not be able to dictate people's intimate sexual encounters and that this standard will not actually prevent sexual assault (Young 2014). The debate over legislating consent is ongoing.

RAPE SURVIVORS, DOUBLE VICTIMIZATION, AND VICTIMIZATION LANGUAGE Survivors of rape do not all respond in the same way to their experience. Some respond immediately, others delay, while others experience feelings of denial. Denial is the process of not accepting what has happened, downplaying the intensity, and is more common when the perpetrator is someone the survivor knew and trusted. Some survivors are impacted for life. Several studies show that rape trauma victims have one of the highest risks of developing posttraumatic stress disorder (PTSD), with symptoms such as reexperiencing the trauma, social withdrawal, hyperalertness, hypervigilance, depression, and severe anxiety (Chivers-Wilson 2006). In one study, 94 percent of women met symptomatic criteria for PTSD in the first 12 days after the sexual assault (Rothbaum et al. 1992). In addition to the high likelihood of PTSD, rape victims can potentially suffer from a wide range of emotional and social problems such as higher levels of sexual dysfunction, disordered eating, sleep problems, and higher rates of substance abuse and suicide (Kilpatrick et al. 2007).

Society's treatment of survivors of sexual assault is often negative, especially those who report or speak out about their experiences of sexual assault. As already mentioned, rape myths that blame the victim can cause double victimization by the police, medical personnel, friends, and family and significantly stunt a victim's recovery. In some cases these types of negative responses silence victims completely (Ahrens 2006). This is one of the reasons why most rapes and sexual assaults against women are not reported to the police. According to the U.S. Bureau of Justice Statistics, only 36 percent of rapes and 26 percent of sexual assaults were reported to police between the years of 1992 and 2000 (Rennison 2002). This means the majority of perpetrators face no legal consequences for their actions.

Some survivors do not report rape or sexual assault because they do not identify with a "victim" identity (Weiss 2011). The *victimization framework*, or the institutionalized use of the term "victim" to describe someone who has been sexually assaulted, was emphasized by feminist activists in the 1980s and '90s as a way to bring to light the high prevalence of rape in U.S. culture and the severe emotional, physical, and social impact it has on women. In many ways, this framework brought significant changes in social views on rape and has been beneficial for victims. However, some feminists question the language used within the victimization framework: Are they victims or

An image of a Take Back the Night rally in Portland, MA, 2012. These are held on college campuses across the country every spring to protest the epidemic of sexual violence on college campuses.
Source: AP Photo/Portland Press Herald/Tim Greenway.

survivors? For some, gaining validation from society that you were, in fact, "victimized" can speed healing and recovery. For others, the term "victim" contributes to a feeling of powerlessness and a term that emphasizes women's strength is preferred, such as "survivor." Moreover, some argue that in a culture that promotes individualism, the language of victimization can inspire backlash discourse (Gavey 2014).

CAMPUS RAPE In 2015, the Association of American Universities conducted a large-scale study of campus sexual assault and misconduct. The study surveyed 150,000 students at 27 colleges and universities, including all of the Ivy League schools, except Princeton. Findings revealed 23.1 percent of female undergraduate student respondents reported experiencing sexual assault and sexual misconduct ranging from physical force, threats of physical force, or incapacitation, including 10.8 percent who experienced unwanted penetration (Cantor et al. 2015). This study was backed up in 2016 by the Bureau of Justice Statistics which found an average of 21 percent of female undergraduates claimed to have been sexually assaulted since starting college. This means that nearly one in four women on campus is at risk of sexual assault (Krebs et al. 2016).

Many aspects of college campus culture are considered risk factors for sexual assault. Alcohol or drug use is commonly associated with campus sexual assault, and women who drink are at higher risk of sexual victimization. According to the U.S. Justice Department, students who live in sorority houses and on-campus dormitories are more likely to experience rape than students who live off campus (Krebs et al. 2007). Sorority membership itself is a risk factor for sexual assault. This is partly because sorority women are more likely to drink, but also because they are more likely to associate with fraternity men. Fraternity men are three times more likely to rape than other men on college campuses (Foubert, Newberry, and Tatum 2007). This is because fraternities promote a group culture that accepts and promotes highly masculine behaviors and ideologies, such as the sexual coercion of women (Martin and Hummer 2009).

Studies on fraternities show that a range of activities promote a highly masculinized, fraternity, group culture. Activities include recruiting practices, an emphasis on group loyalty, the sexual objectification of women, and a discourse of sexual conquest (Martin and

Hummer 2009). Fraternities recruit men who exhibit masculine gender traits of aggression, competition, and heterosexuality. Pledges are often mistreated and taught that loyalty to the brotherhood and abuse of alcohol is expected. "Little sisters" are women who serve as hostesses for parties and help with service projects for fraternities; they are often treated as sexual objects and used as bait to recruit new members or women to parties. Peggy Reeves Sanday's (2015) research on fraternity brothers' sexual discourse reveals a sexual ideology that encourages some men to resort to coercive tactics she calls "working a yes out," or encouraging or forcing a woman to consent to sex either by talking her into it or using alcohol. The fraternity brothers in her study did not see this as coercion, but as seduction. Sanday critiques this lack of self-reflection as irresponsible, phallocentric behavior.

While the incidence rate for sexual assault on campuses is high, the reporting is very low. Sixty four percent of college women will disclose to a friend, roommate, or family member; but only 12 percent report sexual assault to authorities (Krebs et al. 2016). When they do report, they are not always met with support. Many colleges and universities have denied, dismissed, or blamed the victim upon reporting in order to protect their and the young man's reputation (Krakauer 2015). While colleges and universities are required by federal law to investigate when a student reports sexual misconduct, it is handled differently across campuses. Some schools hold their own disciplinary hearings, often made up of students and faculty who are not trained for this type of tribunal. If found guilty in such hearings, often the perpetrator is barely punished with sentences like summer suspensions or community service. This results in the victim being forced to encounter her perpetrator on a potentially daily basis. Ultimately, colleges are businesses with a brand and a fiscal budget. They do not want to lose business from anyone, even a sexual predator; nor do they want the stain of a student arrest or conviction for sexual assault that took place on their campus to hamper their brand.

Congress passed the *Campus Sexual Assault Victims' Bill of Rights* in 1992, mandating that schools provide the same opportunities for the accuser and the accused, and that survivors should be informed of their options to notify law enforcement, seek counseling services, and change living situations. According to Title IX, a school that receives federal funding is required to protect students from sex discrimination. Sex discrimination includes sexual battery, sexual assault, rape, and any other behaviors that could keep a victim from attaining education. When a campus does not report sexual assault to the local police, this becomes a federal violation. Some students and campus groups have filed Title IX complaints to the federal government against their schools for lack of protection and inadequate follow through and investigations by campus officials. Antirape activists and feminists across the country are insisting college campuses take more direct action to end sexual assault.

SEXUAL VIOLENCE IN CONFLICT: WARTIME RAPE Sexual violence against women escalates during wartime. Women and girls living in military conflict zones are often displaced or suffer economic disparities, increasing their vulnerability for sexual violence. ***Wartime sexual violence*** is any type of sexual violence committed by combatants during war. Systematic ***wartime rape*** is a gender-based form of violence in which women are used as a "weapon of war." It is a psychological and gender-based type of warfare in which the goal is to torture and degrade the enemy's women as a way to humiliate the enemy's men (Nagel 2014). Men are also raped in wartime as a form of gender-based violence, again, in which the psychological goal is humiliation. This is particularly harsh for victims in areas where homosexuality is highly stigmatized.

The United Nations identifies four types of war rape: genocidal, opportunistic, political, and forced concubinage (Burn 2011). Genocidal rape, as seen in ethnic cleansing wars in Rwanda and the Balkans, is intended to destroy ethnic or political groups. Opportunistic rape is when men take advantage of the chaos of wartime to inflict sexual violence on women because they know they will most likely not face criminal prosecution. Political rape punishes groups for not having the same politic views; and forced concubinage is when girls and women are kidnapped and forced to have sex with

BOX 12.1

GLOBAL/TRANSNATIONAL PERSPECTIVES ON SEXUALITY:
SEXUAL VIOLENCE AND FEMICIDE IN CIUDAD JUAREZ, MEXICO

Since the mid-1990s, hundreds, perhaps thousands, of women have disappeared or have been found murdered in the border town of Ciudad Juarez, Mexico—or, as some call it, "the capital of murdered women." The shocking reports involve not only murder, but also rape and sexual torture. The exact number of victims is difficult to estimate due to lack of consistent record keeping by officials. Sociologist Julia Monarrez Fragoso has been analyzing and keeping records for more than 20 years. According to Fragoso, between 1993 and 2012, 1,481 murders of women and girls were registered (Driver 2015). Feminists and activists call this level of women-killing *femicide*, a term to describe the murder of girls and women, specifically because of their sex or gender.

Femicide is a gender-based hate crime specific to cultural context. In Juarez, most murdered women's bodies revealed grotesque sexual violence, torture, and even mutilation. The majority of the women killed in Ciudad Juarez are young and poor; and many are *maquiladoras*, or workers in one of the many transnational factories located in the city. When trade barriers were lowered after the passage of the North American Trade Agreement (NAFTA), many global corporations opened factories in Ciudad Juarez to take advantage of low-cost labor. This increased the migration of rural, farming families, including a large number of women, to the city for work. In addition to changing gender roles, the violent misogyny in Juarez is also due to an increase in drug cartels, gang activity, sex trafficking, and police corruption.

Many families choose not to report their daughters' disappearance or murder due to the lack of police arrests, victim blaming by authorities and media, and even the termination of investigations by police and the Mexican government. Instead, by the late 1990s, mothers of murdered daughters began organizing and drew attention from human rights groups and feminist organizations worldwide (Staudt and Mendez 2015). Groups such as the United Nations, Amnesty International, and the International Human Rights Federation have investigated and reported that law enforcement needs to improve its response to the killings. In 2012, 21 bodies of young women between the ages of 15 and 21 were found in a dry riverbed outside the city; and 11 of the bodies matched DNA with mothers in Juarez with missing daughters from 2009 and 2010. In 2015, five gang members were sentenced to 697 years each for the kidnapping, trafficking, and murder of these women (Chaparro 2015). The women had been forced into prostitution before being murdered. This ruling recognizes gender-based violence in the area; and, while there are still many more missing and many murdered without justice, this is a sign of progress.

soldiers. It is only in recent years that prosecution of rapists during wartime began to occur. The United Nations passed resolutions in 2008 and 2013 against wartime rape, declaring it a war crime; and, in support of survivors, declaring the need for full access to sexual and reproductive services.

FEMINIST PERSPECTIVES ON RAPE Feminists have long argued rape is a cultural problem rooted in gender inequality. They argue rape is a logical result of an androcentric and patriarchal culture in which men are granted the sex/gender role of aggressive, sexual pursuer, and women the role of sexual submissive (Brownmiller 1975; Griffin 1979). Radical feminists argue rape is further supported by an undercurrent of misogynistic ideologies woven into almost every social institution, making rape a gender hate crime (MacKinnon 2006). Radical feminists argue that male control over women's bodies in regard to sexuality and reproduction is central to maintaining male sexual dominance; rape is a violent extension of that control. Feminists argue society, as a whole, contributes to a culture of violence against women. Hierarchies built on race, class, ethnicity, and sexuality intersect with male privilege to maintain sexual violence against women (Crenshaw 1989; Davis 2015).

Feminists have long argued that rape is a personal, psychological problem, too. Rape is about power over another, not about uncontrollable sexual urges or overwhelming sexual attraction. While it cannot be denied that rape is a sexual act and can be driven by sexual gratification, the violence inherent in rape is a result of unequal power equations, both real and perceived, between men and women. It is a violation of another person's agency and identity, and it is about complete subjugation and control over another person's body (Cahill 2001). So while the cultural argument is important, the complexity of individual relations is also relevant.

Solutions for ending rape must take place at both the cultural and individual levels. Feminists acknowledge we live in a society in which the message to women is, "Don't get raped" instead of telling men, "Don't rape." This message implies women are responsible for their own victimization, which explains why so many rape victims report feelings of guilt after being assaulted. One of the most effective actions in addressing rape has been the establishment of rape crisis centers across the United States, which began in the 1970s. The critical resources these centers provide for survivors are of utmost importance to ending rape.

Antiviolence prevention measures, including work that is centered on the attitudes and behaviors of boys and men, is also extremely important. Jackson Katz (2006) argues that gender-based violence is not a woman's issue, but a "man's issue," since most perpetrators are male. Naming sexual violence, discussing victim blaming, reexamining gender roles and relationships, busting rape myths, and talking about consent are ways popular discourse and attitudes can shift toward a safe and rape-free culture. On the individual level, when survivors share their stories, in safe environments, they are reclaiming their subjectivity. Personal narrative is a powerful tool for cultural change.

Child Sexual Abuse

The sexual abuse of children is considered a social taboo, or morally wrong; yet it is a significant problem. ***Child sexual abuse*** is a broad term that includes all offences that involve sexually touching, sexual exploitation, sexual assault, or any form of sexual contact with a child. Sometimes the term ***child molestation*** is used to describe when a child is forced, coerced, or threatened to engage in any form of sexual contact. Statistics on child sexual abuse are difficult to determine because it is often not reported. While exact numbers are difficult to pin down, some factors consistently place certain groups at higher risk for child sexual abuse: being female, coming from a low-income family, or being a victim of other forms of violence and abuse. Perpetrators also share commonalities. Most child sexual abuse offenders are men, with a large percentage being juveniles or young adults under the age of 30. Most perpetrators know their victims and are often family members.

Sexual contact that occurs between family members is also referred to as ***incest***, and is considered a form of child sexual abuse. Direct incest can include rape, sexual touching, fondling, kissing, and other direct physical forms of abuse. Indirect incest includes sexualizing statements or jokes, staring at the child's body, or speaking to the child as if they are a surrogate spouse (Shaw and Lee 2012). Whether it is child sex abuse or incest, like other forms of sexual violence, power is always involved because the victims, children, are the least powerful group in society, and adults hold authority in a child's life. When this power dynamic is abused or betrayed by an adult, the effects can be devastating and lifelong. Not only are child sex abuse victims more likely to suffer from anxiety, depression, substance abuse, and disordered eating; but the ability to trust others and form healthy attachments to people is often impaired.

There are laws in every state against child sexual abuse, yet law enforcement and prosecutors often misunderstand the dynamics of sexual abuse, leading to improper handling and prosecution of cases. Confusing dynamics include perpetrators' grooming tactics, in which the victim and the victim's caretakers are "groomed" to develop both a false sense of trust and love for the offender, and reactions such as guilt and pity for the offender. Grooming and familiarity with the abuser is one of the reasons child sexual abuse is extremely underreported. It is often referred to as a "silent and secretive crime" because so many victims do not tell about their abuse. Or, if they do disclose, it is usually to a friend or family member, not to the police. Family members sometimes feel enough loyalty toward the perpetrator that the child's claim is not believed.

The impact of sexual abuse on children is devastating and long lasting. Child sex abusers have higher rates of sexual victimization themselves compared to the general population, with 35 percent of perpetrators reporting being sexual abused as children compared to 11 percent of nonperpetrators (Glasser et al. 2001). Such findings led to the popular idea of the *victim-offender cycle*, or the idea that child sex abusers were victimized as children, which explains why they grow up to become victimizers. While this is sometimes the case, it is not always the case. There are some factors that increase the chances of a victim going on to become an offender such as whether pleasure was connected to the abuse, whether they were physically abused in addition to being sexually abused, whether they witnessed severe violence in the home, and whether support from family or external forms of support were offered in coping with the abuse (Wilcox, Richards, and O'Keefe 2004). Critics of the victim-offender cycle argue it stigmatizes victims by assuming they might go on to offend.

A popular myth is that child abuse leads to LGBTQ identification. While studies do indicate that LGBTQ individuals report higher rates of childhood sexual abuse than heterosexuals, there is no empirical evidence that childhood sexual abuse influences sexual orientation. However, there is a correlation between child sexual abuse and adult sexual trauma experiences. Both heterosexual and LGBTQ victims of child sexual abuse are more likely to report revictimization of sexual violence as adults (Fortier et al. 2009; Heidt, Marx, and Gold 2005).

IS PEDOPHILIA A SEXUAL ORIENTATION? For many, the very idea of this question is insulting; however, let's look at the medical and social aspects of this issue. A *pedophile* is someone with sexual preference for, interest in, or attraction to children. Some question if pedophilia would be better understood as a *sexual age orientation*, or sexual orientation toward a specific age group (Seto 2015). Sexual orientation, as you have learned in previous chapters, is considered a sexual interest or preference; and, for some, it is considered something an individual is born with and cannot change. In many legal and social contexts, sexual orientation is equated with homosexuality. For example, "sexual orientation" is legally protected under many laws against discrimination (see Chapter Five). Most agree, these laws were not intended to protect pedophiles.

So the question is: Are pedophiles born with a sexual attraction to children? In its manual on mental illness, the American Psychiatric Association (APA) defined pedophilic disorder as a sexual orientation, until 2013, when many began questioning this definition. In a press release, the APA said this was an error and that sexual orientation should be described as a "sexual interest" in children instead (American Psychiatric Association 2013). What we do know is that behaviors are often choices. And we do know that some, but not all pedophiles, act on their attractions and victimize children. Yet, some do not. Treatments for pedophilia primarily consist of hormone blockers that stop the sex drive (Dreger 2013). More research is needed in order to better understand pedophilia and how to stop it.

CHILD SEXUAL ABUSE CRISIS IN THE CATHOLIC CHURCH A child sexual abuse crisis exists on a global scale in the Catholic Church. According to the United States Conference of

This victim of sexual abuse by a Catholic priest is wearing a picture of himself at the age he was abused as he meets with reporters in Rome.
Source: AP Photo/Alessandra Tarantino.

Catholic Bishops, between 1950 and 2012, 16,787 people in the U.S. came forward to report they were sexually abused by priests as children (Childress 2014). This data does not include accusations the church determined were "not credible." People began coming forward in large numbers in the 1970s and '80s. By 1992, Catholic dioceses had spent $400 million settling hundreds of cases in which the victims were financially compensated for their injuries and paid to sign nondisclosure agreements (Stille 2016). In other words, the victims were paid to keep quiet. For decades the Church failed to adopt a specific policy for addressing child sex abuse or for helping victims. Instead, local bishops and archbishops were required to handle the cases privately. The U.N. Committee on the Rights of the Child accused the Church of placing the Church's reputation above the interest of children's safety (Childress 2014). In 2016, Pope Francis amended Vatican Law to specify that sexual violence against children is a crime (Childress 2014).

Unfortunately, child sex abuse happens in almost any institution in which children and adults gather, including schools, camps, and Protestant churches. There are many different explanations as to why child sex abuse is such an immense problem specifically in the Catholic Church. Laurie Goodstein (2016), the national religion correspondent for *The New York Times*, and a journalist who covered the sex abuse scandal in the Catholic Church for over twenty years, says there are a few characteristics that make it more conducive to abuse. For one, priests in the Catholic Church are exalted, acting "in persona of Christ," and their actions and behaviors are rarely questioned. It is assumed they would never be capable of a crime. Another factor is that Catholic priests are required to be celibate. For some, this has led to covert sexual relationships. Secret sexual relationships sometimes lead to further sexual deviance. Finally, the Catholic Church requires priests be male. No females are allowed in the clergy. While it is completely possible that women can also be abusers, some question if more women in the priesthood would instill more accountability and sensitivity (see Chapter Eight).

RACIALIZED HOMOPHOBIC AND TRANSPHOBIC VIOLENCE

There is an epidemic of transphobic and homophobic violence that is disproportionately affecting LGBTQ people of color (see Figure 12.1). According to the National Coalition of Anti-Violence Programs (NCAVP), homophobic and transphobic violence has increased dramatically. The severity of violence against LGBTQ people is increasing as well; and it often involves torture, mutilation, castration, sexual assault, and murder (Hequembourg 2014; Perry 2013). LGBTQ people of color are at the greatest risk for such violence. Despite making up less than 1 percent of the world's population, a transgender woman is killed every 29 hours (Busey 2016). The Black Lives Matter movement is well known for protesting against and drawing attention to the extrajudicial killings of unarmed black men, but what is less well known is that they are equally concerned about the epidemic of homophobic and transphobic violence against people of color.

There is a cultural invisibility surrounding racialized homophobic and transphobic violence, including the media coverage of the mass shooting at Pulse nightclub in Orlando, Florida, on June 12, 2016. As mentioned previously, the shooter was an American Muslim, Omar Mateen, who murdered 49 people and injured another 53. While the media framed the story as a shooting at a gay nightclub, the predominant race/ethnicity of the victims went unacknowledged. Almost all victims were people of color, overwhelmingly Latinos, since it was Latin night at the club. The media chose to use a color-blind narrative, despite the fact that Mateen had been a semiregular at the club, and likely knew it was Latin night.

Understanding homophobic and transphobic violence requires we pay attention to intersectionality, the ways multiple systems of oppression intersect, creating unique forms of oppression (Crenshaw 1989; see Chapter One). In this section, we focus on the ways gender, sexuality, and race intersect and result in increased risk of violent victimization for LGBTQ people of color. Their violent victimization is about more than homophobia. It is a racialized homophobia; and for lesbians and transwomen, it is gendered as well (Fitzgerald 2017).

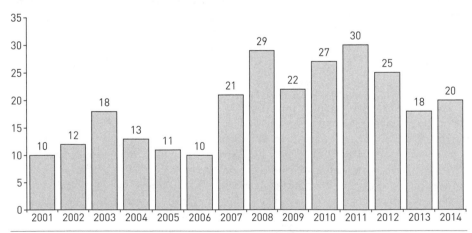

FIGURE 12.1 ■ Hate Violence Homicides of LGBTQ and HIV+ People by Year, 2001–2014

LGBTQ and HIV+ people are some of the most targeted for hate crimes, particularly homicides, as this graph shows.

Source: A Report from the National Coalition of Anti-Violence Programs: Lesbian, Gay, Bisexual, Transgender, and HIV-Affected Hate Violence in 2014 (2015). http://www.avp.org/storage/documents/Reports/2014_HV_Report-Final.pdf.

Despite the epidemic levels of violence faced by LGBTQ people of color, much of this violence is ignored in the mainstream media. Researchers refer to this as ***intersectional invisibility***, when people with multiple subordinate identities do not fit stereotypes associated with any of the respective groups to which they belong and, thus, are not seen (Purdie-Vaughns and Eibach 2008). An example of intersectional invisibility is the fact that white and middle-class gay men experience violence at lower rates than impoverished gay men and transgender people of color; yet white, middle-class gay men's experiences, like that of Matthew Shepard, dominate the media coverage of LGBTQ violence (Meyer 2015).

It is estimated that 30 percent of reported hate crimes involve sexual orientation, with LGBTQ people as the most victimized of any minority group (Hequembourg 2014). Within this group, transgender people experience the highest rates of victimization, with transwomen of color as the most victimized of all. This violence prompted a Transgender Day of Remembrance in 2013, which is now celebrated annually on November 20th.

The epidemic of transphobic violence is also global. In January of 2016, there were 48 murders of transgender people in Brazil, a country described as having the highest rates of transphobic violence in the world. It is a country where gender-nonconforming people are unlikely to live past the age of 30, despite the fact that the life expectancy for the average Brazilian is 75 years. The targeting of transgender people in Brazil is rooted in Brazil's military dictatorship under President João Goulart, in power between 1964 and 1985. During this period, gender-variant people were targeted by the military as a threat to the family (Bowater and Moraes 2015). This added a layer of legitimacy to transphobia that has lingered long after the regime change.

In 2013, 72 percent of LGBTQ murders in the U.S. were of transgender women of color (Tannehill 2015). The year 2015 was the most violent year on record for transgender people in the United States: 22 were murdered, 19 of whom were black or Latina (Michaels 2015). The first seven months of 2016 witnessed a continuation of this epidemic with the murders of 16 transgender people, almost all of whom have been people of color, overwhelmingly African American. These numbers are assumed to be an undercount, as they do not include people who have been misgendered by police or media; nor do they include deaths that have not been reported or investigated (Albeni and Malpani 2016). Since so many LGBTQ youth, particularly youth of color, are homeless, there is a greater likelihood that their murders go unreported or uninvestigated.

Sexual Assault of LGBTQ People

Studies show that sexual violence inflicted on LGBTQ individuals occurs more frequently than for heterosexuals (Black et al. 2010; Rothman, Exner, and Baughman 2011). Approximately 44 percent of lesbian women, 61 percent of bisexual women, and 26 percent of gay men report experiencing sexual violence in their lifetime. Rates are even higher for transgender people, with 64 percent experiencing sexual assault in their lifetimes (Black et al. 2010). This trend continues on college campuses, where LGBTQ students report higher rates of sexual assault and sexual harassment than their heterosexual peers. According to a study by the Association of American Universities, 9 percent of LGBTQ respondents said they experienced sexual assault involving penetration (Cantor et al. 2015).

LGBTQ people are at greater risk for sexual assault due to higher rates of poverty, stigma, and marginalization. Sexual violence against LGBTQ individuals is often a dimension of a hate crime, homophobia, or transphobia. Gay and bisexual men are at more risk of rape than heterosexual men because, like women, they are at risk of being raped by dates or while in relationships with men (Walker, Archer, and Davies 2014). Many LGBTQ survivors do not report sexual assault. LGBTQ victims of violence report the violence to police only about 52 percent of the time, according to the National Coalition of Anti-Violence Programs (NCAVP). The discrimination they face in society often prohibits them from wanting to talk to police, hospitals, or rape crisis centers, for fear of double victimization. Evidence of such double victimization exists: When they do report, they find police officers are indifferent 38 percent of the time, and 18 percent of the time they are openly hostile to them (Mitchell 2013). As it stands now, many criminal rape and sexual assault statutes do not specifically accommodate nonheterosexual violence. In some cases, same-gender assaults are reduced from felonies to misdemeanors. More research on the rates, causes, and reporting of sexual violence against LGBTQ people is still needed due to layered intersections of various forms of discrimination that exacerbate the issue: sexism, racism, heterosexism, and ableism.

Criminalization of LGBTQ People

LGBTQ people of color are more likely to face institutional violence at the hands of law enforcement and the criminal justice system than white LGBTQ people or heterosexuals. Thus, there is a long-standing lack of trust between police departments and LGBTQ communities of color. According to Mogul, Ritchie, and Whitlock, "the same criminalizing archetypes that permeate the treatment of queers in other contexts also profoundly inform police approaches to LGBT victims of crime" (2011:120). As a society, we have recently begun reflecting on mass incarceration and the damage it causes, particularly for communities of color. However, the disproportionate incarceration rates of LGBTQ people and their sexual victimization has drawn less attention (discussed below). Due to the threat of violence they face at the hands of authorities, as racial minorities and sexual- and gender-nonconforming people, LGBTQ people of color are less able to turn to the legal system for protection (Fitzgerald 2017).

The kinds of state violence LGBTQ people disproportionately face include being more likely to be prosecuted for defending themselves against violence, and being targeted by police (Mogul, Ritchie, and Whitlock 2011). One study found 38 percent of black, transgender respondents were harassed by police, 15 percent were assaulted, and 7 percent were sexually assaulted by police (Grant et al. 2011). Police officers commonly assume that transgender women are sex workers; and this assumption results in their oversurveillance, arrest, and prosecution (Flaherty 2013; Pemberton 2013).

CARCERAL SEXUALITY

For the last 40 years, the United States has been engaged in a dramatic social experiment: mass incarceration. Over 2.3 million Americans are behind bars; and entire communities are affected, rather than just a small number of deviant individuals. In a nation where 95 percent of prisoners are eventually released because they have served their time and over 600,000 prisoners are released every year, it behooves us to look more closely at the effects of incarceration on prisoners (Carson 2014; Pager 2007).

While incarcerated, prisoners are denied their sexual citizenship, rights related to sexual agency and expression that are sanctioned and legitimated by the state (Richardson 2000; see Chapter Ten). Prisoners are denied sexual rights; and, at the same time, they are in an environment where their odds of experiencing sexual violence increase dramatically. This section of the chapter explores *carceral sexuality*, any and all sexual encounters that happen to incarcerated persons, including consensual sexual encounters between inmates; nonconsensual sexual encounters, or rape; and sexual encounters between incarcerated persons and corrections staff—all of which violate prison rules in the United States.

While you may or may not have given any thought to prison sexuality, due to mass incarceration, we need mainstream attention directed at the seriousness of this topic—and not just as the punch line of homophobic jokes. It is important to consider what kind of environment prisoners experience (predatory or humane?) and how this will affect their reentry into society. Considered in this light, prison sexuality should concern us all. Additionally, the inmate population is disproportionately composed of African Americans and Latinos. This fuels sexual stereotypes of black men as violent sexual predators (Mogul, Ritchie, and Whitlock 2011).

Prison officials police same-sex sexuality intensely. Some go so far as to brand queer prisoners as sex offenders, forcing them to wear different colored uniforms, even when their convictions are not for sex crimes. In other prisons, rules prohibit same-sex kissing and hugging by prisoners and their visitors, a rule that does not exist for heterosexuals. In states that allow conjugal visits, four out of five of them deny conjugal visits to LGBTQ prisoners. Finally, many prisons even ban gay- and lesbian-themed books and periodicals (Mogul, Ritchie, and Whitlock 2011).

When prison sex is a topic of conversation, it is generally part of a joke rooted in both homophobia and rape culture. For instance, if you read online comments on news stories about the conviction of a criminal, especially if it is a particularly heinous crime or a crime against a child, you will see repeated references to the criminal being raped, becoming someone's "wife," and getting what he "deserves" when he goes to prison. Images of prison rape proliferate in popular culture as well. In one of his stand-up routines, comedian Chris Rock suggests that the presence of the "Tossed Salad" man would be a good deterrent to crime. The term "Tossed Salad" man is a reference to a particular sexual act, anilingual contact with condiments, which an inmate presumably insists new inmates perform on him. Rock argues that men will do anything to avoid such an experience; thus, they will avoid criminal behavior (Byrne and Hummer 2007). Whether "tossed salad" men exist or the extent of such behavior in prisons is unknown and beside the point. The fact that this has become a cultural meme and is included in a major comedian's repertoire is what is significant for our purposes. Research finds the threat of sexual assault and specifically the fear of being labeled a homosexual very much informs prison life (Richmond 1978).

Research on carceral sexuality has a long history, beginning in the early 1900s, yet it is still considered an understudied phenomena (Hensley, Struckman-Johnson, and Eigenberg 2000). Our understandings of prison sex and rape have changed substantially over the generations. Research from the early to mid-twentieth century viewed all prison sex as a form of ***situational homosexuality,*** a term scholars used to refer to an otherwise heterosexual person engaging in homosexual acts in situations where access to members of the opposite sex was constrained (Fishman 1934, 1951; Scacco 1975; Vedder and King 1967; Weiss and Friar 1974). The term situational homosexuality is rarely used by scholars today, and the body of research that falls within this tradition is flawed on a number of levels. First, the term situational homosexuality blurs the lines between consensual and nonconsensual sexual activity, in that scholars used the term to refer to heterosexual inmates who were "seduced" by promises of protection or gifts into homosexual activity while in prison. This form of seduction can also be interpreted as coercion, and coercion is rape; yet this was not acknowledged in the research. Additionally, the concept of situational homosexuality blinded researchers to the possibility of truly consensual sexual relations between prisoners. In this chapter, we are going to follow the criminological literature and use the phrase "consensual sex" instead of just "sex," which, by definition, must be consensual, in order to differentiate between sexual assault and sex in prisons.

Second, the literature on situational homosexuality shifts the blame from the perpetrator, or the aggressor, to the victims, who are also known as "punks." This is because victims are stereotyped as feminine, possibly even homosexual, and as someone who "asked for it" (Buffum 1972; Eigenberg 2000; Kirkham 1971; Sykes 1958). As sexual aggressors, perpetrators are stereotyped as "real men" who are satiating their normally high sex drives in the abnormal situation where there are no available females. In fact, the aggressors "escape stigmatization as the attitude 'boys will be boys' prevails" (Eigenberg 2000:437).

The burgeoning approach to understanding prison rape during the 1980s involved critiquing existing prohibitions on sex and arguing for allowing for masturbation, conjugal visits, and consensual sexual activity between inmates (Scacco 1982). The problem with this humanitarian solution to the prison rape crisis is it assumes rape is about sex rather than about power and domination (Eigenberg 2000). As already discussed in this chapter, feminists have long emphasized rape is about male domination over women. Thus, viewing prison rape as a result of sex deprivation is misleading. While these solutions might result in expanding sexual citizenship to inmates, they will not address the true problem of prison rape.

Today, our understanding of carceral sexuality includes a distinction between prison rape and consensual sex between inmates and an increasing emphasis on eradicating prison rape. In the 1994 Supreme Court decision *Farmer v. Brenan,* the justices ruled that prisons must protect their inmates from sexual assault, as it represents cruel and unusual punishment, which is prohibited by the Constitution (Struckman-Johnson and Struckman-Johnson 2013). In 2003, the *Prison Rape Elimination Act* (PREA) was passed unanimously by Congress and signed into law by President George W. Bush. This legislation garnered incredible support for a number of reasons. First, members of Congress heard testimony from a prison rape survivor and were convinced it was a widespread problem that needed to be addressed. Second, there was significant fear that rape in prison would spread HIV/AIDS among prisoners who would, in turn, spread it to others when they were released from prison. Others insist PREA passed because American correctional institutions failed to address prison rape on their own (Struckman-Johnson and Struckman-Johnson 2013).

With the passage of PREA, eliminating prison rape became a top priority for American correctional institutions. As of 2015, nine states are in full compliance with the PREA standards. Texas, a state with a high rate of reported sexual abuse against inmates, was financially penalized in 2015 for a second straight year for failing to follow established procedures for eliminating rape in prison (Sontag 2015).

LGBTQ Prisoners

No data on the exact number of incarcerated LGBTQ people exists, but the data that is available indicates transgender and gender-nonconforming people are disproportionately represented among the U.S. prison population (Mogul, Ritchie, and Whitlock 2011). Much like the sports world, prisons are sex segregated, which creates particular dilemmas for transgender and intersex inmates. In 2007, researchers estimated there were at least 750 transgender prisoners in U.S. prisons, and the vast majority were transgender women placed in men's prisons (Brown and McDuffie 2009).

Prisoners perceived to be gay or gender-nonconforming are more likely to be raped, assaulted, and harassed than sexual- and gender-conforming prisoners in both male and female prisons. Since male prisons are hypermasculine environments, transgender prisoners, especially those perceived as feminine, become targets of verbal, physical, and sexual abuse. The rape and sexual assault faced by transgender women in men's prisons puts them at great risk of contracting life threatening diseases such as HIV and hepatitis C, due to the high incidences of these diseases among prisoners and due to prohibitions on condoms in most prisons (Pemberton 2013). Some research finds sexual orientation is the greatest determinant of experiencing sexual violence in prison. In fact, in one study, 67 percent of LGBTQ prisoners experienced sexual assault by another inmate during their incarceration, which is 15 times higher than the heterosexual prison population. Additionally, once an inmate is raped, they become targets of further sexual violence (Mogul, Ritchie, and Whitlock 2011).

Prisons enforce gender conformity through sex-segregated housing that is a genitalia-based placement. Thus, for some transgender prisoners, their placement is rather subjective. For instance, where should a transgender woman who has had a penectomy (surgical removal of the penis) but not a vaginoplasty (surgical construction of a vagina) be housed (Pemberton 2013)? At most prisons in the United States, officials refuse to acknowledge transgender prisoners' chosen names and gender identities. Prison rules concerning appearance reinforce sex/gender stereotypes by denying access to clothing that matches gender identity and penalizing inmates for hairstyles that do not conform to their birth sex (Pemberton 2013). Transgender women in male prisons are denied access to cosmetics, while transgender men in women's prisons are forced to wear female clothing (Mogul, Ritchie, and Whitlock 2011).

Prison Rape

Prison rape is defined as unwanted sexual contact experienced by men and women who are incarcerated (Struckman-Johnson and Struckman-Johnson 2013). It is hard to get accurate data on the extent of rape in prison because inmates fear reporting the assault; there is shame and stigma connected to being sexually victimized; and there is a fear that if it is known they were victimized, it will put them at risk for future assaults. Despite the limitations of the data, it is important to highlight the existing research on prison rape.

Research by Weiss and Friar (1974) concluded sexual assault was rampant in men's prisons, while Davis's (1982) research on sexual coercion between men in prison found only three percent of men were sexually assaulted. Lockwood's (1980) research found 28 percent of male prisoners had been the target of sexual aggression, and 1.3 percent had been raped. Wooden and Parker (1982) found 14 percent of the inmates they surveyed had been sexually assaulted. One of the possible explanations for the differential findings between Wooden and Parker's research and other studies may be that their study was conducted in a California State prison facility that held a high percentage of homosexual inmates who were more likely to be targeted for sexual assault, as we have already discussed (Hensley et al. 2000). In 2010, the Department of Justice estimated that 88,500 inmates (4.4 percent in prisons and 3.1 percent in jails) were victims of prison rape in the previous year (Beck and Harrison 2010). It is assumed these are underestimates, as rape is one of the most underreported crimes—and it is estimated to be especially so in prisons, where they are likely to face retaliation from prison officials or other inmates for reporting the abuse (Mogul, Ritchie, and Whitlock 2011).

Research finds that prison culture influences how prisoners define sexual violence, which can explain the varying rates of prison rape found in the data. Sometimes an act will be defined as rape, while other times prisoners may interpret an act of sexual violence to be simply the emergence of someone's true homosexual nature. Inmates make references to the emergence of an inner homosexual with statements such as "time will get you," implying that

This image shows a 2016 protest against prison rape, specifically at Rikers Island, New York.
Source: AP Photo/Sipa.

> "[M]any incarcerated men and women engage in consensual, loving, sexual relationships and friendships as a form of resistance to the isolation and violent dehumanization of prisons, as a tool of survival within them, to affirm their humanity or simply as an exercise of basic human desire" (Mogul, Ritchie, and Whitlock 2011:95).

longer prison terms will weaken one's resistance to their inner homosexual (Fleisher and Krienert 2009).

RAPE, HOMOPHOBIA, AND CORRECTIONAL STAFF There is evidence of significant homophobia among correctional staff, which can inhibit prison rape reporting and reform (Eigenberg 1989; Struckman-Johnson and Struckman-Johnson 2013). In the 1930s, prison guards would draw a large yellow "D" on the backs of men caught having sex together, signaling they were degenerates (Fishman 1934). More recent research notes correctional officers' jokes, sarcasm, and hostility surrounding homosexual incidents (Scacco 1982). Some research evidence suggests that corrections officers struggle to distinguish between rape and consensual homosexuality (Eigenberg 2000; Wooden and Parker 1982).

Homophobic corrections officers are also more likely to blame the victims, claiming they ask for it or enjoy it (Eigenberg 2000; Mogul, Ritchie, and Whitlock 2011). In one study of correctional officers, they found most did not blame the victim for their rape; however, 12 percent did believe that some prisoners deserved to be raped because of the way they acted, 16 percent suggested they deserved to be raped if they were homosexual, and 17 percent felt they deserved rape if they talked in feminine ways. Additionally, 25 percent of the officers believed inmates deserved to be raped if they had previously engaged in consensual sexual acts in prison or if they had taken money or cigarettes for consensual acts previously (Eigenberg 2000). Ultimately, "correctional officers' definitions of rape may not correspond to the reality experienced by inmates" (Eigenberg 2000:445).

Consensual Sexual Relations

The data on consensual sexual activity within prisons is rather unreliable for a number of reasons. First, the topic is not studied to the same extent that sexual violence is studied. Second, prison administrators can be an obstacle to reliable data on sex between inmates because they may fear being held responsible for evidence of sexual activity and any consequences of it, such as spread of sexually transmitted diseases. Finally, inmates are likely hesitant to talk about their same-sex sexual activity due to the fact that it is stigmatized and the fact that they can be punished for it since it is prohibited (Tewksbury and Connor 2014).

With those caveats in mind, we provide a summary of the research on consensual sexual activity in prisons, beginning with the research on men. Most of the research on sex between men in prison has focused on situational homosexuality and sexual violence instead of consensual sex. Research on sex between incarcerated women avoided the topic of sexual violence until the 1990s, focusing instead on consensual sexual relations between female prisoners (Hensley et al. 2000).

SEXUALITY AND MALE PRISONERS Estimates on the extent of consensual sex between men in prison vary. Tewksbury's (1989) research found between 25 and 40 percent of male inmates who considered themselves heterosexual had engaged in consensual sex with another man while incarcerated. Wooden and Parker (1982) found 65 percent of inmates had a sexual experience with another man while in prison, and most identified as heterosexual. Hensley's (2001) research found 80 percent of the sample considered themselves to be heterosexual; yet 23 percent of inmates performed or received oral sex from another inmate, 23 percent rubbed their bodies against another inmate in a sexual manner or allowed another inmate to do that to them, and 20 percent engaged in anal sex with another inmate (Tewksbury and Connor 2014).

SEXUALITY AND FEMALE PRISONERS Researchers have established a typology of sex and sexuality in women's prisons, which includes suppressed sexuality, autoeroticism, true homosexuality, situational homosexuality, and sexual violence (Pardue, Arrigo, and Murphy 2011). *Suppressed sexuality* refers to the absence of sexual behaviors as an adaptive response to the prison environment. Sometimes female offenders make the conscious decision not to engage in any sexual behavior while in prison as a way to stay faithful to a partner outside of prison, or simply as a lifestyle choice (Hensley, Tewksbury, and Koscheski 2001). Interestingly, the research on sexuality in men's prisons does not acknowledge the potential for suppressed sexuality. Of course, since suppressed sexuality is nonproblematic from a prison administrator perspective, it is rarely studied empirically as most of the research instead focuses on sexual behaviors, both consensual and nonconsensual, which are prohibited. The absence of attention to suppressed sexuality among men may also simply be an extension of gendered assumptions, specifically the idea that it is impossible for "real men" to suppress their sexuality.

The second category of sexual activity in women's prisons is *autoeroticism*, or masturbation, which is condemned by prison officials. We have very little research on the extent of masturbation that occurs in prisons. One study of female inmates found that 65.5 percent had masturbated while incarcerated, 18.6 percent report engaging in autoeroticism two to three times per week, and prisoners who were sexually active in same-sex relationships actually engaged in this behavior the most frequently (Hensley et al. 2001).

The next category, true homosexuality, refers to consensual same-sex behavior by prisoners who identified as lesbian prior to their incarceration. Some research finds that same-sex sexual behavior prior to prison was one of the best predictors of such behavior while in prison (Koscheski and Hensley 2001), while other research clarifies that preprison homosexuality does not positively correlate with homosexual behavior while incarcerated, as some lesbians chose to remain faithful to their nonincarcerated partners (Pardue et al. 2011; Ward and Kassebaum 1964).

The third category is consensual situational homosexuality. This refers to when an inmate is introduced to same-sex sexual behaviors while in prison due to the lack of heterosexual options (Pardue et al. 2011). These individuals have historically been referred to as "jailhouse turnouts" (Ward and Kassebaum 1964). It is estimated that 90 percent of women who engage in same-sex sexual relations while in prison are engaging in situational homosexuality and return to heterosexual relationships postincarceration (Ward and Kassebaum 1964). More current research finds that while 8 percent of female inmates report being a lesbian and 28 percent claim to be bisexual when they enter prison; while in prison, 13 percent report being lesbian and 31 percent report being bisexual (Koscheski and Hensley 2001). Of course, the core of these assumptions is essentialist rather than constructionist; there is an assumption that people have an essential, innate sexuality (Chapter One).

The final category is sexual violence, a topic that was not studied in female correctional institutions prior to 1996 (Pardue et al. 2011). As mentioned previously, sexual violence refers to sexually aggressive behaviors such as coercion; assault, including strip searches; rape; child molestation/pedophilia; and manipulation, specifically threats and intimidation (Herberle and Grace 2009; La Fond 2005; Pardue et al. 2011). The specific unequal power relationships incarcerated women find themselves in make them susceptible to manipulation involving sex—sex as a bartering tool in exchange for goods, like drugs or cigarettes, or services, like cell assignments.

Sexual violence can occur between prisoners or between a correctional worker and a prisoner (Pardue et al. 2011). The U.S. Department of Justice estimates that in 2007, there were 22,600 instances of unwanted sexual activity between correctional staff and inmates (Beck and Harrison 2010). In other research, 27 percent of female inmates experienced sexual coercion during their incarceration; and half of these actions were perpetrated by male correctional staff (Struckman-Johnson and Struckman-Johnson 2002). Rates of sexual victimization are higher for female prisoners than for women in general (Blackburn, Mullings, and Marquart 2008).

CONCLUSION

In conclusion, sexual violence is a problem, not only in the United States, but across the globe. Sexual violence is gendered and racialized, resulting in particular populations of people being disproportionately victimized. While the United States currently perpetuates a rape culture, ideally, we will transform into an antirape society with laws, beliefs, and ideologies that prevent sexual violence against women, children, LGBTQ people, and all marginalized groups. Understanding the high incidence of rape in certain environments like college campuses and prisons is the first step toward prevention. Child sex abuse must be addressed in order to minimize the stigma surrounding it and move toward change. Finally, exploring prison sexuality challenges us to think about the idea of sexual citizenship and why prison sexuality should be an issue that concerns us all.

Key Terms and Concepts

Acquaintance rape 260
Affirmative consent
    standard 261
Autoeroticism 275
Carceral sexuality 270
Child molestation 265
Child sexual abuse 265
Consent 260
Date rape 260
Date rape drug 260

Double victimization 259
Incest 265
Intersectional invisibility 269
Pedophile 266
Prison rape 273
Rape 259
Rape culture 257
Rape myths 259
Sexual age orientation 266
Sexual assault 259

Sexual violence 257
Situational
    homosexuality 271
Statutory rape 260
Suppressed sexuality 275
Victimization
    framework 261
Victim-offender cycle 266
Wartime rape 263
Wartime sexual violence 263

Critical Thinking Questions

1. Feminists claim rape is a tool for dominance and social control over women. How does the threat of rape and sexual violence exert social control over women? What limitations or fears exist surrounding sexual violence? In what way might your sex/gender shape your views on this subject?

2. Describe how social myths promote shame, stigma, and silence around sexual violence, particularly child sex abuse. What are the results of widespread social silence on issues such as violence and abuse?

3. Explain the ways homophobia and racism manifest as violence against LGBTQ people of color, including institutionalized homophobia in organized religion, schools, and the media.

4. Explain how carceral sexuality, including the denial of sexual citizenship to prisoners, contributes to sexual violence outside prisons.

Activities

1. Find out if your college or university campus has a rape crisis center. Visit the center and gather as much information as you can on how the center works and what resources it has to offer. Write a one-page persuasive paper on the advantages for rape and sexual assault survivors on campus to visit the rape crisis center.

2. Study the language of consent. Learn ways that even young children can understand and express control over their own bodies, such as learning that everyone has to ask before touching another person. Create a list of the various ways consent can be expressed.

Essential Readings

Harding, Kate. 2015. *Asking For It: The Alarming Rise of Rape Culture and What We Can Do About It.* Boston: Perseus Books.

Katz, Jackson. 2006. *The Macho Paradox: Why Some Men Hurt Women and How All Men Can Help.* Naperville, IL: Sourcebooks.

Krakauer, Doug. 2015. *Missoula: Rape and the Justice System in a College Town.* New York: Doubleday.

Meyer, Doug. 2015. *Violence against Queer People: Race, Class, Gender, and the Persistence of Anti-LGBT Discrimination.* New Brunswick, NJ: Rutgers University Press.

Mogul, Joey L., Andrea J. Ritchie, and Kay Whitlock. 2011. *Queer (In)Justice: The Criminalization of LGBT People in the United States.* Boston, MA: Beacon Press.

Patterson, Jennifer. 2016. *Queering Sexual Violence: Radical Voices from Within the Anti-Violence Movement.* Riverdale, New York: Magnus Imprint Books.

Wooden, W. and J. Parker. 1982. *Men Behind Bars: Sexual Exploitation in Prison.* New York: Plenum.

Recommended Films

Accessory to Murder: Our Culture's Complicity in the Death of Ryan Skipper (2008). Directed and Produced by Vicki Nantz and Mary Meeks. Uses the murder of 25-year-old, rural Florida resident Ryan Skipper to explore the extent of institutionalized homophobia in our culture, from religion to education to law enforcement. In addition to Ryan's brutal murder, the homophobia of local law enforcement was on full display when the sheriff declared Ryan to be responsible for his own murder, an assertion the media failed to challenge.

The Hunting Ground (2015). Kirby Dick, Director, and Amy Ziering, Producer. This documentary explores the epidemic of sexual assaults and rapes on college campuses. It highlights specific individual's stories of sexual assault and the generally impotent response of college administrators, who appear to be more concerned with their campus rape statistics than with protecting young women on their campuses. While most of the narratives are from young women who were victims of sexual assault and/or rape, this documentary also features male victims of sexual assault as well and their specific struggles getting justice.

The Invisible War (2012). Kirby Dick, Director, and produced by Amy Ziering and Tanner King Barklow. This award-winning documentary explores rape and sexual assault in the U.S. military. The film highlights the stories of a number of people sexually assaulted, across all four branches of the military, and the obstacles to justice they experienced. The experience has life-long consequences for the victims, yet the perpetrators experience ongoing career advancement.

Suggested Multimedia

National Coalition of Anti-Violence Programs provides research, prevention measures, and responses to violence against LGBTQ communities. http://www.avp.org/

National Sexual Violence Resource Center is a web site dedicated to responding to and preventing sexual violence by providing collaborations, research, and information on the subject. http://www.nsvrc.org/

V-Day is a global movement to stop violence against women and girls. This web site serves to increase awareness on sexual violence and organize antiviolence events. http://www.vday.org/

REFERENCES

"2015 Word of the Year Is Singular 'They.'" 2016. *American Dialect Society*, January 8. Retrieved July 24, 2016. (http://www.americandialect .org/2015-word-of-the-year-is-singular-they).

Abbott, D. and J. Howarth. 2007. "Still Off-Limits? Staff Views on Supporting Gay, Lesbian, and Bisexual People with Intellectual Disabilities to Develop Sexual and Intimate Relationships?" *Journal of Applied Research in Intellectual Disabilities* 20:116–26.

Abelove, Henry, Michele Aina Barale, and David M. Halperin, eds. 1993. "Introduction." Pp. xv–xvii in *The Lesbian and Gay Studies Reader*. London. England: Routledge.

Ackard, Diann M., Ann Kearney-Cooke, and Carol B. Peterson. 2000. "Effect of Body Image and Self-image on Women's Sexual Behaviors." *International Journal of Eating Disorders* 28(4):422–29.

Adam, Barry D. 2006. "Relationship Innovation in Male Couples." *Sexualities* 9(1):5–26.

Adams, Adi, Eric Anderson, and Mark McCormack. 2010. "Establishing and Challenging Masculinity: The Influence of Gendered Discourses in Organized Sports." *The Journal of Language and Social Psychology* 29(3):278–300.

Ahrens, Courtney E. 2006. "Being Silenced: The Impact of Negative Social Reactions on the Disclosure of Rape." *American Journal of Community Psychology* 38(3–4): 263–74. Retrieved July 14, 2016 (http://www.ncbi.nlm.nih.gov/pmc/ articles/PMC1705531/).

Albeni, Cleis and Aashna Malpani. 2016. "These are the Trans People Killed in 2016." *The Advocate*, May 16. Retrieved May 27, 2016

(http://www.advocate.com/ transgender/2016/5/16/these-are-trans-people-killed-2016).

Albright, Julie M. 2008. "Sex in America Online: An Exploration of Sex, Marital Status, and Sexual Identity in Internet Sex Seeking and its Impacts." *Journal of Sex Research* 45(2):175–86.

Alioto, Anthony M. and John McHale. 2014. *Saintly Sex: Saint John Paul II, Sex, Gender and the Catholic Church*. Dubuque, IA: Kendall Hunt Publishing.

Allen, K.R. and D.H. Demo. 1995. "Families of Lesbian and Gay Men." *Journal of Marriage and Family* 57(1):111–27.

Allyn, David. 2000. *Make Love, Not War: The Sexual Revolution: An Unfettered History*. New York: Routledge.

Alpert, Rebecca. 2003. "Sex in Jewish Law and Culture." Pp. 177–202 in *Sexuality and The World's Religions*, edited by David W. Machacek and Melissa M. Wilcox. Santa Barbara, CA: ABC-CLIO.

American Psychiatric Association. 1980. *Diagnostic and Statistical Manual of Mental Disorders*, 3rd ed. Washington, DC: American Psychiatric Association.

American Psychiatric Association. 2013. "APA Statement on DSM-5 Text Error." New Release, October 13. Retrieved July 18, 2016 (http://www.dsm5 .org/Documents/13-67-DSM-Correction-103113.pdf).

American Psychological Association, Task Force on the Sexualization of Girls. 2007. "Report of the APA Task Force on the Sexualization of Girls." Retrieved July 24, 2016 (http://www .apa.org/pi/women/programs/girls/ report-full.pdf).

American Society for Reproductive Medicine. 2015. "Disparities in Access to Effective Treatment for Infertility in the United States: An Ethic Committee Opinion." *Fertility and Sterility* 104(5):1104–10.

Anderson, Eric. 2002. "Openly Gay Athletes: Contesting Hegemonic Masculinity in a Homophobic Environment." *Gender and Society* 16(6):860–77.

Anderson, Eric. 2005. *In the Game: Gay Athletes and the Cult of Masculinity*. Albany, NY: State University of New York Press.

Anderson, Eric. 2009. *Inclusive Masculinity: The Changing Nature of Masculinities*. London, England: Routledge.

Anderson, Eric, Mark McCormack, and Matt Ripley. 2013. "Men, Masculinities, and Sexualities." Pp. 31–54 in *Sexual Minorities in Sports: Prejudice at Play*, edited by Melanie L. Sartore-Baldwin. Boulder, CO: Lynne Rienner Publishers.

Anderson, M., J.M. Croteau, Y.B. Chung, and T.M. DiStefano. 2001. "Developing an Assessment of Sexual Identity Management for Lesbian and Gay Workers." *Journal of Career Assessment* 9:243–60.

Anderson, Terry H. 2012. *The Sixties*, 4th ed. Boston: Pearson.

Andre, Amy. 2006. "Bisexual Cowboys in Love." *American Sexuality Magazine*. Retrieved September 15, 2014 (http://nsrc.stsu .edu/MagArticle.cfm?Article=554).

Appleford, Steve. 2013. "Q&A: Joan Jett on Writing and Thriving During Her 'Decade of Death.'" *Rolling Stone Magazine*, August 3. Retrieved July 24, 2016 (http://www.rolling stone.com/music/news/q-a-joan-jett-on-writing-and-thriving-during-her-decade-of-death-20130803).

Asencio, Marysol and Katie Acosta. 2010. "Introduction: Mapping Latino/a Sexualities Research and Scholarship." Pp. 1–12 in *Latina/o Sexualities: Probing Powers, Passions, Practices, and Policies*, edited by Marysol Asencio. New Brunswick, NJ: Rutgers University Press.

Assistant Secretary for Public Affairs. 2015. "The Affordable Health Care Act and Maternity Care." Washington D.C.: U.S. Department of Health & Human Services. Retrieved July 22, 2016 (http://www.hhs.gov/healthcare/facts-and-features/fact-sheets/aca-and-maternity-care/index.html).

Attwood, Feona. 2002. "Reading Porn: The Paradigm Shift in Pornography Research." *Sexualities* 5(1):91–105.

Attwood, Feona. 2006. "Sexed Up: Theorizing the Sexualization of Culture." *Sexualities* 9(1):77–94.

Aubrey, Jennifer Stevens and Cynthia M. Frisby. 2011. "Sexual Objectification in Music Videos: A Content Analysis Comparing Gender and Genre." *Mass Communication and Society* 14(4):475–501.

Ayoola, Adejoke B., Gail L. Zandee, and Yenupini J. Adams. 2016. "Women's Knowledge of Ovulation, the Menstrual Cycle, and Its Associated Reproductive Changes." *Birth: Issues in Perinatal Care* 43(3):255–62.

Bacigalupi, Alexia. 2016. "Meet the Women Rocking Rio." *Refinery 29* July 18. Retrieved July 30, 2016. (http://www.refinery29.com/2016/07/116389/female-athletes-olympics-2016#slide).

Bagley, Chris and Loretta Young. 1987. "Juvenile Prostitution and Child Sexual Abuse: A Controlled Study." *Canadian Journal of Community Mental Health* 6(1):5–26

Bailey, Michael, and Richard C. Pillard. 1991. "A Genetic Study of Male Sexual Orientation." *Archives of General Psychiatry* 48:1089–96.

Bailey, S. M. 1993. "The Current Status of Gender Equity Research in American Schools." *Educational Psychologist*. 28(4):321.

Balthazart, Jacques. 2011. "Minireview: Hormones and Human Sexual Orientation." *Endocrinology* 152(8):2937–47. Retrieved July 24, 2016 (http://www.ncbi.nlm.nih.gov/pmc/articles/PMC3138231/).

Bancroft, J. 2004. "Alfred C. Kinsey and the Politics of Sex Research." *Annual Review of Sex Research* 15:1–39.

Banks, Ingrid. 2009. "Hair Still Matters." Pp. 142–150 in *Feminist Frontiers*, 8th ed., edited by Verta Taylor, Nancy Whittier, and Leila Rupp. New York: McGraw Hill.

Barker, Meg. 2005. "This is My Partner, and This is My . . . Partner's Partner: Constructing a Polyamorous Identity in a Monogamous World." *Journal of Constructivist Psychology* 18(1):75–88.

Barker, Meg and Darren Langdridge. 2015. "Whatever Happened to Non-Monogamies? Critical Reflections on Recent Research and Theory." Pp. 348–65 in *Sexualities: Identities, Behaviors, and Society*, 2nd ed., edited by Michael Kimmel and the Stony Brook Sexualities Research Group. New York: Oxford University Press.

Barrett, Betty Jo and Melissa St. Pierre. 2013. "Intimate Partner Violence Reported by Lesbian-, Gay- and Bisexual-Identified Individuals Living in Canada: An Exploration of Within Group Variations." *Journal of Gay and Lesbian Social Services* 25:1–23

Barry, Ellen. 2016. "A Year after Earthquake, Nepal's Recovery Is Just Beginning." *The New York Times*, April 30. Retrieved July 25, 2016 (http://www.nytimes.com/2016/05/01/world/asia/nepals-earthquake-recovery-remains-in-disarray-a-year-later.html?mtrref=www.google.com&gwh=FC5DDBCB9EC7B202F4995E74B873B4E6&gwt=pay).

Barry, Kathleen. 1996. *The Prostitution of Sexuality*. New York: New York University Press.

Barton, Bernadette. 2012. *Pray the Gay Away: The Extraordinary Lives of Bible Belt Gays*. New York: New York University Press.

Bartz, Deborah and James A Greenberg. 2008. "Sterilization in the United States." *Reviews in Obstetrics and Gynecology* 1(1):23–32.

Basson R. 2001. "Human Sex-Response Cycles." *Journal of Sex Marital Therapy* 27:33–43.

Bastian, L. D., Lancaster, A. R. and H. E. Reist. 1996. *Department of Defense 1995 Sexual Harassment Survey*. Report No 96–114. Arlington, VA: Defense Manpower Data Center.

Baumle, Amanda and D'Lane Compton. 2015. *Legalizing LGBT Families: How the Law Shapes Parenthood*. New York: New York University Press.

Baylies, Carolyn, Janet Bujra, and the Gender and AIDS Group. 2000. *AIDS, Sexuality and Gender in Africa: Collective Strategies and Struggles in Tanzania and Zambia*. New York: Routledge.

Bazelon, Emily. 2016a. "Oppression or Profession?" The

New York Times Magazine, May 8, Pp. 34–43, 55.

Bazelon, Emily. 2016b. "Should Prostitution Be a Crime?" *The New York Times Magazine*, May 5. Retrieved July 7, 2016 (http://www.nytimes.com/2016/05/08/magazine/should-prostitution-be-a-crime.html?_r=0).

Bearak, Max and Darla Cameron. 2016. "Here Are the 10 Countries Where Homosexuality May Be Punished by Death." *The Washington Post*, June 16. Retrieved July 28, 2016 (https://www.washingtonpost.com/news/worldviews/wp/2016/06/13/here-are-the-10-countries-where-homosexuality-may-be-punished-by-death-2/).

Beatty, J. E. and S. L. Kirby. 2006. "Beyond the Legal Environment: How Stigma Influences Invisible Identity Groups in the Workplace." *Employee Responsibilities and Rights Journal* 18(1):29–44.

Beck, Allen J. and Paige M. Harrison. 2010. *Sexual Victimization in Prisons and Jails Reported by Inmates, 2008–09.* Washington, DC: Bureau of Justice Statistics.

Becker, Ron. 2006. *Gay TV and Straight America.* New Brunswick, NJ: Rutgers University Press.

Beemyn, Genny. 2015. "Leaving No Trans College Student Behind." *The Chronicle of Higher Education* 62(8):1–4

Beemyn, Genny and Sue Rankin. 2011. "Introduction of the Special Issue on 'LGBTQ Campus Experiences.'" *Journal of Homosexuality* 58:115–964.

Begun, Stephanie and N. Eugene Walls. 2015. "Pedestal or Gutter: Exploring Ambivalent Sexism's Relationship with Abortion Attitudes." *Affilia* 30(2):200–15.

Beirne, Rebecca. 2008. *Televising Queer Women: A Reader.* New York: Palgrave Macmillan.

Beisel, William R. 1996. "Nutrition and Immune Function: Overview." *The Journal of Nutrition* 126(10):2611S–2615S.

Belkin, Aaron and Geoffrey Bateman. 2003. *Don't Ask, Don't Tell: Debating the Gay Ban in the Military.* Boulder, CO: Lynne Rienner Publishers.

Bem, Sandra L. 1983. "Gender Schema Theory and Its Implications for Child Development: Raising Gender Aschematic Children in a Gender-Schematic Society." *Signs* 8(4):598–616.

Bendery, Jennifer. 2014. "Obama Finally Ready to Sign Executive Order Targeting LGBT Job Discrimination." *The Huffington Post,* July 7. Retrieved January 20, 2016 (http://www.huffingtonpost.com/2014/07/18/obama-gay-rights_n_5600100.html).

Benedict, Jeff. 1997. *Public Heroes, Private Felons: Athletes and Crimes against Women.* Boston: Northeastern University Press.

Benedict, Jeff. 2004. *Out of Bounds: Inside the NBA's Culture of Rape, Violence, and Crime.* New York: HarperCollins.

Benedict, Jeff and Don Yaeger. 1998. *Pros and Cons: The Criminals Who Play in the NFL.* New York: Warner.

Benjamin, Harry and R. E. L. Masters. 1964. *Prostitution and Morality: A Definitive Report on the Prostitute in Contemporary Society and an Analysis of the Causes and Effects of the Suppression of Prostitution.* New York: The Julian Press.

Bennett, C. and A. Coyle. 2007. "A Minority within a Minority: Experiences of Gay Men with Intellectual Disabilities." Pp. 125–45 in *Out in Psychology: Lesbian, Gay, Bisexual, Trans, and Queer Perspectives,* edited by V. Clarke and E. Peel. Chichester, UK: Wiley.

Berensen, Tessa. 2015a. "Laverne Cox Says Transgender People Need More Than Just Media Visibility." *Time.com,* April 25. Retrieved June 5, 2016 (http://time.com/3835554/laverne-cox-time-people-party-transgender/).

Berensen, Tessa. 2015b. "These Are Some of the Top Catholic Lawmakers in U.S." *Time Magazine*, September 24. Retrieved July 20, 2016 (http://time.com/4040450/pope-francis-us-visit-catholic-lawmakers/).

Berger, Peter L. and Thomas Luckmann. [1966] 1991. *The Social Construction of Reality.* New York: Penguin Books.

Berman, Laura A., Jennifer R. Berman, Sachin Chhabra, and Irwin Goldstein. 2001. "Novel Approaches to Female Sexual Dysfunction." *Expert Opinion on Investigational Drugs* 10(1):85–95.

Bernstein, Jacob. 2015. "Caitlyn Jenner's Secret-Sharer." *The New York Times*, December 19. Retrieved July 25, 2016 (http://www.nytimes.com/2015/12/20/fashion/caitlyn-jenner-alan-nierob-crisis-manager.html?_r=0).

Bernstein, Mary. 2005. "Identity Politics." *Annual Review of Sociology* 31:47–74.

Berube, Allan. 1990. *Coming Out Under Fire: The History of Gay Men and Women in World War Two.* New York: The Free Press.

Bettie, Julie. 2003. *Women without Class: Girls, Race, and Identity.* Berkeley: University of California Press.

Bieber, Irving. 1962. *Homosexuality: A Psychoanalytical Study.* New York: Vintage Books.

Biegel, Stuart. 2010. *The Right to Be Out: Sexual Orientation and Gender Identity in America's Public Schools.* Minneapolis: University of Minnesota Press.

Birgisson, N. E., Q. Zhao, G. M. Secura, T. Madden, and J. F. Peipert. 2015. "Preventing Unintended Pregnancy: The Contraceptive CHOICE Project in Review." *Journal of Women's Health* 24(5):349–53.

Bissinger, Buzz. 2015. "Caitlyn Jenner: The Full Story." *Vanity Fair,* July. Retrieved July 24, 2016 (http://www.vanityfair .com/hollywood/2015/06/ caitlyn-jenner-bruce-cover-annie-leibovitz).

Bitler, Marianne and Lucie Schmidt. 2006. "Health Disparities and Infertility: Impacts of State-level Insurance Mandates." *Fertility and Sterility* 85(4):858–65.

Black, Michele C., Kathleen C. Basile, Matthew J. Breiding, Sharon G. Smith, Mikel L. Walters, Melissa T. Merrick, Jieru Chen, and Mark R. Stevens. 2010. *The National Intimate Partner and Sexual Violence Survey: 2010 Summary Report.* Atlanta, GA: National Center for Injury Prevention and Control, Centers for Disease Control and Prevention.

Blackburn, A. G., J. L. Mullings, and J. W. Marquart. 2008. "Sexual Assault In Prison and Beyond: Toward an Understanding of Lifetime Sexual Assault among Incarcerated Women." *The Prison Journal* 88:351–77.

Blank, Hanne. 2012. *Straight: The Surprisingly Short History of Heterosexuality.* Boston: Beacon Press.

Blee, Kathleen M. and Kimberly A. Creasap. 2010. *Conservative and Right-Wing Movements.* Annual Review of Sociology Series.

Block, Pamela. 2007. "Feeble Excuses: Public Representations of Gender, Sexuality, and Disability." Pp. 162–71 in *Sex Matters: The Sexuality and Society Reader,* 2nd ed., edited by Mindy Stombler, Dawn M. Baunach, Elisabeth O. Burgess, Denise Donnelly, and Wendy Simonds. Boston: Pearson.

Bloom, Alexander and Wini Breines, eds. 2015. *Takin' It to The Streets: A Sixties Reader.* New York: Oxford University Press.

Bluhm, Julia. 2012. "Seventeen Magazine: Give Girls Images of Real Girls!" Petition to Photo Director, Seventeen Magazine Jordan Barnes. Retrieved July 26, 2016 (https://www .change.org/p/seventeen-magazine-give-girls-images-of-real-girls#delivered-to).

Blumstein, Philip and Pepper Schwartz. 1983. *American Couples: Money, Work, and Sex.* New York: William Morrow & Company.

Bogaert, A. F. 2006. "Toward a Conceptual Understanding of Asexuality." *Review of General Psychology* 10(3):241–50.

Bogle, Kathleen A. 2008. *Hooking Up: Sex, Dating, and Relationships on Campus.* New York: New York University Press.

Boles, J. and K. W. Elifson. 1994. "The Social Organization of Transvestite Prostitution and AIDS." *Social Science and Medicine* 39(1):85–93.

Bolich, D. G. G. 2008. *Crossdressing in Context: Transgender and Religion* 4. Raleigh, NC: Psyche's Press.

Boonstra, Heather D. 2007. "Young People Need Help in Preventing Pregnancy and HIV. How Will the World Respond?" *Guttmacher Policy Review* 10(3). Retrieved July 31, 2016 (https:// www.guttmacher.org/about/ gpr/2007/08/young-people-need-help-preventing-pregnancy-and-hiv-how-will-world-respond).

Boonstra, Heather D. 2011. "Teen Pregnancy among Women in Foster Care: A Primer." *Guttmacher Policy Review* 14(2). Retrieved July 22, 2016 (https:// www.guttmacher.org/about/ gpr/2011/06/teen-pregnancy-among-young-women-foster-care-primer).

Bordo, Susan. 2004. *Unbearable Weight: Feminism, Western Culture and The Body.* 2nd ed., Tenth Anniversary Edition. Berkeley: University of California Press;

Boswell, John. 2005. *Christianity, Social Tolerance, and Homosexuality: Gay People in Western Europe from the Beginning of the Christian Era to the Fourteenth Century.* Chicago: University of Chicago Press.

Bowater, Donna and Priscilla Moraes. 2015. "Brazil: Targeting Trans People with Impunity." *AlJazeera,* April 22, 2015. Retrieved May 27, 2016 (http://www.aljazeera.com/ indepth/features/2015/04/ brazil-targeting-trans-people-impunity-150413210248222 .html)

Boykin, Keith. 2005. *Beyond the Down Low: Sex, Lies, and Denial in Black America.* New York: Carroll & Graf.

Boynton, P. 2003. "'I'm Just a Girl Who Can't Say No?' Women, Consent, and Sex Research." *Journal of Sex and Marital Therapy* 29:23–32.

Brady, S. and B. Halperin-Felsher. 2007. "Adolescents' Reported Consequences of Having Oral Sex versus Vaginal Sex." *Pediatrics* 199:292–36.

Brake, Deborah L. 2015. "On *Not* 'Having it Both Ways' and Still Losing: Reflections on Fifty Years of Pregnancy Litigation under Title VII." *Boston University Law Review* 95(3):995–1014.

Branigan, Tania. 2013. "Typhoon Haiyan: Children in Disaster Zone Are Vulnerable, Warns UNICEF." *The Guardian,* November 20. Retrieved July 25, 2016 (https://www.theguardian.com/world/2013/nov/20/typhoon-haiyan-children-vulnerable-unicef).

Branson-Potts, Hailey. 2015. "Transgender Teen Who Spoke on YouTube of Bullying Takes Her Own Life." *Los Angeles Times,* April 9. Retrieved July 10, 2016 (http://www.latimes.com/local/lanow/la-me-ln-transgender-teen-suicide-20150409-story.html).

Brawn, Kara Marie and Dominique Roe-Sepowitz. 2008. "Female Juvenile Prostitutes: Exploring the Relationship to Substance Use." *Children and Youth Services Review* 30(12): 1395–1402.

Brighe, Mari. 2016. "Miss. Nurse Dee Whigham Becomes 16th Transperson Murdered in 2016." *The Advocate,* July 26. Retrieved July 27, 2016 (http://www.advocate.com/transgender/2016/7/26/mississippi-nurse-dee-whigham-becomes-16th-trans-person-murdered-2016).

Brody, Jane E. 2000. "PERSONAL HEALTH; Exposing the Perils of Eating Disorders." *The New York Times.* Retrieved July 26, 2016 (http://www.nytimes.com/2000/12/12/health/personal-health-exposing-the-perils-of-eating-disorders.html).

Brooks, Virginia. 1981. *Minority Stress: Minority Stress and Lesbian Women.* Lexington, MA: Lexington Books.

Brown, Amy L., Maria Testa, and Terri L. Messman-Moore. 2009. "Psychological Consequences of Sexual Victimization Resulting from Force, Incapacitation, or Verbal Coercion." *Violence against Women* 15(8):898–919. Retrieved July 14, 2016 (http://www.ncbi.nlm.nih.gov/pmc/articles/PMC2761643/).

Brown, George and Everett McDuffie. 2009. "Health Care Policies Addressing Transgender Inmates in Prison Systems in the U.S." *Journal of Correctional Health Care* 15(4):280–91.

Brown, Helen Gurley. 1962. *Sex and the Single Girl.* New York: Bernard Geis Associates.

Brown, Jane. 2002. "Mass Media Influences on Sexuality." *The Journal of Sex Research* 39(1):42–45.

Brown, Jonathan A. C. 2015. "Muslim Scholar on How Islam Really Views Homosexuality." *Variety,* June 30. Retrieved July 28, 2016 (http://variety.com/2015/voices/opinion/islam-gay-marriage-beliefs-muslim-religion-1201531047/).

Brownmiller, Susan. 1975. *Against Our Will: Men, Women, and Rape.* New York: Fawcett Books.

Bryant-Waugh, Rachel and Bryan Lask. 2013. "Overview of Eating Disorders in Childhood and Adolescence." Pp. 33–49 in *Eating Disorders in Childhood and Adolescence,* 4th ed., edited by Rachel Bryant-Waugh and Bryan Lask. New York: Routledge.

Brydum, Sunnivie. 2015. "U.S. Military's Transgender Ban Begins to Fall Monday." *The Advocate,* July 30. Retrieved Jan. 9, 2016 (http://www.advocate.com/transgender/2015/07/30/us-militarys-transgender-ban-begins-fall-monday).

Bryson, Lois. 1990. "Challenges to Male Hegemony in Sport." Pp. 173–84 in *Sport, Men and the Gender Order: Critical Feminist Perspectives,* edited by Don Sabo and Michael A. Messner. Champaign, IL: Human Kinetics.

Buchanan, NiCole T., Isis H. Settles, Angela T. Hall, and Rachel C. O'Connor. 2014. "A Review of Organizational Strategies for Reducing Sexual Harassment: Insights from the U.S. Military." *Journal of Social Issues* 70(4): 687–702.

Buddel, Neil. 2011. "Queering the Workplace." *Journal of Gay and Lesbian Social Sciences* 23:131–46.

Budgeon, Shelley. 2014. "The Dynamics of Gender Hegemony: Femininities, Masculinities and Social Change." *Sociology* 48(2):317–34.

Buffum, P. 1972. *Homosexuality in Prisons.* Washington, DC: U.S. Department of Justice, Law Enforcement Assistance Administration.

Bullingham, Rachael, Rory Magrath, and Eric Anderson. 2014. "Changing the Game: Sport and a Cultural Shift Away from Homohysteria." Pp. 275–82 in *Routledge Handbook of Sport, Gender, and Sexuality,* edited by Jennifer Hargreaves and Eric Anderson. New York: Routledge.

Bullough, Vern. 2004. "Sex Will Never Be the Same: The Contributions of Alfred C. Kinsey." *Arch of Sexual Behavior* 33(3):277–86.

Bullough, Vern. 2007. "Alfred Kinsey and the Kinsey Report." Pp. 60–67 in *Sex Matters: The Sexuality and Society Reader,* 2nd ed., edited by Mindy Stombler, Dawn M. Baunach, Elisabeth O. Burgess, Denise Donnelly, and Wendy Simonds. Boston: Pearson.

Burn, Shawn Meghan. 2011. *Women Across Cultures: A Global Perspective,* Third Edition. New York: McGraw-Hill.

Burns, Crosby and Jeff Krehely. 2011. "Gay and Transgender People Face High Rates of Workplace Discrimination and Harassment." The Center for American Progress, June 2. Retrieved July 31, 2016. (https://www.americanprogress.org/issues/lgbt/news/2011/06/02/9872/gay-and-transgender-people-face-high-rates-of-workplace-discrimination-and-harassment/).

Burns, Crosby and Philip Ross. 2011. "Gay and Transgender Discrimination Outside the Workplace." The Center for American Progress, July 19. Retrieved May 14, 2015 (https://www.americanprogress.org/issues/lgbt/report/2011/07/19/9927/gay-and-transgender-discrimination-outside-the-workplace/).

Burns, Jan and Danielle Davies. 2011. "Same-Sex Relationships and Women With Intellectual Disabilities." *Journal of Applied Research in Intellectual Disabilities* 24:351–60.

Burrowes, N. 2013. *Responding to the Challenge of Rape Myths in Court.* London, England: NB Research. Retrieved July 13, 2016 (http://www.nb-research.co.uk/index.php/projects-2/).

Busey, Kelli. 2016. "A Transgender Person is Murdered Every 29 Hours. Can You Stop Killing Us for Just One Week?" *Planet Transgender,* February 23. Retrieved May 27, 2016 (http://planettransgender.com/trans-people-ban-together-and-ask-can-you-stop-killing-us-for-one-week/).

Butler, Judith. 1990. *Gender Trouble.* New York: Routledge.

Buzuvis, Erin E. 2013. "Transsexual and Intersex Athletes." Pp. 55–71 in *Sexual Minorities in Sports: Prejudice at Play,* edited by Melanie L. Sartore-Baldwin, Editor. Boulder, CO: Lynne Rienner Publishers.

Byrne, James and Don Hummer. 2007. "In Search of the 'Tossed Salad Man' (and Others Involved in Prison Violence): New Strategies for Predicting And Controlling Violence in Prison." *Aggression and Violent Behavior* 12:531–41.

Cabosky, Joseph. 2015. "'For Your Consideration': A Critical Analysis of LGBT-Themed Film Award Campaign Advertisements: 1990-2005." *Journalism History* 41:2.

Cahill, Ann J. 2001. *Rethinking Rape.* Ithaca, NY: Cornell University Press.

Cahn, Susan K. 1994. *Coming On Strong: Gender and Sexuality in Twentieth-Century Women's Sport.* New York: The Free Press.

Cahn, Susan K. 2007. "Coming on Strong: Gender and Sexuality in Twentieth-Century Sports."

Pp. 9–13 in *Equal Play: Title IX and Social Change,* edited by Nancy Hogshead-Makar and Andrew Zimbalist. Philadelphia, PA: Temple University Press.

Calefati, Jennifer. 2008. "Gay High Schools Offer a Haven From Bullies." *U.S. News and World Report,* December 31. Retrieved March 12, 2016.http://www.usnews.com/education/articles/2008/12/31/gay-high-schools-offer-a-haven-from-bullies?page=2.

Campus Sexual Assault Victims' Bill of Rights. 20 U.S.C. 1092(f) (8) (1992).

Cantor, David, Bonnie Fisher, Susan Chibnall, Reanne Townsend, Hyunshik Lee, Carol Bruce, and Gail Thomas. 2015. *Report on the AAU Campus Climate Survey on Sexual Assault and Sexual Misconduct.* The Association of American Universities. Rockville, Maryland: Westat.

Carby, H. V. 1998. *Race Men.* Cambridge, Mass: Harvard University Press.

Carleton, Gregory. 2005. *Sexual Revolution in Bolshevik Russia.* Pittsburgh, PA: University of Pittsburgh Press.

Carmichael, Karie and Edwin Scharlau 2011. *Unfit: Ward v. Ward.* DVD. San Antonio.

Caron, Simone. 2008. *Who Chooses? American Reproductive History since 1830.* Gainesville, FL: University Press of Florida.

Carpenter, Laura M. 2001. "The Ambiguity of 'Having Sex': The Subjective Experience of Virginity Loss in the United States." *The Journal of Sex Research* 38(2): 127–39.

Carpenter, Laura M. 2011. "Like a Virgin ... Again? Secondary Virginity as an Ongoing Gendered

Social Construction." *Sexuality and Culture* 15:115–40.

Carpenter, Laura M. 2013. "The Ambiguity of Sex and Virginity Loss: Insights from Feminist Research Methods." Pp. 41–48 in *Sex, Gender, and Sexuality: The New Basics,* 2nd ed., edited by Abby L. Ferber, Kimberly Holcomb, and Tre Wentling. New York: Oxford University Press.

Carrigan, Mark. 2015. "There's More to Life Than Sex? Difference and Commonality within the Asexual Community." Pp. 336–47 in *Sexualities: Identities, Behaviors, and Society,* 2nd ed., edited by Michael Kimmel and the Stony Brook Sexualities Research Group. New York: Oxford University Press.

Carroll, Jason S., Laura M. Padilla-Walker, Larry J. Nelson, Chad D. Olson, Carolyn McNamara Barry, and Stephanie D. Madsen. 2008. "Generation XXX: Pornography Acceptance and Use Among Emerging Adults." *Journal of Adolescent Research* 23(1):6–30.

Carson, E. Ann. 2014. *Prisoners in 2013.* Bureau of Justice Statistics Bulletin. Washington, DC: US Department of Justice.

Carter, Vednita and Evelina Giobbe. 1999. "Duet: Prostitution, Racism and Feminist Discourse." *Hastings Women's Law Journal* 10(1):37–57.

Cascais, Antonio Fernando and Daniel Cardoso. 2012. "'Loving Many:' Polyamorous Love, Gender, and Identity." Pp. 21–29 in *Gender and Love: Interdisciplinary Perspectives,* 2nd ed., edited by N. de Haro Garcia and M. Tseliou. Oxford, UK: Interdisciplinary Press.

Cavendish, James C. 2003. "The Vatican and the Laity: Diverging

Paths in Catholic Understanding of Sexuality." Pp. 203–30 in *Sexuality and The World's Religions*, edited by David W. Machacek and Melissa M. Wilcox. Santa Barbara, CA: ABC-CLIO.

Center for Women's Global Leadership. 2015. *Sixteen Days of Action, Take Action Kit.* New Jersey: Rutgers, State University of New Jersey. Retrieved June 10, 2016 (http://16dayscwgl.rutgers.edu/2015-campaign/take-action-kit).

Centers for Disease Control and Prevention. 2008. "Youth Risk Behavior Surveillance: United States, 2007." *Morbidity and Mortality Weekly Report* 57:1–131.

Centers for Disease Control and Prevention. 2014. "LGBT Youth." Retrieved July 7, 2016 (http://www.cdc.gov/lgbthealth/youth.htm).

Centers for Disease Control and Prevention. 2016. "CDC Fact Sheet: Reported STDs in the United States, 2014." Retrieved July 23, 2016 (https://www.cdc.gov/std/stats14/std-trends-508.pdf).

Central Intelligence Agency. 2010. "Country Comparison: Maternal Mortality Rate." The World Factbook: Central Intelligence Agency. Retrieved July 22, 2016 (https://www.cia.gov/library/publications/the-world-factbook/rankorder/2223rank.html).

Chambers, Samuel A. 2009. *The Queer Politics of Television.* London, England: I.B. Tauris.

Chan, Connie S. 1988. "Asian-American Women: Psychological Responses to Sexual Exploitation and Cultural Stereotypes." *Women & Therapy* 6(4):33–38.

Chancer, Lynn S. 1992. *Sadomasochism in Everyday Life: The Dynamics of Power and*

Powerlessness. Rutgers, NJ: Rutgers University Press.

Chandra, Anjani, Casey E. Copen, and Elizabeth Hervey Stephen. 2013. "Infertility and Impaired Fecundity in the United States, 1982-2010: Data from the National Survey of Family Growth." U.S. Department of Health and Human Services, Centers for Disease Control and Prevention, National Center for Health Statistics, Number 67. August 14.

Chaparro, Luis. 2015. "Cartel Gangsters Face 697 Years Behind Bars in Historic Femicide Case in Juarez, Mexico." *Vice News*, July 28. Retrieved July 20, 2016 (https://news.vice.com/article/cartel-gangsters-face-697-years-behind-bars-in-historic-femicide-case-in-juarez-mexico).

Chase, Elaine and June Statham. 2005. "Commercial and Sexual Exploitation of Children and Young People in the UK—A Review." *Child Abuse Review* 14(1):4–25.

Chen, Michelle. 2015. "Nepal's Double Disaster: Long before the Quake, Nepal Suffered the Rupturing Shocks of Global Capitalism." *The Nation*, May 8. Retrieved July 25, 2016 (https://www.thenation.com/article/nepals-double-disaster/).

Chen, Stephanie. 2009. "'John Schools' Try to Change Attitudes About Paid Sex." *CNN blog*, August 28. Retrieved June 28, 2016 (http://www.cnn.com/2009/CRIME/08/27/tennessee.john.school/index.html?eref=rss_us).

Cherry, Kittredge and Douglas Blanchard. 2014. *The Passion of Christ: A Gay Vision.* Berkeley, CA: Apocryphile Press.

Child, Ben. 2015. "Fifty Shades of Grey Hits $500 Million at the

Global Box Office." *The Guardian*, March 6. Retrieved July 24, 2016 (http://www.theguardian.com/film/2015/mar/06/fifty-shades-of-grey-hits-500-million-at-the-global-box-office)

"Children and HIV/AIDS." 2016. (n.a.). *AVERT: AVERTing HIV/AIDS*. Retrieved July 22, 2016. (http://www.avert.org/professionals/hiv-social-issues/key-affected-populations/children).

Childress, Sarah. 2014. "What's the State of the Church's Child Abuse Crisis?" *PBS Frontline*, February 24. Retrieved July 18, 2016 (http://www.pbs.org/wgbh/frontline/article/whats-the-state-of-the-churchs-child-abuse-crisis/).

Childs, Anna. 2016. "Why Child Trafficking Surges after Natural Disasters." CNN News, March 23. Retrieved July 25, 2016 (http://www.cnn.com/2016/03/23/opinions/child-trafficking-natural-disasters/).

Chivers-Wilson, Kaitlin A. 2006. "Sexual Assault and Posttraumatic Stress Disorder: A Review of the Biological, Psychological and Sociological Factors and Treatments." *McGill Journal of Medicine* 9(2):111–18. Retrieved July 14, 2016 (http://www.ncbi.nlm.nih.gov/pmc/articles/PMC2323517/).

Cho, Seo-Young, Axel Dreher, and Eric Neumayer. 2013. *World Development* 41:67–82.

Chou, Rosalind. 2012. *Asian American Sexual Politics*. Lanham, MD: Rowman and Littlefield.

Church Gibson, Pamela. 1993. *Dirty Looks: Women, Pornography, Power*. London, England: British Film Institute.

Cianciotto, Jason and Sean Cahill. 2012. *LGBT Youth in America's Schools*. Ann Arbor, MI: The University of Michigan Press.

Cline, Carrier. 2010. "Gay Couple Encounters Housing Discrimination." WSAZ Newschannel 3, February 22. Retrieved June 29, 2016. http://www.wsaz.com/news/headlines/84994592.html

Coad, David. 2008. *The Metrosexual: Gender, Sexuality, and Sport*. Albany, NY: SUNY Press.

Coates, John M., Mark Gurnell, and Zultan Sarnyai. 2010. "From Molecule to Market: Steroid Hormones and Financial Risk-taking." *Philosophical Transactions of the Royal Society B* 365:331–43.

Coelho, Tony. 2011. "Hearts, Groins, and the Intricacies of Gay Male Open Relationships: Sexual Desire and Liberation Revisited." *Sexualities* 14(6):653–68.

Cohen, Adam. 2016. *Imbeciles: The Supreme Court, American Eugenics, and the Sterilization of Carrie Buck*. New York: Penguin Press.

Cohen, Elizabeth. 2013. "North Carolina Lawmakers OK Payments for Victims of Forced Sterilization." *CNN*, July 28. Retrieved July 20, 2016 (http://www.cnn.com/2013/07/26/us/north-carolina-sterilization-payments/).

Cohen, Stanley. 1972. *Folk Devils and Moral Panics: The Creation of Mods and Rockers*. Oxford, UK: Basil.

Colapinto, John. 2005. "The Harvey Milk High School Has No Right to Exist. Discuss." *New York Magazine*, Feb. 7. Retrieved March 12, 2016 (http://nymag.com/nymetro/news/features/10970/).

Collins, Patricia Hill. 1991. *Black Feminist Thought: Knowledge, Consciousness, and the Politics of Empowerment*. New York: Routledge.

Collins, Patricia Hill. 2000. *Black Feminist Thought: Knowledge, Consciousness, and the Politics of Empowerment*. 2nd ed. New York: Routledge.

Collins, Patricia Hill. 2005. *Black Sexual Politics: African Americans, Gender, and the New Racism*. New York: Routledge.

Collins, Rebecca L., Marc N. Elliott, Sandra H. Berry, David E. Kanouse, Dale Kunkel, Sarah B. Hunter, and Angela Miu. 2004. "Watching Sex on Television Predicts Adolescent Initiation of Sexual Behavior." *Pediatrics* 114(3):280–89.

Commonwealth of Australia. 2008. "Sexualisation of Children in the Contemporary Media." Retrieved March 15, 2016 (http://www.aph.gov.au/binaries/senate/committee/eca_ctte/sexualisation_of_children/report/report.pdf).

Conger, George. 2015. "The Episcopal Church Approves Religious Weddings for Gay Couples After Controversial Debate." *Washington Post*, July 1. Retrieved July 28, 2016 (https://www.washingtonpost.com/news/acts-of-faith/wp/2015/07/01/why-the-episcopal-church-is-still-debating-gay-marriage/).

Connell, Catherine. 2015. *School's Out: Gay and Lesbian Teachers in the Classroom*. Berkeley: University of California Press.

Connell, R.W. 1987. *Gender & Power: Society, the Person, and Sexual Politics*. Stanford, CA: Stanford University Press.

Connell, R.W. 1995. *Masculinities*. Berkeley, CA: University of California Press.

Connell, R. W. and James W. Messerschmidt. 2005. "Hegemonic Masculinity: Rethinking the Concept." *Gender & Society* 19(6):829–59.

Conrad, Peter and Kristen K. Barker. 2010. "The Social Construction of Illness: Key Insights and Policy Implications." *Journal of Health and Social Behavior* 51(S):S67–S79.

Coontz, Stephanie. 2011. "Historical Perspectives on Family Diversity." Pp. 42–58 in *Shifting the Center: Understanding Contemporary Families,* 4th ed., edited by Susan J. Ferguson. New York: McGraw-Hill.

Corey, Daniel Webster. 1951. *The Homosexual in America.* New York: Arno Press.

Corprew, Charles S, Jamaal S Matthews, and Avery Devell Mitchell. 2014. "Men at the Crossroads: A Profile Analysis of Hypermasculinity in Emerging Adulthood." *The Journal of Men's Studies* 20(2):105–21.

Coscarelli, Joe. 2014. "Mike Huckabee Has Thoughts on Women's Libidos." *New York Magazine,* January 23. Retrieved July 20, 2016 (http://nymag .com/daily/intelligencer/2014/01/ mike-huckabee-has-thoughts-on-womens-libidos.html).

Covert, Bryce and Mike Konczal. 2015. "Guilty of Pregnancy." *The Nation,* July 6/13:5. Retrieved January 10, 2015 (http:// web.b.ebscohost.com.libproxy .tulane.edu:2048/ehost/pdfviewer/ pdfviewer?vid=3&sid=dca81631-a0b3-4261-a0aa-f036c147ebcf% 40sessionmgr198&hid=124).

Cowan, Gloria, Carole Lee, Daniella Levy, and Debra Snyder. 1988. "Dominance and Inequality in X-rated Videocassettes."

Psychology of Women Quarterly 12(3):299–311.

Crary, David and Brady Mccombs. 2016. "Boy Scouts Faring Well a Year after Voting to Ease Ban on Gay Adults." *The Times-Picayune,* Sunday, July 24, p. A14.

Crenshaw, Kimberle. 1989. "Demarginalizing the Intersection of Race and Sex: A Black Feminist Critique of Antidiscrimination Doctrine, Feminist Theory and Antiracist Politics." *The University of Chicago Legal Forum* 140:139–67.

Crooks, Robert and Karla Baur. 2011. *Our Sexuality.* 11th ed. Belmont, CA: Wadsworth/ Cengage Learning.

Crozier, P. 2012. "Parental Rights after Relationship Dissolution." Pp. 105–30 in *Transgender Family Law: A Guide to Effective Advocacy,* edited by J.L. Levi and E. E. Monnin-Browder. Bloomington, IN: AuthorHouse.

Cruikshank, Margaret. 1992. *The Gay and Lesbian Liberation Movement.* New York: Routledge.

Cruz, Jamie Santa. 2014. "Body-Image Pressure Increasingly Affects Boys." *The Atlantic,* March 10. Retrieved July 24, 2016 (http:// www.theatlantic.com/health/ archive/2014/03/body-image-pressure-increasingly-affects-boys/283897/).

Cummings, Judith. 1987. "Disabled Model Defies Sexual Stereotypes." *The New York Times,* June 8. Retrieved July 23, 2016 (http://www.nytimes.com/1987/ 06/08/style/disabled-model-defies-sexual-stereotypes.html).

Currah, Paisley, Richard M. Juang, and Shannon P. Minter, Editors. 2006. *Transgender Rights.*

Minneapolis: University of Minnesota Press.

Cutway, Adrienne. 2015. "Florida Couple Accused of Running Sex Tourism Business." *Orlando Sentinel,* September 14. Retrieved July 24, 2016 (http://www .orlandosentinel.com/features/ gone-viral/os-sex-tourism-business-20150914-post.html).

Dabbs, James M. Jr., Timothy S. Carr, Robert L. Frady, and Jasmin K. Riad. 1995. "Testosterone, Crime, and Misbehavior among 692 Male Prison-inmates." *Personality and Individual Differences* 18(5):627–33.

Dalla, R. L. 2002. "Night Moves: A Qualitative Investigation of Street-level Sex Work." *Psychology of Women Quarterly* 26(1):63–73.

Dank, Meredith, Bilal Khan, P. Mitchell Downey, Cybele Kotonias, Deborah Mayer, Colleen Owens, Laura Pacifici, and Lilly Yu. 2014. "Estimating the Size and Structure of the Underground Commercial Sex Economy in Eight Major US Cities." Research Report: The Urban Institute. Retrieved July 11, 2016 (http://www.urban.org/sites/ default/files/alfresco/publication-pdfs/413047-Estimating-the-Size-and-Structure-of-the-Underground-Commercial-Sex-Economy-in-Eight-Major-US-Cities.PDF).

Dart Center for Journalism and Trauma. 2016. "Sexual Violence." Columbia Journalism School. Retrieved July 26, 2016 (http:// dartcenter.org/topic/sexual-violence).

Darwin, Charles. [1859] 2009. *On the Origin of Species: By Means of Natural Selection.* Auckland, NZ: The Floating Press.

Das, Aniruddha and Edward O. Laumann. 2015. "How to Get Valid Answers from Survey

Questions." Pp. 32–47 in *Sexualities: Identities, Behaviors, and Society,* 2nd ed., edited by Michael Kimmel and The Stony Brook Sexualities Research Group. New York: Oxford University Press.

David, Deborah and Robert Brannon. 1976. *The Forty-Nine Percent Majority: The Male Sex Role.* Boston: Addison-Wesley.

Davidson, Julia O'Connell. 2005. *Children in the Global Sex Trade.* Cambridge, United Kingdom: Polity.

Davis, A. J. 1982. "Sexual Assaults in the Philadelphia Prison System and Sheriff's Vans." Pp. 107–120 in *Male Rape: A Casebook of Sexual Aggressions,* edited by A.M. Scacco. New York: AMS Press.

Davis, Angela. 1981. *Women, Race and Class.* New York: Random House.

Davis, Angela Y. 2015. "Rape, Racism, and the Myth of the Black Rapist." Pp. 575–86 in *Sexualities: Identities, Behaviors, and Society,* 2nd ed., edited by Michael Kimmel and The Stony Brook Sexualities Research Group. New York: Oxford University Press.

Davis, Georgiann. 2015. *Contesting Intersex:The Dubious Diagnosis.* New York: New York University Press.

Davis, Kingsley. 1937. "The Sociology of Prostitution." *American Sociological Review* 2(5):744–55.

Davis-Floyd, Robbie. 2004. *Birth as an American Rite of Passage.* Oakland, CA: University of California Press.

Davy, Zowie and Eliza Steinbock. 2012. "'Sexing Up' Bodily Aesthetics: Notes towards Theorizing Trans Sexuality." Pp. 266–85 in *Sexualities: Past*

Reflections, Future Directions, edited by S. Hines and Y. Taylor. London, England: Palgrave Macmillan.

Day, Allison. 2009. "Feminism and Pornography after the Sex Wars: Diversifying Pornography." UCLA Center for the Study of Women. UCLA: UCLA Center for the Study of Women. Retrieved on July 1, 2016 (http://escholarship .org/uc/item/61k265vv).

de Albuquerque, K. 1998. "Sex, Beach Boys and Female Tourists in the Caribbean." Pp. 87–112 in *Sex Work and Sex Workers: Sexuality and Culture,* edited by Barry Michael Dank and Roberto Refinetti. Piscataway, NJ: Transaction Publishers.

DeLamater, J., J. Hyde, and M. Fong. 2008. "Sexual Satisfaction in the Seventh Decade of Life." *Journal of Sex and Marital Therapy* 34:439–54.

Demetriou, Demetrakis Z. June 2001. "Connell's Concept of Hegemonic Masculinity: A Critique." *Theory and Society* 30(3): 337–61.

D'Emilio, John. 1983. *Sexual Politics, Sexual Communities: The Making of a Homosexual Minority in the United States, 1940–1970.* Chicago: The University of Chicago Press.

D'Emilio, John and Estelle B. Freedman. 2012. *Intimate Matters: A History of Sexuality in America.* 3rd ed. Chicago: University of Chicago Press.

Denisoff, R. Serge and Richard A. Peterson. 1972. *The Sounds of Social Change: Studies in Popular Culture.* New York: Rand McNally & Company.

De Tocqueville, Alexis. 1956. *The Old Regime and the French Revolution.* New York: Harper Brothers.

Dhana, Ashar, Stanley Luchters, Lizzie Moore, Yves Lafort, Anuradha Roy, Fiona Scorgie, and Matthew Chersich. 2014. "Systematic Review of Facility-based Sexual and Reproductive Health Services for Female Sex Workers in Africa." *Globalization and Health* 10:46. Retrieved July 11, 2016 (http://globalizationandhealth .biomedcentral.com/articles /10.1186/1744 8603 10 46).

Diaz, Rafael. 1997. *Latino Gay Men and HIV: Culture, Sexuality, and Risk Behavior.* New York: Routledge.

Dick-Read, Grantly. [1942] 2013. *Childbirth Without Fear: The Principles and Practice of Natural Childbirth,* 2nd Edition. London, England: Pinter and Martin Ltd.

Dienst, Jonathan. 2015. "Feds Take down Rentboy.com, 'World's Largest Male Escort Site,' in Manhattan; 7 Arrested." *NBC News New York*, Aug. 31. Retrieved July 24, 2016 (http://www .nbcnewyork.com/news/local/ Rentboy-Male-Escort-Website-Manhattan-Arrest-Takedown-Federal-Agent-Police–322826271. html).

Dignity USA: Gay, Lesbian, Bisexual & Transgender Catholics. 2016. "Home." Retrieved July 28, 2016 (https:// dignityusa.org/).

Dines, Gail. 2010. *Pornland: How Porn Has Hijacked Our Sexuality.* Boston: Beacon Press.

"Discrimination." n.d. *SAGE: Services and Advocacy for Gay, Lesbian, Bisexual, and Transgender Elders.* Retrieved July 25, 2016 (https://www.sageusa.org/issues/ general.cfm).

Dittmar, Helga, Suzanne Ive, and Emma Halliwell. 2006. "Does Barbie Make Girls Want to Be Thin? The Effect of Experimental Exposure to Images of Dolls on the Body Image of 5- to 8-Year-Old Girls." *Developmental Psychology* 42(2):283–92.

Division of Nutrition, Physical Activity, and Obesity. 2013. "Breastfeeding Report Card United States 2013." Atlanta, GA: National Center for Chronic Disease Prevention. Retrieved July 22, 2016 (https://www.cdc.gov/breastfeeding/pdf/2013breastfeedingreportcard.pdf).

Dockterman, Eliana. 2014. "5 Things Women Need to Know about the Hobby Lobby Ruling." *Time Magazine*, July 1. Retrieved July 18, 2016 (http://time.com/2941323/supreme-court-contraception-ruling-hobby-lobby/).

Doka, Kenneth J. 1997. *AIDS, Fear, and Society: Challenging the Dreaded Disease.* London, England: Taylor and Francis.

Douglas, E.M. and D.A. Hines. 2011. "The Helpseeking Experiences of Men Who Sustain Intimate Partner Violence: An Overlooked Population and Implications for Practice. *Journal of Family Violence* 26(6):473–85.

Downs, A.C. and S.E. James. 2006. "Gay, Lesbian, and Bisexual Foster Parents: Strengths and Challenges for the Child Welfare System." *Child Welfare* 85(2): 281–98.

Drache, Daniel and Jennifer Velagic. 2013. "A Report on Sexual Violence Journalism in Four Leading Indian English Language Publications Before and After the Delhi Bus Rape." Retrieved July 26, 2016 (http://dx.doi.org/10.2139/ssrn.2277310).

Drape, Joe. 2012. "Sandusky Guilty of Sexual Abuse of 10 Young Boys." *The New York Times*, June 22. Retrieved July 20, 2016 (http://www.nytimes.com/2012/06/23/sports/ncaafootball/jerry-sandusky-convicted-of-sexually-abusing-boys.html).

Dreger, Alice. 2013. "What Can Be Done About Pedophilia?" *The Atlantic*, August 26. Retrieved July 18, 2016 (http://www.theatlantic.com/health/archive/2013/08/what-can-be-done-about-pedophilia/279024/).

Driver, Alice. 2015. *More or Less Dead: Feminicide, Haunting, and the Ethics of Representation in Mexico.* Tucson: The University of Arizona Press.

Duncombe, J., K. Harrison, G. Allan, and D. Marsden, eds. 2004. *The State of Affairs: Explorations in Infidelity and Commitment.* Mahwah, NJ: Lawrence Erlbaum.

Dunne, Gillian. A. 1997. *Lesbian Lifestyles: Women's Work and the Politics of Sexuality.* Toronto, Canada: University of Toronto Press.

Durham, Gigi M. 2008. *The Lolita Effect: The Media Sexualization of Young Girls and What We Can Do About It.* Woodstock, NY: The Overlook Press, Peter Mayer Publishers, Inc.

Dworkin, Andrea. 1993. "Speech, Equality and Harm: Feminist Legal Perspectives on Pornography and Hate Propaganda" Conference speech at the University of Chicago Law School, March 6, 1993. Retrieved June 18, 2016 (http://www.nostatusquo.com/ACLU/dworkin/MichLawJourI.html).

Dworkin, Andrea. 1997. *Life and Death: Unapologetic Writings on the Continuing War against Women.* New York: The Free Press.

Dworkin, Andrea. 2006. *Intercourse.* New York: Basic Books.

Easton, Dossie and Janet Hardy. 2009. *The Ethical Slut: A Practical Guide to Polyamory, Open Relationships, and Other Adventures.* Berkeley, CA: Celestial Arts.

Eberhardt, Judith, Anna van Wersch, and Neil Meikle. 2009. "Attitudes Towards the Male Contraceptive Pill in Men and Women in Casual and Stable Sexual Relationships." *Journal of Family Planning & Reproductive Health Care* 35(3):161–65.

Edwards, Katie M., Jessica A. Turchik, Christina M. Dardis, Nicole Reynolds, and Christine A. Gidycz. 2014. "Rape Myths." Pp. 597–607 in *Sex Matters: The Sexuality and Society Reader,* 4th ed., edited by Mindy Stombler, Dawn M. Baunach, and Wendy Simonds. New York: W.W. Norton & Company.

Ehrensaft, Diane. 2008. "Just Molly and Me, and Donor Makes Three: Lesbian Motherhood in the Age of Assisted Reproductive Technology." *Journal of Lesbian Studies* 12(2-3):161–78.

Eig, Jonathan. 2014. *The Birth of the Pill: How Four Crusaders Reinvented Sex and Launched a Revolution.* New York: W. W. Norton & Company.

Eigenberg, Helen M. 1989. "Male Rape: An Empirical Examination of Correctional Officers' Attitudes Toward Rape in Prison." *The Prison Journal* 69(2):39–56.

Eigenberg, Helen M. 2000. "Correctional Officers' Definitions of Rape in Male Prisons." *Journal of Criminal Justice* 28:435–49.

Eisenbach, David. 2006. *Gay Power: An American Revolution.* New York: Carroll & Graf.

Eisler, Riane. 1988. *The Chalice and The Blade: Our History, Our Future.* Pacific Grove, CA: HarperCollins.

Eisner, Shiri. 2013. *Bi: Notes for a Bisexual Revolution.* Berkeley CA: Seal Press.

Eitzen, D. Stanley and George H. Sage. 2003. *Sociology of North American Sport,* 7th ed. Boston: McGraw Hill.

Elifson K.W., J. Boles, E. Posey, M. Sweat, W. Darrow, and W. Elsea. 1993. "Male Transvestite Prostitutes and HIV Risk." *American Journal of Public Health* 83(2):260–2.

Elliott, Sinikka. 2012. *Not My Kid: What Parents Believe about the Sex Lives of Their Teenagers.* New York: New York University Press.

Embrick, David, Carol Walther, and C.M. Wickens. 2007. "Working Class Masculinity: Keeping Gay Men and Lesbians Out of the Workplace." *Sex Roles* 56:757–66.

Eng, Thomas R. and William T. Butler, Editors. 1997. *The Hidden Epidemic: Confronting Sexually Transmitted Diseases.* Washington, DC: National Academy Press.

Enloe, Cynthia. 2014. *Bananas, Beaches and Bases: Making Feminist Sense of International Politics.* Berkeley: University of California Press.

Ephron, Dan. 2009. 'Don't Ask Too Fast." *Newsweek,* January 12, 153(2):46.

Epstein, Rob and Jeffrey Friedman, Directors. 2000. *Paragraph 175.*

Erdmans, Mary Patrice and Timothy Black. 2015. *On Becoming a Teen Mom: Life Before Pregnancy.* Oakland: University of California Press.

"Erectile Dysfunction Drugs: Market is Expected to Reach USD 34 Billion Globally in 2019." 2013. *PRN Newswire,* October 21. Retrieved July 19, 2016. (http://www.prnewswire .com/news-releases/erectile- dysfunction-drugs-market-is- expected-to-reach-usd-34-billion- globally-in-2019-transparency- market-research-228593931 .html).

Ettlebrick, Paula. 1989. "Since When is Marriage a Path to Liberation?" *Out/Look: National Lesbian and Gay Quarterly* 6:9,14–17.

Evans, Tom. 2010. "Traffickers Targeting Haiti's Children, Human Organs, PM Says." *CNN News,* January 28. Retrieved July 25, 2016 (http://edition .cnn.com/2010/WORLD/ americas/01/27/haiti.earthquake .orphans/).

Eyal, Keren and Tali Te'eni-Harari. 2013. "Explaining the Relationship between Media Exposure and Early Adolescents' Body Image Perceptions: The Role of Favorite Characters." *Journal of Media Psychology: Theories, Methods, and Applications* 25(3):129–41.

Eyerman, Ron and Andrew Jamison. 1998. *Music and Social Movements: Mobilizing Traditions in the Twentieth Century.* Cambridge, New York, and Melbourne: Cambridge University Press.

Falicov, Celia Jaes. 2010. "Changing Constructions of Machismo for Latino Men in Therapy: 'The Devil Never Sleeps.'" *Family Process* 49(3):309–29.

Farias, Cristian. 2016. "Supreme Court Sides with Lesbian Mom Denied Adoption Rights in Alabama." *The Huffington Post,* March 7. Retrieved May 10, 2016 (http://www.huffingtonpost.com/

entry/supreme-court-lgbt- adoption_us_56dd92b7e4b03a 4056791e4f?ir=Queer+Voices &section=us_queer-voices& utm_hp_ref=queer-voices).

Farley, John. 2005. *Majority- Minority Relations,* 5th ed. Upper Saddle River, NJ: Prentice Hall.

Farley, Melissa, Jacqueline Lynne, and Ann J. Cotton. 2005. "Prostitution in Vancouver: Violence and the Colonization of First Nations Women." *Transcultural Psychiatry* 42:242–71.

Farley, Melissa, Jacqueline M. Golding, Emily Schuckman Matthews, Neil M. Malamuth, and Laura Jarrett. 2015. "Comparing Sex Buyers with Men Who Do Not Buy Sex: New Data on Prostitution and Trafficking." *Journal of Interpersonal Violence,* published online before print August 31, 2015, doi:10.1177/0886260515600874.

Fausto-Sterling, Anne. 2000. *Sexing the Body: Gender Politics and the Construction of Sexuality.* New York: Basic Books.

Fausto-Sterling, Anne. 2013. "Dueling Dualisms." Pp. 6–21 in *Sex, Gender, and Sexuality: The New Basics,* 2nd ed., edited by Abby L. Ferber, Kimberly Holcomb, and Tre Wentling. New York: Oxford University Press.

Feinberg, E. C., F. W. Larsen, W. H. Catherino, J. Zhang, and A. Y. Armstrong. 2006. "Comparison of Assisted Reproductive Technology Utilization and Outcomes Between Caucasian and African American Patients in an Equal-Access-to- Care Setting." *Fertility and Sterility* 85(4):888–94.

Ferber, Abby L. 2007. "The Construction of Black Masculinity: White Supremacy Now and Then "

Journal of Sport and Social Issues 31(1):11–24.

Ferber, Marianne A. and Jane W. Loeb. 1997. *Academic Couples: Problems and Promises.* Champaign: University of Illinois Press.

Ferguson, R. 2000. *A Diagnostic Analysis of Black-White GPA Disparities in Shaker Heights, OH.* Washington, DC: Brookings Institution.

Ferguson, Susan J., Ed. 2011. *Shifting the Center: Understanding Contemporary Families,* 4th Ed. New York: McGraw-Hill.

Fetner, Tina. 2008. *How the Religious Right Shaped Lesbian and Gay Activism.* Minneapolis: University of Minnesota Press.

Fetner, Tina and Kristin Kush. 2003. "Gay-Straight Alliances in High Schools: An Emerging Form of LGBTQ Youth Activism." Unpublished paper presented at the American Sociological Society Annual Meetings, August 2004.

Field, A.E., K.R. Sonneville, R.D. Crosby, S.A. Swanson, K.T. Eddy, C.A. Camargo Jr., N.J. Horton, and N. Micali N. 2014. "Prospective Associations of Concerns about Physique and the Development of Obesity, Binge Drinking, and Drug Use among Adolescent Boys and Young Adult Men." *JAMA Pediatric* 168(1):34–9.

Fields, Jessica. 2005. "'Children Having Children': Race, Innocence, and Sexuality Education." *Social Problems* 52(4):549–71.

Filene, Peter G. 1975. *Him/Her/ Self: Sex Roles in Modern America.* New York: Harcourt Brace Jovanovich.

Fine, Michelle. 1988. "Sexuality, Schooling, and Adolescent Females: The Missing Discourse of Desire." *Harvard Educational Review* 58:29–53.

Finer, Lawrence and Mia R. Zolna. 2016. "Declines in Unintended Pregnancy in the United States, 2008-2011." *New England Journal of Medicine* 374:843–52.

Firestone, Shulamith. 1970. *The Dialectic of Sex: The Case for Feminist Revolution.* New York: Farrar, Straus and Giroux.

Fishman, J. F. 1934. *Sex in Prison: Revealing Sex Conditions in American Prisons.* New York: National Library.

Fishman, J. F. 1951. *Sex in Prison.* London, England: John Lane, The Bodley Head.

Fitzgerald, Kathleen J. 2014. *Recognizing Race and Ethnicity: Power, Privilege, and Inequality.* Boulder, CO: Westview Press.

Fitzgerald, Kathleen J. 2017. "Understanding Racialized Homophobic and Transphobic Violence." In *Violence against Black Bodies,* edited by Sandra Weissinger, Elwood Watson, and Dwayne Mack. New York: Routledge.

Fitzgerald, Kathleen J. and Diane M. Rodgers. 2000. "Radical Social Movement Organizations: A Theoretical Model." *The Sociological Quarterly* 41(4):573–92.

Fitzgerald, Nora and Vladimir Ruvinsky. 2015. "The Fear of Being Gay in Russia." *Politico. com,* March 22. Retrieved July 21, 2015 (http://www.politico.com/ magazine/story/2015/03/russia-putin-lgbt-violence-116202.html# .Va_TLPlVhBc).

Fitzpatrick, J.D. 1988. "AIDS Is a Moral Issue." Pp. 32–36 in *AIDS: Opposing Viewpoints,* edited by L. Hall and T. Modl. St. Paul, MN: Greenhaven Press.

Flaherty, Jordan. 2010. "Her Crime? Sex Work in New Orleans." *Colorlines,* January 13. Retrieved May 20, 2015 (http://www .colorlines.com/articles/her-crime-sex-work-new-orleans).

Flaherty, Jordan. 2013. "Are Police Profiling Transgender Americans?" *Aljezeera America,* October 16. Retrieved July 20, 2016. (http:// america.aljazeera.com/watch/ shows/america-tonight/america-tonight-blog/2013/10/16/rise-in-tra nsgenderharassmentviolencebypoli celinkedtoprofiling.html).

Fleisher, Mark S. and Jessie L. Krienert. 2009. *The Myth of Prison Rape: Sexual Culture in American Prisons.* Lanham, MD: Rowman and Littlefield.

Flowers, Barri R. 2001. *Runaway Kids and Teenage Prostitution.* Westport, CT: Greenwood Publishing Group.

Flynn, Taylor. 2006. "The Ties That (Don't) Bind: Transgender Family Law and the Unmaking of Families." Pp. 32–50 in *Transgender Rights,* edited by Paisley Currah, Richard M. Juang, and Shannon Price Minter. Minneapolis: University of Minnesota Press.

Fortier, Michelle A., David DiLillo, Terri L. Messman-Moore, James Peugh, Kathleen A. DeNardi, and Kathryn J. Gaffey. 2009. "Severity of Child Sexual Abuse and Revictimization: The Mediating Role of Coping and Trauma Symptoms." *Psychology of Women Quarterly* 33(3):308–20.

Foubert, J. D., J.T. Newberry, and J. Tatum. 2007. "Behavior Differences Seven Months Later: Effects of a Rape Prevention Program." *Journal of Student Affairs Research and Practice* 44:728–49.

Foucault, Michel. 1978. *The History of Sexuality.* Vols. 1–3. New York: Vintage Books.

Fox, Maggie. 2014. "U.S. Pregnancy Rate Hits Record Low, Data Shows." NBC News, December 11. Retrieved July 17, 2016 (http://www.nbcnews.com/health/womens-health/u-s-pregnancy-rate-hits-record-low-data-shows-n478381).

Franiuk, R., J.L. Seefelt, and J.A. Vandello. 2008. "Prevalence of Rape Myths in Headlines and Their Effects on Attitudes Toward Rape Victims." *Sex Roles* 58:790–801.

Frank, Alex. 2015. "Drag Race Is Back! RuPaul on What Makes a Queen a Star." *Vogue Magazine,* March 2. Retrieved July 24, 2016 (http://www.vogue.com/12041424/rupaul-drag-queen-race-interview/).

Frank, Nathaniel. 2009. *Unfriendly Fire: How the Gay Ban Undermines the Military and Weakens America.* New York: St. Martin's Press.

Freud, Sigmund. [1949, 1906] 2011. *Three Essays on the Theory of Sexuality.* Translated by James Strachey. London, England: Martino Fine Books.

Fricke, David. 2015. "Joan Jett: Built to Rock." *Rolling Stone,* April 24. Retrieved July 24, 2016 (http://www.rollingstone.com/music/features/joan-jett-built-to-rock-20150424).

Fruhstuck, Sabine. 2003. *Colonizing Sex: Sexology and Social Control in Modern Japan.* Berkeley: University of California Press.

Fung, Richard. 1991. "Looking for My Penis: The Eroticized Asian in Gay Video Porn." Pp. 145–68 in *How Do I Look? Queer Film & Video,* edited by Bad Object-Choices. Seattle, WA: Bay Press.

Fyson, Rachel, and Louise Townson. 2015. "Promoting Sexualities and Protecting from Abuse." Pp. 163–72 in *Sexuality and Relationships in the Lives of People with Intellectual Disabilities,* edited by Rohhss Chapman, Sue Ledger, and Louis Townson, with Daniel Docherty. London, England: Jessica Kingsley Publishers.

Gagnon, John H. and William Simon. 1973. *Sexual Conduct: The Social Sources of Human Sexuality.* Newark, NJ: Aldine.

Gaillard, Eric. 2016. "FBI's New Approach to Crack Down on Super Bowl Sex Trafficking." *CBS News,* Jan. 12. Retrieved July 24, 2016 (http://www.cbsnews.com/news/fbi-trying-new-approach-to-crack-down-on-super-bowl-sex-trafficking/).

Gallagher, Delia and Daniel Burke. 2016. "Pope Says Christians Should Apologize to Gay People." *CNN World News,* June 27. Retrieved July 28, 2016 (http://www.cnn.com/2016/06/26/world/pope-apologize-gays/).

Gamson, Joshua. 1998. *Freaks Talk Back: Tabloid Talk Shows and Sexual Nonconformity.* Chicago, IL: The University of Chicago Press.

Garfinkle, Harold. 1967. *Studies in Ethnomethodology.* Englewood Cliffs, NJ: Prentice Hall.

Garner, Abigail. 2005. *Families Like Mine: Children of Gay Parents Tell it Like it Is.* New York: Perennial Currents.

Gaskin, Ina May. 2002. *Spiritual Midwifery.* Summertown, TN: Book Publishing Company.

Gates, G. J., M. Badgett, J. E. Macomber, and K. Chambers. 2007. *Adoption and Foster Care by Gay and Lesbian Parents in the United States.* Los Angeles, CA: The Williams Institute.

Gates, Gary. 2013. "LGBT Parenting in the United States." Los Angeles, CA: The Williams Institute. Retrieved July 31, 2016. (http://williamsinstitute.law.ucla.edu/wp-content/uploads/LGBT-Parenting.pdf).

Gates, Gary. 2015. "Marriage and Family: LGBT Individuals and Same Sex Couples." *The Future of the Children* 25(2):67–87.

Gates, Gary J. and Frank Newport. 2012. "Special Report: 3.4% of U.S. Adults Identify as LGBT: Inaugural Gallup Findings Based on More than 120,000 Interviews." *Gallup Politics.* Retrieved August 10, 2015 (http://www.gallup.com/poll/158066/special-report-adults-identify-lgbt.aspx).

Gavey, Nicole. 2014. "'I Wasn't Raped, but . . .': Revisiting Definitional Problems in Sexual Victimization." Pp. 583–92 in *Sex Matters: the Sexuality and Society Reader,* 4th ed., edited by Mindy Stombler, Dawn M. Baunach, Wendy Simonds, Elroi J. Windsor, and Elisabeth O. Burgess. New York: W.W. Norton & Company.

"Gay Marriage Around the World." 2013. Pew Research Center. Retrieved June 10, 2016 (http://www.pewforum.org/2015/06/26/gay-marriage-around-the-world-2013/#ireland).

Gebhard, Paul J. 1977. "Designated Discussion." In *Ethical Issues in Sex Therapy and Research,* edited by William H. Masters, Virginia E. Johnson, and Robert C. Kolodny. Boston: Little, Brown.

General Assembly of North Carolina. 2016. *Public Facilities Privacy & Security Act.* DRH40005-TC-1B, Second Extra Session. Retrieved July 28, 2016 (http://www.ncleg.net/

Sessions/2015E2/Bills/House/PDF/H2v0.pdf).

George, Lianne. 2007. "Why Are We Dressing our Daughters Like This? Eight-year-olds in Fishnets, Padded 'Bralettes' and Thong Panties: Welcome to the Junior Miss Version of Raunch Culture." *Macleans Magazine* Jan 1:37–40.

Gerbner, George. 1978. "The Dynamics of Cultural Resistance." Pp 46–50 in *Hearth and Home Images of Women in the Mass Media*, edited by Gaye Tuchman, Arlene Kaplan Daniels, and James Benet. New York: Oxford University Press.

Geronimus, A. T. 1991. "Teenage Childbearing and Social and Reproductive Disadvantage: The Evolution of Complex Questions and the Demise of Simple Answers." *Family Relations* 40(4):463–71.

Gershick, Thomas J. 2011. "The Body, Disability, and Sexuality." Pp. 75–83 in *Introducing the New Sexuality Studies,* 2nd ed., edited by Steven Seidman, Nancy Fischer, and Chet Meeks. New York: Routledge.

Getlin, Josh. 2005. "Pregnant and Unwed: Teacher Fights Church." *The Los Angeles Times,* November 26. Retrieved April 20, 2016 (http://articles.latimes.com/2005/nov/26/nation/na-teacher26).

Gettleman, Jeffrey. 2010. "Americans' Role Seen in Uganda Anti-Gay Push." *New York Times,* January 3. Retrieved May 10, 2016 (http://www.nytimes.com/2010/01/04/world/africa/04uganda.html?_r=0).

Ghaziani, Amin. 2008. *The Dividends of Dissent: How Conflict and Culture Work in Lesbian and Gay Marches on Washington.*

Chicago, IL: The University of Chicago Press.

Ghaziani, Amin. 2014. *There Goes the Gayborhood?* Princeton, NJ: Princeton University Press.

Gill, Michael. 2015. *Already Doing It: Intellectual Disability and Sexual Agency.* Minneapolis, MN: University of Minnesota Press.

Gillen, M. M., and E. S. Lefkowitz, and C. L. Shearer. 2006. "Does Body Image Play a Role in Risky Sexual Behavior and Attitudes?" *Journal of Youth and Adolescence* 35:243–55.

Gilreath, Shannon. 2011. *The End of Straight Supremacy.* New York: Cambridge University Press.

Gimbutas, Maria. 2001. *The Language of the Goddess.* New York: Thames & Hudson.

Giscombe, Cheryl L. and Marci Lobel. 2005. "Explaining Disproportionately High Rates of Adverse Birth Outcomes Among African Americans: The Impact of Stress, Racism, and Related Factors in Pregnancy." *Psychological Bulletin* 131(5):662–83.

Giuffre, Patti A. 1997. *Labeling Sexual Harassment in Hospitals: A Case Study of Doctors and Nurses.* Presented at the Sociologists Against Sexual Harassment Annual Meeting, Toronto.

Giuffre, Patti A., Kirsten Dellinger, and Christine L. Williams. 2008. "'No Retribution for Being Gay?' Inequality in Gay-Friendly Workplaces." *Sociological Spectrum* 28:254–77.

GLAAD. 2012. "Where We Are on T.V. Overview." Retrieved July 26, 2016 (http://www.glaad.org/publications/whereweareontv11/overview).

Glasser, M., I. Kolvin, D. Campbell, A. Glasser, I. Leitch, and S. Farrelly. 2001. "Cycle of Child Sexual Abuse: Links Between Being a Victim and Becoming a Perpetrator." *The British Journal of Psychiatry* 179(6):482–94. Retrieved July 18, 2016 (http://bjp.rcpsych.org/content/179/6/482).

Glick, P. and Fiske, S.T. 2001. "An Ambivalent Alliance: Hostile and Benevolent Sexism as Complementary Justifications for Gender Inequality." *American Psychologist* 56:109–18.

Glicksman, Eve. 2013. "Transgender Today." *Monitor on Psychology* 44(4). Retrieved July 24, 2016 (http://www.apa.org/monitor/2013/04/transgender.aspx).

GLSEN (Gay, Lesbian, Straight Education Network). 2014. Retrieved July 31, 2016. (http://www.glsen.org/).

Goffman, Erving. 1963. *Stigma: Notes on the Management of Spoiled Identity.* New York: Simon and Schuster.

Gold, Rachel Benson and Peters D. Willson. 1981. "Depo-Provera: New Developments in a Decade Old Controversy." *Family Planning Perspectives* 13(1):35–39.

Goldin, Claudia and Lawrence F. Katz. 2002. "The Power of the Pill: Oral Contraceptives and Women's Career and Marriage Decisions." *Journal of Political Economy,* 110(4):730–70.

Gonzalez, M. Alfredo. 2007. "Latinos on Da Down Low: The Limitations of Sexual Identity in Public Health." *Latino Studies* 5 (1): 25–52.

Goodstein, Laurie. 2016. "Sex Abuse and the Catholic Church: Why Is It Still a Story?" *The New*

York Times, April 20. Retrieved online July 18, 2016 (http://www.nytimes.com/2016/04/20/insider/sex-abuse-and-the-catholic-church-why-is-it-still-a-story.html).

Grant, Jaime, Lisa Mottet, Justin Tanis, Jack Harrison, Jody Herman, and Mara Keisling. 2011. "Injustice at Every Turn: A Report of the National Transgender Discrimination Survey." Washington, DC: National Center for Transgender Equality and National Gay and Lesbian Task Force.

Grant, Melissa Gira. 2014. *Playing the Whore: The Work of Sex Work*. London, England: Verso Books.

Green, Emma. 2015. "The Real Christian Debate on Transgender Identity." *The Atlantic*, June 4. Retrieved December 1, 2016 (http://www.theatlantic.com/politics/archive/2015/06/the-christian-debate-on-transgender-identity/394796/).

Greenberg, K. 2012. "Still Hidden in the Closet: Trans Women and Domestic Violence." *Berkeley Journal of Gender, Law, & Justice* 28:198–251.

Greene, K. and S. Faulkner. 2005. "Gender, Belief in the Sexual Double-Standard, and Sexual Talk in Heterosexual Dating Relationships." *Sex Roles: A Journal of Research* 53:239–51.

Greenfield, Rebecca. 2012. "Runner Caster Semenya Looks a Lot More Feminine than She Did in 2009." *The Wire,* June 12. Retrieved Feb. 8, 2016 (http://www.thewire.com/entertainment/2012/06/runner-caster-semenya-looks-lot-more-feminine-she-did-2009/53446/).

Gregory, Alice. 2015. "Has the Fashion Industry Reached a

Transgender Turning Point?" *Vogue Magazine*, April 21. Retrieved July 26, 2016 (http://www.vogue.com/13253741/andreja-pejic-transgender-model/).

Greil, Arthur L., Kathleen Slauson-Blevins, and Julia McQuillan. 2010. "The Experience of Infertility: A Review of Recent Literature." *Sociology of Health and Illness* 32(1):140–62.

Griffin, P. 1992. "From Hiding Out to Coming Out: Empowering Lesbian and Gay Educators." Pp. 167–96 in *Coming Out of the Classroom Closet*, edited by K. M. Harbeck. Binghamton, NY: Harrington Park Press.

Griffin, P. 2014. "Overcoming Sexism and Homophobia in Women's Sports: Two Steps Forward and One Step Back." Pp. 265–74 in *Routledge Handbook of Sport, Gender, and Sexuality*, edited by Jennifer Hargreaves and Eric Anderson. New York: Routledge.

Griffin, Pat. 1998. *Strong Women, Deep Closets: Lesbians and Homophobia in Sport*. Champaign, IL: Human Kinetics.

Griffin, Susan. 1979. *Rape, The Power of Consciousness*. New York: Harper & Row.

Griggs, Brandon. 2015. "America's Transgender Moment." *CNN News*, June 1. Retrieved July 26, 2016 (http://www.cnn.com/2015/04/23/living/transgender-moment-jenner-feat/).

Grimm, Andy. 2015. "Lake Charles Transgender Man Sues Tower Loan after Boss Insists He Dress as a Woman." *The Times Picayune,* April 13. Retrieved Jan. 26, 2016 (http://www.nola.com/crime/index.ssf/2015/04/lake_charles_transgender_man_s.html).

Grinberg, Emanuella. 2015. "Online Survey Finds 8 in 10

Adults Have Engaged in Sexting." CNN News, August 8. Retrieved July 9, 2016 (http://www.cnn.com/2015/08/08/health/sexting-adults-online-survey-feat/).

Grossman, A. H. and A. R. D'Augelli. 2007. "Transgender Youth and Life-threatening Behaviors." *Suicide & Life Threatening Behavior* 37(5):527–537. doi:10.1521/suli.2007.37.5.527.

"Groundbreaking High School for LGBT Students to Open." 2016. *Yahoo,* January 5. Retrieved April 2, 2016. (https://www.yahoo.com/parenting/groundbreaking-high-school-for-lgbt-students-to-171414115.html).

Grove, Joshua. 2011. "Christianity and the Regulation of Sexuality in the United States." Pp. 415–20 in *Introducing the New Sexuality Studies,* 2nd ed., edited by Steven Seidman, Nancy Fischer, and Chet Meeks. New York: Routledge.

Guadalupe-Diaz, Xavier. 2016. "Disclosure of Same-Sex Intimate Partner Violence to Police among Lesbians, Gays, and Bisexuals." *Social Currents* 3(2):160–71.

Gullette, Margaret Morganroth. 2011. *Agewise: Fighting the New Ageism in America*. Chicago, IL: The University of Chicago Press.

Gunn Allen, Paula. 2009. "Where I Come from Is Like This." Pp. 18–21 in *Feminist Frontiers*, 8th ed., edited by Verta Taylor, Nancy Whittier, and Leila Rupp. New York: McGraw Hill.

Gurr, Ted R. 1970. *Why Men Rebel*. Princeton, NJ: Princeton University Press.

Gutierrez, Nova. 2013. "Visions of Community for GLBT Youth: Resisting Fragmentation, Living Whole: Four Female Transgender Students of Color Speak about School." Pp. 359–64 in *Sex,*

Gender, and Sexuality: The New Basics, 2nd ed., edited by Abby L. Ferber, Kimberly Holcomb, and Tre Wentling. New York: Oxford University Press.

Guttmacher Institute. 2016. "Unintended Pregnancy in the United States." New York: Guttmacher Institute. Retrieved on July 21, 2016 (https://www .guttmacher.org/fact-sheet/ unintended-pregnancy-united-states).

Guzder, Deena. 2011. "Thailand: The World's Sex Tourism Capital." *The Huffington Post,* May 25. Retrieved July 25, 2016 (http:// www.huffingtonpost.com/ wires/2009/08/14/thailand-the-worlds-sex-t_ws_259562.html).

Haffner, D. and J. Wagoner. 1999. "Vast Majority of Americans Support Sexuality Education." *SIECUS Report* 27(6):22–23.

Hagedorn, J. 1994. "Asian American Women in Film: No Joy, No Luck." *Ms.* January/February: 74–79.

Hagerty, Barbara Bradley. 2010. "Nun Excommunicated for Allowing Abortion." *National Public Radio,* May 19. Retrieved July 20, 2016 (http://www.npr .org/templates/story/story.php? storyId=126985072).

Hald, Gert Martin, Neil N. Malamuth, and Theis Lange. 2013. "Pornography and Sexist Attitudes Among Heterosexuals." *Journal of Communication* 63(4):638–60.

Hallowell, Billy. 2016. "'Who Does President Barack Obama Think He Is?' Evangelist Franklin Graham Issues Blistering Reaction to Transgender Bathroom Directive." *The Blaze,* May 16. Retrieved July 28, 2016 (http:// www.theblaze.com/stories/2016/ 05/16/who-does-president-barack-obama-think-he-is-evangelist-franklin-graham-issues-blistering-reaction-to-transgender-bathroom-directive/).

Halperin-Felsher, B., J. Cornell, R. Kropp, and J. Tschann. 2006. "Oral versus Vaginal Sex among Adolescents: Perceptions, Attitudes, and Behaviors." *Pediatrics* 44(115):845–51;1023–24.

Hamer, Dean, S. Hu, V.L. Magnuson, N. Hu, A.M. Pattatucci. 1993. "A Link Between DNA Markers on the X Chromosome and Male Sexual Orientation." *Science* 261(5119):321–7.

Hamilton Brady E., Joyce A. Martin, Michelle J.K. Osterman, Sally C. Curtin, and T.J. Mathews. 2015. "Births: Final Data for 2014." *National Vital Statistics Report* 64(12):1–64.

Han, C. Winter. 2015. *Geisha of a Different Kind: Race and Sexuality in Gaysian America.* New York: New York University Press.

Harding, Kate. 2015. *Asking For It: The Alarming Rise of Rape Culture and What We Can Do About It.* Boston: Perseus Books.

Hart, Patrick-Kylo R. 2000. "Representing Gay Men on American Television." *The Journal of Men's Studies,* 9(1):59–79.

Hartinger, Jeffrey. 2011. "Triumphs and Setbacks of Gay-Straight Alliances." *The Advocate,* August 1, 2011. Retrieved March 21, 2016 (http://www .advocate.com/society/education/ 2011/08/01/triumphs-and-setbacks-gay-straight-alliances-1).

Hartsock, Nancy C. 1987. "The Feminist Standpoint: Developing the Ground for a Specifically Feminist Historical Materialism." Pp. 157–180 in *Feminism & Methodology.* Edited by Sandra Harding. Bloomington: Indiana University Press.

Hatton, Erin and Mary Nell Trautner. 2011. "Equal Opportunity Objectification? The Sexualization of Men and Women on the Cover of Rolling Stone." *Sexuality & Culture* 15:256–78.

Haworth, Abigail. 2014. "Virginity for Sale: Inside Cambodia's Shocking Trade." *The Guardian,* July 6. Retrieved July 25, 2016 (https://www.theguardian.com/ society/2014/jul/06/virginity-for-sale-cambodia-sex-trade).

Hearn, Jeff and Wendy Parkin. 1987. *"Sex at Work": The Power and Paradox of Organizational Sexuality.* New York: St. Martin's Press.

Heidt, Jennifer M., Brian P. Marx, and Sari D. Gold. 2005. "Sexual Revictimization Among Sexual Minorities: A Preliminary Study." *Journal of Traumatic Stress* 18(5):533–40.

Heimer, Carol A. 2007. "Old Inequalities, New Disease: HIV/ AIDS in Sub-Saharan Africa." *Annual Review of Sociology* 33:551–77.

Heineman, Elizabeth D. 2005. "Sexuality and Nazism: The Doubly Unspeakable?" Pp. 23–66 in *Sexuality and German Fascism,* edited by Dagmar Herzog. New York: Berghahn Books.

Heinemann, Katja and Naomi Schegloff. n.d. "The Graying of AIDS: Stories from An Aging Epidemic." *LGBT Aging Center.* Retrieved July 23, 2016 (http://www .lgbtagingcenter.org/resources/pdfs/ GrayingofAIDS_032011.pdf).

Heinemann, Klaas, Farid Saad, Martin Wiesemes, Steven White, and Lothar Heinemann. 2005. "Attitudes Towards Male Fertility

Control: Results of a Multinational Survey on Four Continents." *Human Reproduction* 20(2): 549–56.

Heiner, Robert. 2015. *Social Problems: An Introduction to Critical Constructionism,* 5th Edition. New York: Oxford University Press.

Hekma, G. 1998. "'As Long as They Don't Make an Issue of it . . . ' Gay Men and Lesbians in Organized Sports in the Netherlands." *Journal of Homosexuality* 35(1):1–23.

Henig, Robin Marantz. 2001. "Consensual Homosexual Activity in Male Prisons." *Corrections Compendium* 26(1):1–4.

Henig, Robin Marantz. 2014. "Transgender Men Who Become Pregnant Face Social, Health Challenges." National Public Radio, November 7. Retrieved July 14, 2016 (http://www.npr.org/sections/health-shots/2014/11/07/362269036/transgender-men-who-become-pregnant-face-health-challenges).

Hensley, Christopher, Cindy Struckman-Johnson, and Helen M. Eigenberg. 2000."Introduction: The History of Prison Sex Research." *The Prison Journal* 80(4):360–67.

Hensley, Christopher, R. Tewksbury, and M. Koscheski. 2001. "Masturbation Uncovered: Autoeroticism in a Female Prison." *The Prison Journal* 81:491–501.

Henson, Melissa. 2011. "'Toddlers and Tiaras' and Sexualizing 3-year-olds." *CNN*, Sept. 13. Retrieved [date] (http://www.cnn.com/2011/09/12/opinion/henson-toddlers-tiaras/)

Hequembourg, Amy. 2014. "Victimization among Special Populations: Sexual Minorities/

LGBTs." NIJ Technical Working Group on Violent Victimization Research. Retrieved Feb. 19, 2016 (http://www.nij.gov/topics/victims-victimization/Documents/violent-victimization-twg-2015-hequembourg.pdf).

Herberle, R.J. and V. Grace. 2009. *Theorizing Sexual Violence.* New York: Routledge.

Herman, Didi. 2005. "'I'm Gay': Declarations, Desire and Coming Out on Prime-Time Television." *Sexualities* 8(1): 7–29.

Hernández-Truyol, Berta E. and Jane E. Larson. 2006. "Sexual Labor and Human Rights." *Columbia Human Rights Law Review*, 37:391–445. Retrieved October 13, 2016. (http://scholarship.law.ufl.edu/facultypub/193).

Herold, Edward, Rafael Garcia, and Tony DeMoya. 2001. "Female Tourists and Beach Boys: Romance or Sex Tourism?" *Annals of Tourism Research* 28(4):978–97.

Herzog, Dagmar. 2005. "Hubris and Hypocrisy, Incitement and Disavowal: Sexuality and German Fascism." Pp. 1–21 in *Sexuality and German Fascism,* edited by Dagmar Herzog. New York: Berghahn Books.

Higgins, Daryl. 2010. "Sexuality, Human Rights, and Safety for People with Disabilities: The Challenge of Intersecting Identities." *Sexual and Relationship Therapy* 25(3):245–57.

Hildebrand, Meagen M. and Cynthia Najdowski. 2015. "The Potential Impact of Rape Culture on Juror Decision Making: Implication for Wrongful Acquittals in Sexual Assault Trials." *Albany Law Review* 78(3):1059–86.

Hill, R.J. 2009. "Incorporating Queers: Blowback, Backlash, and

Other Forms of Resistance to Workplace Diversity Initiatives that Support Sexual Minorities." *Advances in Developing Human Resources* 11(1):37–53.

"HIV/AIDS Fact Sheet." 2016. (n.a.). *World Health Organization* Retrieved July 19, 2016. (http://www.who.int/mediacentre/factsheets/fs360/en/).

"HIV Among People Aged 50 and Over," 2016. Centers for Disease Control and Prevention. Retrieved July 31, 2016. (http://www.cdc.gov/hiv/group/age/olderamericans/index.html).

Ho, P. S. Y. 2006. "The (Charmed) Circle Game: Reflections on Sexual Hierarchy through Multiple Sexual Relationships." *Sexualities* 9(5):547–64.

Hoffman, Jan. 2011. "A Girl's Nude Photo, and Altered Lives." *The New York Times*, March 26. Retrieved July 9, 2016 (http://www.nytimes.com/2011/03/27/us/27sexting.html).

Hoffman, Saul D. and Rebecca A. Maynard. 2008. "The Study, the Context, and the Findings in Brief." Pp. 1–24 in *Kids Having Kids: Economic Costs and Social Consequences of Teen Pregnancy,* edited by Saul D. Hoffman and Rebecca A. Maynard. Washington, DC: Urban Institute Press.

Hogshead-Makar, Nancy and Andrew Zimbalist. 2007. "Introduction." Pp. 1–8 in *Equal Play: Title IX and Social Change,* edited by Nancy Hogshead-Makar and Andrew Zimbalist. Philadelphia: Temple University Press.

hooks, bell. 1992. *Black Looks: Race and Representation.* Boston: South End Press.

hooks, bell. 2014. "Selling Hot Pussy: Representations of Black

Female Sexuality in the Cultural Marketplace." Pp. 61–77 in *Black Looks: Race and Representation.* New York: Routledge.

Howland, C. and D. Rintala. 2001. "Dating Behaviors of Women with Physical Disabilities." *Sexuality and Disability* 19:41–70.

Hubbard, Jim and Sarah Schulman. 2012. *United In Anger: A History of ACT UP.* DVD. New York.

Hudson, David. 2014. "President Obama Signs a New Executive Order to Protect LGBT Workers." Whitehouse.gov, July 21. Retrieved September 30, 2016. https://www .whitehouse.gov/blog/2014/07/21/ president-obama-signs-new- executive-order-protect-lgbt- workers

Hudson, James, Eva Hiripi, Harrison G. Pope, Jr., and Ronald C. Kessler. 2007. "The Prevalence and Correlates of Eating Disorders in the National Comorbidity Survey Replication." *Biol Psychiatry* 61(3):348–58.

Hughes, Donna M., Katherine Y. Chon, and Derek P. Ellerman. 2007. "Modern-Day Comfort Women: The US Military, Transnational Crime, and the Trafficking of Women." *Violence against Women* 13(9):901–22.

Hulin, C. L., Fitzgerald, L. F., and F. Drasgow. 1996. "Organizational Influences on Sexual Harassment." Pp. 127–50 in *Sexual Harassment in the Workplace: Perspectives, Frontiers, and Response Strategies,* edited by Margaret S. Stockdale. Thousand Oaks, CA: Sage.

Humphrey, Mary Ann. 1990. *My Country, My Right to Serve: Experiences of Gay Men and Women in the Military, World War II to the Present.* New York: HarperCollins Publishers.

Humphreys, Laud. 1970. *Tearoom Trade: A Study of Homosexual Encounters in Public Places.* London, England: Gerald Duckworth and Company.

Hunt, Ronald. 1999. *Historical Dictionary of the Gay Liberation Movement: Gay Men and the Quest for Social Justice.* Lanham, MD: Scarecrow Press.

Hunter, James Davison. 1991. *Culture Wars: The Struggle to Define America.* New York: Basic Books.

Hunter, Mic. 2007. *Honor Betrayed: Sexual Abuse in America's Military.* Fort Lee, NJ: Barricade.

Hunter, S.K. 1994. "Prostitution is Cruelty and Abuse to Women and Children." *Michigan Journal of Gender and Law* 1(1):1–14.

Hurst, Charles E. 2004. *Social Inequality: Forms, Causes, and Consequences,* 5th ed. Boston: Pearson.

Ilies, R., N. Hauserman, S. Schwochau, and J. Stibal. 2003. "Reported Incidence Rates of Work-Related Sexual Harassment in the United States: Using Meta-Analysis to Explain Reported Rate Disparities." *Personnel Psychology* 56:607–31.

Imperato-McGinley J., L. Guerrero, T. Gautier, and R.E. Peterson. 1974. "Steroid 5alpha-Reductase Deficiency in Man: An Inherited Form of Male Pseudohermaphroditism." *Science* 186(4170):1213–5.

International Labor Organization. 2016. "Forced Labor, Human Trafficking and Slavery." Retrieved July 25, 2016 (http://www.ilo.org/ global/topics/forced-labour/lang-- en/index.htm).

Irigaray, Luce. [1977 in French] 1985. *This Sex Which Is Not*

One. Ithaca, New York: Cornell University Press.

Irvine, Janice M. 2015. "The Other Sex Work: Stigma in Sexuality Research." *Social Currents* 2(2):116–25.

Israel, Josh. 2014. "Texas Restaurant Bans Gay Couple Because 'We Do Not Like Fags.'" *The Nation of Change,* May 29. Retrieved May 15, 2015 (http:// www.nationofchange.org/ texas-restaurant-bans-gay-couple- because-we-do-not-f).

Jackson, Stevi, and Sue Scott. 2015. "Conceptualizing Sexuality." Pp. 9–21 in *Sexualities: Identities, Behaviors, and Society,* 2nd ed., edited by Michael Kimmel and The Stony Brook Sexualities Research Group. New York: Oxford University Press.

Jackson, Sue and Tamsyn Gilbertson. 2009. "'Hot Lesbians': Young People's Talk about Representations of Lesbianism." *Sexualities* 12(2):199–224.

Jackson, Sue and Tina Vares. 2015. "'Perfect Skin', 'Pretty Skinny': Girls' Embodied Identities and Post-feminist Popular Culture." *Journal of Gender Studies* 24(3):347–60.

Jacobs, James B. 2009. "Foreword." Pp. ix–x in *The Myth of Prison Rape: Sexual Culture in American Prisons,* edited by Mark S. Fleisher and Jessie L. Krienert. Lanham, MD: Rowman and Littlefield.

Jacobs, Sue-Ellen, Wesley Thomas, and Sabine Lang. 1997. *Two-Spirit People: Native American Gender Identity, Sexuality, and Spirituality.* Urbana: University of Illinois Press.

Jaimes, M. A. and T. Halsey. 1992. "American Indian Women: At the Center of Indigenous Resistance in North America." Pp. 311–44 in *The State of Native America:*

Genocide, Colonization, and Resistance, edited by M. S. Jaimes. Boston: South End Press.

Jain, Tarun and Mark D. Hornstein. 2005. "Disparities in Access to Infertility Services in a State with Mandated Insurance Coverage." *Fertility and Sterility* 84(1):221–23.

Janssen, D. 2007. "First Stirrings: Cultural Notes on Orgasm, Ejaculation, and Wet Dreams." *Journal of Sex Research* 44:122–34.

Jenkins, J. Craig and Craig M. Eckert. 1986. "Channeling Black Insurgency: Elite Patronage and Professional Social Movement Organizations in the Development of the Black Movement." *American Sociological Review* 51(6):812–29.

Jenks, R. J. 1998. "Swinging: A Review of the Literature." *Archives of Sexual Behavior* 27:507–21.

Jhally, Sut. 1984. "The Spectacle of Accumulation: Material and Cultural Factors in the Evolution of the Sports/Media Complex." *The Insurgent Sociologist* 12(3):41–57.

Jhally, Sut. 1990. *The Codes of Advertising: Fetishism and the Political Economy of Meaning.* New York: Routledge.

Jhally, Sut. 1995. *DREAMWORLDS 3 (Unabridged) Desire, Sex & Power in Music Video.* Written, Narrated, and Edited by Sut Jhally.

Jjuuko, A. and F. Tumwesige. 2013."The Implications of the Anti-Homosexuality Bill 2009 on Uganda's Legal System." IDS Evidence Report 44. United Kingdom: Institute of Development Studies.

Johnson, M.P. 1995. "Patriarchal Terrorism and Common Couple Violence: Two Forms of Violence

Against Women." *Journal of Marriage and Family* 57:283–94.

Jones, C. Sarah. 2006. "The Extent and Effect of Sex Tourism and Sexual Exploitation of Children on the Kenyan Coast." United Nations Children's Fund (UNICEF), 1418.

Jones, Jo, William Mosher, and Kimberly Daniels. 2012. *Current Contraceptive Use in the United States, 2006–2010, and Changes in Patterns of Use since 1995.* National Health Statistics Report, 60. U.S. Department of Health and Human Services.

Jung, C. G. 1947. *On the Nature of the Psyche.* London, England: Ark Paperbacks.

Junior, Nyasha. 2014. "He. She. Zhe." *Inside Higher Ed,* September 19. Retrieved October 20, 2015. (https://www.insidehighered.com/advice/2014/09/19/simple-classroom-change-make-trans-students-feel-home-essay).

Kakissis, Joanna. 2011. "Birth and Death: Afghanistan's Struggles with Maternal Mortality." *Time Magazine,* October 11. Retrieved July 16, 2016 (http://content.time.com/time/world/article/0,8599,2094031,00.html).

Kane, Paul and Nia-Malika Henderson. 2012. "Todd Akin Rape Comments Prompt GOP to Pull Campaign Funding, Calls to Exit Race." *Washington Post,* August 20. Retrieved July 12, 2016 (https://www.washingtonpost.com/politics/with-todd-akins-rape-comments-abortion-is-back-in-the-campaign-spotlight/2012/08/20/c497bae4-eac7-11e1-a80b-9f898562d010_story.html).

Kanter, Rosabeth Moss. 1977. *Men and Women of the Corporation.* New York: Basic Books.

Kaplan, Laura. 1997. *The Story of Jane: The Legendary Underground Feminist Abortion Service.* Chicago: University of Chicago Press.

Kara, Siddharth. 2009. *Sex Trafficking: Inside the Business of Modern Slavery.* New York: Columbia University Press.

Katz, Jackson. 2006. *The Macho Paradox: Why Some Men Hurt Women and How All Men Can Help.* Naperville, Illinois, Sourcebooks.

Katz, Jonathan Ned. 1995. *The Invention of Heterosexuality.* Chicago, IL: The University of Chicago Press.

Keenan, Sandy. 2015. "Affirmative Consent: Are Students Really Asking?" *The New York Times,* July 28. Retrieved July 14, 2016 (http://www.nytimes.com/2015/08/02/education/edlife/affirmative-consent-are-students-really-asking.html).

Kellaway, Mitch. 2015. "Facebook Now Allows Users to Define Custom Gender." *Advocate,* February 27. Retrieved July 24, 2016 (http://www.advocate.com/politics/transgender/2015/02/27/facebook-now-allows-users-define-custom-gender).

Kelley, Elizabeth. 2005. "The Guevedoces: Gender Metamorphosis at Work." *Issues Berkeley Medical Journal at UC Berkeley* 23(1). Retrieved online July 24, 2016 (https://www.ocf.berkeley.edu/~issues/articles/13.1_Kelley_E_The_Guevedoces.html).

Kelly, Michael J. 2003. "Reducing the Vulnerability of Africa's Children to HIV/AIDS." Pp. 59–84 in *The Children of Africa Confront*

AIDS, edited by Arvind Singhal and W. Stephen Howard. Athens: Ohio University Press.

Kempadoo, Kamala. 2013. "Women of Color and the Global Sex Trade." Pp. 313–23 in *Sex, Gender, and Sexuality,* 2nd ed., edited by Abby L. Ferber, Kimberly Holcomb, and Tre Wentling. New York: Oxford University Press.

Kendall, Todd D. 2006. "Pornography, Rape and the Internet." The John E. Walker Department of Economics at Clemson University. Retrieved June 20, 2016 (http://idei.fr/sites/default/files/medias/doc/conf/sic/papers_2007/kendall.pdf).

Kerrigan, Deanna, Andrea Wirtz, Stefan Baral, Michele Decker, Laura Murray, Tonia Poteat, Carel Pretorius, Susan Sherman, Mike Sweat, Iris Semini, N'Della N'Jie, Anderson Stanciole, Jenny Butler, Sutayut Osornprasop, Robert Oelrichs, and Chris Beyrer. 2013. "The Global HIV Epidemics among Sex Workers." Washington DC: The World Bank.

Kessler, Suzanne and Wendy McKenna. 1978. *Gender: An Ethnomethodological Approach.* Chicago, IL: Chicago University Press.

Khaleeli, Homa. 2015. "One Billion Rising: How can Public Dancing End Violence against Women?" *The Guardian,* February 13. Retrieved July 20, 2016 (https://www.theguardian.com/lifeandstyle/womens-blog/2015/feb/13/one-billion-rising-public-dancing-violence-women-eve-ensler).

Khalid, Asma. 2011. "Lifting the Veil: Muslim Women Explain Their Choice." *National Public Radio.* Retrieved July 28, 2016 (http://www.npr.org/2011/04/21/135523680/

lifting-the-veil-muslim-women-explain-their-choice).

Khan, Fahd, Saheel Mukhtar, Ian K. Dickinson, and Seshadri Sriprasad. 2013. "The Story of the Condom." *Indian Journal of Urology* 29(1):12–15.

Kilbourne, Jean. 1999. *Deadly Persuasion: Why Women and Girls Must Fight the Deadly Power of Advertising.* New York: Simon & Schuster.

Kilpatrick, Dean G., Heidi S. Resnick, Kenneth J. Ruggiero, Lauren M. Conoscenti, and Jenna McCauley. 2007. "Drug-facilitated, Incapacitated, and Forcible Rape: A National Study." Medical University of South Carolina: U.S. Department of Justice. Retrieved July 14, 2016 (https://www.ncjrs.gov/pdffiles1/nij/grants/219181.pdf).

Kim, Daniel and Adrianna Saada. 2013. "The Social Determinants of Infant Mortality and Birth Outcomes in Western Developed Nations: A Cross-Country Systematic Review." *International Journal of Environmental Research and Public Health* 10(6):2296–335.

Kim, Janna L. and L. Monique Ward. 2004. "Pleasure Reading: Associations Between Young Women's Sexual Attitudes And Their Reading Of Contemporary Women's Magazines." *Psychology of Women Quarterly* 28(1):48–58.

Kimmel, D. 1980. "Life History Interviews of Aging Gay Men." *International Journal of Aging and Human Development* 10:239–48.

Kimmel, M. 1994. "Masculinity as Homophobia: Fear, Shame and Silence in the Construction of Gender Identity." Pp. 119–41 in *Theorizing Masculinities,* edited by H. Brod and M. Kaufman. Newbury Park, CA: Sage.

Kimmel, Michael and The Stony Brook Sexualities Research Group. 2015. *Sexualities: Identities, Behaviors, and Society,* 2nd Ed. New York: Oxford University Press.

Kimport, Katrina. 2014. *Queering Marriage: Challenging Family Formation in the United States.* New Brunswick, NJ: Rutgers University Press.

King, J. L. 2004. *On the Down Low: A Journey into the Lives of "Straight" Black Men Who Sleep with Men.* New York: Harmony.

Kinsey, Alfred C., Wardell B. Pomeroy, and Clyde E. Martin. 1948. *Sexual Behavior in the Human Male.* Philadelphia: W. B. Saunders Co.

Kinsey, Alfred C., Wardell B. Pomeroy, Clyde E. Martin, and Paul H. Gebhard. 1953. *Sexual Behavior in the Human Female.* Bloomington: Indiana University Press.

Kirkham, G. 1971. "Homosexuality in Prison." Pp. 325–44 in *Studies in the Sociology of Sex,* edited by J. Henslin. New York: Appleton-Century-Crofts.

Kitzinger, Jenny. 2004. Framing Abuse: Media Influence and Public Understanding of Sexual Violence against Children. London, England: Pluto Press.

Klaassen, Marlene J. E. and Jochen Peter. 2015. "Gender (In)equality in Internet Pornography: A Content Analysis of Popular Pornographic Internet Videos." *Journal of Sex Research* 52(7): 721–35.

Kline, Wendy. 2010. *Bodies of Knowledge: Sexuality, Reproduction, and Women's Health in the Second Wave.* Chicago: The University of Chicago Press.

Kohlberg, Lawrence. 1966. "A Cognitive-Developmental Analysis of Children's Sex-role Concepts and Attitudes." In The Development of Sex Differences. E. E. Maccody, editor. Stanford, CA: Stanford University Press.

Kohner, Claire-Renee. 2015. "Pride Month Started With Transgender People, and Transgender Progress Needs to Be a Focus of the Events." Bustle, June 17. Retrieved July 24, 2016 (http://www.bustle.com/articles/87988-pride-month-started-with-transgender-people-and-transgender-progress-needs-to-be-a-focus-of-the).

Kon, Igor S. 1995. The Sexual Revolution in Russia: From the Age of the Czars to Today. New York: The Free Press.

Kong, T. S. K. 2002. "The Seduction of the Golden Boy: The Sexual Politics of Hong Kong Gay Men." Body and Society 8(1):29–48.

Koon, David. 2015. "Ruth Coker Burns, The Cemetery Angel." The Arkansas Times, January 8. Retrieved July 22, 2016. (http://www.arktimes.com/arkansas/ruth-coker-burks-the-cemetery-angel/Content?oid=3602959).

Koscheski, M. and C. Hensley. 2001. "Inmate Homosexual Behavior in a Southern Female Correctional Facility." American Journal of Criminal Justice 25:269–77.

Kosciw, Joseph G., Emily A. Gretak, Neal A. Palmer, and Madelyn J. Boesen. 2014. The 2013 National School Climate Survey: The Experiences of Lesbian, Gay, Bisexual, and Transgender Youth in Our Nation's Schools. New York: GLSEN.

Krabill, Ron. 2010. Starring Mandela and Cosby: Media and the End(s) of Apartheid. Chicago: The University of Chicago Press.

Krafft-Ebing, R. von. [1886] 1965. Psychopathia Sexualis. New York: Putnam.

Krakauer, Doug. 2015. Missoula: Rape and the Justice System in a College Town. New York: Doubleday.

Krane, V. 1997. "Homonegativism Experienced by Lesbian Collegiate Athletes." Women in Sport & Physical Activity Journal 6:141–64.

Krebs, Christopher, Christine Lindquist, Marcus Berzofsky, Bonnie Shook-Sa, and Kimberly Peterson. 2016. Campus Climate Survey Validation Study Final Technical Report. Bureau of Justice Statistics Research and Development Series, R&DP-2015:04, NCJ 249545. Washington DC: Bureau of Justice Statistics.

Krebs, Christopher P., Christine H. Lindquist, Tara D. Warner, Bonnie S. Fisher, Sandra L. Martin. 2007. The Campus Sexual Assault (CSA) Study. U.S. Department of Justice, 221153. Washington DC: National Institute of Justice.

Kumar, Bal KC, Govind Subedi Yogendra Bahadur Gurung, and Keshab Prasad Adhikari. 2001. "Investigating the Worst Forms of Child Labour No. 2, Nepal: Trafficking in Girls with Special Reference to Prostitution: A Rapid Assessment." Geneva, Switzerland: Central Department on Population Studies (CDPS), International Labour Organization, International Programme on the Elimination of Child Labour (IPEC). Retrieved July 25, 2016 (file:///C:/Users/kgrossman/Downloads/2001_ra_02_np_traff.pdf).

La Fond, J.Q. 2005. Preventing Sexual Violence: How Society Should Cope with Sex Offenders. Washington, DC: American Psychological Association.

Lal, Prerna. 2013. "How Queer Undocumented Youth Built the Immigrant Rights Movement." The Huffington Post, March 28. Retrieved February 14, 2016. http://www.huffingtonpost.com/prerna-lal/how-queer-undocumented_b_2973670.html

Langdridge, Darren. 2011. "The Time of the Sadomasochist: Hunting With(in) the 'Tribus'." Pp. 372–79 in Introducing the New Sexuality Studies, 2nd ed., edited by Steven Seidman, Nancy Fischer, and Chet Meeks. New York: Routledge.

Langdridge, Darren and T. Butt. 2004. "A Hermeneutic Phenomenological Investigation of the Construction of Sadomasochistic Identities." Sexualities 7(10):31–53.

Laqueur, Thomas W. 2004. Solitary Sex: A Cultural History of Masturbation. Brooklyn, NY: Zone Books.

Larson, Meredith. 2010. "Don't Know Much About Biology: Courts and the Rights of Non-Biological Parents in Same-Sex Partnerships." The Georgetown Journal of Gender and the Law XI:869–86.

Laumann, Edward. 2011. "Surveying Sex." Pp. 20–23 in Introducing the New Sexuality Studies, 2nd ed., edited by Steven Seidman, Nancy Fischer, and Chet Meeks. New York: Routledge.

Laumann, Edward O., John H. Gagnon, Robert T. Michael, and Stuart Michaels. 1994. The Social Organization of Sexuality: Sexual Practices in the United States.

Chicago, IL: University of Chicago Press.

Laumann, Edward, A. Paik, and R. Rosen. 1999. "Sexual Dysfunction in the United States." *Journal of the American Medical Association* 281:537–44.

Lehman, Peter. 2006. *Pornography: Film and Culture.* New Brunswick, NJ: Rutgers University Press.

Leiblum, S. and Goldmeier, D. 2008. "Persistent Genital Arousal Disorder in Women: Case Reports of Association with Antidepressant Usage." *Journal of Sex and Marital Therapy* 34:150–9.

Leidholdt, Dorchen A. 2013. "Human Trafficking and Domestic Violence A Primer for Judges." *The Judges Journal* 52(1). Retrieved July 25, 2016 (http://www.americanbar.org/publications/judges_journal/2013/winter/human_trafficking_and_domestic_violence_a_primer_for_judges.html).

Leigh, Carol. 1997. "Inventing Sex Work." Pp. 225–31 in *Whores and Other Feminists*, edited by Jill Nagle. New York: Routledge.

Leitenberg, H., M. Detzer, and D. Srebnick. 1993. "Gender Differences in Masturbation and the Relation of Masturbation Experience in Preadolescence and/or Early Adolescence to Sexual Behavior and Sexual Adjustment in Young Adulthood." *Archives of Sexual Behavior* 22:87–98.

Lenhart, Amanda, Kristen Purcell, Aaron Smith, and Kathryn Zickuhr. 2010. "Social Media and Mobile Internet Use Among Teens and Young Adults." Pew Internet and American Life, 2010. Retrieved May 24, 2016. (http://www.pewinternet.org/).

Lepowsky, Maria. 1994. *Fruit of the Motherland: Gender in an Egalitarian Society.* Madison, WI: University of Wisconsin.

Leuchtag, Alice. 2003. "Human Rights Sex Trafficking and Prostitution (Perspectives on Prostitution)." *The Humanist.* American Humanist Association. HighBeam Research. Retrieved July 10, 2016 (https://www.highbeam.com/doc/1G1-96417147.html).

Lev, A.I. 2004. *Transgender Emergence: Therapeutic Guidelines for Working with Gender-Variant People and Their Families.* New York: Routledge.

Lever, J., & Dolnick, D. 2000. "Clients and Call Girls: Seeking Sex and Intimacy." Pp. 85–100 in *Sex for Sale: Prostitution, Pornography, and the Sex Industry,* edited by R. Weitzer. New York: Routledge.

Levin, Diane E. and Jean Kilbourne. 2008. *So Sexy So Soon: The New Sexualized Childhood, and what Parents Can Do to Protect Their Kids.* New York: Ballantine Books.

Levy, Ariel. 2009. "Either/Or: Sports, Sex, and the Case of Caster Semenya." *The New Yorker,* November 30. Retrieved February 8, 2016 (http://www.newyorker.com/magazine/2009/11/30/eitheror).

Levy, Judith A. 1994. "Sex and Sexuality in Later Life Stages." Pp. 287–309 in *Sexuality across the Life Course,* edited by Alice S. Rossi. Chicago: University of Chicago Press.

Lewin, Ellen. 1993. *Lesbian Mothers: Accounts of Gender in American Culture.* Ithaca, NY: Cornell University Press.

Lewin, Ellen and William L. Leap. 1996. *Out in the Field: Reflections of Lesbian and Gay Anthropologists.*

Urbana, IL: University of Illinois Press.

Lindee, Kirsten M. 2007. "Love, Honor, or Control: Domestic Violence, Trafficking, and the Question of How to Regulate the Mail-Order Bride Industry." *Columbia Journal of Gender and Law* 16(2). Retrieved July 25, 2016 (http://cjgl.cdrs.columbia.edu/article/love-honor-or-control-domestic-violence-trafficking-and-the-question-of-how-to-regulate-the-mail-order-bride-industry/).

Lipka, Sara. 2011. "For Gay Students, More Room on Campuses." *The Chronicle of Higher Education*, March 6. Retrieved June 22, 2016 (http://www.chronicle.com/article/For-Gay-Students-More-Room-on/126608/).

Lipsyte, Robert. 1975. *Sportsworld: An American Dreamland.* New York: Quadrangle.

Lira, Natalie and Alexandra Minna Stern. 2014. "Mexican Americans and Eugenic Sterilization: Resisting Reproductive Injustice in California, 1920–1950." *Aztlan: A Journal of Chicano Studies* 39(2):9–34.

Lisak, David, Lori Gardinier, Sarah C. Nicksa, and Ashley M. Cote. 2010. "False Allegations of Sexual Assualt: An Analysis of Ten Years of Reported Cases." *Violence Against Women* 16(12):1318–34.

Liss-Schultz, Nina. 2016. "An Indiana Court Just Said Women Can't be Jailed for Ending Their Own Pregnancies." *Mother Jones*, July 22. Retrieved July 24, 2016 (http://www.motherjones.com/politics/2016/07/purvi-patel-indiana-abortion-feticide-charges-dropped).

Living Hope Ministries. 2016. "Our Mission." Retrieved July 28, 2016 (https://livehope.org/).

Lo, Clarence. 1982. *Small Property versus Big Government: Social Origins of the Property Tax Revolt.* Berkeley, CA: University of California Press.

Lobasz, Jennifer. 2009. "Beyond Border Security: Feminist Approaches to Human Trafficking." *Security Studies* 18:319–44.

Lock, James. 1998. "Case Study: Treatment of Homophobia in a Gay Male Adolescent." *American Journal of Psychotherapy* 52(2):202 14.

Lockwood, D. 1980. *Prison Sexual Violence.* New York: Elsevier North-Holland.

Lofgren-Martenson, L. 2009. "The Invisibility of Young Homosexual Women and Men with Intellectual Disabilities." *Sexuality and Disability* 27:21–26.

Logue, Josh. 2016. "Restroom Unrest." *Inside Higher Ed,* March 28. Retrieved July 29, 2016. (https://www.insidehighered.com/news/2016/03/28/north-carolina-bathroom-law-could-change-practices-public-colleges-and-universities).

Lorber, Judith. 1994. *Paradoxes of Gender.* New Haven, CT: Yale University Press.

Lorde, Audre. [1984] 2007. "Uses of the Erotic. The Erotic as Power" Pp. 53–59 reprinted in *Sister Outsider: Essays and Speeches.* Freedom, CA: Crossing Press.

Lowe, Pam. 2009. "A 'Snip' in the Right Direction? Vasectomy and Gender Equality." Pp. 70–85 in *Feminism and the Body: Interdisciplinary Perspectives*, edited by Catherine Kevin. Cambridge,

UK: Cambridge Scholars Publishing.

Lucal, Betsy. 1999. "What It Means to Be Gendered Me: Life on the Boundaries of A Dichotomous Gender System." *Gender & Society* 13(6):781–97.

Luker, Kristin. 1997. *Dubious Conceptions: The Politics of Teenage Pregnancy.* Cambridge, MA: Harvard University Press.

Luker, Kristin. 2006. *When Sex Goes to School.* New York: W.W. Norton.

Lundsberg, L. S., L Pal, A. M. Gariepy, X. Xu, M. C. Chu, and J. L. Illuzi. 2014. "Knowledge, Attitudes, and Practices Regarding Conception and Fertility: A Population-based Survey Among Reproductive-age United States Women." *Fertility & Sterility* 1010(3):767–74.

Lykke, Lucia C., and Philip N. Cohen. 2015. "The Widening Gender Gap in Opposition to Pornography, 1975-2012." *Social Currents* 2(4):307–23.

MacDorman, M. F., E. Declercq, F. Menacker, and M. H. Malloy. 2006. "Infant and Neonatal Mortality for Primary Cesarean and Vaginal Births to Women with 'No Indicated Risk,' United States, 1998-2001 Birth Cohorts." *Birth* 33(3):175–82.

MacDougall, J. and S. Morin. 1979. "Sexual Attitudes and Self-Reported Behavior of Congenitally Disabled Adults." *Canadian Journal of Behavioral Science* 11:189–204.

Macgillivray, Ian K. and Todd Jennings. 2008. "A Content Analysis Exploring Lesbian, Gay, Bisexual, and Transgender Topics in Foundations of Education Textbooks." *Journal of Teacher Education* 59(2):170–88.

Mackelprang, R. W. and R. O. Salsgiver. 1999. *Disability: A Diversity Model Approach in Human Service Practice,* 2nd ed. Washington, DC: Lyceum.

MacKinnon, Catharine. 1989a. "Sexuality, Pornography, and Method: Pleasure under Patriarchy." *Ethics*, 99(2):314–46.

MacKinnon, Catharine. 1989b. *Toward a Feminist Theory of the State.* Cambridge, MA: Harvard University Press

MacKinnon, Catharine. 1993. "Prostitution and Civil Rights." *Michigan Journal of Gender and Law*, 13. Originally a Speech Presented at the Michigan Journal of Gender and Law Symposium on October 31, 1992. Retrieved July 11, 2016 (http://www.prostitutionresearch.com/MacKinnon%20Prostitution%20and%20Civil%20Rights.pdf).

MacKinnon, Catharine. 2006. *Are Women Human? And Other International Dialogues.* Cambridge, MA: Harvard University Press.

Madden, Mary, Amanda Lenhart, Maeve Duggan, Sandra Cortesi, and Urs Gasser. 2013. "Teens and Technology 2013." Pew Research Center and The Berkman Center for Internet and Society at Harvard University. Retrieved July 11, 2016 (http://www.pewinternet.org/files/old-media/Files/Reports/2013/PIP_TeensandTechnology2013.pdf).

Magid, Larry. 2009. "Study: 30 Percent of Youths Report Sexting." CBS News, December 3. Retrieved July 9, 2016 (http://www.cbsnews.com/news/study-30-percent-of-youths-report-sexting/).

Maines, Rachel P. 2001. *The Technology of Orgasm: "Hysteria," The Vibrator, and Women's Sexual*

Satisfaction. Baltimore, MD: John Hopkins University Press.

Malamuth, Neil. M and John Briere. 1986. "Sexual Violence in the Media: Indirect Effects on Aggression Against Women." *Journal of Social Issues* 42(3): 75–92.

Malamuth, Neil, Ilana Reisin, and Barry Spinner. 1979. *Exposure to Pornography and Reactions to Rape.* Paper Presented at the 87th Annual Convention of the American Psychological Association, New York. Retrieved July 11, 2016 (http://escholarship.org/uc/item/7437d1qp#page-1).

Mallon, G.P. 2004. *Gay Men Choosing Parenthood.* New York: Columbia University Press.

Mallon, G.P. 2011. "The Home Study Assessment Process for Gay, Lesbian, Bisexual, and Transgender Foster and Adoptive Families." *Journal of GLBT Family Studies* 7(1-2):9–29

Mann, Susan Archer. 2012. *Doing Feminist Theory: From Modernity to Postmodernity.* New York: Oxford University Press.

Marcotte, Amanda. 2015. "The 12 Most Ludicrous Ideas About Women's Health from the GOP Field." *Salon Magazine*, August 23. Retrieved July 12, 2016 (http://www.salon.com/2015/08/23/14051679_partner/).

Marhoefer, Laurie. 2011. "Degeneration, Sexual Freedom, and the Politics of the Weimar Republic, 1918–1933." *German Studies Review* 34(3):529–49.

Marine, Susan B. 2011. "'Our College is Changing, Women's College Student Affairs Administrators and Transgender Students." *Journal of Homosexuality* 58:1165–86.

Massengill, D. and D.J. Peterson. 1995. "Legal Challenges to No Fraternization Rules." *Labor Law* 46:429–35.

Martin, C. W., R. A. Anderson, L. Cheng, P. C. Ho, Z. van der Spuy, K. B. Smith, A. F. Glasier, D. Everington, and D. T. Baird. 2000. "Potential Impact of Hormonal Male Contraception: Cross-cultural Implication for Development of Novel Preparations." *Human Reproduction* 15(3):637–45.

Martin, Emily. 2001. *The Woman in the Body: A Cultural Analysis of Reproduction.* Boston: Beacon Press.

Martin, Karin A. 1998. "Becoming a Gendered Body: Practices of Preschools." *American Sociological Review.* Vol. 63: 494–511.

Martin, Patricia Yancey and Robert A. Hummer. 2009. "Fraternities and Rape on Campus." Pp. 471–80 in *Feminist Frontiers,* 8th ed., edited by Verta Taylor, Nancy Whittier, and Leila Rupp. Boston: McGraw-Hill.

Marvasti, Amir B. and Karyn D. McKinney. 2004. *Middle Eastern Lives in America.* New York: Rowman & Littlefield.

Mass, Lawrence. 2011. "Pioneers Who Began as Volunteers in the AIDS Epidemic." GMHC.org. June 2. Retrieved June 29, 2016. http://www.gmhc.org/news-and-events/press-releases/pioneers-who-began-as-volunteers-in-the-aids-epidemic-by-larry-mass-md.

Masters, W. H. and V. E. Johnson. 1979. *Homosexuality in Perspective.* Toronto: Bantam Books.

Matheson, Kathy. 2013. "Catholic School Fires Gay Teacher, Drawing Protest." *The Huffington Post,* December 13, 2013. Retrieved January 25, 2016

(http://www.huffingtonpost.com/2013/12/13/michael-griffin-protests_n_4440060.html).

Mathews, T. J. and Marian F. MacDorman. 2008. "Infant Mortality Statistics from the 2005 Period Linked Birth/Infant Death Data Set." *National Division of Vital Statistics Center for Disease Control*, 57:2. Retrieved July 13, 2016 (http://www.cdc.gov/nchs/data/nvsr/nvsr57/nvsr57_02.pdf).

Maxwell, Sheila R. and Christopher D. Maxwell. 2000. "Examining the 'Criminal Careers' of Prostitutes Within the Nexus of Drug Use, Drug Selling, and Other Illicit Activities." *Criminology* 38:787–809.

McAdam, Doug. 1982. *Political Process and the Development of Black Insurgency, 1930–1970.* Chicago, IL: University of Chicago Press.

McCabe, M. 1993. "Sex Education Programs for People with Mental Retardation." *Mental Retardation* 31:377–87.

McCabe, M. and A. Schreck. 1992. "Before Sex Education: An Evaluation of the Sexual Knowledge, Experience, Feelings and Needs of People with Mild Intellectual Disabilities." *Australia and New Zealand Journal of Developmental Disabilities* 18:75–82.

McCarthy, M. 1999. *Sexuality and Women With Learning Disabilities.* London, England: Jessica Kingsley Publishers.

McCaughey, Martha. 2008. *The Caveman Mystique: Pop-Darwinism and the Debates over Sex, Violence, and Science.* New York: Routledge.

McCormack, Mark. 2014. "Contextualizing Homophobic Language in Sport." Pp. 283–91 in *Routledge Handbook of Sport, Gender, and Sexuality,* edited by Jennifer Hargreaves and Eric Anderson. New York: Routledge.

McDermott, E. Roen, K., and Scourfield, J. 2008. "Avoiding Shame: Youth LGBT People, Homophobia, and Self-Destructive Behavior." *Culture, Health, and Sexuality* 10:815–29.

McGann, P. J. 2011. "Healing (Disorderly) Desire: Medical-Therapeutic Regulation of Sexuality." Pp. 427–37 in *Introducing the New Sexuality Studies*, 2nd Ed. Steven Seidman, Nancy Fischer, and Chet Meeks, Editors. New York: Routledge.

McGregor, Jena. 2013. "United States Ranks Worse This Year on Gender Gap." *Washington Post*, October 24. Retrieved July 24, 2016 (https://www .washingtonpost.com/news/on-leadership/wp/2013/10/24/united-states-ranks-worse-this-year-on-gender-gap/).

McIntosh, Mary. 1968. "The Homosexual Role." *Social Problems* 16(2):182–92.

McKelvie, M. and S. Gold. 1994. "Hyperfemininity: Further Definition of the Construct." *The Journal of Sex Research* 31(3):219–28. Retrieved September 30, 2016. http://www.jstor.org/ stable/3812915

McKinney, Laura and Kelly Austin. 2015. "Ecological Losses are Harming Women: A Structural Analysis of Female HIV Prevalence and Life Expectancy in Less Developed Countries." *Social Problems* 62(4):529–49.

McNeil, Donald G. 2014. "Are We Ready for H.I.V's Sexual Revolution?" *The New York Times* Sunday, May 25, Review:6–7.

McNeil, Donald G. 2016. "HIV Arrived in the US Long Before 'Patient Zero.'" The New York

Times, October. 26. Retrieved December 20, 2016. (http://www .nytimes.com/2016/10/27/health/ hiv-patient-zero-genetic-analysis .html?_r=0).

Meem, Deborah T., Michelle A. Gibson, and Jonathan F. Alexander. 2010. *Finding Out: An Introduction to LGBT Studies*. Thousand Oaks, CA: Sage.

Melton, E. Nicole. 2013. "Women and the Lesbian Stigma." Pp. 11–30 in *Sexual Minorities in Sports: Prejudice at Play*, edited by Melanie L. Sartore-Baldwin. Boulder, CO: Lynne Rienner Publishers.

Ménard, Dana A. and Peggy J. Kleinplatz. 2008. "Twenty-one Moves Guaranteed to Make His Thighs Go Up in Flames: Depictions of 'Great Sex' in Popular Magazines." *Sexuality and Culture* 12:1–20

Merdian, Hannah L., Nima Moghaddam, Douglas P. Boer, Nick Wilson, Jo Thakker, Cate Curtis, and Dave Dawson. 2016. "Fantasy-Driven Versus Contact-Driven Users of Child Sexual Exploitation Material: Offender Classification and Implications for Their Risk Assessment." *Sex Abuse*. Published online before print April 6, 2016. Retrieved July 10, 2016 (http://sax.sagepub.com/ content/early/2016/04/05/ 1079063216641109.abstract).

Merevick, Tony. 2014. "West Virginia DMV Refused to Photograph Two Transgender Women Until They Removed Their Makeup." *Buzz Feed*, July 7. Retrieved April 20, 2016. (https:// www.buzzfeed.com/tonymerevick/ west-virginia-dmv-refused-to-photograph-two-transgender-wome?utm_term=.pq1mQ0m|8# .fhddypd8q).

Merritt, Jonathan. 2015. "How Christians Turned Against Gay Conversion Therapy." *The Atlantic*, April 15. Retrieved July 28, 2016 (http://www.theatlantic.com/ politics/archive/2015/04/how-christians-turned-against-gay-conversion-therapy/390570/).

Messner, Michael and Donald F. Sabo, eds. 1990. *Sport, Men and Gender Order: Critical Feminist Perspectives*. Champaign, IL: Human Kinetics Publishers.

Messner, Michael, Michele Dunbar, and Darnell Hunt. 2007. "The Televised Sports Manhood Formula." Pp. 139–54 in *Out of Play: Critical Essays on Gender and Sport*, edited by Michael Messner. Albany, NY: SUNY Press.

Messner, Michael, Margaret Carlisle Duncan, and Nicole Willms. 2007. "This Revolution is Not Being Televised." Pp. 155–66 in *Out of Play: Critical Essays on Gender and Sport*, edited by Michael Messner. Albany, NY: SUNY Press.

Messner, Michael A. 1992. *Power at Play: Sports and the Problem of Masculinity*. Boston: Beacon Press.

Messner, Michael A. 2007. *Out of Play: Critical Essays on Gender and Sport*. Albany, NY: SUNY Press.

Meyer, Doug. 2015. *Violence against Queer People: Race, Class, Gender and the Persistence of Anti-LGBT Discrimination*. New Brunswick, NJ: Rutgers University Press.

Meyer, I. H. 2003. "Prejudice, Social Stress, and Mental Health in Lesbian, Gay, and Bisexual Populations: Conceptual Issues and Research Evidence." *Psychological Bulletin* 129:674–97.

Meyer, L.H. 1995. "Minority Stress and Mental Health in Gay Men." *Journal of Health Sciences and Social Behavior* 36:38–56.

Mezey, Nancy J. 2008. *New Choices, New Families: How Lesbians Decide about Motherhood.* Baltimore, MD: The Johns Hopkins University Press.

Mezey, Nancy J. 2013. "How Lesbians and Gay Men Decide to Become Parents or Remain Childfree." Pp. 5–69 in *LGBT-Parent Families: Innovations in Research and Implications for Practice,* edited by A. E. Goldberg and K.R. Allen. New York: Springer.

Mezey, Nancy J. 2015. *LGBT Families.* Thousand Oaks, CA: Sage.

Miall, Charlene E. 1994. "Community Constructs of Involuntary Childlessness: Sympathy, Stigma, and Social Support." *Canadian Review of Sociology* 31:(4)392–421. doi:10.1111/ j.1755-618X.1994.tb00828.

Miceli, Melinda. 2005. *Standing Out, Standing Together: The Social and Political Impact of Gay-Straight Alliances.* New York: Routledge.

Michael, R. T., J. H. Gagnon, E. O. Laumann, and G. Kolata. 1994. *Sex in America: A Definitive Survey.* Boston: Little, Brown.

Michaels, Samantha. 2015. "More Transgender People Have Been Killed in 2015 Than Any Other Year on Record." November 20. Retrieved November 20, 2016. (www.motherjones.com/ mojo/2015/11/more-transgender-people-have-been-murdered-2015-any-other-year-record).

Micheler, Stefan. 2005. "Homophobic Propaganda and the Denunciation of Same-Sex Desiring Men under National Socialism." Pp. 95–130 in *Sexuality and German Fascism,* edited by Dagmar Herzog. New York: Berghahn Books.

Miller, Claire Cain. 2014. "Where Are the Gay Chief Executives?" *New York Times,* Sunday, May 18:SR4.

Miller, Geoffrey. 2001. *The Mating Mind: How Sexual Choice Shaped the Evolution of Human Nature.* New York: First Anchor Books Edition.

Miller, Michael E. 2015. "N.C. Just Prosecuted a Teenage Couple for Making Child Porn — of Themselves." *The Washington Post,* September 21. Retrieved July 24, 2016 (https://www.washington post.com/news/morning-mix/ wp/2015/09/21/n-c-just-prosecuted-a-teenage-couple-for-making-child-porn-of-themselves/).

Miller, Patricia. 2014. *Good Catholics: The Battle Over Abortion in the Catholic Church.* California: University of California Press.

Mint, Pepper. 2004. "The Power Dynamics of Cheating: Effects on Polyamory and Bisexuality." *Journal of Bisexuality* 4(3–4):55–76.

Minter, Shannon Price. 2006. "Do Transsexuals Dream of Gay Rights? Getting Real about Transgender Inclusion." Pp. 141–70 in *Transgender Rights,* edited by Paisley Currah, Richard M. Juang, and Shannon Price Minter. Minneapolis: University of Minnesota Press.

Mitchell, Kimberly J., David Finkelhor, and Janis Wolak. 2003. "The Exposure of Youth to Unwanted Sexual Material on the Internet: A National Survey of Risk, Impact, and Prevention." *Youth and Society* 34(3):330–58.

Mitchell, Koritha. 2013. "Love in Action: Noting Similarities between Lynching Then and Anti-LGBT Violence Now." *Callaloo* 36(3):688–717.

Mogul, Joey L., Andrea J. Ritchie, and Kay Whitlock. 2011. *Queer (In)Justice: The Criminalization of LGBT People in the United States.* Boston: Beacon Press.

Mollow, Anna and Robert McRuer. 2012. "Introduction." Pp. 1–35 in *Sex and Disability,* edited by Anna Mollow and Robert McRuer. Durham, NC: Duke University Press.

Monk, Lee-Ann and Louise Townson. 2015. "Intimacy and Oppression: A Historical Perspective." Pp. 46–64 in *Sexuality and Relationships in the Lives of People with Intellectual Disabilities,* edited by Rohhss Chapman, Sue Ledger, and Louise Townson, with Daniel Docherty. London, England: Jessica Kingsley Publishers.

Montgomery, Kathryn. 2006. "Gay Activists and Networks." *Journal of Communication* 31:49–57.

Monto, Martin A. and Joseph N. McRee. 2005. "A Comparison of the Male Customers of Female Street Prostitutes with National Samples of Men." *International Journal of Offender Therapy and Comparative Criminology* 49(5):505–29.

Moore, Mignon. 2011. *Invisible Families: Gay Identities, Relationships, and Motherhood among Black Women.* Berkeley, CA: University of California Press.

Moraga, Cherrie. 1997. *Waiting in the Wings: Portrait of a Queer Motherhood.* Ann Arbor, MI: Firebrand Books. Retrieved June 20, 2016. (http://www .amazon.com/Waiting-Wings-Portrait-Queer-Motherhood/ dp/1563410923).

Moran, Rachel. 2013. *Paid for: My Journey Through Prostitution.*

Dublin, Ireland: Gill & MacMillan.

Morris, Aldon. 1984. *The Origins of the Civil Rights Movement: Black Communities Organizing for Change.* New York: Free Press.

Morris, Chris. 2015. "Transgender Porn Quickly Growing in Popularity." *CNBC News*, August 27. Retrieved July 24, 2016 (http://www.cnbc.com/2015/08/27/transgender-porn-quickly-growing-in-popularity.html).

Mosbacher, Dee and Fawn Yacker, Directors. 2009. *Training Rules.* A Woman Vision Production.

Mosendz, Polly. 2015. "7 Arrested After Seeking Ordination of Female Priests Protests Pope Francis in Washington." *Newsweek*, September 23. Retrieved July 28, 2016 (http://www.newsweek.com/catholic-church-pope-pope-francis-female-priests-catholic-women-washington-375606).

Mosher, Donald L. and Mark Sirkin. 1984. "Mark Measuring a Macho Personality Constellation." *Journal of Research in Personality* 18(2):150–63.

Mosher, William and Jo Jones. 2010. *Use of Contraception in the United States: 1982–2008.* National Center for Health Statistics. Vital and Health Statistics 23(29).

Moslener, Sara. 2015a. *Virgin Nation: Sexual Purity and American Adolescence.* Oxford, England: Oxford University Press.

Moslener, Sara. 2015b. "Evangelical 'Sexual Purity' Is Not About Sex—It's About Power." Religion Dispatches, June 29. Retrieved July 26, 2016 (http://religiondispatches.org/evangelical-sexual-purity-is-not-about-sex-its-about-power/).

Moynihan, Ray. 2003. "The Making of a Disease: Female Sexual Dysfunction." *BMJ* 326, Jan. 4:45–47.

Mulvey, Laura. 1999. "Visual Pleasure and Narrative Cinema." Pp. 833–44 in *Film Theory and Criticism: Introductory Readings,* edited by Leo Braudy and Marshall Cohen. New York: Oxford University Press.

Mumtaz, Z., U. Shahid, and A. Levay. 2013. "Understanding the Impact of Gendered Roles on the Experiences of Infertility Amongst Men and Women in Punjab." *Reproductive Health* 10(3).

Murnen, Sarah K. and Donn Byrne. Aug. 1991. "Hyperfeminity: Measurement and Initial Validation of the Construct." *The Journal of Sex Research* 28(3):479–89.

Murphy, G.H. and A. O'Callaghan. 2004. "Capacity of Adults with Intellectual Disabilities to Consent to Sexual Relationships." *Psychological Medicine* 34:134–757.

Mustapha, Marda and Aiah A. Gbakima. 2003. "Civil Conflict, Sexual Violence, and HIV/AIDS: Challenges for Children in Sierre Leone." Pp. 40–50 in *The Children of Africa Confront AIDS,* edited by Arvind Singhal and W. Stephen Howard. Athens: Ohio University Press.

Nack, Adina. 2008. *Damaged Goods: Women Living with Incurable Sexually Transmitted Diseases.* Philadelphia, PA: Temple University Press.

Nadon, Susan M., Catherine Koverola, and Eduard H. Schludermann. 1998. "Antecedents to Prostitution: Childhood Victimization." *Journal of Interpersonal Violence* 13(2): 206–21.

Nagel, Joane. 2000. "States of Arousal/Fantasy Islands: Race, Sex, and Romance in the Global Economy of Desire." *American Studies* 41(2/3):159–81.

Nagel, Joane. 2003. *Race, Ethnicity, and Sexuality: Intimate Intersections, Forbidden Frontiers.* Oxford, UK: Oxford University Press.

Nagel, Joane. 2014. "Rape and War: Fighting Men and Comfort Women." Pp. 641–48 in *Sex Matters: the Sexuality & Society Reader,* edited by Mindy Stombler, Dawn M. Baunach, Wendy Simonds, Elroi J. Windsor, and Elisabeth O. Burgess. New York: W.W. Norton & Company.

Nashrulla, Tasneem. 2016. "Two University of Oregon Fraternities Begin Accepting Transgender Men." *Buzzfeed News,* February 19. (http://www.buzzfeed.com/tasneemnashrulla/two-university-of-oregon-fraternaties-begin-accepting-transg#.ut0E5KJQZ).

National Human Trafficking Resource Center. 2015. "National Human Trafficking Resource Center (HHTRC) Data Breakdown." Retrieved July 25, 2016 (http://traffickingresourcecenter.org/sites/default/files/NHTRC%202015%20United%20States%20Report%20-%20USA%20-%2001.01.15%20-%2012.31.15_OTIP_Edited_06-09-16.pdf).

National Report on Hate Violence Against Lesbian, Gay, Bisexual, Transgender, Queer and HIV-Affected Communities. 2014. National Coalition of Anti-Violence Programs. Retrieved July 24, 2016 (http://www.avp.org/storage/documents/2013_mr_ncavp_hvreport.pdf).

National Sexual Violence Resource Center. 2015. *Media Packet on Sexual Violence.* Funded by Centers For Disease Control and Prevention's Division of Violence Prevention. Retrieved online July 13, 2016 (http://www .nsvrc.org/publications/nsvrc-publications-information-packets/ media-packet).

"National School Climate Survey." 2014. *GLSEN Gay, Lesbian, Straight, Education Network.* Retrieved June 10, 2016. (http:// www.glsen.org/article/2013-national-school-climate-survey).

Nebehay, Stephanie. 2009. "Afghanistan Is World's Worst Place to Be Born: U.N." *Reuters,* November 20. Retrieved July 22, 2016 (http://www.reuters.com/ article/us-afghanistan-children-un-idUSTRE5AI4QC20091120? sp=true).

Nemoto, T., D. Operario, J. Keatley, and D. Villegas. 2004. "Social Context of HIV Risk Behaviours Among Male-to-Female Transgenders of Colour." *AIDS Care* 16(6):724–35.

Netzley, Sara Baker. 2010. "Visibility That Demystifies: Gays, Gender, and Sex on Television." *Journal of Homosexuality* 57(8): 968–86.

Neumayer, Eric. 2004. "HIV/AIDS and Cross-National Convergence of Life Expectancy." *Population Development and Review* 30(4):727–42.

Nichols, Francine H. 2000. "History of the Women's Health Movement in the 20th Century." *Journal of Obstetric, Gynecologic, & Neonatal Nursing* 29(1):56–64.

Nikolic-Ristanovic, Vesna. 2003. "Sex Trafficking: The Impact of War, Militarism and Globalization in Eastern Europe." *Gender and*

Globalisms 17. Ann Arbor, MI: University of Michigan Library. Retrieved July 11, 2016 (http:// quod.lib.umich.edu/cgi/t/text/text-idx?cc=mfsfront;c=mfs;c=mfsfront;i dno=ark5583.0017.001;g=mfsg;rgn =main;view=text;xc=1).

Noonan, R.J. 1984. *Sex Surrogates: A Clarification of Their Functions.* New York: SexQuest/The Sex Institute.

North, Gary. 2012. "Legacy: Looking Back at the Queer/ Bi Movement and the Road Ahead." *The Huffington Post,* May 15. Retrieved July 20, 2015 (http://www.huffingtonpost. com/gary-north/bi-movement-legacy_b_1511760.html).

Norton-Hawk, Maureen. 2004. "A Comparison of Pimp- and Non-Pimp Controlled Women." *Violence Against Women* 10(2):189–94.

Nsiah-Jefferson, Laurie. 2003. "Reproductive Laws, Women of Color, and Low Income Women." Pp. 363–70 in *Feminist Frontiers,* 6th ed., edited by Verta Taylor, Nancy Whittier, and Leila J. Rupp. New York: McGraw Hill.

Nwe, Yin Yin. 2005. "Children and the Tsunami, a Year On." UNICEF. Retrieved July 25, 2016 (http://www.unicef.org/files/ WhatWorked.pdf).

NYC Commission on Human Rights Legal Enforcement Guidance on the Discrimination on the Basis of Gender Identity or Expression. 2002. Local Law No. 3, N.Y.C. Admin. Code § 8-102(23).

Nylund, David. 2006. "Deconstructing Patriarchy and Masculinity with Teen Fathers: A Narrative Approach." Pp. 150–9 in *Teenage Pregnancy and Parenthood: Global Perspective, Issues and Interventions,* edited by Helen S. Holgate, Roy Evans, and

Francis K.O. Yuen. New York: Routledge.

Obedin-Maliver, Juno and Harvey J. Makadon. 2015. "Transgender Men and Pregnancy." *Obstetric Medicine,* Published online before print October 28, doi: 10.1177/1753495X15612658.

O'Donnell, Jayne. 2016. "Huge Racial Disparities Persist Despite Slow Infant Mortality Drop." *USA Today,* March 9. Retrieved July 20, 2016 (http://www.usatoday.com/ story/news/nation/2016/03/07/ racial-disparities-infant-mortality/81003686/).

Ogawa, Scott. 2014. "100 Missing Men: Participation, Selection, and Silence of Gay Athletes." Pp. 291–300 in *Routledge Handbook of Sport, Gender, and Sexuality* edited by Jennifer Hargreaves and Eric Anderson. New York: Routledge.

Okazaki, Sumie. 2002. "Influences of Culture on Asian Americans' Sexuality." *Journal of Sex Research* 39(1):34–41.

"One in 4 Teen Girls Has Sexually Transmitted Disease." 2008. N.a. *NBC News,* March 11. Retrieved July 18, 2016. (http://www .nbcnews.com/id/23574940/ ns/health-childrens_health/t/ teen-girls-has-sexually-transmitted-disease/#.V46fkbgrIhc).

Ontario Ministry of Education. 1989. "Media Literacy" Chapter One, *Media Literacy Resource Guide.*

Oosterhuis, Harry. 2012. "Sexual Modernity in the Works of Richard von Krafft-Ebing and Albert Moll." *Medical History* 56(2):133–55.

Orenstein, Peggy. 2016. *Girls and Sex: Navigating the Complicated New Landscape.* New York: Harper Collins.

Oritz, Erik and Nick Bogert. 2015. "Jared Fogle, Ex-Subway Pitchman, Gets 15 Years in Prison for Child Porn Charges." *NBC News,* November 19. Retrieved July 24, 206 (http://www.nbcnews.com/news/us-news/jared-fogle-ex-subway-pitchman-pleads-guilty-child-porn-sex-n466256).

Osterman, Michelle J. K. and Joyce A. Martin. 2014. *Trends in Low-risk Cesarean Delivery in the United States, 1990-2013.* National Center for Health Statistics, National Vital Statistics Reports 63(6).

Oudshoorn, Nelly. 2003. *The Male Pill: A Biography of a Technology in the Making.* London, England: Duke University Press.

Owens, Ernst. 2015. "Op-Ed: The LGBT Movement Needs to Diversify or Die." *The Advocate.com*, July 21. Retrieved July 21, 2015 (http://www.advocate.com/commentary/2015/07/21/op-ed-lgbt-movement-needs-diversify-or-die).

Owens, Tuppy. 2014. *Supporting Disabled People with their Sexual Lives.* London, England: Jessica Kingsley Publishers.

Padawer, Ruth. 2014. "When Women Become Men at Wellesley." *The New York Times Magazine,* October 15. Retrieved April 2, 2016 (http://www.nytimes.com/2014/10/19/magazine/when-women-become-men-at-wellesley-college.html?_r=0).

Pager, Devah. 2007. *Marked: Race, Crime, and Finding Work in an Era of Mass Incarceration.* Chicago, IL: The University of Chicago Press.

Palmer, Brian. 2011. "What's the Difference Between 'Rape' and 'Sexual Assault'?" *Slate Magazine,* February 17. Retrieved online July 19, 2016 (http://www.slate.com/articles/news_and_politics/explainer/2011/02/whats_the_difference_between_rape_and_sexual_assault.html).

Papadopoulos, Linda. 2010. "The Sexualization of Young People Review." London, England: Home Office Publication, Retrieved at: http://www.homeoffice.gov.uk/documents/Sexualisation-young-people.

Pardue, Angela, Bruce A. Arrigo, and Daniel S. Murphy. 2011. "Sex and Sexuality in Women's Prisons: A Preliminary Typological Investigation." *The Prison Journal* 91(3):279–304.

Pardun, Carol J, Kelly Ladin L'Engle, and Jane D Brown. 2005. "Linking Exposure to Outcomes: Early Adolescents' Consumption of Sexual Content in Six Media." *Mass Communication & Society* 8(2):75–91.

Park, Ju-Min. 2014. "Former Korean 'Comfort Women' for U.S. Troops Sue Own Government." Reuters News Agency, July 11. Retrieved July 3, 2016 (http://www.reuters.com/article/us-southkorea-usa-military-idUSKBN0FG0VV20140711).

Parker, Christopher, Boris B. Bates, Scott A. Young, Joseph W. Huff, Robert A. Altman, Heather A. LaCost, and Joanne E. Roberts. 2003. "Relationships Between Psychological Climate Perceptions and Work Outcomes: A Meta-Analytic Review." *Journal of Organizational Behavior* 24(4):389–416.

Parks, C. and J.F. Peipert. 2016. "Eliminating Health Disparities in Unintended Pregnancy with Long-Acting Reversible Contraception (LARC)." *American Journal of Obstetrics and Gynecology* 214(6):681–8.

Pascoe, C. J. 2007. *Dude, You're a Fag: Masculinity and Sexuality in High School.* Berkeley, CA: University of California Press.

Patterson, Amy S. 2003. "AIDS, Orphans, and the Future of Democracy in Africa." Pp. 13–39 in *The Children of Africa Confront AIDS,* edited by Arvind Singhal and W. Stephen Howard. Athens: Ohio University Press.

Patterson, C. 1995. "Sexual Orientation and Human Development: An Overview." *Developmental Psychology* 31:3–11

Patterson, Jennifer. 2016. *Queering Sexual Violence: Radical Voices from Within the Anti-Violence Movement.* Riverdale, New York: Magnus Imprint Books.

Payne, Elizabeth and Melissa Smith. 2012. "Rethinking Safe Schools Approaches for LGBTQ Students: Changing the Questions We Ask." *Multicultural Perspectives* 14(4):187–93.

Peipert, Jeffrey F., Tessa Madden, Jenifer E. Allsworth, and Gina Secura. 2012. "Preventing Unintended Pregnancies by Providing No-Cost Contraception." *Obstetrics and Gynecology* 120(6):1291–7.

Pemberton, Sarah. 2013. "Enforcing Gender: The Constitution of Sex and Gender in Prison Regimes." *Signs: Journal of Women in Culture and Society* 39(1):153–75.

Perez-Pena, Richard. 2015. "Union for Reform Judaism Adopts Transgender Rights Policy." *New York Times*, November 5. Retrieved July 28, 2016 (http://www.nytimes.com/2015/11/06/us/union-for-reform-judaism-adopts-transgender-rights-policy.html?_r=0).

Perry, Barbara. 2013. "Doing Gender and Doing Gender

Inappropriately: Violence against Women, Gay Men, and Lesbians." Pp. 333–50 in *Sex, Gender, and Sexuality: The New Basics,* 2nd ed., edited by Abby Ferber, Kimberly Holcomb, and Tre Wentling. New York: Oxford University Press.

Perry, Samuel L. 2013. "Multiracial Church Attendance and Support for Same-Sex Romantic and Family Relationships." *Sociological Inquiry* 83(2):259–85.

Pew Research Center. 2014. "U.S. Religious Landscape Study." Retrieved July 28, 2016 (http:// www.pewforum.org/about-the-religious-landscape-study).

Pewewardy, Cornel. 1997. "The Pocahontas Paradox: A Cautionary Tale for Educators." *Journal of Navajo Education.* Fall/Winter 1996/1997. Retrieved July 26, 2016 (http://www.hanksville .org/storytellers/pewe/writing/ Pocahontas.htm).

Phillips, S. 2010. "There Were Three in the Bed: Discursive Desire and the Sex Lives of Swingers." Pp. 82–86 in *Understanding Non-Monogamies,* edited by Meg Barker and Darren Langdridge. New York: Routledge.

Pierce, K. 1993. "Socialization of Teenage Girls through Teen-magazine Fiction: The Making of a New Woman or an Old Lady?" *Sex Roles* 29 (1/2):59–68.

Pierceson, Jason. 2016. *Sexual Minorities and Politics: An Introduction.* Lanham, MD: Rowman and Littlefield.

Pizer, Jennifer, Brad Sears, Christy Mallory, and Nan D. Hunter. 2012. "Evidence of Pervasive Workplace Discrimination against LGBT People: The Need for Federal Legislation Prohibiting Discrimination and Providing for Equal Employment Benefits."

Loyola of Los Angeles Law Review 45(3):715–79.

Planty, Michael, Lynn Langton, Christopher Krebs, Marcus Bersofsky and Hope Smiley-McDonald. 2013. *Special Report Female Victims of Sexual Violence 1994–2010.* Bureau of Justice Statistics. Washington, D.C.: U.S. Department of Justice. Retrieved July 26, 2016 (http:// www.bs.gov/content/pub/pdf/ fvsv9410.pdf).

Plaskow, Judith. 2005. *The Coming of Lilith: Essays on Feminism, Judaism, and Sexual Ethics, 1972–2003.* Boston: Beacon Press.

Plaud, J., G. Gaither, H. Hegstad, and L. Rowan. 1999. "Volunteer Bias in Human Psychophysiological Sexual Arousal Research: To Whom Do Our Research Results Apply?" *Journal of Sex Research* 36:171–79.

Plummer, Kenneth. 1975. *Sexual Stigma: An Interactionist Approach.* London, England: Routledge and Kegan Paul.

Polletta, Francesca and James M. Jasper. 2001. "Collective Identity and Social Movements." *Annual Review of Sociology* 27:283–305.

Potter, J. 1998. *Media Literacy.* Thousand Oaks, CA: Sage.

Potterat, John J., Devon D. Brewer, Stephen Q. Muth, Richard B. Rothenberg, Donald E. Woodhouse, John B. Muth, Heather K. Stites, and Stuart Brody. 2004. "Mortality in a Long-term Open Cohort of Prostitute Women." *American Journal of Epidemiology* 159(8):778–85.

Potts, Annie. 2000. "'The Essence of the Hard On:' Hegemonic Masculinity and the Cultural Construction of 'Erectile Dysfunction.'" *Men and Masculinities* 3(1):85–103.

Povoledo, Elisabetta. 2016. "Italy Approves Same Sex Unions." *The New York Times,* May 11. Retrieved June 23, 2016. (http://www .nytimes.com/2016/05/12/world/ europe/italy-gay-same-sex-unions .html?_r=0).

Pregnancy Related Deaths. 2013. "Pregnancy Mortality Surveillance System." Center for Disease Control and Prevention. Retrieved July 23, 2016 (http:// www.cdc.gov/reproductivehealth/ maternalinfanthealth/pmss.html).

Pronger, Brian. 1990. *The Arena of Masculinity: Sports, Homosexuality, and the Meaning of Sex.* New York: St. Martin's.

Pruitt, Deborah and Suzanne LaFont. 1995. "For Love and Money: Romance Tourism in Jamaica." *Annals of Tourism Research* 22(2):422–40.

Purdie-Vaughns, V. and R.P. Eibach. 2008. "Intersectional Invisibility: The Distinctive Advantages and Disadvantages of Multiple Subordinate Group Identities." *Sex Roles* 59:377–91.

Purtill, Corinne. 2015. "World's Biggest Human Rights Group Wants to Legalize Prostitution," *USA Today,* August 13, Retrieved June 22, 2016. (http://www .usatoday.com/story/news/ world/2015/08/13/globalpost-why-worlds-biggest-human-rights-group-wants-legalize-prostitution/31616205/).

"Putin Won't Meet Elton John to Discuss Gay Rights in Russia." *The Huffington Post,* May 26. Retrieved July 30, 2016. (http:// www.huffingtonpost.com/entry/ elton-john-putin-meeting_ us_5746fe8fe4b0dacf7ad409f4).

Pyke, Karen D. and Denise L. Johnson. 2003. "Asian American Women and Racialized

Femininities: 'Doing' Gender Across Cultural Worlds." *Gender & Society* 17(1):33–53.

Pyne, J. 2014. "Gender Independent Kids: A Paradigm Shift in Approaches to Gender Non-conforming Children." *Canadian Journal of Human Sexuality* 23(1):18.

Quarmby, Katharine. 2015. "Disabled and Fighting for a Sex Life." *The Atlantic,* March 11. Retrieved July 18, 2016 (http://www.theatlantic.com/health/archive/2015/03/sex-and-disability/386866/)

"Queer Nation NY History." n.d. Retrieved Jan. 12, 2016 (http://queernationny.org/history).

"Queering Schools." 2014, *Rethinking Schools* Spring: 5–7.

Raby, Rebecca. 2010. "'Tank Tops Are Okay but I Don't Want to See Her Thong.' Girls' Engagements With Secondary School Dress Codes." *Youth and Society* 41(3):333–56.

Rainey, Sarah Smith. 2011. *Love, Sex, and Disability: The Pleasures of Care.* Boulder, CO: Lynne Rienner Publishers.

Raley, Gabrielle. 2008. "Avenue to Adulthood." Pp. 338–50 in *American Families: A Multicultural Reader,* edited by Stephanie Coontz. New York: Routledge.

Rankin, Sue. 2005. "Campus Climates for Sexual Minorities." *New Directions for Student Services* 111:17–24.

Rankin, Sue and Genny Beemyn. 2012. "Beyond a Binary: The Lives of Gender-Nonconforming Youth." *About Campus,* September-October:2–10.

Rapp, Rayna. 2000. *Testing Women, Testing the Fetus: The Social*

Impact of Amniocentesis in America. New York: Routledge.

Raque-Bogdan, Trisha L. and Mary Ann Hoffman. 2015. "The Relationship Among Infertility, Self-compassion, and Well-being for Women With Primary or Secondary Infertility." *Psychology of Women Quarterly* 39(4):484–96.

Raymond, Janice G. 2004. "Prostitution on Demand: Legalizing the Buyers as Sexual Consumers." *Violence Against Women* 10(10):115–686.

Reis, Elizabeth. 2007. "Divergence or Disorder?: The Politics of Naming Intersex." Perspectives in Biology and Medicine, 50(4):535–45.

Rennison, Callie Marie. 2002. "Rape and Sexual Assault: Reporting to Police and Medical Attention, 1992–2000." Bureau of Justice Statistics: U.S. Department of Justice. Retrieved online July 14, 2016 (http://www.bjs.gov/content/pub/pdf/rsarp00.pdf).

Renzetti, Claire M. 2011. "Toward a Better Understanding of Lesbian Battering." Pp. 595–606 in *Shifting the Center: Understanding Contemporary Families,* 4th ed., edited by Susan J. Ferguson. New York: McGraw-Hill.

Rich, Adrienne. 1980. "Compulsory Heterosexuality and Lesbian Existence." *Signs* 5(4):631–60.

Richardson, Diane. 2000. "Constructing Sexual Citizenship: Theorizing Sexual Rights." *Critical Social Policy* 20(1):105–35.

Richman, K.D. 2009. *Courting Change: Queer Parents, Judges, and the Transformation of American Family Law.* New York: New York University Press.

Richmond, K. 1978. "Fear of Homosexuality and Modes of Rationalization in Male Prisons." *Australian and New Zealand Journal of Sociology* 14(1):51–57.

Richters, Juliet. 2011. "Orgasms." Pp. 100–105 in *Introducing the New Sexuality Studies,* 2nd ed., edited by Steven Seidman, Nancy Fischer, and Chet Meeks. New York: Routledge.

Rideout, Victoria J, Ulla G. Foehr, and Donald F. Roberts. 2010. *Generation M2: Media in the Lives of 8- to 18-Year-Olds.* Kaiser Family Foundation. Retrieved March 2016 (https://kaiserfamilyfoundation.files.wordpress.com/2013/01/8010.pdf).

Riley, James C. 2005. "The Timing and Pace of Health Transitions Around the World." *Population Development and Review* 31(4):741–64.

Rimmerman, Craig A. 2015. *The Lesbian and Gay Movements: Assimilation or Liberation?* 2nd Edition. Boulder, CO: Westview Press.

Ring, Trudy. "Gay-Straight Alliance Arouses Controversy in Rural Tennessee." *The Advocate,* February 8, 2016. Retrieved March 23, 2016 (http://www.advocate.com/youth/2016/2/08/gay-straight-alliance-arouses-controversy-rural-tennessee).

Ringdal, Nils Johan. 2004. *Love For Sale: A World History of Prostitution.* New York: Grove Press.

Rippeyoung, Phyllis L. F. and Mary C. Noonan. 2012. "Is Breastfeeding Truly Cost Free? Income Consequences of Breastfeeding for Women." *American Sociological Review* 77(2):244–67.

Risman, Barbara. 2004. "Gender as a Social Structure: Theory

Wrestling with Activism." *Gender and Society* 18(4):429–50.

Rivers, Daniel Winunwe. 2013. *Radical Relations: Lesbian Mothers, Gay Fathers, and Their Children in the United States Since World War II*. Chapel Hill, NC: The University of North Carolina Press.

Rivers-Moore, Megan. 2016. *Gringo Gulch: Sex, Tourism, and Social Mobility in Costa Rica*. Chicago, IL: The University of Chicago Press.

Roberts, Dorothy. 1997. *Killing the Black Body: Race, Reproduction, and the Meaning of Liberty*. New York: Vintage Books.

Roberts, Ron E. and Robert Marsh Kloss. 1974. *Social Movements: Between the Balcony and the Barricade*. Saint Louis, MO: The C.V. Mosby Company.

Robinson, Margaret. 2002. "Bisexuality and the Seduction by the Uncertain," Course paper, University of Toronto.

Romans, Sarah, Rose Clarkson, Gillian Einstein, Michele Petrovic, and Donna Stewart. 2012. "Mood and the Menstrual Cycle: A Review of Prospective Data Studies." *Gender and Medicine* 9(5):361–84.

Rosenbaum, Talli, Ronit Aloni, and Rafi Heruti. 2014. "Surrogate Partner Therapy: Ethical Considerations in Sexual Medicine." *Journal of Sexual Medicine* 11:321–9.

Rosenthal, Elisabeth. 2013. "American Way of Birth, Costliest in the World." *The New York Times*, June 30. Retrieved July 18, 2016 (http://www.nytimes.com/2013/07/01/health/american-way-of-birth-costliest-in-the-world.html?pagewanted=all).

Rothbaum, Barbara Olasov, Edna B. Foa, David S. Riggs, Tamera Murdock, and William Walsh. 1992. "A Prospective Examination of Post-traumatic Stress Disorder in Rape Victims." *Journal of Traumatic Stress* 5(3):455–75.

Rothman, E.F., D. Exner, A.L. Baughman. 2011. "The Prevalence of Sexual Assault Against People Who Identify as Gay, Lesbian, or Bisexual in the United States: A Systematic Review." *Trauma Violence Abuse* 12(2):55–66. Retrieved online July 18, 2016 (http://www.ncbi.nlm.nih.gov/pmc/articles/PMC3118668/).

Rothstein, Mark A., Serge A. Martinez, and W. Paul McKinney. 2002. "Using Established Medical Criteria to Define Disability: A Proposal to Amend the American With Disabilities Act." *Washington ULQ* 80:243.

Roughgarden, Joan. 2013. *Evolution's Rainbow: Diversity, Gender, and Sexuality in Nature and People,* 10th ed. Berkeley: University of California Press.

Rowland, Debran. 2004. *The Boundaries of Her Body: The Troubling History of Women's Rights in America*. Naperville, IL: Sphinx Publishing.

Rubin, Gayle. [1975] 2005. "The Traffic in Women: Notes on the 'Political Economy' of 'Sex'." Pp. 273–88 in *Feminist Theory: A Reader,* 2nd ed., edited by Wendy Kolmar and Frances Bartkowski. Boston: McGraw-Hill.

Rubin, Gayle. 1993. "Thinking Sex: Notes for a Radical Theory of the Politics of Sexuality." Pp. 3–44 in *The Lesbian and Gay Studies Reader,* edited by Henry Abelove, Michele Aina Barale, and David M. Halpern. New York: Routledge.

Rudolph, Jennifer. 2012. *Embodying Latino Masculinities: Producing Masculinidad*. U.S.: Palgrave Macmillan.

Rudy, Kathy. 1998. *Sex and the Church: Gender, Homosexuality, and the Transformation of Christian Ethics*. Boston: Beacon Press.

Rushton, J. Philippe. 1988. "Race Differences in Behavior: A Review and Evolutionary Analysis." *Personality and Individual Differences* 9:1009–24.

Russell, Stephen T. 2003. "Sexual Minority Youth and Suicide Risk." *American Behavioral Scientist*, 46(9): 1241–57. doi: 10.1177/0002764202250667.

"Russian Gay Activists Detained after Unsanctioned LGBT Rights Rally in Moscow." 2015. *The Huffington Post,* May 30. Retrieved July 21, 2015 (http://www.huffingtonpost.com/2015/05/31/russia-gay-rights-rally-_n_7475404.html).

Russo, Vito. 1987. *The Celluloid Closet: Homosexuality in the Movies*. New York: Harper & Row.

Ryan, C., D. Hueebner, R. Diaz, and J. Sanchez. 2009. "Family Rejection as a Predictor of Negative Health Outcomes in White and Latino Lesbian, Gay, and Bisexual Adults. *Pediatrics* 123:346–52.

Ryan, Christopher and Cacilda Jetha. 2010. *Sex at Dawn: How We Mate, Why We Stray, and What It Means for Modern Relationships*. New York: Harper Collins.

Ryan, G. 2000. "Childhood Sexuality: A Decade of Study. Part 1. Research and Curriculum Development." *Child Abuse and Neglect* 24:33–48.

Sadovsky, R. and M. Nussbaum. 2006. "Sexual Health Inquiry and

Support is a Primary Care Priority." *Journal of Sexual Medicine* 3:3–11

Sanday, Peggy Reeves. 2015. "Working a Yes Out." Pp. 145–54 in *Sexualities: Identities, Behaviors, and Society,* 2nd ed., edited by Michael Kimmel and The Stony Brook Sexualities Research Group. New York: Oxford University Press.

Sanger, Alexander. 2007. "Eugenics, Race, and Margaret Sanger Revisited: Reproductive Freedom for All?" *Hypatia* 22(2):210–7.

Sarracino, Carmine and Kevin M. Scott. 2009. *The Porning of America: The Rise of Porn Culture, What It Means, and Where We Go from Here.* Boston MA: Beacon Press.

Sartore, Melanie L. and G. Cunningham. 2009. "Gender, Sexual Prejudice, and Sport Participation: Implications for Sexual Minorities." *Sex Roles* 60(1):100–13.

Sartore, Melanie L. and G. Cunningham. 2010. "The Lesbian Label as a Component of Women's Stigmatization in Sport Organizations: An Exploration of Two Health and Kinesiology Departments." *Journal of Sport Management* 24:481–501.

Sausa L.A., J. Keatley, and D. Operario. 2007. "Perceived Risks and Benefits of Sex Work among Transgender Women of Color in San Francisco." *Archives of Sexual Behavior* 36(6):768–77.

Savin-Williams, Ritch. 2015. "Dating and Romantic Relationships among Gay, Lesbian, and Bisexual Youths." Pp. 112–22 in *Sexualities: Identities, Behaviors, and Society,* 2nd ed., edited by Michael Kimmel and The Stony Brook Sexualities Research Group.

New York: Oxford University Press.

Saxton, Marsha. 1998. "Disability Rights and Selective Abortion." Pp. 374–94 in *Abortion Wars, A Half Century of Struggle: 1950 to 2000,* edited by Rickie Solinger. Berkeley: University of California Press.

Scacco, A. 1975. *Rape in Prisons.* Springfield, IL: Charles C. Thomas.

Scacco, A. 1982. *Male Rape: A Casebook of Sexual Aggression.* New York: AMS Press.

Scelfo, Julie. 2015. "A University Recognizes a Third Gender: Neutral." *The New York Times,* February 3. Retrieved February 14, 2016 (http://www.nytimes .com/2015/02/08/education/ edlife/a-university-recognizes-a-third-gender-neutral.html?_r=0)

Scelles, Fondation. 2014. "Sexual Exploitation: A Growing Menace" 3rd Global Report. Under the direction of Yves Charpenel. France: Economica. Retrieved June 10, 2016 (http:// www.fondationscelles.org/pdf/ rapport_mondial/Book_Sexual_ exploitation_A%20growing%20 menace_Fondation%20Scelles .pdf).

Schilt, Kristen and Laurel Westbrook. 2009. "Doing Gender, Doing Heteronormativity: 'Gender Normals,' Transgender People, and the Social Maintenance of Heterosexuality." Peer Reviewed Articles. Paper 7. Retrieved from http://scholarworks.gvsu.edu/ soc_articles/7/

Schippers, Mimi. 2002. *Rockin' Out of the Box: Gender Maneuvering in Alternative Hard Rock.* New Brunswick: NJ: Rutgers University Press.

Schippers, Mimi. 2007. "Recovering the Feminine Other: Masculinity, Femininity, and Gender Hegemony." *Theory and Society* 36(1):85–102.

Schippers, Mimi. 2016. *Beyond Monogamy: Polyamory and the Future of Polyqueer Sexualities.* New York: New York University Press.

Schmidt, J. 2001. "Redefining Fa'afafine: Western Discourses and the Construction of Transgenderism in Samoa." *Intersections: Gender and Sexuality in Asia and the Pacific,* Issue 6.

Schwarz, Hunter. 2014. "Following Reports of Forced Sterilization of Female Prison Inmates, California Passes Ban." *The Washington Post,* September 26. Retrieved July 13, 2016 (https://www .washingtonpost.com/blogs/ govbeat/wp/2014/09/26/following-reports-of-forced-sterilization-of-female-prison-inmates-california-passes ban/).

Schwirtz, Michael. 2010. "Revolution? Da Sexual? Nyet." *The New York Times,* July 15. Retrieved December 26, 2015 (www.nytimes.com/2010/07/15/ fashion/15sex.html?_r=0).

Scott, Eugene. 2016. "Joe Biden Pens Open Letter to Stanford Rape Victim." *CNN News,* June 9. Retrieved July 20, 2016 (http:// www.cnn.com/2016/06/09/ politics/joe-biden-brock-turner-rape/).

Scrimshaw, Nevin S. 2003. "Historical Concepts of Interactions, Synergism, and Antagonism between Nutrition and Infection." *The Journal of Nutrition* 133(1):316S–21S.

Scrimshaw, Nevin S. and John Paul SanGiovanni. 1997. "Synergism of Nutrition, Infection and Immunity: An Overview." *The American Journal of Clinical Nutrition* 66(2):464S–77S.

Scully, Judith A. M. 2004. "Eugenics, Women of Color and Reproductive Health: The Sage Continues." *Africalogical Perspectives* 1:167–91.

Sears, Clare. 2008. "Electric Brilliancy: Cross-Dressing Law and Freak Show Displays in Nineteenth-Century San Francisco." *Women's Studies Quarterly* 36(3-4):170–87.

Sears, J. T. 1991. *Growing Up Gay in the South: Race, Gender, and Journeys of the Spirit.* New York: Harrington Park Press.

Secura, Gina, Tessa Madden, Colleen McNicholas, Jennifer Mullersman, Christina M. Buckel, Qiuhong Zhao, and Jeffrey F. Peipert. 2014. "Provision of No-Cost, Long-Acting Contraception and Teenage Pregnancy." *The New England Journal of Medicine* 371:1316–23.

Seidman, Steven. 1997. *Difference Troubles: Queering Social Theory and Sexual Politics.* Cambridge, UK: Cambridge University Press.

Seidman, Steven. 2004. *Contested Knowledge: Social Theory Today.* 3rd ed. Oxford, UK: Blackwell.

Seidman, Steven. 2015. *The Social Construction of Sexuality.* 3rd ed. New York: W.W. Norton.

Servais, L. 2006. "Sexual Health Care in Persons With Intellectual Disabilities." *Mental Retardation and Developmental Disabilities Research Reviews* 12:48–56.

Seto, Michael C. 2015. "Is Pedophilia a Sexual Orientation." Pp. 366–72 in *Sexualities: Identities, Behaviors, and Society,* 2nd ed., edited by Michael Kimmel and The Stony Brook Sexualities Research Group. New York: Oxford University Press.

Shakti Samuha. 2016. "Recent News." Retrieved July 29, 2016 (http://shaktisamuha.org.np/).

Shapiro, Eve. 2015. *Gender Circuits: Bodies and Identities in a Technological Age,* 2nd Edition. New York: Routledge.

Shapiro, Lila. 2013. "Gay Adoption Bill Pushed by Lawmakers, Families." *The Huffington Post,* May 5. Retrieved May 10, 2016 (http://www .huffingtonpost.com/2013/05/07/ gay-adoption-bill-_n_3232545 .html).

Shaw, Susan M. and Janet Lee. 2012. *Women's Voices Feminist Visions: Classic and Contemporary Readings,* Fifth Edition. New York: McGraw-Hill.

Sheff, Elisabeth. 2013. *The Polyamorists Next Door: Inside Multiple-Partner Relationships and Families.* Lanham, MD: Rowman and Littlefield.

Shilts, Randy. 1987. *And the Band Played On: Politics, People, and the AIDS Epidemic.* New York: Penguin Books.

Shilts, Randy. 1993. *Conduct Unbecoming: Lesbians and Gays in the U.S. Military from Vietnam to the Persian Gulf.* New York: St. Martin's Press.

Shimizu, Celine Parrenas. 2012. *Straightjacket Sexualities: Unbinding Asian American Manhoods in the Movies.* California: Stanford University Press.

Shuttleworth, Russell, Nikki Wedgewood, and Nathan Wilson. 2012. "The Dilemma of Disabled Masculinity." *Men and Masculinities* 15(2): 174–94.

Sico, Rachelle. 2013. "In the Name of "Love": Mail Order Brides-The Dangerous Legitimization of Sex, Human and Labor Trafficking." *Public Interest Law Report* 18(3):199–206.

Silbert, M. and A.M. Pines, 1981. "Sexual Child Abuse as an Antecedent to Prostitution." *Child Abuse and Neglect* 5(4):407–11.

Silverstein, C. 1981. *Man to Man: Gay Couples in America.* New York: William Morrow.

Simmons Catherine A., Peter Lehman, and Shannon Collier-Tenison. 2008. "Linking Male Use of the Sex Industry to Controlling Behaviors in Violent Relationships: An Exploratory Analysis." *Violence Against Women* 14(4):406–17.

Simon, William and John H. Gagnon. 1967. *Sexual Deviance: A Reader.* New York: Harper and Row Publishers.

Simons, Ronald L. and Les B. Whitbeck. 1991. "Sexual Abuse as a Precursor to Prostitution and Victimization Among Adolescent and Adult Homeless Women." *Journal of Family Issues* 12(3):361–79.

Smith, Andrea. 2009. "Beyond Pro-Choice versus Pro-Life: Women of Color and Reproductive Justice." Pp. 446–57 in *Feminist Frontiers,* 8th ed., edited by Verta Taylor, Nancy Whittier, and Leila J. Rupp. Boston: McGraw Hill.

Smith, Sharon. 2009. "Black Feminism and Intersectionality." *International Socialist Review* 63(Jan). Retrieved July 31, 2016. (http://isreview.org/issue/91/black-feminism-and-intersectionality).

Snorton, C. Riley. 2014. *Nobody Is Supposed to Know: Black Sexuality on the Down Low.* Minneapolis: University of Minnesota Press.

Snow, David. 2013. "Identity Dilemmas, Discursive Fields, Identity Work, and Mobilization: Clarifying the Identity-Movement Nexus." In *The Future of Social Movement Research: Dynamics, Mechanisms, and Processes.* Jacquelien van Stekelenburg, Conny Roggeband, and Bert Klandermans, Editors. Minneapolis, MN: University of Minnesota Press.

Snyder-Hall, Claire R. 2010. "Third-Wave Feminism and the Defense of 'Choice'." *Perspectives on Politics* 8(1):255–61.

Sommers-Flanagan, Rita, and John Sommers-Flanagan, and Britta Davis. 1993. "What's Happening on Music Television? A Gender Role Content Analysis." *Sex Roles* 28:11–12.

Sondy, Amanullah De. 2016. "LGBT Muslims Do Exist, and They Are Grieving, It's Time for Acceptance." *The Washington Post*, June 13. Retrieved July 28, 2016 (https://www.washingtonpost.com/news/acts-of-faith/wp/2016/06/13/lgbt-muslims-do-exist-and-they-are-grieving-its-time-for-acceptance/).

Sontag, Deborah. 2015. "U.S. Spars with Texas on Ending Prison Rapes." *The New York Times,* May 22. Retrieved June 10, 2016. (http://www.nytimes.com/2015/05/23/us/texas-and-us-spar-over-rules-to-stop-prison-rape.html?_r=0).

Span, S. and L. Vidal. 2003. "Cross-Cultural Differences in Female University Students' Attitudes Toward Homosexuals: A Preliminary Study." *Psychological Reports* 92:565–72.

Spector, Jessica. 2006. *Prostitution and Pornography: Philosophical Debate about the Sex Industry.*

Stanford California: Stanford University Press.

Spettigue, Wendy and Katherine A. Henderson. 2004. "Eating Disorders and the Role of the Media." *Journal of the Canadian Academy of Child and Adolescent Psychiatry* 13(1):16–19.

Springer, Kimberly. 2008. "Queering Black Female Heterosexuality." Pp. 77–92 in *Yes Means Yes! Visions of Female Sexual Power and a World Without Rape,* edited by Jaclyn Friedman and Jessica Valentis. Berkeley, CA: Seal Press.

Stacey, Judith. 1996. *In the Name of the Family: Rethinking Family Values in the Postmodern Age.* Boston: Beacon Press.

Stacey, Judith. 2011. *Unhitched: Love, Marriage, and Family Values from West Hollywood to Western China.* New York: New York University Press.

Stacey, Judith and Timothy Biblarz. 2001. "(How) Does the Sexual Orientation of Parents Matter?" *American Sociological Review* 66(2):159–83.

Standards of Care for the Health of Transexual, Transgender, and Gender Non-conforming People, 7th Version. 2012. World Professional Association for Transgender Health. Retrieved July 24, 2016 (http://www.wpath.org/site_page.cfm?pk_association_webpage_menu=1351).

Staples, Robert. 2006. *Exploring Black Sexuality.* Lanham, MD: Rowman and Littlefield.

Staudt, Kathleen and Zulma Y. Mendez. 2015. *Courage, Resistance, and Women in Ciudad Juarez: Challenges to Militarization.* Austin, Texas: University of Texas Press.

Stein, Edward. 1999. *The Mismeasure of Desire: The Science, Theory, and Ethics of Sexual Orientation.* New York: Oxford University Press.

Steinem, Gloria. 2015. "Activist/Author Gloria Steinem." [Interview transcript]. Tavis Smiley Show. Los Angeles, CA: PBS. Retrieved July 22, 2016 (http://www.pbs.org/wnet/tavissmiley/interviews/author-gloria-steinem/).

Steingraber, Sandra. 2007. *The Falling Age of Puberty in U.S. Girls: What We Know, What We Need to Know.* San Francisco: The Breast Cancer Fund.

Steinhauer, Jennifer. 2014. "White House to Press Colleges to Do More to Combat Rape." *The New York Times*, April 28. Retrieved July 20, 2016 (http://www.nytimes.com/2014/04/29/us/tougher-battle-on-sex-assault-on-campus-urged.html?_r=0).

Stevens, Emily E., Thelma E. Patrick, and Rita Pickler. 2009. "A History of Infant Feeding." *Journal of Perinatal Education* 18(2):32–39.

Stille, Alexander. 2016. "What Pope Benedict Knew about Abuse in the Catholic Church." *The New Yorker,* January 14. Retrieved online July 18, 2016 (http://www.newyorker.com/news/news-desk/what-pope-benedict-knew-about-abuse-in-the-catholic-church).

Stillwaggon, Eileen. 2006. *AIDS and the Ecology of Poverty.* Oxford, UK: Oxford University Press.

Stombler, Mindy and Amanda M. Jungels. 2014. "Challenges of Funding Sex Research." Pp. 108–11 in *Sex Matters: The Sexuality and Society Reader,* 4th ed., edited by Mindy Stombler, Dawn B. Baunach, Wendy Simonds, Elroi J. Windsor, and Elisabeth O.

Burgess. New York: W.W. Norton & Company.

Stone, Merlin. 1978. *When God Was a Woman*. New York: A Harvest Book, Harcourt Brace & Company.

Story, Louise. 2007. "Anywhere the Eye Can See, It's Likely to See an Ad." *The New York Times*, January 15. Retrieved July 24, 2016 (http://www.nytimes .com/2007/01/15/business/ media/15everywhere.html?_r=0).

Stotzer, Rebecca L. 2009. "Violence Against Transgender People: A Review of United States Data." *Aggression and Violent Behavior* 14:170–9.

Strauss, Susan L. 2012. *Sexual Harassment and Bullying: A Guide to Keeping Kids Safe and Holding Schools Accountable*. Lanham, MD: Rowman and Littlefield Press.

Strayhorn, Joseph M. and Jillian C. Strayhorn. 2009. "Religiosity and Teen Birth Rate in the United States." *Reproductive Health* 6, 14–20. doi: 10.1186/1742-4755-6-14.

Struckman-Johnson, Cindy and Dave Struckman-Johnson. 2002. "Sexual Coercion Reported by Women in Three Midwestern Prisons." *Journal of Sex Research* 39:217–27.

Struckman-Johnson, Cindy and Dave Struckman-Johnson. 2013. "Stopping Prison Rape: The Evolution of Standards Recommended by PREA's National Prison Rape Elimination Commission." *The Prison Journal* 93(3):335–354.

Stuart, Elizabeth. 2003. *Gay & Lesbian Theologies: Repetitions with Critical Difference*. Burlington VT: Ashgate Publishing Company.

Stubbs, M. L. 2008. "Cultural Perceptions and Practices Around Menarche and Adolescent Menstruation in the United States." *Annals of the New York Academy of Science* 1135:58–66.

Sullivan, Maureen. 2011. "The Emergence of Lesbian-Coparent Families in Postmodern Society." Pp. 20–33 in *Shifting the Center: Understanding Contemporary Families,* 4th ed., edited by Susan J. Ferguson. New York: McGraw-Hill.

Sullivan, Rebecca and Alan McKee. 2015. *Pornography: Structures, Agency and Performance*. Cambridge, UK: Polity Press.

Summers, A. K. 2014. *Pregnant Butch: Nine Long Months Spent in Drag*. Berkeley, CA: Soft Skull Press.

Sutton, M. J., J. D. Brown, K. M. Wilson, and J. D. Klein. 2002. "Shaking the Tree of Knowledge for Forbidden Fruit: Where Adolescents Learn about Sexuality and Contraception." Pp. 25–55 in *Sexual Teens, Sexual Media*, edited by J. D. Brown, J. R. Steele, and K. Walsh-Childers. Mahwah, NJ: Lawrence Erlbaum.

Sweet, Ken. 2014. "LGBT Baby Boomers Face Retirement Hurdles." *The Times-Picayune* A-5, Dec. 1.

Sykes, G. 1958. *The Society of Captives: A Study of a Maximum Security Prison*. Princeton, NJ: Princeton University Press.

Symons, Caroline. 2007. "Challenging Homophobia and Heterosexism in Sport: The Promise of the Gay Games." Pp. 140–59 in *Sport and Gender Identities: Masculinities, Femininities, and Sexualities,* edited by Cara Carmichael Aitchison. New York: Routledge.

Symons, Caroline. 2013. "The Gay Games." Pp. 87–114 in *Sexual Minorities in Sports: Prejudice at Play,* edited by Melanie L. Sartore-Baldwin. Boulder, CO: Lynne Rienner Publishers.

Symons, Caroline and D. Hemphill. 2006. "Transgendering Sex and Sport in the Gay Games." Pp. 109–29 in *Sport, Sexualities and Queer/Theory*, edited by J. Caudwell. London, England: Routledge.

Taibi, Catherine. 2014. "Don Lemon Asks Bill Cosby Accuser Why She Didn't Bite His Penis To Stop Her Rape." *The Huffington Post*, November 19. Retrieved July 20, 2016 (http://www .huffingtonpost.com/2014/11/19/ don-lemon-bill-cosby-rape-accuser-bite-oral-sex_n_6184618.html).

Taleporos, George. 2001."Sexuality and Physical Disability." Pp. 155–66 in *Sexual Positions: An Australian View,* edited by C. Wood. Melbourne, AU: Hill of Content Publishing.

Taleporos, George and Marita P. McCabe. 2001. "Physical Disability and Sexual Esteem." *Sexuality and Disability* 19:159–76.

Taleporos, George and Marita P. McCabe. 2015. "Relationships, Sexuality, and Adjustment among People with Physical Disabilities." Pp. 214–32 in *Sexualities: Identities, Behaviors, and Society,* 2nd ed., edited by Michael Kimmel and The Stony Brook Sexualities Research Group. New York: Oxford University Press.

Tannehill, Brynn. 2015. "Ohio and the Epidemic of Transgender Violence." *The Huffington Post,* February 20. Retrieved May 20, 2015 (http://www.huffingtonpost .com/brynn-tannehill/ohio-and-the-epidemic-of-_b_6720892 .html).

Taormino, Tristan. 2008. *Opening Up: A Guide to Polyamory: Creating and Sustaining Open Relationships.* San Francisco, CA: Cleis Press.

Taylor, Verta. 2013. "Social Movement Participation in the Global Society: Identity, Networks, and Emotions." Pp. 37–57 in *The Future of Social Movement Research: Dynamics, Mechanisms, and Processes,* edited by Jacquelien van Stekelenburg, Conny Roggeband, and Bert Klandermans. Minneapolis, MN: University of Minnesota Press.

Tejeda, M. J. 2006. "Nondiscrimination Policies and Sexual Identity Disclosure: Do They Make a Difference in Employee Outcomes?" *Employee Responsibilities and Rights Journal* 18(1):45–59.

Tepper, Mitchell S. 2000. "Sexuality and Disability: The Missing Discourse of Pleasure." *Sexuality and Disability* 18(4):283–90.

Tepperman, Lorne. 2006. *Deviance, Crime, and Control: Beyond the Straight and Narrow.* New York: Oxford University Press.

Terkel, Amanda. 2015. "Marriage Equality in Germany 'Not a Goal' for Angela Merkel." *The Huffington Post,* May 27. Retrieved May 30, 2016. (http://www.huffingtonpost.com/2015/05/27/angela-merkel-marriage-equality_n_7454090.html).

Tetreault, Patricia, Ryan Fette, Peter Meidlinger, and Debra Hope. 2013. "Perceptions of Campus Climate by Sexual Minorities." *Journal of Homosexuality* 60:947–64.

Tewksbury, Richard. 1989. "Fear of Sexual Assault in Prison Inmates." *The Prison Journal* 69(1):62–71.

Tewksbury, Richard and David Patrick Connor. 2014. "Who is Having Sex Inside Prison?" *Deviant Behavior* 35:993–1005.

Thanasiu, P. 2004. "Childhood Sexuality: Discerning Healthy from Abnormal Sexual Behaviors." *Journal of Mental Health Counseling* 26:309–19.

The American College of Obstetricians and Gynecologists and Society for Maternal-Fetal Medicine. 2014. "Obstetric Care Consensus no. 1: Safe Prevention of the Primary Cesarean Delivery." *Obstetrics and Gynecology* 123(3):693–711.

"The Extraordinary Case of the Guevedoces." 2015. *BBC News,* Sept. 20. Retrieved July 25, 2016 (http://www.bbc.com/news/magazine-34290981).

The Louisiana Human Trafficking Report. 2014. Loyola University Modern Slavery Research Project and New Orleans Human Trafficking Working Group. Loyola, LA: Loyola University New Orleans.

"Thirty Years of HIV/AIDS: Snapshots of an Epidemic." 2016. *Amfar: Making AIDS History.* Retrieved July 8, 2016. (http://www.amfar.org/thirty-years-of-hiv/aids-snapshots-of-an-epidemic/).

Thomas, June. 2011. "The Gay Bar: Why the Gay Rights Movement was Born in One." *Slate.com.* Retrieved June 27, 2015 (http://www.slate.com/articles/life/the_gay_bar/2011/06/the_gay_bar_4.html).

Thompson, Becky Wangsgaard. 2012. "'A Way Outa No Way': Eating Problems among African-American, Latina, and White Women." Pp. 340–48 in *Feminist Frontiers,* 9th ed., edited by Verta

Taylor, Nancy Whittier, Leila J. Rupp. New York: McGraw Hill.

Thompson, Edward H. and Kaitlyn Barnes. 2013. "Meaning of Sexual Performance Among Men With and Without Erectile Dysfunction." *Psychology of Men and Masculinity* 14(3):271–80.

Thompson, S.A. 2003. "Subversive Political Praxis: Supporting Choice, Power and Control for People with Learning Difficulties." *Disability and Society* 18:719–36.

Thorne, Barrie. 2009. "Girls and Boys Together . . . But Mostly Apart: Gender Arrangement in Elementary Schools." Pp. 176–86 in *Feminist Frontiers,* 8th ed., edited by Verta Taylor, Nancy Whittier, and Leila J. Rupp. Boston: McGraw Hill.

Thornhill, Randy and Craig T. Palmer. 2000. *A Natural History of Rape: Biological Bases of Sexual Coercion.* Cambridge, MA: MIT Press.

Thrasher, Steven W. 2014. "For Gay and Lesbian Parents, Equality Is a Myth When it Comes to Custody Cases." *The Guardian,* Monday, April 21. Retrieved Jan. 29, 2016 (http://www.theguardian.com/commentisfree/2014/apr/21/gay-lesbian-parents-equality-myth-custody-cases).

Tibbals, Chauntelle Anne. 2013. "Gonzo, Trannys, and Teens– Current Trends in US Adult Content Production, Distribution and Consumption." *Porn Studies* 1(1-2):127–35.

Tieffer, Leonore. 1995. *Sex is Not a Natural Act and Other Essays.* Boulder, CO: Westview.

Tilly, Charles. 1974. "The Chaos of the Living City." Pp. 86–108 in *The Urban World,* edited by Charles Tilly. Boston: Little Brown.

Tjaden, P. and N. Thoennes. 2000. *Extent, Nature, and Consequences of Intimate Partner Violence: Findings from the National Violence Against Women Survey.* Washington, DC.

Tolman, Deborah L. 1991. "Adolescent Girls, Women and Sexuality: Discerning Dilemmas of Desire." *Women & Therapy* 11(3–4):55–69.

Tolman, Deborah L. 1994. "Doing Desire: Adolescent Girls' Struggles for/with Sexuality." *Gender and Society* 8(3):324–42.

Touraine, Alain. 1985. "An Introduction to the Study of Social Movements." *Social Research* 52:749–87.

Trafficking in Persons Report. 2016. U.S. Department of State. Retrieved July 25, 2016 (http://www.state.gov/j/tip/rls/tiprpt/2016/).

Travis, Cheryl Brown and Jacquelyn White. 2000. *Sexuality, Society, and Feminism.* Washington, DC: American Psychological Association.

Travis, Melissa. 2007. "Asexuality." Pp. 336–338 in *Sex Matters: The Sexuality and Society Reader,* 2nd ed., edited by Mindy Stombler, Dawn M. Baunach, Elisabeth O. Burgess, Denise Donnelly, and Wendy Simonds. Boston: Pearson.

Trudell, Bonnie Nelson. 1993. *Doing Sex Education: Gender Politics and Schooling.* New York: Routledge.

Trujillo, Nick. 1995. "Machines, Missiles, and Men: Images of the Male Body on ABC's Monday Night Football." *Sociology of Sport Journal* 12(4):419.

Truven Health Analytics. 2013. *The Cost of Having a Baby in the United States: Truven Health Analytics Marketscan Study.* Pg. 3. Retrieved online January 20, 2017 (http://transform.childbirthconnection.org/wp-content/uploads/2013/01/Cost-of-Having-a-Baby-Executive-Summary.pdf)

Tuchman, Gaye. 1978. "Introduction: The Symbolic Annihilation of Women by the Mass Media." Pp 3–38 in *Hearth and Home Images of Women in the Mass Media,* edited by Gaye Tuchman, Arlene Kaplan Daniels and James Benet. New York: Oxford University Press.

Tucker, Myra J., Cynthia J. Berg, William M. Callaghan, and Jason Hsia. 2007. "The Black–White Disparity in Pregnancy-Related Mortality From 5 Conditions: Differences in Prevalence and Case-Fatality Rates." *American Journal of Public Health* 97(2):247–51.

Turchik, Jessica A. and Susan M. Wilson. 2009. "Sexual Assault in the U.S. Military: A Review of the Literature and Recommendations for the Future." Aggression and Violent Behavior. Elsevier Publishing.

Turrell, S.C. 2000. "A Descriptive Analysis of Same-Sex Relationship Violence For a Diverse Sample." *Journal of Family Violence* 15(3):281–93.

United Nations. 2002. "Optional Protocol to Convention on the Rights of the Child on the Sale of Children, Child Prostitution and Child Pornography" Entry into force: 18 January 2002. Chapter IV, Human Rights, United Nations. Retrieved online July 11, 2016 (http://www.ohchr.org/EN/ProfessionalInterest/Pages/OPSCCRC.aspx).

United Nations. 2014. *International Conference on Population and Development Programme of Action: 20th Anniversary Edition,* UNFPA. Retrieved July 12, 2016 (http://www.unfpa.org/sites/default/files/pub-pdf/programme_of_action_Web%20ENGLISH.pdf).

United States Conference of Catholic Bishops. 2009. "Ethical and Religious Directives for Catholic Health Care Services." Washington D.C.: United States Conference of Catholic Bishops. Retrieved online July 22, 2016 (http://www.usccb.org/issues-and-action/human-life-and-dignity/health-care/upload/Ethical-Religious-Directives-Catholic-Health-Care-Services-fifth-edition-2009.pdf).

United States Department of Justice. 2012. An Updated Definition of Rape: Office of Public Affairs, Briefing Room, Justice Blogs. Retrieved online July 13, 2016 (https://www.justice.gov/opa/blog/updated-definition-rape).

U.S. Congress. House of Representatives. *Victims of Trafficking and Violence Protection Act of 2000.* H.R. 3244 106th Congress, 1999–2000. Retrieved July 25, 2016 (https://www.congress.gov/bill/106th-congress/house-bill/3244).

U.S. Congress. House of Representatives. *International Marriage Broker Regulation Act of 2005.* S. 1618, 109th Congress, 2005–2006. Retrieved July 25, 2016 (https://www.congress.gov/bill/109th-congress/senate-bill/1618/text).

Vaccaro, Annemarie, Gerri August, and Megan S. Kennedy. 2012. *Safe Spaces: Making Schools and Communities Welcoming to LGBT Youth.* Santa Barbara, CA: Praeger.

Vandiver, Donna M. and Jessie L. Krienert. 2007. "An Assessment of a Cross-National Sample of Men and Women Arrested for Prostitution." *Southwest Journal of Criminal Justice* 4(2):89–105.

Vedder, C. and P. King. 1967. *Problems of Homosexuality in Corrections.* Springfield, IL: Charles C Thomas Publishing.

Vendituolie, Monica. 2014. "Senator McCaskill Plans Legislation to Improve Response to Campus Sexual Violence." *The Chronicle of Higher Education* June 3. Retrieved June 3, 2016. http://www.chronicle.com/article/ Senator-McCaskill-Plans/146895/

Vine, David. 2015. *Base Nation: How U.S. Military Bases Abroad Harm America and the World.* New York: Metropolitan Books Henry Holt and Company, LLC.

Vostral, Sharra L. 2010. *Under Wraps: A History of Menstrual Hygiene Technology.* New York: Lexington Books.

Wadud, Amina. 1999. *Qur'an and Woman: Rereading the Sacred Text from a Woman's Perspective.* New York: Oxford University Press.

Walker, Jayne, John Archer, and Michelle Davies. 2014. "Effects of Rape on Men: A Descriptive Analysis." Pp. 628–39 in *Sex Matters: The Sexuality and Society Reader,* 4th ed., edited by Mindy Stombler, Dawn M. Baunach, Wendy Simonds, Elroi J. Windsor, and Elisabeth O. Burgess. New York: W.W. Norton & Company.

Walls, N., S. Freedenthal and H. Wisneski. 2008. "Suicidal Ideation and Attempts Among Sexual Minority Youths Receiving Social Services. *Social Work* 53:21–29.

Ward, D.A. and G.G. Kassebaum. 1964. "Homosexuality: A Mode of Adaptation in Prison for Women." *Social Problems* 12:159–77.

Ward, Jane. 2015. *Not Gay: Sex between Straight White Men.* New York: New York University Press.

Ward, L.M. 2003. "Understanding the Role of Entertainment Media in the Sexual Socialization of American Youth: A Review of Empirical Research." *Developmental Review* 23: 347–88.

Wardle, Lynn D. 1997. "The Potential Impact of Homosexual Parenting on Children." *University of Illinois Law Review* 1997: 833–919.

Warner, Michael. 1991. "Introduction: Fear of a Queer Planet." *Social Text* 29:3 –17.

Warner, Michael. 1999. *The Trouble With Normal: Sex, Politics, and the Ethics of Queer Life.* Cambridge, MA: Harvard University Press.

Weeks, Jeffrey. 1977. *Coming Out: Homosexual Politics in Britain from the Nineteenth Century to the Present.* London, England: Quartet Books.

Weeks, Jeffrey. 1981. *Sex, Politics, and Society.* London, England: Longman Publishers.

Weeks, Jeffrey. 2011. "The Social Construction of Sexuality." Pp. 13–19 in *Introducing the New Sexuality Studies,* 2nd ed., edited by Steven Seidman, Nancy Fischer, and Chet Meeks. New York: Routledge.

Weeks, Jeffrey. 2012. *Sex, Politics, and Society: The Regulation of Sexuality Since 1800,* 3rd Edition. Harlow, UK: Pearson Education Limited.

Weiss, C. and D.J. Friar. 1974. *Terror in Prisons: Homosexual Rape and Why Society Condones It.* New York: Bobbs-Merrill.

Weiss, Karen G. 2011. "Neutralizing Sexual Victimization: A Typology of Victims' Non-reporting Accounts." *Theoretical Criminology* 15(4):445–67.

Weitzer, Ronald. 2005. "New Directions in Research on Prostitution." *Crime, Law & Social Change* 43:211–35.

Weitzer, Ronald. 2007. "The Social Construction of Sex Trafficking: Ideology and Institutionalization of a Moral Crusade." *Politics & Society* 35(3):447–75.

Weitzer, Ronald. 2012. *Legalizing Prostitution: From Illicit Vice to Lawful Business.* New York University Press.

West, Candace and Sarah Fenstermaker. 1995. "Doing Difference." *Gender and Society.* 9(1): 8–37.

West, Candace and Don H. Zimmerman. 1987. "Doing Gender." *Gender and Society* 1:125.

West, Cornel. 1994. *Race Matters.* New York: Vintage Press.

West, Donald J. 1993. *Male Prostitution.* New York: Routledge.

Western Oregon University. "Preferred Gender Pronoun/ Personal Pronouns" Retrieved July 26, 2016 (https://www.wou. edu/wp/safezone/terminology/ pronouns/).

Weston, Kath. 1991. *Families We Choose: Lesbians, Gays, and Kinship.* New York: Columbia University Press.

Wheaton, Elizabeth M., Edward J. Schauer, and Thomas V. Galli. 2010. "Economics of Human Trafficking." *International Migration* 48(4):114–41.

Wheeler, Jennifer and William H. George. 2005. "Race and Sexual

Offending." Pp. 391–402 in *Race, Culture, Psychology and Law,* edited by Kimberly Holt Barrett and William H. George. Thousand Oaks, CA: Sage.

Wheeler, M. 1991. "Physical Changes of Puberty." *Endocrinology and Metabolism Clinics of North America* 20:1–14.

Whipple B. and K. Brash-McGreer. 1997. "Management of Female Sexual Dysfunction." Pp. 509–34 in *Sexual Function in People with Disability and Chronic Illness,* edited by Marca L. Sipski and Craig J. Alexander. Gaithersburg, MD: Aspen Publishers.

White, M.J., D.H. Rintala, K.A. Hart, and M.J. Fuhrer. 1993. "Sexual Activities, Concerns, and Interests of Women with Spinal Cord Injury Living in the Community. *American Journal of Physical Medicine and Rehabilitation* 72:372–78.

Whiteman, Honor. 2015. "'Female Viagra' Approved by FDA." *Medical News Today,* August 19, Retrieved July 19, 2016. (http://www.medical newstoday.com/articles/298349 .php).

Widom, C. S. and J. B. Kuhns. 1996. "Childhood Victimization and Subsequent Risk for Promiscuity, Prostitution, and Teenage Pregnancy: A Prospective Study." *American Journal of Public Health* 86(11):1607–12.

Wieckowski, E., P. Hartsoe, A. Mayer, and J. Shortz. 1998. Deviant Sexual Behavior in Children and Young Adolescents: Frequency and Patterns. *Sexual Abuse: A Journal of Research and Treatment* 10(4):293–304.

Wiederman, Michael W. 2000. "Women's Body Image Self

Consciousness During Physical Intimacy with a Partner." *Journal of Sex Research* 37:60–68.

Wilcox, Daniel T., Fiona Richards, Zerine C. O'Keefe. 2004. "Resilience and Risk Factors Associated with Experiencing Childhood Sexual Abuse." *Child Abuse Review* 13:338–52.

Williams, Christine L., Patti A. Giuffre, and Kirsten Dellinger. 1999. "Sexuality in the Workplace: Organizational Control, Sexual Harassment, and the Pursuit of Pleasure." *Annual Review of Sociology* 25:73–93.

Williams, Linda. 1999. *Hard Core: Power, Pleasure, and the "Frenzy of the Visible."* Berkeley, CA: University of California Press.

Williamson, Celia and Terry Cluse-Tolar. 2002. "Pimp-Controlled Prostitution: Still an Integral Part of Street Life." *Violence Against Women* 8(9):107–492.

Wilson, William Julius. 1973. *Power, Racism, and Privilege.* New York: Free Press.

Wilson, William Julius. 1978. *The Declining Significance of Race: Blacks and Changing American Institutions.* Chicago, IL: University of Chicago Press.

"Winning the Freedom to Marry Nationwide." n.d. Retrieved July 25, 2016. (http://www .freedomtomarry.org/).

Winter, Sam. 2003. Research and discussion paper: "Language and Identity in Transgender: Gender Wars and the Case of the Thai Kathoey." Paper presented at the Hawaii conference on Social Sciences, Waikiki, HI.

Woan, Sunny. 2008. "White Sexual Imperialism: A Theory of Asian Feminist Jurisprudence."

Washington and Lee Journal of Civil Rights and Social Justice 14(2):275–301.

Wolak, Janis, David Finkelhor, and Kimberly J. Mitchell. 2012. "Trends in Arrests for Child Pornography Production: The Third National Juvenile Online Victimization Study (NJOV-3)." Crimes Against Children Research Center: University of New Hampshire. Retrieved July 8, 2016 (http://www.unh.edu/ccrc/ pdf/CV270_Child%20Porn%20 Production%20Bulletin_4-13-12 .pdf).

Wolf, Naomi. 2002. *The Beauty Myth: How Images of Beauty Are Used Against Women.* New York: HarperCollins.

Wolfe, Nathan. 2012. *The Viral Storm: The Dawn of a New Pandemic Age.* New York: St. Martin's Griffin.

Wood, James L. and Maurice Jackson. 1982. *Social Movements: Development, Participation, and Dynamics.* Belmont, CA: Wadsworth Publishing Company.

Wooden, W. and J. Parker. 1982. *Men Behind Bars: Sexual Exploitation in Prison.* New York: Plenum.

World Health Organization. 2015. "Maternal Mortality Ratio (Modeled Estimate, Per 100,000 Live Births)." Retrieved July 14, 2016 (http://data.worldbank.org/ indicator/SH.STA.MMRT).

Wright, Paul J. and Michelle Funk. 2013. "Pornography Consumption and Opposition to Affirmative Action for Women: A Prospective Study." *Psychology of Women Quarterly.* Retrieved July 11, 2016 (http://pwq.sagepub.com/content/ early/2013/08/20/0361684 313498853.abstract#cited-by).

Wykes, Maggie and Barrie Gunter. 2005. *The Media and Body Image: If Looks Could Kill*. London, England: Sage Publications.

Yan, Holly and Dave Alsup. 2014. "NFL Draft: Reactions Heat Up after Michael Sam Kisses Boyfriend on TV." *CNN*. Tuesday, May 13. Retrieved May 8, 2015 (http://www.cnn.com/2014/05/12/us/michael-sam-nfl-kiss-reaction/index.html).

Yang, M., E. Fullwood, J. Goldstein, and J. Mink. 2005. "Masturbation in Infancy and Early Childhood Presenting as a Movement Disorder: 12 Cases and a Review of the Literature." *Pediatrics* 116:1427–52.

Ybarra, Michele and Kimberly Mitchell. 2005. "Exposure to Internet Pornography among Children and Adolescents: A National Survey." *Cyberpsychology & Behavior* 8(5):473–86.

Young, Cathy. 2014. "Campus Rape: The Problem with 'Yes Means Yes,'" *Time Magazine*, August 29. Retrieved July 14, 2016 (http://time.com/3222176/campus-rape-the-problem-with-yes-means-yes/).

Young, Iris Marion. 2005. *On Female Body Experience: "Throwing Like a Girl" and Other Essays*. Oxford, United Kingdom: Oxford University Press.

Zald, Mayer N. and John D. McCarthy. 1975. "Organizational Intellectuals and the Criticism of Society." *Social Service Research* 49:344–62.

Zimmerman, Jonathan. 2015. *Too Hot To Handle: A Global History of Sex Education*. Princeton, NJ: Princeton University Press.

Zurbriggen, Eileen L., Laura R. Ramsey, and Beth K. Jaworski. 2011. "Self- and Partner-objectification in Romantic Relationships: Associations with Media Consumption and Relationship Satisfaction." *Sex Roles* 64(7): 449–62.

INDEX

ABOUT THE AUTHORS

Kathleen J. Fitzgerald, PhD, is a visiting associate professor of Sociology at Tulane University. Her research and teaching interests are in social stratification; specifically, race/ethnicity, gender, and sexuality. She is the author of *Recognizing Race and Ethnicity: Power, Privilege, and Inequality,* 2nd ed. (2017); and *Beyond White Ethnicity: Developing a Sociological Understanding of Native American Identity Reclamation* (2007); in addition to numerous journal articles. She has been teaching the sociology of inequalities for over 24 years. Dr. Fitzgerald earned all her degrees in sociology: her PhD from the University of Missouri, her MA from Southern Illinois University at Edwardsville, and her bachelor's degree from St. Louis University.

Kandice L. Grossman, MA, is a teaching assistant and doctoral student in sociology at the University of Missouri. She earned her master's degree from University of Manchester, UK (2000), in women's studies with a focus on feminist research methodologies. She is an adjunct professor of gender and sexuality studies and sociology at Stephens College and Columbia College in Columbia, Missouri, and has more than 14 years of teaching experience.